The Utopian Alternative

The Utopian Alternative

FOURIERISM IN NINETEENTH-CENTURY AMERICA

Carl J. Guarneri

Cornell University Press

Ithaca and London

This book has been supported by a grant from
the National Endowment for the Humanities,
an independent federal agency.

First published 1991 by Cornell University Press.
First printing, Cornell Paperbacks, 1994.

Library of Congress Cataloging-in-Publication Data

Guarneri, Carl, 1950–
    The utopian alternative : Fourierism in nineteenth-century America / by Carl J.
Guarneri.
        p.   cm.
    Includes bibliographical references and index.
    ISBN 0-8014-2467-4 (cloth : alk. paper) ISBN 0-8014-8197-x (paper : alk. paper)
    1. Utopian socialism—United States—History—19th century.   2. Collective settle-
ments—United States—History—19th century.   3. Fourier, Charles, 1772–1837—Influence—History—19th century.   I. Title.
HX654.G82   1991
335′.23′097309034—dc20   90-56085

*To my father and the
memory of my mother*

Contents

vii

Illustrations

ix

Preface

This book describes a "road not taken" in our past. What used to be called the Middle Period of American history, roughly from 1820 to 1880, was an era of profound social and economic changes—changes that became intertwined with the calamity of the Civil War but began independently and continued after the fighting stopped. As the nation expanded, sprouted factories and cities, and sorted into antagonistic social classes, the extent to which free-labor capitalism would be the organizing principle of its development became the subject of widespread public discussion. In an atmosphere of anxious expectation, several political and reform world views informed by sectional, class, and ethnic differences competed to shape the emerging society and define America's destiny. The communitarian movement, which for a long time has been viewed as an entertaining sideshow to this main event, was in the thick of the contest for the nation's future. In its most popular guise, the Fourierist or Associationist crusade, utopian socialism enlisted thousands of supporters, spurred the creation of dozens of cooperative experiments, and made surprising inroads into northern public opinion—all in the hope of leading America's competitive society peacefully to a communal alternative. The utopians failed badly in this, their highest ambition; but their initial appeal, their spectacular collapse, and their enduring influence provide a unique window on the great nineteenth-century transformation of America: its nearly irresistible momentum, its missed opportunities, its legacy of dissent as well as accommodation. That is the largest meaning of the detailed narrative that follows.

With the luxury of hindsight, I can see that studying communitarianism represented a natural convergence of my early interests in radicalism, comparative history, and the history of ideas. As a student activist during the Vietnam War years, I resolved to look for guidance to the history of

European socialism—a focus stimulated by the sense of social engagement and intellectual excitement in the classes of Robert Rosen at the University of Pennsylvania. Jack Reese, another Penn professor, challenged me to take on the more problematic field of the United States. Moving away from the traditional question of why there is no socialism in America, I began to ask what kind of radical traditions Americans *did* have. I was struck by the American penchant for cooperative and communal experiments, a tradition that extended from the Shakers to the communes of the 1960s. Fourierism, the most popular and dynamic secular communitarianism of the nineteenth century, was an important but neglected subject. There was an additional payoff: the study of an imported communitarian creed with a substantial indigenous following seemed an ideal opportunity to examine the meeting ground of American and European movements for social change. As I pursued the subject over the years, my initial approach gained a complexity and balance that better represents historical truth yet I hope has retained its underlying sense of engagement. Intellectual history absorbed the techniques of social history to trace and analyze the communitarian movement; comparative history became a nuanced study of similarities and differences rather than a blanket assertion or condemnation of American "exceptionalism"; and the search for a usable past yielded as many discontinuities as links with the present.

A book so big and so long in gestation represents an enormous number of debts. It is a pleasure finally to acknowledge them, just as it is fitting that a communitarian scholar recall that research and writing are cooperative enterprises.

My greatest intellectual debt is to John Higham, under whose direction at Johns Hopkins University my investigation took shape. From the outset Professor Higham's insights, his confidence in me and my subject, his advice in professional matters, and his friendship have been indispensable. His own works are models of judicious interpretation and elegant prose—models that I despair of emulating. Ronald Walters gave an early version of the manuscript an exceptionally close and helpful reading and has maintained a friendly interest in the emerging book. I am also grateful to Gerald Linderman of the University of Michigan, William Freehling of Johns Hopkins, and Rush Welter of Bennington College for their advice and encouragement during the initial stages of research.

Graduate fellowships from Michigan and Johns Hopkins sustained the early work; and an academic year at the Charles Warren Center for Studies in American History at Harvard, financed by the Warren Center and the American Council of Learned Societies, enabled me to complete much of the research that led from the history of ideas to the chronicling of a social movement. A National Endowment for the Humanities Summer Stipend allowed me to write key sections of the book. The Saint Mary's College Faculty Development Fund has covered various convention and photocopying expenses, and an Alumni Faculty Development Award supported my research on Edward Bellamy.

Librarians and archivists in the United States and France have been wonderfully generous with their time and resources. Among those to single out are Gary J. Arnold of the Ohio Historical Society, John Hoffman of the Illinois Historical Survey, Pierre Petitmengin of the Bibliothèque de l'Ecole Normale Supérieure in Paris, and Joan Winterkorn of Cornell University Libraries, all of whom mined collections for me and provided copies of their treasure. Especially helpful in locating materials were staff members at Abernethy Library of Middlebury College, Vermont; Bentley Historical Library and William L. Clements Library, University of Michigan; Columbia University Library; Houghton Library, Harvard University; the Monmouth County (New Jersey) Historical Society; Southern Historical Collections, University of North Carolina at Chapel Hill; the State Historical Society of Wisconsin; and the Warren–Trumbull County (Ohio) Public Library. Interlibrary loan services at Harvard, Johns Hopkins, and the Library of Congress brought me obscure utopian socialist tracts from around the country. Thanks also go to Brigitte Mazon, archivist of the Ecole des Hautes Etudes en Sciences Sociales, who exchanged research tasks with me, combing the Archives Sociétaires at the French National Archives while I found materials for her at the Houghton Library. It was an episode of transatlantic cooperation the Fourierists would have applauded.

To get to various archives and to stay temporarily nearby, I have relied upon many relatives and friends. Robert Carey, Lawrence and Shirsten Danielson, Carol Mooney and George Efta, Theresa and Joseph Gould, Paul and Joann Guarneri, Stewart Jacoby, Michael Mooney, and Stephen Weller were unfailingly gracious in putting me up and putting up with me during these research blitzes. I am especially indebted to my inlaws, George and Alice Weller, for their warm hospitality and cheerful encouragement over the years.

Helpful communitarian scholars have shared sources and findings with me. Glenn Conrad provided information on John Wilkins; the late Rondel Davidson allowed me to see his book manuscript on Victor Considerant, now published; Russell Jones sent information on the Considerant manuscripts at the Ecole Normale Supérieure; and Edward Spann helped me locate some reclusive Parke Godwin letters. Arthur Bestor, the dean of communitarian scholars, generously deposited his notes, bibliographies, and copies of various documents for public use in the Illinois Historical Survey, University of Illinois.

Several friends and colleagues besides those already mentioned read and commented on sections of the manuscript at various stages. My colleagues at Saint Mary's College—Ben Frankel, Ronald Isetti, Katherine Roper, and Paul Zingg—asked probing questions about a draft of my introduction. Professor Roper offered cogent advice on writing and has extended numerous courtesies as friend and as department chairperson.

At the Charles Warren Center, Daniel Kevles encouraged me to write the ambitious book I had in mind, and Tony Freyer tested my ideas against his formidable knowledge of the nineteenth-century economy. Jonathan Beecher saved me from several factual errors on the French Fourierists. Glenna Matthews served as an expert "reality check" for the sections on women and family in utopia. Tony Fels gave the entire manuscript a careful and characteristically perceptive reading. Lawrence Foster, Stephen Nissenbaum, and Thomas Mallon followed my progress closely and at a crucial time (when an attempt was made to plagiarize my work) lent decisive support. Throughout the project, conversations with my close friends Stewart Jacoby and Andrew Rotter clarified my thoughts and sent me back to work with renewed energy, while baseball with Gerald and Misha Eisman provided welcome escape.

At Cornell University Press, editor Peter Agree shepherded the book toward publication with exceptional tact and efficiency, and Patricia Sterling did a meticulous job of copyediting. I benefited greatly from the comments and suggestions of Iver Bernstein and Michael Fellman, who read the initial manuscript submitted to Cornell.

Portions of this book have appeared in earlier versions as articles. Parts of Chapter 4 were published as "Importing Fourierism to America," *Journal of the History of Ideas* 43 (October–December 1982): 581–94, and "The Associationists: Forging a Christian Socialism in Antebellum America," *Church History* 52 (March 1983): 36–49. Chapter 6 includes a revision of "Who Were the Utopian Socialists? Patterns of Membership in American Fourierist Communities," *Communal Societies* 5 (1985): 65–81. A section of Chapter 9 appeared as "Two Utopian Socialist Plans for Emancipation in Antebellum Louisiana," *Louisiana History* 24 (Winter 1983): 5–24. All are reprinted by permission.

I am both dismayed and gratified that this book's writing spanned the decade between the typewriter era and the age of computers. Robin Smith, Patricia Denault, and Eleanor Kitchen typed various chapter drafts. Gerald Eisman helped me transfer text from pages to disks, and Jim Hunter and Joan Halperin generously lent me computer equipment while I was convalescing at home.

My profoundest debt is to my immediate family. My daughters, Julia and Anna, don't know what life is like without "daddy's book," but they suspect it will be more relaxed. They have been patient and inquisitive in just the right mixture. My wife, Valerie Weller, does remember life before this book and deserves to return to it. I alone know all the things she has done to make this work possible. When I write, she is in my mind as a model of empathetic understanding and a critic of pedantry; when I am not writing, she takes over my heart as well.

CARL J. GUARNERI

Oakland, California

The Utopian Alternative

A state of mind is utopian when it is incongruous
with the state of reality within which it occurs. . . .
[Utopias] tend to shatter, either partially or wholly,
the order of things prevailing at the time.
              —Karl Mannheim, *Ideology and Utopia*

Subordinate groups could identify with the
dominant culture—often for sound reasons—even
as they sought to challenge it. And the challenge
could be undermined by that identification.
                      —T. J. Jackson Lears, "The Concept
                          of Cultural Hegemony"

Introduction

Born in 1772 in Besançon, France, during an era of political and social turbulence, Charles Fourier proclaimed with self-confidence verging on madness that his mission was to bring order and justice to humanity. During a long career as a traveling salesman and a modest commercial employee, Fourier saw at first hand the duplicities of mercantile life: adulteration, loan sharking, speculation in paper money, and the creation of artificial shortages that left rice rotting on the docks at Marseilles while people starved in the streets. In Lyons, the misery of silk workers in conflict with master mechanics over declining wages gave Fourier his first inkling of the coming Industrial Revolution. He came to believe that an entire economic system based on the anarchy of free competition was wrong. A radical change was imperative, but it must be constructive, orderly, and peaceful. Having lost his inheritance in the French Revolution when Parisian troops destroyed his stock of goods during the siege of Lyons, Fourier abhorred social conflict and dreamed instead of a society guaranteeing class harmony through scientific organization.

For all his idiosyncrasies, Fourier was not alone. As Friedrich Engels later put it, "the historical situation" of 1800 (by which he meant the surfacing of class conflict in the early stages of industrial capitalism) inspired several "utopian socialists": "The solution of the social problems, which as yet lay hidden in undeveloped economic conditions, the utopians attempted to evolve out of the human brain. Society presented nothing but wrongs; to remove these was the task of reason. It was necessary, then, to discover a new and more perfect system of social order and to impose this upon society from without by propaganda, and wherever it was possible, by the example of model experiments."[1] Each of these utopians—Fourier, Henri de Saint-Simon, and Robert Owen—criticized the emerging order from his peculiar vantage point and projected a "new world" as its obverse image. Saint-Simon saw the gulf between the propertied and propertyless in postrevolutionary France and envisioned a scientific elite, sanctified by a "new Christianity," as the saviors of humanity and administrators of the coming society. Robert Owen, living in the most advanced industrial society of the age, experimented with social engineering at his own factory in New Lanark, Scotland; there he evolved his plan for rational communism, which would later spread throughout Great Britain. Fourier's special subject was bourgeois society: with relentless sarcasm he exposed the "respectable" crimes of competition and the hypocrisy of conventional morality; and with the precision of a true visionary he foresaw a "harmonic" society in which social equity would automatically be taken care of so that persons could devote their energies to expressing their inmost selves creatively, even if this meant traversing the boundaries of contemporary morality.

About the same time that Saint-Simon issued his call for a new technological order and Owen was turning New Lanark into a model factory town, Fourier decided that the cure for the evils of competitive society was the establishment of small cooperative communities to unite persons of all types and classes so successfully that such experiments would spread rapidly throughout the world. By intricately analyzing the "passions" of human personality, Fourier deduced that each of these ideal communities, which he named "phalanxes," would be composed of 1,620 persons inhabiting a huge central dwelling, or "phalanstery," surrounded by the workshops, fields, and cultural institutions necessary to a varied and fulfilling existence for each resident. Operating under the scientific laws of unity that Fourier believed he had discovered, all communal activities would necessarily contribute to social harmony and progress. In 1808 this strange utopian began expounding his social philosophy, embellished by often tangential "scientific" findings, in large and difficult tomes. His writings went virtually unread until after the July Revolution of 1830, when a small group of French intellectuals made them the basis for a humanitarian reform movement.

It was in the United States, not Europe, that Fourier's theory had its greatest practical impact. In 1832 a young American student named Albert Brisbane met the Frenchman, by then a frustrated and bitter old prophet, and was promptly converted. When Brisbane returned to America, his energetic and persistent propagandizing—boosted immeasurably by Horace Greeley of the *New York Tribune*—created a burst of Fourierist activity in the northern states almost overnight. In the decade following 1842 nearly thirty American phalanxes were established from Massachusetts to Iowa. What came to be the most famous of these communities, Brook Farm, in West Roxbury, Massachusetts, had been founded by George Ripley in 1841 as an offshoot of Transcendentalism and had already attracted Hawthorne, Emerson and Margaret Fuller to its orbit before it converted to Fourierism in 1844.

But communal experiments were only one manifestation of the Fourierist movement. Nondenominational utopian socialist churches were established in Boston, Philadelphia, and Cincinnati. New England and New York Fourierists allied themselves with the emerging labor movement of the 1840s to promote producer and consumer cooperatives. In more than two dozen cities and towns "unions" or clubs gathered utopian socialists to hear lectures, discuss Fourier's ideas, and plan scaled-down Fourierist projects such as cooperative stores and urban communes. In 1846 these groups were federated into the American Union of Associationists, headquartered in New York. AUA officers there and at Brook Farm decided official policy, gathered information on the phalanxes, and published a weekly magazine called *The Harbinger*. Counting such luminaries as Ripley, William Henry Channing, Parke Godwin, and Henry James, Sr., among its regular contributors, *The Harbinger* spread its influence far beyond its circulation of a few thousand. From the phalanxes and the American Union there also poured a pamphlet and book literature of more than seventy titles elaborating Fourier's ideas and proclaiming the birth of a "New Industrial World" in America.

Introduced with fanfare and enlisting as many as 100,000 supporters, the New Industrial World died in its childhood. By the mid-1850s all but one of the phalanxes had perished, most the victims of internal discord or inefficient production. None of the "unions" was still active; the Fourierist labor movement was in disarray; and *The Harbinger* and its successors had ceased publication. The few Americans who still used Fourier's name were lending assistance to a French Fourierist colony struggling to survive on the Texas prairie. Their former colleagues had either sunk back into the world of competitive strife or shifted their reform energies from the attack on "wage slavery" to the crusade against chattel slavery.

Such a wildly ambitious program and so meteoric a career lend themselves easily to caricature. Fourierists themselves, with their fantastic predictions of global bliss, their short-lived phalanxes (critics called members "four-year-ites"), and their alien vocabulary, gave humorists plenty of ammunition. Several contemporary accounts, and some historical ones, simply chalk Fourierism up as another of the "fads," "delusions," or "follies" of an era when reformers peddled new pseudosciences and panaceas like snake oil.[2] Although most historians have taken American Fourierism more seriously than this, they do not take it seriously enough to see it on its own terms and in its largest context. The result has been a series of partial perspectives that interpret the movement in relation to, or as an aspect of, other social and intellectual developments.[3] One perspective has considered Fourierism merely one episode of a long-standing American "communitarian tradition" stretching from the eighteenth-century sectarian colonies of the Moravians and Shakers to the communes of the 1960s. Another has analyzed antebellum communities in relation to the westward movement and the frontier. Standard socialist accounts, following Marx and Engels, treat Fourierism as a "utopian" (and hence doomed) forerunner of "scientific" socialism. To traditional historians of American labor, the Fourierists were misguided middle-class intellectuals trying to steer workingmen away from realistic trade unionism. For their part, historians of reform movements before the Civil War have stressed perfectionist rhetoric and propaganda methods that link Fourierists with the mainstream of American "romantic reform." Finally, an approach hinted at in recent works places American Fourierism in the context of modernization and institutional innovation in Jacksonian America.[4]

Certainly these approaches have been valuable. To cite one instance: Arthur Bestor's pathbreaking research into communitarianism—and its belief in progress through imitation of successful social experiments—as a key element in nineteenth-century reform opened new vistas for students of social change in the United States.[5] Readers will find the standard interpretive contexts incorporated into this book when appropriate. Yet because they do not consider Fourierism as a whole and on its own terms, these interpretations are not sufficient. Both socialist and capitalist labor historians, for example, are interested in Fourierist ideas only as "forerunners," early and defective versions of ideologies that took definitive form half a century later, ideologies whose terminology and assumptions were not those of the Associationists. Although the communitarian approach is more sensitive historically, it too is inadequate. Fourierism encompassed other methods of reform besides phalanxes; more important, because communitarianism is only a method of enacting reform (that is, through pilot colonies), it leaves open the question of what specific institutions should prevail in the future. The content of communitarian theories matters at least as much as the envelope. As for the frontier, Fourierist ideologues insisted that they were motivated by fears that "industrial feudalism" was arising in existing towns and cities, not by any anxiety concerning the future of the unsettled West. Finally, interpretations that blend Fourierism with antebellum reform or institutional innovation are also deceptive. Although the Fourierists endorsed fellow reformers' goals and shared their vision of social improvement, their insistence on total structural change in society marked them as radicals apart.

It was this notion of a complete reconstruction of society that informed the Fourierists' writings and activities, however specialized or reformist their individual focus. Fourierism meant different things to different people: to middle-class professionals it could appeal as "scientific" social engineering; to ministers it presented itself as practical Christianity. Craft workers emphasized its opposition to "wage slavery" and support for cooperative workshops. There was even a small group of southern planters opposed to slavery who were attracted to Fourier's plan as a paternalist alternative to "free society." But in its most ambitious form—the form endorsed by the phalanxes and the national leaders—Fourierism proposed a peaceful but total revolution. As "utopianism," it presented a detailed blueprint of the ideal society; as a "critical-utopian socialism" (the full label Marx and Engels used in *The Communist Manifesto*), it based this blueprint on a sweeping, historically informed critique of contemporary social and economic developments.[6] By whatever name we call it, we should recognize that Fourierism offered a comprehensive revolutionary vision, and instead of confining it within specialized frames of reference, we need to see it whole.

To give the Fourierists the serious hearing they deserve, we have to discard one more burden of previous historical writing: the notion that historical change is inexorable or inherently progressive. Applied to industrialization, this notion assumes a series of inevitable stages to which the "impractical" or "visionary" failed to adjust. Thus the modern champions of corporate capitalism and state socialism, though differing in many ideas and values, both view the centralization of production and capital as a "necessary" historical stage and hence they agree that "backward-looking," "utopian" Fourierism failed to face historical "reality."[7] Their interpretation misunderstands the Fourierists' attitude toward industrialism and its components. But quite apart from this misconception, both socialists and capitalists are crippled by doctrinaire assumptions about "reality." Marx's claim that the utopians' plan for social cooperation was "doomed" by virulent class antagonism may have made sense for France in 1848, but it simply does not fit the movement's experience in the more open society of antebellum America.[8] For their part, the apologists of competitive industrialism fail to recall that in its turbulent early years its success was by no means assured. As Eric Hobsbawm reminds us:

> Looking back on the 1840s it is easy to think that the socialists who predicted the imminent final collapse of capitalism were dreamers confusing their hopes with realistic prospects. For in fact what followed was not the breakdown of capitalism, but its most rapid and unchallenged period of expansion and triumph. Yet in the 1830s and 1840s it was far from evident that the new economy could or would overcome its difficulties, which merely seemed to increase with its power to produce larger and larger quantities of goods by more and more revolutionary methods.[9]

Until we look at the processes of modernization and industrialization through the eyes of participants, we risk ignoring the range of possible outcomes those developments held for the future. And unless we recover this sense of plasticity in history, we cannot understand the urgency of the utopian socialists' rhetoric, the importance of their short-lived achievements, and the implications of their demise for the way later Americans thought and lived.

This book, the first full-scale history of American Fourierism, attempts to move beyond partial or deterministic interpretations and reach a new understanding of utopian socialism's dimensions and its role in the

United States. It analyzes the social, economic, and intellectual roots of the Fourierist movement, the ideas its members advocated, and the path they pursued in building a network of cooperative institutions linked by a national organization. Throughout the narrative, even in the many passages critical of the Fourierists, I have tried to respect the utopian socialists' distinctively large ambitions and to portray them as makers of history rather than its fugitives. Seen this way, the Fourierist movement is of interest not as a historical anachronism or a "precursor" of later radicalism but as an important participant in a central episode in American history: the contest over the future of American society which spanned the years of early urban industrialism and the Civil War.

From the 1830s to the 1860s rapid national expansion and the takeoff of industrial capitalism highlighted the distance the United States had traveled from the agrarian republic of the Founders, compelling Americans to reexamine inherited social ideals. The eventual revision of the nation's social identity, with the subsequent spread of that new definition's hegemony, is perhaps the central cultural development of the Civil War era. Conflicting interpretations of the nature and future of American society emerged in an important debate that raged in political forums, workplaces, and presses for more than two decades. Ultimately, the dispute was carried to the battlefield between North and South as sectional differences polarized ideological positions and escalated tensions to the breaking point; but before the guns fired on Fort Sumter, northerners themselves closed one area of contention by coming to agree on the basic soundness of their society.

The most controversial position in the debate centered on a reactionary defense of southern slavery. When a vocal group of proslavery theorists, led by George Fitzhugh and George Frederick Holmes, developed a stinging critique of northern "free society," they raised a fundamental challenge to the ideology of expansive capitalism. Privately, Fitzhugh and Holmes were more ambivalent, and we should be skeptical about how deeply their "Reactionary Enlightenment" took root in the South; but by proclaiming an essential, irreconcilable antagonism between northern and southern social systems and by suggesting that the only alternative to the hidden "wage slavery" of the North was the formalized chattel slavery of the South, Fitzhugh and his colleagues appeared directly to threaten the northern way of life. To Lincoln, Seward, and other Republicans, the proslavery argument spoke for a regressive, authoritarian society that stood in the way of democratic and commercial progress. Without doubt the proslavery position fueled the sectional tensions that led to war.[10]

The defense of slave society was so out of step with nineteenth-century ideas of progress, and its consequences were so traumatic, that it has tended to divert attention from the important quest for alternatives going on *within* northern society at the same time. Under the sway of Louis Hartz and other "consensus" historians, the older Progressive idea that the Democratic and Whig parties, as well as social reformers and conservatives, represented fundamentally different constituencies and world views was discredited. Other contexts for viewing antebellum politics and reform—ethno-cultural analyses, pyschohistory, myth-and-symbol approaches, modernization theory—have largely failed to restore a sense of drama and significance to the debate over social transformation taking place in the antebellum North. Yet the importance of that debate is once again being recognized. Taking their cue from Bernard Bailyn, Gordon Wood, and Eric Foner, historians are finding conflicting versions of republican ideology persisting in the nineteenth century.

A recent study of Jacksonian-era political ideology by John Ashworth describes "aristocratic" and "agrarian" brands of republicanism vying to shape national policy and social evolution in the 1840s. Analyses of working-class development in northern cities, most notably Sean Wilentz's *Chants Democratic*, argue that radical artisans advocated a distinctive variant of the ideology of republicanism bequeathed by the generation of the Founders. Interpreting "independence" in line with craft traditions and envisioning a "commonwealth" more like the workshop than the trading house, these men, Wilentz claims, espoused a fuzzy but powerful "artisan republicanism" that set them against commercial capitalism, at least until their movement collapsed in disarray in the 1850s. A third important book, Anthony F. C. Wallace's *Rockdale*, portrays the struggle between "infidel" Owenite utopians and their evangelical enemies for control of the hearts and minds of workers in the industrial towns of Pennsylvania in the 1830s and 1840s, and by implication for the future direction of American capitalism.[11]

Far more explicitly than Wilentz's artisans or Wallace's factory workers, with whom they shared a dissenting brand of republicanism, the Fourierists saw themselves as a third voice in the debate over the social meaning of America. Opposed both to the free-labor system of northern capitalists and the slave-labor system of the South, their communitarian movement sought to transform both into systems of *cooperative* labor—and to convince Americans that their mission was to make their nation the socialist Promised Land.

From the early nineteenth century, small communal experiments had been initiated in the Northeast and Midwest, often in the wake of religious revivalism. Between 1825 and 1860 thousands of Americans formed almost a hundred new utopias or joined colonies established earlier by millennial religious sects. Communities set up by Shakers, Owenites, and Fourierists and independent experiments such as Hopedale and Oneida varied greatly in their ideas and organizations; they spanned a spectrum from religious to secular in their orientation, from "free love" to celibacy in their sexual practices, and from community of property to relative individualism in their economic arrangements. Yet virtually all such groups shared a deep yearning to evolve a more equitable and communal society than members saw around them, and several voiced the conviction that successful pilot communities could transform American life through their example. The United States of the 1830s and 1840s was young and pliant enough that within a few generations, it was believed, model colonies could peacefully reshape its competitive society into an order resembling the Christian ideal of universal brotherhood.[12]

Fourierism occupied the most prominent and in many ways the most radical position in this loosely organized communitarian movement. Its detailed blueprint was the most popular plan during the great wave of community building in the 1840s. Unlike other antebellum communitarians, American Fourierists offered a comprehensive "social science," adapted not only from Fourier but other European theorists, which gave them a decidedly modern and radical outlook.

Three aspects of this world view particularly stand apart from the conventional reform wisdom of the era, providing key themes in this study. First, the Fourierists' pioneering critique of American society approached social problems from a sociological rather than a moralistic perspective. Using Fourier's definition and indictment of "Civilization"— a term of disapproval in his vocabulary—these utopians viewed the seemingly free and formless American environment as in fact an evolving structure of socioeconomic relations.

Second, Fourierism was by no means a retreat from modernization and industrialism into an impossible agrarian or village past.[13] Unlike many other reformers the Fourierists did not reject the new forces of the Industrial Revolution—large-scale enterprise, the division of labor, machinery, joint-stock organization—but simply proposed to harness them for group benefit rather than individual exploitation. Their complex "scientific" blueprint sought to recreate a lost world of community and integrity through a modern and rational system of social engineering.

Third, the Fourierists committed themselves more fully than any contemporaries to the utopian vision of "universal reform." In contrast to most communitarian groups, they supported transitional reforms—such as mutual insurance and producers' cooperatives—by which those living outside communities could also hasten the social millennium. And whereas other communitarians' religious creeds tended to limit membership to middle-class Protestants, the Fourierists were non-sectarian and emphatically committed to uniting all classes and creeds in cooperative harmony. "Universal reform," as the Fourierists envisioned it, meant a program of voluntary cross-class cooperation, begun by the middle class, which would peacefully revolutionize every aspect of social existence. This is precisely what Marx and Engels found so "utopian" about their socialism.

Fourierism was not just a communitarian program, then, but a new and penetrating way of examining American society which achieved a level of influence far beyond that of its short-lived phalanxes. As a system of ideas, American Fourierism stood near the very center of the antebellum debate over the future of the Republic. Publicized throughout the country, its terms and categories so dominated discourse about the emerging commercial and industrial society that F. O. Mathiessen labeled the two decades before the Civil War "the Age of Fourier" in American social thought.[14] Though the Fourierists obviously failed to convert their contemporaries, important sectors of American intellectual life honed their beliefs in response to Fourier's theory. In the North, Emerson and other writers developed the concepts of "self-reliance," "individualism," and "free labor" in explicit opposition to the utopian socialist challenge. Abolitionists debated the utopians over the merits of the capitalist system into which slaves were to be liberated. Southerners such as Fitzhugh used Fourierist concepts to criticize the northern way of life. Even the radical artisans whom Wilentz and others have discovered adopted Fourierist rhetoric and turned to Fourierist communities or cooperatives in lieu of disastrous strikes. Fourierists played a key part in the dialectic out of which the American national creed emerged, though they utterly failed to control the outcome of that dialectic.

Both as communitarian movement and as social criticism, Fourierism set out to challenge America's competitive structure and the damaging cultural consequences it had produced. But the Fourierists were not totally alienated from American life. For all their imported theory and radical aspirations they were also products of American culture, firm believers in many of its basic values and steeped in its rhetoric. Arthur Bestor is right when he contends that Fourierism won a widespread hearing on this side of the Atlantic because it clarified and extended ideas and tendencies already present in many American minds.[15] The traditions of American politics, Transcendentalism, millennial Christianity, and native reform all shared common presuppositions and ideals which, galvanized by the conditions of the 1840s, cleared the path to communitarian socialism. Fourierists drew upon these native promptings for their ideals and rhetoric. They argued that far from repudiating American values, utopian socialism was merely a more effective way to realize the goals of republicanism, democracy, Christianity, and missionary nationalism. They promised that the new order would bring an abundant, satisfying, and equal society without renouncing conventional ways or liberal beliefs. And their phalanxes incorporated familiar capitalist features such as private property, interest, and a modified wage system inside the communitarian frame. In this sense the Fourierists were proposing not just a cooperative substitute for competitive capitalism but an alternative, more community-minded version of the American Dream. Viewed this way, their history not only holds implications for the course of nineteenth-century society; it becomes a comment on the possibilities and the limitations of American culture.

Fourierism was neither a radically alien presence in American life nor a completely characteristic expression of native reform. It represented an alternative, socialistic way of life yet one suffused with American ideas and promptings. This special configuration accounted in large measure for its spectacular rise in the 1840s, when the convulsions of nascent industrial capitalism challenged more conventional formulations of the American Dream—but the Fourierist accommodation to American culture also contributed to the movement's rapid demise. Why Fourierism failed, as both an intellectual and a social movement, is a complex question whose multiple answers can emerge only from the kind of detailed history presented in this book. Certainly the quick collapse of the phalanxes and the return of national prosperity in the 1850s combined to prevent utopian socialism from taking deep root among the farmers, artisans, and professionals drawn to it. Just as important was the diversion of reformers into the antislavery crusade, whose critique of the South's "peculiar institution" served to affirm existing northern society. In the long run, of course, the communitarian method itself became outmoded as the urban and industrial infrastructure reached a size and complexity that could not be accommodated by colonies of no more than two thousand settlers. By the 1870s the communitarian moment had passed.

Yet even before this, the Fourierist program had ceased to be a vital alternative. Beneath the collapse and dispersal of the movement lay a two-pronged ideological dilemma. The very features that drew enthusiastic support—Fourierism's semicapitalistic community plan, and its dissenting-but-loyal system of thought—prevented the movement from realizing its goals. In the first place, the Fourierist blueprint proved incapable of building the New Industrial World. Individualist and capitalist features made the American phalanxes seedbeds of division and communal life impossible to sustain. Attracted by glib promises of instant wealth, many members joined the communities with selfish motives or unrealistic expectations, and divisive conflicts or rapid disillusionment ensued. Built on the sandy foundations of economic boosterism and millennial optimism, the phalanxes were unable to satisfy members' inflated hopes or to compel their dogged persistence. And Fourier's theory, which scientifically guaranteed success, could not adequately explain the communities' rapid collapse.

A second, related aspect of the utopian socialist dilemma was that beneath their manifestos and jeremiads, the Fourierists' basic commitment to the ideals and values of northern society vitiated their social criticism and undermined the movement. Their belief in democracy, property, Protestant morality, and peaceful progress gave legitimacy to mainstream American society even as they attempted to supplant it. Their promise of freedom, harmony, and abundance was too close to prevailing ideals to compel lasting commitment once economic prospects in the larger society brightened. To make matters worse, American Fourierists developed an evolutionary version of the Fourierist scenario that permitted them to see Fourierist ideals in such seemingly progressive institutions as apartment houses, business corporations, and the Republican party of the 1850s. When asked to choose between free-labor and slave societies, most Fourierists did not hesitate but abandoned their critique of competitive Civilization for a celebration of northern capitalism. Fatally compromised by its affinity with mainstream practice, utopian socialism was co-opted and absorbed into an emerging national consensus.

In the years before the Civil War, as American capitalism was experiencing disturbing growing pains, Fourierism's brand of dissent attracted many into opposition but was not distinctive or strong enough to hold them there. In the final analysis, utopian socialism proved too similar to the northern capitalist society it attempted to buck. The painful irony was that the very components of American Fourierism's massive appeal made it especially vulnerable to defeat.

It is too easy, however, simply to blame antebellum utopians for the failure of their protest; one must appreciate the immense difficulty of their mission and recognize the significant achievements they did manage. Their creative and sophisticated critique of competitive society, unmatched in their time and place, illuminated virtually every area of social life under early industrial capitalism. If their communities proved disappointingly unstable and impermanent institutions, they did for a time provide congenial refuge for Americans dissatisfied with mainstream society, and they conducted fascinating and partially successful experiments in social democracy. The communitarian experience nurtured commitments that carried over into several post–Civil War crusades as well as such practical reforms as cooperatives and life insurance. Nor should we underestimate the powerful obstacle that a booming economy placed in the way of nineteenth-century American radicals, who were fighting not so much a repressive state as the pervasive—and often plausible—hegemony of capitalist values.

Whether we criticize the Fourierists as fatally flawed dissenters or see them as the noble vanguard of a cooperative version of American industrialism, we should not deny their seriousness or their relevance to our world. During the era of American Fourierism (1840–80) American development was at a crucial turningpoint: in the course of little more than a generation, a nation of rural households and independent laborers moved decisively toward an urban and industrial society in which labor was subordinated to capital. The Fourierist movement provides a revealing glimpse into this transformation: its critique illuminates the processes and the human costs involved; its failure suggests important reasons why that transformation was possible. The Fourierists' criticisms of our world in its infancy and the questions they posed have remained troubling throughout the twentieth century. Even if the utopian socialists' methods seem antiquated and their shortcomings obvious, their aspirations and limited achievements should compel the attention of all who desire an industrial society consonant with communal ideals.

I

Origins of American Fourierism

I come as the possessor of the book of Destiny to banish political and moral darkness and to erect the theory of universal harmony upon the ruins of the uncertain sciences.

—Charles Fourier, *Théorie des quatre mouvements et des destinées générales*

We are all a little wild here with numberless projects of social reform. Not a reading man but has a draft of a new community in his waistcoat pocket.

—Ralph Waldo Emerson to Thomas Carlyle, 1840

1

Fourierism Crosses the Atlantic

Fourierism was a doctrine adopted by Americans to explain native conditions and point the way to an American utopia. Yet however "strictly American" the communitarian movement of the 1840s appears, French ancestry is a crucial element of its history.[1] Fourier's theory provides a baseline from which to measure his disciples' diversions, omissions, and innovations. Fourierism's transplantation to America, moreover, began not with dry translations but with the colorful European experience of the American Albert Brisbane. That Brisbane and ultimately many antebellum Americans adopted Fourier's ideas suggests a convergence of feeling among reformers on both sides of the Atlantic in the middle third of the nineteenth century: a common sense of disorientation induced by rapid social change combined with a romantic belief in infinite human possibility. Over time, Fourierist movements on the two continents took on different emphases and had essentially separate histories, but they grew from shared feelings, assumptions, and language. At points they even borrowed ideas and strategies from each other. Fourier's theory and the movement his French followers created formed an essential background to American Fourierism and continued to influence its history in the 1840s.

Fourier and His Theory

Dining in a Parisian restaurant in the 1790s, Charles Fourier was aghast that an apple cost fourteen sous, the price of a hundred apples in the countryside. From that moment, he later testified, he began to analyze the evils of the contemporary economy and to plot its overthrow. The apple became one of four that changed the course of history: "Two were famous by the disasters they caused, those of Adam and of Paris, and

15

two by services rendered to mankind, Newton's and my own," Fourier boasted. If Adam's apple abruptly ended the Edenic phase of human existence and Paris's introduced total warfare to Western civilization, Fourier's was designed to propel humanity to a new golden age, a millennial paradise. And while Newton had determined the laws of gravitational attraction, Fourier was the first to discover the law of "passional attraction," which would "guide the human race to opulence, sensual pleasures, to the unity of the globe."[2]

The apple episode, one of several anecdotes Fourier used to explain how his theorizing began, captured the essence of his philosophical mission: its prosaic biographical background, its key elements, and its almost unbelievably daring scope. The "theory of universal unity" originated in his disillusionment with the "crimes" of competitive capitalism, centered in his theory of the passions (modeled on Newton), and culminated in his vision of a new world that would recapture the abundance and innocence of Eden.

Little in Fourier's background presaged such intellectual ambitions.[3] The son of a successful clothing merchant in the town of Besançon, Fourier was expected to continue the family business and live a quiet and moderately prosperous provincial existence. But the upheaval of the French Revolution, during which most of his inheritance was requisitioned, and his own sensitive and obsessively curious personality prevented such a life. Instead, he shifted from job to job in commercial houses, developing an intense hatred for economic competition, earning just enough money to support his modest but precise habits and to allow a few hours to write each day. His formal education had stopped at age sixteen, when he graduated from the Collège de Besançon; after that he read haphazardly and sporadically, with the selective but acute memory of an autodidact. In the late 1790s Fourier was regaling public officials with proposals to reform everything from military supply operations to city planning. By 1799 his studies had evolved into a complete theory of psychology and history which, he claimed, solved the riddle of human existence. Four years later he announced in a Lyons journal his discovery of the laws of "universal harmony," and the rest of his life was devoted to elaborating and publicizing this "mathematical theory concerning the destinies of all the globes and their inhabitants"—though few of his contemporaries paid attention.[4]

Despite a mostly solitary existence in hotels and boarding-houses, Fourier seized upon the experiences that came his way and spun theories out of them. Jobs as bookkeeper, clerk, and salesman taught him about the "crimes of commerce." A brief stay in Lyons introduced him to unemployment and mass poverty. A disastrous stint as guardian of three promiscuous nieces taught him the hypocrisy of sentimental love. Daily strolls through Paris boulevards and the Palais Royal conjured up visions of the "unitary architecture" of the future. His life was somewhat more eventful and varied than legend relates, but it requires no sophisticated psychological probing to see that into his writings went hatreds, fantasies, and aspirations that compensated for his dull work, drab lifestyle, and lack of recognition by contemporaries. Embarrassed by his limited education, Fourier compared his humble origins to Christ's and taunted the learned philosophers who had failed to solve humanity's problems in two thousand years of trying. Stung by the neglect of Parisian journals, he named Constantinople the capital of his future world and gave the seat of the French Empire to tiny Nevers. The "attractive labor" in Fourier's ideal community put to shame the oppression and monotony of commercial employment, just as the frantic pace and constant sensual delights of the phalanx were the daydreams of an obsessed and lonely bachelor.[5] Whatever private satisfactions Fourier derived from this kind of sublimation, his condemnation of contemporary society and utopian vision for the future eventually struck a responsive chord in the early industrial age. In the 1830s and 1840s dreamers and dissenters on both sides of the Atlantic, armed with Fourier's theory, rejected liberal capitalism at its takeoff point and championed in its place his "New Industrial World" of justice, harmony, and personal fulfillment.

Fourier's starting point was his critique of "Civilization," his pejorative label for contemporary society.[6] Based upon fraud, waste, and exploitation, the modern social order had created incomparable unhappiness along with unprecedented abundance. Fourier's attack left no stone unturned, surveying dozens of "permanent vices"—from degrading work under the wage system to priestly superstitions to "climatic excesses"— all of which indicated that Civilization was not merely imperfect but totally unacceptable.[7] Such evils Fourier exposed with the contempt of a man not bound by conventional wisdom and determined to lift the veil of smugness and prejudice concealing flagrant wrongs under the rubric of progress. For all its rage, Fourier's critique was animated by no single theme or principle. He condemned particular institutions wherever they were most vulnerable: the "isolated household" for its inefficiency, the bourgeois family for its repressive hypocrisy, philosophers and moralists for their wrongheadedness, the rich for oppressing the poor, and the commercial system for torturing both. It was left to Fourier's disciples to supply the idea of competitive individualism as an organizing principle for this critique. But the increase in coherence meant the loss of Fourier's incredible range and mastery of detail. Pronouncing the entire Catholic Church corrupt and rejecting 400,000 volumes of philosophy and morality as moribund, Fourier could also descend to specific lists of thirty-six kinds of bankruptcy and seventy-six types of cuckoldry in Civilization.[8] It was a sweeping and stunning indictment.

There was still hope for humanity, however, because he saw Civilization as but a transient stage of human history. When he fleshed out his historical viewpoint, Fourier concluded that humankind would evolve through no less than thirty-two phases covering the 80,000-year life span of the globe. Starting in Edenism, human history had developed through

Savagery, Patriarchate, and Barbarism before reaching the "perverse" period of Civilization. Each phase had its own distinct material and ideological features and was particularly marked by the social position given to women. Despite its enslavement of women in monogamy, Civilization was a pivotal period because in it were planted the cooperative seeds that would evolve into Guarantism, Sociantism, and eventually the glorious stage of Harmony, a new golden age that would introduce a 60,000-year period of creativity and happiness. Harmonic society represented the full maturity of the race; it would be so long and happy that Fourier virtually ignored the remaining 10,000 years of decline and regression which, in his historical outline, would mark humanity's return to primeval chaos. In fact, the enchantment of Harmony could last even longer if Civilized society would simply skip the sixth and seventh stages of evolution; to do so, it was necessary only to follow Fourier's blueprint for the establishment of model communities.

The key to these communities, or phalanxes, and the heart of his entire system was Fourier's theory of the passions, the springs of motivation, which he insisted governed all human activity. Despite the historical progression of the race, the passions remained the same everywhere; they were instinctive, not rational; their operation was "the drive given us by nature prior to any reflection."[9] In true Rousseauean fashion Fourier believed that the passions were inherently good and the only constructive and harmonious society one that gratified rather than repressed them. To decipher the passions and to design a society that would allow them full development was to discover the "divine social code" for human happiness. Here was the basis for Fourier's claim to have extended the work of Newton by discovering mathematical laws of human behavior akin to those governing the movements of planets and stars. "Passional attraction" was the human equivalent of gravity; individuals' attractions were "proportional" to their destinies; and the orderly and harmonious Newtonian universe could be duplicated in the social sphere.[10]

There were, according to Fourier, twelve basic passions grouped on three branches of the "passional tree." The "luxurious" passions were the five senses, material cravings that required gratification and refinement: sight, taste, smell, touch, and hearing. The "affective" passions, by contrast, addressed people's social needs: friendship, love, ambition, and familism (or parenthood). The most sophisticated—and most neglected in Civilization—were the "distributive" passions, which regulated all the others: the cabalist or intriguing passion; the butterfly or passion for variety; and the composite, the pure enthusiasm that came from a mixture of physical and spiritual pleasures. The tree's trunk Fourier called "unityism," a synthesis of the twelve passions that could best be described as "universal fellow feeling" or benevolence.[11]

Frustrated and perverted in Civilization, the passions would be allowed full rein in Harmony, where attraction would govern all relations. Fourier's ideal community, housed in an impressive hotellike "phalanstery" set in the pastoral countryside, would contain 1,620 persons, exactly twice the 810 basic personality types Fourier extrapolated from his theory of the passions. Its residents would come from different classes and be rewarded differently according to their labor, capital, and skill; yet the phalanx's abundant resources, guaranteed income, and especially its attractive work arrangements would promote the welfare of all. Phalansterians were to be organized in mathematically arranged groups and series according to their passional makeup. As they moved from activity to activity, individuals would develop their unique talents and replace the competition of Civilization with intertwined interests and fraternal feelings. Even their sexual relations would reconcile complete liberation with a communal ethos: in book passages that his disciples later excised and in manuscripts on the "New Amorous World," which remained unpublished until 1967, Fourier delighted in the degrees of promiscuity to be practiced by phalansterians and the fanciful codes and institutions governing Harmonian love.[12] The phalanx (its unfortunate name evoking military order rather than passional freedom) was Fourier's alternative to a fragmented and repressive Civilization and the building block of the Harmonian world.

Once the example of model phalanxes became irresistible, the planet would be covered with over two million communities whose vast regional associations would supersede current nations. As humans abandoned the destructive ways of Civilization, the earth would return to a fertile and creative equilibrium. Fourier's imagination soared—and his critics snickered—as he predicted that diseases would no longer ravage the population, humans would live for 144 years, Siberians would enjoy an Italian climate, new species of docile animals such as "anti-lions" would help Harmonians cultivate the globe, and—most astonishing of all— human beings would develop long and "infinitely useful" tails.[13] Nor was this the limit of Fourier's investigations and fantasies. His writings include a theory of metempsychosis accounting for the migration of souls between material and "aromal" worlds, adventures in cosmogony describing the copulation of planets, and a science of universal analogy uncovering correspondences between the human passions and the phenomena of nature.

It is evident that Fourier's vast and eccentric system incorporated far more than a vision of ideal society. His followers later pruned his theory to a program for the "organization of labor," with some historical and psychological ideas retained as supporting arguments; Marx and Engels reduced his system to a plan of "utopian socialism." But Fourier intended to unfold a comprehensive science of nature and humanity. In his own words, he sought not only "the future and past destinies of human societies" but "the plans adopted by God . . . including everything from the cosmogony of the universes [sic] and the invisible stars to the most minute alterations of matter in the animal, vegetable, and mineral kingdoms."[14]

Nevertheless, after he moved to Paris in 1822, Fourier ceased to draw from his immense "reservoir of ideas" and instead became increasingly absorbed in the effort to "realize" his social doctrines. After this there were virtually no new scientific probings. His writings were devoted to simplifying the "industrial" part of the theory, presenting it as attractively as possible, and persuading some wealthy official or philanthropist to finance a phalanx experiment. "In essence if not in literal fact," writes his biographer, Jonathan Beecher, "the Fourier of the 1820s and 1830s is the Fourier described in [Pierre Jean de] Béranger's famous anecdote: the man who was so obsessed by his vision that he made a point of returning home every day at noon because that was the hour he had set for the rendezvous with his benefactor."[15]

The Early Years of Fourierism in France

Only near the end of Fourier's life did his publicity achieve notable results. During the 1820s his ideas attracted a small band of provincial devotees, mostly in his native Besançon. Just Muiron, a faithful but plodding government functionary, proselytized for Fourier in the Franche-Comté, and a young widow named Clarisse Vigoreux pledged her sizable fortune to disseminate Fourier's theory. The most important early convert was Victor Considerant, a talented student at the Collège de Besançon and later at the prestigious Ecole Polytechnique, who introduced Fourierist "social science" among his fellows.[16] Yet Fourier's scheme might never have emerged into general public discussion but for two key events of the next decade. The first was the revolution of July 1830, which overthrew the Bourbon King Charles X and gave rise to a general social and political awakening. As the new constitutional monarchy loosened restrictions on the press and public gatherings, republican clubs were revived, industrial workers broke out in strikes and demonstrations, and—most important to utopian theorists—book and journal publishers welcomed writings on the problems of industrialization and urbanization.

The second event had to do with one of the most publicized social theorists during these years, Count Henri de Saint-Simon, Fourier's elder rival and Parisian neighbor. A veteran of Yorktown who abdicated his noble title during the French Revolution, Saint-Simon lived the kind of colorful existence Fourier fantasized about.[17] He passed successively through careers as a military officer, revolutionary politician, financial speculator, and fashionable salon host before retiring to a shabby-genteel life of utopian speculation. By the mid-1820s he was husbanding his small pension in the same dingy neighborhood surrounding the Paris Bourse where Fourier lived. Like Fourier, Saint-Simon was obsessed with a personal mission to reorganize a European society rent by the French and Industrial revolutions. Yet while Marx and Engels later classified him with Fourier and Owen as a "utopian socialist," Saint-Simon promoted no communitarian system. Instead, in his pamphlets and especially his brilliant conversations, he uttered vague but impressive prophecies about the coming new society. Nor was Saint-Simon constant in his enthusiasms. Early in his public life he prodded intellectuals to evolve a universal scientific theory based on the Newtonian model. During the Restoration years he abandoned this project for more practical concerns, promoting plans for an industrial society led by an entrepreneurial and artisan elite dedicated to maximum productivity. This position made him an unofficial apologist for the rising liberal bourgeoisie and was the basis for the profound influence his ideas later exerted on the banking, railroad, and canal projects of the Second Empire. Toward the end of his life Saint-Simon's thought was increasingly colored by romantic and humanitarian sentiments. He appealed for a loving "New Christianity" to join the special talents of scientists, workers, and artists into an organic society that would reconcile all classes and improve especially the condition of the poorest.

It was this last aspect that attracted a brilliant young group of disciples to Saint-Simon's side before his death in 1825. Many were graduates of the Ecole Polytechnique who shared the master's faith in the power of science to reorganize society efficiently. But what especially drew them was the promise of brotherly love and social harmony suggested by his "New Christianity." After Saint-Simon's death these disciples developed his ideas on history, industry, and love into a quasi-religious "doctrine" codified in public "sermons" and presented with all the fervor of a religious revival. In December 1829 they officially formed a "church" under the direction of two "supreme fathers," Saint-Amand Bazard and Prosper Enfantin. To bond this hierarchical "family" more closely, the Saint-Simonians soon added other trappings of a sectarian cult: a unique costume (most adepts wore a blue tunic, white trousers, and red vest, symbolizing respectively faith, love, and labor), distinctive rituals, and a separate communal existence.[18]

Contemporary critics mocked the Saint-Simonians' monastic rules and public confessionals; the cultists in fact gave satirists a field day by embarking on a futile comic-opera search for a "Female Messiah" in the Middle East. But the Saint-Simonian religion of selflessness evoked a deep response among the restless young students and professionals whose liberal ideas and social conscience began to stir under the restored European monarchies of the 1830s. Not only in France but in Belgium, Germany, and even Russia the Saint-Simonians' romantic idealism awakened hopes that became the basis for liberal political movements and social reform enthusiasms.[19] Among Americans their influence was less direct but still significant. One New Yorker captivated by their passionate humanitarianism testified that "for twenty years I have been a Saint-Simonian in my inner being." In Boston the crusading intellectual Orestes Brownson introduced Saint-Simonian philosophical concepts to his Transcendentalist friends.[20] Most important, as we will shortly see, the founder

of American Fourierism launched his reform career by converting to the
Saint-Simonian religion.

However influential, the Saint-Simonian sect was a fragile creation,
wracked by internal disputes and besieged by governmental repression.
As early as the middle of 1831 there were signs that the group was in
trouble. Its funds were short, and its journal, *Le Globe,* faced termination.
In the months that followed, disputes over religion and authority shat-
tered the movement. Under the influence of the charismatic Enfantin
many Saint-Simonians began to preach an androgynous deity and advocate the "rehabilitation of the flesh" through sexual freedom. In November 1831 Bazard withdrew in anger from the sect, and Enfantin led the
faithful remnant to Ménilmontant, outside Paris, where he set up a
regime of manual labor and monastic isolation. Meanwhile, the French
government's harassment of the sect culminated in a bizarre trial and
stiff sentences for Enfantin and Michel Chevalier.[21]

From the Fourierists' point of view, the schism in Saint-Simonian ranks
was the second crucial development of the early 1830s. Fourier himself
had launched vehement attacks on the Saint-Simonians, accusing them
on one hand of propagating a phony new religion and on the other
of plagiarizing key elements of his new science. These assaults mainly
revealed Fourier's paranoid delusions and his misunderstanding of Saint-
Simonian ideas; fortunately for him, they had little negative impact on
Saint-Simon's followers.[22] Instead, several disaffected Saint-Simonians
who had heard of Fourier through his polemics now gave his works a
careful reading, and soon many became converts. The first and most
important was the ebullient, independent-minded Jules Lechevalier, who
within weeks of his apostasy began distilling Fourier's theory into the sort
of clear and engaging summary the master himself was incapable of.
Lechevalier's lectures and writings won a hearing for Fourierism among
the respectable public, and his example paved the way for other Saint-
Simonians—most notably, Abel Transon, Hippolyte Renaud, Amédée
Paget, and Charles Pellarin—to join the Fourierist camp. These converts
professed to find in Fourier's theory the concrete plan that could fulfill
Saint-Simon's vague promises of noble work, personal freedom, and class
harmony.[23]

Fortified by the influx of energetic and talented Saint-Simonians, the
Fourierists founded their first journal, the weekly *Phalanstère,* and began
a serious propaganda campaign. To the disciples, a key prerequisite for
success was to select from Fourier's vast and eccentric storehouse of ideas
a coherent and practical "social science," while expunging or otherwise
dissociating their movement from more controversial aspects. In the
Phalanstère and numerous tracts and lectures, French Fourierists set
about creating a respectable reform creed. Such extravagances as plane-
tary copulation, human tails, seas turned to lemonade, and sexual orgies
were subjected to what one Fourierist called a "useful weeding-out" from
the doctrine of association. Not surprisingly, the headstrong theorist of

"universal unity" protested against attempts to segment his theory or water it down for bourgeois audiences. Fourier labeled Pellarin and other followers "bumbling friends who are assassinating me while they think they are increasing my reputation." There were additional sources of tension between master and disciples. Fourier was a crude polemicist who mocked his critics, used savage invective, and perplexed readers with an ever shifting display of topics, tables, and new terminology, whereas his disciples tried to form alliances with other liberals and win audiences through appeals to their sympathy as well as clear and reasoned persuasion. In temperament and ideological bent, the crotchety Enlightenment philosopher and his young romantic followers coexisted uneasily. Beneath their exasperated complaints about Fourier's behavior one can sense the conviction that their master had outlived his usefulness.[24]

One thing Fourier and his disciples agreed upon was the necessity of founding a trial phalanx. In the heady days of the early 1830s they were as intent on "realizing" the doctrine as on propagating it through journals. An opportunity came almost immediately, when in the fall of 1832 Alexandre-François Baudet-Dulary, a deputy from Seine-et-Oise, teamed with a landowning friend to offer the Fourierists a farm of about 750 acres in the commune of Condé-sur-Vesgre, thirty-five miles southwest of Paris. The "Societary Colony" at Condé, organized as a joint-stock company, was to be capitalized at 1,200,000 francs and accommodate six hundred Fourierists. Land was cleared and buildings were begun by an advance crew; but poor soil, delays in construction, and especially a dramatic shortfall of capital forced a premature end to the experiment, despite the commitment of Baudet-Dulary, who dug deeply into his personal fortune to keep operations going. Plans were laid to transform the site into a phalanx housing two hundred children, but when even this scaled-down experiment proved beyond the disciples' financial reach, Baudet-Dulary officially dissolved the company in 1836.[25]

Fourier at first approved the venture at Condé, but as its prospects dimmed, he complained that the leaders were incompetent and divorced the community from his theory. After Condé, Fourier and his immediate circle of disciples became wary of hastily organized experiments—so wary that the issue of trial phalanxes provoked a serious rift among French Fourierists. Several utopians from the provinces accused the Paris Fourierists, led by Considerant, of being elitists more interested in refining doctrine and scoring points among intellectuals than in organizing an effective social movement or undertaking practical experiments. (A strikingly similar tension between cosmopolitan theorists and pragmatic provincials would later haunt the American Fourierist movement.) These dissidents were dealt a severe blow when the aged Fourier threw his support to Considerant and the "orthodox" theorists. Nevertheless, in 1837, the year of Fourier's death, the dissidents began publishing their own journal, the *Correspondance Harmonienne*, and they and other scattered enthusiasts continued to propose new communitarian projects.[26]

In 1841 the English philanthropist Arthur Young, already a patron of French Fourierist publications, purchased the medieval abbey at Citeaux and attempted, against Considerant's advice, to transform it into a phalanx. The community disbanded three years later.[27] Two other experimental French phalanxes, one in Brazil (1841–45) and one in Algeria (1846), met similar fates. All three attempts—which, along with Condé, were the only French phalanxes prior to 1855—were disavowed by the official Fourierist school centered in Paris.[28]

After the mid-1830s this Ecole Sociétaire, headed by Fourier's anointed successor Considerant, settled down to an extended period of propaganda and fund raising. Considerant and his circle became involved in reformist political agitation under the regime of Louis Philippe, and their newspaper, the *Démocratie Pacifique,* printed several phalanx proposals. But in the main the Paris leaders continued to elaborate Fourierist doctrine and to await the day when greater popularity and ample funds would permit a "true" phalanx attempt.

In all this French Fourierist agitating and organizing, there was little thought of the United States, either as target for proselytizing or as potential site for a Fourierist colony. During the first two decades of their movement neither Fourier nor his closest disciples were seriously interested in America. It is true that Fourier did occasionally express the hope that the United States would initiate a trial phalanx. In 1823, as part of his campaign to find a "candidate," he sent a copy of his treatise on "domestic and agricultural association" to the American consul in Paris. Fourier always tried to engage potential backers' self-interest; in this case he suggested that a model community would attract the American Indians to agriculture and thus prove the best way to pacify them. (The consul merely forwarded the book to a friend, surmising that the work was "either a genuine curiosity or the emanation of a disturbed brain.") Again in 1835 Fourier hinted with tantalizing off-handedness that his system could prevent a sectional split between North and South and reduce the threat of a slave uprising in the United States.[29] There is no evidence, however, that he went out of his way to study life in America or that he seriously considered his theory's prospects there. Unlike many European contemporaries, Fourier cherished no conception of the New World as the hope of the future, a "new golden land" upon which an ideal society might easily be planted. One of the great ironies of his life was that this "universal" theoretician was steadfastly nationalistic at the core, taking on traditional French loyalties and hatreds (such as Anglophobia and anti-Semitism) and designing his proposed phalanstery to look like Versailles. Whatever his motives, Fourier never replied to American disciples' repeated urgings that he—the "new Columbus," they called him—personally cross the Atlantic to direct a phalanx experiment in the hospitable New World. He died in 1837 without ever setting foot on American soil, the Newton but not the Columbus of the new social world.[30]

Fourier's French disciples were somewhat more international in outlook, but the Ecole Sociétaire took no initiative in transmitting the master's ideas to an American audience. Fourierism, as Arthur Bestor first noted, was not exported by Frenchmen but imported by Americans.[31] The circumstances that led to its phenomenal but brief popularity in the United States had their roots in native developments, and the job of introducing Fourierism and adapting it to the American scene was undertaken by a small but remarkable group of American disciples.

The Odyssey of Albert Brisbane

The disciple responsible for bringing Fourier's theory across the Atlantic was Albert Brisbane, an abrasive but determined American student who encountered Fourier in France in 1832. In many respects, Brisbane was a poor candidate for reform leadership. The idealistic son of a wealthy New York merchant and landowner, he was devoted to communitarianism but reluctant to spend his inheritance on it, and he was hopelessly impractical as a community organizer. Walt Whitman, who encountered Brisbane often on the street, described him as a comic Dickensian reformer: "A tall, slender man, round-shouldered, chin stuck out, deep-set eyes, sack-coat. His step is quick, and his arms swing awkwardly, as if he were trying to knock his elbows together behind him. . . . Somehow or other he always looks as if he were attempting to think out some problem a little too hard for him."[32]

Intellectually ambitious but incapable of profundity, Brisbane was by temperament a disciple. His version of Fourier was glib and doctrinaire to the point of irritating many colleagues. Yet to a remarkable extent Brisbane overcame these deficiencies with his tremendous energy and perseverance. Preaching Fourier to anyone who would listen, whether fellow passengers on a steamboat or Concord philosophers in their studies, he grew in stature under the master's spell and, for all his impracticality, proved shrewd enough to adjust Fourierism persuasively to American conditions and tastes.

Until recently, little was known about Brisbane's early development outside of a problematic autobiography dictated to his wife when he was in his seventies. By then he was more prone than ever to self-serving memory lapses, wild exaggerations, and rigid categorical thinking. In this narrative the aging utopian conceived his development as a schematic "mental biography," in which the young student of life discovers one by one the leading ideas of Fourierism. Reality is rarely so neat. The actual record of the 1830s, discovered in Brisbane's correspondence and travel diaries, tells a more untidy story of intellectual meandering, identity struggles, and ultimate fulfillment in the embrace of Fourierism as doctrine and lifestyle. The documents also show that for all his doctrinaire rationalism, Brisbane first came to utopian socialism through the essentially emotional lure of Saint-Simonianism.[33]

Brisbane's early years were spent in the small town of Batavia in western New York. His father, once an agent of the Holland Land Company and later Batavia's sole storekeeper, accumulated property with such skill that when he died in 1851, he beqeathed an estate of almost half a million dollars to his two sons. Brisbane's mother was an amateur scholar who thrilled the boys with astronomical mysteries and vivid accounts of ancient civilizations. This family background was to leave important traces on Brisbane's later life: a habit of independence from worldly cares, a passion for speculation ("both mental and monetary," T. D. Seymour Bassett shrewdly notes), and indifference to organized religion: neither parent was a church member, and his father was an active skeptic.[34] Yet because he matured far from home, the channels in which Brisbane's thinking flowed were alien to Batavia. While people back home were being "burned over" by Finneyite revivalism, this native son was on a long journey toward a foreign, secular reform creed.

The starting point for Brisbane's intellectual manhood was New York City, where his father sent him in 1826, at the age of seventeen, for schooling. With the encouragement of Jean Manesca, the elderly refugee from the Santo Domingo slave insurrections who was his language teacher, the young Brisbane absorbed the spirit of the Enlightenment and pledged to forsake "finite" and mundane matters for scientific knowledge. "The frenzy to KNOW," he later recalled, "had now taken complete possession of me."[35]

It sent him to Europe. Armed with money, ambition, and the mandate of the philosophes, Brisbane sailed from New York in 1828 to begin what amounted to six years of study and travel. To study at the University of Berlin and to travel through Asia Minor were rare occurrences for Jacksonian Americans.[36] The range of acquaintances Brisbane made during his tour was impressive: it included Felix Mendelssohn, Franz Liszt, Heinrich Heine, the eminent German professors Eduard Gans and Karl Ludwig Michelet, James Fenimore Cooper, and the American sculptor Horatio Greenough. But what gave Brisbane's journey coherence was his obsessive search for an intellectual system to engage his energies. In his ready though superficial absorption of ideas, Brisbane whirled through several of the major trends in contemporary social philosophy (his friend Greenough aptly called him a metaphysical "windmill")[37] before coming to rest in Fourierism. At the end of his quest, like important French colleagues, Brisbane switched from Saint-Simonianism to Fourier's theory. More broadly, his journey from philosophical idealism through what David O. Evans has called "social romanticism" to Fourierist "social science" encapsulated the evolution of a generation of utopian reformers on both sides of the Atlantic.[38]

Brisbane began his search at the Sorbonne lectures of Victor Cousin, whose eclectic philosophy was to become a conduit of German thought to American Transcendentalists. Though attracted by Cousin's promise of bringing past systems of thought into harmonic unity, Brisbane soon felt that he was dealing with an abridged translation instead of the rich and complex original.[39] After learning German, he enrolled at the University of Berlin to hear the great Hegel in person. In his autobiography Brisbane claimed that his Berlin studies failed to satisfy his consuming passion for a progressive philosophy consonant with "the democratic institutions of a republic," so "putting down to the credit side a melancholy row of zeroes," he turned his thoughts to a new move. In actuality, when Brisbane left Berlin in the spring of 1830, he was very much a Hegelian disciple, admittedly "obsessed" with the idea of universal principles in history. During the travels that followed he noted in Hegelian fashion that each "civilization" has its own "ideas," which determine its character and act themselves out over time.[40]

Gradually, however, Hegel's airy abstractions were eclipsed by direct and often sobering experience. After departing from Berlin, Brisbane headed eastward to Vienna, Trieste, and eventually Constantinople, traveling partway on horseback. He returned by way of Greece, where he spent four months surveying the ravages of its recent war of independence, then proceeded to Malta, Sicily, Naples, Rome, and finally over the Alps to Paris in the early summer of 1831. The young American had seen a remarkable variety of social and geographical conditions. In his diary he noted that preoccupation with "exterior" social and economic details had dimmed his fascination with metaphysics. More than that, the encounter with desperate poverty was leading him toward social reform. Brisbane's faith in republicanism remained intact, but his attention was diverted from the political to the social struggle. As he saw Greeks and Turks scraping a living with rudimentary tools from a poor soil, Brisbane concluded that the masses must have material needs satisfied before one could expect them to be politically or intellectually sophisticated. In the developing notion that politics and culture might be "of secondary importance" to socioeconomic phenomena lay an important seed of his later reform thought.[41]

The student's education in Mediterranean Europe had a sexual dimension as well, though his autobiography is understandably silent on the subject. In Paris and perhaps Berlin the young American had embarked on sexual affairs whose memories lingered in the guilt-inspired reflections of his diary. When his ship was quarantined at Malta, he "sent a man off to see about getting a girl." In Sicily he successfully propositioned his chambermaid and other young women. By then, though all of twenty-one, Brisbane could write with affected world-weariness: "I never slept with a woman, whom I could support afterwards." Rationalizing such disdainful promiscuity, Brisbane concluded that commitment to a life of reflection and reform put him above "finite" and fleeting social conventions. The disinterested reformer could enjoy a liberated moral code but must avoid entangling romantic attachments and "remain alone, without feelings, or cares of a personal nature."[42] Brisbane's impersonal devotion to progress belied—and legitimated—his opportunistic dealings with fellow reformers and sleazy manipulations in private life. The pattern of casually taking on women as concubines and then dropping them when the relationship no longer suited him continued through his adulthood, though it did not become public knowledge during the antebellum Fourierist movement.[43] His pronounced "butterfly" passion for changing sexual partners was the unrevealed side of his attraction to Fourier's scheme.

The next step to a reform career came as Brisbane was returning to Paris in the summer of 1831. In Holland he encountered Saint-Simon's theories through a book by the disciples; by the time he reached the French capital, the Saint-Simonians were lecturing before large public audiences and running their own newspaper. There he heard a full exposition from Enfantin, Charles Duveyrier, and his friend from student days in Berlin, Jules Lechevalier. Brisbane attended their soirees, heard their professions of faith, and even witnessed the first Saint-Simonian wedding. Several of the Saint-Simonians' absorptions appealed to Brisbane: their promotion of machinery, their interest in reforming sexual relations, and the idea of a ruling scientific elite. But what attracted him most was the notion of a new order based on an ethic of "social love." The incessant theorizer was won to reform through the emotions rather than the intellect. Brisbane thrilled to the idea that voluntary reform could bring "an immense social change." He agreed that "the actual social system tends to organize hatred, and distrust in society instead of love and confidence" and was impressed by way the Saint-Simonians adopted the rhetoric and form of the family to counter such trends. Here was a secular religion to replace an outworn Christianity and inspire the devotion needed to transform the globe. In his initial enthusiasm Brisbane sent Saint-Simonian books to his tutor Manesca, who in turn urged him to bring the cause to the New World—an idea that especially "excited" the ambitious young American.[44]

Saint-Simonianism challenged his devotion to Hegel and metaphysics. Philosophy no longer seemed "the most noble science" but a lifeless self-absorption; a philosopher was like "a boy, who having nothing to do sucks his thumb." Gone, too, was Brisbane's confidence in the liberal program of evolutionary political progress. The idea of a republic seemed "small and insignificant" next to the Saint-Simonian future; besides, Saint-Simon confirmed his impression from Mediterranean Europe that "the industrial activity of men" rather than politics controlled the conditions of life. The whole social organization needed to be changed.[45]

Old ideas were not easy to give up, especially for a reform "religion" that required full commitment and struck many as absurd. For a time Brisbane wondered aloud whether he had "the stuff in me to join the S.S. with heart, and soul," and he fretted over losing his comfortable independence. But when he returned to Berlin in the fall of 1831, he aired the new doctrine among German friends. In Paris self-doubt had held him back from joining the Saint-Simonian "family"; in Berlin he found it easier to profess the new gospel without formal commitment and beyond the ears of the doctrine's guardians.[46] During the winter of 1831–32 Brisbane succeeded in bringing Saint-Simonianism to the circle of his friend Rahel Varnhagen von Ense, who presided over the most famous of the Jewish salons around which Berlin's intellectual life revolved during the Old Regime. Frau Varnhagen acknowledged the persuasiveness of the "young but not handsome" American and told Heinrich Heine that Saint-Simonian writings had become her "nourishment, conversation, occupation." From Paris the Saint-Simonian Michel Chevalier congratulated Brisbane on his important converts.[47]

To Brisbane it was now clear that "the highest science is the social science" and implementing it "the highest object, which can be given the activity and efforts of the individual." But was Saint-Simon's the right social science to champion? In Berlin, Brisbane received reports of the emerging schism in Saint-Simonian ranks. At first, despite misgivings about Enfantin's authoritarian rule and the school's artificial "church," Brisbane believed the quarrel "stupid" and urged conciliation in his letters.[48] But as the infighting continued, the key event turning him from the Saint-Simonians was probably the withdrawal of his friend Lechevalier in November 1831, following the split between Bazard and Enfantin.[49]

For Brisbane as for others, the collapse of Saint-Simonianism left an opening for Fourier's theory to fill. Brisbane's autobiography tells dramatically how this happened:

> In my letters to Lechevalier I had frequently requested him to send me all that was published on social ideas in Paris. . . . I had been in Berlin about three months when there arrived one day a package containing two large volumes. On opening one of the volumes I read on the title page: "*L'Association Domestique-Agricole, par Charles Fourier.*" . . . I took up the first volume carelessly and began running over the introduction; soon I came to the following phrase, printed in large type: "Attractive Industry." Those two words made on me an indescribable impression. In the few lines of explanation that followed, I saw that the author conceived the idea of so organizing human labor as to dignify it and render it attractive. I sprang to my feet, threw down the book, and began pacing the floor in a tumult of emotion. I was carried away into a world of new conceptions.[50]

Brisbane had heard of Fourier in Paris, through his attacks on the Saint-Simonians during 1831, but did not read his works until Lechevalier sent them the following spring.[51] "I swear to you," he wrote Lechevalier halfway through the first volume, "that I am astonished by this book and have the greatest admiration for it. What a mind that man must have!" Fourier's "profound truths" would capture the public's imagination before long, and Brisbane himself would return to Paris in November to study them in depth. He had relinquished republicanism and backward-looking German philosophy for the new French socialism: "I fully accept this world of new ideas which is emerging in France, and the grand and

glorious future it promises. We must do away with present society in all
its aspects. I renounce liberalism, and republicanism . . . and German
science."[52] When Brisbane reached Paris, he avoided the Saint-Simonian
enclave at Ménilmontant and went instead to the office of the Fourierist
press. There Lechevalier introduced him to Charles Fourier.

Like anyone who approached the austere and paranoid Fourier, Brisbane was initially received with a stately reserve bordering on aloofness.
Those seeking enlightenment were referred to Fourier's books rather
than given explanations. "He is a dry man," Brisbane reported to friends
in Berlin, "uncommunicative, defiant, always fearful that others will plagiarize his work." And "during the . . . three years of my association with
Fourier," he later recalled, "I never saw him smile." But the young
American used a characteristically blunt device to win Fourier over: he
offered the shabby socialist five francs an hour to tutor him in the theory.
For the next month and a half Brisbane received two hour-long lessons
a week on this basis. He had freer access to the master than most of the
French followers, and though all his doubts were not yet put to rest, he
was "overwhelmed" by Fourier's cosmic theories. He had become the first
American disciple.[53]

The discovery of Fourierism culminated the young Brisbane's search
for the key to human destiny. Fourier's conviction that the new society
had to conform to the essentially good nature of man turned Enlightenment psychology into a positive social plan. The Frenchman's system was
as vast as Hegel's but directed toward the future rather than the status
quo. In contrast to Saint-Simon's inspiring but vague religion, here was
a scientific formula for the new order as exact as the laws of the universe.
In Fourier's idea of "attractive industry" Brisbane saw the working principle of the productive and harmonious new world the Saint-Simonians
were predicting.[54] To Brisbane's mind, Fourier's theory had brought
Enlightenment science, Hegelian order, and Saint-Simonian love into a
grand and inspiring utopian synthesis. In his search for a usable ideal,
Brisbane had encountered a perfectionist religion; now he found in
Fourierism a "science" with which to implement it. He could not know it
at the time, but his conversion would soon be reenacted by many reform-
minded Americans back home.

Beginnings of American Fourierism

By 1833 Brisbane had decided that Fourierism had given him his
life's work. His "sole thought," he wrote his old friend Manesca, was to
"transmit the thought of Charles Fourier to my countrymen."[55] For the
next year and a half he remained in Paris, studying Fourier's writings
and discussing the master's theories with Lechevalier, Considerant, and
other members of the Fourierist school. Finally, in the spring of 1834,
Brisbane returned to upstate New York, proclaiming to Fourier his inten-

tion to translate the master's works, give lectures, and start a Fourierist periodical. Yet it was not until 1839, five years later, that his public promotion of Fourierism actually began. His autobiography attributes this delay to illness, but the same account has him holding currency reform meetings during those years.[56] Marital problems may have held him up: Brisbane returned from Europe with a Bavarian bride, a reputed countess named Adèle le Brun whom he had met in 1831 and married two years later. For some reason—perhaps because his family disapproved of her Catholicism—they separated, and she returned to Europe in 1838.[57]

The most likely reason for the delay, however, was that Brisbane was immersed in land speculation for the Fourierist cause. In 1836 he confided to Fourier that he hoped to earn in two or three years the cost of an entire phalanx; to Considerant he predicted enough profits to set up ten journals and put fifty men to work: "I am determined . . . to individually realize Fourier's system. Instead of asking for subscriptions let us ourselves earn the necessary funds. Fourier would do the same if he had come to this country."[58] Apparently Brisbane conceived of himself as the rich "candidate" Fourier had been searching for among the princes and merchants of Europe, a philanthropist who would endow the first trial phalanx.[59]

The enormous sums he promised never materialized. More likely than not, the Panic of 1837 burst Brisbane's speculative bubble, as it did many others. Extravagant financial visions periodically reappeared to him during his reform career—when his father died in 1851, Brisbane invested his inheritance heavily in railroads, gold, and canals with the idea of financing publications and phalanxes—but for the time being he retreated to the modest but more advisable plan of translating Fourier's works and initiating a journal.[60] The pressure of the economic crisis may well have been responsible for Fourierism's introduction in America as a grassroots reform rather than a philanthropic movement.

While Brisbane schemed, his old tutor Jean Manesca took the first halting steps to spread Fourier's doctrines in the United States. In 1833 Brisbane had sent the master's works across the Atlantic to Manesca, who shortly declared allegiance to these "magnificent conceptions" in a letter to Fourier. Within a couple of years Manesca in turn converted two French-Americans, Frederick Grain and Frederick Gauvain, to the cause. This small group of New Yorkers issued a prospectus for a Fourierist journal—without success—and urged Fourier to come and assess the prospects for an American trial phalanx.[61] In the fall of 1837, their numbers augmented by a few other transplanted Europeans, they succeeded in forming a Fourier (or "Fourienne") Society of New York, with the aged Manesca as secretary. The society published the first installment of *Two Essays on the Social System of Charles Fourier* (1838), but neither their meetings nor this pamphlet attracted much attention. When Manesca died in September 1838, a new secretary, Charles J. Hempel, was duly elected, but New York Fourierism continued to occupy a marginal and precarious status.[62]

In 1839 Brisbane was finally ready to begin his propaganda campaign. He had in mind a broad appeal to the American public, not simply to French-speaking enclaves or prominent philanthropists. He believed, as he told French Fourierists, that America was destined to realize the first successful phalanx, and he intended to pave the way with lectures, translations of Fourier's works, and a popular journal. His first step was to provide a clear and substantial summary of Fourier's ideas. In the early autumn of 1840 he published the *Social Destiny of Man; or, Association and Reorganization of Industry*, a 480-page exposition, half the text translated from Fourier's writings and the other half his own original elaborations and applications.[63] It was the most complete and authoritative account of Fourierism to appear in English during the 1840s. *Social Destiny* was widely noticed in American periodicals, and although it was difficult to digest, its influence grew as those drawn to Fourierism through lectures and newspaper columns sought deeper enlightenment. Brisbane himself peddled the book avidly, leaving copies with prominent Americans such as Ralph Waldo Emerson and Nicholas Biddle (the former director of the National Bank) and discussing its contents with Orestes Brownson and John C. Calhoun.[64] His efforts prompted several reviews of the book and enabled him to place additional articles on Fourierism in such respected magazines as the *Democratic Review*, Brownson's *Boston Quarterly Review*, and the Transcendentalist *Dial*.[65]

Brisbane's plan to publish a periodical took longer to reach fruition but eventually became the key to his success. At the celebration of Fourier's birthday in New York in April 1839, Brisbane was introduced as the master's "personal friend" and early disciple, and the Fourienne Society announced its intention to found an English-language journal that year. When this project failed, Brisbane transferred his efforts to his native western New York. There he persuaded a couple of converts, the Buffalo sarsaparilla manufacturer C. C. Bristol and a young man named Charles Drake Ferris, to launch a weekly journal. In the fall of 1840 *The Phalanx* appeared (not to be confused with the later semimonthly). It was the first American Fourierist periodical, but it lasted a mere six weeks before Brisbane and Bristol had to withdraw their backing.[66]

In the meantime, Brisbane made his most important contact in the journalistic world: the colorful reform editor Horace Greeley, who was then just beginning his newspaper career. As editor of the weekly *New Yorker*, Greeley had reviewed Brisbane's book, and soon thereafter the two began a personal acquaintance that resulted in Greeley's increasing adoption of Fourierist views. At the end of January 1841, Greeley's printing office issued a new Fourierist periodical. *The Future*, "Devoted to the Cause of Association and a Reorganization of Society," was endorsed by Greeley and written largely by Brisbane. The paper lasted only eight issues, most of them bunched in June and July 1841, but it had two important results: through it Brisbane was able to revive the New York Fourier group, and, more important, it cemented the Brisbane-Greeley journalistic alliance. Late that spring *The Future* announced the inauguration of weekly Fourierist meetings and lectures; at their culmination in June the Fourienne Society was reorganized as the Fourier Association of the City of New York. Its list of officers, which included Thomas Whitley, Osborne Macdaniel, and Edward Giles—all to become veteran Fourierist publicists or community members—indicates that Brisbane had moved beyond local French-speaking circles and recruited committed American-born reformers and professionals. A crucial step in the Americanization of Fourierism had been taken.[67]

When *The Future* was about to be discontinued, the Fourier Association urged Brisbane to secure a daily newspaper column for the cause, and he turned once again to Greeley—with spectacular results. In March 1842 Greeley allowed Brisbane to purchase a front-page column in his new daily paper, the *New York Tribune* for $500. It was an independent podium from which to expound Fourier's theory every day (the column's editorship was clearly stated to be "distinct from that of The Tribune")—not only an arrangement unprecedented in American journalism but, as Arthur Bestor noted, "a magnificent opportunity" to present Fourier's doctrine to a sympathetic but as yet uninformed audience. Brisbane took full advantage of his chance. Dropping the long-winded expositions of Fourier's theory that bloated *Social Destiny* and even *The Future,* he wrote succinct and varied columns that related Fourierism to American traditions and contemporary reform movements, outlined its practical arrangements, and reported on Fourierist meetings and conventions in the United States and France. As Greeley's penny daily grew in circulation and his *Weekly Tribune* reprinted the columns for out-of-town readers, Brisbane was able to reach thousands of reform-minded Americans throughout the northern states frequently and inexpensively. Running from March 1842 to September 1843 and quoted by more than forty other newspapers, the *Tribune* column—titled "Association; or, Principles of a True Organization of Society"—was an extremely effective propaganda weapon.[68] Brisbane further expanded its audience by combining several columns into a pamphlet, *A Concise Exposition of the Practical Part of Fourier's Social Science,* which sold 10,000 copies, more than any other Fourierist publication in America.[69]

By the time the subsidized column ended, Greeley and the *Tribune* had been won completely to Fourierism, and Brisbane's publicity was sparking a burgeoning American Fourierist movement. His lectures locally and in upstate New York, announced in the *Tribune,* attracted large audiences. A converted band of Brooklyn mechanics became the first Americans to organize a miniature phalanx. As popular enthusiasm spread to New England, western New York, and the Ohio Valley, local societies disseminated Fourier's ideas, called regional conventions, and planned new communities. Enough support existed by October 1843 for Brisbane to found an exclusively Fourierist periodical, *The Phalanx*, which was to endure in various forms for six years as the chief organ of a national Fourierist movement.

Brisbane's skill was a crucial factor in the rise of American Fourierism, but his propaganda, however well-conceived and widely dispersed, could not have attracted such attention had not the ideas he imported resonated with contemporary social trends and intellectual currents. The awkward vocabulary and fantastic claims of Fourierism won a hearing because they addressed the needs and aspirations of many antebellum Americans. The next two chapters attempt to understand this resonance by examining the social and intellectual climate that led prominent reformers as well as ordinary farmers, mechanics, and businessmen to welcome the strange doctrine Albert Brisbane had brought back from France.

2

Apostles of Association

It was only appropriate that Brisbane, the "first apostle" of American Fourierism, recruited eleven others to spread the new gospel.[1] The chief proponents of the Fourierist doctrine of "Association" included four New Yorkers (Brisbane, Greeley, Osborne Macdaniel, and Parke Godwin) and eight men associated with Brook Farm in Massachusetts: Transcendentalist ministers George Ripley, William Henry Channing, and John Dwight; the efficient Charles Dana and the mystical Marx Edgeworth Lazarus; labor activist Lewis Ryckman; and itinerant lecturers John Orvis and John Allen. The writings and speeches of these twelve kept Fourierism in the reform spotlight; their decisions shaped movement policy, and their endorsement lent intellectual prestige to the cause.

The conversion of influential intellectual figures accentuates important reverberations between utopian socialism and prevailing American modes of thought. Specifically, Greeley's and Godwin's attraction indicates that Fourierism and American political ideologies had significant affinities, and the Brook Farmers' adoption of Fourierism precipitated one of the most interesting ideological experiments of the nineteenth century: the joining of American Transcendentalism and European utopian socialism in a communal venture. The apostles' careers illustrate that reform ideas firmly embedded in antebellum culture had the potential—given the right stimuli—to reach out to new theories and methods. Starting out from the perspectives of Transcendentalism, American politics, and Christian reform, these writers shared a strain of utopianism—belief in human perfectibility, romantic faith in brotherhood, and confidence that a natural order of society could reconcile intense individual expression with strong communal values—which pushed them toward communitarian socialism. Fourierism won their allegiance because it clarified and extended tendencies already in their minds; at the same time, the

35

version of Fourierism each professed was colored by the rhetoric and the ideals he brought to it. In this way as in others, American Fourierism issued from an ongoing dialogue between imported doctrine and native needs and sensibilities.

Horace Greeley: Association and the Whigs

The twentieth century has not treated Horace Greeley kindly. The most influential journalist of the antebellum era and a cultural hero to many contemporaries, Greeley is now remembered condescendingly as a fuzzy-minded crusader and comic-tragic presidential candidate. His best biographer, Glyndon Van Deusen, finds him impractical and contradictory, as intellectually disheveled as his trademark white coat and wispy hair. Greeley's support for Fourierism is especially good grist for this critical mill: unable to see how utopian socialism squared with Greeley's other allegiances, exasperated commentators have interpreted it variously as a political gambit, a puzzling foray into radicalism, a flight of sentimental escapism, or simply another example of personal eccentricity.[2] Yet Greeley was a serious and practical man who, despite an immersion in three decades of daily journalism, showed a determined consistency in his political and intellectual convictions.

Certainly there can be no doubting his commitment to Association. In addition to publishing Brisbane, Greeley's *Tribune* endorsed Fourierism editorially, constantly defended it against critics, and printed news of Fourierist meetings and community experiments. Greeley frequently attended Fourierist conventions, served as president of the national organization, and guided the founding of several phalanxes. Always generous with his money, he invested thousands of dollars in four communities—the Sylvania Association, the Clermont Phalanx, Brook Farm, and the North American Phalanx—losing all he contributed in every case but one. In the late 1840s he used his considerable prestige among workingmen to promote Fourierist cooperatives. Brisbane was not far from the truth when he testified that Greeley "has done for us what we never could have done. He has created the cause on this continent."[3]

The best way to view Greeley's Fourierism is as a communitarian complement to the economic and social beliefs embedded in what one historian calls "the political culture of the American Whigs." As Greeley interpreted it, Fourierism was a welcome addition to his beloved Whig program, one intended to address the nagging problems of capitalist society without overturning either capitalist practices or the Whigs' faith in social cohesion. From this perspective the phalanx—like the corporation, the common school, and the free homestead—illustrated the Whigs' (and Greeley's) penchant for institutional reform that reconciled "progressive measures" with "conservative objectives."[4]

Greeley's social and economic philosophy, broadcast in innumerable speeches and editorials, proclaimed the ideal of collective capitalism that historians customarily identify with Whig ideology in the 1840s.[5] Calling for vigorous federal intervention through a national bank, protective tariff, and internal improvements to promote economic development, the Whig platform envisioned the kind of demographic, industrial, and technological progress associated with what social scientists call modernization. The Whigs' social and moral principles, with their emphasis on work, thrift, and self-discipline, complemented this commitment to economic growth. Taken by themselves, these policies and prescriptions could readily serve the interests of a financial and industrial elite, but the Whigs invested managed capitalism with a democratic aura by stressing the common purpose of all social groups, the benefits of shared prosperity, and the ease of social mobility. Whigs contended that capital and labor, as allies in the common enterprise of production, had essentially the same interests. Capitalist investment benefited all by making more goods available at lower prices; through industry, frugality, and ingenuity laborers could become employers themselves. With production humming and mobility widespread, permanent disparities of condition were impossible.

To this conventional description of Whig ideology should be added a strong dose of Christian moralism. Like many other Whigs, Greeley held to an ethic of paternalism and mutual responsibility. Wealth entailed the obligation to help the less fortunate elevate themselves. Under the influence of the romantic, evangelical Christianity of the age, Greeley expected feelings of brotherly love to overcome class hostility. As the conviction spread that men were equals under God, society would become "a true and essential Brotherhood," an "embodiment . . . of the great Law of Love."[6]

What gave the Whigs' outlook an indelibly conservative tint was their confidence that contemporary America embodied, or was smoothly progressing toward, this model of prosperity, mobility, and social harmony. Formed in the booming 1830s, Greeley's social vision expressed boundless faith in American progress. He felt certain that the United States, unlike Europe, offered wide-open avenues to advancement for the virtuous and ambitious; his own dramatic rise from a penurious boyhood in Vermont and tough times as a journeyman printer in New York City to editorship, prosperity, and national influence was concrete evidence. Here, too, the factory system could be introduced without bringing horrible working conditions and a permanent proletariat. When Greeley visited the famous mills at Lowell, he found conditions there practically idyllic. With its productivity, paternalism, and eminently moral arrangements, Lowell accommodated the machine to order and virtue while spreading opportunity to the poor.[7]

Beginning in 1837, social and economic trends darkened this rosy picture. As factory wages plummeted with immigration and greater competition among manufacturers, it became clear to Greeley that American industry would not escape the European menace so easily. In Greeley's own New York, artisans increasingly driven into competition with large shop production embarked on a series of bitter and fruitless strikes. As editor of an urban daily paper Greeley had a personal view of the Panic of 1837 and the depression that ensued. Aiding local relief efforts in the winter of 1837–38, he discovered that thousands of New Yorkers lived in destitution and disease, and he recorded the pleas of the able-bodied for employment. As poverty and unemployment belied the Whigs' utopian confidence and the depression dragged on, he sought a deeper and more thoroughgoing diagnosis than party slogans provided.[8]

Greeley turned to European social philosophers for guidance. Thomas Carlyle, the pugnacious Scot whom Greeley called "the keenest observer and among the deepest thinkers of our time," graphically portrayed in *Past and Present* (1843) the misery that industrialism brought to workers and the cruel indifference of the new capitalists to it. His indictment of laissez faire obviously dovetailed with Greeley's protectionism, but Carlyle taught Greeley to be suspicious of "free trade" in the largest sense of the term. Free-market capitalism appeared to link wealth and poverty in a "chain of cause and effect," a chain getting larger and heavier with each improvement in technology. Unemployment, which Greeley regarded as the Achilles heel of his capitalist society, was the worst symptom. But decreased wages were also fearsome, for a growing population meant that more laborers competed for the same jobs, and wages declined correspondingly. To Greeley's mind these evils threatened to come to America in the 1840s as urban population mushroomed, factory owners dropped paternalistic policies, and the business cycle heaved and ebbed violently.[9]

Carlyle's reform proposals—migration back to the land and a labor aristocracy building an amicable partnership with capitalists—fit Greeley's conservative biases and eventually entered his agenda, but these seemed unsatisfactory in a time of emergency.[10] He sought an immediate and detailed program that would counter ruinous competition and reopen avenues to advancement, but without impinging upon property rights or fueling class resentment. Charles Fourier's phalanx offered the thorough but "reconciling" remedy Greeley was looking for. Through a process of voluntary association not unlike that of forming a business corporation, Fourier's cooperative communities could solve capitalism's problem of unemployment, decreasing wages, and social instability. Greeley saw the phalanx as a bustling beehive, its wide variety of productive enterprises guaranteeing employment to all members and promising to match each person's faculties with the most appropriate tasks. Work in groups and series would mean maximum efficiency, while the pooling of child care and housework would cut expenditures and free women for more directly productive activities. Here were analogues to the elaborate division of labor and the economies of scale that Greeley admired in the factory system. Though he sometimes called the Fourierists' doctrine of Association a radical break with existing arrangements, at bottom Greeley saw it as the best example of "association," the term the Whig economist Henry Carey used to denote the increased specialization and interdependence of all industrial societies.[11]

Like Carey and Whigs generally, Greeley believed that greater productivity and social cohesion should be complementary. In the phalanx, Whig ideas about the rights of labor and capital and the harmony of interests were given mathematical precision. With community profits distributed in fixed ratios to labor, capital, and skill, each group would receive its due. Fourier's plan, Greeley rejoiced, "increases rather than diminishes the wealth and enjoyments of the rich"; at the same time, through shareholding and dividends, workers would be elevated to "a position of partnership and recognized . . . helpfulness." Without fully relinquishing paternalism and inequality, the Fourierist system defused social tensions by substituting order for anarchy, cooperation for strikes, joint prosperity for competition. To Greeley this class conciliation, along with the phalanx's guaranteed maintenance for the disabled and its sharing of manual and intellectual labor, meant that Fourierism was "based on a profound sentiment of Human Brotherhood."[12]

A scaled-down Fourierist plan that Greeley also endorsed was the producers' cooperative. Even without living in a phalanx, workers could pool talent and money to create cooperative workshops in the Fourierist mold. The producers' association seemed an ingenious way for workers to bypass confrontation with employers and avoid suicidal strikes. As a worker-owned and -generated corporation it was a constructive form of self-help such as Greeley and Whig spokesmen had always advocated. Associative techniques opened channels for upward mobility that were increasingly closed to individual craftsmen and wage earners.[13]

Whichever form it took, the phalanx or the cooperative workshop, Greeley's Fourierist model was, as Daniel Walker Howe points out, "a supplement to capitalism, not a substitute for it."[14] To even the most reform-minded Whig leaders, Association was a cooperative alternative meant to coexist in a competitive world rather than the germ of a radically new way of life, as Fourier himself intended. Greeley carefully avoided describing Fourierism in terms suggesting complete social reconstruction. When challenged in debate by other journalists and reformers, he repudiated Fourier's idea that competitive Civilization had corrupted all areas of life, from medicine to marital relations. And in the phalanxes he helped finance, Greeley warned against any tampering with organized Christianity, the conventional family, or accepted capitalistic practices.[15] Fourierism has been criticized for its conservative tendencies, but it was precisely the prospect of restoring opportunities to labor without disrupting social conventions or treading on the interests of capital that won Greeley's support. Stripped of its militant rhetoric and detached from a program of sweeping cultural change, cooperative production simply extended Greeley's Whig faith in collective capitalism into voluntary economic reform at a time of social crisis.

Parke Godwin and the Failure of Democratic Ideology

Parke Godwin was a Democrat, not a Whig; his version of Fourierism was more radical than Greeley's, and his path to it took him further from party platforms. Arriving in New York City as a young lawyer early in 1837, the idealistic and opinionated Godwin was drawn to journalism. After publishing a few pieces on legal reform, he became a reporter and later assistant editor for William Cullen Bryant's *Evening Post*. A clear and forceful polemicist, Godwin quickly absorbed the nationalistic and ultra-democratic ideas of Bryant (whose daughter he married) and especially the *Post*'s William Leggett, a fiery theorist of Locofoco Democracy. Like many radical Democrats, Godwin had a combative temperament, was devoted to democratic principles, and nursed an ambition to become a recognized spokesman for workingmen and the underprivileged. With other Jacksonians he condemned the national bank and Whig-dominated commercial interests, and he proposed to eliminate the influence of "the privileged classes" in government by abolishing "unequal legislation": lowering the tariff, curtailing federal support for internal improvements, and eliminating monopolies. A decentralized and open society under minimal government, he believed, best assured the free play and equal treatment that democracy demanded.[16]

Writing for the *Democratic Review* in the late 1830s and early 1840s, Godwin amplified this basic Democratic program with the ideas of Christianity and missionary nationalism. Influenced by the American Transcendentalists and fellow Democrat George Bancroft, he maintained that Christianity and Democracy were natural allies because both posited "the essential *equality* of all humanity" under God. The combination of liberal Christianity, an open economy, and representative government would fulfill the American Revolution at home and, by force of example, disseminate purified republican institutions throughout the world. Godwin's expansionist and Christian version of democracy—shared by *Democratic Review* editor John L. O'Sullivan, "Progressive" Democrats, and the jingoistic "Young America" group—was an ebullient updating of the Democrats' traditional ideals of individual freedom and equal opportunity.[17]

Yet Godwin's outlook had a side that distanced him from these Democrats' libertarian and entrepreneurial principles. Born into a wealthy New Jersey family with a Federalist background, he felt a strong need for order and responsibility in social relations and assumed that society should be run by men of education and ideas. His notion of the journalist as the "guardian and guide of public morals" reflected traditional ideals of Christian stewardship.[18] A lifelong concern with social equilibrium, which reflected the classical republican notion that the ideal polity was a delicate balance of social forces and tendencies, countered his libertarian bent. Wide reading in contemporary romantic literature and criticism further heightened the moralistic and communal strain in his thinking. Three sources in particular played an important role. Contact with Transcendentalism, first through the sermons of its forerunner, William Ellery Channing, and then through friendship with Channing's nephew William Henry Channing, exposed Godwin to a Christian democracy that advocated spiritual rather than economic self-development. Godwin was especially impressed by the younger Channing's "Christian Union," a New York congregation that condemned the "Civilization of Selfishness" and aimed to apply gospel principles to social relations.[19] Like Greeley, Godwin was drawn to the Tory socialism of Carlyle, whose fervent appeal for liberation and authenticity was balanced by an equal concern to recover the social bonds lost with the decline of religious and feudal ties. The Scot's bitter condemnation of laissez-faire philosophy pushed Godwin to reconsider his attachment to the Jacksonian definition of economic democracy.[20] To Carlyle's sarcasm was added the more positive voice of utopian socialism. By 1840 Godwin knew something of Robert Owen and had probably read the *Democratic Review*'s notice of Brisbane's treatise, if not the book itself. Not until 1842 was he to examine the ideas of Owen, Saint-Simon, and Fourier with care, but Godwin realized immediately that the utopians' "principle of *Combination*" and their attack on individualism posed a fundamental challenge to the Democratic philosophy.[21]

Faced with these calls for a more communal public order, Godwin attempted awkwardly to incorporate collectivist thinking within the Democrats' world view. For a time his writings alternately invoked Adam Smith's "unseen hand" and the Golden Rule to explain how free competition might foster the same common welfare it urged practitioners to ignore. The marriage of laissez faire and benevolence proved difficult to maintain.[22] What eventually tore Godwin from his Democratic moorings, however, was no theoretical contradiction but his growing sense that the Democrats' program was utterly inadequate to realize the social objectives he identified with it. After the high point of Jackson's presidency Godwin saw a huge gap between Democratic rhetoric and performance. The party's politicians seemed petty opportunists, and not men of virtue, vision, or principle. When New York's Democratic governor called out troops in 1838 to suppress an important railway strike, Godwin began to doubt whether the Democrats really championed the laboring classes. With the infamous "Log Cabin" campaign of 1840, party principle hit a new low. As Democrats and Whigs turned electioneering into show business, Godwin complained to Channing that both were seeking only the "spoils of office" and ignoring vital needs and issues. Among the most urgent problems, according to Godwin, was the mounting social inequality highlighted by the depression of the 1840s. At first he blamed the Panic of 1837 on the Whigs, but soon Godwin came to see that the Democrats' program of minimal government did nothing—on principle—to remedy the crisis. "Our politics and our political parties are stupendous and cruel humbugs," he declared early in 1843. The debasement of political discourse and the perception that corrupt and virtually interchangeable administrations had little effect on social problems turned Godwin from politics to the literature of social reform.[23]

Led by Fourier and Owen, Godwin began to locate the source of class distinctions not in legislation but in "economical arrangements," specifically the same competitive institutions Democrats praised so lavishly. The American economy, newly liberated by deregulated banking and general incorporation laws, was breeding anarchy rather than order, conflict instead of harmony. Far from encouraging mutual respect, free competition was accelerating acquisitive selfishness to the point of trampling all moral feelings. To Godwin, American conditions increasingly confirmed Carlyle and the utopians' claim that liberated capitalism only freed the wealthy from social responsibility and blocked the average worker's opportunity to advance. In his dissatisfaction with Jacksonian economics, Godwin undertook an intensive reading in European political economy; the most salient conclusion, which he drew from the followers of David Ricardo, was the devastating effect of free competition on wages, a bleak forecast that the depression appeared to illustrate. Between the business cycle and the "iron law of wages," Godwin wrote, modern workers were like Sisyphus, condemned to a life of exerting every muscle without ever gaining safe ground.[24]

The Democrats had been pushing for a more competitive economy, but Godwin now argued that laissez faire was the problem, not the solution. If the relatively open New World economy had evolved toward inequality and oppression, removing all remaining restrictions would "make the rich richer and the poor poorer" and entrench the same financial and industrial elite that Jacksonians had been battling for a decade.[25] By mid-1843 Godwin had become convinced that instead of competitive capitalism, Americans needed an entirely new social polity. Since inequality was "organic," social relations had to be restructured. In a series of popular tracts he began to elaborate Fourier's critique of competition and advocate the phalanx as the totalistic solution to America's problems.[26]

Like Horace Greeley, Godwin apparently embraced Fourierism as an alternative path to the version of progress his political beliefs projected but appeared unable to realize by more normal means. While Greeley found that Fourier's community system resonated with the Whigs' devotion to property rights and the "harmony of interests," Godwin saw in it the Democratic society of "equal rights" and minimum coercion. But the phalanx was not simply a more efficient route to Democratic freedoms. Endorsing Fourierism meant that Godwin repudiated the Democrats' laissez-faire program, but it also transformed the meaning of Democratic ideals. His Fourierism infused "equal rights" and liberty with an ethic of mutual responsibility, so that equal treatment metamorphosed into entitlement, and freedom into participation. By designing a society "in which the least individual shall have his rights acknowledged, and the means and opportunities for the fullest expansion of his faculties guaran-

teed," the phalanx promised a new and "true" Democracy. In a proliferation of cooperative Fourierist "townships" Godwin envisioned decentralized democracy evolving into an updated, ideal version of the New
England village. The principles of Locofocoism had been drastically
revised for a modern, interdependent society: rather than destructive
individualism, Fourier proposed (as the title of one of Godwin's tracts
proclaimed) "constructive and pacific democracy."[27]

Does the fact that Greeley's Fourierism complemented his Whig platform while Godwin's repudiated his Democratic heritage mean that,
as several historians allege, Associationism was merely the old wine of
Whiggery in a new bottle?[28] The Fourierists' own decidedly mixed party
allegiances (discussed later) suggest otherwise. One plausible reformula-
tion might be that the Fourierists' critique of social trends lay close
to Democratic ideology, whereas their communitarian program shared
more with the Whigs. Godwin fretted far more than Greeley about economic inequality and often used the rhetoric of class struggle, while
the *Tribune* editor confidently predicted society's progressive evolution
toward cooperation. This interpretation accords with Marvin Meyers's
judgment in *The Jacksonian Persuasion* that the Democrats appealed to
Americans' fears, the Whigs to their hopes.[29] Yet it is also simplistic; it
ignores, for example, the Fourierist critique's Whiggish fear of class
warfare and the phalanx's affinity with Jeffersonian agrarianism. Perhaps
the most accurate assessment is to acknowledge that Fourierism was
susceptible to both reformist and radical interpretations. In this case the
Democratic Godwin, who rejected Greeley's piecemeal cooperatives for
a future dominated by phalanxes and who accepted the sweeping implications of "passional attraction" for much of social life, was the radical
utopian. But division among Fourierists cut across political backgrounds,
as we shall see.

For all their differences in ideology and temperament, Greeley and
Godwin shared an underlying sense that American society should combine the greatest possible opportunities for individual advancement with
an equally strong sense of cultural and moral unity. Greeley called himself
"a mediator, an interpreter, a reconciler, between Conservativism and
Radicalism"; Godwin viewed his own role in precisely the same way; and
both specifically testified that Fourierism's ingenious reconciliation of
freedom and order, individual rights and communal duties, was (in the
florid prose of Greeley) "a feature of the system which has won for it my
sympathies, and enlisted . . . my earnest and hopeful exertions."[30] This
basic congruence has important implications for the question of how
Fourierism related to American politics. First of all, Greeley's and Godwin's insistence upon interdependence and the organic unity of society
suggests that there was a lingering strain of corporatism inside American
political ideologies that smoothed the way for some adherents to accept
communitarian socialism. The New Yorkers' Federalist background,
their evangelical Protestantism, and, to a lesser extent, the shared inheri-

tance of republicanism helped attach them to an ideal of community and social equilibrium which found its most explicit expression in Fourier's phalanx.

Perhaps less obvious but even more important for understanding Fourierism's appeal, antebellum Democrats and Whigs alike believed that, at least in America, individual pursuits and social destinies need not conflict. Both parties shared the conviction that whether through the invisible hand of Democrats' economic dogma or the more visible institutions favored by Whigs, sound social policy would channel private actions to the common good and, politically, steer the republic safely from the extremes of anarchy or despotism. In the intensely optimistic environment of early nineteenth-century America, moreover, this faith in the common good and an implied middle course became something entirely different. Greeley's and Godwin's ideals show how the boundless optimism of the age transformed the classical republican belief in balanced social objectives into a romantic-evangelical vision of a perfect society. In the broadest sense, the political culture of antebellum America shared many ideas and attitudes with Fourierism: the belief in material progress and voluntary association, faith in human nature, a distinctly millennial tone. But the utopian notion that unfettered individual effort and a communal ethos could be reconciled in a perfect social order was their most basic and influential common assumption. Searching for a new model for society, Greeley and Godwin gravitated to Fourier because in his writings they heard a fresh version of the utopian promise their political creeds had voiced, in different ways, during days of greater confidence.

Transcendentalists and Utopia

A similar revision of ideals moved the Transcendentalists of Brook Farm to experiment with Fourierism. When the Brook Farmers decided in the winter of 1843–44 to adopt Fourier's theory, American Fourierism was given a dramatic boost, both as a noteworthy system of ideas and as a reform movement. The community's leader, George Ripley, was a close friend of Emerson and a charter member of the Transcendental Club. Around the new society in its early years some of the leading minds of Transcendentalism had gathered: Theodore Parker, William Henry Channing, Orestes Brownson, Elizabeth Peabody, Margaret Fuller, and John S. Dwight. With the exception of Brownson, all remained as members or loyal friends after Brook Farm's conversion into a Fourierist phalanx. Their reputation gave Fourierist ideas new prestige in intellectual circles. The efforts particularly of Ripley, Channing, Dwight, and Charles Dana made Brook Farm the propaganda center of the American Fourierist movement in the mid-1840s.

That Transcendentalists should support a communal venture at all has struck historians as a "curious paradox." How could nonconformists who preached self-reliance and were hostile to any compromise of individual freedom take part in a community experiment such as Brook Farm? Part of the answer lies in recognizing that Ripley and his colleagues did not abandon Transcendentalist ideals; they simply built an institution to implement them more effectively. Brook Farm's arrangements were designed specifically to enhance and spread opportunities for self-expression and personal integration. Cooperative living would eliminate the obstacles to spiritual growth presented by an acquisitive, unequal, compartmentalized society and make the means of Transcendentalist "self-culture" available to more individuals.[31]

Yet putting self-culture in a collective context *was* a crucial shift of emphasis for Transcendentalists. The fact was that Brook Farm resulted from an important divergence in the Transcendentalist movement over strategies and goals. By the end of the 1830s a sizable segment of ministers and intellectuals led by Ripley, Brownson, and Channing broke from Emerson's leadership and began calling for a Christianized society achieved not through self-reliance but through immersion in the lives of others and ultimately through social reorganization. These "fraternity people," as Emerson called them, escalated the Transcendentalist call for self-realization into the demand for a society acknowledging the right to labor and education for all.[32] They interpreted biblical prophecy and human intuition to forecast a society of equality and love which could be realized only in communal form. By insisting upon a group environment for self-development, early Brook Farm was thus both an expression of Transcendentalist individualism and a reaction against it.

Ripley, a gentle, modest, and somewhat bookish Unitarian minister, adopted increasingly militant and reformist ideas as the Transcendentalists' controversy with orthodox religion heated during the 1830s and his awareness of social problems heightened. Defending the new theology against Andrews Norton, the "Unitarian Pope" of Boston, Ripley developed the democratic and reformist implications of the Transcendentalists' reliance upon intuition rather than doctrine and ritual. True Christianity, he came to believe, posited the ability of each person to hear the voice of God and thus affirmed the "intrinsic equality and brotherhood of man." The task of the minister was not to protect dead doctrine against heresy but to identify with the lives of common people, to "comprehend their destiny and secure its accomplishment."[33] In 1836 Ripley's friend and fellow Transcendentalist Orestes Brownson proclaimed that the divinity of human nature forecast a "New Church" that would be not a formal congregation but the infusion of Christian morality into society as a whole. Ripley, who later credited Brownson with the inspiration for Brook Farm, came to agree. Following upon the heels of Brownson's writings, Ripley's *Discourses on the Philosophy of Religion* (1836) presented Christianity "as a system adopted to produce the most magnificent changes in the heart of man and the fortunes of the world."[34]

Social circumstances in Ripley's America seemed to compel religious attention to what he called "the abuses that prevail in modern society." The feverish acquisitiveness of the 1830s was transforming men into profitmaking machines and drowning out Transcendentalist talk of noble ideals, Ripley complained to Thomas Carlyle in 1836. His concern grew as he watched the Boston slums creep toward his Purchase Street Church after the Panic of 1837. Ripley's parishioners did little beyond lamenting the invasion of their neighborhood and the decline of church attendance. Frustrated by their apathy, he told them he could not "behold the degradation, the ignorance, the poverty, the vice, the ruin of the soul which is everywhere displayed . . . in our own city" without doing something.[35] As Ripley's Transcendentalist mission encountered economic privation, it came to include the working class and began to center on social reform. His evolution toward social activism was stimulated by the proposals of such friends as George Bancroft, Brownson, and Edward Palmer. Though he hesitated to join any reform organization, by the time he left the ministry he called himself "a peace man, a temperance man, an abolitionist, . . . [and] a friend of radical reform in our social institutions."[36]

The gospel of brotherhood that Ripley and his colleagues began to preach was not the exclusive preserve of American reformers. The blunt voice of Carlyle played a part in forming the Transcendentalists' conscience, as it did Greeley's and Godwin's, but the example of French utopianism was especially prominent. Brownson knew of Fourier as early as 1839, and Ripley read Brisbane's *Social Destiny* in 1840, but both at first were too put off by the Frenchman's numerical formulas and pseudoscientific prose to hear the language of fraternal sympathy in it.[37] Instead, it was Saint-Simonianism that warmed their hearts, as it had Albert Brisbane's, with invocations of human brotherhood. Brownson testified that his *New Views of Christianity, Society, and the Church* (1836) was influenced "in almost every page" by the Saint-Simonians. In it he argued that the true mission of religion was the "redemption of the race" and that the Saint-Simonians' "New Christianity" was but another name for the social millennium. Despite divergent traditions and vocabularies, Saint-Simonianism and reform Transcendentalism drew upon a common early nineteeth-century sensibility of "social romanticism" that pushed adherents toward utopian projects.[38] By the late 1830s Ripley and his Transcendentalist friends Parker and Channing had also read the Saint-Simonians and reflected their influence in espousing a mystical and communal version of Christian morality.[39]

A key facet of the evolution toward communitarian reform was the break with Emerson's individualist version of Transcendentalism. In contrast to Emerson's belief that through self-culture the individual could transcend material circumstances, Ripley contended that true freedom was impossible in a depersonalized and unequal society. Whereas Emerson interpreted the internal spark of divine life as a call to personal integrity and self-reliance, Ripley saw it as a "sympathetic chain which binds heart with heart." "As a Christian," he testified, "I could not feel that my duty was accomplished while there was one human being, within the sphere of my influence, held to unrequited labor at the will of another, destitute of the means of education, or doomed to penury, degradation and vice by the misfortune of his birth."[40] Ripley harbored hopes for Emerson's conversion to "fraternity"; he was too tactful to confront his mentor, but Channing expressed his thoughts when he charged that Emerson's poet-hero was a cold-hearted egotist rather than "a self-forgetting minister to men."[41]

The Brook Farmers' frequent complaints that Emerson lacked social sympathies, as well as Emerson's admitted inability to be "thawed" by Ripley's reform plans, suggests that varying degrees of personal warmth existed among the opponents of "corpse-cold" Unitarianism.[42] Emerson's American scholar was the natural product of a determinedly self-contained intellectual, just as Channing's reformer was driven by an effusive need for others. Ripley's best biographer, Charles Crowe, suggests that the shy and emotionally limited young minister turned to communal life in part to overcome the sense of isolation that characterized his personal life. Ripley's relationships were restrained and formal, even with Sophia, his wife. She in turn longed desperately for greater intimacy, sought it in a variety of friends, and eventually found solace in the Catholic Church. Quite possibly it was Ripley's unspoken desire for companionship, repressed in his personal life, that surfaced in his quest for a "religion of humanity" and his sensitivity to social suffering. It may also be, as Anne Rose has speculated, that in experimenting among themselves with new ways of living, Ripley and the social Transcendentalists were attempting to compensate for their exclusion from the local religious and social establishment.[43]

In any event, in 1840 Ripley told Emerson that he felt bound to sacrifice his cherished privacy "in the hope of a great social good." Resigning from his congregation, he declared in a farewell letter that "the purpose of Christianity is to redeem society as well as the individual from all sin."[44] In the fall he brought plans for a communal experiment before the Transcendental Club and discussed them with Emerson, Bronson Alcott, Margaret Fuller, and Elizabeth Peabody. He and Sophia had boarded at a lovely farm outside Boston the previous summer; now they proposed to join with several friends and their families in purchasing it. As Ripley explained to Emerson, the idea was to build a small model society, primarily agricultural, which would provide its members economic security and cultural stimulation in a free environment:

Our objects, as you know, are to insure a more natural union between intellectual and manual labor than now exists; to combine the thinker and the worker, as far as possible, in the same individual; to guarantee the highest mental freedom, by providing all with labor, adapted to their tastes and talents, and securing them the fruits of their industry; to do away with the necessity of menial services, by opening the benefits of eduation and the profits of labor to all; and thus to prepare a society of liberal, intelligent, and cultivated persons, whose relations with each other would permit a more simple and wholesome life, than can be led amidst the pressure of our competitive institutions.[45]

Here, in the most succinct summary of early Brook Farm's aims, was an undeniably Transcendentalist program promising freedom, self-culture, the integration of thought and labor, and humane relationships. The basic idea, that of creating "whole" personalities by developing both intellectual and practical aptitudes, Ripley derived from Emerson's own address on "The American Scholar." No wonder Emerson declined Ripley's invitation to join "very slowly and I may almost say penitentially."[46]

Like other Transcendentalists, Emerson had become increasingly interested in manual labor as a source of dignity and wholeness. Distrust of the cash nexus made him forgo house servants, and his move to Concord had simplified his life and deepened his friendships. But all that Brook Farm promised Emerson felt he could accomplish at home, where Concord offered an informal community that respected his freedom more than Brook Farm's "hive" would do. Equally important, as his journal indicates, Emerson realized that to join Brook Farm would be to repudiate his "long trumpeted theory, and the instinct which spoke from it, that one man is a counterpoise to a city . . . that his solitude is more prevalent and beneficent than the concert of crowds."[47] In fact, after his difficult decision against Brook Farm, Emerson's defense of the intellectual stiffened, and his championing of individualism became more extreme. In "Self-Reliance," an essay completed in the same month during which he attended planning discussions for Brook Farm, he defined society in necessary opposition to the individual—"a joint-stock company, in which the members agree, for the better securing of his bread to each shareholder, to surrender the liberty and culture of the eater"—and disclaimed any personal responsibility for social problems. In "New England Reformers" he acknowledged that communal experiments were awakening the world to the idea of union but contended that their methods were wrongheaded: the truest community was the simple affinity of isolated workers, an ideal "union . . . in actual individualism."[48] It was testimony to Brook Farm's pull on his conscience that Emerson's confrontation with the communitarians occasioned his landmark statements of American individualism. Time and again during the 1840s he returned in his journals to the subject of Brook Farm (and, later, Fourierism and socialism), his defensiveness eventually giving way to a habitual condescension.

Despite Emerson's misgivings, however, early Brook Farm's highest priority was given to individual expression and spiritual interests. In April 1841 the Ripleys moved to the domain in West Roxbury, nine miles west of Boston, with fifteen others, including Nathaniel Hawthorne.

Hawthorne's presence testified to the personal freedom Brook Farm seemed to offer: he viewed associated labor primarily as a way to open up time for writing. Though he quickly found that "a man's soul may be buried and perish under a dungheap or in a furrow of the field, just as well as under a pile of money," for most members Brook Farm took on the relaxed air of a retreat.[49] Ripley's informal leadership and low-key demeanor made it a quiet community of teachers and scholars who concentrated on the daily activities of farm, boarding school, and leisure. Though accommodations were makeshift, the farm offered a simple and basically comfortable life where members could pursue intellectual and spiritual growth, through either private studies or group activities such as reading circles, musical performances, and dramatic presentations. In contrast to many residents of Puritan Boston, members delighted in spontaneity and fun. To John Sears, a student in Brook Farm's school, Transcendentalism was the "philosophy of the Here and Now," a thirst for heightened immediate experience which could be equally satisfied by a lecture or a costume party.[50] Transcendentalists might dispute this definition, but several found Brook Farm's friendly atmosphere and spiritual focus particularly congenial. One third of the original stockholders were self-proclaimed Transcendentalists, and though few became members, Transcendentalists were frequent visitors in the first few years, particularly Emerson, Channing, Parker, and Fuller. Some sent children to the Brook Farmers' school—most notably Fuller's brother, Emerson's nephew, and Brownson's son—and recommended their friends as boarders.[51]

Brook Farm's practical arrangements were designed with self-culture in mind. The community's joint-stock basis preserved property ownership, which Ripley regarded as essential to freedom. Abolishing private property, he wrote to a member of another communal experiment, would "so far destroy the independence of the individual as to interfere with the great object of all social reforms: namely, the development . . . of a race of free, noble, holy men and women instead of the dwarfish and mutilated specimens which now cover the earth."[52] While part of Ripley's goal was to unite all classes, membership was dependent on ownership of shares, a provision that limited early Brook Farm's working-class ranks to a few well-to-do farmers and artisans. If this compromised the social model, it nevertheless gave Brook Farm a pleasing homogeneity and made it easier to create Ripley's society of "cultivated persons." Ripley's choice of agriculture as the chief industry was also a preference for self-culture: as one historian notes, the Transcendentalists "saw farming as the occupation most favorable to personal growth because of its distance from the market, proximity to nature, and promise of a subsistence to protect moral independence."[53] To become whole persons and augment leisure time, Brook Farm leaders alternated teaching with milking cows or working in the fields. With the community's varied chores, its informal work schedules, and relaxed attitude toward sojourns to the outside world, communal harmony depended upon good will far more than organization.

Yet early Brook Farm's principles, as Elizabeth Peabody articulated them, included "cooperation in social matters" as well as "individual self-unfolding." In light of the later turn to Fourierism, it is important to note that the communal impulse formed a significant if secondary part of Brook Farm's aims and organization from the beginning. In his letter to Emerson, Ripley envisioned Brook Farm as "a society of educated friends, working, thinking, and living together, with no strife, except that of each to contribute the most to the benefit of all." The experiment's earliest Articles of Association, dated September 1841, reflect a modest collectivism. Members provided free room and board to all under ten years old or over seventy as well as to the sick and disabled. Medical care was available free to everyone. All residents earned the same pay per hour, and were charged equally for room and board. Such arrangements suggest that from the outset Brook Farmers valued working, eating, and living together both as a material expression of unity and as a way of life.[54]

Two young Transcendentalist followers who joined Brook Farm in its first year reinforced this communal orientation, though in very different ways. John Sullivan Dwight, at whose ordination Ripley preached in 1840, found at Brook Farm a sense of belonging that had eluded him in early manhood. Graduating from Harvard Divinity School in 1836, the diminutive Dwight preached at various places for four years before assuming the ministry in Northampton, where his religious doubts, shyness, and general "lack of fitness for the profession" became apparent; he resigned after a year.[55] Painfully insecure and longing for sensitive kindred spirits, Dwight instinctively saw the essence of Transcendentalism as "the embodying of Christian love in practical life" rather than self-reliance. Emerson styled him a "good, susceptible, yearning soul, not so apt to create as to receive with the freest allowance." Dwight's sketch of Mozart—a vulnerable manchild "whose life was one intense longing to be loved"—was probably autobiographical.[56] At Brook Farm he found congenial souls and even a measure of triumph in instilling the love of music in the students, reorganizing the school, and creating distinctive communal rituals. Escaping an unrespectable family background, resolving, at least for a time, the difficulty of a calling, and finding his niche as resident musician, Dwight became the most eloquent spokesman for the communal spirit among Brook Farm writers.

Sophia Ripley's young cousin Charles Dana was Dwight's opposite, with practical skills and a disarming self-assurance that belied his youth. In 1841 Dana was forced to leave his studies at Harvard, where he had shared the Transcendentalist enthusiasm, because of deteriorating eyesight. In the fall he moved to Brook Farm to teach Greek and German; his dignified demeanor quickly earned him the nickname "Professor." But Dana was far from absentminded: he brought a shrewd business sense and surprisingly thorough knowledge of horticulture to the community's farming operation. Slim and energetic, with an executive bearing and a genius for organization, Dana quickly became Ripley's right-hand man and an advocate of greater discipline and efficiency at Brook Farm.[57] If Dwight took his place as a natural Harmonian, Dana was a born member of Fourier's ruling council, or "Areopagus." Both played important roles in evolving Brook Farm into a phalanx.

The "Unnatural Union" of Brook Farm and Fourierism

Much ink has been spent on the issue of whether the decision to adopt Fourierism represented a sharp break from the initial Transcendentalist period of Brook Farm's existence or instead flowed directly from the early community's goals and ideas. The issue was initially joined when a few members who left during the reorganization complained that Brook Farm was losing its charm and high-mindedness. From the Fourierist side some stalwarts like James Kay complained that Transcendentalism and Fourierism constituted an "unnatural union" that would never last. The most influential critique of Fourierism's role was voiced by Lindsay Swift, who found the shift to Fourierism out of character—indeed, almost inexplicable—and labeled Brisbane the "evil genius" who destroyed Brook Farm. Swift's formulation was seconded by Perry Miller and has been repeated in most popular accounts of American utopias.[58] On the other hand, John Codman later recalled that the transition to Fourierism was natural and not divisive, an opinion that is supported by some recent scholars. One of them, Charles Crowe, goes so far as to say that "the ideology of Brook Farm leaders was from the beginning closer to Fourierism than to Transcendentalism."[59]

The debate is really a conflation of several important questions, some factual and others interpretive: the extent to which Brook Farm was manipulated by Fourierist leaders in New York; the degree to which Fourierism departed from Brook Farm's Transcendentalist ideas and goals; the amount of dispute the conversion engendered; and the impact of the conversion on the social and economic life of Brook Farm. Considering these issues sequentially is perhaps the best way to ascertain why the community adopted Fourierism and how much change was involved.

Though Ripley and a few Brook Farmers had heard of Fourier as early as 1840, it was only after Brisbane and other New York apostles visited the community and lobbied there that signs of definite interest began to appear. Brisbane pressed Fourier's views upon Ripley with increasing success; his visits to Brook Farm began in May 1843 and led to a lecture series in Boston in August, followed by a meeting to form a Fourier society, at which Ripley presided.[60] Greeley initiated Charles Dana's conversion. During his first visit to Brook Farm in 1842 he discussed reform with Dana; in later correspondence he criticized the "cant of exclusiveness" he had detected at Brook Farm and warned Dana that the community's naive expectation of members' "angelic natures" would prove fatal. Fourier's system, he said, avoided these problems by embracing all classes and erecting "a rampart of exact justice behind that of philanthropy."[61] Parke Godwin became a confidant of Dana's after visiting Brook Farm; Dana at first hesitated to embrace Fourierism, but eventually the two exchanged letters testifying to its validity.[62] The New Yorkers had another key ally at the community: in January 1843 Lewis Ryckman, a cordwainer who had been a member of the New York Fourier Society, was admitted to Brook Farm.[63] Ryckman set in motion plans to introduce craft industries at the community. With such close contacts and insistent proselytizing, it is tempting to conclude—as some hostile accounts imply—that the conversion of Brook Farm was the result of an outside conspiracy hatched among the New York Fourierist leaders.

Nevertheless, it is clear that the main impetus came from the Brook Farmers themselves. In several crucial ways Fourierism was the logical culmination of Brook Farm's development. There was, to begin with, an undeniable affinity between certain of the Brook Farmers' ideas and goals and the philosophy of Fourier. Fourier's philosophy of human nature matched the Transcendentalists' sense of the innate goodness of human promptings. His affirmation that the beneficent divine law governing the universe could be extended to social relations corresponded to their faith in "universal unity." Brook Farm's social arrangements already embodied some of Fourier's key ideas: the vision of a community harmoniously uniting middle and working classes; the belief in "integral education" of body and mind; guarantees of minimum maintenance for the sick and aged; division of ownership into joint-stock shares; and the desire to make labor attractive through camaraderie and variation.[64] It is not so much that early Brook Farm was closer to Fourierism than to Transcendentalism (one can only say this by equating Transcendentalism with Emerson) but rather that Ripley's "fraternal" or social version of Transcendentalism meshed remarkably well with Fourierist ideas. It may have been true, as John Dwight contended, that "Socialism . . . in New England did not take its first impulse from France or Fourier, as much as from the . . . liberal movement in theology." Yet in fleshing out their experiment's social and economic features the Brook Farmers, as one member recounted, "had fallen unwittingly . . . on ideas that coincided with those of Charles Fourier."[65]

Where Fourierism differed most clearly from early Brook Farm was in its systematic character and the very explicitness of its blueprint. Starting from an elaborate taxonomy of human nature, Fourier fashioned a minutely detailed organizational plan that enmeshed phalansterians in a web of work teams and timetables. Transcendentalist critics of Fourier were bothered not only by the philosophical determinism underlying such a scheme but by its straitjacketing of individual expression. Ripley's friend Convers Frances, noting Brook Farm's evolution toward Fourier, felt a "distrust" of such plans; Fourierism seemed "too much like applying mathematics & mechanism to a free soul." This is what Emerson meant when he wrote that "Fourier had skipped no fact but one, namely life," for human nature "spawns and scorns systems and system-makers, . . . eludes all conditions, . . . [and] makes or supplants a thousand phalanxes and New Harmonys with each pulsation." Fourier's attempt to mold phalansterians was a misguided attempt to impose system on the messy vitality of life and to place communal needs ahead of the individual's. Even Ripley, in a letter to the *New York Tribune* in August 1842, expressed reservations about a social science that "starts with definite rules for every possible case."[66]

Yet more systematic organization and a heightened communal focus were precisely what most Brook Farmers were seeking by the third year of their experiment. Increasingly, Ripley and his colleagues looked to Fourierist mechanisms to help solve the practical problems of labor, economics, and organization at Brook Farm. By the winter of 1842–43 it was clear that the farm was not prospering. Ripley complained to one member that "the realization of our idea is constantly thwarted by outward impediments," mainly the lack of enough members, buildings, and capital to sustain large-scale cooperative enterprise.[67] Symptoms of inefficiency and disorganization included the irregularity of workers' schedules, the confusion of scattered living quarters, and the need to take out a second mortgage in 1843. Brook Farm leaders responded to the crisis with a host of new measures, including the prohibition of buying on credit and a "retrenchment" at the dinner table. But the most important changes were four actions that put them directly on the road to Fourierism.

First, Brook Farm leaders moved to tighten the community's labor requirements. As of January 1843 the expected work week became sixty hours, and each person's hours of labor were to be recorded. To recognize the better workers, the directors began to consider replacing Brook Farm's provision for equal credit for all labor with Fourier's wage differentials, a measure they finally adopted in 1844.[68]

Second, productive operations were diversified. Farming many have been a "wholesome" occupation, but the community's stony soil resisted utopian aspirations, and Brook Farmers began exploring other sorts of production. Early in 1843 Lewis Ryckman arranged with community leaders to set up a shoemaking workshop. Undertaking a deliberate change in policy, Brook Farm advanced Ryckman around $100 to begin operations and recruited other shoemakers to join him. Brisbane's version of Fourierism advocated mixed industry in the phalanx, and the involvement of Ryckman suggests that Fourierism was a factor in changing the Brook Farmers' outlook on this score. But as Anne Rose comments on the shoemaking venture, Fourierist economic ideas "would have had little appeal to the Brook Farmers had they not been ready to move in a different direction."[69]

A third change was the decision to erect a large unitary dwelling for community members. Brook Farmers found that scattering members in several cottages and buildings not only hampered communications but divided utopians into two groups: private families nestled comfortably in apartments, and single persons huddled in garrets. Each became a subculture, undermining the community's belief that family feeling should be shared by all. And each member paid the same rent, no matter what size his or her lodgings. Faced with such problems, Ripley and Dana began to look favorably upon Fourier's phalanstery, which combined service rooms, meeting rooms, and living quarters in an efficient whole, endorsed differential rents, and also promised to extend the "isolated family."[70]

The fourth move, a concerted effort to attract outside capital, put Brook Farmers in direct contact with New York Fourierists. In the summer of 1843 Ripley told Minot Pratt that "comparatively a small sum of money" would make the difference between communal failure and physical expansion. That fall Ripley met frequently with Brook Farm's Boston sponsors, who were asked to underwrite community craft operations; most significantly, he also traveled to New York to cultivate investors among Brisbane's Fourierist friends.[71] Ripley's New York sojourn demonstrated the Brook Farmers' new desire to link themselves to the burgeoning communitarian movement. Increasingly, they felt not only that Fourierist patrons might provide much-needed capital but that an alliance with utopian socialists would revise Brook Farm's image from that of an elite private retreat to the status of an important public cause. At the outset Ripley had been reticent to publicize Brook Farm, leaving that job to Peabody and Brownson and other friends, and made only modest claims for the experiment as a social model. By mid-1843 Brook Farm leaders had become convinced that despite their precarious finances they had proved it possible to live a better life than that afforded by competitive institutions. The time had come to escalate this potential into a full-fledged challenge to the existing society.

The switch to Fourierism was possible because at the same time that they were addressing practical considerations, the Brook Farmers had been warming to Fourierism as an intellectual system. The process was complex, but although Brook Farm correspondence hints at the steps it involved, community members were too engrossed in everyday affairs to leave a full accounting. Instead, the movement toward communal theory became most clearly visible in the writings of their revered friend William Henry Channing.

The young Channing shared his famous uncle's progressive leanings but replaced the elder man's reserve with sentimental sweetness and unabashed enthusiasm for reform.[72] After graduating from Harvard Divinity School in 1833, Channing developed his own brand of Transcendentalism, which interpreted the "new spirit" of Christianity as a call to philanthropy and, within a decade, to communitarian socialism. In 1837 Channing served as a minister-at-large in New York City; two years later he moved to Cincinnati, where he presided over the Unitarian church and also sharpened his differences with Emersonian individualism. By 1843 he had returned to New York to organize the "Christian Union" as an independent congregation; Fourierists Greeley, Godwin, and Henry James, Sr., were among his admiring parishioners. There he also published a journal, *The Present,* in which he worked out his Christian socialist approach to religious and social problems. In 1845 Channing resigned his New York ministry and moved to West Roxbury to be close to Brook Farm. Community members were won over by his personal warmth and sincere devotion to the mission of "divine humanity." One Brook Farmer later recalled how the slim and delicate Channing, his burning, deep-set eyes those of a mystic, delivered inspirational sermons with "an earnestness that seemed almost painful."[73] For two years Channing served as the community's unofficial chaplain, living at Brook Farm in late 1845, preaching to Theodore Parker's congregation nearby, and organizing a socialist church among in Fourierists in 1846.

In his conversations, his sermons, and his writings in *The Present,* Channing cleared the way for Brook Farmers to accept Fourierism as an intellectual system. His explorations followed three complementary lines of inquiry: adopting the notion of "solidarity" as an expression of the communal ethos; calling for a "science of unity" to reconcile the individual and the group; and attempting to add a moral dimension to Fourier's mechanistic structure.

From the outset Channing, like George Ripley, considered the idea of human "likeness to God" a reminder of common "sonship" and thus infused Transcendentalism with the "sentiment of love for all who breathe, of sympathy for all who suffer."[74] A further step to a communal rather than individual context for spirituality—and a key step toward Fourierism—came when Channing and then the Brook Farmers adopted the doctrine of the "solidarity of the race." In June 1842 Channing told Theodore Parker that "one conviction" had become "the ground of my Christian faith—and my reconciliation with the Church": "That the Race is inspired as well as the Individual; that Humanity is a growth from a Divine Life as well as Man; and indeed that the true advancement of the individual is dependent upon the advancement of a generation."[75] He had heard this conviction voiced in *De l'humanité* (1840) by Pierre Leroux, the Saint-Simonian who had been the first French writer to use the word "socialism." According to Leroux's doctrine of solidarity, a mystical bond of divine life linked persons throughout time and space, demonstrating both the interdependence of humanity and the reality of racial progress. From Channing and Orestes Brownson, who ran an exegesis of Leroux's book in the *Boston Quarterly Review,* the concept passed to Parke Godwin and the Brook Farmers.[76]

With typically absolutist logic, Brownson followed the organicist implications of Leroux's doctrine into Catholic conservatism. But Channing and the Brook Farmers interpreted Leroux to endorse the utopian socialist program. The notion that humans possessed divine life jointly seemed to move the powerful self of Transcendentalism off center stage. As Dwight explained, since "part of me is in you [and] in every fellow being . . . we are real *persons* only entering into true relations with other beings. . . . [Hence] only all men sharing each other's life, co-operating with and completing one another, can ever realize . . .the full meaning of the idea of man." Here was a religious sanction for communitarian reform. Moreover, as they came to adopt Fourier's plan and his critique of individualism, the Brook Farmers turned to solidarity as their organic image of the perfect society. It became, one community member later recalled, "the doctrine they taught above all others . . . that the human race was one creation, bound together by indissoluble ties," and thus that society should reflect "one heart, one brain, one purpose."[77]

Fourier's phalanx embodied this ideal nicely, Brook Farmers decided. Through joint-stock organization and the elaborate system of work in shifting teams, Fourier assured that in economic terms utopian socialists would be "members one of another." With such interlocking interests, declared Channing, "all will seek to give the most favorable opportunities to each, and each will find his highest joy in blending his energies with the best designs of all."[78] The phalanx proclaimed collective responsibility by providing a guaranteed income and free medical care to all, as well as free room and board to the sick and aged. To Christian socialists Fourier's communal arrangements were a material expression of the "solidarity of the race."

But how could such a heightened communal ethos be reconciled with the Brook Farmers' commitment to individual "self-unfolding"? Would not greater discipline and organization smother the fragile flower of spontaneity and creativity? In his running commentary on Brook Farm, Orestes Brownson posed the question of community versus individualism, then gloomily pronounced the needs of individual and group irreconcilable without compromise or submission. But Channing, in true utopian fashion, was convinced that Brook Farmers could have it both ways. In a series of articles in *The Present* he called for a "Science of Unity" to restore through reason the natural harmony between personal initiative and collective unity which had been destroyed by a corrupt society. At the series' end he declared that Fourierism dissolved the central dilemma of Transcendentalist communalism: the phalanx accommodated choice and spontaneity by channeling them into socially constructive activities, and its elaborate parceling of community profits ensured social justice without destroying individual property. In a community based on divine law, instinct and duty merged into the simple living out of a Christian social life.[79]

There were, of course, some problems with swallowing Fourier whole. Not just Emerson but sympathetic friends such as James Freeman Clarke and Elizabeth Peabody expressed serious reservations about Fourier's plan, specifically its deterministic assumptions and its utilitarian accep-

tance of self-interest.[80] To Channing these obstacles were not insur-
mountable. Rather than endorsing or rejecting Fourierism in toto, he
attempted to make room within it for what Richard Francis has called a
"moral superstructure."[81] By injecting spiritual regeneration and self-
sacrifice into communitarian economic reform, Channing's articles of
1843–44 showed the way for Brook Farmers to Christianize Fourierism
as they adopted it (see Chapter 4). His writings were—to use Zoltan
Haraszti's happy image—"the bridge on which the Brook Farmers
crossed over to Fourierism."[82]

The culmination of these trends at Brook Farm—social, economic, and
intellectual—was a lively and well-attended convention held in Boston
on December 27 and 28, 1843. Addressed "To the Friends of Social
Reform," its announcement indicated that the gathering, though an
eclectic mix of abolitionists and communitarians of all stripes, was intended to cheer the progress of the "TRUTHS of Social Science discovered by CHARLES FOURIER." National Fourierist leaders issued the
call, but the Brook Farmers were intensely involved. Lewis Ryckman
signed the announcement, as did future Brook Farmers John Orvis, John
Allen, and Fred Cabot. Channing attended and gave a stirring speech in
favor of communities; Ripley and Dana were elected convention officers
and participated in debates.[83]

The convention was a rousing success for the Fourierists. The presence
of delegates from the independent Hopedale and Northampton communities as well as prominent abolitionists William Lloyd Garrison and
Frederick Douglass gave Fourierism new respectability. Channing reported that the gathering was a turningpoint in New England's history
and marked the phalanx as "an experiment which deserves the most
systematic and energetic trial."[84]

Brook Farm then took its first official steps toward Fourierism: immediately after the convention the community appointed Ripley, Dana, and
Ryckman to draft new articles of association. On January 18, 1844, Brook
Farm's new constitution, quickly approved by the membership, was presented to the public. A long introductory statement explained the rationale for the change. Acknowledging that Brook Farm had so far taken
"the character of a private experiment," the directors pointed out that
the community's moral if not financial success, along with contemporaries' "deep interest in the doctrine of Association," indicated that the social
millennium was near and the time for silence had passed. They professed
the community's "unqualified assent" to Fourier's doctrine of universal
unity and testified that their experience had shown the wisdom of his
"practical arrangements." Brook Farmers hoped to concentrate local
Fourierist efforts on their experiment and intended to progress into a
full model phalanx.[85]

The most dramatic development the transition to Fourierism brought
was a change of members. By 1844 Brook Farm's core of veterans had
been reduced to a mere dozen—not so much because of defection by

those objecting to Fourierism, as some chroniclers suggest, but mainly because significant numbers became dissatisfied with life on the farm or discovered new vocational or reform outlets. A few departing Brook Farmers did complain about Fourierism. George W. Curtis bemoaned the community's transformation from a "congregation of calm scholars and poets" to a full-fledged reform association; he preferred the earlier "severance from the world" and the pleasure of doing one thing well rather than rotating from job to job, as Fourier prescribed.[86] Yet others who left during the transition, among them Fred Cabot and Georgianna Bruce, continued to preach Fourierism in their new locations.[87] Vacancies were more than filled by a rapid influx of new members, proof of the Brook Farmers' desire to widen their social base and expand the community's scale. Sixty-seven newcomers became members of Brook Farm in 1844, more than two times those who had joined previously. Further, whereas early Brook Farm had been a community of ministers, teachers, and students, the new members were mostly working class: carpenters, shoemakers, printers, seamstresses, and other craftspersons.[88]

As these occupations and the community's new name—the Brook Farm Association for Industry and Education—implied, manufacturing was now put on an equal footing with farming. By March 1844 the community had built a large two-story workshop with a steam engine to accommodate new trades. In addition to expanding Ryckman's shoe operations, members initiated new lines of production such as a sash and blind business and a women's "fancy group" making caps and collars for sale in Boston. Carpenters were employed in building the new phalanstery, which would provide an orderly "unitary dwelling" for the phalanx. The new constitution arranged Brook Farm workers in agricultural, mechanical, and domestic series composed of several specialized work groups. Each group handled its schedules and elected its leaders in a democratic manner; discipline was maintained by co-workers backed by the directors as a court of appeal. This system proved a welcome alternative to the individual caprices and informal controls of early Brook Farm.

Whether all the Fourierist changes were beneficial is difficult to tell. Probably no system could have rescued Brook Farm's economy, for its chief problems were limited resources: lack of capital, infertile land, and poor access to markets. That 1844 was the first year Brook Farm turned a profit testified to some Fourierist efficiencies and the modest boost in outside support that resulted from the conversion. No doubt some of the spontaneity of the early community was smothered in the Fourierist mechanism: even so ardent a defender of Fourier as John Codman complained that his cumbersome organization acted as a "dead weight" on the group, preoccupying members with schedules and meetings rather than the release of creative energies.[89] Perhaps the most accurate assessment is that the adoption of Fourierism involved a deliberate tradeoff of charm for social relevance. By embracing Fourier, Brook Farm took a risky but calculated leap out of the insular world of Transcendentalist

Boston into the wider world of American—and transatlantic—utopianism. Begun as a relatively private and elite idyll, it became a full-fledged social experiment engaged in its times and part of a growing communitarian movement. After 1844 its history merged with that of American Fourierism.

3

Roots of Popular Participation

Through the efforts of Brisbane, Greeley, Godwin, and the Brook Farmers, Fourierism became the most popular secular communitarian movement of the nineteenth century. Even though utopian socialism never spawned the mass movement its leaders hoped for, it was an unprecedented overnight success. At the end of 1843 Brisbane rejoiced that "the name of FOURIER is now heard from the Atlantic to the Mississippi" thanks to the *Tribune* and Fourierist writings and lectures. Within four years, twenty-six miniature phalanxes were founded across northern states and territories from Massachusetts to Iowa, and two dozen Fourierist clubs or "unions" met in the cities. If Arthur Bestor's estimate of fifteen to twenty followers for every community member is a reliable guide, the Associationist movement attracted as many as 100,000 Americans.[1]

The prestige and propaganda skills of Fourierist leaders, however impressive, could not alone account for such results. In the biographies of the "apostles" there are glimpses of the larger forces that form the background to the movement. The romantic and liberal Christianity that inspired Brook Farm Transcendentalists was part of a general evangelical awakening of the 1830s which provided many recruits for communitarian reform. The economic crisis of the early 1840s, which disturbed Greeley and Godwin, pushed others who were more venturous or desperate into communal experiments. This chapter explores some of the social and cultural factors that combined to make American Fourierism a popular antebellum movement and to shape its development. By situating individual biographies and the record of the movement within the larger historical context, we can assess the impact of social and religious transformation upon the utopians and examine their links to other reform and communitarian groups.

Aside from the specific connections and influences discussed in the following pages, two simple factors accounted more than any others for the Fourierist craze. The first was timing. Fourierism could not have entered the American public arena at a more auspicious moment. By 1840 a major depression was shaking American society, making bankrupt farmers and unemployed artisans potential recruits for economic experiments and prompting many Americans to search for a theory to explain their plight. The Second Great Awakening had peaked in the 1830s in impatient crusades to transform moribund churches and rid society of such ills as poverty, intemperance, and slavery. National expansion highlighted the momentous potential of the American future and the necessity of shaping it immediately in new regions. Communal experimentation was in the air, as Transcendentalist discussions, popular interest in the Shakers, and comments in reform journals indicated. The example of successful religious communal groups lay before the reform public, and enough time had passed since Robert Owen's fiasco at New Harmony, Indiana, to allow the followers of Fourier to dissociate their theory from Owen's free-thought doctrines. The Fourierists' spectacular success had little to do with building an environment conducive to reform discussion or creating the right preconditions for communal experiments; rather, they were able to harness an already existing enthusiasm for model institutions and reform causes and direct it to their specific communitarian plan.[2]

The Fourierists accomplished this largely because theirs was a "universal" ideology that promised to incorporate all legitimate reform goals and reconcile the conflicting interests of social groups. The remarkable elasticity of Fourierist doctrine was the second key to their early success. At a time of crisis and questioning the Associationist alternative became the repository for many groups' hopes and dreams. In its radical yet reassuring program each constituency found something for itself. Workers interpreted Fourier's plan as a system of self-help cooperatives that promised economic security and an alternative to wage labor; to wealthy philanthropists and professionals Fourierism appealed as a paternalistic "social science" that could restructure production with rational efficiency, guarantee class harmony, and even return a profit. Religious reformers embraced Fourierism as the social expression of Christian brotherhood; secular communitarians saw in it, according to Bestor, "a way of achieving the prosperity, the security, and the peace of a Shaker village without subjecting themselves to the [rigid] Shaker theology."[3] Feminists and marital reformers sought greater independence for women in the phalanx and in some cases questioned gender and family conventions; other phalanx joiners wanted the economic benefits of association without challenging the family structure or child-rearing practices.

Clearly, Fourierism meant different things to different persons. In fact, despite a common doctrinal core there were several versions of Fourierism, ranging from capitalistic to socialistic, libertarian to authoritarian, reformist to revolutionary. Ultimately, they collided in the tensions, disputes, and defections which form a large part of the history of the movement. But in the heady days of the early 1840s all things seemed possible: the phalanx had a "scientific" blueprint for success, and Fourierism appeared to many to be the swiftest and safest route to the coming social millennium.

Social Transformation and Economic Crisis

American communitarianism has been identified as a movement shaped by the continuing nineteenth-century process of westward expansion.[4] This perspective helps explain certain aspects of the Fourierist movement: an interest in colonization schemes, a penchant for land speculation, and confidence in the ability to "plant" new social institutions. But Fourierism's direct roots lay instead in a dynamic but disturbing cluster of changes overtaking the American Northeast in the second quarter of the nineteenth century. Long-term trends of population growth, urbanization, and industrialization accelerated in the antebellum era, reaching the point of producing important qualitative changes in many Americans' way of life. Thanks to a steady natural increase and the influx of immigrants from England, Ireland, and Germany, the nation's population grew by almost 30 percent each decade. The proportion of the workforce engaged in agriculture began to decline, and urban population (defined as those living in places with more than 2,500 people) rose from 5 percent in 1820 to 20 percent by 1860. New York and Philadelphia each became a metropolis of over half a million persons, while inland centers such as Cincinnati and Chicago became important staging points for westward migration. Through banks, mercantile houses, and the "transportation revolution" wrought by steamboats, canals, and railroads, such cities established greater economic control over the hinterland. Most Americans still lived on farms, but as cities took in migrants and extended their cultural influence, they came to house a distinctive way of life—fast-paced, heterogeneous, atomistic, and unequal—which promised (or threatened) to become the American norm.[5]

The pace of industrial growth was equally rapid. Factory towns using water power to run mills sprang up on inland rivers in the 1820s. In the following decades steam engines allowed industry to locate in the large cities, where a sizable unskilled labor pool was available. In this transitional age industrial organization ranged from small handcraft workshops under merchant control to huge, fully mechanized corporate factories, with variations such the "putting out" system and sweatshops. Especially in the Northeast, new production techniques combined with improvements in transportation and cheap labor to fuel industrial growth. In New England manufacturing began to replace agriculture as the dominant sector when the soil became exhausted and western farms increased their output; New York, with its upstate mill towns and New York City workshops, became the country's leading industrial state. Manufacturing was still regionally concentrated, and the typical enterprise employed only a few workers, but the factory, like the big city, loomed in America's future.

Economic expansion in the antebellum North, often encapsulated by general labels such as "urbanization," "modernization," or "early industrialism," was in fact specifically conditioned by an open and undisciplined capitalist economy.[6] Thus social change proceeded in a special way that reflected the uncertainty and inequality of competitive individualism. As capitalist relations extended into household and workshop economies, farmers and craftsmen faced competition from larger units, were required to specialize production, and found themselves dependent upon unpredictable external forces for their livelihood. The vagaries of competition were multiplied by decentralized and poorly regulated credit conditions, which exaggerated the ups and downs of the business cycle. Prices, interest rates, and unemployment swung wildly as the economic boom of the 1830s—fueled by small banks, land speculation, and reckless entrepreneurs—collapsed in 1837 and brought the worst depression the nation had seen.[7]

A huge body of evidence has by now documented serious and growing inequalities of wealth in the "era of the common man." When powerful new instruments of production and distribution—urban banks, machinery, corporations, railroads—were introduced into an environment of private capitalism, they widened the gap between rich and poor. Financiers, merchants, industrial entrepreneurs, and professionals might benefit from the new technology, but down the occupational ladder there were many casualties. Lacking capital or the requisite specialized skills, immigrant and native workers lowered their occupational horizons, accepted wage-earner status (which by the Civil War encompassed perhaps 60 percent of the labor force), and at times experienced unemployment and outright poverty.[8] Independent artisans and small craftsmen also faced the threat of permanent "wage slavery" when merchant capitalists reorganized workshop production for greater efficiency and profit. The most advanced example of this dilution of craft skills and loss of independence was the new factory system in the mill towns of New England, New York, and the Middle Atlantic states, where discipline was rigid, tasks were extremely simple, and wages gradually declined to what the market would bear. Despite the rosy predictions of Whig champions of progress, urbanization and industrialization sharpened rather than eliminated class distinctions in the antebellum North.[9]

Unsettling trends in the larger economy had their counterparts in changes in the smaller world of family, household, and community. In the early nineteenth century most northerners lived in what Mary P. Ryan has called a corporate family household.[10] The family was an economic unit that produced goods for its own consumption as well as for the market. The home was the center of production not simply for farmers but for the craftsman who kept his workshop in a lean-to, for the shopkeeper whose family lived upstairs, and for women and children engaged in handicrafts. Husband and wife shared productive roles, though the male head of household wielded superior authority. Outside its doors the family was enmeshed in a complex network of support and discipline that included the local Protestant church and town government.

This entire preindustrial social pattern changed in a few decades with the development of commercial agriculture and industrial production, the reorganization of urban space, the spread of wage labor, and an explosion of geographic mobility. Production exclusively for the market tied farmers and workers to impersonal forces and sent the latter to work in shops and factories owned by others. The separation of work and home and the decline of home crafts not only robbed the family of some of its independence; it sharpened the division between sex roles. Increasingly, men worked in the competitive outside world while women assumed sole responsibility for managing the home and raising children. Geographic mobility increasingly separated individuals from parental and community ties; when combined with urban growth and the emergence of impersonal, large-scale institutions such as corporations, this meant that individuals felt fewer ties to the traditional support structure of family, church, and community.

Not everyone in the antebellum North was troubled by such developments; those who were concerned often idealized the past as a benchmark against which to measure change. More broadly speaking, however, many Americans worried over the apparent transformation of a village-oriented society, where class lines were blurry and groups shared communal responsibility, to an urbanized, competitive, and unequal society dominated by footloose and selfish entrepreneurs. This transformation was felt with a special intensity near rapidly growing cities—Boston, New York, and Cincinnati—and in the "Burned-Over District" of western New York state. The latter region, where the opening of the Erie Canal telescoped development from frontier to factory into one generation, became the nation's "storm center," the place where economic and social change led to a spectacular flowering of new religious and social movements. Revivalism, Mormonism, spiritualism, feminism, and communitarian experiments took root and prospered in this fertile ground of anxiety and expectation, though historians differ on the precise ways they did so.[11]

Like these other movements, Fourierism derived much of its meaning from the complex social transformation of antebellum America. Fourier's theory originated across the Atlantic under circumstances only partly analogous to American developments, but the doctrine of Association that Brisbane promoted and the movement it inspired were shaped by early industrial capitalism in America. Utopian socialists shared the new society's zeal for efficiency and organization, applauded its improvements in communication and transportation, and endorsed the goal of material prosperity. But they also believed that the competitive economy was channeling social change into a disastrous course. Spiritual restlessness, economic insecurity, and family instability were not separate problems but the related products of a specific stage of social evolution. Much of the appeal of Fourierism came from its ability to incorporate isolated complaints against social change into a coherent, historically informed critique of social structures. Behind the materialism, rootlessness, and inequality of the antebellum era, Fourierists detected the false system of "Civilization" based on competitive individualism. Under the influence of banks, corporations and land monopolies this system would evolve toward a brutal new "industrial feudalism" unless Americans intervened immediately. With alluring scientific precision, Fourierism not only diagnosed social ills but prescribed a detailed cure. Communitarian experiments modeled on Fourier's plan of Association would reshape social development according to old ideals of freedom and commonwealth.

Fourierists made a special appeal to two of the groups most disoriented by antebellum social change: middle-class family members and traditional artisans. Beneath utopian socialist fulminations against Civilization's individualism lay the same fear of social fragmentation as that felt by families attenuated by geographic mobility or cut off from traditional church and community ties. Brisbane's indictment of the "isolated household" with its privatism and separate spheres pointed out the dark side of the emerging ideology of domesticity. Like other communitarian groups, the Fourierists sought to recapture the larger social nexus of family, church, and village in a modern and more egalitarian setting. Their goal, according to John Humphrey Noyes of the Oneida Community, was "the enlargement of home" beyond the private circle to the group. The phalanx and its "unitary dwelling" would replace isolation with an "association of families," extending ties of kinship and friendship and purifying them by eliminating material concerns.[12] Though the Fourierist communities renounced "free love" or any radical tampering with conventional morality, they did promise a larger and more fulfilling environment for middle-class family members. Demographic data reviewed later in this book show that the American phalanxes attracted enough extended families, families broken by death or separation, and unmarried adults seeking companionship to testify to this formula's appeal.

Though Fourierism originated with the middle class, artisans were a sizable portion of the utopian socialist constitutency and in some phalanxes made up the majority of members. Most utopian socialist workers had not been either labor agitators or factory operatives; instead, they came from the ranks of traditional craftsmen.[13] Whether independent or employed by skilled masters, they felt increasing competitive pressure from large-scale workshops and feared the prospect of permanent wage-earner status. To such men the phalanx and Fourierist "producers' associations" were an appealing alternative. At a time when self-employment was increasingly difficult, the Fourierists plan for private ownership, profit-sharing, and small-scale production replicated craft traditions in a cooperative environment. Association promised to hold at bay the relentless march of "wage slavery."

Fourierist ideology spoke eloquently to the large themes of social and economic dislocation in the antebellum period. But the most immediate stimulus to communitarian reform came from a major depression in the early 1840s which drove home the Fourierist lesson and multiplied its appeal. In 1837 the commercial and industrial boom of the preceding decades was abruptly terminated by a bank panic whose origins lay in unbridled speculation in cotton, public land, and internal improvements. Within two years credit virtually dried up, banks and state governments defaulted, businesses went bankrupt, farm commodity prices plummeted, and urban unemployment skyrocketed.[14] Brisbane's recollection that "scarcely a dozen men" between Albany and Buffalo escaped bankruptcy was grossly exaggerated, as were reports that nine-tenths of eastern factories had closed. But in the first months of the panic wages fell by as much as half in New England textile mills, and over a third of New York City's workforce was unemployed. The depression lingered until the end of 1843, and even then the hardship continued for most workers as the cost of living rose more rapidly than wages.[15]

Hard times drove many northerners to Association as a practical way to pool their resources and find employment and security. Especially in the early 1840s, workers rushed to join phalanxes or in some cases to organize them. Hard-pressed urban mechanics, mainly from New York City, Brooklyn, and Albany, predominated at the Sylvania, Morehouse Union, and Social Reform Unity communities. After interviewing veterans from the last, A. J. Macdonald concluded that "business [had been] dull and the times were hard; so that working-men were mostly unemployed, and many of them were glad to try an apparently reasonable plan for bettering their condition." The depression's impact on trades helps account for the many urban craftsmen—especially carpenters— from Albany, Boston, Providence, and New York City who joined Brook Farm and the North American Phalanx. Carpenters and masons entering the Wisconsin Phalanx were also reacting to the slowdown in building activity along the Great Lakes after the western land boom collapsed.[16]

The depression set farmers equally adrift. As those in western New York and the Middle West began to produce for regional or national markets in the 1820s and 1830s, they extended their credit to make capital improvements or to speculate in additional land. When crop prices fell to a pre–Civil War low in 1843, farmers found themselves unable to pay mortgages or generate needed cash. According to Brisbane, the financial squeeze was "well calculated to awaken the poor farmers to the hardships of their condition and to lead them to catch eagerly at any scheme for their relief."[17] West of the Appalachians the Fourierist communities enlisted large numbers of farmers, many of them recent migrants from New England's declining agriculture. More than two-thirds of the residents of the Sodus Bay Phalanx in western New York were country dwellers. In Pennsylvania, neighboring farmers simply pooled their land to form a phalanx domain. Fourierist farmers in Ohio, Michigan, and Wisconsin took a different route, turning their land over to the community for resale and exchanging cattle and farm equipment for phalanx shares.[18]

Interest in Fourierism was further heightened by the inability of either major political party to combat the depression or even to understand it. The Democrats may have contributed to the Panic of 1837 by encouraging unregulated state banks and then requiring that public lands be purchased with gold—Jackson's notorious Specie Circular of 1836. But just as recent analyses of the panic stress the importance of impersonal economic forces such as declining British investment in the United States, so too many contemporaries felt, in the words of one historian, that "something beyond the sphere of politics was wrong with the system."[19] In any case, the frenetic imagemaking and sloganeering of the 1840 presidential campaign showed all too clearly that both parties preferred to avoid direct responses to the crisis of unemployment and credit. As Parke Godwin's experience suggested, the Fourierist movement fed upon reform advocates' increasing disillusionment with party positions and their skepticism about legislative solutions.

The Fourierists' response to the depression also set them apart from prominent ministers, benevolent reformers, romantic novelists, and other shapers of northern opinion. By and large these public figures, while concerned about the depression's impact, saw poverty as an individual responsibility and not the result of systematic social forces. Most repeated timeworn moralistic strictures against middle-class "materialism" and urged hard-pressed workers to practice thrift, patience, and industry.[20] Even as sensitive an observer as William Ellery Channing, in his 1840 speech "On the Elevation of the Laboring Classes" before the mechanics of Boston, concluded that workers suffered "not from outward necessity, not from the irresistible obstacles abroad, but chiefly from the fault or ignorance of the sufferers themselves": mainly intemperance, laziness, and wastefulness.[21] In contrast, Fourierism put the panic and the depression in a larger and novel structural perspective: Brisbane and his colleagues indicted the competitive economic system for bringing hard times. Equipped with their master's taxonomy of historical stages, the Fourierists confidently located for bewildered contemporaries the exact transition point between early "Civilization" and "Industrial Feudalism" which the crisis heralded. Utopians claimed that the return to prosperity required more collective action than self-discipline, and scientific organization rather than moral exhortation. So persuasive did their "social science" seem as an alternative paradigm that many Americans joined Fourierist leaders in expressing "gratitude to Charles Fourier for having opened a whole new world of study, hope and action."[22]

Revivalism, Evangelical Religion, and Social Reform

Besides addressing social and economic fears, the Fourierists successfully invoked the blessing of liberal Christianity upon their cause. Like
the Fourierist movement, the Second Great Awakening confronted antebellum anxieties with a dynamic and fundamentally optimistic message.
This creative break with dour Calvinist orthodoxy reached its frenzied
peak in the revivalist atmosphere of the 1830s, radiating into several
different religious movements and spilling over into social reform. When
zealous Protestants began to preach that people could effect their own
salvation and bring the kingdom of God to earth in the process, the gate
was opened for a rich variety of movements and creeds, including not
just religious revivals but mysticism, "come-outerism," perfectionism, and
new millennial sects. American Fourierism drew from several particular
currents in this flood, most notably Transcendentalism, the come-outer
impulse, and the revivals. But the most potent religious underpinning of
communitarianism was the most general: a widespread expectation of an
imminent kingdom of heaven on earth. Reform millennialism took root
among the wide range of liberal Protestants who were the Fourierists'
primary constituents. Blurring the boundary between religious and secular worlds, it transformed evangelical Christianity from a conservative to
a radical social force.

The communitarian wave of the 1840s was given a crucial push by the
evangelical revivalism of the preceding years. John Humphrey Noyes
drew a direct line from the revivals of Charles Finney to the socialistic
"excitement" of the next decade. The "Fourier revival" repeated "the
same confident predictions of the coming of Christ's kingdom" that
evangelicals had first voiced. Whitney Cross's study of western New
York's Burned-Over District interpreted Fourierism as the "aftermath"
of religious revivalism in the region. Cross agreed with Noyes that the
Fourierist agitation "reached the proportions and acquired many of the
characteristics of a religious revival."[23]

In actuality, the evangelicals' legacy to the Fourierists, like the social
implications of the revivals themselves, was ambiguous. Recent studies
of the social roots of the revivals interpret them as a middle-class means
of coping with the problem of class, legitimacy, and order in the early
stages of the Industrial Revolution. According to Paul Johnson's study
of Rochester, New York, the revivals of the 1830s spread through manufacturing towns as new industrialists and their middle-class allies adopted
religious methods of instilling labor discipline and individualist values
in the preindustrial workforce. Democratic, pietistic religion helped to
legitimate the rapid transition from a paternalistic, preindustrial ethos
to a capitalist, free-labor society. Anthony F. C. Wallace's brilliant portrait
of industrial villages in eastern Pennsylvania reveals a similar scenario.
There the evangelical campaign, begun as an attack on "infidel" Owenite
labor agitators, culminated in general acceptance of what Wallace calls

"Christian capitalism," a pro-enterprise attitude much like the economic tenets of contemporary Whiggism. Coming together in churches and religious associations, employers and workers pledged allegiance to industrial growth, government by wealthy "stewards," and harmony between classes. Thus the evangelical campaign of the 1830s gave Christianity's endorsement to the growing hegemony of capitalist values.[24]

It would be foolish, however, to reduce the revivals to a capitalist plot. Religious ideas and emotions, however generated, can often lead believers in unforeseen directions. There was a close relationship between the religious perfectionism of revivalists such as Finney and the genesis of the "romantic" reform movements that came to challenge middle-class faith in churches, government, and even property. Revivals may have begun by serving a middle-class desire to discipline and control a dynamic society, but evangelicals' emphasis on human agency, distinterested benevolence, and especially the possibility of social perfectionism through mass conversions proved explosive. Evangelical enthusiasm inspired a crusading moral fervor, an antiinstitutional animus, and a millennial expectancy that eventually brought avid recruits to reform movements like abolitionism and Fourierism.[25]

Because the Fourierists rejected the militant skepticism of the Owenites, their communitarianism had a far broader appeal among evangelical Protestants and was more susceptible to their influence. But the relation between Fourierism and the evangelicals was double-edged. To a certain extent, the Fourierists drew upon the conservative roots of the evangelical impulse. Middle-class in its origins, the Fourierist movement shared the evangelicals' fear of social distintegration, their rage for order, and their dream of class conciliation. At the same time, the utopians adopted the millennial rhetoric of the evangelicals to condemn the competitive system that "Christian capitalists" praised and to argue for a cooperative economic order. Fourierist spokesmen denounced hard-line evangelicals for fostering a "self-involved pietism" inimical to social reform. The revivals, one wrote, served only to "neutralize much of the energy which would otherwise have been available for the mitigation of human suffering." The ambivalent relationship was reflected by Noyes's comment that although revivalism and socialism ought to be complementary, evangelicals and socialists tended to "despise each other."[26]

Both in personnel and in chronology, in fact, there was no simple equation between religious revivalism and Fourierist activity. While Fourierism attracted adherents in the revival-prone regions of New York and the Middle West, many Associationists came from other areas and creeds. Fourierism was popular in the diverse environment of New York City, in Unitarian Boston, and in Ohio Valley cities such as Pittsburgh and Cincinnati which had been strongholds of free-thought Owenism. Cross concluded that most Fourierist leaders in the Burned-Over District came from backgrounds of Quakerism and Universalism, liberal denominations that ignored or were even hostile to the revivals; a more recent study found that Rochester's Fourierists had fewer ties to evangelical churches—or any churches, for that matter—than other local reformers.[27] The urbane Brook Farmers were of course temperamentally distant from the emotional display of revivalism. But even in frontier experiments in Michigan and Wisconsin fervent pietism never took hold; hardline evangelical minorities were outvoted on such issues as Sabbath observance. H. R. Schetterly, the Universalist leader of the Alphadelphia Association, published articles in religious journals condemning revivals for inducing "mental delusions" and frightening believers into a false and temporary virtue.[28]

There was also a revealing time lag between the revivals and the Fourierist movement. Revivalist agitation in western New York peaked more than a half-dozen years before the Fourierist craze. In the interim, the Panic of 1837 drained the coffers of the pious merchants who had financed the revivals and made economic questions as pressing as religious ones. Within a few years, moreover, some of those touched by the revivals passed on to such "ultra" positions as come-outerism and perfectionism. In 1838 the former animated a convention of revivalist veterans in Syracuse who advocated union churches that would "annihilate the existing denominational distinctions," a sentiment that drew George Ripley's endorsement.[29] The latter was demonstrated by the career of John Humphrey Noyes, himself converted at a revival meeting in his native Vermont. Noyes's views evolved toward a radical version of the doctrine of perfectionism. Whereas Charles Finney believed that the sanctified Christian could approach perfection by following traditional church strictures, Noyes became convinced that true holiness necessitated communal living and the abolition of monogamy. In 1844 he gathered three dozen followers to practice "Bible Communism" in Putney, Vermont, but when faced with local hostility four years later, the group relocated as the Oneida Community near Syracuse. Edwin A. Stillman, for a time a member of Noyes's perfectionist circle, became active in the Fourierist movement in the Burned-Over District, founding the Bloomfield Union Association and serving as secretary to several regional Fourierist conventions.[30]

Outside New York, communitarianism may also have picked up restless revival converts, as the experience of Joseph Cooke of Providence demonstrated. Cooke was a spiritually lax businessman brought to the anxious seat in 1840 by a Baptist revivalist. Eventually, his new-found desire to "live religion" made him dissatisfied with formal church ties and with the Baptists' hedging on social issues from pauperism to slavery. At this point he decided that Fourierist reform, which he had earlier dismissed, would "eradicate all evil, and . . . bring the Christian Millennium."[31]

Cooke's experience and the chronology of Fourierism in upstate New York suggest that revivalism heightened aspirations for godly living which evangelical pietism could not itself fulfill. As the initial excitement tapered off, converts who became impatient with church rules and a

narrow focus on individual conversion sought new outlets for their millennial hopes.[32] Fourierists fed their discontent by criticizing revivalism
as superficial, sectarian, and "essentially anti-social" in its absorption
with personal piety. Communitarianism was a practical alternative to the
"failure" of Christian evangelism, whether in its traditional forms or
in revivalism's "new measures."[33] The collapse of the revivals in the
depression atmosphere of the early 1840s completed the transition. As
erstwhile born-again Christians defected to the Fourierists, the utopians,
like the land reformers and abolitionists, benefited from religious enthusiasm redirected to social reform.

The revivals were only one symptom of a general religious awakening
whose various manifestations sent representatives into the communitarian movement. On the fringe of religious agitation a colorful array of
religious seekers and mystics, among them A. B. Smolnikar and H. H.
Van Amringe, brought their idiosyncratic millennial beliefs into the Fourierist movement. A Pittsburgh lawyer and amateur theologian, Van
Amringe claimed to have divined the "inner sense" of the Book of Revelation: a history of Christianity's doctrinal and spiritual degeneration after
the apostolic age, and a glorious prophecy of universal salvation through
Christ's second coming into human hearts. For eight years Van Amringe
constituted a one-man religious sect—until he saw in Fourier's plan the
millennial kingdom prefigured by his biblical studies. Inflamed with
communitarian zeal, he lectured in the Middle West and helped to direct
two Ohio phalanxes.[34] Smolnikar was doubtless the most eccentric of
these religious pilgrims. A former Benedictine monk and biblical studies
professor in Austria, he determined that the scriptures had appointed
him to inaugurate the "Universal Republic of Peace" in America. He
crossed the Atlantic in 1837, published five volumes on his revelations,
and established a short-lived "Peace-Union" settlement in Warren
County, Pennsylvania. Smolnikar's community efforts and his interest in
Fourier gained him a vice-presidency at the 1844 General Convention of
Associationists, and thereafter he wandered from phalanx to phalanx
preaching his highly personalized millennial gospel.[35]

Fourierism also attracted members from the numerous small sects
energized by the antebellum awakening. In the quickened atmosphere
even liberal denominations rooted in rational theology and wary of revivalist methods felt called to intensified faith and more systematic social
action. Universalism, the country cousin of Unitarianism, voiced the same
belief in the divinity of all humans which led George Ripley and his
friends to the Brook Farm experiment. Just as Transcendentalists—and
ultimately Brook Farmers—were the products of a Unitarian "revival,"
Universalists licked by nearby evangelical flames shed their Yankee reticence and eagerly embraced reform causes. Universalist contingents
could be found at virtually every phalanx. There was, in addition, a
noticeable connection between the Fourierists and the Society of Friends.
As early as 1828 revivalist agitation split the Quakers into two factions:

an Orthodox group adopting the evangelicals' emphasis on scriptural truths, and the followers of Elias Hicks, who, like liberal evangelicals, preached a subjective faith criticizing the authority of church elders. Hicksite Quakers had been prominent in the Owenite movement in Ohio and Indiana; two decades later liberal Friends became leaders at the Clarkson and Sodus Bay phalanxes in western New York, and a handful surfaced as members of other Fourierist communities. A third group, more evangelical in background, was the Disciples of Christ, founded by Alexander Campbell, an independent preacher at one time affiliated with the Baptists. Disciples looked toward the reunion of Christians in a universal church as the event that would inaugurate the millennium, and communitarianism seemed a natural vehicle for such aspirations. Theophilus Sweet, the leader of the Fourierist Sangamon Association of Illinois, was a Campbellite preacher; Campbellite Baptists predominated at the Integral Phalanx, which merged with Sangamon; and most members of the Trumbull Phalanx were Disciples.[36]

Perhaps the sectarians closest to the Fourierists were the Swedenborgians. Emanuel Swedenborg (1688–1772) was a Scandinavian scientist and mystic whose visionary theology became the basis for a "New Church"; its first American society was established in 1792. Swedenborgians had been drawn to Owenism in the 1820s and two decades later developed so close a relationship with Fourierism that Noyes claimed flatly, "Fourierism had Swedenborgianism for its state religion."[37] Swedenborgian ministers were responsible for two American phalanxes—the Leraysville and Canton communities—and were active in propagating Fourierist doctrine in Ohio, New York City, and Philadelphia. A western New Church journalist claimed to recognize names of fellow churchmen in "nearly all published proceedings of Fourier meetings."[38] Those who embraced Fourier were not, however, in the mainstream of the New Church, which interpreted Swedenborg's ideas in a Calvinistic mode and established a formal ecclesiastical body with its own doctrine and sacraments. Rather, they were either liberal New Churchmen who had caught the reform fever or independents who had developed a millennial interpretation of Swedenborg's writings.

The most celebrated and influential example of the latter group was Henry James, Sr., who was raised as a Presbyterian. When James experienced a sudden nervous breakdown during a sojourn in England in 1844, a friend confided that his exhaustion and emptiness were what Swedenborg had described as the prelude to enlightenment. James turned to the Swedish thinker's voluminous revelations and was converted. From the beginning, however, he interpreted Swedenborg's idea of a "new church" not as an ecclesiastical organization but as a new dispensation that would perfect social relations and allow spontaneous expression of the divine instincts within all humans. This millennial view, as well as impatience with New Church "quietism," led James directly to the Fourierist movement, for which he became an important publicist.[39]

Like James, the evangelicals, religious liberals, and personal seekers who came to Fourierism held an urgent, reforming conception of Christianity whose demands could not be met by conventional church forms and creeds. To some reformers the churches' toleration of slavery was the most telling indicator of institutional resistance to godliness and was thus an important stimulus toward utopian experiment. When blocked by their respective churches, come-outer abolitionists such as Adin Ballou, John Collins, and George Benson left them to build communities exempt from the world's corruption.[40] Another notorious come-outer, the outspoken abolitionist editor Henry Clapp, Jr., of Lynn, Massachusetts, found a temporary home for his "no-organization" principles among the Fourierists before forming his own anarchist circle in New York City. The antislavery New Yorker George Throop, who delighted to see such men "throw off the shakles [sic] and expose the hypocrisy of the churches," tried to organize a phalanx near Hamilton in 1844. But the Fourierists' most important come-outer convert was the tireless lecturer John Allen, a Universalist minister from Vermont who felt he must denounce slavery. When his congregation barred the subject from the pulpit, he packed off for Brook Farm, which, although it did not share his abolitionist fervor, did promise a society immune from the influence and thus the compromises of slavery.[41]

By far the most important religious impetus to Fourierism—more influential than any specific religious movement, sect, or impulse of these years—was the general millennial culture that the era of evangelical ascendancy fostered. American Fourierism took shape at a time when expectations of an impending millennium had become so pervasive as to be almost an assumption. Predictions of the coming kingdom were voiced not only by revivalists (Charles Finney at one point believed the revivals would bring the Second Coming in five years) but an astonishing spectrum of Americans, ranging from fringe sects such as the Millerites, who expected a cataclysmic Last Judgment in 1843, to mainstream Fourth of July orators celebrating American political and economic progress. Believers divided generally into pessimistic premillennialists, who held that religious turmoil and social disasters would precede the Final Days, and optimistic postmillennialists, who thought that the thousand-year Kingdom of God would come gradually through the efforts of committed Christians. Most of those touched by the Second Great Awakening were postmillennialists: just as the revivals emphasized a benevolent deity and the importance of human effort, nineteenth- century evangelicals tended to believe that spiritual renewal would manifest itself in virtuous behavior, which would in turn assure social improvement. Religious evangelism and social reform went hand in hand; the goal of both became a perfected society whose attributes depended upon the particular reform one espoused. In its various reform guises, postmillennialism provided a congenial meeting ground for secular and religious concerns, giving rise to a blurry but nonetheless potent vision that rationalist reformers and devout evangelicals could share.[42]

Among antebellum reformers the Fourierists were especially skillful at assimilating the rhetoric of millennial Christianity. Like the Bible, Fourierism envisioned a centuries-long reign of love in humanity's future; the social utopia to be created by phalanxes became identical in Fourierist minds to the millennial kingdom. Communitarianism appealed to antiformalist and antidogmatic Christian reformers as "practical Christianity," the embodiment of the Golden Rule in social relations. With the exception of Van Amringe and a few others, Fourierist leaders wisely avoided detailed scriptural explication, which might alienate deists or orthodox Protestants, in favor of stirring perfectionist rhetoric. Lectures and tracts cast the Fourierists as prophets heralding a New Jerusalem where human instincts would be guided to cooperative harmony and become truly divine. William Henry Channing announced that "a new era in Humanity is opening, and sounds forth more fully than ever before the venerable yet new gospel, that the kingdom of HEAVEN IS AT HAND." Christ's second coming would take the form of a society swathed in comfort and love. By grafting the progressive eschatology of utopian socialism onto Christian "salvation history," the Fourierists transferred to their movement the breathless urgency, prophetic power, and inspiring optimism of the evangelical awakening.[43]

For hundreds of antebellum utopians, Fourierist communitarianism became the culminating phase of the evangelical dynamic. The general religious awakening of the era and its millennial culture aroused expectations of imminent perfection which were ripe for communitarians to harvest. Purist zeal, initially invested in self-discipline and moral reform, turned increasingly to collective attempts to build small models of the perfect society. By that time, of course, it had become something quite different. Beneath their religious rhetoric Fourierist spokesmen remained committed to an Enlightenment "social science" that took issue with the evangelicals' fundamentally moralistic perspective on social problems. Utopian socialist spokesmen attributed poverty and immorality to faulty socioeconomic relations, warned against relying on individual regeneration, and portrayed themselves as "the only TRUE PERFECTIONISTS" because of their environmental realism.[44] When Fourierists adopted the evangelical language of the age, they refashioned it from an injunction to self-discipline or an occasion of cultural self-congratulation into a persuasive call for social and economic reform.

Fourierism and Antebellum Reform

It was Fourierism's good fortune to arrive in America at a time when reform agitation was at high tide. Energized by evangelical Protestantism, the spread of democratic principles, and a romantic belief in moral progress, yet also troubled by the dislocations of early industrial society, a sense of urgency and hope dominated much of middle-class discussion in the antebellum North. Conventional institutions and habits were subjected to intense scrutiny, and reform panaceas were hatched which

promised to purify American society and pave the way for a social millennium. "In the history of the world," Emerson wrote in 1841, "the doctrine
of Reform had never such scope as at the present hour. . . . all things . . .
hear the trumpet, and must rush to judgment,—Christianity, the laws,
commerce, schools, the farm, the laboratory; and not a kingdom, town,
statute, rite, calling, man, or woman, but is threatened by the new spirit."[45]
Abolitionists, peace reformers, temperance advocates, prison reformers,
women's rights protesters, public school promoters, and a host of other
groups filled newspapers and lecture halls with impassioned pleas to
apply the ideals of individual liberty, middle-class propriety, and Christian benevolence to American life. The utopian socialists, who took their
place as the most comprehensive of these reform groups, never achieved
the massive popularity of antislavery or temperance reformers. But Fourierists profited from the general agitation even as they defined themselves against it.

By the time Fourierism was introduced, the techniques of agitation
and the social role of the reformer had already been established. The
"benevolent empire" of the revivalists—with its tract and missionary
societies and their offspring—spread in the 1820s and 1830s through
mechanisms that secular reformers later adopted. Reform tracts replaced
Bibles as abolitionists or temperance lecturers—secular versions of itinerant evangelists—toured towns and villages preaching the new gospel.
Reform conventions analogous to camp meetings stirred enthusiasm that
soon became institutionalized in local societies functioning much like new
churches. Those societies joined in a national network, which financed
yet more agitation and took official positions on public issues.[46] Secular
reformers also benefited from important innovations in mass communications in the antebellum era. Steam-powered cylindrical presses made
possible cheap journals and newspapers, which in turn created a mass
audience for reform. The increasing popularity of lyceum speakers and
public lectures among the Jacksonian era's common men and women
provided a convenient forum for reform spokesmen. Both lecturers and
publications were able to reach potential converts through the rapidly
growing network of canals, steamboat routes, and railroads that brought
a "transportation revolution" to early nineteenth-century America.[47]

Fourierism owed no small measure of its success to these methods and
innovations, which utopians eagerly seized upon. It was Horace Greeley's
penny newspaper that distributed the doctrine of Association quickly
and cheaply to thousands of northern households. Greeley, Godwin,
Channing, and Dana became popular lecturers on the lyceum circuit.
Brisbane used his *Tribune* columns for speeches, and Greeley collected
his lectures into a best-selling book; thus, lectures and publications fed
each other's success.[48] Brisbane, Dana, Ripley, and other national leaders
frequently boarded railroads, stages, and steamboats to reach regional
conventions or visit fledgling phalanxes. In 1848 oceangoing steamers
brought the latest letters from Brisbane and Dana assessing the progress

of socialism in Europe. Even the new telegraph came into play as Fourier-ist clubs exchanged greetings on important anniversaries. The transportation revolution made Fourierist spokesmen career itinerants: on a visit to America in 1853 Victor Considerant noted with amazement that Brisbane had spent the last fifteen years on railroads and steamboats, his actual home more "on the highways he travels than in his native village."[49]

The abolitionist and moral reform societies also became, at least in part, the model for Fourierist organizing. It was the reform press that impressed Brisbane, upon his return to America in 1834, with the need to establish a Fourierist journal. Like other reform organs, *The Phalanx* and *The Harbinger* featured not simply news of the cause's progress but angry exposés of social ills, personal testimony from escapees of the bondage of "Civilization," and sentimental poems and stories dramatizing the regeneration of society. Local Fourierist agitation often began with presentations to church groups or deliberately controversial lectures by Brisbane or other traveling speakers. Like the American Anti-Slavery Society, the American Union of Associationists, established in 1846, was a national federation of affiliated local and regional groups that met in an annual convention to set policy and review the movement's successes and failures. As the union grew moderately prosperous, it was able to print pamphlets, command dues from members, and send lecturers into the field. Fourierist women, forming an auxiliary society akin to the abolitionists', raised money at utopian socialist fairs and bazaars that sold goods produced by "free laborers" rather than "wage slaves."

By the 1840s the work of publicity and organization had so progressed that for the first time in American history, reform became a viable profession. Veteran agitators such as William Lloyd Garrison, Wendell Phillips, and Horace Mann defined the parameters of the reformer's role, and a younger generation of idealists eagerly accepted it as the resolution of their own career dilemmas. Ralph Waldo Emerson was shrewder than most contemporaries when he traced the roots of reform to "the practical impediments that stand in the way of virtuous young men." Not only had commercial employment grown "selfish to the borders of theft," but the law, the ministry, and "each of the professions has its own wrongs. Each finds a tender and very intelligent conscience a disqualification for success." Nothing was left to the man of integrity, declared Emerson, but to "assume his own vows, . . . call the institutions of society to account," and "begin the world anew."[50]

As a communitarian faith, Fourierism offered adherents a reform career in a special double sense. Outside the phalanxes publicists such as Brisbane and Godwin, while continuing to receive income from business and journalistic ventures, devoted most of their time to lectures and writings intended to win new converts. Brisbane, unswervingly attached to Fourierist doctrine but reluctant to lead an experiment himself, was the quintessential career agitator. For nearly half a century his prime concern was to publish Fourier's writings, hatch new communal schemes,

and present informal expositions of Fourierism to any reformer or states-
man who might listen. Life inside a Fourierist phalanx offered a second
set of communitarians a chance to find occupational fulfillment in a world
begun anew. For sensitive young men such as John Dwight of Brook
Farm, Warren Chase of the Wisconsin Phalanx, and Marx Lazarus of the
North American Phalanx, communal living opened up important new
roles as members of the reform vanguard. Their experience was shared
by others who remain nameless, as the following triumphant report from
The Harbinger indicates:

> Three attorneys-at-law have left that profession and joined the Integral
> Phalanx, not, as they say, that they could not make a living, if they would
> stick to it and do their share of the dirty work, but because by doing so they
> must sacrifice their consciences, as the practice of the law, in many instances,
> is but stealing under another name. They are elevating themselves by learn-
> ing honest and useful trades, so as to become producers in Association.[51]

Unsuccessful in business or unable to live with the pressures and compromises of the outside world, fledgling ministers, lawyers, clerks, and artisans found congenial places in Fourier's New Industrial World as teachers, farmers, and administrators. Nothing testified to the appeal of this
commitment more than the remarkable careers of such life-long utopians
as Stephen Young, reportedly a veteran of five phalanxes and a handful
of other communities of the 1840s and 1850s; and Alcander Longley of
the North American Phalanx, who after the breakup of that experiment
founded a succession of ill-fated communitarian ventures over the next
fifty years in Indiana, Michigan, Ohio, and Missouri.[52] By calling for
members to separate from others and instill cooperative values in their
daily lives, communitarianism gave new meaning to the notion of reform
as a career.

Antebellum reform groups shared not simply organizing methods and
social roles but also values, sympathies, and sometimes members. Both
southern critics of seemingly contagious "isms" and bemused northern
observers such as Emerson recognized a general reform frame of mind
which produced alliances and even mergers. Among the values that
Fourierists shared with other reformers, probably the most important
were their belief in social perfectibility and their commitment to America's special destiny. It is customary to label antebellum reformers as
"moral" or "social" according to whether their tactical emphasis lay upon
individual "suasion" or such methods as institution building and legislation. This can be a useful distinction, but it begins to break down when
we admit that "suasion" abolitionists used such methods as economic
boycotts and communitarians began with appeals to the individual conscience. Both groups expected personal conversions to radiate outward
and purify social relations. John Humphrey Noyes recognized that the
Fourierists and religious reformers, often perceived as antagonists, were

in fact "closely related" in their devotion to perfectibility. While evangelical reformers "had for their great idea the regeneration of the soul," utopian socialists preached "the regeneration of society, which is the soul's environment." This common commitment to redeem their society led reformers on what Noyes called parallel "lines of labor."[53]

The reform mission was doubly compelling because most antebellum reformers believed the United States had a unique role to play in guiding the world to enlightenment. They saw republican political foundations, material prosperity, and a Protestant orientation as giving tremendous advantages to Americans and thus imposing a heavy responsibility. Abolitionists, pacifists, and communitarians professed disillusionment with American society, but their dissent—and their dreams—were based upon familiar ideals, which they berated other Americans for forsaking. Like ministers preaching jeremiads, they recalled wayward members of the flock to agreed-upon values. To be sure, the connotative meaning of such ideals is malleable and ever changing. Efforts to recast or redefine shared ideologies are part of the constant dialogue in which reformers engage their society as groups struggle to dominate the terms of public discourse and hence its outcome. Each coterie of reformers attached a particular emphasis to common American terms such as liberty and republicanism and in the process attempted to shape and transform them. Fourierists especially were intent upon making room within traditional American concepts for a foreign-bred communitarian program that challenged some dominant American patterns of thinking and acting. I will have more to say about the nature of this dialectic; the important point here is the remarkable extent to which all reformers—utopians included—shared basic nationalist notions of democracy, republicanism, and Christianity as premises for their quest to purify the nation for the coming millennium.[54]

Fourierists were also susceptible to trends that affected other reform groups' development. The wave of "immediatism" that swept through temperance, peace, and abolitionist reform in the 1830s cleared the way for discussion of projects for total social reconstruction.[55] Indeed, the rise of Fourierism was part of a general reform shift to secular issues and interventionist methods in the wake of the Panic of 1837 and the ensuing depression. As poverty mounted in northern centers, proposals for economic reform—ten-hour movements, land reform, and trade unionism—began to attract as much public attention as did the "moral reform" causes of home missions and abolitionism.[56] Workers turned increasingly to self-help strategies when the depression persisted, forming their own temperance crusade in the Washingtonian movement and establishing cooperatives and mutual benefit societies when strikes proved useless. Fourierists bent to these prevailing winds when they promoted consumer and producer cooperatives among labor groups in the mid-1840s. And like other reformers, the Fourierists spent much time after the Mexican War addressing the increasingly threatening issue of slavery.

At times, relations between reform movements were cordial and even cooperative. Numerous groups and individuals called for general councils; reform conventions frequently endorsed a full menu of proposals; and prominent crusaders— Theodore Parker, Horace Greeley, Gerrit Smith—embraced a generous sampling of causes that ranged from antislavery and land reform to temperance, vegetarianism, and women's rights. Many Fourierists shared this attitude. William Throop reported that within a month he attended abolition, Washingtonian, and Fourier meetings, "all in one sense aiming at the same great center": "first make all *sober* then equal & the philosophy of Fourier carried out will do the rest." Boston and Providence Associationists also regularly attended local antislavery meetings.[57] As a group, the Fourierists preached a brand of "universal" and reconciling reform that was professedly open to other causes. Boston Fourierists held their conventions during the reform societies' "anniversary week" so that participants could attend other meetings. The American Union of Associationists appointed delegates to an international peace convention in Frankfort. Fourierist groups sent representatives to meetings of the New England Workingmen's Association; Brisbane and other leaders addressed the annual Industrial Congress intended to coordinate labor reform initiatives.

Nevertheless, there was usually a competitive edge to such apparent cooperation. Like Nathaniel Hawthorne's Hollingsworth in *The Blithedale Romance,* reformers tended to commit themselves to one great cause and subsume others under it. From this vantage point other crusades appeared as rivals that might siphon off members' support or divert public attention. Even when they acted jointly, most reform groups remained interested in preserving their exclusive turf or else gaining adherents from other causes. Fourierists, who believed that their "social science" contained the key to human betterment, were especially prone to this doctrinaire frame of mind. Their relation to a few of the antebellum reform groups—most notably the abolitionists and land reformers—was substantial and important enough to merit closer analysis later on, but for the most part their interaction with other reformers fell into a consistent pattern. In the beginning the Fourierists sought allies among established communitarian and reform groups; cooperation was again the watchword when their movement waned and they endeavored to hitch it to such rising causes as free soil and European republicanism. In the main, however, during the few years the Fourierists led a popular social movement, they stressed their distinctiveness and superiority, confidently standing apart from other groups and trying simply to lure their members. After a brief period of openness Fourierist conventions became exclusive affairs, ritual gatherings of the already committed which were opened to the public only for evening lectures. Like most reformers, utopians sought cooperation on their own terms.

Fourierists argued that theirs was an "integral" reform encompassing all the "partial" reforms of the era. They chided land reformers, abolitionists, and temperance advocates as myopic "one-idea" men concentrating on "fragmentary" projects. Fourierist propaganda aimed to show reformers that their various causes "all naturally and necessarily tend to central Social Reorganization." True abolition required an end to "the serfdom of wages" as well as physical bondage; peace reform could never succeed until the Harmonic order arrived; intemperance could be traced to the "monotonous employments, . . . wretched homes, . . . [and] anxieties" of competitive Civilization; prostitution stemmed from the legal and economic dependence of women; health reform required totally overhauled work and living arrangements. By professing sympathy with virtually all reform goals and stressing the necessity of their own totalistic approach, they hoped to establish their cause as the "Reform of Reforms," the logical culmination of perfectionist efforts.[58] Only a reorganized society would provide the proper environment for a just, harmonious, and pure social life, and model communities established on Fourierist principles were the way to begin.

The Communitarian Tradition

In advocating reform through pilot communities, the Fourierists adopted a secularized version of the old religious concept that a small enclave of believers could best achieve a godly life. If a community withdrew from the corrupt society around it, the task of liberating personality and establishing social cooperation could be pursued with enough concentration and control to ensure success. Even though such experiments separated true believers from the world, ultimately they would transform it; once perfected, the phalanx would "serve as a model for, and induce the rapid establishment of others," Brisbane assured readers. "If we can substitute peaceably and gradually Associations . . . in the place of present falsely and defectively organized townships, we can effect quietly and easily . . . a social transformation and a mighty reform."[59] This plan to reconstruct society through model townships was the essence of what Arthur Bestor calls the "communitarian point of view."[60]

Precedents for miniature Christian societies existed in dozens of sectarian religious communities established on American soil in the eighteenth and nineteenth centuries. The vision of America as an earthly paradise and the lure of religious toleration and cheap land drew Shakers from England as well as Moravians, Inspirationists, Harmonists, and other German Anabaptist sects. Some brought with them the primitive Christian practice of sharing goods communally; others, like the Shakers, adopted it after their arrival to institutionalize and fortify their faith. In the late 1830s at least three German pietist and nineteen Shaker villages were still in operation, mostly in the northeastern and midwestern United States.[61]

Though Albert Brisbane insisted that the Fourierist phalanx not be compared with sectarian religious communities, there is no doubt that the American Fourierists were influenced by them. Two years before they established Brook Farm, George and Sophia Ripley visited several western Shaker and Zoarite communities and were impressed by their lack of class distinctions and the prevailing atmosphere of self-sacrifice. Around the same time, Horace Greeley wrote of spending "a Sabbath with the Shakers," respectfully described their ritual, and portrayed their life as happy and blameless. It was surely no coincidence that the first extensive prospectus for Brook Farm alluded to the example of the Shakers, Rappites, and Moravians, or that almost all Fourierist phalanxes, as Bestor pointed out, were located within sixty miles of a preexisting Shaker or German community. (One Fourierist group in western New York simply purchased a former Shaker village for its domain.)[62] The literature of American Fourierism contains many references to the Shakers and Rappites; Brisbane and prominent phalanx leaders such as Charles Sears of the North American Phalanx studied their communal arrangements. Conversely, religious communitarians Frederick Evans of the Shakers and John Humphrey Noyes were well acquainted with Fourierism. Noyes acknowledged a special debt to Brook Farm, calling his Oneida Community a "continuation" of that Fourierist experiment. Oneida may also have adopted details of its economic organization and building design from the North American Phalanx.[63]

Ties between the communal sects and secular communitarians were also suggested by patterns of migration. As Bestor points out, the social idealism of communitarians was powerful enough at times to draw adherents across the line dividing theocratic communities from secular ones.[64] One recent study of intergroup migration among nineteenth-century utopian communities found that most groups drew some members from other communities or saw them migrate to others. Though sectarians most often moved from one religious community to another and secular veterans migrated to other nonreligious groups, a few individuals even transferred their allegiance across sectarian lines.[65] Fourierists reflected these patterns: many moved quite freely from phalanx to phalanx; others migrated to or from other secular groups; and a few had connections to religious sectarians (see Appendix Figure 1). As noted above, E. A. Stillman of the Bloomfield Union had been one of Noyes's perfectionist followers at Putney. Peter Kaufmann of the Trumbull Phalanx had lived at a Rappite community called Economy. The Alphadelphia Association counted a former Shaker among its members. One member of the North American Phalanx came from the religious community of Hopedale; another left to practice "Bible Communism" at Oneida; and a third had been a Shaker and returned to that celibate sect when the phalanx disbanded.[66]

The deepest impression that sectarian communities made upon the Fourierists came not from the transfer of members or ideas but from their living example of a thriving communal life. The religious societies taught secular socialists that small cooperative communities could be economically successful. To the Fourierists, the industrious Shaker and Rappite villages proved that with cooperative labor "a greater quantity of wealth is procured with fewer hours of toil, and without any degradation of the laborer." In much the same way that Friedrich Engels contended that the Shakers' success vindicated Communist economic principles, the Fourierists announced that the prosperity of the religious sectarians was "an invincible argument for Association."[67] The Shakers' principles of common property and strict equality were actually much closer to Engels's Communism than to the ideals of the Fourierists, who condemned Shaker doctrines as profoundly anti-libertarian. But at the level of public opinion such distinctions may not have been important, and even liberal communitarians could profit from the favorable image that admiring journalists painted of the religious groups. As Bestor points out, practically every observer took for granted that the experimental communities of the antebellum era were "manifestations of a single movement." Americans found the continuing vigor of the religious sects persuasive enough that they believed in the possibility of success at Robert Owen's New Harmony in 1825 and, even after Owen's disastrous failure, turned again to communitarian reform during the 1840s. Noyes claimed that the religious communities' success was "the 'specie basis' that has upheld all the paper theories, and counteracted the failures, of the French and English schools" of socialism. Bestor goes so far as to say that the "continuing communitive tradition" was "the most important single factor behind the American enthusiasm for Owenism and Fourierism" in the 1830s and 40s.[68]

But the unity of the communitarian movement should not be exaggerated. Noyes was wrong when he doubted that Fourierism "would ever have existed" without the Shakers' precedent and when he reduced experiments of the 1840s to "echoes of Shakerism" that grew "fainter and fainter, as the time-distance increased."[69] In France and America, Fourierism arose independent of religious groups such as the Shakers; the American movement attracted few communitarian veterans of the 1820s and 1830s, whether devout theocrats or free-thinking Owenites; and Fourierists generally kept a respectful distance from contemporary communitarians, whom they considered rivals as much as allies. Though they benefited from the moral capital that religious groups such as the Shakers had accrued with reformers, the Fourierists disavowed any similarity between the phalanx and the ascetic, conformist sectarian societies. The Shaker, John Dwight complained, "wants the spiritual without the material, not the spiritual *in* the material. Life without passion, law without attraction, and purity by sheer simplistic abstinence are no solution, but in reality an evasion of the grand life-problem. . . . These sectarians unite men by leaving out a vast deal that is human."[70]

Religious "communism" and secular "communitarianism" were different things. It seems unlikely that, as Bestor contends, it was sectarian groups that "suggested to [secular utopians] the possibility of social reform by means of . . . [model] colonies." Fourierists consistently described the religious communities as retreats from the world rather than aggressive levers for overturning society. Considering that the German sects made almost no attempt to convert English-speaking Americans, and considering the Shakers' celibacy, peculiar theology, and distrust of "the world," social reformers understandably regarded these communities as reactionary and otherworldly. Only after they endorsed communitarian reform did Fourierists such as Dwight, Sears, Godwin, and Marcus Spring begin to look at the religious communities seriously. Typically, the lessons they drew from studies and visits had nothing to do with the communitarian idea but echoed the standard admiration of sectarian prosperity, now coupled with a smug assertion of Fourierism's "scientific" superiority. "If, in spite of their ignorance," Godwin wrote, "these societies . . . have succeeded in accumulating immeasurable wealth, what might have been done by a Community having a right principle of organization and composed of intellectual . . . men?"[71]

Utopian socialism, not the religious sects, introduced Ripley, Godwin, Channing, and their fellow reformers to the idea that small communities could be progressive models for a profound social transformation. Owen's New Harmony experiment of 1825–27 was the first modern exemplar of the communitarian idea. Most Fourierists were too young to have witnessed its brief and troubled life, but Owen himself, who continued writing in the 1830s and toured the United States in 1844, remained in their consciousness.[72] When George Ripley first encountered Fourier's system in 1840, he recognized it as a scheme of social reorganization akin to Owen's. That same year Ripley's friend Samuel Osgood referred to the infant Brook Farm project as "a New Harmony."[73] More decisive than the lingering influence of Owenism, however, was Brisbane's Fourierist treatise of 1840, *Social Destiny of Man*. Even before the organization of any avowedly Fourierist phalanx, Brisbane's writings played a crucial role in kindling communitarian plans. Ripley introduced his own proposal for Brook Farm to the Transcendental Club just a few weeks after his review of *Social Destiny* in *The Dial* had praised Brisbane's plan to remove "the practical evils of society" through a model community. Fourierism may not have shaped early Brook Farm's specific internal arrangements, but Brisbane's book, appearing at a critical moment, crystallized Ripley's vague reform aspirations around the idea that a small community could be "a house, which would ere long become the desire of nations."[74] As Brisbane's and then Ripley's proposals circulated through Massachusetts at the end of 1840, they awakened communitarian sentiments in such reform journals as *The Liberator* and helped inspire the establishment of independent experiments such as Hopedale (1842) and Northampton (1842). Brisbane's *New York Tribune* column of 1842–43 then spread the fever nationally, so that communitarian activity, which had virtually ceased in the mid-1830s, attained an unprecedented pace. Between 1842 and 1849 fifty-five community experiments were founded, and though only about half were officially Fourierist communities, the Fourierist program had been their immediate inspiration.

The Brisbane–Brook Farm organizing of the early 1840s was the precipitant, but the communitarian idea found widespread acceptance largely because it embodied long-held and deep-seated American ways of thinking, ways that especially appealed to Americans in the second quarter of the nineteenth century.[75] Communitarianism's distrust of government action was shared generally by Americans, whose country had begun in a revolution against tyranny and who shied away from powerful central governments. This bias was reinforced among many antebellum reformers by the sense that American politics had degenerated since the Founders' time into interest-group squabbling and cowardly evasion of such important issues as poverty and slavery. Fourierism proposed a congenial way to bypass such an institutional roadblock. In banding together to build the New Industrial World, communitarians exercised the characteristic American habit of forming voluntary associations. Reform associations were voluntary in a double sense: not only were they formed without specific recognition or sanction from the government, but they did not rely on legal coercion to achieve their goals. Fourierists might argue with evangelicals over reform strategies, but at bottom they also counted upon personal conversion to bring the good society. "Just as the moral reformers appealed to right conduct and conscience in individuals," historian John L. Thomas has noted, "the communitarians sought to erect models of collective conscience to educate Americans." Like evangelicals, Garrisonian abolitionists, and other "romantic reformers" of the age, communitarians preferred publicity and "suasion" to politics.[76]

Another congruence between the communitarian idea and American practice was the phalanx system's parallel with federalism. The Fourierists' faith that a community of several hundred members could serve as the germ of social reconstruction accorded with American experience that the "township" was the element from which larger social organizations evolved. Like townships, phalanxes could be planted at regular intervals and federated into larger regional administrative and economic units. More than this, the township system was uniquely suited for social experimentation. Commentators on the American political system have noted that federalism enabled Americans to try experiments in legislation and administration on the safer and smaller scale of the state or county. In a similar way, social reformers claimed that a model "associative township" would be a perfect scientific laboratory. On the one hand, it was small enough to permit precision in its blueprint and to control noxious consequences should the experiment fail; on the other, it was large enough to contain the requisite components of a typical society. Like a scientific demonstration, its success would be replicable indefinitely.[77]

On the broadest level, the communitarian program accorded with nineteenth-century Americans' sense of the extreme plasticity of their society. Ultimately, social reform rested on the faith that people could simply remake their institutions by making rational decisions. This faith came easily to many nineteenth-century Americans, who believed that their ancestors had established a "new order of the ages" through deliberation and a constitution. Communitarians took this belief in social pliancy to an extreme, for their doctrine assumed that "institutions of world-wide scope might grow from tiny seeds deliberately planted." Such an asssumption, implausible in an old and settled country, was almost taken for granted by those who watched social institutions began anew at each western outpost. Popular movements such as home missionary crusades, antislavery, and land reform were built upon the twin assumption that new settlements represented the American future and that social patterns were indelibly shaped by early decisions and projects. Communitarianism, which envisioned a fresh start in all walks of life, was the radical culmination of this mode of thought. Fourier's assurance that social transformation would spread gradually from model settlements thus corresponded to pervasive nineteenth-century American ideas about social change, especially as shaped by westward expansion.[78] In actuality only a few Fourierist phalanxes set up as colonies on the frontier; like other antebellum communitarians, the Fourierists favored more settled agricultural and commercial regions. Yet all such groups profited from a habit of mind, fostered by the frontier, which saw American society as young, fluid, and perfectible. Reformers were concerned that an impersonal and competitive urban society was usurping the traditional village ideal; why not start over while there was still time and room to create new villages whose example would prove irresistible?

To those setting out to build the ideal society, then, communitarianism was a remarkably congenial strategy. It remained, however, only a strategy, leaving open the crucial question of what specific form the model community would take. As reformers pondered the internal arrangements of their proposed experiments, they gravitated toward the idea that a "science of society" would reveal the natural laws of organization necessary for perfecting both the individual and the group.

"Social Science" and the Search for Order

Although the notion of a science of society originated in the Enlightenment, the term "social science" emerged only after 1828, when British Owenites and French Saint-Simonians and Fourierists laid claim to the title for their respective systems.[79] The concept found its way to America with the communitarian ferment of the 1840s. Orestes Brownson made a passing reference to "social science" in his 1840 essay "The Laboring Classes," but the Fourierists popularized the term by attaching it to their master's system. In *Social Destiny of Man* (1840) Brisbane presented Fourier's community blueprint as a "Divine Social Code" that conformed to God's laws for the harmony of all creation. By the spring of 1842 the American disciple identified Fourier's system as the true "Social Science." Fourierism, John Codman later recalled, first exposed the Brook Farmers to the idea of "science applied to society."[80]

Fourierist "social science" grew out of the Enlightenment quest for natural laws that would reveal not simply the workings of the planets or elements but the physical, moral, and intellectual nature of humanity. Just as Newton discerned the laws of gravitation and Copernicus founded the science of astronomy, Brisbane claimed, Fourier ascertained "the laws and organization of a Social Order, which is based upon fixed laws in the moral or intellectual world, and which can be demonstrated with the precision of a mathematical problem."[81] Fourierism was thus "discovered," not invented; it was *the* science of society rather than one methodological approach. Because Fourier derived the blueprint of the perfect society from his discovery of the God-given passions of human nature, his phalanxes were technically not "experiments" meant to test a theory but demonstrations intended to illustrate the workings of divine and natural law. Fourier's conviction that nature and revelation were identical and accessible to all was a crucial link between his "social science" and the assumptions of many nineteenth-century Americans, whether members of liberal Protestant and rational sects or advocates of new "scientific" credos (such as phrenology) contending for legitimacy. At the same time, the utopians' claim to mathematical precision proved irresistible to many philanthropists and reformers seeking a scientific model of the good society.

During a century that was making a slow and often painful transition from religious to secular modes of thought, Fourierism marked a smooth path by claiming to harmonize reason and revelation in an optimistic synthesis. A rational yet professedly devout "science" of social unity appealed to liberal sects such as Unitarians and Universalists as well as to deists and freethinkers. Even before confronting Fourier, the Transcendentalists had agreed with French eclectic philosophers that their age would replace the Enlightenment's skeptical empiricism with a constructive credo abolishing all dualisms. Mind and matter, man and nature, self and society would be married in a systematic philosophy illustrating the unity of the universe under God, their manifestos proclaimed.[82] Not just Transcendentalists but liberal Protestants generally expected to find in philosophy both confirmation of divine law and clues to social harmony. "Reason meets religion at the same altar, which is faith in Unity," wrote John Dwight. If Providence manifested itself in natural law, increased scientific knowledge would provide revealing glimpses of the ordained "divine plan" for the universe. Believing that such a plan or code would also govern human relations, Fourierists were convinced that, as one tract proclaimed, "There Exists a Social Law, or a Divine Order of Human Society." Brook Farmers voiced the idea common to many nineteenth-century thinkers that each element in nature inevitably functions for the whole, and the whole for the good of each. For many liberal Protestants and their freethinking allies, this became the ideal to be realized among humans through "social science."[83]

Several of the antebellum era's unorthodox scientific systems and practices—later generations would label them pseudosciences—undertook a quest similar to Fourierism's junction of reason, revelation, and reform. Mesmerism, clairvoyance, and spiritualism, all claiming to expand knowledge of the mind's operations, at the same time provided tantalizing but reassuring glimpses of divine life. Séances and hypnotic trances, duplicable "experiments" performed before reputable witnesses, offered apparently scientific proof of a benign spiritual universe analogous to earthly existence. Phrenology, which sought to discern mental faculties and character traits by examining the shape of the skull, was decidedly less "spiritual" in its approach and more deterministic in implication. But like the other new sciences it had the tendency to expand outward toward a synthesis of science and moral philosophy bent upon human improvement.[84] Ambitious practitioners such as Joseph Rodes Buchanan interpreted phrenology as merely one part of a comprehensive "science of man" that included metaphysics and social history, and publicists such as Orson Fowler popularized it as a complement to other systems of self-knowledge based on "universal principles." Devotees of these new "sciences" often felt a kinship with utopian socialism for its scientific air, its rejection of orthodoxy, and its faith in all-encompassing explanatory systems. Their shared belief in an intimate relation between human affairs and natural processes engendered hope that men could engineer a perfect social order. Buchanan devoured Robert Owen's works as a child and maintained close contact with the Fourierists. Clairvoyants and spiritualists appeared at several phalanxes. And Fourierist writers found a hearty welcome at Fowlers and Wells, the preferred publishing house of phrenologists and spiritualists.[85]

The closest connection between "social science" and other new "sciences" was in medicine. Fourierism's philosophical trappings and its emphasis on the prevention of ill health fit well with a rising interest in health and dietary reform. The large number of doctors and health advocates among prominent Fourierists included several professors of unorthodox theories and proponents of dietary reform. Medical reformers, outcasts, and cranks were all drawn by the Fourierists' claim to be working with nature rather than against it and by their criticism of conventional practitioners as inept and greedy. Among leading Fourierists involved with health, Thomas Low Nichols and Mary Gove Nichols were dietary reformers and proponents of "hydropathy," or watercure; Buchanan and George Calvert were medical doctors who turned to phrenology and mesmerism; and C. J. Hempel, Charles Neidhard, and Marx Lazarus were pioneer homeopaths.[86]

Homeopathy was particularly appropriate to Fourierism because it was "the Medicine of Analogy." Homeopathic treatment involved combatting disease with a natural drug that produced similar but milder symptoms. Hempel and Lazarus thus could hail the new system as medical proof of the Fourier-Swedenborg doctrine of "correspondence" or "universal analogy," which linked mind and matter in close one-to-one relationships.[87] One of the more fanciful parts of Fourier's theory held that analogies between humans and plants, like similarities between colors and moods, highlighted distinctive human characteristics while also demonstrating the unity of creation.

Connections to reform metaphysics and unorthodox new "sciences" served to increase Fourierism's disreputable aura among social and religious conservatives and no doubt kept utopians off the list of many wealthy benefactors. Yet the Fourierists succeeded in attracting their own elite corps of financial backers among reform-minded patricians, and the appeal of "social science" had much to do with that success. Several prominent merchants and professional men were drawn to Fourierism because it promised to put philanthropy on a scientific basis. Instead of the often-temporary religious conversions that the evangelical crusade depended upon, utopian socialism pledged enduring reform; for the piecemeal, localized efforts of traditional benefactors of hospitals and colleges it substituted nothing less than a national transformation. Fourierism was sufficiently complex, philosophical, and revolutionary to attract a maverick professional elite; yet the revolution it envisioned was comfortably distant, and meanwhile its leaders assured a fair return to investors. Perhaps most important to such sponsors was the Fourierist program of class conciliation. Patrician reformers sought greater social justice without endorsing complete equality or encouraging class antagonisms. Utopian socialism filled the bill, its blueprint "scientifically" reconciling conflicting interests and guaranteeing prosperity for all yet preserving distinctions of wealth and talent. Fourierism was a Christian socialism, yet it incorporated enough features of "Christian capitalism" to appeal to philanthropically inclined capitalists—not the new industrialists who eagerly supported revivals among their workers but the more disinterested old-family merchants and landowners.[88]

Early utopian socialism often took on aspects of paternalistic social engineering. Owenism was rooted directly in its founder's philanthropic experiment in the New Lanark mills, where he improved working conditions, ran model schools, and restricted child labor. Charles Fourier, who had little money himself, was obsessed by the search for wealthy patrons who might finance a complete model phalanx. Though he failed miserably in this quest, the two phalanxes undertaken in France when his writings attracted wide attention were paid for by wealthy landowner-philanthropists, the French legislator Baudet-Dulary and the Englishman Arthur Young. It is clear from the history of these experiments as well as from Fourier's writings that French Fourierist leaders viewed themselves as enlightened absentee directors creating scientifically sound arrangements for their pliable subjects.[89]

American Fourierists were necessarily more democratic, yet even after Brisbane fashioned Associationism as a grassroots movement relying primarily on volunteer work and modest contributions from members, he continued to court the wealthy. Benevolent patrons and financial "angels" were warmly welcomed by Fourierist leaders, if not by the rank and file. Fourierist clubs and churches in Boston, New York, and Philadelphia were subsidized by a few wealthy local merchants, who also became absentee stockholders of several phalanxes.[90] When a group of New York City patrons who financed expansion of the North American Phalanx tried to wield the power of trustees, and when a few large landowners offered their domains to communal groups, tensions often simmered between hard-working resident members and these rich outsiders who also had voting rights, believed themselves more enlightened Fourierists, and stood to profit from the group's success.[91] Only one American Fourierist experiment deliberately adopted the philanthropic model; significantly, it was an isolated attempt run by a French landowner who invited working-class families to his Kansas farm in the 1870s and ruled the community as a benevolent patriarch.[92]

Unlike the French, Americans had no long tradition of social engineering through model institutions such as schools, hospitals, and asylums, whether state-owned or privately financed. But by the 1830s they were creating a republican version of such a tradition so effectively that the French themselves sent liberal aristocrat Alexis de Tocqueville to inspect new American prisons. During the Jacksonian period there was a widespread perception that the traditional networks of church, family, and community had broken down and were being replaced by an atomistic and violently disordered society; new institutions were needed to instill habits of virtue and self-discipline and serve as models for a free but orderly republican society. In this urge to create model institutions that would maintain social order yet also prepare individuals for responsible and fulfilling freedom lay the main impetus behind popular reform movements advocating model prisons, state-run asylums, and common schools.[93] Fourierism was part of this institution-building trend, which had radical as well as conservative implications. A few utopian socialists, such as common-school advocate Thomas Palmer of Vermont, were leaders in other institutional crusades.[94] More often the connection was indirect: the journalists, doctors, and ministers who led the Fourierist movement perceived the phalanx as a communitarian analogue to the model school or prison. Though they were more concerned about exploitation than crime or intemperance and more interested in passional liberation than self-discipline, these professionals turned to Fourierism in part because they expected communal experiments governed by "social science" to impose a rational and reconciling order on a dangerously fragmented society.

For those committed to communitarianism, much of the appeal of "social science" arose from the practical problem of reconciling productivity and "attraction," private and universal love in a society without coercion. How could communitarians harmonize the apparently antagonistic claims of the individual and the group without sacrificing or diminishing either? Determined to achieve "community with individuality," the Brook Farmers and their allies had scanned contemporary experiments for what Channing called "the clue out of our scientific labyrinth," but they were disappointed.[95] Anarchistic communal experiments such as John Collins's "no-government" Skaneateles and Bronson Alcott's quirky Fruitlands were fatally centrifugal, setting members adrift to pursue their own brand of purity in disruptive fads and manias; Shakers and other religious communitarians seemed to achieve communal peace only through dull conformity and blind obedience.[96] In Fourier's system the secular utopians believed they had found the scientific formula to accommodate all desirable social objectives. Other groups' communal arrangements may have been ingenious inventions—"patent-office models of the good society," as Bestor labels them—but Fourier's elaborate social mathematics was grounded in divine and natural law. Those who embraced his blueprint succumbed to what John L. Thomas called "the myth of the mathematically precise arrangement": they combed Fourier's writings "searching for the perfect number or the exact size, plotting the precise disposition of working forces and living space, and combining these in a formula which would ensure perfect concord." The phalanx was to be a self-adjusting mechanism in which the very institutions fostering cooperation made possible the fullest self-development. Through the community's intricate organization of work in groups and series, its joint-stock foundation, and its complex distributive system, utopians would achieve a dynamic equilibrium where "attractions" always equaled "destinies."[97] To liberal communitarians, the irresistible lure of "social science" lay in its confident claim to reconcile in a rational plan the reaction against "individualism" and the quest for true "individuality."

II

The
Doctrine of
Association

Our plans are revolutionary. . . . But the revolution they contemplate is not violent, nor unjust, nor destructive. . . . Fourier's doctrine possesses a particular value to our minds because it seems to us to be Universal and consequently Reconciling and Pacific. It is both conservative and radical.

—Parke Godwin, *A Popular View of
the Doctrines of Charles Fourier*

4

Association and American Society

When antebellum reformers embraced Fourier's system, they brought native reform promptings face to face with a divergent European tradition. Americanizing Fourierism meant paring it down to a practical community plan, but it also entailed more complex changes and explanations. As a universal, secular, and socialistic ideology, Fourier's theory presented serious difficulties to Americans applying it to their own environment and eager to win converts. Responding to the challenge, Brisbane and his colleagues tried to reconcile Fourierism with American ideas and practices, partly by modifying the theory they had imported and partly by explaining its consistency with the noblest aims of national life. At the same time, Associationist leaders used Fourier's theory to develop a pioneering critique of their own society which applied the Frenchman's indictment of "Civilization" to democratic politics and a freewheeling capitalist economy. The process of Americanization was thus a two-way street. It involved strategies not just to conform communitarian socialism to American conditions and values but also to reshape the reformers' liberal and republican ideological inheritance. The result was a fascinating ideological hybrid called "Association," neither a totally alien presence in American life nor a typical expression of antebellum reform. Radical in its critique but moderate in its program, it appealed as a cooperative and "scientific" version of the American dream at a time when jarring social and economic changes were challenging conventional formulations.

Fourierism and "Association"

The first problem the Americans faced was to edit Fourier's philosophy. The phalanx answered their need for an organized community

93

blueprint, but communitarianism formed only one segment of a huge and intricate philosophical system that included an analysis of the human "passions," ideas about the origins and demise of the solar system, a description of the thirty-two stages of humanity's 80,000-year history, and a program of scientific investigation through analogy. Vast in scope, unique in its categories, and often bizarre, it appeared too unwieldy and eccentric to serve a practical social movement.[1]

The problem had a second aspect, for according to Fourier the same scientific principles dictating phalanx organization predicted sweeping changes in religion, government, and social life. In his "Harmonic" society of the future, organized religion was to be replaced by unconscious obedience to natural law. A global federation of two million phalanxes would supplant existing states and governments. Most distressing to many reformers was Fourier's prediction of a "New Amorous World" that would give full scope to human sexual "attractions" by organizing love in a series of graded "corporations" ranging from "vestalic" virginity to complete promiscuity, both heterosexual and homosexual.

Clearly, Fourierism required pruning, but to extract from it a practical and well-grounded communitarian program called for a delicate balancing act. On the one hand, Albert Brisbane and the Americans separated what they regarded as absurdities and immoralities from the communal plan scattered throughout Fourier's writings. On the other, they preserved enough of Fourier's theory to demonstrate that the phalanx was part of the divine law governing all aspects of nature. The process by which Brisbane carefully selected the most practical and uncontroversial elements of Fourier's theory for an American doctrine of Association has been outlined by Arthur Bestor.[2] Yet because Bestor and other students of American Fourierism have overlooked the influence of Fourier's French disciples on Brisbane and his peers, a truly comparative perspective on the Americanization of Fourier's theory has been lacking. Correspondence, the reading and translating of French Fourierist publications, and the European visits of Brisbane, Charles Dana, and James T. Fisher kept American Fourierists abreast of the strategic and doctrinal modifications that French Fourierists introduced after their master's death in 1837.[3] In discussing the American editing of Fourier in the 1840s, then, we must differentiate between mere echoes of French Fourierism and real divergence.

Not surprisingly, given French precedence and the similarity of the two movements' aims, American Fourierists tended to follow the strategy outlined by the French. Instead of simply translating Fourier's works, French and American disciples wrote their own tracts which in the guise of summarizing his ideas limited them to his philosophy of history, theory of the passions, and plan for model communities. Brisbane's *Social Destiny of Man* (1840), the founding text of the American movement, established virtually the same boundaries on Fourier's theory as did Jules Lechevalier's *Etudes sur la science sociale* (1834), Amédée Paget's *Introduction à l'étude de la science sociale* (1838), and especially Victor Considerant's *Destinée sociale* (1838). *Social Destiny of Man* was by no means a copy of Considerant's book, but from it Brisbane borrowed not simply the title but quotations, drawings, and indeed the whole notion that "industrial reform" was the primary focus of the Fourierist movement.[4]

It is unclear whether Brisbane expected eventually to reveal the deleted parts of Fourier's theory. *Social Destiny* hinted that Fourierism would bring "a fundamental change in the Intellectual and Passional existence of mankind" but then frankly passed over "this dangerous ground" because it might "open a field to controversy." Within a few years, however, attacks in the American press forced Brisbane to act. Some critics pounced upon his exposition to warn that passional psychology legitimated free love or criminality. Others served up juicy excerpts from Fourier's own writings, fueling suspicion that Brisbane and his American converts were hiding Fourier's—and their own—true beliefs. To counteract such criticism, Brisbane and American spokesmen adopted the French Fourierist strategy of revealing the exotic and futuristic sections of Fourier's thought but renouncing the movement's adherence to them.[5]

Three tactics implemented this strategy. First, the portions of Fourier's theory outside approved limits were declared not integral to American Fourierism, which had "the Organization of Labor" as its "exclusive aim." At the Fourierists' New York convention of 1844, a key resolution stated that "we do not receive all the parts of his [Fourier's] theories, which in the publications of the [French] Fourier school are denominated 'Conjectural.'" Specifically, the American movement denied responsibility for Fourier's views "relating to cosmogony and the future manner of society."[6] Second, social reformers repudiated the term "Fourierism" in favor of labels less suggestive of discipleship. French tracts of the 1830s preferred *science sociale*, and Brisbane later subtitled his *Phalanx* the "Journal of Social Science." In the 1840s, French Fourierists vacillated indecisively among *science sociale, la doctrine phalanstérienne*, and *la théorie sociétaire* (the associative theory). Americans preferred the last, agreed upon "Association" in 1844 as the definitive label for their creed, and insisted upon being called "Associationists."[7] Finally, the Americans adopted the idea of an Associative "School" from the Ecole Sociétaire in Paris, the official French decisionmaking body on doctrinal and strategic issues. The Associationists' annual conventions, begun in 1844, were intended to be the "centre" of the American movement, not only for formulating strategy but also for "establishing principles and deciding upon doctrinal questions." Doctrinal statements not sanctioned by this "school" were merely individual opinions rather than articles of Associative faith.[8]

All this does not mean there was nothing peculiarly American about the way American reformers selected from Fourier. In his *Tribune* column and his pamphlet *Association* of 1843, Brisbane created a distinctly American "edition" of Fourierism. In effect, he stripped the master's theory to its bare-boned "practical part," as the pamphlet's subtitle labeled it. To maximize propaganda impact, Brisbane virtually eliminated all theoretical arguments for the phalanx. Out with abstruse passages and analytical tables went Fourier's psychology and theory of history. Instead, Brisbane hinged his argument on the simple and obvious contrast between Associative abundance and present scarcity. In the remaining three-fourths of the pamphlet he concentrated on describing the practical details of phalanx organization and operation. The whole culminated, logically enough, in an invitation to establish a "North American Phalanx"—not Fourier's grand community of 1,620 persons but a far more modest outpost of 400, based upon one of Fourier's scaled-down models. A sample constitution was appended.[9]

Nowhere in French Fourierism did such an insistently practical version appear. Considerant's *Exposition abrégée* (1841), the French precursor to Brisbane's "concise exposition," seems windy and theoretical by comparison, with its vague phalanx description, its abstruse opening section on the "general character of science," and its warning that phalanx trials should be delayed indefinitely until substantial financial backing was available. Especially after their initial failure at Condé-sur-Vesgre, French leaders retreated to fund-raising for a huge phalanx "realization" based on Fourier's full-blown plan. While patiently accruing the capital for a socialist Versailles, they repudiated smaller phalanx attempts by provincial supporters as unauthorized and rudimentary.[10]

In contrast, American Associationists were convinced that Fourierism was best presented as an immediately operative small-scale reform. Their letters to French colleagues and propaganda at home emphasized that Americans had the pragmatic, venturous spirit and the available land to implement the phalanx idea. Largely because they streamlined the Fourierist gospel accordingly, they were able to spawn a popular community movement. They might later express doubts about too hasty construction of miniature phalanxes, but American leaders initially answered the question "What is Association?" with a succinct summary of Fourier's smallest community plan, entreating farmers, artisans, and professionals to drop their doings and begin cooperative working and living.[11]

In a more subtle—and unrecognized—fashion Americans also differed from the French by putting extra distance between their movement and Fourier's controversial ideas about sex and cosmology. Like the French, Associationists differentiated between "official" and "speculative" Fourierist theory, but they went further by hiding the latter from the public or disavowing it totally. Fourier's works were available in France as they were written; French disciples supplemented them with glosses on their master's more abstruse or controversial notions and even published some of his manuscripts, which, though edited with a heavy hand, nonetheless gave a fair idea of his sexual theories. Yet not until most of the New World phalanxes had already been established did Americans begin to reveal Fourier's speculations and predictions to the public. And never in the course of their movement did Americans publish more than one severely abridged volume of Fourier's own writings.[12]

American revelations were thus not only late but incomplete and hedged. Parke Godwin's *Popular View of the Doctrines of Fourier* (1844) purported finally to reveal the scope of Fourier's thought. Since most of Godwin's book was a translation of a French Fourierist tract by Hippolyte Renaud, a brief comparison is instructive. Godwin did reveal certain theories and predictions hitherto unpublished in America. A section on "cosmogony," for example, presented Fourier's notion that planets are "intelligent . . . beings" who create new worlds through intercourse and his idea that men begin life anew in an analogous "aromal" world after death. But Godwin edited Renaud's account of future sexual relations, blurring the French writer's already generalized portrait of sexual freedom in the phalanx, and at some points changed Renaud's text in order to tone down Fourier's sexual radicalism. For example, he transformed Renaud's statement that most future phalansterians would go beyond marital fidelity to freer relations into an assertion that most would *stop* at virtuous "constancy." And where Renaud, in spite of offical Ecole Sociétaire policy, claimed that Fourier's predictions were "ELEVATED AND CLEAR TRUTHS, which I believe with total conviction," Godwin repudiated them as "highly repugnant," "erroneous" and "false" and inserted additional disclaimers divorcing them from official Associationism.[13]

Wariness in revealing Fourier's futurology—especially the future of sex—and extra emphasis in disclaiming it were typical of the American movement's leadership. One by one, Brook Farmers and other propagandists issued notices personally repudiating "speculative" elements of Fourier's theory. Charles Dana told an audience that even in his own limited study of Fourier's works he found "many things" he could not "agree to or even approve." Henry Van Amringe called Fourier's theory of metempsychosis "unsubstantial and unphilosophical" and charged that the Frenchman's loosening of conjugal ties violated both biblical ordinance and natural law. According to John Dwight, it was uncertain whether *any* prominent Associationist accepted all of Fourier's views on love and marriage.[14] Those few who harbored doubts about this sexual conservatism, such as E. P. Grant of the Ohio Phalanx, expressed them only in private. Not until 1849, when American Fourierism was in disarray, did a group of latecomers to the movement venture to discuss the founder's sexual theories in greater detail and even endorse them.[15]

The practicality of American Fourierist doctrine and the moral conservatism of American propagandizing suggest that within a wide-ranging utopian theory Americans established the boundaries that best reflected their aspirations and accommodated their culture. By honing Fourier's theory down to a workable blueprint, Brisbane and his colleagues were able to channel the antebellum outburst of social perfectionism into a specifically Fourierist mold. The overwhelming response to their message in the early 1840s confirmed their doctrinal achievement. But the sad fate of the miniature phalanxes they inspired also showed that Fourierist leaders' willingness to promote small and underfinanced experiments could threaten the very movement it created.

The strategy of dividing Fourier's theory in two and making only one part "official" policy had a more clearly positive result. It helped dissociate Fourierists from the stigma of free love attached to the Owenites, enabling them to concentrate on the social critique and communitarian plan that formed the heart of their utopian socialism. It also allowed Associationist leaders to present a united front to the public, despite internal disagreements over theory. Of course, since Fourier's phalanx and his prediction of a "new amorous world" were equally grounded in his psychology of the "passions," Associationists were vulnerable to the charge of being closet free-lovers. But by publicly disclaiming adherence to Fourier's sexual agenda and by setting up relatively conventional arrangements in their phalanxes, the Americans tried to minimize the damage that Fourier's orgiastic visions could bring.

Civilization, American Style

The writings of American Fourierists, though hardly as "impoverished" as one French historian claims, are not as voluminous or theoretically sophisticated as their French counterparts.[16] The practical nature of the American movement and its shorter life precluded their being so. Yet it is this "occasional" character and specific reference to social context that make Associationist propaganda uniquely significant. To look to American Fourierists for refinement of Fourier's theory of the "passions" or for further explorations into the abstruse "Law of the Series" is to miss the basic importance of their undertaking. In their books, pamphlets, and periodicals, Associationists made the first extensive attempt to apply socialistic ideas to the American scene.

As a product of the Enlightenment, Fourier's theory—like the "scientific" socialism that followed it—repudiated the idea of national uniqueness. His philosophy outlined the stages of "Man" in the past, present, and future rather than the phases of various distinctive cultures. Built upon this metahistorical foundation and rising from Fourier's analysis of human nature, the phalanx purported to solve the problems of humanity, not Frenchmen. In view of this determined universalism, Fourier's critique of "Civilization" took on special importance. When Fourier indicted Civilization's competitive economy, he was pointing his finger at the social order in which much of the populated world was enmeshed and toward which the remainder was evolving by inexorable law. Likewise, when Fourier predicted that in later stages of Civilization large manufacturing and agricultural corporations would create a new feudalism, he was warning the entire world that unless it adopted his phalanx system, it would suffer increasing misery.

Such sweeping conceptual power came from isolated deduction rather than exhaustive empiricism. Having moved from French particulars to a dizzying level of generalization, Fourier felt no need to descend again to apply his critique to specific societies or explain their deviations; he merely decreed them subservient to his discovered laws. Since Fourier virtually ignored American society and his French disciples were almost as indifferent, it was left to Americans to apply his ideas to this country, determine its place in his system, and argue the prospects for socialism here.

At the outset they denied the fundamental uniqueness of American social and economic institutions. Associationists insisted that Fourier's critique of Civilization applied to the United States, and they presented evidence that "Industrial Feudalism" was coming to the New World as to the Old. Even after a century of socialist interpretations of the United States, their critique seems startlingly fresh. Not only were Associationists virtually unique among antebellum reformers in denying America's exemption from European-style poverty and class warfare, but few American radicals of the entire century—entranced as they were by the idea of laissez faire—joined them in denouncing competitive individualism so thoroughly.[17] Yet for all their European radicalism the Associationists were in many ways characteristically American, and their version of Fourierism was an emphatically American creed. When they turned from social criticism to social ideals, Associationists argued that far from repudiating American pieties, the phalanx order was merely a more effective way of realizing the ideals of democracy, Christianity, and missionary nationalism. And when they assessed the prospects for Fourierism here, Associationists spun out a new version of American "exceptionalism": America as the Promised Land of Socialism. Theirs was a radical critique of American institutions which was nevertheless animated by a strongly nationalistic vision of utopia.

In presenting their argument, Associationists relied most heavily on Fourier's own theory, but they also drew from Carlyle, British economists, and the Saint-Simonians. A new world of discourse about society was emerging in Europe in the second third of the nineteenth century, a world that Fourier's theory had helped to build. "Individualism," "socialism," "communism," "solidarity," "wage slavery"—these terms were coined in Europe during an era when class consciousness was crystallized by industrialism (another contemporary coinage) and study of society as a distinct organization was born.[18] Acquaintance with Saint-Simonian and Tory socialist literature had helped draw such reformers as Godwin and Channing to Fourierism, and they found these ideas useful in elaborating a Fourierist analysis of American society. European influences were not adopted wholesale, however; rather, they were used to elucidate and extend qualms about American society already being voiced by Transcendentalists, evangelicals, and Jacksonian artisans. In the complex, creative resonance between foreign ideologies and indigenous reform lay the unique appeal of American Association.

American Fourierists began by repudiating the widespread contemporary belief that American social and economic forms differed so drastically from European that different categories and strategies were required to address them. The American Revolution had introduced a new form of government, but it had left oppressive Old World social institutions intact: "We have the same repugnant, degrading and ill-requited system of Industry as Europe; the same system of Free Competition, or false rivalry and envious strife and anarchy in the field of commerce and industry; the same menial system of Hired Labor or Labor for Wages; the same wasteful, intricate and grasping system of Trade; the same exclusive ownership of machinery by capital . . . and the same system of isolated or separate Households."[19]

And the one exception was for the worse: chattel slavery, a relic from the period of "Barbarism" that lingered in the American South after its abolition in Europe (see Chapter 9). Apart from this anachronism, in both the Old and New Worlds society had passed through "Edenism," "Savagery," "Patriarchy," and "Barbarism" to arrive at the crucial stage called "Civilization"—from which it might either continue its "subversive" development or make the sudden leap directly into the eighth or "Harmonic" period of human existence.

Civilization's "pivotal" feature and the root of most of its evils was that "system of Free Competition" which—in the absence of restraints upon greed or economic forms channeling self-interest into the common good—degenerated into wholesale economic warfare. According to Associationists, Civilization resembled nothing so much as a Bunyanesque "City of Antagonism." First, capital vied with capital for a larger share of the market. In the process of rivalry among manufacturers and other suppliers, enormous funds were wasted, services duplicated, and the economy subjected to the periodic shock of business failure. The struggle to achieve a monopoly through either ruthless competition or—as Jacksonians feared—legislative privileges victimized the public with high prices and encouraged bribery, fraud, and other dishonest practices.[20]

Second, in quest of supremacy over competitors, capitalists regularly preyed upon labor. Like radical Jacksonian Democrats, Associationists held to a moral version of the labor theory of value; they saw capital siphoning off the wealth that labor produced in an unfair process of "spoliation." Two "civilized" institutions served as vehicles for this exploitation. The system of labor for wages set up a contract between laborer and employer in which the latter held all the power and hired at the lowest possible rates. As a result, the nominally free laborer was held in a dependent "vassalage" that resembled feudal relations but was even worse because it lacked guarantees and responsibilities on the part of the powerful. Associationists adopted the term "wage slavery" from British workingmen's movements and French socialism to dramatize the workers' fall from dignity, craftsmanship, and economic independence to employment under rigid work discipline by merchant capitalists or manufacturers.[21]

What capital could not appropriate through the wage system it took through commerce. Fourier had aimed his dissecting knife at the bankers, speculators, and merchants who epitomized to him the grasping, fraudulent dealings of Civilization. American Associationists echoed his disdain for middlemen. Like many contemporaries in the liberal and republican traditions, they made an invidious distinction between real "producers" of wealth and "nonproducing" distributors of it, between "virtue" and "commerce." In this spirit Charles Dana deplored the fleecing of the public through "monopolies, adulterations, periodical crises and bankruptcies, and fifty other instruments of the same sort." Other indictments added usury and speculation to the list of commercial predations.[22]

Civilized competition was "glossed over by an appearance of equity and justice," declared Brisbane and Godwin, but underneath there was parasitism and exploitation: "The producing multitude toil and drudge to create the means of sustaining in ease and idleness a favored minority." Even "in this most democratic of countries" a pernicious "aristocratic order" ruled. Associationist attacks on aristocracy, commerce, and wages echoed clearly the rhetoric of "country ideology" and Jacksonian radicalism. Yet because they believed that the wage system and commercial oppression were outgrowths rather than usurpers of "free trade" and "equal rights," Fourierists were able to turn egalitarian and laissez-faire arguments against the order they had helped to build.[23]

A third and particularly galling conflict of interests was among laborers themselves. The wage system arrayed worker against worker in the bid to undersell one another's labor, cutting wages "to the lowest point which will sustain existence, and thus reduc[ing] themselves by their own incoherent strife to poverty and destitution." Associationists accepted David Ricardo's "iron law of wages" as a legitimate description of labor's plight under Civilization, contending that pauperism arose in different countries in direct ratio to their implementation of unregulated wage labor. Torn by multiple layers of competition, Civilization thus amounted to nothing less than an "insane war of efforts and interests" destructive to all social classes but especially to the workers. And such a "war" was raging in America as well as in Europe.[24]

This was not simply rhetoric. To Brisbane, Godwin, and Channing, Fourier's critique of Civilization helped account for the persistence of deprivation in America, despite its political freedom, by tying American social ills into a general theory of social organization. Impressed by Fourierist "social science" and sensitized to American shortcomings, they firmly believed in the basic and pernicious similarity of American and European societies under Civilization's competitive system. Above that basic structure, however, they had to recognize that actual conditions diverged significantly. Critics charged the Associationists with misapplying theories born in strife-torn Europe to a peaceful, prosperous America, and in fact the economic evils of Civilization simply were not as apparent in antebellum America as across the Atlantic. Despite the depression of the early 1840s, for instance, really desperate poverty was confined to small pockets in a few major cities. And Associationists believed that cheap lands in the West functioned as a safety valve by providing an outlet for urban malcontents and keeping the eastern wage scale above subsistence levels. There was no doubt even to Fourierists that American society was more fluid and the condition of the masses "much above what it is in Europe."[25]

To Americanize the Fourierist critique, Associationists sought to incorporate their country's apparent social advantages into Fourierism without denying Fourier's universal typology. One way was to stress the moral and psychological damage rather than the strictly economic injustices of competitive capitalism. Such an emphasis grew naturally out of antebellum reformers' moralistic rather than economic habit of thought, but it also reflected their perception of American differences. Whereas they usually described European conditions in terms of straight economic deprivation, Associationists most often spoke of the American economy with reference to the psychology of mobility and moral "culture":

> Our whole system of Commerce and Industry has become a round of killing cares, harassing anxieties, hopes blasted, and unforeseen reverses and ruin. The business world is . . . a school for the most callous selfishness and duplicity; its spirit has rendered business tact . . . and petty cunning the most important of qualifications, . . . set up wealth as the standard of excellence and respectability, and rendered its acquisition a mania, to which all the higher and more noble aims of life are sacrificed.[26]

The opening "our" is the cue for the words particularly relevant to the American scene: "anxiety" rather than "misery," "acquisition" rather than "exploitation." The distinction is betrayed rather than stated outright through comparison with Europe, but it is noticeable and significant all the same.

Emphasizing psychology and personality was not renouncing Fourier, who had edified readers with long lists detailing the deceits, frustrations, and anxieties that commerce inflicted on the common man.[27] Associationists were merely stressing the one aspect of the Fourierist critique of Civilization peculiarly appropriate to America. Unbridled capitalism's business cycle seemed to breed a new kind of confusion and helplessness along the social spectrum. The absence of traditional hierarchies whetted Americans' appetite for distinction through wealth, but economic fluctuations continually frustrated it. "Eagerness to acquire" quickly turned into "dread to lose." Periodic commercial crises, credit shortages, and bank failures left workingmen jobless and threatened the middle and upper classes with sudden ruin. Actual deprivation might be less prevalent than in Europe, Horace Greeley admitted, but the nagging fear of being "cut off from any opportunity to acquire and possess" wore upon the American population.[28]

Talk about bank panics and economic uncertainty seemed more relevant in the American 1840s than tirades on behalf of a proletariat. Furthermore, by stressing the psychological costs of Civilization, Associationists were tapping central antebellum currents of thought. The obsessed and careworn American achiever had already become a common figure among commentators who were having second thoughts about New World enterprise. Had not James Fenimore Cooper and domestic novelists such as Sarah Josepha Hale and Harriet Beecher Stowe berated Americans for their single-minded pursuit of wealth? Even the *American Whig Review* featured an essay suggesting that "the trading spirit" was making Americans tense and dull. It was left to the brilliant French visitor Alexis de Tocqueville, of course, to create the most resonant and influential description of how general equality had turned Americans into anxious competers.[29]

Some Associationists were more concerned about moral corruption than about insecurity; in warning against selfishness and dishonesty under competition, these utopians drew directly on evangelical or Transcendentalist arguments against an obsession with moneymaking. When Fourierists of the Burned-Over District condemned Americans' slavish devotion to wealth, they were echoing the revivalist thunderings against Mammon which had sounded through western New York a decade earlier. In much the same way, when Brook Farm Fourierists complained that materialism nipped spirituality in the bud and that the modern economy compartmentalized life, they were summoning their Transcendentalist past to testify for Fourier's plan. By then they claimed to realize, however, that Christian reformation and charity were inadequate because immorality was structural. As long as one took part in competitive commercial transactions, a life of "complete . . . Christian honesty" was "impossible."[30]

Civilization's selfishness also mocked the Christian ideal of solidarity through its privatization of economic and social life. Individuals approached each other in the marketplace with such calculation and suspicion that older republican notions of justice and civic responsibility were virtually forgotten. "Men have lost all confidence in each other," lamented one phalansterian. Furthermore, because the business world was corrupt and labor no longer satisfying, civilizees had set aside the home as a retreat from work and the repository of virtue. Associationists were one of the few antebellum groups to see social dangers in the growing Victorian glorification of the privatized family. The ideology of domesticity, they argued, actually reinforced civilized selfishness. From the private hearth arose a "family-selfishness" that concentrated "all affections and hopes within its own little circle," leaving "the heart indifferent to the woes and sufferings of mankind."[31]

Through laissez-faire economics and the "isolated household," Civilization made "individualism" the "be all and the end all of social life" and obstructed the important idea that "men . . . are brothers and not competitors."[32] In the concept of individualism Associationists found an important bridge between their gospel of fraternity and a sociological indictment of Civilization. As Yehoshua Arieli has shown, the term was coined by the Saint-Simonians in the 1830s to denote the ethos of modern fragmented and uprooted society, in contrast to the developing concept of "socialism." From the Saint-Simonians the word spread to French Fourierists, then to Tocqueville and others. Associationists absorbed the Fourierist usage through Brisbane, whose *Social Destiny* organized its critique of Civilization around the concept. According to Brisbane, individualism was a spirit of rootlessness, anarchy and selfishness which had gathered force in Western minds since the Reformation. It underlay the growth of capitalism, all the while masking its pernicious effects with spurious claims about liberty. Its influence sustained free competition, encouraged workers to fight for status and wealth, hardened their sympathies, and prevented cooperation.[33]

Thus applied, the concept of individualism was a potent one. While incorporating the utopians' critique of social divisiveness and materialism it helped shift their terms of discourse from moralism to sociology. It showed that selfishness, rather than having a "permanent basis in the nature of man," was one of "the poisonous weeds a false system . . . has produced." The problem was not attitudes so much as a social organization that gave rise to them. And when Fourierists distinguished "individualism" from "individuality"—the name they gave to legitimate self-expression—they argued that full development of social, moral, and aesthetic faculties could take place only in a noncompetitive society.[34]

The final focal point of Associationists' personality-oriented critique of Civilization was the nature of work. Fourier's path-breaking idea that work must be an "attractive" and integral part of life meshed with the Transcendentalists' longing to ennoble everyday activity, as well as with labor reformers' resistance to industrial work discipline. As competition led to increased specialization, work was becoming monotonous and alienated. Confined to one task, men were no longer "whole": Associationists pointed to the use of the term "hands" to designate laborers as a typical symptom of the fragmentation of civilized life. Similarly, factory workers were mere "operatives": under a system of work for wages and strict shop discipline, men had become things rather than persons. Manual labor and intellectual activity, which Brook Farmers felt should fertilize each other, had drawn apart with the advent of a sophisticated market economy. The result was that workers were denied their natural right to culture, while the educated lacked the practical knowhow needed to make them complete. Associationists also added a communal dimension to their critique of modern work when they complained that specialized labor "separates men . . . during the long hours of the day" from the "sympathy" and "companionship" their nature requires.[35] Such arguments echoed on a theoretical level the practical fears of artisans that industrial capitalism was destroying the independence and personalism of traditional workshop production.

Toward a Modern Feudalism

In spelling out the moral and psychological implications of Civilization, Associationists protested that despite its relative prosperity the American competitive order made life intolerable. Fourier's theory of history provided a second way to incorporate local conditions into utopian socialist categories. Fourier had predicted that in the late stages of Civilization a growing "Commercial and Industrial Feudalism" would place producers in bondage to large corporations and banking houses; American utopians saw this warning coming true in scattered "symptoms" of a frightful urban-industrial order "close at our doors."[36] Since Thomas Jefferson, Americans had wondered whether their society could remain immune to the contrasts of Europe's cities or the permanent proletariat of its industrial centers. To the Associationists' heightened sensitivities, New York—where one of every seven residents required charity—and other commercial cities were already infected. In the mode of Dickens, Parke Godwin led readers from the luxurious comfort of a merchant's "marble palace" to the destitution of a slum alley, suggesting that urban life both created and cruelly juxtaposed such extremes. This kind of sensationalized reportage was perfected by two Fourierist fellow travelers: George ("Gaslight") Foster, whose journalistic "slices" of New York were excerpted in The Harbinger, and George Lippard, the combative young Philadelphian whose lurid populist novels proclaimed a Fourieristic association of workers as the only antidote to an approaching urban apocalypse. Lippard and Foster wrote neo-Gothic tales, modeled on Eugène Sue's phenomenally successful Mystères de Paris (1844), in which they announced the migration of a dangerous urban underworld of poverty and crime from Europe to the New World.[37]

Early American factory towns such as Lowell, Massachusetts, were deliberately planned as rural manufacturing utopias to allay the public's fears of misery and disorder. England, with its vast industrial hells, polluted rivers, and "two nations," was particularly the example to avoid; like other Americans, Fourierists were horrified by reports from Manchester and followed the revealing Parliamentary debates on Factory bills. Yet when they examined the Lowell mills, Associationists found them nearer to Manchester than to the rosy pictures such visitors as Daniel Webster and Michel Chevalier painted. Returned from a visit to Lowell and Manchester, New Hampshire, Brisbane described the tyrannical working conditions: operatives forced to be silent, subjected to poor ventilation and lighting, governed by ringing bells, and tending machines twelve to fourteen hours per day. John Allen recounted similar impressions to audiences in Boston and Cincinnati.[38] Even in industries not yet fully mechanized, industrial concentration had begun. Associationists complained that shoe, hat, and furniture manufacturing houses set up by wholesale merchants throughout the East were destroying independent artisans. "It has come to this," Dana concluded, "that the Moneyed Feudalism, which in the old world grinds out the very life of men, stupifies their souls, and ruins their bodies, . . . is laying its unrelaxing hand upon our own brothers."[39]

Structurally, this new feudalism meant that the introduction of modern commercial and industrial mechanisms—banks, machinery, factories, corporations—was hardening the evils of competitive Civilization into systematic oppression. Injecting these forms into "free competition" increased the power of the haves at the expense of the have-nots. Parke Godwin revived Jacksonian arguments against large-scale banks and other beneficiaries of "special legislation," citing them as examples of how institutions that might be useful in other contexts only deepened the inequalities of competition. The "great producing establishments" going up everywhere were similarly good seeds planted in the wrong soil. As advocates of a rational "organization of industry" the Associationists appreciated economies of scale, efficiencies of planning, and the orderly division of labor; for them the problem lay in the application of these new forces within Civilization. Because of competition factory owners reduced wages to a minimum, required iron discipline, and designed their buildings to speed production rather than to promote worker satisfaction. Large corporations depersonalized relationships between master and worker: in the small workshop "the instinctive sense of brotherhood" limited the employer's perogatives, wrote Dana, but "when the employer, instead of being a man is a company," the worker's situation deteriorated as the power of capital increased. Introducing rhetoric that would be revived by Populists and socialists fifty years later, Dana proclaimed that "a corporation has no heart, no human sympathies: it has a rule to be rigidly followed, a treasury to fill . . . it is not a part of Humanity, it is a machine for making money." Corporations showed the benefits of coordinated organization, but they represented "a false system of Association," the inverted image of the phalanx ideal. If not channeled away from "subversive" competitive forms, the efficiency impulse threatened to bring the new feudalism.[40]

The Fourierist position on mechanization was analogous. Dana, Godwin, Greeley, and Van Amringe noted with Carlyle, Marx, and other nineteenth-century critics that productive machinery exposed a painful contradiction of competitive capitalism: "The sufferings of the masses are aggravated in the precise ratio in which the means of satisfying every desire become more plentiful," Dana complained. Yet Associationists did not wish to turn back the clock and recreate the preindustrial village. Far more than Fourier, American utopians accepted mechanical invention as a potential boon to humanity. The crucial problem was ownership: machinery was potentially liberating, but "when monopolized by Capital," it became "at once the enemy and scourge of the laboring multitude, working against instead of for them." Only when workers became owners and owners workers would all reap the rewards of mechanical improvements. At that point, "the more aid Associationists get from machinery, the better for them."[41] Association as outlined by its major spokesmen was not, as has been claimed, a philosophy of retreat from industrialism.[42] Fourierists did not reject the new forces of the Industrial Revolution; they deplored their use to bolster the exploitation and inequalities of competition. As long as social and economic institutions legitimated this free-for-all, the advance of commerce and manufacturing in America would tend "to separate society into two classes—the rich and the poor," and make "the rich grow richer and the poor poorer, in equal proportions."[43]

When opponents protested that Associationists were mistakenly transplanting complaints against European conditions to the less developed and more nearly equal society of America, Fourierists disagreed. "The discerning mind" could see that the pieces accumulating in America fit into Fourier's puzzle. Dwight compared the Fourierist picture of American Industrial Feudalism to the portrait of Hawthorne's two lovers in "The Prophetic Pictures": "At first it bore no likeness to them and displeased them; but . . . as they lived together month after month . . . they grew like the picture; for the painter had painted deeper than the surface and painted the essential fact of their two characters."[44] The United States simply lagged in acting out Fourier's universal law of social development. Crowded old Europe had had thousands of years in which to build oppression; in more recently discovered America the "sparse population" and "vast extent of soil" were "accidental" and "temporary" conditions that merely delayed the arrival of the new feudalism. Since America differed from Europe "only as the plant of spring differs from the mature product of autumn," time would tell its equivalent fate.[45]

The common belief that cheap lands provided a safety valve for labor discontent implied danger when the supply ran out. Associationists confirmed Orestes Brownson's point that western homesteads already were beyond the financial reach of eastern workers. Not only was population pressure driving up prices, but western farmlands were increasingly coming under the control of wealthy individuals and companies as either absentee owners or mortgage holders. Land monopoly was entering the United States as an integral feature of the new feudalism. With Fourier's help, Associationists accurately predicted what twentieth-century Americans would call "agribusiness": Brisbane, Van Amringe, and others envisioned that wealthy joint-stock corporations in alliance with investment bankers would take over agriculture and run huge mechanized farms much as they did factories.[46]

Between booming eastern cities and "Agricultural Feudalism" encroaching in the West, said Godwin, America would have its own "social hell" within two or three generations.[47] At that juncture, either the toiling masses would succumb to the new feudalism or they would break out in violence against its lords. Because they were better attuned than Fourier to the Industrial Revolution and radical working-class ideologies, French and American Fourierists feared a "Civil War between Producers and Capitalists" more than their master had. Revolutionary upheaval was a plausible alternative to the voluntary servitude of industrial feudalism, or perhaps would serve as a bloody prelude to it. Leaders among American Associationists whose outlook was conciliatory rather than pugnacious, Whig rather than Democratic, tended to be most afraid. Channing and Greeley saw an American "war of classes" as "plainly threatened" and even "partially commenced."[48] Godwin and Dana were closer to the belligerent rhetoric of the workingmen's movement, but even their threats and warnings were meant to move the middle class toward a reconciliatory socialism rather than to incite workers. No Associationist wanted class violence, but most feared it possible in the not too distant future.

Yet if the crisis was still a couple of generations away, why were Associationists so alarmed? One cause was the "immediatist" attitude and millennial expectations that Fourierists shared with other antebellum reformers. To Christian idealists the present social order was sinful and should be replaced at once, regardless of whether it had reached its crisis point. "The question," George Ripley asserted, "is not whether we in the United States are some few degrees worse or better off than Europeans or others. Rather, the question is whether the social organization in which we live is that intended by the Creator."[49]

Within the Fourierists' view of social development, however, lay an equally compelling reason for their impatience. Just as nineteenth-century communitarians believed that small colonies planted on the frontier might well become the dominant social institutions of later generations, the developmental habit of thought gave special significance to the form taken by the industrial towns and commercial centers expanding on the eastern seaboard and along major transportation routes: a single factory town or urban slum might determine the course of a region's future or even the nation's. Lowell and New York City's notorious Five Points district might well be harbingers of an approaching feudal order. To the mid-nineteenth-century mind, "potentialities were among the most real of all things."[50] Associationists sincerely believed their society to be at a critical turningpoint, when new competitive industrial and commercial forms had to be reshaped before they became permanently entrenched.

In a sense, the Associationists' warning that a new feudal order was coming to America gave voice to an anxious undercurrent of the seemingly confident Jacksonian years: a muted but growing chorus of fears that Old World inequality and corruption were crossing the Atlantic. Historians have found its expression in sources ranging from artisan protests to popular literature, from art to the rhetoric of western expansionism.[51] Fourierists were only expressing in a more extreme form the anxiety many Americans felt about growing competition, urbanization, and industrialization. What Fourier's theory did was to attach these indigenous criticisms convincingly to a coherent radical critique of American social organization.

The Failure of Republican Politics

The Fourierists responded to the situation of American politics with a similar revision of American concepts. On one hand, they argued that the strategies of democratic politics were thoroughly inadequate solutions to the mounting ills of Civilization; on the other, they presented social reorganization as the completion of the noble ideals voiced by the Founding Fathers and the republican tradition.

Because America's revolution had been political, and because democratic politics appeared responsible for national prosperity, many nineteenth-century Americans believed that the ballot could correct any lingering social ills. Following Fourier, Associationists pronounced this faith in politics "illusory." "Our evils are SOCIAL, not POLITICAL," proclaimed Brisbane's *Social Destiny of Man*. Politics was only the "superstructure" atop deeper social developments that determined measures and institutions "as a stream carries . . . objects floating on its surface."[52] Fierce electoral struggles between parties simply reflected Civilization's social war brewing beneath them: "They are dignified, it is true, with the name of battles for principles, but in reality . . . they are battles on narrow, selfish ground, of class against class, of locality against locality, of business against business. . . . success . . . consists of putting one set of men out of office and another in, and substituting one series of selfish interests for another."[53]

Complaints against "factions" and selfish politicians were common in the Jacksonian era, when the emergence of rough-and-tumble democratic politics seemed to question an older republican tradition of civic virtue and patrician rule.[54] Fourierists voiced them, however, not to return political debate to civility and grand principles but to denigrate political activity itself. Endless sterile debates over the tariff and internal improvements convinced most Associationists that the communitarian method of sidestepping politics was a far better alternative than pressing for social legislation. There were some exceptions: Horace Greeley remained committed to the Whig Party and exempt from antipolitical rhetoric, and even Brisbane at times appeared eager to have politicians address Fourierist issues. In the early 1840s Brisbane buttonholed John C. Calhoun and Caleb Cushing and actually made a convert of Nicholas

Trist, James Polk's negotiator of the Mexican War treaty.[55] But for the most part, Associationists refrained from active participation in politics during the communitarian agitation and recommended against reaching the social millennium through the ballot box. Only when the phalanx idea was petering out and land reform and antislavery beckoned as plausible interim measures did Fourierists revive their political interests.[56]

According to Brisbane, in the half-century since America had established the world's most advanced democratic government, there had been little progress in extending opportunity and security to all. This proved that political measures could not bring meaningful social improvement:

> The best talent of the country has been devoted to Politics; various parties—Federal and Democratic—have had the ascendancy; different policies—Hamiltonian and Jeffersonian—have been carried out; the labors of from thirteen to twenty-six State Legislatures, of a National Congress and an unshackled Press, have been devoted to the work of improvement, and after all, what great results have been attained? Are the people happier? are they more elevated, morally and socially? have they pleasing and encouraging prospects before them? No, far from it . . . poverty and dependence, anxiety . . . and instability . . . have increased . . . with marked rapidity.[57]

These were hardly mathematical proofs, but beneath the utopians' hyperbole lay two important new insights. First, and more simply, in rejecting politics Associationists detached social conflicts from political life. The dominant "republican" ideological framework of the young United States tended to consider social groups less as economic classes than as categories of citizens, interpreting "privileges" and "monopolies" as creations of unfair legislation rather than the products of a particular economic system.[58] In contrast, as forerunners of modern sociology, utopians viewed society as an independently functioning system of individual and class conflict, a system inherently unequal and one subject to reform without reference to politics. Other antebellum reformers, particularly those pursuing an evangelical agenda, separated reform from politics, but they dealt with society as an aggregate of individuals to be addressed by moral appeals rather than a social structure to be overhauled. Fourierism gave reformers a vocabulary and a strategy for addressing social ills as structural problems independent of politics.

Second, through utopian "social science" Associationists challenged the contemporary American dogma (held even by abolitionists, as Reconstruction would prove) that civil and political rights were sufficient guarantors of freedom. Fourierist social theory taught that classes could use democratic politics to support oppression and that mere legislation did not eliminate basic economic antagonisms. Not only could "political freedom" coexist with "social slavery," but a belief in the right to vote or the right of *habeus corpus* as "the sum of all good" helped disguise the essentially false basis of society. Under democratic government men could well think themselves free when in reality they were the "slaves of labor."[59]

Elaborating these basic insights, Associationists analyzed American party positions with a sharp eye on how they related to underlying social developments. Parke Godwin led the attack on his former Democratic allies. In much the same way that Marx and Engels combined historical materialism with Ricardian theory, Godwin used history and economics to label the Democrats' laissez-faire program dangerously anachronistic. The Democrats noticed encroaching monopoly, he wrote, but proposed a remedy that dated from the eighteenth-century assault on feudal privileges and mercantile policies. To abolish restraining laws and repeal government-sanctioned monopolies in the nineteenth century was to give "free scope" to greed and exploitation, "accelerate the formation of that Aristocracy of Wealth" which Democrats deplored, and oppress the unpropertied even further. In the modern era, growing inequality and class polarization were the *results* of free competition, not symptoms it would cure. Because new feudal forms were gaining hold right within Civilized competition, laissez faire was only a pernicious mask for "the subjection and robbery of the masses." Charles Dana amplified Godwin's point when he contended that Democratic opposition to the national bank and tariff had delayed a government-sponsored American feudalism but that the party's cherished principle of "unlimited competition" would bring it about anyway, through the private sector. Add to this the fact that the Democrats sanctioned slavery, and one had to conclude that the party's "democracy" was "a humbug."[60]

Whigs fared little better in Associationist propaganda. Greeley, of course, supported Association as a supplement to the Whig program of protectionism and economic growth. But most leading Fourierists identified the Whigs as the party of capital, whose tariff and bank measures would codify the tendency toward a new feudalism. Whig economic policy may have been similar to Fourierism in several ways: as benevolent capitalists the Whigs promoted conciliation between labor and capital, praised joint-stock production, acknowledged public responsibility for employment, and argued for a regionally diversified economy somewhat akin to the phalanx vision. And certainly the Whigs' aggressive Protestantism and their sympathy for reform were congenial to many Associationists.[61] Yet the Fourierists believed a "harmony of interests" impossible under competitive capitalism, whereas the Whigs proclaimed it an operative reality. Because they endorsed competition, the Whigs advocated the "false" association of corporations and the new feudal order rather than "true" cooperative socialism. According to Associationists, Whig spokesmen simply sugarcoated competitive exploitation when they promised abundance for all and depicted factory owners and workers as "partners."[62]

On the basis of such factors as Greeley's endorsement, the Fourierists' ideology, their geographic distribution, and their eventual migration to

Republicanism, several historians judge that "participating Associationists were largely Whigs."[63] But all these grounds for such a conclusion can be questioned or qualified. Solid evidence of voting preference or party allegiance is difficult to come by—a fact that underscores Fourierism's origins in disaffection from politics and also suggests that Associationists acted seriously on the policy to "take sides with no party." What evidence there is indicates that prior to the Mexican War and the Free Soil movement, Associationist leaders were evenly split between Whig and Democratic backgrounds. This matches Warren Chase's report that Wisconsin Phalanx members were "about equally divided, and vote accordingly, but generally believe both parties culpable for many of the political evils of the day." The important point is that in joining the movement, Fourierists put strong political allegiances aside. Virtually all their spokesmen professed hostility to both major parties of the 1840s, an attitude based on their specific platforms as well as the general position that political measures would not ameliorate social conditions.[64]

When they denounced political liberty and republican politics, Associationists used strong language. Dana charged that republican institutions produced only "a universal system of demagogueism, gaining its base ends by bribery, by lying and unblushing intrigue"; he complained that equal rights and democracy had become "empty words." Yet Associationists were capable of sincere praise for republicanism. In an official statement of 1846 the American Union of Associationists referred to representative government as "the greatest step of modern political improvement" and a key instrument of providential progress. Godwin rejoiced that "the objects for which the liberal minds of other nations are so painfully struggling, have been long since conquered by the American people," and he called Fourierists "decided republicans."[65] The apparent discrepancy dissolves when we realize that Associationists were condemning not republican principles per se but rather the widespread conviction that political rights were adequate to ensure social progress and equality. Fourierist antirepublicanism was a strategy rather than a deep conviction. The idea of a republic was a noble one, but when political liberty became the final item on the progressive agenda or legislation the preferred means of reform, Associationists objected strenuously.

The Socialist Promised Land

A republican form of government, however praiseworthy, could not prevent America from following Europe's road to ruin. The idea that American social and economic problems were in fact attributes of all modern societies gave the Fourierists' perspective the flavor of a modern socialist critique. Nevertheless, when they turned from diagnosing those ills and refuting conventional remedies to the more hopeful task of promoting the Fourierist antidote, Associationists did a startling about-face on the question of American exceptionalism. At the same time that they dismissed the lag between Europe and America on the road to industrial feudalism as "temporary" and "accidental," they suggested that American backwardness was a unique and crucial asset. Controverting both Fourier and his French disciples, Associationists proclaimed that Europe was already enslaved by monopoly and industrialism, while the infeudation of America was just beginning. Thanks to its late discovery and vast domain, the United States had been granted a crucial grace period before the onset of industrial capitalism. The "great object" of its citizens was thus "to take advantage of our favorable position, and effect peacefully a Social Reform before we sink into the poverty and ignorance in which Europe is plunged." If the public acted quickly, while institutions were still malleable and class antagonisms not yet hardened, America could lead the way to the Harmonic future. Indeed, since Europeans had already capitulated, it was up to America alone to save the world for utopian socialism. The United States was mankind's second chance, the "savior" of the world's oppressed, the Promised Land of socialism.[66]

This was a long way from denying American uniqueness. Simply but effectively, Associationists modified Fourierism to fit the common American theme of the contrast between the tired, decaying Old World and the fresh New World. In so doing they found a special place within utopian socialism for American exceptionalism. As utopian critics they initially repudiated nationalist prejudices; as utopian planners they brought nationalism in the back door, this time clothed as a communitarian. Once that back door was opened, the familiar vocabulary of America's beneficent uniqueness rushed in. The same vast space and sparse population that could only temporarily postpone social disaster provided a golden opportunity for communitarian reform: since land was cheap and pestilent institutions not yet victorious, there was still room for experimentation. The frontier, moreover, encouraged venturousness, practicality, and respect for hard work—traits that would benefit first-generation phalansterians. When in 1844 the Americans opened an official correspondence with French Fourierists, they could not resist compiling a list of American "advantages" that ought to compel the French to abandon Old World propagandism for New World realization. These included "the absence of oppressive institutions," "the universal habits of associated efforts in financial, commercial, philanthropic, literary and religious endeavors," and "the inestimable advantage of expansion on virgin soil." Freedom from legalized castes and feudal distinction between nobles and serfs made Americans "a people of WORKING-MEN" who held titled drones in contempt and cherished the ideal of uniting hard work and high culture. In aristocratic France, Fourier had to appeal to princes, capitalists, and wealthy landowners to underwrite a phalanx, but Associationists could depend on the sympathies, skills, and resources of "the great middling classes of American society."[67]

Even American politics, which they frequently criticized as vapid and irrelevant to social problems, gave communitarians unique advantages. Universal male suffrage and representative government fostered general intelligence and a participatory spirit. The constitution guaranteed freedom of thought, speech, and association. And the federal system of townships, counties, and states provided a framework in which phalanxes could multiply and confederate. Republican habits and institutions would play a part in dotting the land with phalanxes.[68]

In this vision of a land dotted with phalanxes, Associationists found the true version of American republicanism. Godwin, Brisbane, and others argued that Fourierism could realize the republican dream by extending its notions of liberty and equality from politics to society. The work of 1776 would culminate in a peaceful social revolution giving birth to a system in which "democracy" meant not the free-for-all of competitive individualism but "a condition of society in which the least individual shall have his rights acknowledged, and the means . . . for the fullest expansion of his faculties guaranteed." By forming a network of small and relatively self-sufficient "townships," Fourierism would also complement the decentralized governmental system the Founding Fathers had established. To Godwin and other Associationists, communitarianism was a kind of socialist federalism implementing the national motto of *E Pluribus Unum*.[69]

In such ways Associationist writings linked Fourierism with an alternative conception of America's mission. Like conventional nationalists they declared that the discovery of the New World indicated a providential hand and contended that the nation's "peculiarly favorable opportunities" imposed exacting "responsibilities and duties." But the Fourierist version of America's destiny was not building an empire or even spreading republican institutions worldwide; instead, the United States was summoned "to manifest before the Nations of the Earth . . . the possibility of human brotherhood." To this putative call to "fulfill the law of love" Associationist spokesmen transferred the covenant rhetoric of their Puritan ancestry. With the skill of a New England patriarch, William Henry Channing pronounced Americans guilty of national "hypocrisy" and a "breach of trust" in their acquisitive way of life, and he warned of imminent social warfare unless they awakened to their fraternal responsibility.[70]

George Ripley voiced a similar appeal:

No half-way measures will remove the impending ruin with which God must visit the rash contemner of his inviolable laws. A merciful Providence is warning us in every way that we are in false relations. He sends us pecuniary distress, awful convulsions in commercial affairs, sickness of body and sickness of soul, a tormenting sense of satiety blended with a tormenting sense of want, in order to show us that we have erred . . . . We must then return to the Lord on whose ordinances we have trampled; we must organize our social relations, in solemn reverence before his law.[71]

Here was a Fourierist version of the jeremiad, the Puritan sermon form which, as Perry Miller and Sacvan Bercovitch have shown, was identified throughout the nineteenth century with conceptions of America's mission. In this case, the jeremiad did not confine dissenters to capitalism's hegemony, or what Bercovitch calls "the norms we have come to associate with the free-enterprise system."[72] The Associationists' commitment to nationalism was an endorsement of America's potential rather than its present; it was inspired by communitarianism, not individualism. Still, Ripley and Channing sensed that the rhythms of the Fourierist scenario were precisely those of millennial nationalism, with its litany of advantages and responsibilities and its alternating visions of impending judgment and heavenly promise. Their writings culminated Associationist efforts to fuse utopian socialism and American nationalism.

Forging a Christian Socialism

Ripley's and Channing's jeremiads suggest a final aspect of the Americanization process: the creation of an explicitly Christian Fourierism. Much like his contemporary Robert Owen, Fourier construed his utopia as an alternative, "rational" religion. Fourier began by assuming that a deity had created the cosmos in perfect order and unity and ended by arguing that his "new industrial world" was consistent with Christian revelation. Yet despite a few bows to scripture, his categories, values, and analytical methods were rooted in the secular "science" of Enlightenment rationalism. On both sides of the Atlantic, Fourier's disciples were members of a later generation: influenced by romanticism and the nineteenth-century revival of Christianity, they were less anticlerical, not so mechanistic in their view of the world, and more open to a devout (if eclectic) faith.[73] French Fourierists tried to align their doctrine with Christianity through abstruse articles on "the religious question" in La Phalange or engraved depictions of Fourier alongside Christ in popular phalansterian almanacs.[74] The connection between American Fourierism and Christianity was even stronger and the religious emphasis more pervasive in the movement's literature. Brook Farmers, Protestant ministers, and Christian reformers were drawn to Association by its promise to embody "practical Christianity," and once there they elaborated Fourierism's religious mission. Inspired by religious commitment to brotherly love and convinced of the essential unity of reason and revelation, they believed that Christianity and socialism were not inevitable antagonists, as critics claimed, but indispensable allies. To demonstrate that alliance, they embarked upon a campaign to enlist Christian ideas and symbols in the Fourierist cause without denying the integrity of either, to harmonize Christian and utopian socialist world views. An examination of antebellum reformers' resolve to move beyond inherited formulas of personal salvation yet maintain continuity with the Christian tradition that nourished their idealism provides a new perspective on what is traditionally labeled "secular" communitarianism.[75]

Liberal Protestants naturally sought to align the new socialism with their Christian inheritance, but there were also strategic reasons to identify Fourierism as a legitimately religious philosophy. Utopian socialism had first come to America allied to the militant free thought of Owen, who shocked contemporaries by denying that the Bible was God's word and publicly issuing a "Declaration of Mental Independence" from all "irrational systems of religion."[76] Thanks to his legacy, communitarian schemes crossing the Atlantic were invariably associated with "infidelity." Fourier's theory was in fact vulnerable to such a charge: despite the Frenchman's protestations of piety, his scheme of social reorganization diverged at key points from traditional Christian ideas and methods, as America's religious press quickly pointed out. To minimize the impact of such criticism, Associationists set out to square Fourierism with the Christian tradition.

An additional spur came from the discontent many Associationists felt with the thoroughly secular version of Fourierism publicized by Albert Brisbane. Fourier had at least argued that his system complemented Christianity, but Brisbane eliminated the master's biblical references and his scientific "proofs" of Christian doctrine when he extracted the "practical part" of Fourier's theory.[77] Moreover, to attract investors and community volunteers, Brisbane deliberately suggested that phalanxes would revolutionize the world not by spreading brotherly love and self-sacrifice but by guaranteeing unparalleled prosperity.[78] Such a pragmatic and materialistic approach distressed spiritually minded Associationists. Behind Brisbane's back they complained that his conception of Fourier trampled upon "the more delicate and beautiful graces of the soul" and expressed fears that his appeal to the profit motive would bring a "crowd of converts who desire to help themselves rather than . . . the movement."[79] With the conversion of Brook Farm to Fourierism near the beginning of 1844 and the accession to leadership of Channing, Godwin, Van Amringe, and other devout spokesmen, Christian socialists in the movement soon outnumbered Brisbane and his allies. When Brisbane departed for further studies in Europe in the spring of 1844, the task of propagating Fourierism shifted decisively to believers.

One way Brook Farmers and their colleagues addressed the religious issue was by turning to Emmanuel Swedenborg. Ralph Waldo Emerson inadvertently led Associationists to Swedenborg's works when he noted the "strange coincidences" between their revelations and Fourier's theory. Within a few years there appeared at least two books and some thirty articles in the Associationist press describing Swedenborg's system as "a beautiful complement" to Fourier's.[80] By invoking Swedenborg as the spiritual counterpart of Fourier, utopians hoped to gain the religious respectability that Fourierism lacked.

Associationists discovered similarities between Swedenborg's idea that the inner life sought outer "uses" and Fourier's notion that the passions governed human actions. Swedenborg's theory that a system of "correspondences" linked material and spiritual worlds in one-to-one relationships seemed to echo Fourier's law of "universal analogy" between different levels of the ladder of creation. To religious liberals eager to harmonize reason and revelation, here was confirmation of the reign of "Divine Order": Fourier, proceeding "by strictly scientific synthesis," and Swedenborg, prompted "by the study of the Scriptures, aided by Divine Illumination," converged in asserting the unity of the universe in unvarying law emanating from God. Finally, the two seers envisioned the kingdom of heaven in remarkably similar terms. Not only did both predict an end to the dualisms of spirit and matter, conscience and instinct, self-love and brotherly love which had plagued the race since the Fall, but Fourier's plan for "Harmonic" society seemed to translate to this world Swedenborg's vision of life among spirits. Charged with millennial expectation, Associationists saw Swedenborg and Fourier as "the Two commissioned by the Great Leader of the Christian Israel, to spy out the Promised Land of Peace and Happiness."[81]

Not all New Churchmen found the two philosophies congruent. To some, the lingering Calvinism of Swedenborg's theories of sin, divine agency, and hell invalidated Fourier's sublime confidence in human potential. And most took Swedenborg's eschatology to describe the Second Coming as the inward revelation of biblical truths to the devout, not as a transformed society. To bring Swedenborgian ideas into their camp, Associationists placed them in a radically new context. To them, Swedenborg's vision of "Divine Order" meant that humans could decipher the "Divine Social Code"; his "New Church" became not a body of believers but a millennial society where work was worship and fraternal love instinctive. By linking Swedenborg and Fourier, then bringing Swedenborg's heaven down to earth, the Fourierists were recruiting an important religious figure to testify on behalf of Association. Viewed from this perspective, Swedenborg emerged as a socialist prophet, and Fourier's phalanx became "the true organization of the New Church."[82]

By far the simplest and most forceful way to identify Fourierism with Christianity was to equate the goal of Association directly with the social millennium so many nineteenth-century Americans anticipated. The urgency of Fourierist rhetoric, its vividly religious imagery, and its swings from pronouncements of doom to visions of heaven were repeated elsewhere in antebellum America, but the Fourierist version of a secularized paradise stands out in its determination to attach millennial meaning to a complete reorganization of American social and economic institutions.

"We have no Theology, i.e. Science of the Divine, worth the name," William Henry Channing told John Dwight, "[but] we have a *religion* to announce to our fellows . . . our watch-cry is . . . in the most emphatic meaning of the words, 'The Kingdom of Heaven upon Earth.' "[83] Channing's sermons portrayed Association as the culmination of perfectionist trends in contemporary churches; the writings of Dwight and Dana supported this claim with a Fourierist intepretation of Christian history. According to Dana's *Lecture on Association in its Relation to Religion* (1844), an important part of Christ's mission had been to prepare humanity for the ultimate reign of divine wisdom and love on earth. Yet his disciples misunderstood or soon forgot his call. Burdened by an infant sect's need to survive, the church retreated into an organization of true believers bent on salvation in the hereafter. In the antebellum age of benevolence and millennial expectation, however, Christ's vision was finally being recalled. From all quarters came appeals to translate divine truths into actual life, but Fourierism alone provided the "scientific" blueprint to realize "peace on earth and good will among men." Dwight argued that Fourierism ended the long-raging conflict between Christian love and daily life. No longer need churches renounce the world or radicals denounce churches' seeming complicity in its evils. In providing the opportunity of "growing into the beauty of Christian fellowship, by the very act which earns us bread," Association reconciled spiritual and material realms. Christianity had withered for centuries for lack of a social "body" but could now find it in Fourier's system. Christ would come a second time in the form of a redeemed society.[84]

Such blending of utopian socialist idealism and Christian teleology was typical of Associationist rhetoric. At Fourierist conventions, addresses abounding in scriptural quotations portrayed utopians as new "apostles" carrying a divinely inspired message to the public, or as biblical prophets foretelling the doom of "Babylon" and the advent of a "New Jerusalem" where human passions would be harmonized in associative unity. Once Association had been realized, Godwin told a Fourierist assembly, "God will manifest to us the immensity of his providence, and . . . the Kingdom of Heaven . . . [will]. . . come to us in this terrestrial world."[85]

Not all facets of utopian socialism were so conveniently blended with Christianity. There was a serious discrepancy between the determinism of Fourier's "social science" and traditional Christian notions of sin and regeneration. Though he disavowed Owen's notorious postulate that "the character of man is formed for and not by him," Fourier denied individual responsibility by blaming social circumstances for corrupting human development. Vicious habits or actions were merely the result of an unnatural society directing innately pure human "passions" into "subversive" channels. Simply implementing the phalanx plan of social reorganization would be sufficient to banish evil from the globe.

Critics from both mainstream and liberal churches charged that Fourier's theory was guilty of "making the invisible, the intangible, and irresponsible condition we call SOCIETY the scape-goat for the sins and sufferings of the visible, tangible, and responsible individuals who compose it." Since social problems were only individual sins compounded, according to these opponents, reform had to begin with the spiritual regeneration of the self, then proceed outward. Because Fourierism merely changed external circumstances, it could never eliminate sin from the world.[86]

Religious opponents also condemned Fourier's utopia for accommodating self-interest. Convinced that every human "passion" had legitimate uses, Fourier envisioned a society that would not repress self-seeking but channel it to benign purposes. His complex community blueprint offered specific assurance that if each member pursued his or her own interest, all others would automatically benefit. Church critics disagreed: in proclaiming that "by a proper arrangement of individuals in whom selfishness is the predominant principle, . . . discords . . . can be avoided, and the whole . . . of life move along . . . harmoniously," they countered, Fourierists were overturning Christ's law of love for an amoral and ultimately ineffective social mechanics. True perfection demanded spiritual awakening and intense self-sacrifice.[87]

Albert Brisbane's doctrinaire devotion to Fourier and thoroughgoing secularism left him helpless before such charges. "False . . . social principles" lay behind the world's ills, he recited from Fourier, and Association's diffusion of wealth would be enough to perfect society: "With prosperity come the means of education, with education refinement and intelligence, and with these the virtues."[88] In their own response, Godwin, Channing, and the Brook Farmers tried to stake out a compromise position between Brisbane's utilitarian dogma and the moralism of traditional Christianity. Insisting upon social reorganization as the most important reform tool, they nevertheless qualified utopian environmentalism by acknowledging that personal wrongdoing contributed to social ills. The chaos of Civilization stemmed from "the substitution in the soul of mankind of a principle of selfishness for a principle of benevolence." With this simple concession, the controversy descended from a clash of opposing world views to a question of tactical emphasis. Believing both that "society is wrong because men are bad" and that "men are bad because society is wrong," Associationists stressed that a corrupted environment had become the primary obstacle to godly living: individual sins could be repented, but "social" or shared sins were embedded in the structure of daily relations, and their abolition required economic reform. Because conventional Christians overlooked these outward relations, their efforts to redeem humankind had been frustrated.[89]

Still, Associationists agreed, simply substituting cooperative mechanisms for competitive ones did not guarantee godliness. Religion was needed to write the law of love in human hearts as well as in constitutions. As Van Amringe put it, "No matter how closely you may bring dead limbs and joints together, by any social system, . . . unless the spirit of God descend and quicken the carcass, it will possess no more life than the fragments of a statue." Christianity and socialism must proceed hand in hand, each "necessary to the other."[90]

Associationists replied to charges of condoning self-interest in the same conciliatory spirit. They acknowledged that Fourier, "in his anxiety to

impress his principles upon the minds of his selfish and sensuous generation," overemphasized materialistic desires. They conceded that phalanx
arrangements permitted self-seeking. But since members of greedy and
competitive Civilization had to be won voluntarily to Association, it was
necessary at first to use material gain to lure the unregenerate. Over
time, by neutralizing self-interested action, phalanx mechanisms would
discourage members from trying to benefit at others' expense. More
positively, the habit of "doing good" instilled by cooperative arrangements would permit phalansterians to see the truth of Christian love.[91]
Again, Fourierism did not exclude spiritual life but merely enlisted material forces in its aid. Given the conjunction of the two, in a few generations
a communal ethos would substitute "Unityism" for selfishness within the
phalanx.[92]

For all its sincerity, the Associationists' attempt to blend Christianity
and utopian socialism was far from problem-free. The highly selective
use they made of Swedenborg, for example, merited Garth Wilkinson's
complaint that in "marrying Fourier to the New Church" they gave the
former "the masculine character in the compact."[93] When Fourierist
leaders envisioned Christian beliefs and forms persisting into the Harmonic future, they opened phalanx doors to sectarian bickering. Perhaps
most important, Associationists never resolved the discrepancy between
socialist and Christian reform strategies. Spiritual regeneration and social
reform may plausibly complement each other, but love and selfishness are
mutually exclusive, and the latter was undeniably embedded in Fourier's
communal structure. Associationists might explain that self-interest was
a temporary legacy from Civilization to Harmony, but their phalanx
mechanisms blurred the distinction between Christian love and utilitarian
cleverness. Nor was this only a theoretical question: George Ripley's
fear that appeals to self-interest rather than to self-sacrifice would bring
undesirable converts proved all too prescient.[94] Frustrated Associationist
leaders watched helplessly in the mid-1840s as the scramble for personal
advantage and material rewards brought phalanx after phalanx to an
early grave. The question of self-interest proved the most intractable
problem facing the Americans trying to build a Christian Fourierism.

5

The Utopian Alternative

The most widely known interpretation of Fourierism is as a pre-Marxian "utopian socialism," a forerunner—along with the ideas of Saint-Simon and Owen—of the tough-minded Communism of Karl Marx. Marx and Engels themselves were largely responsible for this: their polemics, beginning with a section of the *Communist Manifesto* which contrasted "Critical-Utopian Socialism" with Communism and culminating in Engels's pamphlet *Socialism, Utopian and Scientific* (1880), coined the epithet and gave it its negative connotation. The founders of Communism admired the way these theorists "attack[ed] every principle of existing society" and advocated a collectivist lifestyle, but they condemned communal experiments promising "the disappearance of class antagonisms" as "purely utopian" and "contrived." History progressed not through models of social harmony, they said, but according to the violent logic of the class struggle.[1] After 1848, "utopian socialism" stuck as a label for Fourierism, first retaining its pejorative connotation but later becoming a neutral term. An alternative label, "liberal communitarianism," has recently come into use, spurred by Arthur Bestor's resurrection of the nineteenth-century word "communitarianism" to denote social reconstruction through model communities and then popularized in the account of Fourierism by T. D. Seymour Bassett in *Socialism and American Life* (1952). Like Marx and Engels, Bassett distinguished Owenites and Fourierists from Communists, but he did so from a different angle. Contrasting early nineteenth-century communitarians with the deterministic and undemocratic Marxian socialists of later years, Bassett called Fourierists liberals because they believed in "the free play of reason as the universal solvent of all strife," built democratic structures, and tolerated religion.[2]

The full range of Associationist thinking is hard to encompass in any

121

phrase, and surely Fourierists should not be expected to have conformed to the dogmas of a socialism that crystallized a generation later. Still, it is striking that the two best labels for the Fourierist blueprint depict it as a hybrid, paradoxical structure. To Marx and Engels, Fourierism was progressive in its vision of communal life but retrogressive in its "utopian" proposal of revolution by example. Bassett's formulation is in a sense the opposite, since inside the Fourierists' strategy of radical reconstruction he found a great deal of conventional liberal piety. Dissenting and conventional elements are reversed, but both labels encapsulate Association as a dichotomous ideology. In fact, Associationists described themselves this way. "Our plans," Parke Godwin wrote, "certainly are revolutionary, or . . . they would not be worth a moment's thought. . . . But the revolution they contemplate is not violent, nor unjust, nor destructive." Association was "both conservative and radical."[3]

The apparent contradiction derives from Association's presentation both as a communitarian revolution and a "reconciling and universal" social philosophy. Fourierists promised adherents both individual freedom and communal solidarity, capitalist profits and socialist ethics, gradual progress and revolutionary change. The communitarian New Jerusalem would arrive without traumatic social convulsions and would benefit everyone. It seems clear that this sublimely optimistic "both-and" way of thinking was a key to Association's appeal among antebellum Americans, who wanted reform without pain and who were used to hearing similar utopian promises from rival versions of the American dream.

The Fourierists' confident paradoxes gave their program a familiar utopian ring, but their relation to mainstream American culture was actually a complex blend of dissent and loyalty, resistance and accommodation. Emerging from the false and disordered state of American Civilization, their phalanxes were intended to incorporate the best features of liberalism, capitalism, and nationalism into a brave new communal world where humanity's true destiny would be revealed. Inside these communities, complete personal freedom would coexist with social harmony in a way that paralleled capitalism's "enlightened self-interest" as well as America's "collective individualism." The Fourierists' utopian alternative, in short, turned out to be a kind of loyal communitarian opposition, a mixture of dissent and celebration which proved popular among reformers but also extremely vulnerable to absorption and failure.

The World of the Phalanx

The phalanx, the basic socioeconomic unit of the Fourierists' "New Industrial World," was envisioned as a scientifically organized communal village in which future utopians would live, work, and play. Its size stemmed from the variety of characters necessary to ensure the interplay of "passions": Fourier postulated 810 basic character types and multiplied by two for gender. A phalanx of 1,620 men, women, and children would have enough work and recreational "series" to satisfy members' needs and sufficiently interlock their interests. On occasion Fourier countenanced scaled-down versions of two hundred to seven hundred members—particularly children—as rudimentary transitional communities, but he never described them in detail. His heart and virtually all his propaganda efforts went toward a full-blown model community on a domain of some six thousand acres, at the enormous cost of fourteen million francs.[4]

American Associationists were more practical and less patient. Brisbane's texts represented four hundred as the minimum number required for sufficiently varied productive operations; located on a thousand acres and capitalized at $400,000, this would be a full "realization," albeit at a smaller than optimal scale. Even when Associationist leaders protested that the tiny phalanxes of the 1840s were not fair trials of Fourier's theory, they compared them to this reduced "model phalanx" rather than to Fourier's huge plan.[5] Their smaller blueprint meant not only that Associationists were willing to start with limited means but that they took Fourier's economic arrangments more seriously than his psychology. A phalanx of four hundred could still benefit from economies of scale, "unitary" kitchens and dwellings, and collective labor to eliminate inefficiency and waste. Brisbane and Greeley, the most insistent "modernizers" among American Fourierists, particularly stressed the productive advantages of communal living over the "isolated system." Because small phalanxes could not offer the subtly graded occupations and pleasures Fourier intended to gratify all tastes, capital investment and work skills were more important than passional variety in selecting applicants to put phalanxes on a secure footing. Advocating immediate practical reform, the Americans stressed economic opportunity rather than "justice to the passions."[6]

Most Associationists echoed Fourier's dictum that the phalanx locate itself in an agricultural area not far from a large city. Brisbane's proposed North American Phalanx was to be situated between fifty and a hundred miles from New York City, Philadelphia, or Baltimore. A nearby urban center would provide a convenient market for phalanx produce and would supply tools and machinery cheaply. Apart from economic considerations, proximity to the urban press meant greater publicity and hence "more rapid imitation" of a successful model.[7]

Into the moderately settled countryside the phalanx would enter—somewhat incongruously—as a large, bustling community. All members were to live in the phalanstery, the "unitary edifice" that would serve as quarters for most work and leisure as well. Despite advocating a less populous "model Association," American propagandists presented only a slightly simplified version of Fourier's grandiose building and grounds.[8] In their plans, the sprawling phalanstery was a kind of People's Versailles, a symmetrical, multistoried, neoclassical palace with a massive center and two wings. Interior courtyards featured hothouse gardens, and a glass-

covered "street gallery" running the building's length would shelter phalansterians from the weather and make every shift in members' busy
schedules a delightful promenade. Part of the phalanstery was set aside
for production, but most of its space was taken up by members' apartments and by rooms serving group purposes, such as refectories, schools,
and theatres. Especially in living and dining arrangements, diversity was
the precondition of Associative harmony. Apartments were designed to
vary in quality, size, and price, depending on residents' needs and wishes,
and diners could choose among several halls or take their meals in their
own rooms. Outside the phalanstery a huge parade ground spanned
the distance to carefully arranged gardens artfully framing workshops,
stables, and the community's power plant. Beyond the level campus
formed by phalanstery, workshops and grounds, bountiful orchards, and
fields of grain and vegetables extended to the horizon, separated by
forest groves and brambles. These wilder areas would encourage refresh-
ment and serve as picnic or meditation grounds.[9]

The phalanx was thus both city and country. In an era of rapid,
disorienting urban growth and increasing nostalgia for nature, Associationists proposed not a retreat from the city but a reconstructed order
that might "combine all the advantages, resources and enjoyments of city
and country life, and avoid the disadvantages of both." To the modern
viewer the prospect of a gleaming palace set down in a fertile farming
valley may seem ludicrous, but Associationists, like contemporary Owenites and later utopian writers, conceived a reconciling counterpoint of
urban and rural forms on a scale commensurate with progress.[10] They
envisioned their phalanxes as balanced "townships," larger than the average American settlement of the time, dotting the landscape at appropriate
intervals. At certain "pivotal" points, groups of Associations would cluster
to form major administrative, commercial, and cultural centers. There
would indeed be cities in Harmony: their blocks would resemble phalansteries; their streets, clean and wide, would reproduce the phalanx's
parade ground in an urban context. With huge gardens spreading beyond the city limits, Harmonic cities and their environs represented the
phalanx plan writ large.[11]

Such a vision was formal, monumental, and potentially sterile—though
Fourier himself enlivened it with colored banners and tents, a festive
atmosphere, and the songs of marching workers as they changed work
locations. However rigid, the phalanx blueprint effectively rebuts the
theory that Associationists were antimodern reactionaries.[12] Like other
antebellum institutional reformers, the Fourierists aimed to impose a
reconciling order on the atomized, ever changing Jacksonian world.
Even more explicitly than the asylum and the school, the phalanx was a
microcosm scaled between the household and the city; it was meant to
take on the production and socialization functions that family and church
had lost under commercial capitalism without descending to the chaos

and impersonalism of the metropolis. In their dream of reshaping behavior by inventing a controlled new social environment the Fourierists revealed themselves agents of modernization as much as rebels against it.[13]

A similar point can be made about the phalanx's mixed economy. Unlike Owen and Saint-Simon, Fourier had little appreciation for modern technology and cast his utopia in fundamentally preindustrial terms. Agriculture formed the economic basis of Harmonic society, and even his carefully graded work teams were enumerated to match varieties of peaches and pears. One-fourth of phalanx production was to be devoted to manufacturing, but Fourier's "industries" consisted of traditional handicrafts such as shoe- and glassmaking, and Fourier valued these mainly to keep phalansterians busy during the winter months between growing seasons.[14] Associationists agreed that agriculture, "the fundamental source of subsistence," would be primary in the phalanx. The Americans shared Fourier's penchant for a huge domain—critics called it "land mania"—and they repeated his one-fourth formula for manufactures.[15] Nevertheless, American Fourierists sought a greater role for technology in the phalanx, viewing it as an application rather than a repudiation of the principles of nature. Like the phalanx itself, mechanical invention extended man's mastery over nature, brought "riches and abundance" that released humans to cultivate higher needs, and spread fraternity by increasing interchanges between peoples. Fourierists promised that the phalansterian future would apply scientific knowledge to the utmost.[16] Brisbane, Macdaniel, and John Allen were especially entranced by the proposals of J. A. Etzler, the German-born visionary whose promise of *Paradise within the Reach of All Men, without Labor, by Powers of Nature and Machinery* (1842) Henry David Thoreau had dismissed as vulgar hubris. Etzler's plans for solar- and wind-powered machines plowing vast farmlands and uprooting tree stumps represented technology's harnessing of natural forces in the service of agriculture. Associationist leaders endorsed the idea for their phalanxes; Brisbane, himself an inventor of futuristic devices, harbored the dream of a huge mechanized farm for the rest of his life.[17]

The Associationists' enthusiasm for improved transportation, vision of bustling workshops, and praise for Etzler refute charges that they had "no conception of the industrial . . . trends of the time" and merely sought an agrarian refuge. No Fourierist wanted huge factories in Harmony, but an impulse toward mechanical efficiency, collective labor, and specialization linked the phalanx to corporate factory towns such as Lowell, despite the Associationists' disclaimers. This confluence suggests how much industrial capitalism and early socialism shared as harbingers of modernization. But just as Lowell's rural setting and campuslike environment were intended to harmonize agrarian ideals with industrial progress, the Fourierists' suburban "new industrial world" was meant to reconcile the ma-

chine and the garden (to use Leo Marx's terms). Like good utopians—
and many other nineteenth-century Americans—Associationists felt they
could blend old ideals and new techniques.[18]

Division of labor inside the phalanx was to take the form of work
"groups" and "series." Individuals with like interests would spontaneously form a group of at least seven laborers, and groups would range
themselves into a series centered on one dominant occupation such as
carpentry, education, household work, or gardening. Fascinated by numerology, Fourier drew up esoteric tables showing geometric refinements of series organization in which groups were arranged in "ascending and descending wings" according to variations on the central
task. In the largest phalanx, for example, a series might be dedicated to
growing potatoes: each constituent group would work with a different
type; the central and largest team would cultivate the standard, most
popular variety.[19]

With their smaller and simpler communal plans the Americans virtually ignored this obsessive specialization, but they did endorse Fourier's
idea that the "serial organization of labor" would create "attractive industry." Work in groups and series was to be voluntary, varied, and fulfilling.
In theory at least, members would be drawn to work by their "passions"
rather than compelled by scarcity or starvation; every essential job would
entice an adequate number of volunteers; and each element of members'
personalities would find its complement among the wide range of phalanx tasks. Work in groups and series would satisfy the three "distributive" passions of the soul: the "composite" enthusiasm deriving from
stimulation of both mind and body; the "cabalist" fondness for friendly
rivalry between groups; and, most important, the "butterfly" thirst for
change, which dictated that each worker spend no more than two hours
at a task before moving to another. Job rotation and the complex division
of labor meant that phalanxes should organize as many series as possible;
a full phalanx could accommodate more than forty-five, a scaled-down
model about a dozen. The series and their constituent groups, nature's
way of rendering labor attractive, represented the Fourierists' pioneering
solution to the problem of work.[20]

To evangelicals who objected that labor was an inherently repugnant
"duty" or a biblical curse, Associationists replied that teamwork made it
fun and that the unity of creation guaranteed a personality fit for every
job. The phalanx's "Little Hordes" exemplified both principles. Fourier
reasoned that adolescents were naturally attracted to filth, adventure,
and camaraderie; hence, they would form a sort of sanitation knighthood
devoted to removing phalanx garbage, tending animals, cleaning kitchens and butcheries—all for little remuneration except the pleasure of the
work and the gratitude of fellow phalansterians. An adult version of the
Little Hordes, necessarily animated more by the communal spirit than
delight in dirt, was the "Sacred Legion."[21]

Perhaps Civilization's only institution that made work attractive this way was the army, with its varied tasks, outdoor living, reward through honors, and competitive teamwork. The phalanx, instead of destructive, warmaking troops, would substitute huge "industrial armies." These brigades, utopian ancestors of the New Deal's CCC and WPA, would rove the countryside engaging in reforestation, bridge building, and land reclamation. American Fourierists carefully omitted Fourier's fanciful description of amorous "skirmishes" between male and female troops; rather, in the idea of turning Civilization's swords into Harmony's ploughshares they found a fitting symbol of Fourierism's millennial potential.[22]

If organization of work in series ensured phalansterians' personal fulfillment, economic arrangements securing "unity of interests" and social justice provided for communal solidarity. All land, buildings, and phalanx assets were to be owned by the group through shares purchased when individuals entered the community. In the 1840s, joint-stock organization was not yet identified exclusively with capitalist corporations but could be seen as a "mutualist" mechanism, much like workers' benefit societies, which pooled individual risks and resources to enable a common good.[23] Shareholding meant democratic control over community policy and at the same time would give each member a lively proprietary interest in the success of the whole. If a particular group's product could command a high market price—for no phalanx would be wholly self-sufficient—the benefit would redound to all community members. Frequent variation of tasks would also foster social cohesion. As individuals shifted among teams, their roles as workers and managers might be reversed. With self-interest checked through dispersion and erstwhile rivalries replaced with friendships, job rotation would prevent the groups from hardening into selfish enclaves and dominating phalanx decisionmaking. Work in groups and series would serve as an integrating force at the same time it allowed individual capacities to flower.[24]

To guarantee each phalansterian a fair share of the community surplus, Fourier devised a complex remuneration scheme encapsulated by two slogans, "the equitable distribution of profits" and "honors according to usefulness." The first decreed that the annual dividend be divided according to the formula of five-twelfths to labor, four-twelfths to capital, and three-twelfths to skill or talent. Capital's one-third would go toward paying the interest on shares to resident stockholders and absentee investors. Labor's dividend was distributed among the series through a ranking of their work as "necessary," "useful," or "attractive," the first receiving the highest reward and the last the lowest—hence the second slogan. Despite his prediction that all work in Harmony would be attractive, Fourier believed that higher pay for menial labor and other unpleasant tasks served justice and might also lure some phalansterians from genteel but economically unproductive preoccupations. Within each series, remuneration was again graded, with more experienced and esteemed workers allotted a higher return from the dividend to talent than apprentices. Rates and gradings were to be determined by the phalanx's elected councils. All this required an intricate system of bookkeeping and a fair amount of calculation.[25]

Because they advocated more modest experiments, the Associationists necessarily streamlined Fourier's remuneration scheme. Brisbane suggested that in transitional phalanxes the series could simply be paid the market value of their products rather than graded according to types of labor. The most important change concerned the allotment to capital. Almost all Associationists believed that Fourier, in his anxiety to attract wealthy sponsors for the first phalanx, had promised too high a return. The Americans' scaled-down communities relied upon more modest investments; more important, they were warier than Fourier—although not wary enough—of the danger that the same "tyranny" capitalists wielded in Civilization could undermine phalanxes unless labor out-earned capital and most shares were owned by residents. Hence, Brisbane and his colleagues suggested a division of three-twelfths to capital and seven-twelfths to labor.[26]

The "right to labor" and the "social minimum" completed Fourier's phalansterian economic arrangements. The first, a concept brought to center stage in the revolutionary prelude of the 1840s by Fourierists and other French socialists, simply asserted public responsibility for providing full employment. Louis Blanc and Pierre Proudhon used this principle to promote state-supported national workshops and producer cooperatives, but Fourierists pointed out that the phalanx accomplished the same ends without state intervention. Among Americans, Horace Greeley particularly stressed that "every one willing to work has a clear social and moral right to the opportunity to Labor." Phalanx collectivism complemented Greeley's devotion to the work ethic as well as the Whig notion that the group should "protect" the economic welfare of its members.[27] The "social minimum" was essentially a guaranteed annual income for all phalansterians. To provide economic security, level class distinctions, and assure that work would be freely undertaken, Fourierists promised community members and their dependents a minimum provision of food, fuel, and clothing—as long as phalanx finances would allow—and free support during sickness, disability, and old age. Here was concrete proof of Association's commitment to those simply cast aside in the individualistic and profit-oriented world of Civilization.[28]

Above such minimum guarantees, however, phalanx arrangements were hardly premised on the ideal of equal conditions. Fourier scorned the egalitarian radicalism of the Jacobins and the "communism" of Owen, believing that strict economic equality ignored natural differences in intelligence and character. He frankly predicted that phalanxes would have three classes: the rich, the poor, and the middle class.[29] In this, Associationists followed him only part way. To those who protested that capital investment and graded labor dividends brought inequality into utopia, the Americans cited the rights of capital and the justice of rewarding "ingenious, efficient" workers over others. Each individual's passional makeup necessarily produced differences in needs and achievements. Perhaps unaware of how closely they were embracing the tenets of liberal individualism, Associationists declared that once everyone had equal access to labor and education, the remaining disparities would be natural and acceptable. Still, the Americans were more sensitive than the French to the charge that Fourierism was inegalitarian. They reminded readers that the social minimum eliminated privation from Harmony. And they argued that higher pay for manual labor, universal education, the rotation of tasks, and a stipulation that small shareholders eventually receive higher dividend rates than large investors would all tend to equalize incomes in the phalanx.[30]

The fact was that Associationists tolerated inequality because their plan promised unprecedented abundance. How else could Fourierism "improve and elevate the condition of all, without taking from any"? Thanks to phalanx efficiency and economies of scale, all Harmonians would have as much as they wanted. Even in his lecture "Association in Its Relation to Religion," the pragmatic Charles Dana declared that wealth was the "first object" of Fourierists and a "necessary condition" for universal progress. Brisbane characteristically went further, impressing audiences with engravings of Fourier's phalanstery and promising that Association would "produce so much, and so fill the world with wealth," that the question would be "how to consume it all." Small wonder that ministers and other critics professed disgust with the "Oriental magnificence" of Fourier's plan.[31]

The Fourierists' belief that luxury could be compatible with communal virtue represented a key departure from the classical republican tradition, whose cyclical view of history forecast a descent into oblivion for decadent and materialistic peoples.[32] For this bleak scenario the utopians substituted a theory of linear progress guided by reason and Christianity, followed by the "leap" to Harmonic peace and plenty. Yet the specter of decadent luxury in Harmony haunted the more spiritual-minded Associationists. More than once William Henry Channing cautioned that with the phalanx's productive potential and its refinement of tastes, an extravagant appetite for wealth might dominate Harmonic life. Here was another indication that socialism required the moderating influence of religion.[33]

If the pursuit of wealth needed disciplining, legal coercion was not the proper method. The "law of love" was to be written in phalansterians' hearts, not statute books. One is struck by the superficial treatment of phalanx rules and government in Fourierist thought. Politics is by definition the exercise of power, yet the Fourierist scheme, like many utopian programs, assumed that power could largely be eliminated from human relations. Fourier conceived the phalanx as a self-operating mechanism run by "attraction" without legislation and supervised by a tiny and largely honorific corps of officers, mainly the "Areopagus" or Supreme

Council of Industry, which would merely advise members on the scheduling of tasks.[34] American followers looking for a model of phalanx government were thus given little to work with; what they extracted from Fourier's writings was an administrative plan that would essentially result in a workers' republic. Elections were to begin in the work group, with members choosing a new "chief" quarterly or (according to Brisbane) annually. Godwin, following Renaud, foresaw series chiefs electing various phalanx directors; but because Americans envisioned phalanxes so much smaller than Fourier's ideal, Brisbane planned for series chiefs themselves to serve as a council (or directory) of industry. Other councils representing different phalanx functions—finance, administration, education—were to be elected annually by the entire membership.[35]

Fourier's neglect of politics was more than counterbalanced by his vignettes of cultural, social, and domestic life in Harmony, detailed visions of complete passional fulfillment. His writings are crowded with schedules of typical phalanx days, descriptions of rituals and celebrations, accounts of education and childhood in Harmony, and, not least, vivid tours through the phalansterians' liberated sexual lives. But his American disciples, intent on the phalanx's economic and work arrangements, preferred to blanket future social and cultural life under general terms such as "spiritual development," "self-culture," and "congenial social relations."

This reticence was particularly pronounced, as has been suggested, in the matter of sex. Fourier projected a fantastic range of sexual activity once phalansterian freedom had become triumphant. His notebooks described some features of this "organization of love," and his published works hinted enough to make the prudish Emerson label the plan "a calculation how to secure the greatest amount of kissing that the infirmity of the human constitution admitted." Between the ages of fifteen and twenty, phalanx youths—male and female—were either "Vestals" or non-virginal but faithful "Damsels"; upon leaving those "corporations" they would enter Harmony's extremely complicated sexual marketplace, with liaisons of all sorts—from exclusive marriage to polygamy, homosexuality, and even incest—forming and disbanding regularly, presided over by a "Court of Love" to plan festivities and gently scold violators of agreements. Elderly "confessors" would advise phalansterians on the art of matching personalities, and each Harmonian was guaranteed a "sexual minimum" akin to the phalanx's social one.[36] Not surprisingly, though Associationists had ample access to these notions, almost none were described in the movement's own literature.

In somewhat less controversial areas of domestic and social life the Americans gave readers a sense of the Harmonic future. Without repeating Fourier's specific predictions about women's status in utopia, for example, Associationist pronouncements shared his distinctive blend of radical reform and conservative stereotypes. Associationists proclaimed women the equals of men and repeated Fourier's maxim that the progressive character of a society could best be judged by the position it accorded women. Civilization was clearly a failure, for its "isolated household," restrictions on female education, and legal enforcement of women's economic dependence meant that "WOMAN HAS NOT BEEN FREE." In Harmonic society women would benefit from a thorough education, equal access to occupational pursuits, and cooperative work that would virtually eliminate household drudgery.[37] Yet while toasting the "integral independence of woman" and her "co-sovereignty with man," Fourierists were not immune to conventional sex stereotyping. Ever the mathematician, Fourier extrapolated his conception of gender traits into series composed two-thirds of one sex and one-third the other; thus, cooking, cleaning, and other domestic tasks in the phalanx, theoretically open to all, would in practice engage twice as many women as men.[38] Most Associationists did not venture precise predictions, nor did they indulge in what Ripley called "babbling about the proper sphere of woman," but they agreed with Fourier's—and romanticism's—general notion that women best represented the emotional and man the rational side of humanity. Male leaders drew up long lists of conventional male and female attributes and asserted that Association would bring out woman's superiority in "certain branches" of activity corresponding to her traits. Phalansterian women were beautifiers, sympathizers, and spiritualizers; the phalanx would abolish the "isolated household" and its enslavement of women only to replace it with a new version of domesticity: a communal "home" pervaded by women's moral influence.[39] On the "woman question," as on many social and economic issues, the Fourierist plan tried to harmonize a progressive future with familiar roles and values.

A similar reconciliation of old and new characterized Fourierist ideas about child care and education. The socialization of child rearing was an important aspect of the communitarian "enlargement of home," but Associationists cushioned its impact by preserving women's traditional role as caretaker in infancy and by giving parents a choice of child care and educational arrangements.[40] Still, the Fourierists' educational plans were more innovative than conservative in addressing explicitly utopian ends. Phalanx education, like phalanx work arrangements, was designed to develop unique personalities and simultaneously integrate them into a new communal world.

The key features Fourier derived from such goals were communal child rearing from infancy (which would also incidentally help to liberate women), industrial training, friendly and flexible instructional environments, and a monitorial system in which children would learn from peers as much as from adults. To realize this system Fourier prescribed a detailed educational schema of eight phases nurturing phalanx children from birth to age nineteen or twenty. Starting in communal nurseries, children would at age three enter formal training that concentrated on developing physical aptitude; from age nine their conceptual and moral training would become increasingly integrated into regular phalanx activities. By the end of their second decade, phalanx youths would be prepared to graduate from the childhood world of learning to the "industrial" and "amorous" new world of adults.[41]

Here, too, Brisbane simplified and edited Fourier's scheme in presenting it to Americans. *Social Destiny of Man* reduced Fourier's design to three stages or "orders," ignored his obsession with opera and cuisine as teaching tools, and cut off the Frenchman's description before phalanx fifteen-year-olds began to be sorted into the chasers (Damsels) and the chaste (Vestals).[42] Brisbane, John Dwight, and other Associationist spokesmen elaborated three qualities that Harmonic education was to embody. First, it was to be developmental. Civilization impressed a foreign body of knowledge upon children through discipline; phalanx education would instead "develop what is in the child, by placing him in harmonious relations with all about him." In Fourier's ideas about learning through concrete experience and everyday activities, Brook Farmers heard echoes of the Transcendentalist ideal of self-culture. But Transcendentalist "self-ism" created precocious misfits, whereas Fourierist education was "socialized," bonding youngsters to community ways. By acquainting children with adults outside the family, the phalanx would widen their sphere of affection; by mingling educational exercises with communal tasks, children would experience a smooth transition into Associative adulthood, in contrast to the abrupt shock of civilized students encountering "the real world." Finally, Associationists captured both individual and communal dimensions of phalanx schooling in the ideal of "Integral" education. Just as the alternation of moral, intellectual, and physical learning was designed to create well-rounded individuals, it would foster "a more brotherly relation" between the farmer, the scholar, and the mechanic as "members of the same social body."[43]

Integral education was consistent with Associationist ideas about health. Country air, exercise, and a varied workday would contribute to a health-giving harmony between man and nature; the phalanx would eliminate many diseases thought to be inevitable afflictions. Fourier had an ingenious scheme for promoting Harmonians' well-being: he suggested that doctors be rewarded for preventing illness rather than treating it.[44] No American wrote more on health in the phalanx or so clearly demonstrated the link between Association and health reform than Marx Edgeworth Lazarus. The wayward offspring of a prominent North Carolina Jewish family, Lazarus consorted with Fourierists in New York and Boston before joining the North American Phalanx, all the while contributing long, abstruse articles on such topics as "Physiognomy" and "Scriptural Analogies" to *The Harbinger*. In the early 1850s Lazarus published several treatises elaborating his near-mystical blend of medical theory and Fourierist science. To Lazarus, Association was the means by which humans could attain harmony with nature and themselves and hence the foundation for the fullest physical and mental well-being. Adopting Fourier's psychology, he interpreted health as "passional hygiene" and portrayed the phalanx as an "Integral Hygienic Institute" that would recreate the natural existence of Eden. Harmonians would be vegetarians (despite Fourier's own preference for a mixed diet) who would derive great pleasure from eating, working, and bathing (Lazarus's purple passages about the last must have shocked more puritanical Associationists). Water-cure, "Magnetism" and above all homeopathy would extirpate all their physical ills.[45]

Lazarus and others repeated Fourier's claim that Harmonic society would escape Malthusian doom by maintaining an equilibrium between resources and population. As comparative birth rates between rich and poor demonstrated, Providence arranged that "refinement" of the species decreased fertility. Associationists also argued—somewhat contradictorily—that with productive machinery, increased agricultural output, improved climate, and a more evenly distributed population, the phalansterian world could support more people. Those who portray the Fourierists as backward-looking agrarians would be hard-pressed to explain Lazarus's confident prediction that a fully Harmonized Europe would comfortably sustain four and a quarter billion inhabitants![46]

As Associationists turned their eyes to Europe and the rest of the world, they provided occasional glimpses of the global future. Fourier envisioned the Harmonic world as comprising some two million phalanxes linked in associated regional units, with trade passing busily among them. Although nations would have parallel organizations, they would retain clear borders and, in their own version of passional freedom, distinctive characters. Americans were too preoccupied with actual phalanx building to add to Fourier's ideas on future world organization. Their scattered statements generally agreed with Fourier that Harmony would retain contemporary boundaries and national traits, but instead of waging ruinous wars over scarce resources, "nation will vie with nation in generous efforts to enrich and bless humanity." The international community would replicate the easy conjunction of individuality and unity taking place inside the phalanx.[47]

As communitarians, Fourierists believed that this global transformation would come peacefully and rapidly. Once successful, a trial phalanx would be so quickly and easily imitated that a host of cooperative communities would simply replace the competitive order—a process that offered an appealing alternative to violent revolution or gradual political reform.[48] By advocating scaled-down versions of the phalanx, Associationists prolonged the transition into Harmony somewhat beyond Fourier's "sudden leap." Implicit in their willingness to undertake small communities was a more evolutionary model than Fourier's, one in which "partial" experiments would grow into or else inspire full phalanxes. Yet this alteration—one that Fourier himself countenanced late in life—in no way compromised the communitarian program. Brisbane and his colleagues still believed that "the whole question of effecting a Social Reform may be reduced to the establishment of one Association, which will serve as a model for, and induce the rapid establishment of others."[49] In a few years Fourier's new industrial world would become reality, and humanity would meet its true social destiny.

In the ways they modified and presented Fourier's plan, Associationists demonstrated how much their Fourierism was permeated with contemporary attitudes and values. Utopians shared the ambivalent stance of antebellum reformers generally, believing in progress, freedom, and equality but also committed to moral order and discipline.[50] Fourierists accepted the new forces of urban industrialism but sought to reconcile them with familiar values and satisfactions; they justified women's claim to power through the conventions of domesticity; and they gave Fourier's economy a more egalitarian cast even as they accepted inequality of result. Utopians' arguments served the cause of a transformed social order, yet that order closely reflected contemporary aspirations that the widening course of democracy, urbanization, and industrialization be harmonized with traditional values and ideals. The hopeful, "scientific" reconciliation of continuity and change was the essence of the phalanx's message.

The Paradoxes of Liberal Communitarianism

Fourierism as Americans interpreted it was energized—and ultimately enervated—by this ambivalent posture toward social change. Association extended longings for justice and brotherhood into the revolutionary new world of Harmonic society, but its starting point was a community blueprint designed to be acceptable to all "Civilizees." "Not through hatred, collision, and depressing competition," Horace Greeley proclaimed, "not through War, whether of Nation against Nation, Class against Class, or Capital against Labor; but through Union, Harmony, and the reconciling of all Interests . . . is the Renovation of the World, the Elevation of the degraded and suffering Masses of Mankind, to be sought and effected."[51] Phalanx mechanisms would channel Civilizees' desires and interests into a socialist outcome without wrenching disruption or sacrifice. The paradox of Association's "conservative radicalism" ramified into every article of its creed. To be conservative and radical at the same time meant to promise individuality and community, capitalism and socialism, reform and revolution. In sublimely optimistic—indeed "utopian"—fashion, Association claimed to reconcile these apparently contradictory goals within its communal frame. The phalanx would allow reformers to be cautious individualists and radical communitarians at the same time, to have their cake and eat it too.

"As deep as is the prayer of every soul to be made one with every other," John Dwight declared, "so deep also is the demand of each to *be himself* in the full force and freedom of an individual. . . . Honor to the profound mind who has reconciled these seeming opposites!" Associationists insisted that their proposals did not require joiners to give up their selfhood: the "grand object" of the "Combined Order" was "to *enlarge* individual freedom, not to subject it to additional shackles." Readers were warned not to confuse the phalanx with the "monastic" communities of the Rappites and Shakers, which stifled rather than freed human passions. Religious and Owenite utopians also erred when they repudiated individual property and shared goods equally. Fourierist joint-stock ownership was preferable to the "communism" of Shakers and Owenites, which in true liberal fashion Brisbane labeled "the grave of liberty."[52] Fourierists avoided the term "socialism," at least until 1847, precisely because it was identified with the Owenites and communal property. "Agrarianism," the idea of confiscating property and distributing it equally, was similarly repugnant to them.[53]

In contrast, Association secured personal liberty in several ways listed by Brisbane: "satisfaction of all legitimate tastes and inclinations, with variety and change in order—unrestricted personal freedom, when it does not degenerate into license—free choice in occupations and social relations—no sacrifice of the individual to the mass—and adaptation of the social Organization to Man."[54] Brook Farmers, always more poetic, pointed out the subtle ways in which Civilization stamped out unique character traits, then evoked a society "in perfect union with the nature of man," according to Ripley, one "to which every chord in his sensitive and finely-fibred frame will respond; which will call forth, as from a well-tuned instrument, all those exquisite modulations of feeling and intellect, which were aptly termed by Plato, the 'music' of our being."[55]

What would the phalanx's "new man" look like? From Fourier's sketches and their Transcendentalist heritage, Associationist leaders evolved an image of the free and "whole" individual of Harmonian society. At liberty to develop their full potential, phalansterians would move into all spheres of life with sympathy and gusto, learning new trades and skills, enjoying nature as companions, and growing in reverence of God. Yet Harmonians were not selfish individualists, for Associationists believed that the most complete self-fulfillment came from joining interests and love with others. By definition, no such persons could yet exist, although a few great men provided a glimpse of the future. Jesus Christ, whom Associationists claimed came to predict the social millennium, was of course the ideal, which mortals could only approximate. Fourier himself, though he carried a "divine" message, was personally too coarse and crotchety to serve as a model. Carlyle and Daniel Webster, whom Fourierist leaders admired in earlier days, were turning into crabby conservatives. William Ellery Channing had more congenial views but remained a detached and blurry personality. By contrast, one can feel the Brook Farmers' admiration for the serene yet forceful and versatile Emerson even as they criticized their former hero for disavowing Association and thus "Humanity." In much the same way that Brook Farmers evolved a social version of Transcendentalism from Emerson's early manifestos, the "integral" phalansterian would be a warmhearted version of this free, practical—and characteristically American—idealist.[56]

When looking for images of community, Associationists had fewer materials close by to draw upon. The theoretical ideal was that of "solidarity," the mystical notion that there was "one life . . . in all humanity" and only becoming "members one of another" could bring out its fullness.[57] But did Associationists have any actual communal models in mind? Americans owned an authentic community tradition in Puritanism and the New England village. There are veiled suggestions in Ripley and Channing's writings that through Fourierism these men sought to recreate the close-knit Puritan and Federalist villages of their youth.[58] But if unconscious cultural memories surfaced periodically and Puritan forms helped shape their moral vocabulary, Associationists were as yet too near the reaction against Puritanism to appreciate its affinity with communitarian aims.

Another source of community imagery was the republican ideological tradition, whose "commonwealth" vision of equality and civic virtue Associationists recast, as I have already suggested, into the phalanx's promise of Christian brotherhood. By the 1840s, however, the language of republicanism had become diffuse and attenuated enough to serve constituencies ranging from "Bowery boys" to nativists, capitalist entrepreneurs to slaveholders, artisans to their masters.[59] Granting republicanism's lingering rhetorical pull and the need to annoint reform proposals with its holy words, it nevertheless remained too vague and open-ended a vision to encapsulate communitarian goals distinctively and fully. For different reasons, Puritanism and republicanism fell short as satisfactory communal models.

R. J. Wilson has pointed out that nineteenth-century Americans impelled by loose social bonds to search for communal models and metaphors had to go outside their own country to find them. Americans in quest of community turned to Europe, to the distant past, or to exotic or mystical creeds for appropriate images.[60] There was in fact a distinct echo of medievalism in Associationist thought and propaganda. Godwin was fascinated by medieval towns and communes, and Channing confided to Isaac Hecker that he would recreate the Middle Ages in the nineteenth century if it were possible. Fourierist spokesmen compared the Associationists' mission to the Crusades and contrasted the chivalric spirit with the selfish materialism of contemporary life. Associationists admired the profound sense of integration of medieval times: the mutual dependence of feudal relations, the cooperative aspects of guild production, and the unity of religion and everyday life.[61]

Roman Catholic doctrine and institutions carried similar connotations of coherence and community. Seeing the Strasbourg cathedral, the young Brisbane was so awed that Protestant faiths seemed "meager, and starved" by comparison; yet back in the street he recalled that the church had done little to end the pauperism evident all around him. Brisbane's ambivalence was shared by many liberal Protestants who could not swallow reactionary Catholic doctrines yet were lured by the church's continuity, mystery, and promise of spiritual peace. For some the attraction was overpowering: the list of Transcendentalist converts to Catholicism included Orestes Brownson and Brook Farm's Isaac Hecker and Sophia Ripley. At one point Brownson and Hecker felt they had Channing won over. Though he and George Ripley resisted, they, along with John Dwight, continued to find Catholic images and music appropriate symbols of holy community.[62]

In at least a few instances harmony and community were also identified with the exotic East. Marx Lazarus, who learned about oriental mysticism from Emerson and French sources, maintained in a book on Zoroastrianism that Westerners could benefit from the Eastern idea that human lives were only limited "individuations" of a unitary spirit infusing all beings. Realizing this truth would make modern men less self-sufficient and more communal-minded.[63] Far more pervasive was imagery that linked Association to the return of a lost Edenic paradise. According to Fourier, "Edenism" had been humanity's first stage of social existence. "Attractive industry" promised to remove the curse put upon labor by the Fall and thus recover simple joy in work; "passional liberation" could gratify desires without sin. The paradoxical idea of a self-conscious return to a lost golden age surfaced between the lines of several phalanx accounts, especially those penned by the romantic Lazarus. We were "ALL BORN HARMONIANS BEFORE WE WERE EDUCATED AS CIVILIZEES," this devotee of Herman Melville's *Typee* and *Omoo* proclaimed. A southerner, naturalist, and non-Protestant, Lazarus was far more sensual than the repressed New England Fourierists. He and other southern-born Associationists proposed that a model phalanx be undertaken in a lush, subtropical environment where fruits grew by themselves, each human lived as "the darling child of Earth and Sun," and social science would recover Edenic bliss.[64]

Images of medievalism, Catholicism, and Edenism were meant to express the integration of phalansterians with one another and with nature, but the Associationist ideal was to enhance individual growth while attaining this communal oneness. The metaphor of music seemed to come closest to capturing the combination. Fourier declared that the laws of serial organization—the key to establishing complete Harmony—were echoed in musical scales. Brisbane returned to France in 1844 in part to study musical theory, and John Dwight undertook similar work back home. Both marveled at how musical laws harmonized groups of single notes, preserving the individuality of each yet bringing them into perfect union. In the same way, phalanx work and living arrangements, modeled like music on natural laws of proportion, would create a complex and beautiful orchestration of personalities.[65]

How did the phalanx plan compare with Associationists' individualist and communal ideals? Could community arrangements really reconcile the two, as the image of the chorus or orchestra suggested? Archindividualists Emerson and Horatio Greenough complained about Fourierist constraints, but Associationists had a plausible case when they replied that phalanx institutions were premised on personal freedom and guaranteed self-expression in virtually all activities.[66] The far greater problem, as some religious critics perceived, involved the goal of community. There was a fundamental disparity between the Associationists' aspirations for community and the forms they intended to embody it: the goal was organic, the means to achieve it atomistic and mechanistic. Beneath its rhetorical cover the phalanx was a mechanism for assuring cooperative behavior rather than an expression of communal solidarity.

In the first place, the phalanx plan proposed not organic community but voluntary cooperation. This important distinction reflected the gradual transformation in American social thought from Puritanism to the liberal nineteenth-century world view. Basic conceptions of community in America underwent an unmistakable shift between the seventeenth and nineteenth centuries, from those of self-sacrificing individuals governed by a prior commitment to providential authority to those foreseeing the voluntary commitment of free and regenerate individuals. In other words, as the concept of individualism developed in American thought, the ideal of community became diluted and postponed.[67] Associationists espoused an old-fashioned communal bond but advocated new individualistic forms to attain it. For all its collectivism, Fourier's plan began—like voluntary associations or evangelical reform societies—with the solitary, self-determining individual and asked that person to give part of him- or herself (but only part) to others. Like these nineteenth-century expressions of "union," Fourierism envisioned community less as the means to personal fulfillment than the eventual product of individual actions. By addressing the conscience through educational models, by allowing privacy and property, and by treating the social context as a medium for self-culture, the phalanx adapted "the ethics of individualism to larger social units."[68] "Association" and "cooperation" rather than true community were the group forms consonant with nineteenth-century liberalism.

Furthermore, even cooperation in the phalanx was not necessarily voluntary, since the Fourierist blueprint simply channeled self-interested action to the common good. "In Association," Brisbane explained, "*Selfishness* will be rendered *Social,* and be made to serve the interests of the whole." Joint-stock organization and the elaborate system of work in shifting teams were to assure automatically that "each individual can only forward his interests by forwarding those of all the other members, and all the other members can only forward those by forwarding his." Fourier's social mathematics was a "divine formula" that permitted all "to follow exactly and entirely the inclinations of their natures and yet in the process add their share to perfect social harmony."[69] Doctrinaire

Associationists such as Brisbane and George Corselius were content with this mechanistic reconciliation of individual and group; the Brook Farmers, on the other hand, struggled to create a truly cooperative version of Fourierism based on self-sacrifice and spiritual values.[70] Neither plan was organicist, but the second offered the intriguing possibility of resolving the dualism of individual and community within the framework of liberal thought. If Associationists succeeded in attracting self-sacrificing humanitarians rather than self-interested Civilizees, their little communities could hope to approach the harmonic cooperative ideal instead of the benevolent machine of more conventional liberal dreams.

Reconciliation of individual with community interests also placed Fourierists in an ambiguous middle ground somewhere between capitalism and socialism. Largely because the Associationists' economic definition of liberty was "possessive" (that is, proprietarian), their communitarianism retained many capitalistic features. Fourierists regarded the individual's right to hold property as a "sacred" guarantor of freedom and property itself as a means of personal expression. Since capital represented legitimate past labor, it was due a fair return: talk of abolishing interest on investment was a "radical" and "mistaken" notion.[71] Belief in property and capital was implicit in joint-stock holdings divided into dividend-paying shares, and faith in individual achievement meant that the phalanx "wage scale" rewarded harder work with higher pay. All these features functioned as capitalistic incentives toward communal success. Here too the phalanx seemed to solve the problem of individual versus social goals by means of a mechanism. Its elaborate division of labor, complex compensation scheme, and sharehold ownership were ways of bringing about a socialized economy by capitalistic means. Viewed from this angle, Fourierist economics resembled a "visible hand" analogous to the "invisible" one that laissez-faire capitalists believed guided free-market competition to the general good.[72]

Albert Brisbane, himself a rabid speculator, saw nothing wrong in outside investors netting large profits from communal experiments, since he believed that private and public gain coincided. Horace Greeley concurred, predicting that phalanxes would outcompete conventional corporations and offer the most attractive version of Whig managerial capitalism available.[73] It would be unfair, though, to view Associationists merely as more efficient capitalist engineers than their opponents. The Fourierism of Godwin, Dana, and the Brook Farmers, with its egalitarian emphasis and ethic of solidarity, was more militant than Greeley's and less compatible with capitalism. As community-minded radicals, these Associationists did not take on capitalist forms intact but restricted them or else set them in a socialistic context. For example, they advocated measures to prevent the "tyranny" of outside capital over communal experiments; they envisioned all phalansterians as holders of community stock; and they repudiated individual ownership of that uniquely communal and precious property—land.[74] Shareholding, when diffused and nearly equalized, and when workers owned their means of production, was a viable socialist tool. In a similar way the phalanx scheme of remuneration repudiated the market economy by adopting a scale based on the intrinsic quality of work and by rewarding tasks such as housework, which capitalism deemed "unproductive." Finally, rather than endorsing competition, these Associationists hoped that personal ambition would take the form of a friendly rivalry among peers in service to the group.

Even more to the point, one should be wary of positing "capitalism" and "socialism" as timeless categories with fixed and mutually exclusive components. To do so ignores their development over time, the reality of history as process, and in fact the possibility of alternative routes from the past. Just as recent scholarship has returned such terms as "liberalism," "individualism," and "republicanism" to historical contexts, we need to remember that capitalism and socialism evolved in tandem through the nineteenth century and drew ideas and institutions from each other. It was no coincidence that Robert Owen was both benevolent factory owner and socialist communitarian. Early capitalism and early socialism had much in common as ideologies of freedom and agents of modernization: promises of efficiency, abundance and liberation from oppression; a belief in collective enterprise and the division of labor; and an idealistic internationalism. In the 1840s the ideal of efficiency and economic forms such as joint-stock organization still had a flexible and as yet undetermined character: the former was voiced by Saint-Simonians as well as cotton-mill designers; the latter served such promoters of working-class solidarity as mutual benefit societies and producer cooperatives in addition to capitalist corporations. Rather than emulating capitalist methods, such features of Association were often meant to critique them, contest their growing dominance, and appropriate them for socially responsible ends.[75]

Of course, things could, and often did, go the other way. Although this kind of adaptation made the phalanx more familiar and attractive, it brought the risk that capitalist mechanisms might undermine communal objectives. Attempting to lure outside investors, Associationists could find themselves burdened by heavy mortgage and interest obligations. In promising abundance, they might well attract the wrong recruits to struggling communal experiments. And allowing each member a separate entry in phalanx labor records and stock ledgers could promote rather than discourage capitalist self-interest. The Associationists' compromise with capitalism brought into their movement myriad possibilities for internal division, defection, and co-optation, especially as phalanx troubles coincided with the nation's headlong rush into the capitalist boom years of the late 1840s and 1850s. The American economy may have been "contested terrain" in the antebellum years, but the combatants were far from equally matched.

Perhaps the most striking of all paradoxes within Fourierism—and one central to liberal communitarianism—was the idea that humans could move voluntarily toward a radically egalitarian society. Marx and Engels were among the first to charge that Fourier was relying on capitalists to bring the revolution that would eventually topple them. American Fourierists, seeking to build a popular movement rather than depend on wealthy patrons, were even more concerned with consensus than Fourier. The need to reconcile their revolutionary forecast with popular appeal led them to trumpet radical principles yet stress a gradual, voluntary policy of reform. Especially in matters of church, government, and marriage—three institutions dear to conservatives—Associationists criticized contemporary arrangements and hinted at vast and necessary future changes; but they contended that until complete Association was reached, the "restraining principles" of convention were needed to prevent chaos. Their model phalanx was a universal and reconciling structure that would "violate no rights" and bring no controversial changes in social and domestic affairs.[76]

This ambiguity pervaded—and in fact undermined—the utopians' position on religious sects under Association. Fourierists professed that all religious creeds would be respected in the phalanx. Brisbane assured readers that "the most perfect Freedom of Opinion will exist, and . . . every individual will enjoy his religious opinions precisely as he wishes and without restriction." Phalanx halls would serve as churches or meetinghouses where congregations of any persuasion could gather. Associationists proudly pointed out that their ranks included Catholics and Jews as well as all varieties of Protestants.[77]

But could Fourierist toleration be taken at face value? Brisbane and other Associationists predicted that in the Harmonic order, religious sects would wither away and the changed circumstances of life generate a new and diffuse religious context. Sectarian battles were emblematic of the disordered, strife-torn world of Civilization and would find no conscripts in the peace and concord of Association. Instead, with all human passions tuned to the divine harmonies of the universe, work, play and all daily activities would take on a religious aura.[78] Most Fourierist leaders still foresaw some sort of formalized religion in the future, whether to spiritualize the Fourierist mechanism (as Brook Farmers contended) or to give focus to communal rituals. For the Harmonic world they envisioned a "Unitary Church" that would encompass all Harmonians in brotherly love and "contain within itself innumerable minor differences in faith and ritual."[79]

The difference between Brisbane and the Brook Farmers was characteristic but not as wide as it seemed. Whether Association simply eliminated existing churches or incorporated them in a syncretistic new religion mattered little; the choice between obsolescence and trivialization was hardly a meaningful one. Either scenario illustrated the dilemma of an ideology that assured churches' continued existence and also predicted they would disappear.

The same ambiguity between reassuring, conservative policy and disquieting revolutionary principle cut through the Associationist stance on government. Charles Dana told an audience that Association was "possible under any form of civilized government, . . . whether here in Boston, or in Vienna, or London, or St. Petersburg," but in the same lecture contended that Fourierist principles provided a "true theory of government" to replace the contemporary "false state" coercing subjects' obedience. There was no denying that government with only symbolic offices, a peaceful "industrial army," and no legislation would seem strange to Americans of the 1840s. Yet Fourierists saw in the familiar concept of democratic federalism one means of making such changes attractive. Phalanxes corresponded to American townships; linking them into counties and states would simply add an economic dimension to the existing federal system. In a similar vein they contended that phalanx democracy and pacifism were only extensions of cherished American ideals.[80]

Fourierist ambiguity concerning marriage and family under Association was much more controversial and damaging. Defenders of conventional notions of home and family protested that Fourier's "combined households" actually meant "combined wives," or at least would damage the nuclear family tie. Fourierist spokesmen hopped about enough in their statements to give credibility to these charges. Even as they stressed that Associationists did not endorse and were not responsible for Fourier's sexual theories, the Americans repeated many of Fourier's sharpest criticisms of bourgeois mores—not the Frenchman's repudiation of monogamy but his indictment of marriage in Civilization.[81] Its waste of time and resources, its entrapment of women in housework and child rearing, and its promotion of selfishness toward the outside world condemned the "isolated household" to obsolescence. Contemporary marriage was Civilization writ small, and its conflicts echoed the "discords" of an unequal society. True marriage was based upon love, but in Civilization women were often forced to wed—or reluctant to divorce—for financial reasons. Husbands ordered wives about and dictated children's fate with the sanction of church and law. Formed without freedom and condoning injustices ranging from financial bondage to forced seduction, "Civilized" marriage was, according to Associationist propaganda, "legalized prostitution" or "legalized rape."[82]

Such phrases became slogans for radical free-lovers in the 1850s. Yet despite their indictment of conventional marriage, and contrary to reformers who insisted that "the question of the relation of the sexes in Association . . . must be met," Fourierist spokesmen vowed not to "interfere with, or effect any change whatever in . . . institutions relating to the family union or marriage," at least for the foreseeable future.[83] Some, like Greeley and Van Amringe, believed that indissoluble marriage was God's law. Others explained that in Civilization and during the transition to Harmony, "conservative and restraining principles" were necessary because loosening family ties would only encourage immorality and intensify the wrongs inflicted on women. Fourier himself had recognized

this and, unlike Robert Owen, discountenanced immediate domestic revolution.[84] Whatever future changes they foresaw for the family, the Associationists, like most nineteenth-century sex theorists, justified them in
terms of preserving and elevating marriage rather than destroying it.
Association would "correct [Civilization's] evils and give to the Family
Union a purity, elevation and harmony, which it now rarely possesses."
Enjoying complete equality and pecuniary independence, wives and husbands could base their relationship on free and untainted affection. Since
children would be cared for in communal nurseries and schools, parents
could relate to them as advisers and friends rather than disciplinarians.
All would benefit from communalism's opportunities to develop their
talents and interests; they would return to the family apartment more
interesting persons than they had been when they left, thus revitalizing
family ties of love and pleasure.[85]

It is not hard to see how such descriptions, intended to reassure, might
bring the opposite reaction. The fact was that Association was bound to
produce important changes in sex and family matters. Guaranteeing
education to women and opening to them all realms of employment
would encourage their assertion of marital rights as well. Brisbane and
Godwin both frankly predicted looser divorce regulations under Association. When communities took over educational and child-rearing functions, nuclear family bonds would doubtless be weakened, and as Dwight
acknowledged, "the relation of parent and child" would be "modified"
to make room for wider attachments.[86]

On a theoretical level, certainly, there was no denying that passional
psychology justified complete personal freedom in Harmonic society.
Parke Godwin depicted Fourier's scenario in guardedly general terms,
noting that "as society approaches a more organic state, the severity of
its discipline may be relaxed, until finally, having attained social Harmony, men may be left to their native Attractions, which are their only
true guides."[87] Would absolute freedom be extended specifically to marriage and sexual relations? No matter how much Associationists protested
that "passions" and "attractions" had no sexual connotation, Fourier's
theory put them in an impossible dilemma: they could repudiate passional psychology and the phalanx's scientific grounding, or else accept its
radical principles with their implication of sexual freedom. Most leaders
hoped to stave off charges of immorality by disavowing Fourier's "speculative" extrapolations and by arguing that liberation would proceed gradually and by consensus. Such arguments not only left the Fourierists
vulnerable to attack from conservatives; they also failed to pacify communitarians who were impatient for sexual change. Claiming a conciliatory
middle ground for social reform, the Associationists faced difficult pressures from conservatives and radicals alike.

Finally, a marked ambivalence between evolutionary and interventionist scenarios complicated Fourierist ideology and influenced the fate of
the American movement. Like many social philosophers touched by

nineteenth-century historicism, including Marx, Fourier tried simultaneously to enlist history in his cause and transcend it. According to his conception of history, Harmonic society was the inevitable culmination of humanity's progressive development from Edenism through five "unfortunate periods" (including Civilization) to the triumphal reign of Association. Between Civilization and Harmony were at least two transitional stages, Guarantism and Simple Association, during which humankind would work its way slowly to more complete experiments in cooperation. Yet Fourier himself believed these intermediate stages superfluous. Since the "divine social code" had been deciphered and the material conditions for Harmonic abundance were already available, humans could save themselves additional centuries of social misery by establishing a successful phalanx. Was the perfect society to be reached through evolution, or would humanity suddenly leap through history into Harmony?[88]

Associationists acknowledged that there were indeed "two ways to the Phalanstery," one gradual and unconscious, the other rapid and intentional. There was no doubt which scenario they preferred. Fourier's evolutionary schema derived more from a penchant for scientific classification and symmetry than a desire to follow the dialectics of historical change. Nor did this utopian theorist ever envision gradual reform through such "Guarantist" institutions as collective kitchens and communal banks as anything but a last resort. American Associationists followed Fourier's emphasis on the phalanx and even strengthened it. None of their synopses of Association included Fourier's proposals for partial cooperative organizations; according to Godwin's *Popular View*, these were of "secondary importance" and could be "safely left out of the account of the societary Reformer, who should labor for the direct introduction of what is strictly Association."[89]

Still, neither Fourier nor his American followers were willing to dismiss the idea that partial measures might progress toward the phalanx. Gradualist schemes could demonstrate Associative principles, attract those unwilling or unable to join communities, and give reformers institutions to rally around when phalanx trials failed. No reform short of the phalanx was adequate, but producer and consumer cooperatives, mutual insurance plans, savings banks, and joint-stock organizations could awaken the public to the benefits of cooperation.[90] Nor did Associationists relinquish their optimism that even without their efforts the world was evolving inevitably toward the phalanx. The notion that the seeds of Association lay in "Civilized" ground confirmed utopians' belief that their age was one of progress and expanding benevolence. Symptoms of gradual but definite progress toward Association were discernible in the unconscious workings of economy and society. Railroads, steamboats, and the telegraph were "material types" of unity, increasing interchanges between nations, spreading wealth, and quickening the spirit of brotherhood. The proliferation of religious societies, voluntary associations, and business corporations attested to the power of collective organization. By combining in large corporations and trade unions, capitalists and workers were preparing for Harmonic society without even knowing it. Association, wrote one Fourierist, was coming as quickly by society's own momentum as by the strenuous efforts of reformers.[91]

Such praise for progressive "signs of the times" contrasted with the dreary and foreboding picture of Civilization that Associationists usually relied upon to press for radical reform. Just as the phalanx might come through either intervention or evolution, Harmonic society could be presented as either radical break from Civilization or progressive development from contemporary trends. Each perspective had its partisans in the American movement, reflecting various degrees of disenchantment. Brisbane generally portrayed Association in direct opposition to Civilization, whereas to Greeley it was a natural outgrowth of modern progress. (It is revealing that Greeley used "civilization" as a complimentary term.) Most movement spokesmen, including Dana, Godwin, Ripley, and Channing, fluctuated between the two positions. For these and the movement as a whole the tension between evolutionary and interventionist perspectives was salutary. Finding the roots of Harmony within Civilization fit contemporary trends within the Fourierist framework, boosted communitarians' confidence, and helped prevent the embittered isolation reformers always risk. Openness to gradualist reforms attracted moderates' sympathy, stimulated useful debate on movement tactics, and gave utopians realistic goals to strive for while accruing funds for future phalanxes or sorting through the remains of past ones.

Yet there was always the danger that this creative ambiguity might dissolve completely into its evolutionist component. Tired or disillusioned radicals could prove vulnerable to an easy retreat into accommodation or quietude. As long as Fourierism preached that Association was inevitable, gradual measures or even optimistic resignation were there to fall back on when phalanx attempts failed. The notion that Association stemmed from the gradual tendency toward cooperative enterprise left utopians open to the idea that "Association" was but another name for society itself and the development of Civilization ample illustration of Fourierist principles. As the course of the American Fourierist movement was to demonstrate, admitting evolutionary thought into a communitarian framework had its costs as well as advantages.

As "conservative radicals," Associationists sought to bring revolutionary change without destroying what they liked about the present; as "universal" social reformers they tried to win all classes and individuals to a program of social transformation. The ideology that resulted from these needs spun a web of paradox and ambiguity which incorporated elements of opposing social options into a grand and plausible synthesis. In the implication that phalansterians did not have to choose among conflicting options or sacrifice familiar ways but could enjoy the best of all possibilities lay the deeper meaning of Association's utopianism.

"A nation's identity," writes Erik Erikson, "is derived from the ways in which history has, as it were, counterpointed certain opposite potentialities; the ways in which it lifts this counterpoint to a unique style of civilization, or lets it disintegrate into mere contradiction."[92] What Erikson says of a dominant national identity was no less true for the utopian ideology that aimed to supplant it. As a reconciling yet radical alternative, Association had to accommodate static and dynamic social options in a fruitful synthesis. Insofar as its optimistic, ambivalent approach was plausible, Association might generate a popular movement. But once that movement got under way, utopia's theoretical paradoxes faced the test of reality. If communitarian institutions failed to embody the doctrine's tensions creatively, or if ambivalence proved inadequate to direct movement strategy, Associationist paradoxes ran the risk of disintegrating into contradictions and taking the movement with them.

Association as Alternative Americanism

In much the same way that Associationist doctrine was shot through with internal paradoxes, it stood in an ambiguous relation to mainstream American ways of thinking and acting. There was, to be sure, no unitary American "mind" or "ideology" in the 1840s, only diverse voices and rival creeds contending for popular allegiance and control of the nation's institutions.[93] But insofar as opposing groups shared traditions of liberalism, republicanism, and Protestantism, they drew meanings and goals from a common cultural heritage. And articulate northern whites especially, participating in a dynamic capitalist economy not yet drastically rent by divisions of ethnicity and class, shared enough values, habits, and assumptions to suggest that a definite "national character" had emerged after the first half-century of the American experiment.[94]

If we take the more conventional half of each "paradox" discussed above, we see a substantial overlap between the Associationist program and this nineteenth-century cultural mainstream. In one way or another most antebellum northerners, like the Fourierists, championed individual freedom, participated in a capitalist economy, and believed in the democratic process and the inevitability of progress. The communitarian strategy of reforming society through model experiments also had a special appeal to Americans, as has been argued.[95] Its pragmatic tinkering found sympathy with a nation of experimenters, a nation that viewed itself as an experiment; and private reform corresponded to the tendencies toward antistatism and voluntary association which Tocqueville and other foreign visitors found so noticeable. The specifically Fourierist variant of communitarianism resonated with the kind of paeans to nationalism, promises of abundance, and glorious millennial rhetoric already familiar to antebellum audiences from sermons, newspaper editorials, and political speeches.

In such ways Associationist ideology reaffirmed the prejudices and hopes of a wider American culture. The most striking affinity between

Fourierism and what we can loosely call "Americanism" occurred at a level above these specifics. Ideologies are not mere aggregates of individual ideas and attitudes; they can also be seen as structures that organize fears and aspirations into a coherent whole with a distinct tone and purpose. At this structural level there was a remarkable correspondence between Association and American ways of thinking. Just as polarity and tension best characterized Fourierist ideology, the same mode pervades the most persuasive descriptions of an American "creed" or "character." Furthermore, the basic dualisms of Associationist ideology were precisely those most often cited as characteristically American: individualism versus community, idealism versus materialism, conservatism versus change, experiment versus destiny, nationalism versus internationalism.[96] Partly because both sought to be total world views, and partly because of changes wrought by its American interpreters, Association's central issues were those crucial also to "Americanism" but reproduced more intensely and explicitly within a communitarian framework.

Finally and most remarkably, both "Americanism" and Fourierism resolved these polarized options in much the same way. No less than their communitarian rival, "official" nineteenth-century versions of America's nature and destiny tended to be wildly optimistic. Both promised an earthly paradise that would reconcile dualisms of thought and action, and both identified it with the American future. Through a sublime faith—in one case, faith in republican institutions and democratic capitalism; in the other, faith in a scientific model of an ideal society—adherents could achieve seemingly conflicting social goals without choice or sacrifice. Individuality and community, wealth and virtue, freedom and order, the machine and the garden, the city and the country—alternatives that a few native nineteenth-century pessimists, and many European commentators, conceived as mutually exclusive—were possible on American soil. If, as historian T. J. Jackson Lears has suggested, "a dominant culture takes root, not by imposing ideology, but by addressing utopian longings," this was especially true in antebellum America. A large and growing historical literature portrays the popular cast of mind animated by a nearly boundless faith in an all-reconciling utopian future made possible by abundance, space, and diversity.[97] This spirit underlay the implicit utopianism of American political ideologies such as Greeley's Whiggism and Godwin's Democracy, and it provided fertile soil for perfectionist ideas among reformers. Antebellum Americans, in short, were utopians long before they heard of phalanxes and Charles Fourier. When they were introduced, many natives heard the rhythms and rhetoric of the nation's utopian venture within Fourierist rhapsodies.[98]

The Associationists' utopia was of course the phalanx, not the homestead, factory, or township. Fourierist ideology spun out a coherent critique of American exceptionalism and repudiated competitive social relations. Inside the phalanx there was an important strain of communalism represented by the social minimum and arrangements for cooperative work and living. Perhaps most important, the goal of social reconstruction was inherently radical. Always beneath the Associationists' assurance that change would be voluntary and gradual lay the opposing idea that existing political, economic, and social relations would eventually be replaced by a new order reflecting a more free and loving way of life. If Fourierism echoed the American Dream, it did so in the cause of a communitarian revolution rather than an indefinite extension of contemporary progress.

Even so, this "revolution" never took its leaders very far from the American mainstream. Within its communitarian frame Fourierism incorporated many of the assumptions, ideas, and promises of the dominant American culture. Its critique of Civilization may have been dialectical and radical, but its prescription was utopian and liberal. The phalanx plan upon which Associationists based their movement grew from an optimistic belief in individual potential, had several capitalistic features, and was presented as the culmination of Christianity and American nationalism. Association was indeed a utopian alternative, but one so close to American ideas that it was less an alternative *to* American ways of thinking than an alternative version *of* them, a community-minded version of the American Dream. It appeared on the antebellum reform scene not as an irreconcilable enemy of American society but as an attractive rival for the allegiance of Americans and the destiny of their nation.

Characterizing Fourierist doctrine as an "alternative Americanism" helps explain its immediate appeal for thousands of antebellum northerners who were drawn to communitarian reform but reluctant to depart from old beliefs and allegiances. Yet Fourierism's distinctive blend of dissent and moderation also played a crucial role in the failure of the Associationist movement. In a penetrating essay on the concept of cultural "hegemony," Jackson Lears points out that radical movements contesting a ruling group's authority could be undermined by ideological ambivalence: "Subordinate groups could identify with the dominant culture—often for sound reasons—even as they sought to challenge it." Jackson Lears finds such a Gramscian "divided consciousness" among the artisans, farmers, and shopkeepers who rallied around a "producer ideology" in the nineteenth century. These combined egalitarian democracy, republicanism, the labor theory of value, and communal customs into a powerful but unstable force that animated such mass movements as the Knights of Labor.[99]

Even more than the producer ideology, Associationism "contained contradictory elements that promoted internal divisions and pointed toward accommodation as well as resistance." Fourierists staked out a position too close to the American mainstream to survive. Individualist guarantees, capitalist incentives, the belief in class conciliation and inevitable progress—all these were integral features of Fourierist voluntarist socialism. But like liberal inroads into the producer ideology, they constituted "powerful countertendencies" that often subverted "egalitarian and communal aims." Individualism and capitalism rendered the phalanx a "house divided against itself," as Fourierist veteran Alcander Longley complained, and brought Associationist communal experiments brief and troubled lives.[100] And, with one foot in the dominant culture, Associationists were unable to stand apart from economic expansion during the prosperous 1850s and the emerging "free labor" version of Americanism which sanctified northern capitalism. The Fourierists' compromise with American culture made theirs an immensely attractive but highly vulnerable form of dissent.

III

Building the
New Industrial
World

Three wise men of Gotham
Went to sea in a bowl;
If the bowl had been stronger,
My song had been longer.
                    —Mother Goose

Fred [Cabot] said something to which all our hearts responded,
about the happiness we enjoy,—that he would not exchange a
day here for a year in civilization.
                    —Marianne Dwight, *Letters from Brook Farm*

6

The Communitarian Boom and Bust

By joining familiar nineteenth-century ideals to the new ideology of secular communitarianism, the Fourierists struck a responsive chord among restless northerners. As streamlined by Brisbane and his colleagues, the phalanx plan was simple yet systematic and its promise of instant wealth too enticing to pass up. Eventually, Associationists would establish a network of Fourierist clubs and cooperative stores and build coalitions with labor organizations. But in the early 1840s reform audiences clamored for immediate panaceas and rushed into phalanx experiments. One local lecturer estimated only two years after the *Tribune* began publicizing Fourierism that 20,000 converts in western New York were "willing, nay anxious, to take their place in associative unity." A Michigan Associationist reported that at a meeting to organize a local phalanx "the number of members was increased to upwards of 1,300, and more than one hundred applicants were rejected, because there seemed to be no end, and we became almost frightened at the number."[1] In 1843 six American phalanxes were established, and the next year no less than twelve began operations.

With a few exceptions these were struggling, poorly organized experiments doomed to failure. Fourierist leaders spent almost no time preparing the domains or training members, who in many cases were strangers to one another. Instead of large, carefully planned communities in a few central locations, tiny colonies multiplied in odd and sometimes competing locations. The result of such a naive and chaotic charge into communal life was predictable. Of the twenty-four phalanxes founded between 1842 and 1846, five survived for three years and only two lasted more than half a decade (see Appendix Table 1). For most, the cycle from "great hope at the beginning" to the "bitterness of the end" was completed in just one or two years. It was, John Humphrey Noyes later observed, the socialist version of Bull Run—with the difference that the Fourierist army never recovered from its disastrous initial defeat.[2]

The Rush to Utopia

Spread over an area from eastern Massachusetts to Iowa, the phalanxes' locations linked them to the wake of religious revivals, the reach of free-wheeling commercial capitalism, and, more generally, the path of westward settlement (see Appendix Map 1). Brook Farm was the only phalanx in New England, where industrialism had begun, social lines were well established, and population was migrating to the west. One Fourierist community located in New Jersey and three in Pennsylvania; of these all but one were founded by New York City constituents reeling from the depression of the early 1840s. In the Burned-Over District no less than seven phalanxes emerged of the ten or so originally planned. The remainder of the Fourierist communities fanned out in a two-pronged pattern tracing the spread of Yankee settlement along the Great Lakes and, south of that, following the line of the Ohio River where New Englanders, descendants of Scotch-Irish settlers, and German immigrants clustered in bustling commercial ports. Five phalanxes were begun in Ohio; three each were established in Indiana, Illinois, and Wisconsin. Individual experiments in Michigan, Iowa, and Texas rounded out the antebellum group. Western phalanxes tended to be established a year or two after eastern ones, so the founding of communities roughly paralleled the spread of Associative ideas westward from propaganda centers in New England and New York City.

Given the extent of settled country in the 1840s, most of these were not really frontier colonies, as Arthur Bestor first pointed out.[3] Of all the antebellum phalanxes, only four—the Wisconsin, Iowa Pioneer, and Integral phalanxes and the Réunion colony in Texas—involved substantial migration to a western outpost. As Fourier and Brisbane recommended, Associationists usually chose established agricultural locales not far from denser population centers. Sometimes families on nearby farms joined their lands together as at the Leraysville Phalanx, or traded them for shares in a large farmsite nearby as at the Alphadelphia and Trumbull phalanxes. But the most common pattern was a local move by residents of eastern or midwestern towns to a site in the countryside, usually no more than fifty miles away.

Some of the first American phalanxes were based loosely on Fourier's paternalistic model of wealthy patrons and poor but worthy subjects. The Sylvania Association in Pennsylvania was financed by a coalition of New York merchants and professionals, including Horace Greeley and Charles Hempel; the pioneer band was composed mostly of New York and Albany artisans. A. K. Morehouse, an upstate New York landowner and speculator, donated 10,000 acres for another experiment; he recruited workers from New York City and ran the community himself, paying workers in scrip and providing all supplies through his store.[4] By far the most frequent scenario, however, was a broad-based local agitation in which reform-minded citizens, led by doctors, lawyers, and journalists but also including craftsmen, formed Fourierist clubs or reading groups after encountering the doctrine in the *Tribune* or in Brisbane's or Godwin's tracts. Perhaps they also heard one of the Associationists' regional lecturers such as T. C. Leland in upstate New York, H. R. Schetterly in Michigan, Henry Van Amringe in Pittsburgh, or John S. Williams in Ohio. Some clubs published tracts that addressed Fourierist theory to local concerns and drummed up interest in practical experiments.[5]

The most striking aspect of this agitation was the speed with which it resulted in the founding of phalanxes. Conventions quickly organized by local Fourierists in Albany, Rochester, Pittsburgh, Cincinnati, and Bellevue, Michigan, listened to speeches, received the blessings of Brisbane, Greeley, or other national leaders through the mails or sometimes in person, drafted constitutions, and appointed committees to select phalanx sites. In most cases the road from propaganda to the beginnings of community life was traveled in just a few months.

In Southport (now Kenosha), Wisconsin, for example, the local newspaper frequently commented on Brisbane's *Tribune* column, and the Franklin Lyceum took up the subject of Fourierism in a series of debates that attracted large audiences in the final two months of 1843. A group of interested townsmen led by the newspaper editor, small professionals, shopkeepers, and craftsmen then formed a Fourier Club, which resolved in December 1843 to "lose no time" in demonstrating "Fourier's principles of Social Science" through a communal experiment. By the end of March they had drafted a constitution, enlisted fifty subscribers, elected officers, and sent out an agent to find a communal site. The Wisconsin Phalanx was well under way.[6] The Sangamon Association near Springfield, Illinois, was organized following three lectures presenting "The Science of Social Unity" in the winter of 1844–45. Despite the leaders' fear that they had "got up too strong an excitement," by February 1845 the group had chosen officers and purchased five hundred acres of prairie and timberland.[7] In Cincinnati the local Fourier Association formed in 1843 to disseminate Fourier's theory was quickly taken over by impatient members who pushed for formation of a phalanx. Early in 1844 the practical communitarians held two conventions at a local Universalist church. At the first, in late February, delegates heard letters of support from Brisbane, Greeley, and Channing; unanimously passed resolutions to establish a phalanx; and appointed committees to sell shares and select a site. Three weeks later they approved a constitution modeled on Brisbane's for the North American Phalanx. In May the first band of Associationists departed for the domain of the Clermont Phalanx some thirty-five miles up the Ohio River.[8]

Even the most cautious Associationist leaders were swept up in a wave of "immediatism" akin to the one that coursed through the abolition movement.[9] Elijah P. Grant, a Yale-educated Ohio lawyer and a doctrinal purist well-read in Fourier ("our great master"), was determined to establish a full-scale phalanx west of the Appalachians. Hoping to ally with similarly rigorous utopians, he attended the Western Fourier Convention in Pittsburgh in September 1843 but came away disappointed. Delegates wanted to tamper with Fourier's specifications, and "every neighborhood" hatched its own phalanx scheme, refusing to cooperate with others or even consider their proposed sites. It was impossible to unite western Fourierists in one experiment. Yet rather than retreat in despair or bury himself in Fourierist studies, Grant decided to move up his timetable for "the first *genuine* Fourier Association in the West": "I find myself driven forward much faster than I expected," he explained, "and faster indeed than I could desire. The eagerness and zeal of the friends of the cause cannot be restrained, and they are determined to go on." He planned to harness the excitement in a tightly organized phalanx and to persuade Brisbane to become its "despot." Brisbane turned him down, but Grant proceeded nonetheless. By the end of January 1844 he had accepted applications from more than thirty adults, and the next month operations began, though on a scale far short of Brisbane's model. To Horace Greeley, Grant confessed doubt "whether anything we shall experience within two years will deserve the name of Association." In fact his Ohio Phalanx was plagued by lack of capital and by religious disputes and had to be reorganized within a year. In June 1845 Grant resigned the presidency "in complete despair" and more than $1,000 poorer. Complaining that the westerners rushing into phalanxes were "not yet . . . prepared for Association," Grant failed to see how he himself had succumbed to the fever.[10]

Observing this Fourierist bandwagon, Brisbane acknowledged that it was "useless to preach moderation in organizing Associations"; he and other national leaders hoped instead to persuade converts "to avoid small and fragmental undertakings, and unite with the largest one in their section of the country."[11] Yet the local rivalries and ideological splinterings Grant observed in Pittsburgh were the norm for Associationist conventions. Regional delegates failed to agree on the site, the blueprint, or even the leadership of proposed communities. Some wanted to build a model Fourierist phalanx, while others knew little Fourierist doctrine or else sought freedom to experiment. Groups that issued calls to rally around one proposal usually had their own in mind, and rival Fourierists refused to cave in. Each group believed itself best qualified to demonstrate Fourierist principles conclusively. The remarkable thing was how little rancor these disagreements produced. With the Fourierist mania growing each day, communitarians believed there were plenty of applicants and funds to go around; the bitterness would come later. It was a perverse demonstration of Fourier's idea that abundance would produce friendly rivalries rather than brutal competition.

The result was an amazing, and ultimately fatal, balkanization of communitarian projects. Cincinnati Fourierists split into the Clermont and Integral Phalanxes. The Ohio, Trumbull, and Columbian phalanxes competed for support from Associationists in Pittsburgh and eastern Ohio. Even so small a center as Watertown, New York, gave birth to two phalanxes, one that rooted locally and an offshoot that migrated to the Iowa frontier. The worst case was western New York, where a convention in Rochester in August 1843 attracted several hundred enthusiasts eager to begin communal life but disagreeing on "several points of doctrine and expediency." T. C. Leland reported that no less than nine associations were being planned within a fifty-mile radius of Rochester: the Clarkson group was determined to follow Fourier as closely as possible; others were only vaguely committed to the Associationist program. One group was able to purchase a fertile and convenient site that had been a Shaker community, but other locations were promoted by real estate speculators and residents of competing towns. In the end, five different phalanxes arose out of the Rochester convention (the Clarkson, Sodus Bay, Mixville, North Bloomfield, and Ontario Union associations), dividing members' capital and talent into impossibly small portions.[12]

In a few cases (the Washtenaw Phalanx, Beverly Association, and Rochester Industrial Association), fledgling projects were absorbed by nearby communities with better prospects. Other cooperative efforts came after established communities found themselves in trouble and thus proved short-lived. When negotations for a domain north of Cincinnati broke down, the Integral Phalanx moved to Illinois to merge with the Sangamon Association under the Ohio group's name and constitution. The marriage was a rocky one, and disputes between Ohio and Illinois members over community shares dragged on in court long after the phalanx had disbanded. The five western New York phalanxes attempted to form a supporting alliance: in March 1844 they established a unique confederation, the American Industrial Union, at whose meetings delegates hoped to exchange information, standardize the phalanxes' Fourierist arrangements, and stimulate trade among the member communities. But the union had barely gotten under way when its constituent phalanxes began to fold.[13]

The potential for such troubles seems not to have been in members' minds when they first set out for phalanx domains. Each band of phalanx pioneers believed that nature had destined its particular domain to realize Fourier's magnificent vision. Time and again such heady optimism was voiced under the combined influence of material hopes, Fourierist faith, and millennial dreams. No communal experiment began with more fanfare than the Clermont Phalanx. A. J. Macdonald, who steamed up the Ohio River from Cincinnati with the pioneer boatload of Associationists in May 1844, recorded his impressions on the day they took possession of the property:

There were about one hundred and thirty of us. The weather was beautiful, but cool, and the scenery on the river was splendid in its spring dress. . . . We reached the domain about two o'clock P.M., and marched on shore in procession, with a band of music in front, leading the way up a road cut in the high clay bank; and then formed a mass meeting, at which we had praying, music and speech-making. I strolled out with a friend and examined the purchase, and we came to the conclusion that it was a splendid domain. . . . Here . . . was all that could be desired, hill and plain, rich soil, fine scenery, plenty of first-rate timber, a maple-sugar camp, a good commercial situation, convenient to the best market in the West. . .[14]

The festivities were somewhat marred, however, by a foreboding incident. When waiters spread the meal on the table in the ship's cabin, a mad dash for seats ensued; in a few minutes all the food was gone, and those not quick enough—including Macdonald—went hungry. The principle of equality had been overcome by the Fourierist appetite for individualism. Accompanying the second boatload from Cincinnati on July 4, Macdonald noted that the settlers "were in circumstances inferior to what they had been used to."[15] They were enduring hardship with patience, but disagreements had already arisen. Two years later the Clermont Phalanx expired, victim of a flood, a debt of over $15,000, and lawsuits between members.

Problems of Survival

The rough initial period of establishing a viable settlement undid most phalanxes. Although only a few were truly on the edge of national expansion, communitarians tended to settle where cheaper, undeveloped land was available; consequently, several experiments took on pioneer characteristics. For the first months the struggle with nature, not Fourierist ideology, was the central fact of existence. Housing was overcrowded, capital short, and technical knowledge of farming rudimentary. Reports from these groups dealt with the mundane matters of frontier settlement: building cabins, clearing the land, planting and harvesting a profitable crop. Often these tasks were overwhelming enough to postpone discussion of the group's relation to communitarian theory, and some phalanxes never did clear these preliminary hurdles to success. More prosperous frontier experiments, such as the Wisconsin Phalanx, found themselves used as staging grounds where migrants learned farming techniques and gained a foothold in the new country before planting their own "isolated households" in the virgin soil.[16]

Whether on the frontier or closer to civilization, the harsh reality of life in most phalanxes mocked Associationists' hopes and made a demoralizing contrast with their pie-in-the-sky propaganda. Though conditions varied from community to community, the most important reasons for their failing so quickly were quite similar. There were glaring mistakes in planning and organization, serious membership problems, and, at bottom, fatal shortcomings in Fourierist ideology.

One frequent problem was the selection of communal sites. The Sylvania Association, which originated among New York City mechanics, appointed a committee consisting of a landscape painter, a cooper, and a homeopathic physician to procure a suitable domain. In March 1843 these would-be farmers chose a rugged tract of 2,300 acres in the Pocono Mountains of eastern Pennsylvania. Though the ground was covered with snow, they pronounced it "a deep loam, well calculated for tillage and grazing." And whereas Fourierism recommended a site with good access to urban markets, their location was a hundred miles from New York City, forty miles from the nearest railroad, and five miles up a steep and bumpy road from the Delaware and Hudson Canal. The result was predictably disastrous. A late frost destroyed much of what the community first planted, and despite members' heroic efforts to clear and aerate the rocky soil, it yielded less than three bushels of wheat per acre. Members suffered from cold and hunger for a little over a year before disbanding. The Social Reform Unity, also in Pike County, met a similar fate.[17]

Whatever the quality of their land, most Associationists purchased too much for communal experiments of a hundred or so members. The phalanxes averaged over 1200 acres, far more than necessary to feed and house the population. While some extra land might have proved useful for orchards or timber, too much of many domains was uncultivated or otherwise unproductive. Sylvania planted only 30 of its 2,300 acres, and the Alphadelphia Association "improved" 400 of 2,800 acres. The remaining property was subject to mortgages and taxes without contributing income. Moreover, as Noyes pointed out, the lust for cheap land tended to lead utopians too far from railroads and markets; it was no coincidence that the largest Fourierist domains were the ones most isolated from trade routes. Associationist ideology was partly responsible for this "land mania": Fourier's ideal phalanx covered three square miles, and even Brisbane's scaled-down model was planted on a thousand acres.[18] But the oversupply had other sources as well: the characteristic American faith in land ownership as the basis of republican independence and virtue, urban workers' naiveté about farm practice, and several communities' acceptance of land in lieu of cash investments from members.

To purchase these huge farms, communities went into crippling debt. The Social Reform Unity made a down payment of only $100 on $2,500 worth of land; the Clermont paid $1,000 of the $20,000 cost; the Ohio Phalanx put down nothing at all on $69,000.[19] When interest payments or installments on the principal came due, they could not be made, and these phalanxes had to renegotiate terms or else disband. Shortages of capital plagued almost every community. Many members had little cash or did not come through with the amount originally pledged to phalanx stock, but overeager communitarians began operations anyway. Out of the $17,000 originally subscribed, the Clermont Phalanx received only $6,000. Instead of the $400,000 investment specified by Brisbane for starting a true American model, the Social Reform Unity and the Spring Farm Association each began with a pathetic $1,000. Even communities that claimed much better capitalization, such as the Alphadelphia Association, issued a significant portion of their stock in exchange for members' farms or houses, which the phalanxes later found difficult to sell.[20]

Staggering under the weight of such heavy debt, most phalanxes not only failed to turn a profit but were unable to survive even moderate natural or human mishaps. When a frost destroyed Spring Farm's crops, the community immediately dissolved. Brook Farmers had put about $7,000 into their new phalanstery when by accident it caught fire; a fully capitalized phalanx could have absorbed the loss, but it represented about one-quarter of the community's entire assets.[21]

Without funds to buy domains outright, Associationists sometimes had to give away control of their land. In a few cases the property was owned by individuals or families who let Associationists settle on their grounds. Founding families of the Leraysville Phalanx lived comfortably on their homesteads, while the members they recruited boarded with them. Almost immediately friction arose over who was benefiting from such an arrangement. When the phalanx broke up after only eight months, it was charged that the owners had profited from improvements that unpropertied members had made to their farms. Even well-intentioned owners could doom communities by reclaiming their estates. When James Shriver, who had allowed the Ohio Phalanx to build on his land without a down payment, began to despair of ever receiving rent, he simply evicted the members.[22]

Most phalanxes were established under widely held joint-stock arrangements, but even this did not prevent ownership disputes. Especially in communities that failed to incorporate, members wrangled over property rights when individuals sought to leave the group—an occurrence so common among utopian communities that a body of court decisions developed to address the issue.[23] Though New York's Bloomfield Union was prosperous—perhaps *because* it was prosperous—members began to quarrel over who held the land title. They heard different answers from different lawyers: "Some counselors . . . find it in the Committee of Finance, as representatives of the Association; others have discovered that it is vested in them as individuals; others still . . . find, perhaps, that it is in the committee and stockholders jointly; while there are those who profess to find it in neither of these parties, but in the persons of whom the property was purchased, and to whom has been paid its full valuation!"[24]

The nearby Clarkson Association also broke up in a dispute over legal title. When members tried to sell some land to raise capital, they found that the title was tied up in a Board of Trustees whose claim no purchasers would trust. They were forced to disband while the matter was settled in Chancery court.[25] Joint-stock ownership, which Associationists believed would reconcile individual and group property interests, was more complex and troublesome than they anticipated. Only where land values were soaring was agriculture a quick way to wealth, but the Associationists' bloated holdings, heavy indebtedness, and disputes over property ownership made even mere survival impossible for most phalanxes.

Crowded together in close quarters, phalanx members were also vulnerable to contagious diseases. According to one resident, the swampy land, poor diet, and cramped dwellings spread "fever and ague" around the Trumbull Phalanx. The outbreak was severe enough that "three-fourths of the people, both old and young, were shaking with it for months together." In September 1845 John Allen's son returned to Brook Farm from a local trip with symptoms of varioloid, a mild version of smallpox. Once introduced in the communal dwelling, the disease spread quickly to more than thirty members. Brook Farmers were lucky to avoid a fatality, but the epidemic brought the phalanx's productive operations to a virtual standstill.[26]

In spite of all these difficulties, perhaps the largest obstacle to survival was not squalid material conditions but the divided, contentious bands of members these communities recruited. Communitarian groups were notorious for drawing cranks and misfits, but in large measure the Associationists' difficulties stemmed from a distinctively Fourierist ideological problem: their propaganda depicted a social millennium so magnificent and so imminent that thousands clamored to enter communal life without serious reflection on their means or motives. More fundamentally, the Fourierists' ambiguous blend of capitalist means with communitarian ends attracted essentially two different kinds of recruits. One group, only nominally committed to Association, viewed phalanx arrangements as a guaranteed maintenance or even a profitable investment; the other sought a genuine transformation of social relations in a miniature New Jerusalem. The numerous postmortems collected by A. J. Macdonald suggest that though the former rarely outnumbered the latter, their greed could undermine a phalanx. The Philadelphia Industrial Association in Indiana collapsed in a dispute with its president and landowner, who reportedly was interested in "getting his land cleared up and improved for nothing." An Alphadelphia Association stockholder provoked a similar conflict when he insisted that the community build its mill on his portion of the land, anticipating the rise in value should the group disband. Several Wisconsin Phalanx members engaged in outside land speculations and eventually persuaded the others to sell the domain at a sizable profit. According to a longtime member, the community was dissolved by "the love of money, and the want of love for Association." Finally, one "malcontent" from the Trumbull Phalanx told Macdonald an alarming tale of capitalist exploitation in the midst of a community devoted to eradicating it. An acquisitive Yankee doctor established a boardinghouse where he fleeced phalanx residents of their money in return for a floor to sleep on and coffee made from burnt bread, then added insult to injury by presenting exorbitant medical bills for treating their ague.[27] Clearly, the profit motive was the camel let into the Associationist tent.

Still, the damage might have been contained had phalanx leaders been more selective in their admissions. Communities short of labor welcomed members too readily; even the Wisconsin Phalanx, which had a well-organized screening process, accepted over 60 percent of its applications. Those already full took in additional members out of philanthropy or miscalculation. The formal criteria for admission were usually quite minimal: "good moral character" and the approval of resident members. In practice, the more successful communities preferred recruits who were able to invest property or cash (at the Wisconsin Phalanx, at least $100 per family member), had practical work skills, and expressed sympathy with Fourierism.[28] But no phalanx imposed a rigorous ideological test for candidates, and only three put new members through a probation period. It was no coincidence that these—Brook Farm, the North American Phalanx, and the Wisconsin Phalanx—were the longest-lasting Fourierist experiments.

The most extreme result of lax selection methods was visible at the Morehouse Union, whose agent recruited indiscriminately in New York City. One veteran described the membership as "a motley group of ill-assorted materials, as inexperienced as it was heterogeneous":

> We had some specimens of the raw material of human nature, and some of New York manufacture spoiled in the making. There were philosophers and philanthropists, bankrupt merchants and broken-down grocery-keepers; officers who had returned from the Texan army on half-pay; and some who had returned from situations in the New York ten-pin alleys. There were all kinds of ideas, notions, theories, and whims; all kinds of religions; and some persons without any. There was no unanimity of purpose, or congeniality of disposition; but there was plenty of discussion, and an abundance of variety, which is called the spice of life. This spice however constituted the greater part of the fare, as we sometimes had scarcely anything to eat.[29]

Few phalanx groups were such crazy-quilts, but loose admission practices meant that members were "strangers to each other" with shaky prospects for cohesion.[30] Entrants brought widely varying degrees of ideological commitment to Association. When Mary Gove visited the Columbian Phalanx in Ohio, she found the community disastrously split between fifteen Fourierists and the remainder who were "hardly in the alphabet of social science." The Fourierist leader, a former Methodist minister, antagonized the conventional majority by favoring racial equality, working on Sunday, and criticizing Civilized marriage. When they expelled him, the entire Fourierist faction seceded, and the community descended into chaos.[31] Even in phalanxes where all members endorsed Fourier's theory, they often disagreed over how far to implement it.

Out of the phalanxes' unfiltered mixture of strangers arose personal disputes, which did not always overlap with ideological schisms but were equally rancorous. According to Macdonald, members of the Alphadelphia Association disagreed on "nothing of consequence," but records of the community's Council of Arbitration tell a different story. Minutes of several hearings reveal the numerous complaints members brought against one another, ranging from "falsehoods," "profane language," and "insulting and disorderly conduct" to taking community property for personal use and "refusing . . . to do the work."[32] Jealousies and feuds led to lawsuits at the Clermont and Bloomfield Union phalanxes. Several communities reported having disruptive members or factions; a few discovered dishonest treasurers; and suspicion often focused on an individual or clique that seemed to be exempt from the misery of most residents.

It was once thought that a high rate of population turnover was a product of such communal chaos and social tension. A recent study by Lawrence Foster, however, found surprising fluctuations of membership among the Shakers, long considered the most stable of antebellum communitarian groups. During the twelve years of the Sodus Bay Shaker community's existence (1826–38), the number of entries, departures, and deaths ranged from one-fourth to one-half of the total group each year.[33] The longer-lived Fourierist phalanxes show a similar pattern. From fairly complete records, a total of 259 persons can be identified as having been residents of the Wisconsin Phalanx at some point. The community's average residential population was around 150; thus, about one-eighth of the total group came or went in each of its six years. At the North American Phalanx only one-sixth of the probationers remained as full members, which meant that as many as forty newcomers—about a third of the community's total population—came and went each year.[34] Apparently, the longer-lived communitarian experiments were fluid but not necessarily unstable. High turnover may not have been a sign of crisis if the overall population remained level or increased. Each of these communities, moreover, had a faithful core of veteran members who provided continuity and leadership. At the Wisconsin Phalanx, for example, most of the turnover came from probationers; members who survived even a four-month introduction to community life averaged a stay of four years. Over 40 percent of the North American Phalanx's membership of late 1844 was still around for the 1850 census. Such persistence—and even a steady turnover—were privileges enjoyed only by phalanxes that endured more than a few seasons. Most did not last long enough for persistence rates to be established, and as they lurched toward dissolution, they experienced not "turnover" but mass defections not balanced by infusions of newcomers.

A Tale of Two Communities

The phalanxes' sad progression of organizational blunders, economic problems, large-scale defections, and communal collapse is typified by the history of one western New York community, the Sodus Bay Phalanx. The North American Phalanx in New Jersey, on the other hand, provides a refreshing but all too rare glimpse of conditions that made communal survival possible. Since the North American endured for twelve years— twice as long as any other American phalanx—and the Sodus Bay less than two, they present a stark contrast between successful and unsuccessful communal strategies.

The Sodus Bay Phalanx was one of several local communities founded after Fourierism swept through the Burned-Over District in 1843. Such a dispersal of leaders and capital hurt all these efforts, but the prospects of the Sodus Bay Fourierists were still quite promising. Early in 1844 members obtained a tract of 1,400 acres, bordering Lake Ontario, which had formerly been inhabited by a Shaker community. The Fourierists inherited a sawmill, workshops, a meetinghouse, and enough residences to accommodate twenty-five or thirty families. In addition there was a large orchard of apple, peach, pear, and plum trees. To complete the list of advantages, one visitor pronounced the bay itself "the best natural harbor on the whole chain of the Great Lakes." With its strategic location, fertile soil, already planted orchards, and substantial buildings, the Sodus Bay Phalanx seemed poised to lead the Fourierist transformation of western New York. Yet the experiment was a disastrous failure.[35]

Financial problems loomed in the background from the beginning. The first sale of Sodus Bay shares was undersubscribed, but Associationists simply postponed the disaster that this undercapitalization portended. The landowners agreed to require no immediate down payment on the tract's price of $35,000, but two years later a 20 percent down payment would be due in addition to the first interest installment. Given their inability to raise enough money the first time around, it was no surprise that by early 1846 the hefty payment of $9,500 was impossible for Sodus Bay members to meet.

In fact, during its first spring and summer Sodus Bay actually spent $500 more than its capital stock was worth. The phalanx's Articles of Association promised that room and board would be provided free of charge to all residents for one year; at year's end the expenses would simply be subtracted from the community's annual profits. During the hard times of the early 1840s along the Erie Canal this amounted to a blanket invitation to the unemployed or financially strapped to enjoy a year's guaranteed income. In addition to free room and board, Sodus Bay investors were assured a return of "ten or twelve per cent. in a few years."[36] The resulting rush of members was so large and the outlays so generous that the phalanx was virtually out of money several months before the year was out.

More than a few applicants to Sodus Bay were motivated, according to one observer, "not by . . . noble philanthropy, or self-denying enthusiasm, but by the most narrow selfishness." Yet because of loose admissions procedures, large numbers were accepted without character references, sufficient capital, or useful work skills. By the summer of 1844 there were 260 people—some characterized by one critic as "inexperienced, restless, indolent, feeble, and selfish"—crammed into the phalanx's sixty-four rooms. Many may have been naturally lazy, but the overcrowded accommodations further depleted their energies by hastening the spread of typhoid fever. At one point forty-nine members were on the sick list.[37]

Pressured by such troubles, the fragile foundations at Sodus Bay needed only one more burden to collapse. This was added when disputes arose between the community's evangelical Protestants and religious liberals over work on the Sabbath and control of phalanx education. Fourier's dream that discordant individuals would fall naturally into a balance of passions failed to materialize. Instead, according to one observer, the two factions became "opposite and hostile elements, which have no more affinity for each other than water and oil, or fire and gunpowder." By the spring of 1845 most of the evangelicals had left; as they departed, the community sold its crops to repay members for their investments and began to go bankrupt. As A. J. Macdonald accurately reported, "each individual helped himself to the movable property, and . . . some decamped in the night, leaving the remains of the Phalanx to be disposed of in any way which the last men might choose."[38]

After this mass defection the religious liberals reorganized under a new constitution, but saddled with its huge debt, the community could not survive. In April 1846 the thirteen remaining members formally dissolved the Sodus Bay Phalanx. On their domain the problems typical of many phalanxes—poor management, lack of capital, religious quarrels, overcrowding, and disease—had been concentrated in one pathetic Fourierist experiment.

Even though the North American Phalanx (NAP) began with fewer obvious advantages than the Sodus Bay community, it was able to overcome the divisions and problems of its founding years and endure as a stable Fourierist experiment.[39] The phalanx began, confusingly, from the efforts of two geographically and ideologically separate groups. In October 1842 Albert Brisbane announced in his *Tribune* column that he would take stock subscriptions for a "North American Phalanx" to be located near New York City. The following January the Fourier Society of New York drafted a constitution for this model community, and Brisbane and Greeley were empowered to accept investments totaling $200,000. Two months later, however, a group calling itself the Albany Branch of the North American Phalanx was formed, with Brisbane's assistance, to investigate Fourier's theory and cooperate with others in organizing a phalanx. There were immediate tensions between the two groups. While the parent society in New York remained entranced by dreams of a huge model phalanx and organized listlessly, the Albany group committed itself rapidly to practical, even if imperfect, association. By May 1843 they had assumed full responsibility for preparing a communal experiment, and in August they purchased a 673-acre tract of cultivated but unremarkable land about forty miles from New York City near Red Bank, New Jersey. Though Brisbane protested that they had appropriated his name for a community that could not properly be called a phalanx, the Albany group presented him and the other New York leaders with a *fait accompli*.

A second struggle for communal identity followed shortly after the phalanx's families occupied the existing farmhouses in September 1843. Discouraged by the failure of the New York and other Fourierist groups to come through with promised support, members were vulnerable to factional disputes. The most serious was prompted by Allen Warden, the phalanx's president, who sought to wrest control over policy from the Executive Council and specifically opposed the adoption of a Fourierist organization of work into groups and series. The strife between Warden's followers and the "Phalansterian" party was "long and vigorous," according to one member. It was resolved in the spring of 1844 when the Executive Council decided "to form an industrial organization in accordance as far as is practicable with the principles laid down by Fourier." Shortly thereafter, Warden resigned his office and returned to Albany.[40]

These early battles proved to be harbingers of communal health, for they resolved at the outset the kind of rivalries and ideological conflicts that festered for years in other phalanxes. They also separated the true Fourierist wheat from the pretending chaff. Remaining members were nowhere near Brisbane's ideal number—there were ninety after the first year—and their resources were modest: only $7,200 had been raised as the phalanx's working capital and stock. But the residents were reasonably united in their goals and varied in their skills; they worked hard and did not overextend their means. Their small domain cost less than half that of Sodus Bay. Rather than construct a grand phalanstery, they put up a temporary communal dwelling in 1844 to accommodate newcomers and then concentrated on planting crops and building workshops and mills. And whereas Sodus Bay promised subsistence without payment, the North American Phalanx balanced accounts monthly. Through such frugality the New Jersey Fourierists increased their assets enough to pay off $5,000 of the property's $14,000 cost within their first year.

Unlike most phalanxes, the North American carefully screened applicants before admitting them. The Executive Council took seriously its mission to find members who exhibited good character, demonstrated genuine interest in Association, and brought with them capital and a usable skill. Though they sometimes waived the capital requirement, they turned down some wealthy applicants because of doubts about their character or their devotion to Fourierism. The result was the strictest admissions policy of any American phalanx, the acceptance rate fewer than one-third of the applicants.[41] Further, admitted candidates had to pass through a probationery period, which in 1847 was formally divided into three stages covering ten months.

By surviving its early testing times, the NAP achieved a sense of cohesion; and by exploiting nearby New York City as a profitable market for its fruit, vegetables, and flour, the community found a secure basis for survival. To be sure, a serious religious quarrel and a damaging fire lay unforeseen in its future, but by contrast with phalanx failures such as Sodus Bay, the New Jersey community was a prosperous and harmonious experiment that suggested the viability of Fourierist principles. By 1848 the North American was the sole surviving eastern phalanx and—ironically, given its original quarrel with Brisbane—the leading contender for national leaders' support in their drive to create an American "model phalanx."

Unfortunately for Associationists, the Sodus Bay fiasco was far more typical than the limited success of the NAP. Most communities were so plagued by unfavorable conditions and internal divisions that they lasted only a year or two. In addition to the many financial problems, organizational shortcomings, and leadership failures recounted thus far, two less obvious but even more important factors underlay the phalanxes' meteoric career: the social composition of their membership and, ultimately, the flawed ideology of Fourierism itself.

Religion and Class in Utopia

No discussion of the nature and weaknesses of the American phalanxes would be complete without some consideration of the seven or eight thousand residents who at one time or another joined them. What were the ethnic, religious, and socioeconomic backgrounds of phalanx members? Few questions are as important to an understanding of the Associationist movement. Attempting to answer it systematically reveals how successfully the Fourierists fulfilled their mission to organize a "universal" reform crusade. And because membership data point to the significant social and ideological roots of the phalanxes' collapse, they deserve careful analysis, especially with respect to religion and class.

Reliable information about the birthplace and ethnicity of phalanx members, available only for Brook Farm and the North American and Wisconsin phalanxes, suggests the basic boundaries of the Fourierist constituency.[42] The overwhelming majority of these communities' residents were native-born Americans, and all were white. The preponderance of such surnames as Bacon, Strong, French, Barnes, Ash, Clark, Davis, and Wilson indicates primarily English derivation. Of 293 resident members, only 37 foreign-born individuals could be traced, and three-fourths of these were born in England, Scotland, or Canada. Native-born Fourierists were distinctly northeastern in origin, with most adults even at the Wisconsin Phalanx coming from New England and New York families. Of the aggregate total 87 were born in New York, 81 in Massachusetts, and 30 in Vermont; only 2 were born west of Ohio, and 4 south of the Mason-Dixon Line. Outside of these phalanxes some Fourierist leaders, especially in the Midwest, came from non-English stock. There was obvious Scotch-Irish blood in William McDiarmid of Wheeling and Dutch ancestry in Henry Van Amringe of Pittsburgh and Wade Loof-bourrow of the Clermont Phalanx. Alphadelphia's Henry Schetterly had migrated to Michigan from Germany in the early 1830s. Quarreling with Van Amringe and James Thornburg, Elijah Grant complained that there were not enough industrious New Englanders in his Ohio Phalanx. But members whose ancestry was non-English were probably a small minority even in the midwestern communities, as the Wisconsin Phalanx nativity data and a list of Alphadelphia Association residents suggest. The major-ity of American phalansterians were what was loosely called "Yankees."[43] Nevertheless, when religious backgrounds are combined with geographic origins, considerable variety begins to appear, both between the commu-nities and inside them. The Fourierists painfully learned that all Yankees were not the same.

As Chapter 3's discussion of Fourierism's religious roots suggested, phalanx members' religious backgrounds varied dramatically within a basic Protestant consensus. A handful of American phalanxes were each dominated by one religious strain. The Leraysville Phalanx, founded by a New Church minister and his relatives, was a Swedenborgian enclave in Pennsylvania where members frankly aimed to "keep up . . . a prevail-ing New Church influence" in their school and services. At the Integral and Trumbull Phalanxes many members were Campbellite Baptists (or Disciples of Christ). Brook Farm was unified behind Unitarianism.[44]

Most phalanxes attracted a more varied affiliation, however. According to one member, the Clarkson Phalanx housed a colorful "assortment" of religious beliefs: "We had seventy-four praying Christians, including all the sects in America, except Millerites and Mormons. We had one Catho-lic family, . . . one Presbyterian clergyman, and one Universalist. One of our first trustees was a Quaker. We had one Atheist, several Deists . . . but of Nothingarians, none; for being free for the first time in our lives, we spoke out . . . and found that every body did believe something."[45]

Perhaps the greatest religious diversity appeared at the North Ameri-can Phalanx, which not only drew upon New York City's multi-ethnic population but took in remnants from several shorter-lived phalanxes. Its members came from nearly a dozen different denominations: there were Universalists, Unitarians, Presbyterians, Swedenborgians, Baptists, Quakers, Dutch Reformers, Episcopalians, Jews, Roman Catholics, and a former Shaker among them.[46] Overall, the Clarkson and North American pattern of diversity predominated in the movement, and even where certain denominations outnumbered others, there were significant reli-gious minorities.

Far from worrying Associationist leaders, this kind of diversity fulfilled their dream of gathering persons of all characters and creeds under the Fourierist umbrella. Following Brisbane's model, phalanx constitutions promised "perfect religious tolerance," imposed no religious tests, and guaranteed freedom of worship. Each group was permitted to organize and pay for its own services, usually held in the community's meeting hall; those who did not take advantage of this arrangement often organized rides to nearby churches. Such pluralism clearly differentiated the utopian socialists from religious communitarians such as the Shakers, Mormons, or Oneidans, who came from heavily evangelical Protestant backgrounds and made a common profession of faith.[47] Unlike the Shaker United Order or Oneida's Bible Communism, Fourier's communal plan was presented as a neutral blueprint to be adopted by persons of different faiths who were looking for a way to converge toward the millennial New Jerusalem. Baptists, Unitarians, and Jews were expected to submerge creedal differences in Fourier's cooperative mechanics. At bottom, utopian socialism assumed that theological and ritual differences did not matter; under proper arrangments all men and women of good will could get along.

It didn't work out that way. In several phalanxes religious pluralism exploded into conflict over work on Sunday, the frequency and kind of preaching, and standards of personal conduct. The Wisconsin Phalanx, for example, duplicated Sodus Bay's religious troubles. Many members had migrated to the frontier from the Burned-Over District or from similar hotbeds of revivalism in Vermont. These Methodists and Baptists attended weekly services, organized a Bible class and Sunday School, and prohibited alcohol from the domain. Yet a vocal minority of liberals and freethinkers, led by phalanx president Warren Chase, diluted the evangelicals' moral legislation, introduced weekly readings from Swedenborg, and held séances. When two of the community's evangelical leaders left in disgust in 1846, relations between the two groups settled down to an uneasy truce, but religious tensions underlay continuing disputes over such matters as communal meals.[48] At the two Campbellite-dominated phalanxes recurrent quarrels about "infidelity" were recounted by members as "great drawbacks to success." E. P. Grant complained that Swedenborgians who joined western phalanxes were "arrogant and intolerant" fanatics; he blamed the demise of the Ohio Phalanx largely on "religious bigotry," particularly disputes over Sabbath observance and social amusements.[49] Even the comparatively long-lived North American Phalanx succumbed in the end to a dispute with religious groundings (see Chapter 12). Peaceful coexistence of religions, even of different Protestant denominations, proved an elusive Associationist goal.

The class composition of Fourierist communities was similarly diverse and almost as volatile. Traditionally, historians have followed the lead of Marx and Engels and, generalizing from ideology, called Fourierism a "middle-class movement" with few workers involved.[50] Yet as advocates of peaceful social reconstruction, the Associationists invited all classes into the phalanxes. To what extent did they succeed in recruiting a socioeconomically diverse membership? Detailed information on the prior occupations of communitarians can be gathered for four phalanxes and sorted into categories similar to those used by social mobility analysts (see Appendix Table 11).[51] The data are somewhat fragmentary, especially for the Wisconsin Phalanx, and aggregate occupational information for the Alphadelphia Association includes sympathizers and stockholders as well as residents. But the available facts do permit generalizations about the proportion of different groups among phalanx males.

Excluding for a moment the more rural Alphadelphia Association, we find that the urban middle class accounted for an important minority of phalanx members: 10 to 20 percent of the men came from the professional and proprietor category; many Associationist leaders were ministers, lawyers, doctors, and merchants. Their version of Fourierism reflects the desire of clerics and devout laymen to enact practical Christian ethics as well as the lure of a "social science" by which enlightened professional men might bring order to a chaotic world. The next 15 to 20 percent of these communities' adult males were teachers, clerks, journalists, and other white-collar workers, young men whose literacy, idealism, and career uncertainties rendered them likely candidates for reform enterprises.

These two categories provided the bulk of middle-class membership of the phalanxes, yet they constituted at most 40 percent of the total. The data reveal that large numbers of skilled artisans joined these communities: a striking 49 percent of Alphadelphia residents and supporters were craftsmen; at the North American Phalanx 45 percent of identifiable members represented such trades as carpenter, tinsmith, shoemaker, printer, and machinist. Although the Wisconsin Phalanx sample is small, one member's report that "most of the men are mechanics" suggests that the figure of 45 percent does not exaggerate the artisan presence there.[52] Perhaps most surprisingly, a full 67 percent of identifiable Brook Farmers came from artisan or blue-collar backgrounds. The conventional picture of that community, drawn by Lindsay Swift and many others, portrays a cluster of earnest ministers and dreamy intellectuals. The analysis presented here and the recent study by Anne Rose indicate that while Brook Farm in its Transcendentalist phase *was* dominated by ministers, writers, and students, as a Fourierist phalanx it had an artisan majority.[53]

To be sure, the phalanxes recruited artisans more aggressively than any other group. Admissions committees favored applicants with useful trades such as carpentry and blacksmithing, and such skills were often credited in lieu of the capital investment normally required of newcomers. But preferential treatment does not explain the fact that significant numbers of workingmen were drawn to Fourierist communities in the first place. An analysis of applicants to the North American Phalanx, most of whom were not admitted, showed that roughly half came from artisan backgrounds. And in his pioneering study of Fourierism in the Rochester area, Arthur Bestor found that half of those involved in the movement whom he could identify were "working class," mainly carpenters, shoemakers, tailors, and masons.[54]

There is evidence that many phalanx workers had been moderately successful prior to communal life. City directories indicate that a significant proportion, perhaps as many as one-fourth, of Brook Farm and North American Phalanx artisans were self-employed before joining; in the frontier conditions of Wisconsin the percentage was probably higher. Few Brook Farm workers apparently bought stock in the community, but initial investments by craftsmen entering the Wisconsin Phalanx ranged from $25 to $500, and shareholdings of North American Phalanx artisans (after some years of accumulated labor dividends) averaged nearly $400. From these records and impressionistic sources, it appears that many phalanx workingmen came from what one community visitor called the "better class of mechanics": ambitious, relatively independent, and moderately prosperous. For such craftsmen utopian socialism proved a logical choice. At a time when wage labor and mercantile control were expanding rapidly, the phalanx's small cooperative workshops, retaining a measure of autonomy and sharing profits, seemed "the next best thing to self-employment."[55]

In contrast to artisans, lower-status manual workers were seriously underrepresented in the phalanxes. Among all four of the phalanxes for which such data are available, only nine semiskilled or service workers could be located; just five, all at the Alphadelphia Association, were listed as common laborers. The utopian socialist message appealed to few such workers, and community requirements for skills, capital investment, and "reputable character" tended to doom the candidacies of any who did express interest.

Farmers constituted a second disproportionately small group, at least in the eastern phalanxes. Both Brook Farm and the North American Phalanx drew most of their members from nearby urban centers and their satellite towns. Despite the fact that these communities were primarily agricultural enterprises, just over 10 percent of men at Brook Farm and the NAP whose prior occupations can be determined were farmers or farmworkers. Reliance upon city directories brings some bias into the data, and throughout antebellum America men with craft skills in small-town areas were likely to have had some farming experience; still, all available evidence indicates a chronic shortage of skilled farm workers at several eastern phalanxes. A. J. Macdonald noted that Sylvania Association and Social Reform Unity members struggling to wrest a living from the soil were "primarily working people, brought up to a city life." Other communities' minutes record authorizations to hire help with planting or harvest. The census taker found fifteen German- and Swiss-born farm laborers at the North American Phalanx in 1850. Brook Farm agricultural operations were under the control of two ministers and a printer, and George Ripley repeatedly borrowed books to find out what to grow and how to grow it. The shortage of experienced farmers cut into these phalanxes' crop production and, especially at Brook Farm, contributed to economic collapse.[56]

To the west, though phalanx projects often arose from conventions or clubs in such cities as Cleveland, Pittsburgh, and Cincinnati, several communities did attract large contingents of farmers. At the Alphadelphia Association, where many recruits traded their land, livestock, and equipment for phalanx shares, 42 percent of identifiable members and supporters were farmers. The La Grange Phalanx in Illinois enrolled enough farmers to make them the community's largest occupational group.[57]

The phalanxes' occupational profile thus displays somewhat distinct regional variations. While western experiments were led by doctors and lawyers and drew substantial numbers of farmers as recruits, phalanxes on the east coast reflected a more urbanized and industrialized constituency. Sylvania, Brook Farm, the North American Phalanx, and others attracted almost no farmers and instead allied middle-class reformers, artisans, and absentee mercantile and professional investors. Upstate New York communities came closest to a balanced mixture of one-third professionals and shopkeepers, one-third artisans, and one-third farmers.

Even admitting the relative scarcity of unskilled laborers and in some cases of farmers, membership data clearly refute charges that the utopian socialists were middle-class elitists with few connections and little real interest in working people.[58] Fourierism may have originated with middle-class propagandists, but at least in the United States its ideas spread quickly to forge a genuine coalition across class and occupational lines. In France, Fourierist organizations and lectures appealed primarily to urban professionals, reform journalists, and middle-class proprietors; the "communist" utopianism of Etienne Cabet was far more popular among artisans; and neither group apparently attracted many farmers.[59] The American Fourierist movement came much closer to the utopian ideal of uniting all classes in nonsectarian model communities. With its broad constituency and strong working-class support, the Associationist movement deserves to be viewed as a genuine attempt at cooperative social reconstruction rather than a tool of class paternalism or a sideshow of middle-class misfits.

Uniting classes under the communitarian banner was not the same as dismantling the class structure, however. Despite the Associationists' blending of occupational groups, definite class distinctions persisted in their utopia. Like Fourier himself, the Associationists preached harmony between classes rather than the removal of all inequalities of wealth and power. Fearing that "communism" would stifle freedom, they made allowances for gradations in members' investment and accommodations, at the same time designing a remuneration system that favored manual labor and thus, over the long haul, would tend to equalize incomes. In the short run, however, differences rooted in class were often transplanted directly from Civilization and led to disputes in the phalanxes.

At times, class lines paralleled the distinction between residents and nonresidents. The largest financial backers of Brook Farm and the North American Phalanx were wealthy absentee stockholders whose managerial advice was not always welcomed by community dwellers. Relations between merchant supporters and phalanx members were particularly tense at the NAP. Outsiders owned 61 percent of the community's shares; the ten wealthiest held just under 50 percent, including 527 shares owned by a consortium of Fourierist merchants from New York City. These patrons wanted their investment to build an enormous demonstration along Fourier's grandiose lines, but phalanx residents preferred to evolve gradually from small-scale beginnings and decide their own fate.[60]

The question of class fomented divisions inside communities as well. Phalanx agents and officers faced resentment from rank-and-file members who believed that Fourierism was creating a salaried elite. Especially when officers came disproportionately from the ranks of professionals and shopowners, as at Brook Farm and the North American Phalanx, there was much grumbling among artisans about "the aristocratic element."[61] At phalanxes such as Leraysville and Morehouse, where the founders owned the property and furnished members with room and board, a blatant two-tier class system quickly dissolved communal ties. Even in more egalitarian communities the disparities in shareholding gave control to a wealthy elite. According to A. J. Macdonald, a man named Jones owned almost half the shares of the La Grange Phalanx; members considered his behind-the-scenes maneuvering for financial advantage "the chief cause of their failure."[62] Shareholding by Wisconsin Phalanx residents ranged from three to ninety shares, and the distribution of ownership at the North American Phalanx was even more skewed (see Appendix Tables 9 and 10). Well-to-do residents Charles Sears and James Angell owned more than one hundred shares apiece, while most owned fewer than twenty. Until 1848 only stockholders participated in the NAP's Executive Council sessions, and the rule of one vote per share gave enormous influence to such men as Sears and Angell. That year a group of insurgent small shareholders proposed to allow labor an equal voice with capital in governing the phalanx; in December they pushed through a provision giving each resident one vote in the Executive Council, but the weighted system continued at NAP's semiannual meetings.[63]

Elsewhere, class feeling simmered in private comments about appearance or manners. Brook Farm was nominally committed to Christian fellowship, but its middle-class women were clearly uncomfortable with the phalanx's later working-class arrivals. According to Georgianna Bruce's memoirs, when "skilled mechanics" began to replace "transcendental enthusiasts" at Brook Farm, "it was plain that there could be no congeniality between the newcomers and those who had been so united under the first dispensation." Finding "the charm . . . swiftly disspelled," Bruce soon left the community for a teaching post in Illinois. Her friend Marianne Dwight, who remained behind, was undeniably patronizing in her view of working-class members. As she watched one carpenter's wife improve from "coarse" to "charming," Dwight proclaimed: "In her, we see what Association is going to do for the uneducated and rude." Later, Dwight lost her temper when pragmatic workers left Brook Farm after the phalanstery burned in 1846, confiding to a friend that "it always seemed to me a great mistake to admit coarse people on the place."[64] Brook Farm was unusual in its two-phase history and the blueblood background of its educated elite; nevertheless, comments like these support the criticism that communitarians did not accept workers on their own terms but attempted to "elevate" them to middle-class ways.

In 1870 John Humphrey Noyes, who had studied the records of many communitarian groups, concluded that the two most essential prerequisites for communal success were "religious principle" and "previous acquaintance of the members." Noyes found that the secular utopians' religious pluralism, together with their "advertising method" of recruiting members, "necessarily ignores both." These conclusions were echoed a century later in an impressive sociological study. In comparing nineteenth-century utopian communities Rosabeth Kanter found that in successful or long-lived communities, members were very likely to share a common religious background or similar social status and to have had some prior acquaintance with one another before coming together in community.[65] In contrast, a central idea of Fourierism was to gather persons—even strangers—of divergent religions and classes together into communal life, where their differences would be harmonized by natural attraction. The diverse membership of the phalanxes indicates that the Associationists' recruitment efforts were quite successful, but without a tight organizational structure or an ideological bond as compelling as religious belief, the centrifugal pressures of membership were irresistible. The very diversity of Fourierism's appeal probably hastened its communities' disintegration.

Fourierist Ideology and Communal Longevity

Recounting a few of the phalanxes' histories, surveying their problems, and analyzing their membership cannot fully convey the drama of their failure: its devastating effect on the Associationist movement, and especially its tragic impact on individuals who had sacrificed themselves to the cause. "What a story of passion and suffering can be traced in this broken material!" Noyes exclaimed after reviewing the history of one American phalanx: "This human group was made up of husbands and wives, parents and children, brothers and sisters, friends and lovers, and had two hundred hearts, longing for blessedness. Plodding on their weary march of life, Association rises before them like the mirage of the desert. . . . They rush like the thirsty caravan to realize their vision."[66] But instead of restful palaces, Fourierists found themselves huddled together in sheds, driven by hunger and debt, until "that great corporate death" could be put off no longer. If communitarianism was the Fourierists' moral equivalent of war, the casualties were correspondingly high. Many who "formed themselves into Phalanxes and marched into the wilderness to the music of Fourierism" lost everything they had in the battle.[67]

Who or what was responsible for such a fiasco? So many things went wrong in so many communities that it would be difficult to single out one cause for their disastrous collapse. In addition to economic problems, organizational inefficiencies, and tensions over religion and class, surely Associationist leaders were to blame. Albert Brisbane never led or joined a phalanx experiment—he had enough sense to realize his practical shortcomings—but through lectures and writings he converted aspiring phalansterians too superficially, recruited them indiscriminately, and encouraged them to form experiments too hastily. In later years Brisbane confessed he had been "quite unprepared" for the enthusiasm his propaganda created.[68] In fact, he got caught up in the excitement, and only when it was already too late did he warn communitarians to consolidate their efforts and patiently accrue more funds. For their part, the modest and strife-torn phalanxes generated few outstanding leaders. With the possible exception of the North American Phalanx's Charles Sears, no community officer combined ideological commitment with enough personal stature and practical sense to guide an experiment to success, as John Humphrey Noyes was doing at Oneida.

For all their problems of leadership, membership, and organization, at bottom the collapse of the American phalanxes was an ideological one. Beyond and beneath the specific ills of the communities lay the more general problem of a utopian creed that promised too much and required too little of its adherents. American Fourierism was literally too good to be true. Its flawed utopianism came home to roost in the inevitable disparity between the phalanx ideal and communal reality, the mixed motives of phalanx recruits, and the failure of Fourierist social mechanics to create or compel unity.

When American reformers adopted Fourier's imaginings as the basis for a practical social movement, they promised a combination of instant social transformation and magnificent economic abundance that no society could have fulfilled. Their confident predictions of an imminent social millennium, backed by the authority of "social science," attracted eager communitarians with unrealistically inflated expectations. These recruits were totally unprepared for setbacks, and their manic mood swung inevitably to disillusion when communal life proved difficult and progress painfully slow. "If we had known at the commencement what fiery trials were to surround us, we should have hesitated to enter," Noyes paraphrased one phalanx joiner's response.[69] If Associationist ideology failed to prepare adherents to sacrifice or persevere, it also lacked an adequate explanation for the phalanxes' shortcomings. Unlike religious utopians, doctrinaire Fourierists could not explain conflict among community members or examples of individual selfishness by claiming that humans were imperfect or "not yet prepared" in their hearts for Association; Fourier gave his followers no theory of sin. Instead, their excuse that the small phalanxes' material foundations were too rudimentary to give members' "passions" full play not only seemed naive but merely fed members' disillusionment, since Brisbane's formula for a model phalanx of a fully prepared domain, several hundred members, and huge amounts of capital was clearly impossible to meet.

That so many recruits reacted to adversity by leaving or causing disputes can also be blamed on Fourierism's ambiguous blend of capitalism and socialism. Phalanx leaders claimed to want "none who view . . . [communal life] only as a matter of dollars and cents, but those who are Associationists in deed and truth."[70] Yet Fourierist doctrine undermined sincere communitarians by inviting ambitious profit-seekers and capitalist investors to join in building the New Jerusalem. The ongoing tension between capitalist and communal objectives broke out into contradiction when conflict over locations, land titles, and dividends crippled the phalanxes and members traded allegations of incompetence or impure motives. Such disputes, like the Fourierists' diverse religious and occupational backgrounds, were less the result of lax admissions policies than a direct outgrowth of their ideology of class cooperation and universal reconciliation. In the end, devotion to this vague cooperative ideal proved a far less compelling bond among communitarians than a traditionally doctrinal religious faith. Fourierism, in other words, did not inspire a faith strong enough to overcome its own internal contradictions.

Where communal ideals failed to take hold, Fourier's social mathematics was supposed to guarantee harmony. Theoretically, phalansterians could pursue interests and attractions freely, confident that the "visible hand" of joint-stock organization and "attractive industry" would guide the results to the benefit of all. In practice, members' discordant beliefs and selfish behavior sparked debilitating disputes. The Fourierists' confidence that their "scientific" arrangements could quickly and painlessly reconcile religious, ideological, class, and personality differences was perhaps their greatest illusion.

In her now standard sociological examination of nineteenth-century utopias, Kanter concluded that long-lived communal groups such as the Shakers and the Oneida Community had strong "commitment mechanisms" that bound members to a distinctive group set apart from the world. They required a simple and austere lifestyle. They subordinated individual freedom to the group, often to an authoritarian leader. They erected firm boundaries between members and the outside world. They denied individual property rights. And they significantly changed family relations through celibacy, some form of group marriage, or carefully controlled communal child rearing.[71]

The list is remarkable because it is the antithesis of most phalanx ideals and arrangements. Fourierist communities promised substantial wealth and unlimited personal freedom. They accommodated self-interest. Their structure was democratic; their sexual arrangements were comparatively conventional; and access was always open to the society outside. Such features appealed to many Americans, but they also virtually guaranteed a short life for the phalanxes. Fourierism's assurance of personal rights and its promise of automatic abundance encouraged divisive individualism and attracted loafers to a venture whose success required discipline and self-sacrifice. Phalanx democracy produced endless hours of constitution-tinkering, which religious diversity only exacerbated. And without substantially altering domestic ties, the phalanxes proved subject to the same family selfishness that Fourierists condemned in Civilization.

The painful irony of Associationism was that the very features that gave it broad appeal among antebellum Americans militated against lasting communal existence. Democratic, all-embracing, semicapitalistic communities proved popular but inherently unstable. While the Associationists' critique of American society and their vision of its distant future were indeed revolutionary, their immediate practices were not distinctive or radical enough to hold members once the expectation of instant success was disappointed.

There are, however, alternative and equally compelling definitions of a communitarian group's "success" besides the longevity of its experiments. One recent analysis enumerates no less than seven criteria for success which can be found in the literature on intentional communities, ranging from accomplishment of the group's goals, to the degree that its arrangements approach some notion of an ideal society, to more quantifiable criteria such as size, longevity, and influence.[72] The Associationists obviously failed in their largest intention: to transform American society into a cooperative utopia. And no phalanx lasted long enough or grew large enough to fit the most common notions of success. But what about the Fourierists' goal of demonstrating the practical and moral benefits of Association? Did any of their communities evolve an economically viable or morally satisfying way of life? To what extent *were* the phalanxes organized on Fourierist principles? What impact did their arrangements have on members' lives in key areas such as work, sex, family, and education? If we put aside the question of success or failure, at least for the moment, and instead examine the phalanxes' actual arrangements in light of Associationist ideology and antebellum culture, we can better understand the social dynamics and the personal implications of life under Association. This is the intention of the next chapter.

7 | Life in the Phalanxes

Beset by internal schisms and poor economic foundations, most phalanxes were too consumed by the scramble for survival to establish a coherent way of life reflective of members' ideals. Only in the longer-lived communities can one see a distinctive Fourierist regime coming into existence. In attempting to determine how far the American communities put Fourier's ideas into practice and what impact phalanx life had on members' lives, this chapter examines the communities' architectural designs, work and family arrangements, gender roles, and educational systems. The discussion concentrates on the three most important phalanxes—Brook Farm, the North American Phalanx, and the Wisconsin Phalanx. These communities played the largest role in the national Fourierist movement, had the opportunity to implement their plans most fully, and left the best records for later researchers. But wherever it is available I have included information from shorter-lived Fourierist experiments whose arrangements were more rudimentary but more representative of the phalanx experience.

It is not easy to know what went on in nineteenth-century utopian communities. Victorian Americans were reticent about such private matters as sex and family life, and reports of communal arrangements in contemporary journals and newspapers need to be taken with grains of salt. On one hand, as Horace Greeley noted, sympathetic writers were "too apt to blend what they desire or hope to see, with what they actually do see"; on the other, hostile accounts in conservative newspapers or evangelical journals rarely let facts interfere with invective.[1] Fortunately, there exists a widely scattered if not deep collection of reliable sources on the phalanxes. The invaluable documents, descriptions, and interviews collected by A. J. Macdonald, who toured American utopian communities in the early 1850s, have been preserved and are substantially reprinted in John Humphrey Noyes's *History of American Socialisms* (1870). Brook Farm's memoirists, recordkeepers, and correspondents were especially conscientious, but for other phalanxes there survive newspaper sources, published and manuscript reminiscences, a few good collections of letters, and—for the North American, Wisconsin, Sodus Bay, and Alphadelphia phalanxes—community records.

These sources refute the common assertion that Fourier's ideas were not implemented or even well known at the phalanxes. The extent to which Americans understood, endorsed, and applied Fourierism in their communities has been badly underestimated. Generally, commentators accept Macdonald's assertion that most phalanx dwellers knew little of Fourierism but were afflicted with an acute but unfocused communitarian fever. More fundamentally, they share a doctrinaire mentality that identifies "true" Fourierism only with the Frenchman's most grandiose plan and not the scaled-down proposals of Brisbane or Fourier himself. With this purist definition in mind, Noyes declares that in "all the experiments of the Fourier epoch" members' "doings . . . had . . . no semblance of Fourierism," and Arthur Bestor concludes that none of Fourier's "fundamental principles" was carried out in American experiments.[2] Associationist leaders tried to promote just such a conclusion when they beat a hasty retreat to the doctrinaire definition of Fourierism in the mid-1840s and repudiated the struggling phalanxes as "unscientific" trials of the founder's theory. It was a strategy they had learned from the master himself.[3]

Yet familiarity with Fourier's doctrine in the communities was more specific and widespread than these comments imply. When Macdonald charged that "the majority" in the Clermont Phalanx, "as in many others, had no further knowledge of Fourier's principles than that which they had obtained from 'Brisbane's pamphlet' and the paper called the Tribune," he little realized how much he was giving away.[4] Brisbane's *Concise Exposition* and his *Tribune* columns, along with Greeley's editorials, featured succinct outlines of Fourier's theory in addition to detailed practical plans. The version of Fourierism fashioned by Brisbane, Greeley, and Parke Godwin included enough of Fourier's blueprint and the "higher parts" of his theory to link smaller endeavors to the large-scale "scientific" transformation of society. Knowledge of Fourierism at Brook Farm was unusually sophisticated but hardly unique. Bestor's study of western New York phalanxes shows that local Associationists were familiar with Fourier's principles and precise plans and approved most of them.[5] Midwestern phalanx leaders not only subscribed to Associationist periodicals but wrote Fourierist books, pamphlets, and newspaper articles themselves. Phalanx constitutions usually contained a brief exposition of Fourier's theory, and new members were required to sign in agreement. The records of several communities show that members met frequently to discuss Fourier's ideas. Membership applications and minutes of meetings suggest that the rank and file had a fair knowledge of Fourierist principles and plans. They proved their allegiance to Fourierism by joining other phalanxes when their own community disbanded or disappointed them: twenty-three of the twenty-nine American phalanxes either took in members of other phalanxes or sent their own to other Fourierist communities (see Appendix Figure 1).

Appreciation of Fourierism was deeper in the phalanxes than standard histories indicate, but it was the *American* version of Fourierism that members knew and attempted to realize. Certainly the most vivid superficial impression of phalanx histories is the huge gap between Fourier's ideal and the reality of communal life in the American countryside. But American attempts to inaugurate communitarian reform should be judged against the transitional model sketched in Associationist writings rather than the grandiose plans of Fourier himself. Associationists acknowledged that phalanxes in early stages could hardly approach his expectations. Huge injections of capital, grand phalansteries, varied industrial operations, and intricate groups and series could not be expected at the outset, when, as one communal veteran recalled, "bread and butter" were more important than Fourierist "science."[6] Phalansterians intended eventually to institute a full Fourierist organization of labor but recognized the need for a gradual transition and reserved the right to experiment. Their constitutions, bylaws, and public pronouncements repeatedly stipulated that arrangements would follow Fourierist guidelines "as far as practicable." Clarifying the distinction between Fourier's full-blown theory and the more modest aspirations of American communitarians yields a better appreciation of the texture of phalanx life and its achievements and limitations.

Even when committed to Fourierist change, American utopians were hindered by conflicts over the pace or extent of reforms and by the constraints of their poor economic situation. Life in these communities was shaped by material necessity, a recalcitrant cultural inheritance, and demographic accidents perhaps as much as by Fourierist theory. Housing shortages resulted in makeshift arrangements; lack of capital limited the communities' size and industrial base; the need for marketable products focused work on a few activities. The attitudes of Civilization about work, marriage, and women's roles inhibited progress. In addition, each community was given a distinctive flavor by the age, religious, and occupational structure of its membership. The process by which phalanx members attempted to realize a Fourierist vision in such contexts was a revealing commentary on the difficulties of constructing a new way of life within the shell of the old. "The question," Charles Sears of the North American Phalanx later recalled, "was whether the infant Association should . . . be civilisee or Phalansterian." Like most community leaders, Sears was committed to the latter, yet he acknowledged that "to break up habitudes, relinquish prejudices, sunder ties, . . . to adopt new modes of action . . . and readjust . . . to new relations" was a trying agenda.[7] The mixture of new ideas, old habits, and practical constraints permitted phalanx members to take only preliminary steps toward a new way of life.

Building a Fourierist Environment

Fourier's French and American disciples pictured the phalanx as a splendid rural township combining the peace and beauty of country life with the variety and sophistication of cities. Approaching its rolling hills from the city, visitors would drive through sylvan forests, bountiful orchards, and neat rows of crops before arriving at a huge open square formed by workshops on one side and a vast and elegant phalanstery on the other. All elements of this physical environment contributed to Fourier's aim of social harmony through complete passional development. It was an enchanting but impossible dream. As Frederick Grimké noted ruefully, "The picture drawn by . . . Fourier . . . is very flattering, and delightful to look upon; but its fair exterior vanishes at the touch of experience."[8] In the American phalanxes Fourier's environmental ideas were necessarily tempered by economic constraints, the condition of existing land and buildings, and the gradualist strategy of community building. But in modest ways the American communities attempted and sometimes managed to embody the spirit of Harmonic society in their physical environment, even during the phalanxes' short lives.

As Fourier and Brisbane prescribed, most American phalanxes were primarily agricultural communities set in the countryside not far from city markets. Attracted as always by variety and contrasts, the Frenchman recommended that members undertake the most diverse farming operations that a domain would permit, placing special emphasis on horticulture and animal husbandry. Since few communities could produce all they needed, Fourier envisioned an extensive trading network among phalanxes. Like Fourier's Harmonians, American utopians strove to become self-supporting rather than self-sufficient, but they found that economic survival meant engaging extensively in cash-crop agriculture. In many phalanxes large tracts of wheat, rye, corn, and oats were harvested mainly for external markets. A few communities marketed cheese, hides, wool, and vegetables, but in general the greater portion of the phalanxes' livestock, dairy production, and vegetables was reserved for their own tables. The amount of acreage devoted to each crop reflected its relation to commercial farming. In 1845 the Trumbull Phalanx reported sixty-five acres of corn, fifty-five of oats, twenty-four of buckwheat, thirty of wheat, twenty of rye, twelve of potatoes, and smaller gardens for community use. The same year the Wisconsin Phalanx, with the most productive farm of any Fourierist community, reported that members had harvested one hundred acres of wheat and sown another four hundred, "raised sixty acres of corn, twenty acres of potatoes and thirty of beans, peas, roots, etc. . . . [and] cut four hundred tons of hay." The vegetables would later appear in the dining hall, and much of the corn and hay fed the livestock, but wheat sold outside the phalanx was the largest source of community income. Understandably, the Wisconsinites named their fertile township "Ceresco" after the goddess of grain.[9]

The growing of fruit provided Fourier's most detailed descriptions of attractive work in Harmonic society, which were repeated in Associationist writings. Several phalanxes, including Brook Farm, La Grange, Wisconsin, and Alphadelphia, planted extensive orchards; Sodus Bay inherited one from the Shakers. The North American Phalanx had the largest horticultural operation, with over eight thousand trees and vines by 1848 and several thousand more saplings in their nursery. Horticulture was ideologically correct: one environmental historian has noticed that at the NAP "cleared areas were planted in patterns which suggest a tentative attempt to establish Fourier's interlaced system of cultivation": orchards alternating with fields, to enable workers from rival agricultural groups to intermingle. But fruit production also made economic sense a ferry ride away from New York City. In 1849 the community built a brick "Seristery" where members efficiently processed and bottled (later canned) grapes, berries, and tomatoes and dried fruits for nearby urban households. It was among the first such operations in the state and the most profitable of all the phalanx's series.[10]

Bright-colored spring blossoms on neat rows of apple or peach trees provided the sole glimpse of the gardenlike beauty of Harmonic society that most phalanx members would ever see. Struggling colonies and pragmatic western farmers paid little attention to aesthetics. The more urbane communities did attempt to beautify their grounds. Brook Farmers surrounded their communal house with shrubs and flowerbeds, and near a rustic cottage on the domain one member laid out a formal garden stretching over a half-acre. Visitors to the Raritan Bay Union reported that the community's grounds overlooking the Raritan River were "tastefully laid out" with a profusion of flowers. Perhaps the North American Phalanx best developed the picturesque qualities of its site. On the fringes of the community's 673 acres were wooded lands in which members created winding footpaths dotted by rustic benches. At the end of one path a formal garden was laid out, "a most romantic spot on a rising elevation of land overlooking long stretches of meadow land." Wisteria and trumpet vines softened the phalanstery's regular arcade. In front of the dwelling, shade trees were planted, and Trout Brook was dammed to create a pond that not only supplied water to community shops and kitchens but served as a canoeing lake and swimming hole. Still, a few years was hardly enough time to turn conventional farms into lovely Harmonian resorts; utopian leaders such as Victor Considerant, with expectations inflated by Fourier's lavish descriptions of Harmony, might pronounce even the NAP's gardens "sorrowful to the sight." But compared to surrounding farms, Brook Farm and the North American Phalanx were lush oases.[11]

Looking for alternative sources of income and profitable pursuits in winter, the phalanxes turned to craft industries. In updating Fourier's preindustrial utopia for the 1840s, Brisbane emphasized the variety of manufactures that phalanxes should undertake, ranging from furniture, shoes, and clothing to such luxuries as books, musical instruments, and candy. By establishing craft production the Americans also attempted to fulfill their Fourierist commitment to attract the working class to communitarian experiments. The most dramatic example was Brook Farm, where conversion to Fourierism coincided with expansion of the community's industrial program to include tailoring, shoemaking, sash and blind making, and other handcrafts.[12] Most phalanxes erected grist-mills, sawmills and blacksmith shops to serve themselves and their neigh-bors. Several maintained tailoring and shoemaking shops, and a few housed print shops that took on outside jobs. Perhaps the Trumbull Phalanx pursued the most diverse array of "industrial" enterprises: saw- and gristmills, a woolen mill, a tannery, a brickmaking operation, and shops for shoemakers, hatters, tailors, and blacksmiths. Officers boasted that these operations yielded $30 a week.[13] Such extensive operations— and certainly such profits—were unusual. In contrast to Noyes's Oneida Community, the Associationists, like Fourier himself, subordinated craft industry to agricultural production. And since phalanx craft operations were hampered by their small scale, distance from consumer markets, and shortage of skilled workers, most did not repay the sums invested in them.

In fact, despite such varied operations, the output from phalanx farms and workshops was rarely enough to sustain residents well. Members were able to show surpluses only by shaving living expenses to a mini-mum. One key index of this spartan regime was the communal meals, so central in Fourier's version of the good life. North American Phalanx members were proud of their varied menu, which gave members a choice of ham and beef dishes as well as fruits, vegetables, pastries, and such luxuries as chocolate.[14] At less prosperous communities, however, steady diets of potatoes or buckwheat pancakes and milk made a bitter contrast with Fourier's vision of five sumptuous daily meals in Harmonic society. When several families left the Trumbull Phalanx "because they had been in the habit of living on better food," N. C. Meeker warned that early stages of Association required dietary sacrifices of communitarians:

> If they are willing to endure privations, to eat coarse food, sometimes with no meat, but with milk for a substitute (this is a glorious resort for the Grahamites), . . . they may consider themselves fitted for the transition-period. But if they sigh for the flesh pots and leeks and onions of civilization . . . and growl because they cannot have eggs, and honey, and warm biscuit and butter for breakfast, they had better stay where they are, and wait for the advent of perfect industrial Association.[15]

On such grounds alone, Fourier the gourmand would have dismissed the American phalanxes as unworthy of the name.

Given the difficulties of establishing subsistence, the Americans could construct true Fourierist phalansteries only in their imaginations. Fourier's communal dwelling, sketched by Considerant as an opulent palace whose 2,400-foot facade formed a vast parade ground in front and hid delightful garden courtyards inside, was reproduced in Brisbane's books and featured in his lectures. National Fourierist leaders offered a substantial loan if an American community would imitate it. But phalanx residents evolving a communal life were more practical than Associationist leaders looking for a model experiment to subsidize. Scant resources made such an attempt impractical or impossible; where it was even discussed, members foresaw a long evolution before an extravagant edifice was warranted. As NAP spokesmen pointed out, "new forms into which the life of a people shall flow, cannot be determined by merely external conditions and the elaboration of a theory . . . but are matters of growth."[16]

Meanwhile, however, phalanxes had to do something to house the rapid, almost haphazard influx of members, which outstripped development of their physical plants. Overwhelmed by immigration and crippled by too little capital, their buildings were at first makeshift combinations of preexisting farm buildings, nearby houses, and temporary shelters and workshops. Fourierists at Sodus Bay acquired a fine Shaker residence and then divided the old Shaker meetinghouse into nine additional bedrooms. Most phalanxes were less fortunate in inheriting solid structures but equally pragmatic in exploiting usable space. Many crammed members into frame cottages hastily built and farmhouses awkwardly converted into communal dwellings. The Trumbull Phalanx boasted that it had "the only veritable 'log-cabin President' the whole land can show," though most members were "huddled together like brutes" in existing farm buildings. One Sylvania veteran recalled that during the first winter more than a hundred residents were crowded into "mere huts." The Alphadelphia and North American phalanxes quickly built barracks for temporary communal housing, while some members continued to reside in individual dwellings. These "isolated homes," compromising Fourier's communal blueprint, were nearby farms subscribed as stock, local houses purchased by the community, or cottages the phalanxes allowed individual families to build.[17]

Brook Farm's motley collection of buildings strung along adjacent hilltops was probably a representative mixture. The existing clapboard farmhouse, rechristened "The Hive," contained the community's kitchen, dining room, office, and single bedrooms. Two small wings were added for a laundry and day nursery. Across the street the community rented a small building used at different times as a school or a family residence. On the domain an additional house—the Eyrie—was built to accommodate several members as well as the community's library and piano. Meanwhile, members allowed two private homes—the Pilgrim House and the Cottage—to be built on the grounds; after the initial residents departed, these buildings were given over to the primary school, workshops, and additional lodgings. There was not only a jumbling of styles (the Eyrie was an Italianate square box, the Cottage a cruciform gothic retreat, the Pilgrim House an urban-style twin house) but such a shifting and confusing mixture of uses that members gladly embraced plans for a central Fourierist phalanstery.[18]

In time, virtually all the phalanxes built "unitary dwellings," so called to distinguish them from Fourier's grandiose ideal. The American version of the phalanstery was a long wood-frame building based not on neoclassical civic architecture but on prevailing styles of residential construction. Brook Farm's served as a prototype. According to a report in *The Harbinger,* this wooden building was "one hundred and seventy-five feet long, three stories high, with attics divided into pleasant and convenient rooms for single persons. The second and third stories were divided into fourteen houses, independent of each other, with a parlor and three sleeping-rooms in each, connected by piazzas which ran the whole length of the building on both stories. The basement contained a large and commodious kitchen, a dining-hall capable of seating from three to four-hundred persons, two public saloons, and a spacious hall or lecture-room."[19]

Variations on this basic model were surprisingly minor. Phalanxes in Indiana, Michigan, and Illinois built rowhouse-style "mansions" of one or two stories. The Wisconsin Phalanx's Long Home, a 208- by 32-foot series of family suites, had no kitchen but featured exterior galleries on each of its two floors. The Trumbull Phalanx's 200-foot-long dwelling was a story and a half, built around an open courtyard. At the La Grange Phalanx members simply added a 120-foot-long residential wing to an existing farmhouse. Clermont residents awaiting completion of their brick phalanstery lived in a steamboatlike barracks with a long, narrow hallway punctuated by small staterooms for married couples or paired single persons. Perhaps the most unusual phalanstery was the North American's, which was built in three stages. A three-story rectangular building constructed in 1849 contained the community's library, parlor, and office, as well as some upstairs bedrooms. From this central block two extensions were built, giving the phalanstery an L-shape. In the first, completed in 1851, laundry and dairy rooms occupied the basement below the kitchen and an impressive two-story dining hall; fourteen bedrooms were on the third floor. In the second wing, completed a year later, there were eight separate family suites and an open sleeping loft. Outdoor galleries lined two of the facades.[20]

Built in the architectural vernacular without pretensions to grandeur, these unitary dwellings managed to embody Associationist ideals quietly and sometimes efficiently. The concentration of residences allowed for centralized services: communal kitchens, gaslight, central steam heating, and water piped from nearby ponds or streams. Phalanx carpenters compensated for small scale by creating spaces whose use could be varied:

with doors sealed, suites became bedrooms; a dining room with a stage could be rearranged as a dancing or lecture hall. Relatively generous public spaces reflected the percentage of members' time given to communal events such as common meals and business meetings, while private apartments, in some cases separated by brick walls, preserved family freedom and seclusion. The private spaces themselves were sorted into a two-tier system that reflected, and perhaps accentuated, different degrees of loyalty to group life among members: families often occupied first-story suites; single persons slept in barrackslike attics, their beds in a common room or else tiny separate ones. While families entered and exited their private apartments through doors leading to the outside, "bachelor" quarters opened onto hallways, parlors, and other communal spaces. For both groups, however, private rooms were small enough to encourage mingling in the more spacious parlors, libraries, and meeting rooms. And long covered porches—modest echoes of Fourier's "street galleries"—encouraged members to socialize and enjoy the outdoors in a protected way. North American Phalanx members even made an attempt to connect some buildings by roofed passageways.

The main problems were overcrowding and—in some cases—cheap materials, but these were less the fault of the architectural plan than the result of insufficient funds. On the whole, the American phalanstery represented an economical, flexible, and generally comfortable transitional step between the private single residence and the monumental communal hotel advocated by Fourier. Certainly in many ways these "unitary dwellings" were antithetical to the Victorian ideal of privatism; the "Fourierite system" came under attack from such champions of domesticity as Catherine Beecher, who found the communal household more like a Catholic convent than the "true Protestant system" of single-family bliss.[21] Such criticism is worth recalling as a counterweight to charges that Associationists simply reproduced middle-class family life. The genuine achievements of these modest phalansteries as alternative, communal living spaces in early Victorian America should be appreciated, even if they disappointed sexual radicals or doctrinaire Fourierists.

The dream of a Fourierist Versailles persisted through the 1840s, surfacing in campaigns to replace existing buildings with massive edifices. Even Integral Phalanx members, who warned that "the distance between Civilization and Association cannot be passed in one leap," intended to attach their modest unitary dwelling to a phalanstery nearly 6,000 feet long. Not until the 1850s did Associationist leaders get the monumental phalanstery they hoped for: Marcus Spring's building for the Raritan Bay Union (see Chapter 12). This building's failure to unite Raritan Bay and the genuine success of the North American Phalanx's wood-frame additions suggest that communal dwellings worked best when evolved out of members' experiences rather than imposed by theory. Dolores Hayden, a recent critic of Fourier's blueprint, remarks, "There are no architectural shortcuts to Harmony."[22] Horatio Greenough, the American sculptor who had met Brisbane during student days in Europe, denounced the Fourierist scheme as too regular and stultifying: "I hate thy straight lines, and thy arrangements for the elbows, and thy lid that fits over all, with the screws ready in thy hand."[23] But in constructing their physical environment, Associationists of the 1840s did not impose a rigid Fourierist plan. Guided by practical considerations and wary of Fourier's extravagances, they built inexpensive, flexible, and sociable dwellings that at their best proved a viable communal alternative to the middle-class home.

"Attractive Industry" in Association

The Fourierists' plan to make work attractive was probably the most distinctive feature of their theory. The conviction that work could bring complete self-realization set Fourier apart not just from contemporary utopian planners such as Owen and Saint-Simon who promoted work as a social duty but from mainstream nineteenth-century social thinkers who interpreted the urge to work as a form of discipline, self-sacrifice, and productivity.[24] In Harmonic society labor would be motivated by "passional attraction" and contribute to a life of pleasure. Placing work in a communal context and multiplying outlets for individual expression opened up new possibilities for friendship, ambition, and variety. In the work groups of the phalanx the disparate interests and conflicting passions of Civilizees would be harmonized and guided into a subtle coherence. From Fourier's point of view the components of attractive labor, from its organization in voluntary groups and series to its complex distribution of profits and guaranteed minimum income, were not cogs of an efficient machine or planks in a socialist platform but instructions from the divine composer to the human orchestra. It was a strange but alluring kind of aleatory music in which particular notes and players were left to chance "attraction," yet time limits and the arrangement of instruments guaranteed harmony.

Writers in *The Harbinger* could almost hear the glorious music the "passions of the soul" would create. To the Brook Farmers the argument that communal work expanded individual capacities appeared analogous to the Transcendentalist ideal of self-culture. Their constitution of 1844 asserted that work in groups and series was "the law of human nature"; its bylaws envisioned work circles to be formed "by members of the Association who have passional attraction therefor."[25] But most Associationists viewed attractive labor with productivity and social justice more than passional fulfillment in mind. Their expositions of Fourier's plan stressed the economic efficiency of work in groups, the fairness of Fourier's remuneration scheme, and the social cohesion that teamwork would create. Brisbane's and Godwin's handbooks emphasized that Fourier's work arrangements were not fixed law but should vary according to conditions and needs. Individual phalanxes took such advice to heart by modifying Fourier's details when necessary or desirable.[26]

American Associationists believed too strongly in the work ethic to agree with Fourier that everyone in the phalanx, even those unwilling to work, should be guaranteed a minimum income. It was one thing to promise subsistence in the lavishly abundant Harmonic future, quite another to do so in struggling experiments on nineteenth-century farms. The Trumbull Phalanx constitution proclaimed it a "duty" for members to work; Brook Farmers limited their "guarantees" to "members of the Phalanx engaging for the regular time in its occupations"; and other phalanxes enacted similar provisions. A contemporary cartoon satirized phalansterians who refused to work because they belonged to the "eating group," a scenario that reinforced Associationists' fear of invasions of idlers and loafers who would doom their fragile communities. Most American phalanxes limited expression of group solidarity to free education for children and free maintenance for the sick, disabled, and aged. Even here, there was hedging, less from concern about free lunches than from lack of resources. Brook Farm and other communities deducted the cost of support for the elderly and disabled from any community shares they owned. The Wisconsin Phalanx would not cover the cost of outside medical assistance even though there was no doctor on the domain.[27]

Associationists also qualified Fourier's demand that phalanx members have free choice of occupation. Fourier not only envisioned dozens of different work activities in a thriving phalanx; he believed there would be a perfect equilibrium between supply and demand because Harmonians would spontaneously choose the tasks that passional psychology predicted. In the real world the Americans had to balance free choice against community needs, limited opportunities, and variable demand. Thus, Alphadelphia Association bylaws declared that each member could pursue a preferred occupation only "without prejudicing the interest of the Association"; the majority decided when one type of work was inappropriate. In the Sylvania Association work groups drew lots when oversubscribed—a condition that must have occurred rarely at a community where many complained about slackers. Wisconsin Phalanx bylaws empowered the president to select members from other groups when there were not enough volunteers to fill vacancies. Among the Alphadelphia Association papers can be found the most concrete evidence that members' aptitudes and interests were taken into account: a questionnaire asking community women what kind of work they were willing to do.[28] For all the phalanxes, however, the issue of gratifying individual preferences took a back seat to the need for group survival. The formation of work groups and schedules was always subject to officers' approval. Applicants for admission to phalanxes were screened for skills—carpentry, masonry, horticulture—that fit the community's desire to construct buildings or establish profitable enterprises. A final decision to take up a new branch of work such as shoemaking, milling, or silk cultivation was made by community officers with questions of outlay and profitability uppermost in mind.

Associationists more clearly endorsed Fourier's plan for work in groups and series and tried to implement it as far as small numbers and limited industries allowed. Many phalanxes were unable to push such schemes beyond the planning stage. The Trumbull constitution foresaw a wide range of groups and series with elaborate pay differentials. Yet three years after the phalanx was established, one member reported that "the present arrangement is as though we were all in one group; what is earned by the body is divided among individuals according to the amount of labor expended by each." Integral Phalanx members decided not to establish groups and series "until we have the requisite number, have gone through a proper system of training, and erected an edifice sufficient for the accommodation of about four hundred persons." From previous communal failures they had learned to expand operations gradually. Other phalanxes, such as the Sylvania and Sodus Bay communities, apparently adopted rudimentary work groups of three or more persons.[29]

The best opportunity to organize groups and series came in longer-lived phalanxes with the fullest commitment to Fourier's plans. As these communities prospered and their populations increased, division of work into groups and series became more detailed and sophisticated. Progress was charted somewhat unevenly at the Wisconsin Phalanx, which changed its labor arrangements several times in search of the right formula. Early community bylaws envisioned a variety of tasks performed by work groups whose duties, compensation, and command lines were spelled out. But because of a labor shortage and insufficiently diversified operations, the groups were never formed into series. Community records at the end of 1846 show separate three-man committees overseeing work in six areas: agricultural, mechanical, dormitory, finance, education, and applications. Finally, the new bylaws of February 1848 organized members into one large Industrial Series, which elected ten persons from the various work departments to a regulatory Industrial Council. The phalanx still had no true Fourierist series, but work groups and the rudiments of worker government were in place.[30]

The North American Phalanx came closer to Fourierist specifications. When it established worker groups in February 1844, members were lumped into three undifferentiated series: agricultural, manufacturing, and domestic. By 1848 a livestock series had been added, and the four series boasted twenty-five separate work groups of two to fifteen members each. The next year a "festal serie" to organize musical and dramatic events and an education series to run the school, library, and nursery were formed. Eventually, the community added to the agricultural series a "Contingent" group that "looked after the scattering of rubbish" and other repugnant tasks; this and a similar group at Brook Farm were modeled directly on Fourier's "Sacred Legion."[31] The NAP's revised constitution of December 1848 reorganized community government to bring it closer to the Fourier-Brisbane plan of a workers' republic. Elected chiefs of the series formed an Industrial Council, which directed work under supervision of the phalanx's Executive Council; and a Council on Labor Awards, composed equally of series chiefs and members appointed by stockholders, set compensation rates on the domain (see Appendix Figure 2). A similar process evolved at Brook Farm, where the revised constitution of 1845 envisioned more series, an elaborate classification of groups by the nature of their work, and the formation of a Council of Industry composed of series chiefs.[32]

At the NAP, Brook Farm, and a few other phalanxes, residents worked at different tasks and under varying rates as they shifted from team to team, depending on the day, the season, and the community's needs. Labor credits were recorded by the group's chief or foreman and later charged against the cost of room and board. Chiefs were sometimes chosen by community officers but more often elected by group members. The North American's chiefs met each evening to arrange the next day's work schedule, and before retiring, members checked a bulletin board where assignments were posted.[33] No phalanx was large or varied enough to have Fourier's elaborate subdivision of labor between "ascending" and "descending" wings within groups, or even to organize the forty work groups of Brisbane's scaled-down model. But in the few phalanxes where groups were numerous and members alternated among them, the Americans created a reasonable approximation of Fourier's blueprint.

To what extent was there task rotation in the phalanxes? Associationist spokesmen admired the way frequent migration between work groups cleverly integrated personal freedom with communal needs, yet genuine job rotation was hard to achieve in fledgling phalanxes.[34] For one thing, the sexual division of labor limited the range of tasks for men and women. Just as important, certain kinds of work, such as farming, carpentry, and housework, were so vital in communities' initial years that they limited the work experiences available and influenced admissions committees to look for specialized skills among applicants. The phalanxes' urgent need for marketable crops and products left little time for experimentation or training. Labor shortages in some phalanxes were usually remedied by hiring seasonal farmhands rather than drafting workers from "industrial" groups.

For such reasons there was little formal alternation of tasks at many American phalanxes. Yet where commitment to Fourierist principles was greatest and community operations most diversified, genuine rotation between groups was possible. Charles Sears recalled that most North American Phalanx members "belonged to a number of groups whose labors succeeded each other; and in cases of emergency the forces of several series could be concentrated upon one detail to save a crop or bring up an arrear of work."[35] A list of the twenty-five NAP groups in

1848 shows men and women averaging enrollment in more than two each, with some in as many as four. Conditions at Brook Farm were the most favorable for injecting charm and variety into work. The experiment began with the project of combining intellectual and manual labor in "whole persons"; it strove to create an atmosphere of social equality where members shunned no disagreeable tasks; its successful school provided teaching opportunities for several members; and publication of *The Harbinger* absorbed the writing, translating, and editorial talents of no less than ten members. Community leaders Ripley, Dwight, and Dana not only taught in the school, lectured on Association, and wrote for Fourierist periodicals; they also harvested crops, milked cows, and waited on tables. Evening discussions, concerts, and theatrical performances arranged by an "amusement group" engaged members' intellect and refreshed them for the next day's work. At such times Associationists came close to the young Marx's Fourierist-inspired vision of a society in which it would be possible "to do one thing today and another tomorrow, to hunt in the morning, fish in the afternoon, rear cattle in the evening, criticize after dinner, just as I like, without ever becoming a hunter, fisherman, shepherd, or critic."[36]

To be sure, at Brook Farm and the North American Phalanx many members pursued domestic or farm work most of the day. Yet these chores lent themselves readily to frequent change. Marianne Dwight reported the following schedule of the mostly domestic duties typical for Brook Farm women in 1844:

> I wait on the breakfast table (½ hour), help M. A. Ripley clear away breakfast things, etc. (1 ½ hours), go into the dormitory group till eleven o'clock,—dress for dinner—then over to the Eyrie and sew till dinner time,—half past twelve. Then from half past one or two o'clock until ½ past five, I teach drawing in Pilgrim Hall and sew in the Eyrie. At ½ past five go down to the Hive, to help set the tea table, and afterwards I wash tea cups, etc., till about ½ past seven.

Except for the teaching, this was traditional domestic work, but the communal setting and busy schedule had Dwight shifting partners and buildings and thus adding variety and sociability to work that otherwise might verge on boredom. "I make a long day of it," she wrote a friend, "but alternation of work and pleasant company and chats make it pleasant."[37]

For men, too, Fourierism often did less to supplant traditional farmwork than to legitimize its variety and supplement it with a group environment. The labor book of Alphadelphia's Hannibal Taylor, covering March to September 1845 (a rare surviving long-term, day-by-day record of a phalanx worker), shows a range of farm tasks typical of the era. From mid-March to mid-April, Taylor put in nine hours a day boiling sap from maple trees to make syrup and sugar. The remainder of April was spent gardening, putting up fences, chopping wood, and washing. Much of May was devoted to plowing and planting crops, June to maintaining the seedlings in the fields. The leisurely July interlude could be used to gather berries and stone a well, but by August and into September Taylor was busy again with haying and harvesting corn. Through spring and summer his workday varied from two to seventeen hours, averaging six and a half.[38] For workers like Taylor the seasonal rhythms of such preindustrial work and the jack-of-all-trades nature of most phalanx duties set the pace and schedule of labor as much as Fourier's theory did. The Fourierist environment simply contributed coworkers, group meals, and meetings or entertainment in the evenings.

Not surprisingly, the more phalanxes relied on skilled labor to produce marketable goods in their workshops, the less their members were able to enjoy rotating tasks. Surviving records show that carpenters, blacksmiths, printers, and shoemakers often worked a full week on the job without any change except for such minor tasks as waiting tables. When Marianne Dwight became chief of a "fancy group" at Brook Farm, she began spending six or seven hours a day decorating fans and lampshades. Fourier himself foresaw the dangers of manufacturing when he limited its role in Harmony to providing a seasonal complement to agriculture, one that would take no more than a quarter of each phalansterian's worktime.[39]

The final criterion of attractive labor was a just rate of compensation. Like Associationist writers, communitarians found Fourier's allocation of profits through fractional dividends intriguing but complex, controversial, and requiring adaptation to local needs. Most were wary of control by nonresidents and of substantial investments by capitalists with the wrong motives. Instead of Fourier's four-twelfths return to capital—an enormous yield, given the profits Fourier assumed the phalanx would make—communitarians adopted figures more in line with contemporary interest rates, though they varied from phalanx to phalanx. At one end of the spectrum, Wisconsin, Clermont, and Alphadelphia allotted one-fourth of the dividend to capital, as Brisbane recommended; in the Wisconsin case this resulted in yearly yields of 6 to 12 percent. At the other end, the Morehouse Union in western New York declared in advance no dividends for investors for the first five years. Several phalanxes simply promised a flat percentage return, usually 5 or 6 percent. In the end, however, few were able to realize any profits at all for shareholders.[40]

Methods used to assign phalanx workers their share of labor's dividend varied from a simple version of Civilization's wages to Fourierist complexities. Phalanxes in the rudimentary stages of organization simply credited a flat rate of 50 or 75 cents for a day's labor, usually defined as ten hours. More profitable or ambitious communities adopted ratios of compensation based on Fourier's principle of "honors according to usefulness," which took into account the difficulty and disagreeableness of each task. The Sodus Bay and Jefferson Industrial Association presidents rewarded repugnant work with higher pay at their discretion. In 1847 the North American Phalanx rated a day's maximum pay of 84 cents on a scale of twelve points, ranging from haying, digging potatoes, and caring for livestock (which earned a twelve) to serving tables (which earned only a seven). The Wisconsin Phalanx divided work into classes of "Necessity," which included masonry and digging; "Usefulness," which comprised almost all mechanical and agricultural labor as well as washing, tending livestock, and bookkeeping; and "Attractiveness," which included most domestic work and the business of the board of directors. For proper weighting, hours of labor in these classes were to be multiplied by 24, 20, and 15, respectively. In practice, the community simplified this scheme, classing most labor in the category of usefulness.[41]

The most elaborate ranking appeared at the Clarkson Association, which proclaimed its determination "to follow as near the *letter* of Fourier as possible."[42] Each group was assigned a maximum rank based on the attractiveness or difficulty of its task; each worker was assigned a number equal to or less than the group's maximum, based upon individual skill and productiveness. When workers' hours were multiplied by their particular rank, a "quotient" resulted; for every thousand of this quotient, members were allowed to draw on their account for 75 cents' worth of goods. The weekly account of one group looked like this:

SERIES OF TAILORESSES—GROUP NO. 1

Maximum Rank 25.

1844 Rank		Mo.	Tue.	We.	Thu.	Fri.	Sat.	Total hours	Hours & rank
20	M. Weed	6	10	3	–	–	5	24	480
25	J. Peabody	10	10	10	12	10	10	62	1550
20	S. Clark	10	10	10	10	8	–	48	960
25	E. Clark	2	10	10	Sick	–	–	22	550
18	H. Lee	6	4	10	6	4	4	34	612
15	J. Folsom	3	3	2	6	5	3	22	330
12	Eliza Mann	4	4	2	2	6	4	22	264

In such cases the allotment to skill or talent was determined inside groups, as Fourier recommended.[43]

Beginning in 1850 North American Phalanx groups took skill into account by awarding to chiefs or particularly productive members a wage bonus of 10 to 25 percent. Later the NAP adopted an elaborate Fourierist-style scale, with "simple," "mixed," and "compound" degrees of difference in "performance," which rewarded extraordinary skill with as much as 40 percent over standard pay. Brook Farm groups simply multiplied members' hours of labor by a fraction indicative of skill and experience, which ranged in the case of the printers from 0.4 to 1.0. But because the gradient for skill made distinctions by persons rather than by jobs, it was less popular than the ranking of work by attractiveness and was not implemented in many communities. A proposal for foremen to rank group members by skill took effect at the Wisconsin Phalanx in 1844; the plan was dropped within a year because of workers' opposition, but the idea kept resurfacing thereafter. At least one contemporary close to the community pointed to conflict over this issue as a cause of the phalanx's breakup.[44]

Since transitional phalanxes implemented Fourier's work plans only to a degree, no community was able to achieve the economies or productive splendor envisioned by Fourier or Brisbane. Still, several maintained an average workday equal to or lower than the ten-hour standard of contemporary society, and those best organized accumulated modest annual surpluses. Though much credit is due to the reduced expenses of combined living, at least part of this gain can be attributed to increased productivity through "combined industry," which, the Wisconsin Phalanx testified, "accomplished much more than could be done by the same person[s] in an isolated condition." A reporter visiting the North American Phalanx marveled at "how soon work is performed when there are numbers to do it. A building is put up, trees are felled, a crop is planted and gathered, an embankment raised, . . . all this by magic, on the principle of associated effort." His impression may have been exaggerated, but the community's officers proudly pointed out that the farm's profit margin ranked it in the top 2 percent of agricultural enterprises nationally. Fourierism brought clear evidence of discipline to Brook Farm's leisurely work habits and, in 1844, the year the community adopted Fourier's work system, its first annual profit. Both eastern phalanxes adopted the symbol of the beehive to dramatize the productivity of Fourierist communal work.[45]

On the other hand, Fourierist work methods produced annoying inefficiencies. Commuting from task to task was time-consuming; complex remuneration schemes required elaborate bookkeeping, which preoccupied series chiefs and financial officers. Communities also lost time in constant tinkering with group membership lists and work schedules, which, as one Wisconsin Phalanx leader complained, were "complicated, and could never be satisfactorily arranged." NAP members were so absorbed in debating work series, according to Sears, that "our days were spent in labor and our nights in legislation, for the first five years of our associate life."[46]

Making labor attractive was a challenge that some phalanxes met successfully. All those evening meetings at the NAP evidently paid off, for on its modest scale, according to spokesmen, the community "established firmly the Right of Labor . . . [to] constant employment with a fair remuneration, . . . abolished the servile character of labor, and the servile relation of employer and employed," and permitted each member to do "that which he is best qualified by endowment to do, receiving for his labor precisely his share of the product as nearly as it can be ascertained."

Charles Dana, proclaiming Brook Farm a practical success after only two years of Fourierism, was more succinct: "We have established justice to the laborer, and ennobled industry."[47] In this case, rosy public pronouncements were seconded by members' reminiscences. Alcander Longley, who served as a beekeeper, printer, and farmhand at the NAP, recalled that "we could always find something to do, which is not always the case with mechanics and other laborers [in the isolated system] . . . in bad weather, or when they are out of a job." Though farm work was strenuous, "as there were a half dozen of us at it, and I had opportunity to talk with them, the time past [*sic*] pleasantly." Shifting jobs as phalanx business required, Longley "got to be 'jack of all trades' and perhaps master of two or three; at any rate this variety of occupation and associating with different persons in labor . . . added very much to my satisfaction." According to another NAP member, work in teams fostered such an esprit de corps that "in many cases, the work seemed turned into merry making." Visitors reported that phalanx arrangements dignified labor and promoted egalitarianism, since "no activity of any sort draws upon itself scorn, and none is regarded by members as either better or worse."[48]

Nevertheless, the effectiveness of the Fourierist labor system was compromised by inequality in workloads and compensation. For Fourier, the notion that some Harmonians would work less than others demonstrated true passional freedom; life in the American phalanxes, however, required hard work and self-sacrifice. As their communities struggled through indebtedness, chronic shortages, and crop failures, Associationists found themselves undermined by their own propaganda. Promises of security and quick wealth attracted many members who regarded Fourier as "the Messiah of bread buttered on both sides, and of rest earned . . . without labor."[49] The phalanxes never solved the problem of what do to about those who did not assume their share of the work. Fourier was confident that sloppy or disruptive workers could be disciplined through "exclusion from honors," but Marianne Dwight recorded the failure of one such attempt at Brook Farm:

> Yesterday Mr. List and Mr. Reynolds were unanimously expelled from the carpenter's group in consequence of their being discordant elements,—so they went to the general direction requesting to be furnished with work, and that body have set them to work upon the frame of the Phalanstery,—so they are working right in the midst of the group, but not of the group, doing just what they are told to do,—a sort of solitary labor and imprisonment. . . . The group who thought to get rid of their company are foiled in that.[50]

Shunning was too weak a punishment for those who should have been expelled or initially screened out. Loose admissions practices and rarely used expulsion policies made the problem of selfish or lazy members increasingly serious. In theory, the communities' guarantees were limited to full-time workers, but rarely were minimum hours enforced. Given their commitment to occupational freedom, Fourierists frankly admitted there was little they could do about members who preferred to work just enough to meet expenses and no more.[51] In a few communities such loafers poisoned the atmosphere; where they were less prominent, they still caused constant grumbling.

When members worked diligently, the Fourierist compensation system also created hard feelings. Longley noted that the scheme of individual credits "tended to make them count every minute of labor and every cent of charges, and to be continually on the lookout to get their share." Keeping economic interests separate promoted rather than discouraged the selfishness of individualist capitalism.[52] Attractive labor was compromised by its accommodation to inequality as well as to private property. Fourierist ideology assumed that phalanx members could earn differential rewards without feeling resentment; in fact, workers found them disturbing. In addition to the dividend to skill already cited, two provisions caused conflict: the generous allotment to capital and low pay to community artisans. Wisconsin and North American spokesmen considered their dividend of one-fourth the year's output to shareholders "too large and disproportionate." In these thriving communities, large shareholders in residence accrued substantial sums through the property's rise in value; their dividend on capital as well as on labor amounted to a double payment. The division between residents and nonresidents resulted in an even worse gap. Members who left the Wisconsin Phalanx often retained their stock; as the percentage of shares owned by nonresidents became higher, residents increasingly resented the siphoning off of their product to those who had quit. Workers at these communities did at least receive a healthy annual dividend; hard-working members of other phalanxes complained bitterly that investors received the first and in many cases the only share of a meager annual profit.[53]

Phalanxes usually gave craftwork and farmwork the same rank on the scale from "necessary" to "attractive" labor and hence the same pay. Fierce disputes arose at the Wisconsin, Alphadelphia, and North American communities when artisans protested that their skilled work merited higher rewards than farm labor, as was the case outside the phalanx. Mechanics sometimes hired themselves out in nearby towns in order to supplement their income. Opponents countered that farm labor and domestic work were undervalued in Civilization, a wrong it was the duty of Associationists to redress. At all three communities nonartisan members supported existing remuneration scales and pushed through resolutions outlawing prolonged absences without permission. But it was a Pyrrhic victory: the phalanxes suffered such severe shortages of mechanics as a result that they were forced to cut production from mills and workshops and ironically (in the North American's case) hire outside artisans at market wages.[54]

Despite such tensions and conflicts, in phalanxes making a genuine attempt to enact Fourierist principles, the transition to attractive industry was worthwhile and partially successful. Even Dana, looking back from his old age, exempted Brook Farm work arrangements from what had become his customary cynicism: "Each person chose what he wished to do, what groups he would work in, and none . . . tried to shirk. There was more entertainment in doing the duty than in getting away from it." When the groups and series functioned well, there was camaraderie, even joy, in work and a feeling of fairness in rewards. In his post-utopian phase Marx mocked Fourier's belief that work could be made an "amusement," but at their best the American phalanxes proved him wrong.[55]

"The Hive" versus "the Nest": Sex, Marriage, and Family

"The slight allusion in all the writers of the 'Phalansterian' class, to the subject of marriage, is rather remarkable," complained the Englishman Charles Lane, who was living with the Shakers at the time. "They are acute and eloquent in deploring Woman's oppressed and degraded position in past and present times, but are almost silent as to the future."[56] *The Harbinger* echoed Fourier's criticisms of the bourgeois family, but most Associationist writers confined their disapproval to the "isolated house-hold" without extending it to traditional relations between the sexes. Phalanx leaders were even more conservative. Aware of the fate of the Owenites, they dreaded the effect of bad publicity if communities tampered with the conjugal bond. Charles Sears spoke for most when he described the North American Phalanx's hands-off policy: "What the true law of relationship of the sexes is, we don't pretend to determine." The Columbian Phalanx went so far as to expel a leader who had "spoken of civilized marriages very disrepectfully," something the Fourierists' own national lecturers were guilty of.[57]

Associationists could not fully escape the radical implications of Fourier's psychology. As long as they professed that full Association guaranteed passional freedom, they not only invited attacks from angry conservatives but attracted unconventional characters to their phalanxes. The dynamics of communal life and the demographics of membership weakened the walls protecting the isolated home: the phalanxes' jumbling of families in close quarters and their enlistment of many unmarried adults began some movement away from Victorian ideals. Contacts between the sexes were more frequent and informal, family feeling was modestly redirected to the group, and inroads were made upon the privatism of the nuclear family. But even limited changes met with resistance from the upholders of traditional mores—the majority in most phalanxes.[58]

Because Brook Farm originated from a private quest for ethical social relationships rather than national reform agitation, it diverged further from convention than any other phalanx. George Ripley's vision of "a society of liberal, intelligent, and cultivated persons" living "a more simple and wholesome life" than their contemporaries took shape in an atmosphere of freedom, informality, and experiment.[59] Even in its Fourierist phase, when families were actively recruited, Brook Farm was predominantly a singles community. The median age of entry was in the mid-twenties; two-thirds of entering men and over two-fifths of entering women were unmarried. Inevitably, rumors circulated among outsiders about sexual freedom at the farm. A friend asked the Fourierist Henry James how much "concubinage" was going on; and Emerson, seeking to clear "the mists which gossip has made," sought reassurance from community member George Bradford, who told him that "plain dealing was the best defense of manners & morals between the sexes." Actually, Brook Farmers were careful to avoid impropriety. In 1843 one man and woman who may have engaged in sexual misconduct—they were later married—were abruptly asked to leave the community. Members also refused to admit the daughter of controversial sex reformer Mary Gove as a student, both because of the publicity her presence might have generated and because Gove offered to pay tuition by giving lectures on the grounds.[60]

But "plain dealing" meant relations between men and women free of many formalities and restraints expected in Puritan New England. Reminiscences of Brook Farm depict a pleasurable, lighthearted environment where friendships were easily made and social amusements almost constant. Marianne Dwight's letters, the best contemporary source on life at the community, describe how young persons engaged in impromptu parties, frequent room visits, and walks in the evening moonlight. Such casual contacts gave Brook Farm a coed campus atmosphere otherwise unavailable in America of the 1840s. Members later recalled that it promoted healthy friendships across gender lines, free of the sexual tensions of Victorian adolescence. But Dwight's letters indicate that male-female interchange, however frequent and casual, was still governed by sentimental conventions and produced a constant buzz of gossip, flirting, courting, petty jealousies, intrigues, and heartbreaks. Charles Dana jokingly suggested that among Fourierist groups at Brook Farm a "rejected lover's sympathising group" be formed; there were enough successful suitors, however, that Lindsay Swift counted fourteen marriages directly traceable to friendships initiated at the village. Dwight's breathless gossip shows that while Brook Farm's reorganization into a phalanx may have regimented working arrangements and widened the class spectrum, it did not break up this youthful subculture of merry but mostly innocent "dissipation," as one member called it.[61]

As they witnessed the emergence of intensely privatized family life in Victorian America, antebellum communitarians tried to recreate the world they had lost—an integrated nexus of family, economy, and community—under new conditions. Their goal, according to Noyes, was the "enlargement of home—the extension of family union beyond the little

man-and-wife circle to large corporations."[62] The Associationists' indictment of impersonalized life in commercial society and their attack upon
the "isolated household" implied a similar reorientation of affection even
as they denied tampering with conventions. John Dwight, who defended
Fourierism against conservatives' charges, acknowledged that the nuclear
family would "fall somewhat into the background" as social life centered
increasingly on the community. At Brook Farm the high proportion of
unmarried members hastened this process and enabled the phalanx to
seem like an extended family. Without conjugal ties, affections could be
widely shared, and even in communities where single persons did not
predominate, they often viewed fellow members as an adopted family.
Unmarried members who roomed with families began to seem related;
those who lived in bachelor quarters or dormitory-style barracks formed
close brotherly or sisterly bonds. Twenty-year-old Harriot Haven enjoyed
both situations at the Wisconsin Phalanx. When she moved to St. Louis,
she felt she had "left a home," missed the "hospitality and warmheart-
edness" of the group, and could not "bear to be forgotten" by friends
who remained in Ceresco.[63]

Communities also served as surrogate families for widows, widowers,
and single parents, substituting a new homelike environment for older
community and kinship support networks eroded by urbanization and
migration. Isabella Town, a widow living in Milwaukee with two young
sons, joined the Wisconsin Phalanx believing it "an ideal place for bringing up fatherless boys." The phalanx's prohibition of liquor and profanity
and its schools would surround the children with good influences, while
adults living in fraternity would provide good role models.[64] Married
women such as Almira Barlow of Brook Farm found the communities
safe retreats from estranged husbands. In the three phalanxes for which
kinship evidence can be gathered—Brook Farm, the NAP, and the Wisconsin Phalanx—at least seventeen families broken by death or separation reconstructed their lives communally.

To a certain extent, kinship ties linked single and married Fourierists
together. At Brook Farm and the NAP, thirteen unmarried adults were
the children or siblings of other adult members, and several more were
cousins. Members took in elderly sisters or recruited younger brothers or
sisters who needed work or were looking for a home. Like contemporary
factory workers and immigrants, community families established chain
migrations and relied on each other for emotional and economic support
in a society in which impersonal institutions such as banks and corporations grew powerful and families were increasingly dispersed. By their
own migration to phalanxes, Fourierist kin thus both reflected industrial
capitalist trends and resisted them.[65]

Yet there were undeniable differences between families and single
members in the phalanxes, and limits to how far family feeling extended
to the whole community. Even as the communitarian movement got
under way, Charles Lane wondered "whether the existence of the marital

family is compatible with the universal family, which the term 'Community' signifies." Professing doubt that "the affections can be . . . bent with equal ardor, on two objects, so opposed as universal and individual love," Lane challenged Associationists to prove otherwise.[66] Brook Farm and to the lesser extent the North American Phalanx, with their high proportion of single persons, were not fair tests. But conventional families formed the core of the other phalanxes, especially western ones; reports from these groups counted residents by number of families more often than by individuals. The Wisconsin and Alphadelphia communities boasted over three dozen young families averaging two or more children each. Aggregate figures for communities other than Brook Farm and the NAP show that at any one time, between 47 and 64 percent of the resident adult males were married and 75 to 86 percent of adult females (see Appendix Tables 7 and 8). Phalanx officers were usually married, and married Fourierists tended to stay in the communities longer than single members. Phalanx admissions committees explicitly preferred parents, considering them good investors and likely permanent members.

As Lane predicted, however, it was often difficult for couples to consider the phalanx a home and fellow Associationists a family. Conventional nuclear families brought expectations and practices that jarred with communal life. Married women left behind with regret the domestic ideal of what Lane called "the separate fire-side." Warren Chase, for example, reported that his wife opposed moving to the Wisconsin Phalanx. Never a convert to Fourierism, she "gently remonstrated, and then gave up, as she thought a true wife ought to do," ruefully predicting that "we shall not get a home of our own again." Mary Chase's suppressed opposition resurfaced as physical illness: soon after arrival at the phalanx she became "feeble and emaciated" and could recover only through a long stay at her parental homestead in New England.[67]

Once on the domain, families faced a difficult adjustment to "unitary living"; in some cases there was overt resistance. Sylvania Association families, herded together in ramshackle barracks, bickered over "the right to procure for their children all the little indulgences they had been used to." The tie between mother and child that "circumscribes her desire and ambitions to her own immediate family"—whether biologically formed, as Lane believed, or the product of competitive society, as Associationists professed—asserted itself aggressively when survival was at stake. Reviewing the communal squalor of many phalanx beginnings, the Integral Phalanx later concluded that "it is better that the different families should remain separate for five years, than to bring them together under circumstances worse than Civilization."[68]

Even when phalanxes prospered, there was tension over communal living. Some members could not stand the lack of privacy. In the Alphadelphia "mansion" the schoolteacher's fiddling drove another member to complain in doggerel:

> Oh Allen, oh, Allen, how you do torture me,
> Surely you'll kill me as dead as a stone;
> All the while sawing, and rasping, and scraping me,
> Surely you'll scrape all the flesh from my bones.[69]

And Nathan C. Meeker, who lived on the crowded Trumbull domain, left a graphic portrait of one husband's exasperation:

> The rooms where families lived adjoined each other, or were divided by long halls. Young men did not always go to bed early. Perhaps they would be out late sparking, and they returned to their rooms before morning. A man was apt to call to mind the words of the country mouse lamenting that he had left his hollow tree. Sometimes one had a few words to say to his wife when he was not in good humor on account of bad digestion. When some one overheard him, they would . . . keep silent; while others thought that they had a good thing to tell of.[70]

Most phalanxes took over settled farms with several buildings into which members arranged themselves, usually separating families from single members. Conflict arose over plans to concentrate members into phalansteries. At the Wisconsin Phalanx, although unmarried residents zealously promoted Fourier's "unitary plan," several families preferred separate living and dining. When a small majority decided to build a phalanstery, some families refused to submit and continued to live and eat in separate dwellings. Even a few families in the phalanx's Long House prepared and ate meals in their rooms, despite the lack of cooking facilities. Warren Chase explained that such families wanted to control their diets, ask a blessing, oversee their children, or otherwise continue fixed "habits of living." The dual system of boarding generated controversy for several years, and Chase later called it "the apple of discord" that broke up the phalanx.[71] The North American Phalanx presented a similar spectacle of a large central phalanstery surrounded by small family cottages, although the cottages were fewer and without kitchens. Even this compromise was achieved over the objection of some members. Marcia Hammond, a feminist who had come from the Hopedale community, told A. J. Macdonald that "the single-cottage system was wrong, and that woman would never attain her true position in such circumstances."[72]

Like the NAP, most phalanxes found a workable solution in erecting a phalanstery but also offering the option of separate cottages for families—though such a transitional expedient belied the Fourierist critique of isolated households and undermined attempts to make the community a larger family. At Brook Farm, Amelia Russell remembered that an uneasy tension existed between the Hive, the large farmhouse where most members lived, and the Nest, the school cottage at one time inhabited by a family with small children: "It was a pleasant little place, but somehow those who lived there seemed in a degree separated from us, living more by themselves, more like a separate family who visited us as neighbors, and even in that way seldom joining us in our social meetings."[73]

Single phalanx members were not immune to the "nest" syndrome of Civilization. Though they enjoyed the casual camaraderie of communal living they felt a lack of privacy once they were part of an "exclusive alliance." In March 1846 Charles Dana and Eunice Macdaniel, around whom gossip had been raging for months, were secretly married away from Brook Farm. Dana uneasily explained that Eunice's "private movements" required her to be in New York, but George Ripley and other Brook Farmers were troubled by the couple's secrecy—less because it invited nasty speculation than for its violation of the community's tacit right to mark important milestones of members' lives. When the crunch came, Dana—who had criticized Civilization for encouraging family selfishness—apparently preferred private love to associative ideals. His elopement marked him in the eyes of Marianne Dwight as one "who probably will not stop here long." The transfer of allegiance was accentuated by the fact that while he was in New York, Brook Farm's phalanstery burned down, an event that knit witnesses together in their determination to survive.[74]

Dana's awkward escape was only a halfway solution. In their quest for a private utopia, many new phalanx couples left communal life entirely behind. Without an institution like Mormon polygamy or Oneida's "complex marriage" to channel sexual urges to the community as a whole, or at least some special leadership role for families, the phalanxes allowed sentimental and exclusive relationships to disrupt communal life. Young men and women tended to pair off in permanent alliances, then leave the community to start a family homestead. Of the fifteen couples married at the Wisconsin Phalanx, eight left within a few months, and those who stayed built nearly equivalent barriers between themselves and former intimates. Isabella Town married Nathan Hunter in 1845; though the newlyweds initially used the common diningroom Town later recalled that "after our first child was born we had our own private table, and in 1848 moved to our own little home, some three-quarters of a mile away from the phalanx buildings." From "brothers and sisters" with other community members, they had evolved to neighbors.[75]

The gulf between single and married phalanx members was widened by economic pressures. According to complaints in community minutes and members' reminiscences, phalanx families found it especially difficult to meet expenses. Normally given only a partial subsidy for children's clothing and board, parents had to cover the remainder with the same meager "wage" that single persons earned. At the North American Phalanx the issue of raising the "social minimum" for children caused a heated debate, never fully resolved, over the division of responsibility between community and family. Parents, complaining that "with large families and small wages they could not hold their own," expected communal support.[76] On the other side, disillusioned phalanx veterans charged that communities had "too many children" or "too many large families."[77] The actual evidence is mixed. NAP families were somewhat smaller than the national average, and the large number of single adults made children quite a low percentage of the population. At Wisconsin and Alphadelphia there were fewer unmarried adults and more children, particularly young ones, and rough fertility ratios were significantly higher than the national average (see Appendix Table 8). In both cases the results were similar: where children were relatively rare, they were perceived as economic burdens for phalanx parents; where they were numerous, as disastrous sponges on the community. The hardship of building communal life from scratch under poor financial and physical conditions left little surplus to distribute among nonproducers. Especially in the first stages of Associative life, one communal veteran harshly concluded, "the less children the better."[78]

There was a special poignancy in the emotional and economic plight of phalanx families. Married men and women joined Fourierist communities in part because they were assured by promises that cooperative living would bring economic and social advantages without disrupting conventional family arrangements. With their growing families and settled occupations they usually risked more than single members by joining, and they proved to be the most persevering phalanx residents. Yet most married adults found even the limited reforms of "unitary living" too drastic; in practical terms their community lives were more difficult than those of single members and their children an economic liability. Some unmarried members, meanwhile, felt that allowing individual houses and kitchens was selling out to Civilization. On this issue as on others the Associationists, hoping to accommodate all shades of opinion with their gradualist socialism, struck an awkward compromise that satisfied few.

The Status of Women in Phalanxes

It followed from the phalanxes' limited inroads upon family life that gains for community women, though real, were circumscribed by strategic and cultural conservatism. The best way to illustrate the balance sheet is to bring to light the lives of three phalanx women among the few who left records of their experiences.

Family lore—not a reliable source—later had it that Charlotte Haven, a girl of nineteen from New Hampshire, was present in 1840 at the Transcendental Club meeting where George Ripley announced his communal plans. More likely, Charlotte intended to join Brook Farm and was disappointed when the fire curtailed its expansion. During a western trip in the mid-1840s, which included a visit to the Mormon city of Nauvoo, Illinois, Charlotte fell in love with the less restrictive life of pioneer country. In February 1848 she applied for membership in the Wisconsin Phalanx; seven months later, at age twenty-seven, she came to

Ceresco with her eighteen-year-old sister Harriot. They attended community lectures and debates on Fourierism, but mainly their tasks were the social and domestic ones usually reserved for phalanx women. Both belonged to a committee that arranged visitors' accommodations for bi-weekly community dances; otherwise, they kept busy doing laundry, cooking, sewing sacks for community grain, teaching in the school, and caring for phalanx children. Despite their mother's claim that they could earn better wages in New Hampshire and their sister's invitation to teach in St. Louis, Charlotte and Harriot refused to leave "as long as Ceresco offers so many charms."

The fact was that they relished the easy socializing with young men and women at the phalanx. The sisters' room in the crowded Long House made up for its discomfort with the convenience of entertaining new friends. "We have had visitors every evening since we had a room," Charlotte exulted. Boredom and loneliness were impossible, according to Harriot, because "by opening either door we can see and talk to as many people as we care to." They played music, chess, and cards with community men and took almost daily walks on community grounds with mixed groups of unmarried friends. The merry socializing continued when the sisters moved into their own cottage; "old bachelors" visited in the evenings or chatted with them while they sewed. In February 1850, as the community was breaking up, Charlotte married the most persistent of her gentleman callers; they immediately set out for a cottage on government land in nearby Fox River. In the first ten days she had but one visitor: "I anticipate a very peaceful life and I fear my letters henceforth will be void of interest," she told her sister a bit uneasily. Harriot was more pointed; she predicted that in her "isolated" family Charlotte would "miss the noise and excitement after Association and will feel rather lonely some of these fine days."[79]

Just as independent as the Havens but more serious, Mary Paul found economic benefits in Associative life. Determined to earn good money while single, Paul left her family home in Vermont at age fifteen to become a domestic, then labored in the Lowell mills for four years before taking a job as a seamstress. In the Boston area she befriended several Associationists—including Carrie Livingston, who had lived briefly at Brook Farm—and concluded that "their principles are just what I would like to see carried into practice." When Carrie and her husband decided to try out the North American Phalanx, Mary joined them, despite the added distance it put between her and her ailing father. As she explained in seeking his approval, "I can get better pay without working as hard as at any other place. . . . besides I should not be confined to one kind of work but could do almost anything, . . . *Housework* if I choose and that without degrading myself, which is more than I could do anywhere else." At the phalanx it was "different": "*All* work there, and all are paid alike. . . . One can join them with or without funds, and can leave at any time they choose." Given her father's blessing, Paul moved to the phalanx in

May 1854. Her initiation was somewhat disorienting—though the people were pleasant, she had to get used to their "strange ways" and especially the public meals—but the community met her highest expectations. The workday at Lowell had been twelve hours; at the phalanx she could live easily on six, and the work was better for her health than tending spindles or sewing. Unfortunately, the NAP's mill burned down shortly after she joined, and the community began to disband. But Mary stayed to the very end sixteen months later, convinced that Association offered "attractions & advantages which no other life can have." She defended Fourier's theory against her father's criticisms and departed "as strong in the faith as ever."[80]

Married women—the overwhelming majority of phalanx females—might have told a different story. Lizzie Curson, a twenty-three-year-old daughter of a miller from Newburyport, Massachusetts, visited Brook Farm in September 1845 and came to stay three months later. Gracious, charming, and traditionally domestic, Lizzie took little part in community meetings but instead devoted herself to mending, caring for the sick, ironing, doing laundry, and heading the Dormitory Group, which arranged accommodations for Brook Farm's many visitors. Marianne Dwight, who quickly befriended Curson, classified her not as a leader but one who "love[s] the life here"; in fact, Lizzie was among the last to leave the grounds in the spring of 1847. Sometime after Brook Farm closed down, Lizzie married John Hoxie, one of the community's carpenters; and by the time they joined the Raritan Bay Union in New Jersey in the fall of 1853, they had three children. Her world at Brook Farm had been a carefree jumble of single persons; now, as a wife and parent at Raritan Bay, she confided to her mother that "the associating of families" was "a very uncomfortable style" of life. Their rooms were too small, and communal child rearing was not working because of a shortage of women in the domestic series. Her husband was unable to find work profitable enough to sustain the family. Most of all, her time was consumed by the children, cooking, community chores, and caring for the sick. Domestic drudgery was made harder to bear by watching the wealthier families of the community hire servants to cook and wash. Though she cared "a great deal" about Fourier, she could not attend the annual Associationist celebration at the nearby North American Phalanx or participate in Raritan Bay's election-day rituals because of chores and the children. She was sorry when economic need forced them to leave the community in March 1855, but her feeling was regret for abandoning the principle of Association more than nostalgia for any personal "advantages" of communal life.[81]

The Haven sisters' busy socializing, Mary Paul's economic independence, and Lizzie Curson's wifely drudgery suggest the range of phalanx women's experience; their limited sphere of work and separation from community decisionmaking indicate its boundaries. Simply joining communal experiments showed a measure of independence. Paul felt guilty

about leaving her widowed father behind but insisted upon better working conditions. The Havens stayed at Wisconsin despite their siblings'
nagging pleas to leave. Even Lizzie Curson had to face down the disapproval of a mother who neither cared for nor understood her devotion
to Fourierism.[82] Other young women who wanted to join phalanxes, such
as Marianne's Dwight's friend Anna Parsons, were prevented by parental
opposition.

Yet if this assertive spirit continued after women joined, it found
limited outlets. The phalanxes' disorganized and rudimentary economic
conditions made survival rather than social experimentation the highest
priority. More important, most Fourierists harbored profoundly ambivalent attitudes about the role of women in Association, arguing on the one
hand that emancipation left phalanx women free to work, to own, and
to legislate; assuming on the other that women's passional attraction
would lead them into domestic labors, festive celebrations, child rearing,
and religious ceremonies. Rather than consistently questioning paternalistic notions of woman's sphere, Associationists simply envisioned a
broader field for feminine influence than the isolated household. Their
emphasis on community was meant to achieve, perhaps to recover, a
wider and more fulfilling context for domestic life in a fragmented
society. The phalanx would be the communal "home" of the future and
women its guardians. Their liberation would come by elevating and
beautifying the new society.[83]

The transport of such cultural baggage into the utopian future should
not be surprising. Even the antebellum communitarian groups that devised alternatives to sexual conventions were similarly ambivalent. Mormons, Shakers, and Oneidans who rejected sentimental love and the
small nuclear family still voiced typical stereotypes about women and
often institutionalized new forms of male domination.[84] The Associationists' arrangements may well have been less oppressive than those
of their celebrated communal contemporaries. Because the Fourierists
enacted no systematic alternative in sex and family roles, there was some
flexibility in women's position, depending on time and community. And
since women's limited gains occurred in arrangements closer to conventional society, the forms they took were more attractive to contemporary
feminists.

Nevertheless, almost every improvement in women's condition came
with important qualifiers. Women could and did, for example, independently own stock in Fourierist communities. This not only gave them the
right to yearly dividends but, in the case of the Wisconsin Phalanx,
resulted in a substantial acquisition of property when the community
disbanded. Property ownership put phalanx women ahead of contemporary society, where married women's rights were subsumed by their
husbands until 1848, when New York passed the first law giving them
control over property brought into marriage.[85] But patterns of shareholding for the three phalanxes whose records are extant show that women

owned only a small percentage of the communities' stock, 12 percent at the North American Phalanx being the largest. Women shareholders were usually wives of male leaders or else widows; the former owned far fewer shares than their husbands, and in neither case did any female stockholders emerge as powerful policymaking voices.

Voting rights, another traditional locus of male power, varied by community. At the Social Reform Unity women actually had greater rights than men: political participation was determined by entry into the formal workforce, and women began communal labors at age eighteen, men at twenty. At most Fourierist communities women were given the vote on equal terms with men. One Brook Farmer recalled that in community meetings "a proposition could be put, discussed, and voted on, with entire freedom, by women and men alike."[86] Nevertheless, through an unequal application of voting privileges and a Fourierist version of a property requirement, women at many phalanxes found themselves excluded from key community decisions. Wisconsin's bylaws stipulated that only males could vote on expulsion of members; Alphadelphia and the Jefferson Industrial Association prohibited female voting on certain business matters. Most communities made stock ownership a prerequisite for voting at their important annual meetings, a restriction that worked against women. And even female stockholders in the Wisconsin Phalanx could not vote at annual meetings: to ease passage of the community's incorporation law, the phalanx, like the Wisconsin Territory, restricted suffrage to males over twenty-one.[87]

In part because of such voting restrictions, at many phalanxes women held no elected positions. The Wisconsin Phalanx had no female officers in its six years of existence, though women were named to committees relating to kitchen and domestic work. At Brook Farm and the North American Phalanx, which attracted more unmarried and outspoken women, there was more involvement in community politics. At various times Brook Farm women supervised the community's school and domestic series, and they participated in frequent discussions about the community's future. Several female Brook Farmers also attended Fourierist and labor movement gatherings in the Boston area, though they apparently refrained from speaking.[88] Until 1848 the NAP had no women on its numerous committees, but the new constitution of that year gave a more prominent role to the chiefs of the series, and women began to take places on both the Industrial and Executive councils.[89] What was true at the NAP held throughout the movement: as communities expanded and adopted Brisbane's organizational plan in which work leaders formed a "council of industry" they became more likely to have women officers. But all the phalanxes' highest offices—president, vice-president, treasurer, secretary—were held by men.

Voting restrictions only partly explain the dearth of female officers. NAP women bemoaned the lack of a "natural leader" among themselves, and as Brook Farm faced the crisis of its fire, Marianne Dwight wondered:

"Where are the ladies? Where is the *one* . . . around whom might be a rallying?"[90] The Fourierists' most talented and outspoken female friends—Margaret Fuller, Mary Gove, and Elizabeth Cady Stanton—were unwilling to commit themselves to a communitarian experiment, and without such leadership the phalanx women lacked the confidence and experience to play active public roles. An even more important factor was the women's constant immersion in work. Like Lizzie Curson, Fourierist women swamped by domestic duties could find little time for meetings and debates. Lydia Arnold, the NAP president's wife, told Fredrika Bremer that the community's women "had so much to do" with the children and domestic chores that they "troubled [themselves] very little" with community politics. And Gertrude Sears defended the lack of feminist initiative at the NAP by citing "exhausting labor" and consequently "a long arrear of unfulfilled family and personal obligations."[91] Women's status in the phalanxes, then, was held down by the conflict between emancipation and domesticity, between feminist aspirations and the rudimentary conditions of struggling communal ventures.

The fact was that the phalanxes' division of labor paralleled the patterns and inequalities outside the communities. Though phalanx women enjoyed some of the occupational choice that Mary Paul expected, the tasks among which they alternated were the traditional domestic activities of food preparation, cleaning, laundry, sewing, and child rearing. Paul's own account for 1854–55 shows that 92 percent of her earnings came from the "domestic serie," with the remainder comprising "manufacturing" work (probably assisting at the gristmill) and a little teaching and gardening.[92] A roster of the NAP's series in 1848 indicates that only five phalanx women spent worktime outside the domestic series, three in canning fruits and vegetables and two doing dairy work. Men and women did share some tasks on the margins of the domestic role. A few men cooked and washed clothes alongside women, and some waited on tables. Wisconsin Fourierists appointed a committee of three females and three males to aid the sick and bury the dead, though one suspects a division of labor by gender even here.[93] Education was a third area where responsibility was shared. Women dominated the infant and primary levels at most community schools; men taught the more advanced curriculum. Only Brook Farm was an exception: there Marianne Dwight and Sophia Ripley joined male instructors of classical and literary subjects at the college prep level, and Mrs. Ripley and her sister-in-law Marianne Ripley were at various times in charge of the entire school. Variations in the sexual division of labor were not only infrequent but consistent with conventional antebellum conceptions of women's aptitudes and sphere. Indeed, at Brook Farm the conversion to Fourierism served to straitjacket women's roles. During the Transcendentalist phase, gender lines had been informal and relatively loose; once reorganized under the Fourierist aegis, they reflected the Associationists' systematization of stereotypes. John Dwight, full of bookish Fourierist educational theory, succeeded

Marianne Ripley as director of education in January 1845. And the new constitution of that month enacted Fourier's recommendation of a female-dominated Council of Arbiters, which decided cases of "morals and manners."[94]

Female work in most phalanxes was also relatively underpaid. The Sylvania constitution declared flatly that "women shall receive five-eighths the wages of men"; the Jefferson Association's fixed the maximum wage for women at the minimum for men. Even at the North American Phalanx, where Mary Paul exulted that members were paid strictly according to their work, residents in 1843 set an average rate of compensation of 75 cents a day for males and 50 cents for females, a ratio roughly adhered to for almost five years. The most detailed codification of gender inequality appeared in the report of a "Committee to Organize and Equalize Labor" of the Alphadelphia Association. Using eight hours of farmwork as the benchmark, the committee decided that for "male labor" six hours of carpentry or blacksmithing, seven hours of sawing, and eight hours of gardening and clerking equaled the standard; "female labor" required ten hours of weaving or tailoring, twelve hours of cooking, dressmaking, nursing, or dairy work, and sixteen hours of spinning. Among women's tasks only laundry work was paid equally with farming; in the one overlapping occupation, a man's six hours of teaching was deemed equal to a woman's ten.[95] With phalanxes needing to sell products in the outside market and leaders holding traditional stereotypes, domestic work was not considered as "productive" as farming or manufacturing, despite the Fourierists' nominal commitment to rank all work according to its intrinsic qualities.

To this overt discrimination, hidden inequalities were added. Mothers were expected to care for their children when the latter were ill or the community school or nursery was closed. Women were tacitly entrusted with the community's sick and disabled, whether family members or not. At most phalanxes neither of these kinds of work was credited as payable labor. Moreover, since there were more men than women (given the greater number of single males), Fourier's promised economies did not materialize, and women bore a proportionately greater burden of domestic work than in the "isolated family." "There are so many, and so few women to do the work that we have to be nearly all the time about it," Marianne Dwight complained to a correspondent. As Barbara Taylor has noted in connection with British Owenite communities, between the lopsided sex ratios, hordes of overnight visitors, and almost constant reorganizations, the utopians' New Moral World generated even more household drudgery for women than the Old Immoral World.[96]

Yet for all these burdens and the limitations in their role, phalanx women did achieve significant gains over their sisters in antebellum America. Voting rights and property ownership, however restricted, suggested new avenues for women's ambitions. One Brook Farm veteran recalled that voting at the community was her "first delightful experience of 'Woman's Rights.' . . . This new sense of power and responsibility widened my horizon, and included all the benefits I was prepared to take advantage of."[97] At the phalanxes as nowhere else, middle-class women could work outside their immediate household without losing social status. Day nurseries at Brook Farm and the NAP freed mothers to pursue gainful work. Simply to be paid for doing one's own housework was a small revolution that added to women's self-worth. The economic benefits were more tangible. Mary Paul proved her belief that at the North American Phalanx "a woman gets much better pay . . . than elsewhere": in a year she accumulated a surplus equal to several months' pay in the Lowell mills. Alphadelphia labor records reveal that even when paid less per hour than their husbands, several wives regularly outearned them. Most phalanxes did not last long enough for such a rebalance of economic forces to change gender attitudes noticeably. At the NAP, however, once women became accustomed to earning money for household work, they were emboldened to press for greater equality in wages, and in 1848 the Executive Council responded by appointing a committee of three men and three women which narrowed the pay differential between predominantly male and female work.[98]

In some cases, moreover, the kind of economic independence women enjoyed in the phalanx escalated to self-conscious feminism. As Brook Farm set up work groups in the summer of 1844, Marianne Dwight envisioned them as levers of economic autonomy for women. She organized a "fancy group" or sewing circle whose goal was avowedly feminist: "nothing less than the elevation of woman to independence, and an acknowledged equality with man." With the idea that women must "become producers of marketable articles" and earn their own support, Dwight and "a large part" of the Brook Farm women purchased materials to make caps, collars, and undersleeves, which were then sold on commission at a Boston clothier's. They hoped to attract new members to share Brook Farm's housework, thereby freeing their time to expand production to other articles, the proceeds to be applied to "the elevation of women forever." The "fancy group" flourished enough to diversify: in March 1845 a separate team was organized under Dwight's supervision to paint fans and lampshades. In the reorganization after the fire of March 1846, the community consolidated around the farm, school, and printshop. Sewing and painting were abandoned, but Dwight's efforts had laid the groundwork for later organization by Boston Fourierist women.[99]

As if to highlight their sense of independence and sisterhood, some women in the phalanxes wore the bloomer costume popular among antebellum feminists. Its short skirt, dropping two inches below the knee, and loose trousers gathered at the ankle retained modesty while permitting a much wider variety of physical activity than the full dresses featured in *Godey's Ladies Book*. Visitors noticed these outfits at Brook

Farm, the North American Phalanx, and the Raritan Bay Union, though the women were reluctant to wear them off the communities' grounds.[100]

Such steps toward independence, like other women's gains in the phalanxes, were halting and incomplete but nonetheless real. Though Charlotte Haven and Mary Paul soon married after leaving the communities, associative life stretched the interlude between the parental home and their own parenthood and gave them a taste of independence they were unlikely to forget. And though the association of families did not relieve domestic drudgery, work in groups made it easier to bear. Phalanx "sisterhood" was real, but for most community women it was far less a group assertion of rights than a brief idyll of intense friendships and shared domesticity. What they communicated in letters to outsiders and remembered most vividly years later were the happy times of work, play, and talk with community friends, especially other women. Julia Bucklin Giles, a teenager at the North American Phalanx, savored the times "when on hot summer mornings the farmers brought in baskets of peas to be shelled, groups of women and children would gather around the porch by the kitchen door . . . joining in the shelling, and the singing of the sweet old songs that always accompanied such gatherings." Isabella Town of the Wisconsin Phalanx told an interviewer that her "friendships of those days have lasted through all the years."[101] Work groups, communal housing, and social equality, along with the traditional separation of "spheres," encouraged close friendships and other expressions of sisterhood.

Fredrika Bremer told the intriguing story of a young woman "without beauty, but with a lofty, intellectual forehead," who found in such companionship at the North American Phalanx a cure for her victimization by society. Having been driven nearly insane by poverty, poor health, and male oppression, she was received warmly by phalanx women and became a devoted member of the gardening group and a "universal favorite."[102] A feminist today might see in this progression the insidious reprogramming of a social rebel, but that would miss the point. In the Associationists' world view the emancipation of women was joined to the goal of "feminizing" society, creating a nurturing and cooperative atmosphere—without disturbing conventional sex roles—in which women's innate "attractions" found their "destiny" by beautifying and purifying everyday life. The community was the household writ large, where the mothers and daughters infused social relations with cheerfulness and love. Phalanx women's roles and expectations were shaped by domesticity even as they enlarged its frame.

Creating a Communitarian Culture

Like most utopian planners, Fourier believed that cultural atavisms such as the domesticity ideal would quickly disappear under new social arrangements. This process would be especially swift among children, who were less corrupted by Civilization than adults and constituted the first generation raised in the phalanx. Education was central to Fourier's scheme—not in the sense of schools and books aimed at intellectual achievement but rather as plans for communal nurseries, children's series, theatrical performances, miniature workshops, and other means of integrating the youth of Harmony into a new way of life.

Educational reform was a principal aim of at least one American phalanx. Brook Farm began its life as an "Institute of Agriculture and Education," and by the time the community joined the Fourierist movement, its school had become a celebrated center whose new teaching methods and varied curriculum drew the children of wealthy New Englanders and reform-minded parents of other regions. When Brook Farmers read expositions of Fourier's scheme, they found rough confirmation of the system they were already developing. From Fourier's principles John Dwight deduced a three-stage educational process leading toward full communal participation. Infancy, from birth to six years, was the period of "influences," when maternal caretakers and a stimulating environment in the nursery would awaken the child's mind. A period of "pupilage" from age six to ten or twelve would be devoted to increasingly independent "exercises." In the mornings youths would learn concretely in phalanx work groups; in the afternoon they would practice the arts and study rigorous academic subjects. Finally, during a four-year "probation" teeenagers were to participate as full phalanx residents until formally joining the community as adults. Dwight's first two stages corresponded to Brook Farm's infant and primary school departments. The third was simply a future hope; in its place appeared a far more conventional college preparatory course that gave Brook Farm its fine reputation, attracted students from as far away as Louisiana, and helped keep the community financially alive.[103]

It is clear, then, that Fourierism cannot take the main credit for Brook Farm's educational achievements. The school's most successful division diverged furthest from the Fourierist blueprint, and after the community embraced Association, its school was increasingly overshadowed by the expanding farm and handicraft industries. But Fourierism, interpreted in line with the Brook Farmers' Transcendentalist aims, reinforced the community's determination to combine book learning with practical training; even the college prep course put students to work in the fields and workshops. The school endorsed the ideal of teaching through "friendly counsel and assistance . . . without the constraints of arbitrary discipline." Under the Fourierist regime, lessons in music, painting, drawing, and dancing were expanded to bring out pupils' full passional palette. And in keeping with the Fourierist goal of communal child rearing and female independence, Brook Farm's nursery was reorganized more rigorously when the community adopted Associationism.[104]

The Fourierist ideal of "integral education" more directly inspired arrangements at the North American Phalanx. Under the direction of the physician Emile Guillaudeu, the community's education department expanded gradually from a crude one-room affair to a series that enrolled several teachers and sorted out children into separate age groups. Infants were supervised by elderly women, children three to six were tutored in elementary subjects, and older children worked side by side with the phalanx's adults as they learned arithmetic and practical skills. There was also an evening school where working adults absorbed mathematics, music, and languages. The phalanx also achieved the Associationist goal of freeing parents from child care during the day; one visitor in 1846 found mothers especially pleased by this program. Nevertheless, well into the 1850s NAP members felt "the want of a school more in harmony with the [Associative] idea." Although Fourierist friends recommended more rigorous organization and training, community leaders pleaded lack of funds, and some parents were reluctant to cede more control over their children to the group. Whatever the reason, the slow development of its educational program was a major disappointment for the most prominent American showplace of Fourierist principles.[105]

Elsewhere in the movement there were faint echoes of Fourier's educational theory. Raritan Bay Union's founder, Marcus Spring, had been a Brook Farm stockholder; the community's schoolmaster, abolitionist Theodore Weld, though drawing his educational ideas from several sources, sympathized with Fourier's preference that students learn by doing and integrate their subjects with community life. At the Weld school, students learned farming and household skills as well as academic subjects, attended Sunday services and adult lectures, and in general used the entire community as their classroom. The Wisconsin and Trumbull communities supplemented normal schooling with "industrial education" so that boys could be initiated in manual skills, organized into work groups, and given credit for their hours. At Trumbull, one leading mother set up in the family apartment a nursery school believed to be the first in the Western Reserve.[106]

The overwhelming majority of phalanxes, however, established typical one-room schoolhouses with the standard rote curriculum; some of these became the local public schools to which outsiders sent their children. Fourier's educational theory did not circulate as readily among Associationists as his more immediately practical plans; where it was known, quality education required a commitment of members' time and resources that few communities could afford. Absorbed by the struggle to survive, American phalanxes did not have the luxury of creating a Fourierist superstructure.

Associationists came much closer to creating a distinctive communitarian culture in the convivial atmosphere and group rituals of their most successful communities. Fourier's Harmony was an intensely "festive society," as Henri Desroche calls it, with its long days devoted to culinary delights, celebration of work, and musical enjoyment and its nights enlivened by sexual escapades. In their choice to live fully by passional at-traction Harmonians would shatter the boundary between life and art. In much the same way that Harmonic education favored socialization over individual achievement, its artistic and cultural expressions were framed not in the romantic idiom of intense individualism but as part of community ritual. Fourier's phalanx culture would find unique expres-sion in grand parades of series to their fields of work, special fetes celebrating the arrival of visitors or the distribution of honors among members, frequent theatrical and operatic performances—and orgies arranged by the "Court of Love."[107]

American utopians, sidestepping Fourier's frank hedonism and sexual license, recast phalanx festivities in more congenial terms: aesthetic plea-sure, innocent "amusements," moral uplift, and social bonding. Within their limited means, however, many Associationists seemed as deter-mined as the Harmonians to enjoy themselves. The Brook Farmers were the liveliest: Lindsay Swift claimed that "enjoyment . . . formed a part of the curriculum and was a daily habit of life. . . . [Members] made happi-ness a duty, and their high courage held them to harmless fun when fainter souls would have drooped at the whisperings of evil days ahead." Among the many amusements revealed by letters and reminiscences were picnics and boating parties, formal and informal dances, concerts, reading clubs, debates, historical tableaux, and theatrical performances. When the gentle John Dwight first visited the community, he was over-whelmed: "How *fast* you live here; I *like* it, but really my head, my head suffers." To which one member replied that he "could not think of living in the old way again; it seemed like stagnation, vegetation."[108]

Other phalanxes could not approach this frenzied pace. Albert Bris-bane, constitutionally incapable of staying in one place more than a few days, complained that there was "no excitement" at the North American Phalanx; other visitors agreed that the phalanx "neglected the intellectual and aesthetic element."[109] In truth, the North American and most pha-lanxes that lasted more than a year or two tended to take on the provincial air of Yankee farming villages. Members read the *New York Tribune*, agricultural magazines and *Godey's Ladies Book,* and in a half-dozen com-munities produced their own struggling journals. In reporting their progress, they proudly totaled the newspapers and periodicals received and announced new libraries and reading rooms. Those who could play the violin or piano gave lessons or accompanied community choirs. Tem-perance and other reform society agents passed through to lecture and collect donations.

Still, the phalanxes attracted far more visitors than comparable farm settlements, generated more public events, and involved residents more readily in community affairs. Perhaps the sharpest contrast with their New England–bred neighbors was what one member called a "more free and lively enjoyment of society." Though they could not match Brook Farm's amenities, other phalanxes created a convivial atmosphere very much in the Fourierist spirit. One magazine correspondent observed the "animated and charming" after-supper scene at the North American Phalanx:

> Nearly the whole population of the place is out of doors. Happy papas and mamas draw their baby-wagons . . . along the wide walks; groups of little girls and boys frolic in the clover under the big walnut-trees by the side of the pond; some older children and young ladies are out on the water in their light canoes; . . . men and women are standing here and there in groups engaged in conversation, while others are reclining on the soft grass; and several young ladies in their picturesque working and walking costume . . . are strolling down the road toward the shaded avenue which leads to the highway.[110]

The NAP formed a festal series in 1849 which organized musical concerts, dancing, and theatricals; members even gave their fancy dress ball a Fourierist twist by having participants wear costumes representing the stages of history from Barbarism to Harmony.[111] What imparted special charm to life at Brook Farm and the North American and Wisconsin phalanxes was not programmed festivities as much as the impromptu get-togethers that seemed to happen daily: after-dinner walks in the woods, songs at the piano, card games and coffee parties in members' rooms.

Such casual gaiety was a refreshing contrast to the sobriety of evangelical reformers. To be sure, Associationists shared with antebellum contemporaries an affinity for moral purity and health reforms which pitted them against Fourier's hedonism. Many of the phalanxes, including Brook Farm, prohibited alchoholic beverages and provided separate vegetarian tables in their dining rooms. Members' letters contain references to cold baths, homeopathic treatments, and graham bread. Yet for Associationists this quest for healthful personal habits and "the simple life" remained distinct from such issues as dancing, church attendance, and rigid codes of sexual conduct. Like the freer atmosphere of the phalanxes, their penchant for health reforms represented a reaction against cultural straitjacketing in favor of more natural ways of living— a kind of utopian socialist counterculture poking at the boundaries of Victorian America.[112]

But if Fourierist principles gave phalanx life a relaxed and sociable flavor, they failed to create a distinctively Fourierist high culture. *The Harbinger* published pioneering musical criticism by John Dwight and attempted to establish a utopian socialist canon of authors: George Sand, Eugène Sue, Emmanuel Swedenborg. But Fourierist concerts, books, and periodicals featured few original creations, and phalanx life inspired even fewer. The phalanxes had their buildings and grounds captured in appropriately romanticized form by Fourierist artists, yet the most prominent artists associated with the cause—painter Fitz-Hugh Lane, sculptor William Wetmore Story, and engraver John Sartain—neither joined a phalanx (although Sartain came close) nor pursued utopian themes in their work.[113] And though novels by George Lippard and an anonymous visionary of the year 2000 obliquely preached the Fourierist program, only one phalanx dweller, N. C. Meeker of Trumbull, was moved to create a utopian novel (unpublished and unfortunately now lost). And the two dozen poems by Brook Farmers and other Associationists which appeared in *The Harbinger* tended to follow natural, moralistic, and spiritual themes little different from those of contemporaries.[114]

The most distinctive Associationist cultural expressions were not individual creations but group rituals fashioned in the Fourierist spirit. When Marianne Dwight and John Orvis were married at Brook Farm, William Henry Channing bid the attendants form a symbol of universal unity. All stood, held hands in a circle, and pledged themselves to Association, "the cause of God and humanity." For James Martin's funeral, North American Phalanx residents escorted the coffin to the community burial ground in an ordered procession of series, each with tools draped and at rest. Members thus mourned the loss of a "departed brother" but also proclaimed "the true dignity of productive labor." Though Martin's family was remembered in prayers at the graveside, the ritual emphasized instead his role as a coworker in the New Industrial World.[115]

Just as events in individual lifecycles were marked by communal ceremonies, stages in the community's career became occasions of ritual celebration. The North American Phalanx invited friends and absentee stockholders to an annual corn-husking bee to join in communal labor and witness its fruits. The opening of the phalanx's new meeting hall in May 1851 occasioned a busy three-day series of meetings and ceremonies. Channing gave a dedicatory address, friends of the phalanx presented a piano and other gifts, and officers reviewed the community's history and prospects. On a nearby hill members formed a circle around the phalanx's banner and "asked the Divine aid in their fresh reconsecration of this work."[116] The Fourierist penchant for festivities also fixed upon national holidays, which could be used both to legitimate communitarian reform and to recast American ideals in the Associationist mold. Brook Farmers attended Fourth of July celebrations at which labor militantly declared its independence from capital. At the NAP a band played as members marched in double file with the American flag and the phalanx's banner to a picnic in the woods. "We had swinging, singing, speaking, dancing, and a plentiful and delicious supper of the substantials and desserts," one resident reported to a friend. "And at sunset, we returned to the house, where we spent the evening with dancing in the hall, music and sociable intercourse." They had staged an American version of Fourier's fetes.[117]

Most important of all rituals were the celebrations of Fourier's birthday every April 7. Brook Farm's 1845 gathering featured an elaborate symbolic program. A huge banner proclaiming "Universal Unity" was draped across the windows of the community's dining hall. On one wall rainbow colors symbolized the spectrum of human passions; on another the name of Fourier, decorated in immortal evergreen, was flanked by an anchor (suggesting the principles of divine law) and a beehive (the phalanx's own logo). A plaster bust of Fourier given by his French disciples faced a central cross-shaped table, whose floral arrangement featured calla lilies, emblems of unity. After a benediction, half a dozen speeches, toasts to Fourierist ideas and heroes, and favorite songs carried the celebration into the night until all were "at one," as a Phalanx punster declared. Variations on these emblems and themes were played out at similar festivities in the North American and other phalanxes. In such celebrations the Americans rededicated themselves to Association, linked Fourier's theory to the universal truths of Christianity, and anticipated the Harmonic society of the future. Perhaps the most vivid conjuring of the utopia to come occurred at the close of one gathering of the NAP's New York friends. Associationists joined hands, invoked their French colleagues meeting simultaneously across the Atlantic, and recalled one of Fourier's most stirring visions: at dawn each equinox in Harmony, all global inhabitants would link hands and sing a hymn of brotherly love and thanks to God, the birthday song of a regenerated Humanity. Through the ceremonial blending of religious memories and patriotic motifs with Fourierist philosophy, the Associationists attempted to build cultural bridges to the communitarian future.[118]

Fourierist reminiscences left conflicting judgments for later generations to sort out. In the early 1850s, A. J. Macdonald set out to find out why the phalanxes had failed; responses to his questions from disillusioned communitarians, well-publicized by Noyes, chronicle the dashed hopes, monumental mistakes, and intense quarrels all too common in the Associationist ranks. A. D. P. Van Buren, seeking information from former members of the Alphadelphia Association, was told by some: "When we left we banished every memory of the old domain from our minds and have not wished to recall them." Yet there is equally compelling testimony that life in the phalanxes was satisfying and successful. Chester Adkins and Isabella Hunter of the Wisconsin Phalanx separately concurred in old age that their communal years were "among the happiest" of their lives. "We were like brothers and sisters living together in the sweetest harmony. . . . [It was] a little taste of the millennium."[119] And a generation after Brook Farm closed shop, Charles Dana evoked an idyllic memory: "The healthy mixture of manual and intellectual labor, the kindly and unaffected social relations, the absence of anything like assumption or servility, the amusements, the discussions, the ideal and poetical atmosphere which gave a charm to life, all these combined to create a picture towards which the mind turns back as to something distant and beautiful, and not elsewhere met with amid the routine of this world."[120]

Such appreciative evaluations, increasingly colored by nostalgia as the years passed, reflected in part the healing influence of time. As Emerson wrote of Brook Farmers in his own misty dotage, "I suppose they all, at the moment, regarded it as a failure. I do not think they can so regard it now, but probably as an important chapter in their experience which has been of lifelong value."[121] Mainly, the surviving assessments underscore the dichotomy between the many unsuccessful phalanxes and the few successful ones which has run through this chapter. Most American phalanxes suffered such a short and chaotic existence that their Fourierism remained a matter of constitutions and bylaws; members recalled their stay as a nightmare, not an idyll. But when ideological consensus and material conditions came together felicitously, communal experiments endured long enough to establish a distinctive way of life and approach members' Fourierist ideals. At Brook Farm and the North American and Wisconsin phalanxes, utopians enjoyed for a few fleeting years an appealing alternative to the "Civilized" selfishness of antebellum America.

1. Charles Fourier.
Lithograph by Cisneros,
1847, after the portrait by
Jean-François Gigoux.
Photograph courtesy of
Bibliothèque Nationale,
Paris

2. Albert Brisbane at the
age of thirty. Reprinted
from Redelia Brisbane,
*Albert Brisbane: A Mental
Biography* (Boston: Arena,
1893), frontispiece.
Photograph courtesy of
Library Photographic
Service, University of
California, Berkeley

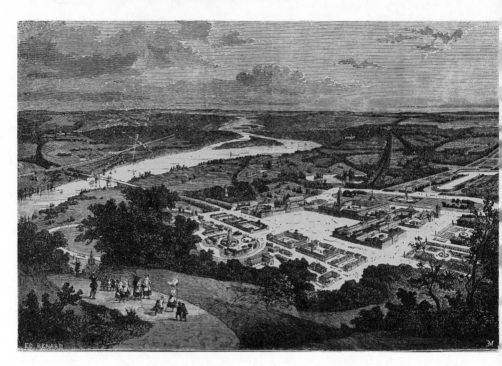

3. General view of a phalanstery. Drawn by Jules Arnoult, published by the Librairie Phalanstérienne, and exhibited by Albert Brisbane in the United States. Photography courtesy of Service Photographique des Archives Nationales, Paris

4. Parke Godwin. Engraving from *Putnam's Monthly* 4 (October 1854): facing p. 345. Courtesy of The Bancroft Library

5. Editorial staff of the *New York Tribune:* George Ripley (seated, right), Horace Greeley (seated, second from right), Charles Dana (standing, center), and others. Daguerreotype, c. 1850. Courtesy of Brady Collection, Library of Congress

6. William Henry Channing. Undated photograph. Courtesy of Unitarian Universalist Association of Congregations

7. Brook Farm. Oil painting by Josiah Wolcott, c. 1846, with ruins of the phalanstery (center, on hillside). Courtesy of Massachusetts Historical Society

8. Shareholding certificate, North American Phalanx. Courtesy of Monmouth County Historical Association, Freehold, New Jersey

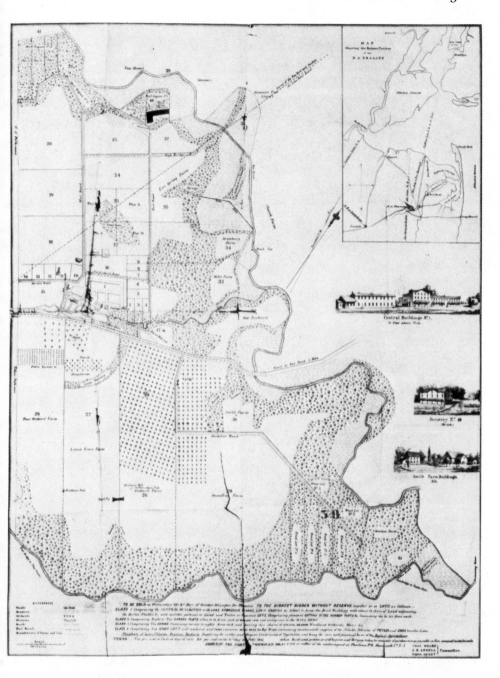

9. Plan and central buildings of the North American Phalanx. From "Map of the Domain of the North American Phalanx," 1855. By permission of the Houghton Library, Harvard University

10. View of the Clermont Phalanx. Ink drawing by A. J. Macdonald, July 1844. From A. J. Macdonald Collection, p. 242. Courtesy of The Beinecke Rare Book and Manuscript Library, Yale University

" COME ALONG AND HELP DIG THEM TATERS!"
" WHY, YOU MUST BE A NEW-COMER IN THIS PHALANSTRY, OR YOU
WOULD KNOW THAT I BELONG TO THE EATING GROUP."

11. "Pictures of Progress": the humor magazine *Yankee Doodle* comments on Fourierism, 19 December 1846. Photograph courtesy of Library Photographic Service, University of California, Berkeley

12. Two Fourierist women: Marianne Dwight (left) and Marie Howland (right). From Marianne Dwight, *Letters from Brook Farm, 1844–1847*, ed. Amy L. Reed (Poughkeepsie, N.Y.: Vassar College, 1928), facing p. 40; and *Social Solutions* 2 (28 May 1886): 1. Photographs courtesy of Library Photographic Service, University of California, Berkeley

Residence of M. Spring, Esqr.

Eagleswood House.

13. Eagleswood House and Spring residence, Raritan Bay Union. From a map of Perth Amboy, Staten Island, and South Amboy, by Thomas A. Hurley, 1858. Courtesy of New Jersey Historical Society

14. Victor Considerant.
Engraving by Jean-Baptiste-
Adolphe Lafosse, 1848.
Photograph courtesy of
Bibliothèque Nationale, Paris

15. View of Silkville. From L. S. Crozier, *Circular Letter, to Those Interested in Silk Culture in Kansas* (Topeka, Kan., 1877), 1. Courtesy of Kansas State Historical Society

8

Organizing a National Movement

In theory, American phalanxes should not have been started until the Fourierists had organized local clubs, rallied public support through systematic propaganda, and amassed a huge building fund. The spontaneous rush into communal life presented Associationist leaders with unforeseen problems. Their response came in two stages. During the surge of phalanx building in 1843 and 1844, Fourierist leaders hoped to harness the movement's momentum by preventing the indiscriminate founding of communities, linking existing phalanxes in confederations, and establishing an official movement center to determine and promote Fourierist doctrine. When this initiative failed, Fourierist leaders attempted to start over by creating a national organization to direct propagandizing through lectures and publications, raise funds, and ultimately concentrate the movement on a single model phalanx. Formed in 1846, the American Union of Associationists spread the influence of Fourierism into remote towns and villages, gained it respect in prominent literary circles, and won support in the labor movement. But its success was too limited and too late. Not until the wave of phalanx building had crashed did Associationist leaders manage to create a viable national network of supporters. By then popular support had dwindled, and adherents were on their way to becoming an elite socialist sect instead of the triumphant communitarian vanguard the movement's spokesmen had envisioned.

Leadership Problems

Given the revivallike wildfire of Fourierism's spread, the profusion of local phalanx projects, and the distance of much agitation from the eastern seaboard, probably no leadership group could have united the movement. To make matters worse, eastern Fourierist leaders were themselves seriously divided. There was constant tension along the New York–Boston axis. New York spokesmen were the first Americans to embrace Fourierism; they published the movement's journalistic organ, *The Phalanx;* and they posed as authorities on the Frenchman's theory. Brisbane, Macdaniel, Godwin, and their friends usually favored "pure" or "scientific" Fourierism, conducting abstruse investigations into the founder's theory while slowly gathering converts for a full-scale experiment according to his specifications. When existing communities were not developing quickly enough, they tended to lose interest. Ever mercurial, Brisbane oscillated between preaching Fourier to any audience he could find and sequestering himself in the study of Fourier's theory. Hopelessly unable to focus on practical matters, at key points in the movement's history he was simply unavailable. Godwin, though a forceful writer, was an ambitious young man who also withdrew periodically to his researches for what was to be the breakthrough book on Fourier. He also maintained connections to the Democratic party, which brought a job at the Customs House and involved him in land reform campaigns. Horace Greeley was far from doctrinaire, but the eclectic and impressionable editor divided his time between Fourierism and several other causes. National spokesmen and propagandists for Association, these New Yorkers were unwilling to join existing communal experiments.

Ripley and the Brook Farmers, by contrast, were full-time communitarians, committed to their phalanx not only as a center of Fourierist influence but as a satisfying refuge from Civilization. Struggling to establish Brook Farm securely, they were more sympathetic than the New Yorkers to embryonic phalanxes fighting for their lives in the Burned-Over District and the west. The Bostonians lobbied for aid to Brook Farm after it became a phalanx and were annoyed when New Yorkers appeared apathetic or favored the nearby North American Phalanx. "Oh, for men who feel this idea to advance humanity by Association burning in their bones," Ripley wrote Isaac Hecker late in 1843. "When shall we see them? . . . Are there not five men in New York city who would dare to venture $200 each in the cause of social reform without being assured of a phalanx for themselves and their children forever? Alas, I know not."[1]

Another source of conflict (treated more fully in later chapters) was the slavery question. New Englanders like Ripley, Channing, John Allen, and James Fisher came from a background of Whig politics and moral reform; from the outset they sympathized with the antislavery movement of the 1840s, even if they subordinated it to communitarian reform. Brisbane, Macdaniel, and especially Godwin, firmly in the Democratic party tradition, favored national expansion whatever the consequences for slavery and criticized abolitionism as a fragmentary reform and irresponsible undertaking. To Middle Atlantic leaders it seemed that New England Fourierists were too prone to the wandering reform fever that had created the temperance, abolition, and vegetarian movements. Ignoring Greeley's various enthusiasms, Godwin and the Philadelphian

James Kay accused the New Englanders of embracing every fad and "ism" that came their way.[2]

Ideological disputes were aggravated by differences in personality and temperament, though these did not always split along Boston–New York lines. Brisbane, for all his work in creating the movement, was a divisive force. Though he was respected for his energy and knowledge, his doctrinaire and almost monomaniacal promotion of Fourier, his condescension toward colleagues, and his practical unreliability alienated most colleagues. Brook Farmers found they could not count on his allegiance and support. Godwin found him intolerable, confessing to Charles Dana his "considerable repugnance to . . . propagation (this is *entre nous*) because it brings me in contact with Brisbane," whose influence he believed "most disastrous" and whose presence he found "a sort of moral torture."[3] Dana exchanged similar complaints about Brisbane with E. P. Grant.[4] The normally reticent George Ripley found Godwin arrogant and "too much of a Caliban" to cooperate on common projects. Ripley confided to friends that Horace Greeley had "none too much love . . . for Boston Associationists" and with the exception of Channing would not "go across the street to save any of us from hell-fire."[5] Dana refused to recommend Marx Lazarus for an editorial post because he found him wildly "impractical."[6] Associationism always threatened to divide at the top among three types: doers (Dana, Kay, Grant), dreamers (Brisbane, Van Amringe, Lazarus), and "disappointers" who had ability but insufficient time or divided commitments (Godwin, Greeley).

What, then, enabled Fourierist leaders to work together at all? The gap between New York and Boston was bridged by several persons: the pragmatic Dana, a Brook Farmer with a New York temperament; Osborne Macdaniel, a protégé of Brisbane whose mother and two sisters were popular Brook Farmers (Dana and Macdaniel in a sense cemented the New York–Boston alliance by marrying each other's sisters); Louis Ryckman, the portly New York shoemaker who headed the "industrial" department at Brook Farm; and William Henry Channing, whose soaring aspirations and soothing religious rhetoric held both groups in rapt admiration—at least until the slavery question became prominent. As an ideology of reconciliation, Fourierism itself encouraged good will and toleration of diversity. As long as writers stayed within the Fourierist fold, the Associationists' periodicals were not afraid to print doctrinal debates and dissenting opinions. Throughout Associationism's history, leaders such as Ripley and Channing worked hard to convince themselves and their readers that "apparently diverging tendencies" in the movement were actually complementary.[7]

At a level deeper than rhetoric there was often genuine camaraderie among Fourierist spokesmen. At times they shared a warm sense of fellowship akin to that of living in community. Associationism's ethos of participation and cooperation was the best part of its "movement culture," in Lawrence Goodwyn's phrase.[8] The New Yorkers' frequent visits to

Brook Farm, like celebrations of Fourier's birthday in the two cities, instilled among Fourierists the heady solidarity of a dedicated band working for the ultimate moral cause. At such times the pledge they shared offered an apparent foretaste of Fourier's universal love. Marianne Dwight's glimpse of an evening "coffee party" at Brook Farm is revealing:

> The spirits of good angels and all lovers of humanity were gathering around us,—the soul of Fourier must have bent lovingly over the heads of our little band . . . [and] the light of love began to beam from all eyes. . . . [Remarks were made by Dana, Brisbane, and John Dwight.] After those present were toasted, beautiful tributes were paid to the absent. Fourier, William H. Channing—the priest and poet of Association—Greeley and other New York friends were remembered. . . . As the speeches became higher and holier and more beautiful and the broadest principles were uttered from golden lips, and our emotions grew more elevated and solemn, . . . Charles Dana spoke of a meeting in New York where they all joined hands and pledged themselves to the cause of Association,—and he called upon us warmly and fervently to do the same. With one impulse we all arose and formed a circle around the little table and hand in hand we vowed "*truth to the cause of God and humanity.*" It was a solemn moment, never to be forgotten.[9]

The push toward national organization benefited from this fervent, almost religious conviction that Fourier's plan was indeed the social destiny of man. Alternately buoyed by the spread of Fourierist principles and challenged by the threat that the movement would disintegrate, this faith enabled the New York publicists and the Brook Farm communitarians—sometimes—to subordinate differences and join in the task of coordinating the movement.

Attempts at Consolidation

The first steps toward harnessing the Fourierist outburst were undertaken not by Brisbane or the New Yorkers but by regional conventions intended to plan large-scale phalanxes or to link existing communities. Toward the end of 1843 there were three such meetings: in the West, upstate New York, and New England. Only the New England group was able to create a lasting organization.

The Western Fourier Convention at Pittsburgh in late September has already been noted. Its intention was to gather regional Fourierists in one "Model Western Association," a venture introduced by E. P. Grant and supported by national leaders Greeley and Brisbane. But localistic rivalries, personality clashes, and religious differences prevented unity. H. H. Van Amringe objected that the final resolutions failed to reflect Fourier's religious millennialism. Cincinnati delegates arrived too late to take part. Several speakers presented rival schemes, and in the end no less than four little phalanxes (Ohio, Trumbull, Clermont, Integral) were set up by contingents at the gathering.[10]

Fourierists in the Midwest were the victims of easterners' neglect as well as their own rivalries. Western phalanxes sent frequent reports to the *Tribune* and *The Phalanx* which were duly reprinted and commented upon. But, prior to 1846, with the exception of E. P. Grant's correspondence, there was little genuine interchange between eastern Associationists and local leaders and phalanxes in the Midwest. Westerners complained about the lack of Fourierist lecturers sent to the region, since they were unable to attend "national" meetings held in distant Boston and New York, and they wanted more eastern investment in their communities.[11] Still, no westerner emerged to fill the leadership vacuum, and no periodical, phalanx, or club generated the resources and authority to control the regional Fourierist movement. Grant and N. C. Meeker of the Trumbull Phalanx went east after their communities failed; Warren Chase of the Wisconsin Phalanx was able but pugnacious and suffering from reform wanderlust; Van Amringe joined the Ohio, the Trumbull, then the Wisconsin Phalanx and lectured throughout the West, but he never earned public confidence and eventually defected to the land reformers.

Prospects for a coordinated movement were somewhat better in western New York, where Rochester emerged in 1843–44 as a regional propaganda center and to which Brisbane and the Brook Farmers could travel more easily. Brisbane's lectures during the fall of 1843 in Utica, Seneca Falls, Syracuse, and Rochester were intended not only to keep Fourierist fires burning there but to consolidate them. In Rochester he attended a planning meeting for the Ontario Phalanx, again urging Fourierists— fruitlessly, as it turned out—to concentrate on one big experiment. During the following winter, local leaders did hold discussions about forming a league of existing New York phalanxes, the sort of confederation that Fourier's writings envisioned. From these discussions the American Industrial Union (AIU), a council of delegates from seven phalanxes, was born early in 1844. Holding their first meeting in March, members intended to help each other to survive economically through cooperative buying and mutual trade, to establish a central office for selling phalanx stock, and to share advice on translating Fourier's theory into practical arrangements. An office was opened in Rochester in May, and some headway was made on doctrinal matters, but the AIU had barely gotten under way when the Burned-Over District phalanxes began to collapse. Nevertheless, the confederation idea remained a preferred strategy for national Fourierist leaders in 1844.[12]

Successful regional organizing really began in New England, and the major impetus was Brook Farm. At the Boston convention of December 1843, at which the Brook Farmers announced their Fourierist leanings, they also took two practical steps to organize beyond the community's boundaries. First, plans were made for Brook Farm and the Hopedale and Northampton communities of Massachusetts to send two delegates each to quarterly meetings at the communities in rotation. On the surface, the idea was to exchange information about the practical arrangements of communal life; Ripley apparently hoped to have the other communities join the Fourierist movement and perhaps affiliate in a regional confederation. The scheme did not work, though conferences were held at Hopedale in May 1844, at Northampton in August, and at Brook Farm in October before the concept was abandoned. Adin Ballou of Hopedale insisted on a religious and pacifist test of membership for any aligned communities; the Northamptonites, on the other hand, were pragmatic cooperators rather than social and religious ideologues. The August meeting degenerated into a platform for reform lectures of various stripes much like the Boston convention. No Northampton delegates showed up for the Brook Farm meeting in October, which proved to be the last.[13]

The second and more lasting result of the Boston convention was the formation of the New England Fourier Society. Brisbane and Channing had remained in Boston, prodding the Brook Farmers to organize regionally, and on January 15 the new society was formed, with Ripley as president, Brook Farmers Dwight and Cabot on the executive committee, and a varied assembly of local supporters as members. The society convened twice again during the winter of 1844 to hear lectures by Brook Farmers, which were promptly published as tracts, and it continued to meet for two years.[14]

In the spring of 1844 the New York leaders, spurred by activity in Boston and western New York, took the first steps toward a national organization that might harness the Fourierist enthusiasm. *The Phalanx* issued a call to a "General Convention of the Friends of Association in the United States," scheduled for April 4–6 in New York City. Its purpose was to celebrate the progress of Fourierism, regularize doctrine, and coordinate the efforts of phalanxes and local Fourier clubs. When the convention gathered at Clinton Hall, a few delegates had come from as far away as Maine and Virginia, and letters were received from Pittsburgh and Ohio Fourierists; nevertheless, the eastern leaders (especially the New Yorkers, who outnumbered all other officers) were clearly in control and imposed their agenda on the group.

The convention's first task was officially to separate "Association" from Fourierism by renouncing the "conjectural" parts of Fourier's theories. As communitarians they endorsed Fourier's plan of practical association and its philosophical rationale; all other theories attrbuted to Fourier or voiced by American followers were declared personal opinions rather than true social science. While acknowledging their debt to Fourier's genius, his disciples sought to free themselves from charges of sectarianism: they wished to be called not "Fourierists" but "the Associationists of the United States."[15]

Next, the delegates addressed the important issue of policy toward existing phalanxes. It was obvious that too many tiny and ill-equipped phalanxes had been established, miniature experiments that were not "scientific" trials of Fourierism. They could not simply be disavowed or abandoned, yet each community's collapse damaged the movement's public image. When delegates learned that even more phalanxes were being planned, they passed two resolutions warning against "rash and fragmentary" attempts undertaken without enough capital or committed members and recommending that Fourierists concentrate their efforts on community experiments already under way.[16]

The New Yorkers were in fact so overwhelmed by the surge of phalanx building that they gave first priority to the consolidation of phalanxes for survival rather than to the merger of Fourierist clubs, communities, and individuals in a national organization. Much of the convention's time and energy went toward promoting the Rochester group's confederation idea: existing phalanxes should form a "Union of Associations" to facilitate trade and cooperation. Delegates from the phalanxes were to attend a meeting in October to forge such a confederation. The convention's other practical achievement was to set up an executive committee to function for the next year. Six community leaders (including Brook Farm's Ripley) and twelve New Yorkers (including Brisbane, Macdaniel, Godwin, and Greeley) were appointed as a group to edit *The Phalanx,* carry out the resolutions, and manage business affairs until the following spring.[17]

No sooner had the convention adjourned than Albert Brisbane, the acknowledged leader of American Fourierism, left for Paris. His motives are something of an enigma. Brisbane's own reminiscences portray him as chastened by the "too hasty propaganda" that had resulted in rapid communal failures and retreating to Paris to study Fourier's theory and manuscripts.[18] But by April 1844 only two or three phalanxes had disbanded, ten were still under way, and several were in the planning stage. The atmosphere among Fourierist leaders was then one of cautious optimism rather than despair; not until the end of the year did the tide clearly turn. More likely, Brisbane felt confident that the movement was progressing and in good hands. With the phalanx idea spreading, perhaps he saw his most useful role as extending American knowledge of Fourier to the "higher and more scientific" discoveries. In particular, the "Law of the Series," which Brisbane intended to decode from Fourier's manuscripts, held the key to the distribution of "harmonies" in nature and, by direct implication, the proper organization of groups and series in phalanxes. No doubt Brisbane's eight-month trip to France seems strange in retrospect; certainly it reflects his lifelong inability to cope with power and responsibility. But Brisbane was apparently convinced, as E. P. Grant told him, that there was "no other way in which . . . [he] could so efficiently promote the cause of *practical* Association." Shortly after his arrival in Paris, Brisbane assured American readers that his theoretical findings as well as practical discussions with the French would be of great help to American phalanxes.[19]

Without Brisbane's energetic presence, the New Yorkers had no full-time organizer to further the April convention's work, and the momentum quickly dissipated. Insofar as anyone was in charge, it was Parke Godwin, who chaired the executive committee. He and Macdaniel now edited *The Phalanx;* his *Popular View of the Doctrine of Fourier,* published in the spring, gave Americans their first glimpse of the range of Fourier's theories while reaffirming the limited doctrines of the American "school." But Godwin had irons in many fires. Convinced that his rival Brisbane would come up with nothing new in France, he feverishly studied Fourier's works for the theory of "classification and method" which underlay its social mathematics. His overtures to the labor movement paid off when the land reformers nominated him for Congress in September 1844. And in the hope of winning a comfortable patronage position, Godwin wrote campaign tracts for Polk and the Democrats for the 1844 election. He was rewarded with an appointment as deputy collector at the New York Customs House, a traditional post for literary men who did hack writing for politicians. The job paid well but took time away from socialist pursuits.[20]

Godwin and Macdaniel did manage to keep *The Phalanx* going, using it to publicize the New York convention and promote Fourierist organizing. They emphasized that the annual convention had been formed as the "center of the movement in the United States" and would thenceforth decide doctrinal questions. They advocated the establishment of local Fourier clubs such as those already meeting in Rochester, Cincinnati, and Bangor. Also, using an anonymous contribution of $500 as a start, they and the executive committee inaugurated a "Fund for the Propagation of Association" to support *The Phalanx,* publish tracts, and obtain newspaper columns. These small steps had few lasting results.[21]

The key organizational measure advocated by the April Convention—the confederation idea—was soon abandoned. Godwin and the executive committee published a model constitution for a nationwide Union of Associations, and *The Phalanx* reprinted American Industrial Union president Alonzo Watson's recommendation that phalanxes confederate for mutual aid during the "transition state" into full Association.[22] Charles Dana visited the western New York phalanxes to gather information and stimulate interest for the meeting on confederation mandated by the April convention. When the meeting convened at Rochester on October 7, Godwin attended as executive committee chair, Dana and Ripley came from Brook Farm, and five New York communities sent delegates, but no other phalanxes were represented. Discouraged by the poor turnout and reports that the western New York communities were failing, and concluding that American phalanxes "were not sufficiently advanced to enter upon the arrangements contemplated," the delegates retreated to a lame resolution that merely suggested trade links between neighboring Associations. Godwin and the Brook Farm Fourierists were able to sal-

vage from the Rochester meeting only two symbolic resolutions recognizing the New York committee's doctrinal authority.[23]

Thus by the fall of 1844 the New Yorkers' campaign for a national
organization had stalled. Word was arriving that several western New
York phalanxes were collapsing, and almost every new Association was
in financial trouble. To make things worse, the Fourierists' publications
were threatened. Response to the propagation fund appeal was disappointing, and in November Godwin confided to Dana that *The Phalanx*
was "sickly—and may be compelled to stop."[24]

In the midst of this crisis, Brisbane returned from Paris. He had spent
the summer and fall studying Fourier's voluminous manuscripts and the
"science of harmony" in music, as well as surveying the Fourierist movement in France. Assuming a triumphal air, Brisbane professed himself
completely satisfied with his studies, but it soon became clear that he had
found no foolproof solution to the riddle of phalanx organization. All he
had to show were notes from lectures and copies from Fourier's manuscripts on abstruse topics of numerology and analogy: "The Modulations
and Transitions of Passional Movement," "The Application of the Arith-
metical Scale to the Life of a Man." The best he could promise was that
further study would provide "a clear synthetic view" of Fourier's theory.[25]

Yet Brisbane did provide some encouragement. For one thing, he
immediately jumped back into agitation. Though he later recalled that
upon his return from France he "turned aside from the sphere of practical action altogether" and retired to his studies,[26] he in fact continued
lecturing and writing on Fourier with his customary zeal for the next two
years. To critics like Godwin this was a mixed blessing, but Brisbane's
visions of the Fourierist future once again captivated the Brook Farmers—even the skeptical Dana admired the "restless, ceaseless flood of
things he pours forth"—and his enthusiasm was infectious. Brisbane
reported that Fourierists in France had succeeded in supporting a daily
newspaper with a respectable circulation (*La Démocratie Pacifique*) and
had converted Eugène Sue, whose melodramatic social novels were being
read by millions. If French socialists could do so well under what Brisbane
depicted as unpromising conditions, then Americans blessed with unparalleled freedom could match their success.[27]

The trip to France revived Brisbane's orthodox belief in a grand phalanx experiment. Fourier's manuscripts and the experience of French
colleagues taught the same painful lesson that American Associationists
were learning by the end of 1844: organizing a phalanx was "a thing of
great *difficulty*" requiring more capital and devoted communitarians than
they had believed. Accompanied by a large French engraving depicting
the magnificent building and grounds of a full phalanx, Brisbane now
took the French movement's stand that Fourierists should strive patiently
to build one grand experiment.[28] For the next few years the idea of
constructing a regulation model phalanx appealed greatly to American

Fourierist leaders, wounded as they were from the failure of premature attempts at community.

Brook Farm and *The Harbinger*

With the New York group's efforts clearly failing, the Brook Farmers took the initiative. Ripley, Dana, and their Boston friends had made important contacts with the New England labor movement; they had kept the New England Fourier Society meeting regularly through the year (it was the only thriving Fourier club at this point); and they represented a vein of literary talent *The Phalanx* had not seriously mined. The New Yorkers now looked to the Brook Farmers for help. Juggling *The Phalanx* with his other obligations, Godwin was anxious to share editorial responsibilities. Macdaniel, who had fallen in love with community life during his frequent visits, wanted to make Brook Farm the American "model phalanx." When Charles Dana proposed a conference of leaders at Brook Farm during the New England Fourier Society's annual meeting of January 1845, the New Yorkers readily agreed. Brisbane himself, newly returned from France, went straight to Brook Farm, stayed for a month, and spoke of "concentrating" the Fourierist movement there.[29]

At the New England Fourier Society's Boston meeting, the New Yorkers and Brook Farmers announced two new undertakings. First, a small group of leaders would investigate the "profounder problems" of Fourier's theory. Brisbane, Godwin, and John Dwight were already studying Fourier's writings and manuscripts—Dwight for the revision of Brook Farm's constitution, which was completed in March 1845; Godwin for his book; and Brisbane (with Ripley) in order to translate Fourier's *Theory of Universal Unity*, a task that would require twelve more years and several other assistants. Brisbane also conducted a series of "scientific classes" on Fourier at Brook Farm during the summer of 1845. Although the formal study group Brisbane envisioned never materialized, he was a catalyst for a deeper reading of the master among the eastern leaders, especially at Brook Farm, and the benefits were soon reflected in a more sophisticated presentation of Fourierism in the movement's literature.[30]

The second measure committed leaders to a new strategy. The Boston convention's executive committee determined that the best way to promote Fourierism was to focus on "one of the associations already established," whose success would "impregnably fortify our arguments and promises." If there was any doubt about what this meant, Macdaniel followed with a resolution endorsing the establishment of a model phalanx and recommending that all Associationists concentrate their efforts on Brook Farm, "as far as is consistent with other interests and connexions [*sic*]." The convention report does not indicate whether the resolution was adopted, but a few weeks later the New York executive committee apparently endorsed it.[31]

Not surprisingly, the idea of a model phalanx met with opposition.

There was the question of whether the model should evolve from an existing one or be set up *de novo* after careful planning—a problem Fourierist leaders debated for the rest of the movement's history. Singling out Brook Farm as the preferred candidate provoked even greater dissent. After the convention report was published, letters came to eastern leaders from western Fourierists proposing their own communities as fitter candidates. The most vehement, John Williams of the Clermont Phalanx, protested that the addition of a few New Yorkers to the New England meeting did not make it a true national convention. "Such humbuggery will prosper no better in Association than in Civilization," Williams wrote, complaining that concentration on Brook Farm would "starve out 13 or 14 other Phalanxes."[32] Nor was it only westerners who disagreed: Greeley, Edmund Tweedy, and other New Yorkers remained committed to the North American Phalanx as the movement's best hope. Brisbane himself was to change his mind about Brook Farm at the end of the year. Nevertheless, the New England meeting's resolution was the first endorsement of the model phalanx idea and had an important impact on the Fourierists' future strategy.

Behind the scenes at the New England meeting, other decisions were shaping the movement's future. One set of discussions, centering on promoting Fourierism through national lectures, eventually resulted in a circular calling for $1,500 in contributions, but the response was too meager to support the project.[33] A second proposal proved far more successful: a plan evolved by Brisbane, Macdaniel, and the Brook Farmers to move *The Phalanx* to Brook Farm. Ripley was to become chief editor, and the paper would be printed at Brook Farm and issued simultaneously in New York and Boston. Godwin, contacted privately, consented, with the proviso that the new paper not represent one community (Brook Farm) or one individual; *The Phalanx*, he said, had been "little more than a vehicle for Brisbane's vanity." He proposed *The Harbinger* as a title better suggesting the movement's broadminded social millennialism.[34] By February, arrangements were finalized as the Brook Farmers bought a press and New York friends raised a thousand dollars. Later that month the New York executive committee formally approved the project, and in June *The Phalanx* gave way to *The Harbinger*. Boston had replaced New York as the propaganda center of the movement and its unofficial headquarters.[35]

Launched on June 14, 1845, and published weekly, *The Harbinger* proved a valuable organ for the movement. Its editorial staff and frequent contributors included the ablest of Fourierist leaders from New York and Boston, and the Brook Farmers drew contributions from prominent friends such as John Greenleaf Whittier, William Wetmore Story, James Russell Lowell, and Thomas Wentworth Higginson. These distinguished literary contributors, along with the regular book and music reviews, made the journal an immediate success. But the journal's primary devotion was to Fourierism. Most issues featured translations from

Fourier and his French disciples, excerpts from social novels by George Sand, Fourierist-inspired commentary on politics and reform movements, and responses to critics of Fourierist doctrine. More practically, the editors printed news of the phalanxes, communications from Fourierists around the country, calls to meetings, and reports of local lectures on social reform. *The Harbinger* was indispensable in providing a semblance of unity to a movement that often appeared little more than a conglomeration of individuals and groups devoted in varying degrees to Association. Circulating inside the movement and out, the publication reached a subscription of over one thousand by mid-July.[36]

Such a following, though encouraging, could not sustain the journal without the labor and materials contributed by the Brook Farmers. But Brook Farm was never prosperous enough to support *The Harbinger* without strain; in fact, the timing of the journal's move was unfortunate. In late 1845 Marianne Dwight reported that Brook Farm had reached its "severest crisis." The community was plagued "by debts, by want of capital to carry on any business to advantage, [and] by want of our Phalanstery or the means to finish it."[37] At this crucial point, Brisbane told Ripley that New York Associationists were leaning toward the North American Phalanx as the movement's best prospect. Brisbane himself wanted to start over with a grand new experiment; he callously suggested "bringing Brook Farm to a close, and making preparations for a trial under more favorable circumstances." Fifteen thousand dollars, he said, "might do a great deal at Brook Farm, but would it do the thing effectually—would it make a trial that would impress the public? And for anything short of that, none of us, I suppose, would labor."[38]

Early in 1846, John Allen and John Orvis lectured on Association throughout Cape Cod, northern Massachusetts, Vermont, and New Hampshire to drum up support for *The Harbinger* and reported fair success.[39] But on the night of March 3, 1846, the Brook Farmers' nearly completed phalanstery burned to the ground. Members rallied to save their community and began retrenching to make each division self-sustaining. Greeley, Marcus Spring, and the New York stockholders—less heartless than Brisbane imagined—generously relinquished their investments; this canceled stock and new contributions saw Brook Farm through the immediate crisis.[40] But the community's life was ebbing away and with it its role as movement headquarters and publisher of *The Harbinger*. Not surprisingly, the commemoration of Fourier's birthday on April 7, that year was private and subdued both at Brook Farm and in New York, where delegates lamented the "apparent cessation of effort" to advance Associationism.[41]

Starting Over: The American Union of Associationists

To spark some action, George Ripley suggested that Fourierists again attempt to use a meeting of the New England Fourier Society to organize nationally; he envisioned a central society with affiliated local clubs and a permanent fund to support lectures and publications. Meanwhile, Ripley visited the North American Phalanx to drum up support, and in May he presented his proposal at a private gathering in Brisbane's New York City home.[42] The New England Fourier Society met in Boston later that month and promptly resolved itself into a "General Convention of the Friends of Association." Ripley, Channing, Brisbane, and Boston Fourierists prepared a constitution that the new organization adopted immediately. The American Union of Associationists (AUA) was to be composed of individual Fourierists and local affiliated societies. Each society, or "union," would elect delegates to the annual convention and pay at least $12 yearly to the national organization. Divided into weekly contributions, these dues would form a "rent fund" (the term was borrowed from the French Fourierists, *rente* meaning "income") to support lectures and publications, including *The Harbinger*. Horace Greeley was elected president, and seven vice-presidents—largely honorary—were chosen to reflect the movement's geographic distribution. The directors, who formed the executive committee that would run the AUA on a daily basis, were all New Yorkers and Brook Farmers: Ripley, Dana, Brisbane, Macdaniel, Tweedy, Allen, and Dwight.[43]

The AUA planned to begin a second, long-term phase of agitation in the United States. According to national leaders the enthusiasm of the early 1840s had resulted in premature phalanxes that poorly reflected Fourier's doctrine yet whose failures discredited Fourierism in the public mind. The movement had to begin again, but on a more solid foundation. The AUA would be a stable, permanent organization dedicated to systematically spreading Associative ideas nationwide. Eventually, public sympathy would return, knowledge of Fourierism would be deepened, and enough disciples and funds accrued to assure successful practical experiments. True Fourierist communities were put off to the future; sympathizers were warned not to undertake any more doomed phalanxes.[44]

Gradually, a concerted program of publicity and fund raising got under way. In mid-June the executive committee voted to send Dana on a lecture tour westward to Ohio, but the trip was canceled for lack of funds.[45] Lectures closer to the eastern seaboard were cheaper and easier to arrange: *The Harbinger* announced that any group of Fourierists who could provide a hall and a place for the lecturer to stay would be visited. In July, Brisbane and Dana lectured at Lowell, Salem, Worcester, and Hingham, Massachusetts, as well as Dover and Portsmouth, New Hampshire.[46] In the fall of 1846, Orvis and Allen undertook an extensive tour through Vermont, giving forty speeches in the last five weeks of the year.

Orvis's and Allen's letters of 1846 and 1847 described the mechanics of such tours and the hardship they entailed. "I wonder if the Executive Committee of the Union have any idea of the nature of lecturing," Orvis wrote to his wife at Brook Farm:

In the first place we have to spend sometimes two days in running about calling upon such persons as we can ascertain take any manner of interest in Association. If we cannot find any of this class, we then ask for reformers of any & all kinds—Nationals [Land Reformers], Protectionists [Protective Union members], Leaguers [members of Gerrit Smith's Liberty League] or anything else. At the end of the second day we can usually get a meeting. Sometimes there will be a dozen & sometimes twice that number at the first meeting. Having got one meeting we determine to push it: to hold on until we make an impression. . . . Much of the time we are obliged to travel all night & catch what sleep we can in a jambed [*sic*] packet-boat, or in the cars of the worst rail-road imaginable.

"This," Orvis wryly concluded, "is a glance at the *attractive industry* of a lecturing group."[47]

After lectures in a church meetinghouse or lyceum, they gathered subscriptions to *The Harbinger,* sold Associationist tracts, and—if interest was sufficient—formed a local Fourierist union. From their letters emerges a detailed picture of successes and failures on the Fourierist lecture trail and of the prejudice Associationists often faced outside major cities. In January, Allen reported that on Cape Cod "we are encountering the 'Rough Realities' of Civilized Life." Though they had made "a most luminous exposé of the principles of Divine harmony" only two dozen listeners occupied a hall that seated a thousand, and none bought a subscription to *The Harbinger.* They were staying with a disapproving Methodist minister who prayed "long and loud" for their souls. A long walk on the beach soothed their ruffled feelings: when they visited a party of gulls, Allen declared it the best social life they had experienced since leaving Brook Farm.[48] In Vermont the next month the two walked miles through the snow, only to find that friends had made no preparations for a meeting; undaunted, they borrowed lamps from a tavern and rang the meeting hall bell. Such impromptu expositions of Fourier attracted meager groups except in a few places: Bennington, Brattleboro, and Putney, where they drew an attentive audience of John Humphrey Noyes and his Perfectionist followers, later the founders of Oneida.[49]

When they lectured again in Vermont at the end of 1846, the results were equally mixed. At Brandon, Clarendon, Pittsford, and Middlebury, Orvis enlisted several *Harbinger* subscriptions and formed unions that pledged weekly dues. But Middlebury struck Orvis as "the very citadel of conservative Congregationalism, of Vermont Chronicles, New York Observerism in this State." Its "two-penny piety" and "six-penny aristocracy" gave no coins to Association.[50] A second tour through eastern Massachusetts early in 1847 got more promising results. Joined by Brisbane and Channing at Newburyport, Orvis and Allen enjoyed "the best audience that have ever been known to attend any kind of popular lecture in this place." Interest in New Bedford was high enough for Orvis and Allen to invite Ripley and Brisbane for a second week of lectures, which resulted in a new affiliated union. Speeches in Providence that spring by the same group made surprising inroads among local abolitionists.[51]

Meanwhile, more sophisticated lectures on "the science of Association" were scheduled in the Associationist leaders' home cities. Boston Fourierists sponsored a January 1847 series that ran the gamut from ideology to practice. Channing expounded "The Destiny of Man on Earth" and Dana, "The Progressive Development of Society"; Greeley spoke on "Tendencies of Modern Civilization," Ripley on "Charles Fourier," Dwight on "The Grounds of Association in the Spiritual Nature of Man," and Brisbane on "Practical Organization of Association"—all before reportedly large audiences. A similar series was offered the following month in New York.[52]

By the end of May 1847, one year after the founding of the AUA, 225 speeches had been delivered in over thirty places by Orvis, Allen, and eight others. Lectures continued in Massachusetts, New Hampshire, and upstate New York later that year. Yet despite leaders' promises to "western friends," there was still no AUA lecture campaign west of Buffalo. Fourierist groups in Cincinnati, Pittsburgh, and Wheeling sent contributions to the American Union, but these tailed off when no speakers appeared. Not until John Allen traveled to Cincinnati in March 1848 did western Fourierist groups get any support from the national organization.[53]

Affiliated Unions and the Gentrification of Fourierism

In the wake of Fourierist lectures, at least twenty-eight "affiliated unions" were founded. Most were located in Massachusetts, Vermont, and upstate New York, the ground Orvis and Allen worked over; the remainder were in the large cities of the eastern seaboard and the Ohio Valley; and one was formed at the Wisconsin Phalanx (see Appendix Table 4). Affiliated unions were expected to pay dues to the AUA, sell Fourierist tracts, sponsor lectures and social events, and meet to discuss Fourier's works. They were also urged by the AUA to adopt such "mutual guarantees" as cooperative stores, sickness and life insurance, subscription libraries, or a common living arrangement. These partial measures were envisioned as a foretaste and first step toward full Association.[54]

The most active union was the Boston club, whose well-preserved records suggest the range of activities clubs could undertake. Founded in December 1846, the society included several former Brook Farmers, who brought with them that community's combination of idealism, practicality, and charm. By 1848 there were fifty-five active members—twenty-one of them women—and a full agenda. The union sponsored lectures and the publication of tracts such as Thomas Palmer's *Plain Lecture on Association* and Channing's *Gospel of To-day*. A "Group of Study and Indoctrination" met weekly to discuss Fourier's *Nouveau monde industriel et sociétaire* (1830) and his manuscripts. A "Group of Social Culture" organized the annual Fourier birthday festival as well as more modest monthly parties. The "Group of Practical Affairs" obtained a meeting hall and debated such projects as organizing a cooperative store, subscribing to sickness and disability insurance, and erecting a "combined house," the Fourierist version of what later became known as apartment hotels.[55]

The Boston Union's relationship to the AUA was ambivalent. *The Harbinger* praised its organization, and the union was the incubator for nationally important Fourierist women's and religious groups. But the Bostonians, especially the Brook Farmers, continued to distrust New York leaders. In 1847 they lobbied hard but unsuccessfully to prevent *The Harbinger* from moving back to New York. Then, after rejecting a proposal to provide the sagging journal extra money, they voted to reserve half their weekly "rent" for local projects, donating the remainder to the AUA only if given more voting delegates at the annual meetings.[56] Their fears that New Yorkers were fair-weather friends were borne out: long after the AUA dissolved, the Boston Union remained a vital organization and continued to meet at least sporadically until 1853.

Unions elsewhere looked to Boston for their model, and though they never matched its activism, they testified that Fourierist ideals lingered after the phalanxes failed. Eight unions sent delegates to the 1848 annual meeting of the AUA; virtually all mailed contributions to the rent fund; and active clubs such as those in Lowell, Philadelphia, and Providence faithfully held weekly meetings and sponsored lecture series by the national leaders. Most planned the kind of practical partial reforms the AUA advocated, and a few succeeded in establishing them: the Albany Union opened a cooperative store and began a mutual insurance plan; Lowell and Nantucket clubs helped to form a thriving network of consumer cooperatives.[57] In response to national leaders' suggestion that unions maintain frequent contacts, the Philadelphia and Boston unions exchanged correspondence, visitors, gifts, and even telegraphic greetings on Fourier's birthday ("As the Magnetic Wire even now secures our fraternal attractions with an instant presence so all physical conditions shall in good time answer to the prophecy of universal unity").[58] The New York Union, as desultory as its leaders, had about thirty members; the Providence Union reported forty-nine members in May 1848; Philadelphia had fifty-six in 1849.[59] In all perhaps seven hundred persons enrolled as members of the AUA's affiliated unions during their heyday.

How many of these were serious Fourierists is a good question. In part, we are dealing here with a faithful remnant left after the phalanxes' demise. Yet as Fourierists once again reached out for converts, they drew newcomers of varied persuasions, including commitments to antislavery and temperance. Almost all reports in *The Harbinger* and private correspondence distinguished between "friendly" or nominal members, and those who could be counted on for dues and Fourierist activities—usually less than half. Orvis and Allen reported that most Albany Union members did "not believe in Association" but joined to benefit from the group's insurance plan and cooperative store. Sometimes attendance at union gatherings was inflated by ecumenical reform appeals: in imitation of French revolutionaries, the Cincinnati Union hosted a "Reform Banquet" on Fourier's birthday in 1848 at which participants toasted "the Peace Movement," "Land Reform," and "the Anti-Slavery Movement" as well as Fourierism. Though the union had only two dozen members, the event attracted a throng of almost five hundred.[60]

Those who joined Fourierist clubs came from a somewhat higher social echelon than those who had entered the phalanxes (see Appendix Table 12). With the exception of places such as Lowell and Fall River, where workers held prominent positions, union officers were primarily ministers, doctors, journalists, lawyers, and businessmen, with a few clerks, artists, and artisans making up the remainder. After excluding ex–Brook Farmers from lists of the Boston Union, an occupational analysis of fifty-two male members shows that eleven were professionals and major proprietors; thirty-one were clerks, white-collar workers, and shopkeepers; and only ten were artisans or service workers—a sharp contrast to the artisan predominance at Brook Farm.[61] Even the Brook Farm contingent was nearly equally split between artisans and higher-status professions, indicating that after the collapse of Brook Farm its craftsmen were as likely to move to the North American Phalanx as to remain in the Boston area as active Fourierists. The occupational profile of Boston Fourierists suggests that working-class Associationists committed themselves disproportionately to such cooperative experiments as Brook Farm and the Protective Union stores, while white-collar Fourierists wrote for communitarian journals, ran local clubs, or helped to sustain Fourierism through monetary contributions. A similar spectrum of affiliation obtained in Rochester, Cincinnati, and New York City.

These membership characteristics thus signaled a class-based division of labor inside the Fourierist movement, though it must be kept in mind that some artisans, reformers, and professionals worked side by side in each organization. Just as important, the relative elitism of the unions reflected an important shift in the Fourierists' core membership after 1846. Mechanics and small farmers began to leave behind the vision of communal life as phalanx experiments failed and local economic conditions improved. Those who remained were leaders rather than followers: idealistic ministers, businessmen, and professionals who had responded more to Fourierism's appeal as a philanthropic social science than to the advantages of cooperative work and living. Brook Farm's conversion to Fourierism and the literary success of *The Harbinger* no doubt accelerated this "gentrification" trend, but the dominant factor was probably the withdrawal of many working-class followers from communitarian projects. On tour for the AUA in upstate New York, Orvis and Allen reported that after the failure of local phalanxes Associationist prospects depended not on the broad spectrum of enthusiasts attracted earlier but on "wealthy farmers" and "professional and mercantile men."[62]

The Philadelphia Union was the most extreme example of the new atmosphere in Fourierist clubs, which its own president criticized as "dilletantism." With no roots in the phalanxes and no connections to local workingmen, the Philadelphia group counted among its members prominent local artists and "several highly cultivated families" who lent a tone of refinement to its weekly meetings. Philadelphia Associationists rejoiced that "a healthy spirit of investigation" was replacing the "blind enthusiasm" of the first converts to Fourierism and that the movement was now enlisting "the most useful members of society." John Sartain drew up an elaborate plan for a "Grand Unitary Dwelling" in the Philadelphia suburbs, with huge wings ending in Mannerist pavilions flanking a central temple portico.[63] Union members hoped to live in its luxurious apartments and commute to work in the city. No doubt Fourier would have been pleased by the grand scale of the proposal, but the project, like the Philadelphia Union and indeed much of the late Fourierist movement, suggested an elite club rather than a coalition of all classes in cooperative labor.

A Socialist Ladies' Auxiliary

The same conservatizing tendency can be seen in the role of women in the Fourierist movement. Once the phalanxes disbanded, the utopian vision of changed relations between the sexes lost its immediacy—in part because the movement's very survival became the top priority and pushed other agendas aside. The change may also have been related to the changing class membership of the unions: just as the affiliated societies enlisted "gentlemen" merchants and lawyers rather than workingmen, their female members were "ladies" rather than women. But the problem was ideological as well: the Fourierist ideal of womanhood was close enough to conventional stereotypes that when alternative institutions failed, it retreated into the glorification of women's peculiar talents and sphere which underlay more limited reforms.

Several letters to *The Harbinger* complained that women were not taking part publicly in the movement. William Henry Channing urged Associationist women to form their own societies or join the American Union.[64] In fact, nationalizing the Fourierist movement through the AUA continued the pattern of women's public silence. Enjoying less free time than men, intimidated by the prospect of public speaking, and unable to travel far from their families, women did not serve as officers or lecturers for the AUA, nor did any appear as appointed delegates to its annual conventions. Only once, in July 1847, were three women (Anna Parsons, Sophia Ripley, and a Mrs. Schetter) recruited for AUA subcommittees to formulate movement policy, mainly on education.[65]

The affiliated unions, however, opened up opportunities for local leadership and involvement. Women made up 40 percent of the Boston Union's members, and two served on the board of directors for a time. Here and in most other unions their role was circumscribed: the positions they most consistently held were corresponding secretary and chief of the Group of Social Culture (responsible for entertainment and festivities). This limitation was not always the result of male chauvinism; even when a more politically responsible role was possible, women themselves often rejected it. The Boston Union's minutes record a revealing episode. When James T. Fisher resigned as treasurer in May 1848, he made "a lengthy speech setting forth the propriety and desirableness of choosing a lady to that office." In response, Mary Bullard declared that she "could not think the proposer of this in earnest & was most decidedly shocked at the idea." Apparently no woman spoke in defense of Fisher's proposal, and after an embarrassed interlude a man was unanimously voted temporary treasurer.[66]

The Philadelphia Union from its inception was dominated by sentimental paternalism. Early in its history the men lamented having no women "to charm the circle of their constant devotion, and sanctify their masculine wisdom by a holy sympathy and love." Union president James Kay regarded the Boston women "as gifts to our movement" and regretted that no such "sisters of charity" could be found in Philadelphia. Kay wondered whether charges of Fourier's immorality were keeping women from joining.[67] A drive to recruit women paid off, however, and by late 1848 the Philadelphians had signed up twenty-one, including the obligatory recording secretary and chief of social culture. The most important female member—later to become a celebrated women's pioneer—was the very first recruit: Elizabeth Blackwell. Coming from a reform-minded family with Quaker connections, Blackwell had been attracted to a colony of New England Transcendentalists settled in Cincinnati. Its leader was William Henry Channing, whom she called "a man of rare moral endowments and eloquence as a speaker"; he introduced her to the writings of Carlyle, Emerson, and above all Fourier. She became a regular subscriber to The Harbinger, whose "bright visions of associated life," she later remembered, "nurtured that faith in co-operation as the necessary future of society which has become one of my articles of faith."[68] Her sister Anna, who had lived at Brook Farm in 1845 and spent time at other phalanxes, joined Elizabeth in Philadelphia in the summer of 1847 as Elizabeth prepared for medical school. The two stayed at the home of William Elder, an attorney and reform lecturer whom they eventually brought into the union.[69] By November, Elizabeth was on her way to Geneva College in New York, the only medical school that would accept her, despite her sterling credentials. "With her," Kay lamented, "went the instrumentalist by whose pivotal aid we closed our meetings with music" (she had been the union's first chief of the Group of Social Culture). Kay consoled fellow Associationists that "we have not lost Miss Blackwell to the cause however. Her devotion deepens with every hour's life; and she hopes by her present plan to contribute largely to our cause hereafter in more ways than one."[70] Blackwell's youth, her sense of reserve, and her medical vocation prevented her from taking a more active role in the movement, but Fourierist ideals and connections played a prominent part in her subsequent medical career and her role as publicist for Christian Socialism in England.

There are indications that in some cities the women of Fourierist clubs were more assertive. In the Bangor (Maine) Union a woman did *not* decline the office of treasurer. In Cincinnati a mixed group met every Saturday to study Fourier's works "translated aloud by a young woman." The strongest female presence was in the Lowell Union (see Chapter 11), which had as many women as men and whose officers were independent women with experience in labor and reform agitation.[71] But the largest and most representative unions set the florid rhetorical tone and provided traditional role models for the rest to follow. In the New York Union, which had no female members at all, the men claimed to miss "that magical . . . refining sympathy which flows from the presence of Woman." The sizable female contingent in Providence organized the festivals and tea socials. In Boston, rather than discuss women's issues or agitate questions of gender politics, union women were content to lend their "blessed influence and sympathy and council [*sic*]" to the work of Fourierist men.[72]

Nowhere were the scaled-down aspirations of Fourierist women so apparent as in the only organization they founded outside the phalanxes: the Woman's Associative Union. Its origins go back to the "fancy group" that Marianne Dwight set up with a feminist agenda at Brook Farm in 1844. While Brook Farm thrived, the group made a stab at economic independence for women, and the community itself created an unusually free social atmosphere. But after the community closed down, even that limited vision of female emancipation was put aside for the exigencies of the Associative movement's survival. During the crisis of 1847 the idea of a women's group again inspired Dwight, who took her plan to Anna Parsons and a dozen Boston Union women in May. The nature of the new organization was significant: instead of a women's caucus inside the AUA or a separate feminist group, it was conceived as a fund-raising auxiliary to the AUA and swathed in the traditional rhetoric of woman's sphere.

In June 1847 *The Harbinger* printed an appeal "To the Women Interested in Association." In flowery language expounding the special role of women it urged Fourierist women to adopt "some collective action" to "cooperate with our brothers and raise money for the movement."[73] The Boston group sent sixty letters to affiliated unions and individuals; over forty replies came back, of which two were particularly revealing. The women of the Trumbull Phalanx encouraged the Boston women but reminded them of the difference between knitting for the AUA and struggling to survive in rudimentary communal life: "Yours is the part to arouse the idle and indifferent . . . by contributing funds to sustain and aid publications. Ours is the part to organize ourselves in all the affairs of life, in the best manner that our imperfect institution will permit." The phalanx women added a none-too-subtle dig at armchair communitarians: "Could all the women fitted to engage in Social Reform be located on one domain, one can not imagine the immense changes that would ensue."[74] A second feminist response applauded the Boston sisters for their desire to have women "*unite together* in their own behalf and that of the human family" but hoped they would go further: Associationist women should "command a Press," establish mutual insurance, and serve the AUA as lecturers. In short, it was "high time that the *Mother of Mankind* should cease to play the *child!*"[75]

Notwithstanding these criticisms, the Woman's Associative Union (WAU) was officially formed in December 1847 and its constitution adopted by fourteen Boston members. Its objects were to support the Associative movement by selling objects or labor to raise funds, to study Fourier's writings, and to institute "mutual guarantees" (insurance) among members. By mid-1848 the WAU had seventeen members and had netted $170 from selling its craftwork (fans, lampshades, paintings, and other "fancy articles") and offering private instruction in music, drawing, and French. These proceeds were distributed among *The Harbinger*, various branches of the AUA, and the mutual insurance fund. Its suggestion that other unions set up women's workshops and stores was apparently taken up at least by the Philadelphia Union.[76]

The establishment of the WAU as an auxiliary did not mean that Associationists had given up aspirations to greater autonomy for women; the later careers of some would prove otherwise. But in the late 1840s the question of women's economic and social independence was subordinated to the urgent goal of keeping the Fourierist movement alive. Furthermore, in those same years, revelations of the free love doctrines implicit in Fourier's writings made it riskier for woman's rights advocates publicly to espouse Fourierism in feminist terms. Elizabeth Blackwell apparently spoke for other women when she told her mother in 1849— just two years after proclaiming Fourierism "the great hope of the world"—that she distrusted Associationists "and their way of discussing some subjects": "I go in whole-souledly for the Divine Marriage institution, and shall always support it by precept, and as soon as I get the chance by example too, and all those who would upset it I consider fools and infidels."[77] For most Associationist women, "universal reform" had never meant abolishing conventional marriage and family arrangements but only purifying them and distributing their burdens equitably.

The AUA and the Limits of International Fourierism

Except for the Woman's Associative Union, the inspiration for measures taken in the mid-1840s to consolidate the Associationist movement—the AUA, the weekly rent, field lecturers, and concentration on a model phalanx—came from French Fourierists. The movement was by no means a centralized or coordinated international one, yet translations of French Fourierist writings, correspondence between leaders across the Atlantic, and the travels of Albert Brisbane gave a cosmopolitan air to American Fourierism and a semblance of unity to utopian socialism in the Old and New Worlds. As the Americans tried to organize a coherent national movement, they absorbed important strategies from the French, who had gone much further in formalizing their movement's structure. French interest in the Americans, on the other hand, remained desultory at best until the failures of 1848 in Europe. Still, the exchanges that did take place in the mid-1840s helped to guide the American movement and, ironically, demonstrated the power of nationalism in shaping even the "universal" ideology of utopian socialism.

The 1844 New York convention designated Brisbane, already intent upon Parisian studies, its official representative to the French Fourierists. When the New Yorker boarded ship after the meeting, he took along two communications. The first, a letter of greeting and solidarity from the Americans, was a mere formality; the second, from the convention's executive committee, was a detailed appeal for advice on important practical matters. Included were questions on how to avoid public controversies over Fourierist doctrine, how to apply the "law of the series" to social relations, and how to link phalanxes together effectively. Also enclosed was a request for model plans and drawings. The French Fourierists' response, characteristically thorough and self-assured, was reprinted with the American letters in *La Phalange,* the French Fourierist monthly, but curiously never appeared in American Fourierist literature. Brisbane did, however, return with an imposing plaster bust of Fourier, some copies of the master's manuscripts—and a huge engraved aerial view of an ideal phalanx, which helped to spread the doctrine to impressionable American audiences.[78]

By 1846, after the first wave of phalanxes had collapsed, the Americans were turning to the French, whose cautious and organization-minded strategy seemed to promise more enduring results. The AUA was explicitly set up to represent an American, federal-style version of the French Ecole Sociétaire. Its system of a weekly "rent" to support publications, headquarters staff, and field lecturers was derived from the French Fourierist program inaugurated in 1845, which within two years boasted over two thousand subscribers who were contributing the equivalent of $21,000 annually. And the idea of building a model phalanx had been orthodox French strategy since before Fourier's death in 1837.[79]

American Fourierists hoped that the AUA would expand French-American contacts, and there was in fact a brief flurry of transatlantic communications. Parke Godwin was appointed foreign corresponding secretary with a charge to inform and consult with the French on the movement's progress. *The Harbinger* stepped up its reporting of political gains and propaganda activities by French Fourierists. A "rich harvest of books and pamphlets" was purchased from the French and advertised in *The Harbinger*. Americans translated half a dozen works of Fourier and his disciples, and the AUA published Victor Considerant's lectures on Fourier as a leading tract in its new propaganda offensive.[80]

Yet French publications gave only intermittent notice to the American movement: some three dozen items compared to hundreds of references in the opposite direction by the Americans. When Godwin sent letters to the *Démocratie Pacifique* on American Fourierism they were not published. Hugh Doherty, an English Fourierist living in Paris, explained that the articles "were not deemed likely to interest the French public," who were "very far from being cosmopolitan in their outlook." Even a prominent French Fourierist complained that the United States was "considered nonexistent" in the movement's press.[81] Until the 1850s, communitarian ideas and influences tended to travel in one direction only.

In part this was only natural. Fourier's theory originated in France, his manuscripts lay there, and his French disciples studied and elaborated upon his works with unparalleled sophistication. Because the French movement predated the American one, it faced most theoretical and practical problems sooner. While the Americans cast themselves as thirsty provincials hoping to learn from French studies and experiences, the French had reason to be preoccupied with developments in their own country: the problems of coordinating a movement in Paris and the provinces, preparations for a trial phalanx, intense public debate over socialism, and—after 1847—the gathering storm of national revolution. There was also the problem of language: their command of English was too poor for most French leaders to read *The Harbinger*, whereas many Associationist spokesmen could read and write in French.

A third deterrent was the French Fourierists' posture as the anointed keepers of Fourier's flame. When Associationists sought advice or information, the French tended to respond with condescending hauteur. Thus the lengthy response to American inquiries in 1844 not only warned the Americans against establishing "embryonic Associations" but reaffirmed Paris as "the general center of the Universal School, where the strongest lights of the School gather by a law of reciprocal attraction."[82] When Parisian Fourierists did share information, it was on their own exacting terms: the agreement Considerant required Brisbane to sign, for example, stipulated that only twenty-four carefully chosen persons (one-third of whom had to be women) could view the American's copies of Fourier's manuscripts.[83] Even dissident Fourierists in the French provinces protested that the Paris center resembled the Vatican and that Considerant had become a kind of socialist pope.[84]

Language difficulties and this pompous attitude notwithstanding, there could have been more French interest in America and more coordination of Fourierist efforts across the Atlantic. During the same period Karl Marx, despite his poor English, kept up a running correspondence with American labor organizers and made intense efforts to keep abreast of American developments in order to integrate them into his system.[85] Beneath the sporadic and disappointing record of French-American contacts lay not only problems of communication and preoccupation with different social contexts but a deep current of nationalism that divided the two branches of the Fourierist movement.

For both theoretical and practical reasons, French Fourierists were committed to their own land. Most were convinced that a successful phalanx had to be near urban centers with the greatest influence rather than in a colony or province. Others argued that socialism, though a universal truth, had risen out of specific conditions in Europe and would have its first triumph there. Then too, under Considerant's leadership the French Fourierists increasingly moved into politics with the goal of persuading the state to subsidize phalanxes and cooperative workshops; Considerant himself was elected to the National Assembly in 1848. These ideas and allegiances all reflected, and in turn reinforced, the French Fourierists' intense nationalism—an attachment to France not only as their home but the historic birthplace of revolutionary social and political progress.[86]

For their part, the Americans professed such a naive and insistent confidence in the New World as the socialist Promised Land that they alienated the French. Associationists interpreted transatlantic cooperation primarily to mean French support for New World phalanxes. As early as 1834, Brisbane had urged Fourier to establish a trial phalanx in America, and through the 1840s he kept up pressure on Considerant either to found a colony here or to contribute members and funds to the fledgling American communities. Among the "resolutions" Brisbane carried to Paris in 1844 was a lengthy argument asserting "the urgent necessity of concentrating all phalansterian efforts on the Associative movement of the United States"; both the American movement's rapid start and the nation's "providential disposition . . . for the combined order" guaranteed its triumph here, and then its example would be "irresistible" in Europe. This was the only resolution the French did not reply to in print.[87]

According to letters in the French national archives, a few French Fourierists did consider an American colony a viable alternative whenever the domestic movement seemed to be lagging. Around 1840 a Fourierist named Pellegrini, having obtained a land grant from the newly formed Republic of Texas, enlisted two hundred French families in a colonization project, but the group could not agree on a constitution and soon disbanded. Seven years later the French utopian communist Etienne Cabet decided to emigrate to Texas to found the colony of Icaria, and this prompted rumors that Fourierists were making similar plans.[88] A letter of this period from French Fourierists to Brisbane (now lost), proposing to combine French and American rent funds, may have been written with a joint trial phalanx in mind.[89]

Considerant and the most influential French leaders strongly resisted such proposals. They were committed to laying the educational groundwork and amassing the funds for a huge phalanx rather than any immediate experiment. They distrusted overseas colonies: in 1841 a doctor from Lyons had founded a French Fourierist colony in Brazil without the official support of the Ecole Sociétaire, and its quick disintegration set a poor precedent for such ventures.[90] Most important, Considerant believed that any experiments had to be near the urban centers of Western civilization—preferably within a short radius of Paris—to have the greatest impact upon European liberals. Not until the failure of the 1848 revolution did French Fourierist leaders reassess their position and begin to take real interest in prospects in the United States. But by then it was too late to aid or even to revive the American Union of Associationists.

The Problem of Slavery

A key part of the Associationists' organizing campaign was their attempt to win rival reformers to Fourierism. The greatest challenge came from abolitionism, the crusade against slavery which predated the Fourierists and in some respects had been a model for their propaganda efforts. At first a fairly abstract problem of morality and economic theory, the question of what to do about slavery became increasingly urgent as slaveholders encouraged war with Mexico and the South's peculiar institution spread to new western territories. Confronting the problem of slavery in the mid-1840s led Associationists to clarify important philosophical differences with abolitionists over the nature and merits of "free" and slave labor systems. But the issue also produced serious internal divisions in the Fourierist movement: was "chattel slavery" or "wage slavery" the worse evil, and which should be attacked first? The Fourierists' response demonstrated both the theoretical strength of their communitarian critique of slavery and the practical weakness of their gradualist approach to emancipation. By the latter half of the 1840s the escalating sectional controversy over slavery not only precluded any Fourierist "solution"; it was threatening to break up the communitarian movement itself.

Associationists versus Abolitionists

Taking their cue from Fourier and his French disciple Charles Dain, Albert Brisbane and American Associationists saw slavery as only one of many "servitudes" inflicted upon humanity by corrupt and immoral social arrangements. Deriving from the age of Barbarism, human bondage had been succeeded by the more sophisticated exploitation of Civilization, in which several forms of "slavery" coexisted. Calling upon Fourierist social science, Brisbane and Osborne Macdaniel listed nine different kinds of slavery in "subversive" forms of society, ranging from chattel slavery, feudal serfdom, and hired labor to domestic service, military conscription, and poverty. Horace Greeley, always a less literal Fourierist, defined slavery to encompass all social relationships in which "one human being exists mainly as a convenience for other human beings"; he included all class systems and land monopolies in that category.[1]

Unlike Fourier, however, American Associationists insisted that slavery was first and foremost a question of the appropriation of labor rather than the denial of elementary freedoms or the stifling of human "passions."[2] In part, they did so because they were faced with competition from abolitionists for reform audiences: to oppose slavery in the name of human rights or racial equality would be to play into abolitionist hands. But the Associationists' perspective was less a calculated strategy than a special point of view assimilated from Fourierist sociology, their own emphasis on economic cooperation, and contemporary workingmen's movements. Defining socialism as the "reorganization of labor," Fourierists contended that all contemporary work was based on coercion and competition and that southern bondage was only another form of the "slavery" existing in the North.

Of the various kinds of servitude, the wage system of competitive capitalism deserved special attention because it was the most prevalent, advanced, and neglected form of coerced labor. To Fourier's analysis Associationists grafted the concept of "wage slavery" to dramatize the evils of hired labor under capitalism. Complaints about workingmen's "slavery" had been part of Owenite rhetoric and had found their way into Anglo-American labor reformers' vocabulary, but a more direct source for leading Associationists was the French Christian socialist Abbé de Lamennais, whose *Le Peuple* (translated in 1839) called the wage system "a prolonged slavery."[3] To arouse indignation against competitive individualism, Fourierists contended that the northern worker was, or would soon be, worse off than the southern slave. Lacking slave society's "guarantees" in case of unemployment, sickness, and old age, northern laborers were increasingly "free" only to compete for wages approaching subsistence levels, to be goaded by fear of starvation rather than the whip, and to long for the chimera of self-employment without the means to attain it. One needed only to look at England, Fourierists claimed, where industrialism had reduced wage earners to a condition "worse and more appalling" than that of southern slaves, to see what was in store for the American North.[4]

Given the Fourierists' preference for reforming northern capitalism, their initial response to abolitionism was cool. Associationists charged abolitionists with blindness or hypocrisy when they attacked distant evils and ignored local ones. As Charles Dana remarked, "It does not become those who daily live by civilized slavery, who have it in their kitchens, their work-shops, and their manufactories, to use loud words of denunciation against those who live by barbarous slavery, which is only the elder sister of the same monstrous family." Greeley declined an invitation to an antislavery convention in Cincinnati by explaining that he was "less troubled concerning the slavery prevalent in Charleston or New-Orleans . . . because I see so much slavery in New-York," and he urged abolitionists to "be at least as ardent in opposing the near as the distant forms of Oppression."[5] When faced with abolitionist countercharges that talk of "wage slavery" palliated the evils of southern bondage, Associationists admitted that the wage system was "less degrading and oppressive" than chattel slavery but insisted that communitarianism was the only way to eliminate both. A "false industrial system" had generated all degrees of slavery and must be uprooted. Pursuit of abolition as a separate, immediate goal was dangerous and self-defeating. The abolitionists' aggressive tactics might inflame slaveholders to secession and bring on civil war; even if successful, their "partial" reform would leave the ills of Civilization intact. General social reconstruction along Fourier's guidelines promised a more peaceful and thorough remedy.[6]

One distinctive result of Fourierists' insistence that both contemporary labor systems were evil was the emphasis they put upon preparing slaves for the harsh freedom of Civilization. Prior to the Civil War, abolitionists tended either to reject as obstructionist the question of what would happen to the slaves when freed or to gloss it over with paeans to self-help and traditional Protestant virtues. Even historians sympathetic to abolitionism have criticized "the almost total failure of the antislavery movement as a whole to provide any direct, organized, sustained, and practical assistance in training the Negro for freedom in white society."[7] Associationists frequently pointed out that immediate emancipation would leave the slaves adrift with few skills and no education, ripe to become dependent "hirelings of Capital."[8]

Associationists urged reformers to devise a gradual emancipation plan based on Fourierist principles and involving larger reform goals. As early as November 1843, Brisbane and Macdaniel spelled out the general criteria for a proper Fourierist scheme. Like Association, emancipation would be peaceful, voluntary, and gradual. The ideal plan would be "satisfactory to all parties," secure the masters "full . . . indemnification," educate the slaves for freedom, and incorporate cooperative mechanisms.[9] Specific proposals were slow in coming, however. In the mid-1840s Greeley, Parke Godwin, and other leaders merely voiced the hope that if free blacks formed successful cooperative townships in the North or became productive members of existing phalanxes, the public would be convinced that peaceful emancipation benefited blacks and would then pressure masters to release their slaves.[10]

At the same time, Fourierists prodded abolitionists to join them or at least to expand antislavery activities to oppose "universal servitude"—white as well as black, capital as well as chattel, soul as well as body. As has often been pointed out, many antebellum labor leaders were hostile or at least indifferent to the abolitionist appeal because they believed that it diverted attention from the serious problems facing northern workers with the onset of industrial capitalism. Brisbane and the Associationists claimed that broadening the abolitionist platform to include attacks on wage slavery would attract greater working-class support for antislavery. A universal crusade against the oppression of all labor would be irresistible.[11]

Abolitionists did not, in fact, totally dismiss the plight of northern workers. By the late 1830s many were attempting to enlist workers' support. *The Liberator* and the *Anti-Slavery Standard* contended that aggrieved workers should oppose slave labor as a first step to improving their own condition, and some political abolitionists—among them William Goodell and Gerrit Smith—actively took up the cause of land reform.[12] During the 1840s a few prominent abolitionists even moved toward an alliance with communitarians and their critique of northern labor relations. John A. Collins, a Garrisonian who converted to labor radicalism during a fund-raising trip to England, returned believing that private property was the root of all evil and founded the anarchist Skaneateles community in western New York. Associationist lecturer John Orvis had been a follower of Collins but eventually left the "No-God, No-Government, . . . No-Money . . . system of Community" for Fourierist "constructive reform" and a lifetime of labor movement leadership. Marcus Spring, founder of the Raritan Bay Union and benefactor of the North American Phalanx, came to New York City in the 1830s with strong abolitionist connections but shifted his allegiance to Association during the depression of the early 1840s.[13]

Perhaps the abolitionists' leading advocate of Association was Elizur Wright, Jr. A former corresponding secretary of the American Anti-Slavery Society, Wright had a brush with poverty in the 1840s which sensitized him to working-class problems. Subsequently, he lashed out at free-labor capitalism and promoted Fourierist cooperatives in his *Boston Daily Chronotype*.[14] Fourierism made some headway among the abolitionist rank and file as well. *The Harbinger* reported that in some New England cities, especially Providence, Associationists found several supporters at Anti-Slavery Society gatherings.[15] Nevertheless, only a tiny minority of abolitionists endorsed Associationism, and those who did tended to leave abolitionist rhetoric and affiliations behind as they joined phalanxes or promoted local Fourierist unions.

At bottom, fundamental ideological differences between Associationists and abolitionists prevented close cooperation. As Aileen Kraditor, Eric Foner, and others have observed, abolitionists conceptualized slavery and freedom in "profoundly individualistic" terms, understanding them as personal and moral situations.[16] But Fourierists viewed them primarily as social and economic arrangements. Thus, whereas abolitionists saw slavery as "a system of arbitrary and illegitimate power exercised by one individual over another," Fourierists interpreted it as a class system and traced its roots to a competitive economy that encouraged groups to subjugate one another. Abolitionists identified freedom as self-ownership—the basic "right of man to himself," as the *Anti-Slavery Standard* put it; Fourierists linked it to economic independence and believed that any meaningful concept of freedom must include employment and welfare "guarantees." Like other labor reformers, Associationists invoked the traditional republican ideals of the farmer and self-employed craftsman to decry the progressive deterioration of labor under the wage system and capitalist competition. But abolitionists believed that northern free labor was inherently sound and emphasized the opportunities and openness of American society: the right to contract his or her labor made the northern worker a free agent in the economy; those who were industrious, abolitionists asserted, would surely improve their material condition. Though competition for jobs could be intense and poverty a possibility for some workers, these rigors were beneficial because they taught temperate behavior and disciplined work habits. Both by the basic categories in which they classified human actions and by their estimate of contemporary trends, the abolitionists believed that the wage system and slavery were not comparable. The Associationists insisted otherwise.[17]

Perhaps nowhere were the abolitionists' belief in American exceptionalism and their confidence in capitalism more strikingly exemplified than in an important exchange between the Associationists and Wendell Phillips, the eloquent Garrisonian agitator. When Phillips acknowledged at an antislavery convention in 1847 that coal from England's mines and textiles from its mills were "the products of unrequited labor," *The Harbinger* rejoiced that he was on the road to Fourierism. Phillips's response in *The Liberator* quashed any idea that he viewed wage and slave labor as comparable: "Except in a few crowded cities and a few manufacturing towns, I believe the terms 'wages slavery' and 'white slavery' would be utterly unintelligible to an audience of laboring people, as applied to themselves."[18]

Phillips distinguished American workers from slaves on two grounds: "First, the laborers, as a class, are neither wronged nor oppressed; and secondly, if they were, they possess ample power to defend themselves, by the exercise of their own acknowledged rights. Does legislation bear hard upon them? Their votes can alter it. Does capital wrong them? Economy will make them capitalists. Does the crowded competition of cities reduce their wages? They have only to stay at home, devoted to other pursuits, and soon diminished supply will bring the remedy." The Associationists erred, Phillips claimed, by "looking at American questions through European spectacles, and transplanting the eloquent complaints against capital and monopoly, which are well-grounded and well applied there, to a state of society here, where they have little meaning or application, and serve only for party watch-words."[19]

Ironically Phillips was to change his opinion after the Civil War, when

he became a prominent speaker at labor reform conventions and denounced free labor as a species of slavery.[20] But in the 1840s his praise
of American free labor was echoed by many abolitionists. Such a rousing
defense of free-market society lends support to the thesis that the spread
of abolitionism had the effect—intended or not—of legitimating competitive capitalism. As historians building upon the penetrating work of
David Brion Davis contend, by glorifying the northern free-labor system
and isolating slavery as an exceptional evil, the abolitionists may well have
bolstered the exploitative character of northern capitalism.[21]

Given the apparently close relation between the antislavery movement
and capitalism, it is understandable that so much attention has been paid
to why abolitionists were practicing "selective compassion" in targeting
southern slavery to the exclusion of northern labor problems. But it is
only fair to reverse the question and ask why the utopians were relatively
indifferent to black slavery. It is true that Fourierists, like other labor
reformers, were more hostile to abolitionists than blind to slavery's evils.
Still, it can be argued that by concentrating upon reconstructing Civilization and by considering slavery a derivative, secondary social problem,
Fourierist ideology did encourage a certain tolerance of slavery among
adherents. The "wage slavery" argument highlighted the erosion of
workers' independence under commercial capitalism, but its assertion
that northern laborers were comparable to southern slaves downplayed
the basic and blatant oppression of human bondage.[22] Did there lie
beneath utopian socialist rhetoric a racial preference for whites which
really accounted for Associationists' relative unconcern about slavery?

The movement's position on slavery followed logically from utopian
socialist premises and was consistent with Associationist policy toward
other reforms. Virtually every Fourierist spokesman condemned slavery
as a social evil; George Ripley and William Henry Channing employed
the full arsenal of evangelical arguments against the sinfulness of the
peculiar institution. Yet for some northern Associationists, race prejudice
clearly contributed to or reinforced the Fourierist position. (For the racial
position of southern-born Fourierists, see the discussion of emancipation
proposals, below.) Although Parke Godwin condemned slavery, he was
not above privately calling abolitionists, whom he blamed for diverting
attention from the evils of capitalism, "nigger-loving and white-man
hating fanatics." One Fourierist sympathizer balked at supporting the
Free-Soilers because he felt they were "not in favour of the freedom of
the 'soil,' but of the freedom of the *negroes*." Even an Ohio Associationist
who urged free blacks to form phalanxes did so because mixed-race
communities, he claimed, would "always produce incompatibility" between members.[23]

Numerous suggestions that the Fourierist movement take in free blacks
were ignored. The most flagrantly squandered opportunity occurred at
the North American Phalanx. Because of New Jersey's extremely gradual
emancipation provisions, slavery persisted in the state until the 1840s.

The Van Mater estate near Red Bank, which NAP members purchased for their communal site, had once quartered nearly a hundred slaves, and several freedmen remained as tenants in 1843. The Associationists made no attempt to incorporate these blacks into the community but apparently evicted them: Van Mater freedmen were never enrolled as members, and the 1850 census taker found some of them living on nearby land outside the phalanx's boundaries.[24] A variety of factors—Fourierist doctrine, an economic conception of freedom, rootedness in labor reform, and reluctance to alienate white supporters by making the slavery issue central—left Associationists more concerned about competitive capitalism than about black slavery. Though it was rarely primary, in some cases racial prejudice added its ugly weight to these forces.

Division over the Mexican War

Despite substantial disagreement between the two movements, there was from the beginning a minority of Fourierists who shared the abolitionists' priorities. As the expansion of slavery became the central political question of the late 1840s, this group became more vocal and powerful. As early as 1846 William Henry Channing noted that there were two Associationist factions on the slavery issue. The first group, while condemning slavery in principle, believed it could be effectively abolished only by replacing competitive arrangements with cooperative communities. This was the movement's "orthodox" position; those who followed it tended to be northern Democrats, westerners, or southerners. The second group, whose members usually came from New England Whig or evangelical backgrounds, believed instead that slavery had to be abolished before the general reorganization of labor could be pursued. Not only did the "logical order" of history dictate that liberation from barbarism precede freedom from capitalism, but—as abolitionists frequently argued—the existence of chattel slavery degraded the status of labor everywhere. Enthusiasm for Association tended to keep all Fourierists from participating in antislavery agitation, but Channing believed that the second class was "rapidly increasing" in numbers and influence. Channing himself, who had come out against slavery before his conversion to Association, continued to speak at abolitionist conventions in the 1840s. By 1846 he was convinced that "the Anti-Slavery victory must be won, before our day of triumph for Association can come" and pledged his primary efforts to the cause.[25]

The issue that crystallized these differences between Fourierists and gave the antislavery faction an enormous boost was the expansion of slavery in the West. Particularly among Brook Farmers, the annexation of Texas in the last days of John Tyler's administration reawakened antislavery sentiment that had slumbered under the Fourierist regime. Several Brook Farmers began attending antislavery meetings at Faneuil Hall, and one (Frederick Cabot) served as the Massachusetts Anti-Slavery

Society's auditor. Brook Farm's Boston benefactors James T. Fisher and Francis G. Shaw helped finance abolitionist propaganda, and Fisher also was appointed to the blue-ribbon Committee of Vigilance formed to protect Boston blacks from slave catchers.[26]

The most vocal antislavery New England Fourierist was Channing, whose magazine *The Present* had opposed "the plot to annex Texas" as early as November 1843. At several antislavery meetings in the summer of 1845, Channing denounced the Texas scheme, and in *The Harbinger* he condemned it as an unconstitutional usurpation by the "Slave Power" conspiracy.[27] When war broke out with Mexico in 1846, Channing's rhetoric reached its fiery peak. Among abolitionists he preached disunion: at the New England Anti-Slavery Convention in May, he offered a resolution asserting "that there is no longer a Union of these States, a National Constitution, [or] a National Executive." Echoing the Garrisonians, he proposed that popular assemblies and new state conventions meet to form a new "Union of Freemen" that would exclude slave states and territories.[28]

Channing's conversion to disunion earned praise from Garrison himself,[29] but his friend and erstwhile mentor Emerson was not pleased. In his celebrated "Ode Inscribed to W. H. Channing" written in June 1846, Emerson, though adamantly opposed to slavery, took issue with the disunionist line:

> What boots thy zeal,
> O glowing friend,
> That would indignant rend
> The northland from the south?
> Wherefore? to what good end?

Four years earlier Channing had reviewed the Divinity School Address and scolded Emerson for "deny[ing] the human race" and attempting to stand "a complete Adam." Now Emerson turned the tables on Channing, suggesting that abolitionists who preached disunion were themselves denying the human race in the South by dissociating themselves from slavery without abolishing it. Their separatist "cant" and destructive rage would never succeed, but a positive, inspired statement of ideals by virtuous men would bring "thousands" who would "for freedom strike and stand."[30]

Channing never broached the dissolution of the Union in *The Harbinger,* but there and in speeches he urged utopians to refuse military service, withhold their taxes, and otherwise resist the war effort. The Mexican War, Channing charged, had been started by Polk in order "to rob a sister republic of province after province that she [the U.S.] may extend over it to the Pacific and the Isthmus of Panama slave institutions and slave labor."[31] With Rhode Island Associationists apparently seconding the charge and Greeley's *Tribune* thundering against the "Mexican Robbery," a sizable wing of the Fourierist movement seemed poised to follow Channing into an alliance with antislaveryites and antiwar dissenters. An important step in this direction came when the American Union of Associationists, meeting in Boston two weeks after war was officially declared, adopted a resolution written by Channing in which Fourierists pledged "in no way to aid the Government of these United States, or of the several States, in carrying on war against Mexico."[32]

Many Associationists outside New England, especially those who were Democrats, had an entirely different view of national expansion. Parke Godwin was their most forceful voice; though he had gone on record against slavery as early as 1843, he was vehemently opposed to identifying Association with antislavery. Like many Fourierists, Godwin believed that supporting the "partial reform" of abolitionism would lead Associationists into sectarian isolation. As a Democrat who had befriended expansionist spokesman John L. O'Sullivan and campaigned for Polk, Godwin was under the spell of Manifest Destiny. Calling the spirit of annexation "the most vital thing that has shown itself in our politics for some years," Godwin heartily endorsed the task of "extending *constitutional republican institutions* over this whole continent."[33] But Godwin was more than a grown-up Young American; he also believed, as historian John Wennersten has written, that "empire and socialism went hand in hand." Annexation would add virgin territory where cooperative communities could take root; just as important to Godwin, expansion would generate popular enthusiasm for the principles of a truly democratic society and thus rekindle discussion of social reform. Against such possibilities the issues of war and slavery were only "incidental" evils that had to be overlooked.[34]

As he read Greeley's editorials and heard rumors that Brook Farm was warming to abolitionist views, Godwin became alarmed. Texas was the most important political question of the day, but the Brook Farmers and their friends were adopting the New England view of it, "the narrowest, meanest and most despicable that a conceited and bigoted intellect could take." Lingering resentment over *The Phalanx's* transfer to Brook Farm and a deep-seated aversion to Yankees added fuel to Godwin's fire. Channing, he claimed, looked at Texas annexation solely through "a miserable anti-slavery fanaticism," and editor Ripley was just as guilty for allowing Channing's articles to appear. As long as *The Harbinger* endorsed such ideas, Godwin would not allow his name to appear as an editor. He convinced himself that opposition to annexation was, unlike his brand of socialism, "unAmerican."[35]

When news of the Mexican War's outbreak reached New York, Godwin unhesitatingly chose Manifest Destiny over antislavery. Fourierist opposition to the war only confirmed his sense that New England antislaveryites were leading the movement to a disastrous split. When the Boston AUA meeting adopted Channing's resolution urging resistance to the war, Godwin penned an angry protest to *The Harbinger* refusing to hold office in the organization unless the "treasonable" resolution was repudiated. Godwin's protest and defense of the war were not published. It would be "unfortunate," the editors confided, to launch the AUA with such "public evidence of . . . dissension" in the movement. Nevertheless, Charles Dana inserted a disclaimer in *The Harbinger* assuring readers that the antiwar resolution was the sentiment of a particular meeting, not the position of the entire Associative School.[36]

The episode strained relations among Associationist leaders almost to the breaking point. Godwin, previously a fervent admirer of Channing, continued to spar with the New Englander in print and did not speak to him for four years.[37] Ripley, miffed by Godwin's crude and overbearing manner, harbored an intense dislike for the New Yorker which escalated through the late 1840s. Though Dana and John Dwight tried to defuse personal and political tensions, the controversy continued into 1847. Channing steered another resolution critical of the war through the January AUA convention; privately he circulated even stronger petitions among Associationists.[38] Godwin and his supporters kept up their protests against the antiwar faction and called for utopian socialist leaders who "respect the Constitution rather than slander it."[39]

Emancipation Plans and the Louisiana Connection

Against this contentious background two Fourierist reformers from the upper South, Osborne Macdaniel and Marx Edgeworth Lazarus, attempted to work out practical proposals that would solve the vexing problem of slavery once and for all and repair the rift in Associationist ranks. Their emancipation plans—by far the most elaborate to emerge from the Associationist movement—are significant because they reveal an intriguing collaboration between national Fourierist leaders and an important but little-known circle of southern sympathizers. These proposals, furthermore, present the most concrete opportunity available to assess the nature and limitations of the utopian socialists' approach to slavery.

Being faithful utopians, Macdaniel and Lazarus believed that cooperative principles could end slavery peacefully, and their preference for sectional conciliation reinforced this faith. Macdaniel, who was raised in the District of Columbia's Georgetown, moved to New York around 1840, where he co-edited *The Phalanx* with Brisbane while his mother and two sisters lived at Brook Farm.[40] Macdaniel's early articles expounded his conservative blend of Fourierism and mild antislavery sentiments: acknowledging the evil of slavery, warning that abolitionism was a "dangerous" reform, recommending Fourierist gradual emancipation, yet outlining no specific scheme. When the Mexican War fueled antislavery passions, Macdaniel spoke more decisively. In *The Harbinger* he contended that despite the war's apparent "knavery," it represented in the long run the triumph of Civilized over Barbarous nations and hence a step toward socialism; he advised Fourierists to remain silent while history ran its course. It was a strategic line parallel to Godwin's.[41] More positively, Macdaniel decided to devise a detailed and foolproof emancipation plan that would eliminate the slavery question and in the process rally the splintering Fourierist movement. To develop it, he journeyed to Louisiana in April 1847.

Macdaniel chose Louisiana because there he could draw upon a remarkable, indeed unique, connection between northern Fourierists and a group of southern sympathizers. John D. Wilkins, whose sugar plantation Macdaniel visited, was an elderly Virginian settled in St. Mary's Parish, the owner of some seventy slaves, and an eccentric philanthropist who had contributed thousands of dollars to the Associationist movement. For two years Wilkins's money had sent *The Phalanx* and *The Harbinger* to every college in the country as well as Fourierist lecturers to cities and towns in the Northeast. At one point Wilkins had to be talked out of mortgaging his plantation for the cause.[42] Robert Wilson, whose weekly *Planter's Banner* reported Macdaniel's doings in Louisiana, had endorsed Fourierism as early as 1844; he had corresponded with and sent gifts to the New York headquarters and expressed interest in joining the Ohio Phalanx.[43] Others in the sugar-growing region sympathetic to Fourierism included Thomas May of St. John the Baptist Parish, who had pledged over a thousand dollars to the movement, and another planter who had sent his son to the school at Brook Farm.[44] In addition, there was a circle of important Fourierists in New Orleans, among them Thomas J. Durant, then a federal attorney and later Louisiana's attorney general during wartime Reconstruction, and T. Wharton Collens, an attorney and city judge active after the Civil War as a Christian Socialist author.[45] It was Durant, Macdaniel's contact in New Orleans, who organized the Louisiana group and channeled its members' money and suggestions to the national Fourierist leaders.

That a circle of established southern planters and attorneys would endorse one of the most reviled of northern "isms" seems little short of bizarre. Some abolitionists predicted that slaveholders might adopt Fourierist arrangements to maximize their profits and assure a loyal work force.[46] But the motives that drew this group to utopian socialism were apparently more complex and less sinister. Like northern Fourierists, the southerners represented a coalition of views and interests. Wilson and Collens were Whigs; Durant was a Democrat; Wilkins was neither. Wilkins approached utopian socialism as a paternalistic philanthropy that promised to end class antagonism and promote efficient production. Durant, though a successful attorney, saw himself as the embattled champion of New Orleans workers. What the Louisiana group shared, evidently, was a commitment to economic progress, plus private dissatisfaction with slavery on humanitarian and economic grounds. Fourier's vision of a slaveless cooperative order to be reached peacefully through social science appealed to southerners who were attracted to liberal ideas but afraid of violently disrupting the old order or of importing the competitive anarchy of the North.

Isolated in a region Durant called "peculiarly unsusceptible to the influence of associative doctrines," these southern utopian socialists kept a low profile. They corresponded and gathered privately, concentrating on collecting weekly contributions for the AUA.[47] Durant and Wilkins also invited Fourierist lecturers to Louisiana but had no illusions about leading a full-fledged utopian movement there. For his part, Macdaniel went south not to win local converts but to assess, with the help of Louisiana colleagues, the prospects for a model emancipation project. From a base in New Orleans, he ranged over southwest Louisiana for six weeks "on foot and horseback," consulting with Wilson, Wilkins, and other residents and scrupulously recording his observations.[48]

What he found pleased him so much that he became a local booster. The experiment of John McDonogh, a stern but philanthropic local planter who had allowed his slaves to earn their freedom by working extra hours for wages, proved that the lure of emancipation stimulated hard work and self-improvement.[49] The Attakapas region of southwestern Louisiana was "the garden spot of the U.S.," a tropical paradise whose excellent soil, delightful climate, and easy access to markets via steamboat made it an ideal location for a trial phalanx. Only the mosquitoes intruded, but these, Macdaniel fourierized, were "rascals [who] belong to civilization and other subversive societies as emblems of lawyers and other kinds of social suckers, and as soon as we get a Phalanstery erected they will not dare to show their *Bills* any more than their prototypes."[50]

After returning to the North and conferring with Brisbane, Macdaniel drew up a detailed plan and introduced it to trusted colleagues. The mechanism he proposed was a Fourierist colony where blacks would work their way to freedom. As the colony's founders, Macdaniel and other Associationists would procure slaves on the understanding that the owners would be paid the slaves' market value from the products of their labor. In the process of constructing the colony's buildings, tilling its fields, and manning its workshops, the blacks would learn practical skills and accumulate the price of their emancipation. It was a theme common to many manumission plans aired in the antebellum era that slaves should "earn" their own freedom,[51] but Macdaniel introduced two novel Fourierist features. First, emancipation would be an object lesson in cooperative labor; rotating work teams and periodic community festivals would add to the slaves' productivity and enjoyment while introducing elements of cooperation. Second, as they worked for their freedom, blacks would be building a model Fourierist phalanx for whites to inhabit and enjoy thereafter. Macdaniel's goal was not simply to emancipate slaves but to "establish Association with the Whites, and [thereby] . . . lead the way to Universal Association." Indeed, he left no doubt which aim was more important: "The abolition of slavery is a great thing, but for itself alone, disconnected with general progress, I am not much concerned. I propose to avail myself of the slaves as agents to accomplish higher purposes than effecting their freedom only, which is incidental."

Brisbane, disappointed with the "unscientific" communal experiments gasping for breath in the North, had been proposing that Fourierists accumulate as much as $500,000 and hire laborers to prepare a regulation phalanx domain.[52] Macdaniel hoped to accomplish the same end by using borrowed slaves. As the phalanx neared completion, whites would gradually be substituted for blacks, and the slaves would move on to build up another site. The process could be continued indefinitely as fresh slaves replaced those earning emancipation and more whites were attracted to new communities. Through this scheme the feudal South would leap directly to socialism without passing through a capitalist phase. The freedmen themselves, having been educated and trained as skilled laborers, would be either colonized somewhere outside the United States or retained as "subordinate" workers whom American whites could hire to clear the frontier wilderness. This blatant racial paternalism aside, the absence of specific provisions for "the continued welfare of the Negroes after they are liberated" meant that Macdaniel failed to satisfy one of his and other Fourierists' stated conditions for sound emancipation.

Marx Edgeworth Lazarus proposed a similar but less sweeping plan. As a child of a slaveholding North Carolina family, he believed that the utopian socialists' mission was to head off abolitionist extremism with conciliatory overtures and practical suggestions for slaveholders.[53] In *The Harbinger* he outlined a program to increase productivity on plantations by substituting Fourierist attractive for coercive labor. As in a phalanx, music would send the workers out to the fields in the morning and greet them when they returned. The most productive would be honored with badges and titles, and on Saturday evenings great feasts would celebrate the week's devoted labor. Most important, slaves would rotate jobs every three or four hours, each time joining a new work group competing with others in the same task; the gains in health, morale, and productivity would be immense.[54] Taken by themselves these changes could be the work of an enlightened despot practicing sophisticated social engineering. Indeed, a few weeks after Lazarus presented his plan, the *Anti-Slavery Standard* warned that slavery and Association could form a sinister alliance: "Slaveholders may resort to social re-organization for their own benefit," abolitionists cautioned, by rationalizing plantation production without relinquishing their ownership of black workers. Jefferson Davis's older brother, inspired by Robert Owen, did conduct just such an experiment on his plantation at Davis Bend, Mississippi.[55]

But Lazarus intended his work reforms to be implemented simultaneously with an emancipation plan like John McDonogh's, in which slaves could work extra hours for wages, using the money to "buy" more time and eventually their freedom. Purchasing free time would become progressively easier: the more freedom gained, the greater the wages earned. Like Macdaniel, Lazarus viewed his scheme as a way of inculcating attitudes and habits that would guarantee the blacks' "energy, fitness for freedom, and ability to sustain themselves" in Civilization. Unlike Macdaniel, however, Lazarus believed that the freedmen's future lay in the American South, where "ties of good will and reciprocal service" would somehow replace coercive relations with their masters. Nor did he envision his model farms as the building blocks of full Association. Plantations adopting his plan would not become phalanxes, and their directors, whether southern planters or abolitionists, need not be utopian socialists, though the colonies' demonstration of Fourierist principles would doubtless benefit the Associationist movement.[56]

Macdaniel's and Lazarus's plans differed in details and were drawn up independently of the Fourierist movement, but their key provisions reflected the utopian socialist approach to emancipation. The gradual replacement of slavery with an alternative labor system, the introduction of cooperative arrangements in transitional colonies, and especially the reliance upon voluntary participation by slaveowners were established Fourierist strategies. Change was to come as slaveowners realized that they had nothing to lose through emancipation and perhaps much to gain. "Slaveholders do not hold slaves for the mere love of the system itself," Thomas Durant advised Brisbane, "but because they have not or they are not yet convinced that they have a better mode of making labor effective. Convince them that there is another and better mode, and you may be sure that they will adopt it."[57] This pragmatic appeal to slaveholders' self-interest suited the cautious path which southern-born antislaveryites, caught between their criticism of slavery and their distrust of the mounting northern crusade against it, tended to follow. The Macdaniel and Lazarus plans suggest a striking convergence between utopian socialism and the kind of conservative opposition to slavery that animated the small minority of southerners who voiced their dissent in the antebellum years. Though such men as Daniel Goodloe, Robert Breckinridge, or even John McDonogh hardly shared the Fourierist dream of transforming planters' mansions into phalansteries, they would have approved the utopians' gradualist strategy, their economic "realism," and their hostility to Garrisonian impatience.[58]

Macdaniel and Lazarus's manipulation of blacks and their not-so-subtle indifference to the oppression of slavery also reflect this conservative pattern. It would be unfair, however, to blame Fourierism for their cavalier attitude. Macdaniel and Lazarus actually ignored Associationist ideology by basing their stance toward blacks on the ground of innate racial traits rather than the devastation of slavery. Blacks were particularly suited for communal experiments, Macdaniel explained, because they are "children . . . grown infants with the muscular power of men . . . [whom] we can lead and wield . . . as we choose." To Lazarus the slaves were sensual, sentimental beings with extremely limited intellectual capacity: he advised planters adopting his plan to forgo the too taxing process of educating slaves to read and write. And though Lazarus rejected colonization, he evidently believed the Negro race doomed to extinction in the New World.[59] Such attitudes were in no sense derived from Fourierism, but they demonstrate how easily the pervasive racial prejudice of nineteenth-century America influenced opponents of slavery, whether northern Free-Soilers, southern dissenters, or utopian socialists.

Reaction to the two plans was revealing, ranging from mild endorsement or indifference among southern utopians to outright hostility among northern Associationists. Not surprisingly, the Fourierists' best friends in the South were unwilling to commit themselves to emancipation. Lazarus's plan was publicly endorsed by a Georgia Fourierist and, thanks to this encouragement, reprinted in books and articles that Lazarus published in the 1850s—but to no avail.[60] And although the Louisiana Fourierists gave Macdaniel advice and perhaps privately approved his scheme, neither Durant nor Wilkins nor any of the others publicly endorsed it. In fact, when Wilkins announced plans in 1850 to form an "Agricultural and Industrial Association" in Texas, he proposed to people it with northern emigrants rather than southern slaves. When he died two years later, he left no instructions to free his own slaves.[61]

Macdaniel, Lazarus, and the Fourierists may have shown more sophistication than abolitionists when they argued that immediate emancipation would leave the slaves totally dependent upon their former masters, but in some ways they were far more naive in their views of the nature of slavery and the slaveholder mentality. By considering chattel slavery simply another form of property ownership, the Fourierists respected the "rights" that guaranteed oppression. And by relying on voluntary emancipation, they doomed their plans to failure. Partly because slavery was very profitable to men like John Wilkins, but also because it was a system of race control as well as a system of labor, no appeals to philanthropy, no "attractions" of a Fourierist experiment, no promises of excellent compensation were enough to induce planters to abandon it.

As for northern Fourierists, by 1847 an increasing number had begun to believe that concessions to slaveowners or coalitions with them were intolerable. Though Macdaniel's plan won Ohio Associationist E. P. Grant's approval as well as Brisbane's, the generally hostile reception of Macdaniel's and Lazarus's ideas among northern Fourierists demonstrated the gains that antislavery attitudes were making in the movement. The Harbinger's editors felt compelled to print Lazarus's scheme, but they immediately disclaimed responsibility for his views of slavery and blacks, which, they regretted, expressed "the point of view prevailing at the South." One New England Fourierist not only declared Lazarus's plan unworkable but compared its compensation for slaveholders to ransom for kidnappers.[62]

Opposition to Macdaniel's Louisiana mission was swift and direct. While Macdaniel was in Louisiana, William Henry Channing introduced a motion at the annual AUA convention which would have required the movement to refuse any monetary contributions connected with slavery. Aimed directly at Wilkins and the Louisiana planters, it was defeated only after a "very animated discussion" during which Brisbane, Lazarus, and others defended a utopian socialist alliance with slaveholders.[63] Then when reports reached the North that in a lecture Macdaniel had criticized the abolitionists as "rash" and informed southern planters that the North's "white slavery" was in some respects worse than black bondage, a storm of protests erupted. It was one thing to air such arguments in Boston, quite another to profess them in Louisiana. Angry letters from antislavery Associationists poured into *The Harbinger* office, complaining that Macdaniel had misrepresented the "true" Fourierist position and that his remarks would serve to "quiet the conscience of the slaveholders . . . and . . . confirm their prejudices against the Abolitionists." According to these critics, the "wage slavery" argument was no longer viable because it carried the sinister implication that chattel slavery was *preferable* to free labor, an implication that proslavery ideologues were already beginning to develop. Slave ownership was so monstrously unjust that the old utopian socialist idea of compensated emancipation now seemed "absurd."[64]

The controversy over Macdaniel's mission demonstrated that the antislavery crusade was making powerful inroads among Northern utopians, just as Macdaniel and Lazarus had feared, and was discrediting the conciliatory economic reform that Fourierism had traditonally advocated and these southern-born utopians still stood for. Rather than absorbing the movement against slavery, the Associationists were themselves being absorbed by it.

10

The Movement Retreats

In the American Union of Associationists, national leaders had finally created a viable organizational structure for the Fourierist movement. AUA lecturers blanketed the Northeast with propaganda, and the affiliated unions promoted local Associationist projects after the lecturers moved on. Enough contributions were collected to publish three AUA-sponsored tracts: a statement refuting religious attacks on Fourierism, a translation of Considerant's lectures, and Godwin's rousing address to the New York convention of 1844.[1] Wealthy patrons Francis G. Shaw of Boston and Edmund Tweedy of New York contributed time and money for other publications, five of them French books translated by Shaw himself.[2] Yet the AUA faced financial difficulties from the outset. Boston and Philadelphia unions paid the weekly rent faithfully, but other dues arrived only sporadically, despite frequent appeals. Godwin and other New Yorkers pledged periodic payments to a permanent "propagation fund" to underwrite tracts and lecturers, but the New York Union could not even keep up its weekly pledge.[3] To make matters worse, Associationist leaders allowed funds to be tied up in speculative ventures. With the executive committee's approval, Brisbane invested a large contribution from John D. Wilkins of Louisiana in a new process for making steel. Apparently the scheme failed, and the money was never seen again.[4] The episode illustrated not just Brisbane's own lifelong weakness for inventions and speculations but the dangers inherent in the Fourierists' flirtation with capitalist practice.

Like the AUA, *The Harbinger* led a precarious financial existence. In June 1846, the same month the executive committee designated it the official organ of the AUA, editor George Ripley urgently appealed for contributions and additional subscribers.[5] Donations from key individuals kept the journal alive until the AUA's annual meeting in New York in 1847, at which New York and Boston Associationists negotiated its future. Each group wanted its city to house *The Harbinger* and the AUA's proposed new central office. It was decided that Bostonians would keep the paper until that fall; meanwhile, the AUA would open an office in New York to serve as the executive committee's headquarters, a library and clearinghouse, and eventually the new home of *The Harbinger*.[6] By October, George Ripley had closed Brook Farm's accounts and, now designated general agent of the AUA, moved to New York to man the AUA desk in the *Tribune* building and to review books for Greeley's paper. The next month *The Harbinger* was transferred to the AUA offices in New York. Parke Godwin was named the new editor, to be assisted by Ripley and Charles Dana in New York and John Dwight and William Henry Channing in Boston. The editors were to be paid a combined salary of $800 per year. Though Ripley complained in melancholy letters to Dwight of his "slavish and shabby" New York existence, he and the other Associationist leaders hoped that the move had put *The Harbinger* and the AUA on a permanent footing.[7]

The Model Phalanx and Deductive Socialism

For all their financial worries, the most crucial problem AUA leaders confronted in 1846–47 was a question of strategy: what to do about the phalanxes still in operation. With popular interest waning, Associationists faced the choice of either throwing their support to those phalanxes— and hoping not to perish with them—or working to amass resources for a new full-scale community closer to Fourier's specifications. The idea of a model phalanx had already been mapped out in 1845 as leaders reacted to the first phalanx failures, and their increasing emphasis on deep study and careful preparation made its creation the logical choice. But would the model be an entirely new experiment? Or would it evolve from an existing community, and if so, which phalanx was the best candidate? The New England Fourier Society had gone on record supporting Brook Farm, but the Massachusetts community was already living on borrowed time following its fire. Choosing another candidate would be especially difficult: Brook Farmers resented New York leaders' partiality to the North American Phalanx; despite promises of support the NAP seemed determined to evolve slowly; and the other major experiments, the Wisconsin and Trumbull phalanxes, were too far removed from the movement's popular base and its leaders' anxious eyes. On the other hand, starting afresh would strand these communities, might alienate faithful supporters, and in itself held no guarantee of success.

John Dwight, torn between his commitment as Fourierist leader and communal memories of West Roxbury, made an emotional plea in *The Harbinger*, for both preserving Brook Farm and undertaking a new trial. But most Associationists knew that a choice had to be made, and a spirited debate ensued privately and in print. On one side partisans of surviving phalanxes insisted that their communities be considered. North American Phalanx members argued that their "progressive mode" of reaching full Association had the best prospects of success. Warren Chase recommended the fertile site of his Wisconsin Phalanx as an asset; its western farmers were hardy souls who realized that the spartan "transition state" would take "many years."[8]

Ironically, the most articulate spokesman for this evolutionary view was the otherwise orthodox Parke Godwin. By 1846 Godwin had privately come to the conclusion that the movement had failed because it "desired to go too fast and too far at once"; he developed this insight into a telling critique of Fourier's teleology: "Model-phalanxes are a pretty idea, . . . but . . . no attempts of this kind could succeed. . . . I do not believe with Fourier that we can skip over all processes of guaranteeism. The most superficial and inconsistent part of his whole theory is where he supposes we can spring at once from Civilization to Association."[9] Godwin suggested that Associationists prepare "a plan for organizing townships,—taking them up as they are, and carrying them on step by step to higher degrees of associative unity," though he had no candidate for such townships among existing communities.[10]

On the other side stood Ripley, Brisbane, and a host of wealthy and impatient Boston, New York, and Philadelphia supporters. Ripley saw the end coming at Brook Farm and was not impressed by the NAP. Though publicly he wished current communities well, he favored a completely new trial somewhere in the East, with $300,000 providing the land and materials for four or five hundred members. Brisbane characteristically was more ambitious and elitist: at least $400,000 would be needed, he said, and hired laborers should prepare the domain for four years before the phalansterians arrived.[11]

Following a Boston meeting in January 1847, the AUA offically announced its aim to establish a model community "which shall illustrate to the world the truth, grandeur, and practicability of the doctrines of Association." The requisite funds would be accumulated in a permanent fund separate from the weekly AUA dues.[12] But would the model phalanx be a completely new experiment? The issue was settled at the AUA annual meeting in May 1847. Delegates rejected a resolution recommending aid to existing phalanxes as the best means of furthering Association and in its place passed a motion to register all those willing to join a new attempt. A committee of thirteen was appointed to study the best means of beginning a practical trial and report at the next annual meeting. Named to the committee were Brisbane and eastern publicists; only Charles Sears of the NAP represented an existing phalanx. In July, subcommittees were established to analyze the failure of recent Associations; to report on the condition of the NAP and the Trumbull and Wisconsin phalanxes, whose arrangements might hold lessons for the model phalanx; and to gather information on those ready to enter a new trial.[13]

Inquiries were placed in *The Harbinger* and sent to affiliated unions and individuals; trusted businessmen Joseph Cooke of Providence and James T. Fisher of Boston were sent to tour the phalanxes.[14] In October 1847 the committee reported that of the three communities visited, only the NAP's condition was "decidedly hopeful"; prospects at the others were "less sanguine."[15] But the AUA had already rejected the North American Phalanx as a model, and the permanent fund was as yet too meager to finance a new phalanx. The disappointing conclusion was inevitable: at the May 1848 annual convention the committee reluctantly reported that it was "not prepared to recommend" that the AUA "become responsible for any Practical Movement at the present time." There the model phalanx question died as an official concern of the American Union of Associationists.[16]

Not only did time-consuming vacillation hurt the model phalanx campaign, but the final decision was probably mistaken: the notion of organizing a new trial phalanx helped to kill the Fourierist movement. Time and energy were wasted in preparing to start over, while existing communities—manned by loyal friends and publicly identified as Fourierist—were left dangling. Their failures continued to discredit the theory, despite Associationist leaders' disclaimers. Meanwhile, putting all the movement's eggs in one (proposed) basket proved just as dangerous as spreading resources too thin among existing groups, since the projected model community was never established.

There was still one circle of influential and wealthy Associationists, however, who opted for the other strategy: evolving an existing phalanx into a full-fledged Fourierist model. In February 1848 this group, which included Greeley and Henry James, Sr., New York merchants Edward Giles, Marcus Spring, and Edmund Tweedy, Philadelphia's James Kay, and Boston's James Fisher, officially formed the Phalansterian Realization Fund Society (PRFS). Most were shareholders in the North American Phalanx, though none was a resident member. These patrons subscribed $35,000 for the "founding, or assisting & carrying forward" of a model association.[17] They had in mind that the North American Phalanx should be developed into a model experiment and could for that purpose draw interest-free loans from their fund. There were two conditions: that the PRFS be formally joined to the NAP under incorporation laws (thus guaranteeing the PRFS more collateral for the loan and a greater voice in NAP affairs), and that several thousand dollars be used to erect a permanent "Grand Unitary Edifice" that would house an expanded membership of five hundred persons.[18]

There was some interest in expansion at the North American Phalanx; during the model phalanx debate the NAP had told *Harbinger* readers that with "more good members and more means," it could make "a more decided demonstration" of Fourierist principles. But most of its members objected to the PRFS scheme. They believed that the community had to grow slowly and selectively; they wanted its fate decided by residents, not outsiders; and they preferred to base expansion on improvements in the community's agricultural and milling operations. After "an animated discussion," the NAP's Executive Council decided in June 1848 that "the interests of this Association will not be best promoted by the appropriation" proposed by the PRFS. Eventually, a compromise was reached in which $2,000 went to begin a "provisional" unitary edifice, $1,400 toward land improvements, and $1,500 for the mill.[19] As Dolores Hayden has noted, "The patrons' dreams of a building on Brisbane Hill with a facade half a mile long had been countered effectively by the members' more practical and comprehensive views."[20] By 1852, NAP members had built a modest wood-frame, three-story residence with additional wings for a dining hall and bedrooms. They had chosen wisely. Their decision to avoid drastic overnight expansion helped keep the community socially and economically cohesive for six more years, whereas outside control and sudden growth would probably have shattered it.

The PRFS loans of 1848–49 were the only organized attempt by national Associationist leaders to subsidize expansion of an existing phalanx into a "true" Fourierist community. But the dream of a huge model phalanx died hard. Again in September 1850 the PRFS tried without success to raise money for upgrading the NAP or undertaking a new Fourierist experiment.[21] Once they had read Fourier's vivid description and had seen the palatial phalanstery in the engraving Brisbane brought back from France, many Associationists found it difficult to praise such modest efforts as the North American Phalanx, however economically viable they appeared. "Orthodox" leaders Brisbane, E. P. Grant and James Kay continued to dream of a utopian socialist version of Versailles on American soil. At the very banquet celebrating the opening of the NAP's new dining hall in 1851, PRFS secretary James Fisher could not resist sketching on his menu a gigantic phalanstery better representing, he felt, the true "social destiny of man." The following year, when Marcus Spring forsook the North American Phalanx to establish the Raritan Bay Union nearby, he began with a monumental stone phalanstery costing $40,000 and built by hired laborers.[22] Long after the Fourierist movement faded, Brisbane remained obsessed with promoting plans for one huge experiment that would demonstrate conclusively the truth of Fourier's theory. For three decades he circulated innumerable proposals, as if one detail changed or another sponsor contacted could make the dream achieve reality.[23]

In actuality, the chances that a model phalanx could succeed, whether built from scratch or evolved more gradually from a smaller community, were remote. It is here that we come upon one of the most vulnerable assumptions of Fourier's theory and of utopian socialism in general: the notion that material arrangements guaranteeing collective harmony could be "scientifically" derived from human nature and then simply applied to living subjects ignored the messy vitality of life, as Emerson had pointed out.[24] All experience argued against starting with fixed, a priori principles and plans that viewed communal life as an illustration of doctrine rather than an evolving experiment. Emerson and several contemporaries voiced this caveat, but it was John Humphrey Noyes of Oneida who developed the most coherent critique in a revealing exchange with Brisbane on "deductive and inductive socialisms" after the Fourierist movement's collapse. After reminding Noyes in timeworn fashion that no phalanx of the 1840s met Fourier's prescribed conditions, Brisbane asserted that a true social science had to be deduced "with the greatest patience and fidelity" from nature's laws of organization. In response, Noyes denied that "cogitation without experiment" could produce communitarian success. Fourier's model phalanx had already proved this: "It was brought before the world with all the advantages that the most brilliant school of modern genius could give it; and it did not win the confidence of scientific men or of capitalists, because they saw . . . that it came from the closet, and not from the world of facts."[25] Noyes had an ax to grind when he favored inductive religious communitarianism over deductive secular socialism, but he put his finger on a crucial flaw in Fourier's theory. The history of Oneida bore out his critique by showing the superiority of evolving, rather than imposing, the conditions for communal life.

Yet whether a "model phalanx" could have succeeded is in a sense a moot issue. The immediate problem was that by adopting it as a goal, Associationists created a strategic cul-de-sac. Brisbane and his colleagues had shown admirable flexibility when they pared down Fourier's grandiose phalanx blueprint and encouraged modest communal ventures, but when they reversed themselves and returned to orthodoxy in the movement's midcareer, they guaranteed disaster. If rudimentary phalanxes had to be repudiated as bogus trials of Fourier's theory, yet a true model phalanx was so elaborate and expensive it could never be set up, then what was left? Here again, Noyes shrewdly saw the pitfalls of deductive social science and thus deserves the last word:

> Practically it [associationism] says to the world—"The experiments of the Shakers and other religious Communities, though successful, are unscientific and worthless; the experiments of the Fourierists that failed so miserably, were illegitimate and prove nothing; . . . the only thing that can be done to realize true Association, is to put together eighteen hundred human beings on a domain three miles square, with a palace and outfit to match. Then you will see the equilibrium of the passions and spontaneous order and industry, insuring infinite success." As these conditions are well known to be impossible, because nobody believes in the promised equilibrium and success, the upshot of this teaching is despair.[26]

Public Opinion and the Decline of Fourierism

At some point in the years 1846 and 1847, the American public must have realized the truth of Noyes's conclusions, for it turned against

Association so decisively that the Fourierists' hope for a national federation of phalanxes was no longer viable. In part, this shift of opinion was simply the result of the nation's return to relative prosperity. As the depression of the early 1840s lifted and the business cycle began its climb, opportunities for employment increased, and workers who had flocked to phalanxes found new options for mobility and security. Public attention was also drawn to the issues of expansion and slavery which the Mexican War made so pressing and controversial. But the increasingly negative response to Fourierism was also prompted by attacks in the nation's magazines and newspapers.

Ever since they had introduced Fourierism in the *New York Tribune* and *The Phalanx,* Associationists had faced criticism in the religious and political press. There were predictable charges that Fourierists, like all radical reformers, were out to overturn property rights and customary social obligations. Arising more out of prejudice than from knowledge of the theory, these could be easily disposed of.[27] Claims that Association was impractical could also be pushed aside by referring critics to thriving communal groups such as the Shakers or by predicting success for phalanx experiments currently underway.[28] More unsettling to Associationist leaders, at least in the period from 1844 to 1846, were criticisms of Fourier's theory from evangelical Protestants. Often carefully reasoned and well documented, published sermons and articles in such journals as the *New York Observer,* the *Universalist Quarterly,* and the *American Whig Review* argued that Fourierism was antithetical to Christianity and charged that Associationists were hiding Fourier's most shocking descriptions of life in Harmony, visions that the Frenchman asserted were necessary extrapolations of his theory.[29]

Associationist responses to these charges have already been discussed, but whether the Fourierists were winning or losing these exchanges is less significant than the fact that they were increasingly being put on the defensive. With community building slowing down, attention turned to a more leisurely examination of Fourierist ideas; as phalanxes began to fail, critics became more confident that they could end the Fourierist mania by destroying the theory. Ironically, Associationist leaders added fuel to the fire by choosing to enter their second stage of propaganda at exactly this moment. Beginning in 1845 *The Phalanx* and then *The Harbinger* printed more detailed accounts of Fourier's "theory of the passions" and its implications for sensitive areas of "civilized" life such as church and family. The movement's critics were donated ammunition just as the war of words escalated.

As a result, far more of *The Harbinger's* pages were devoted to refuting critics than to discussing the mechanics of building an organized Fourierist movement. Such articles as "The Democratic Review and Association" and "The New York Observer on Association" and a long series answering "Objections to Association" crowded out news of the phalanxes and the American Union.[30] The first tract published by the AUA was a formal statement "with reference to recent attacks," in which national leaders again repudiated Fourier's "theories of Marriage . . . and the Immortality of the Soul" and denied advocating *any* change in church and family.[31] Parke Godwin and E. P. Grant, who were not consulted in its preparation, warned that it was "truckling" and "timid." Associationists, wrote Grant, "should shrink from nothing, whether in the present or the future." They should "openly and boldly . . . dissent from the religious dogmas of our prevalent Christianity" and proclaim "the true relations of love and familism." Those who demurred "should be treated as unconverted persons."[32] According to these dissenters, the necessity of placating religious sects and the need to present a united front among Associationist leaders was reducing the movement to platitudes.

Both this debilitating defensiveness and the ticklish ideological problems behind it were dramatized in a nationally publicized debate in 1846–47 between Horace Greeley and Henry J. Raymond of the *New York Courier and Enquirer*. Here the tension between Fourierism and "Association," the radical implications of Fourier's passional psychology, and the awkward timidity of Fourierist leaders were uncomfortably displayed at the worst possible time for the movement.

The contrast between the two opponents could hardly have been greater. On one side stood Greeley, the tall, white-haired, and flinty progressive; on the other was Raymond, a small, black-bearded conservative whose cleverness was more than a match for Greeley's sincerity. As Greeley's assistant in 1841, Raymond had thought the alliance with Fourierism a mistake; now with a rival paper, he saw an opportunity to deflate Greeley's reform enthusiasms and boost circulation in the process. It was a fitting tack for the ambitious young journalist who would later found the *New York Times*.[33]

Raymond opened the debate by attacking phalanx arrangements as unfair and impractical, but when Greeley's defense proved forceful, Raymond turned to the radical underpinnings of Fourierist social science. Passional attraction, he charged, was the most fundamental and pernicious Fourierist law. It substituted human whim for immutable moral laws; it abolished such important disciplining institutions as churches and governments; and it threatened to destroy monogamous marriage and sexual restraint. Greeley replied with the usual disclaimers that Associationists did not swallow Fourier whole and that social reconstruction should be guided by conservative "experience." But Raymond shrewdly noted that such disclaimers left room for substantial social changes and, more important, did not deny the principles upon which Fourierism rested. Associationists could not have it both ways: either Fourierism was *not* grounded in a true "science of man," or its proponents had to acknowledge the radical implications of that science.

Pushed to the wall, Greeley made damaging admissions. He did not endorse the theory of passional attraction, and Fourier erred in applying it to sexual relations. Brisbane's *Social Destiny of Man*, from which Raymond had drawn his ammunition, was the "crudest book ever issued in this country by an Associationist." "No two Associationists" agreed on interpreting Fourier's writings, and Greeley himself did not believe—or even fully understand—Association as a scientific theory: "This thing Assocation, as I hold and advocate it, is a matter of Practice altogether—the simple actualization of the truth of Universal Human Brotherhood." No wonder that as the debate wound down, Raymond proclaimed himself satisfied that he had "*compelled* the Tribune . . . to disavow and abandon, some of the most vital and essential elements of the Association theory."[34]

The Greeley-Raymond debate revealed the huge and uncomfortable gap between what Greeley called "Association as I understand it" and orthodox Fourierism. "Industrial Association" could not be separated from Fourier's entire system unless Associationists were willing to admit that their plan was intuition and guesswork rather than "social science." Most Associationist leaders did not join Greeley in renouncing Fourier's psychology but hoped to stave off critics by declaring sexual relations exempt or favoring the gradual liberation of instinct. Both positions exemplified the nearly unbearable tension between Fourierist principles and Associationist policy: Greeley's stance renounced Fourier in order to remain consistent; the majority position retained Fourier but was hopelessly contradictory. Though few readers may have been able to detect the larger ideological dilemma that the Greeley-Raymond debate exposed, they could not miss Greeley's defensive posture and his abject retreat from Fourierism.

The debate, running from November 1846 to May 1847 and coming on the heels of the AUA's own timid *Statement*, dealt so demoralizing a blow to the Associationist movement that James Parton, writing a few years later, claimed it had "*finished* Fourierism in the United States."[35] Certainly it widely broadcast the coming end. Reprinted in the *Tribune's* weekly and semiweekly editions, it circulated into the very homes and libraries where Association had found its first hearing. Greeley himself seemed to sense the debate's significance. Near the end of the exchange he declined to join the New York Union's celebration of Fourier's birthday, calling himself a "weary soldier . . . not particularly inclined to feasting."[36] Afterwards, he slowly withdrew from the Associative movement. Though he continued as titular head of the American Union and the *Tribune* continued to print news of Fourierist meetings and communities, Greeley shifted his interest to the more practical and gradual measures of land reform and worker cooperatives. The phalanxes had lost an enormously influential and appealing public supporter.

Greeley's defeat and critics' puncturing of Fourier's theory hurt the Associationists, but what really "finished" Fourierism in the United States—at least as a social movement—was the failure of the American phalanxes. Beset by enormous problems mostly of their own making, the overwhelming majority of the communities established during the early Fourierist craze suffered brief and troubled lives. Of the seventeen phalanxes founded in 1843–44, all but five had succumbed by the end of 1846, and three of those disbanded within another two years. In the end it was these ill-fated experiments upon which the outcome of the Fourierist movement hinged. Though Association encompassed much more than the phalanxes, and such leaders as Brisbane and Godwin never joined one, to most observers—then and since—Fourierism was a communitarian movement pure and simple.

The rapid collapse of the phalanxes had a devastating effect. Expectations for success had been raised ridiculously high by the millennial fervor of the early 1840s, and the subsequent disillusionment was proportional. This dynamic could best be seen in New York's Burned-Over District, where, as Arthur Bestor pointed out, there was a closer connection between Fourierist experiments and local public opinion than in large urban centers.[37] By 1847, none of the phalanxes established by Rochester-area Fourierists was still in operation; and Jonathan Grieg, formerly of the Clarkson Phalanx, lamented to Associationist leaders that "I know of no man, except a brother of mine, . . . in this city of 30,000 . . . who dares publicly to advocate the 'Great Truth.' "[38] When John Allen and John Orvis toured upstate New York the following summer as agents of the AUA, they witnessed the permanent damage done by local phalanx failures. Though they had some success in Albany and Utica, the lecturers' task became more and more difficult as they moved westward to the heart of the Burned-Over District. Syracuse they found "blighted" by the failure of John Collins's Skaneateles community, mistakenly identified by many as Fourierist. "Most of the old friends of the cause," they reported, "are disheartened; their hands are hanging down in despair." In Rochester they could get no hearing at all, thanks to "the faded glory of *four* [local] phalanxes." Prospects for meetings there were "less favorable than . . . [in] any place where we have previously visited. . . . The very name of Association is odious with the public, and the unfortunate people who went into these movements in such mad haste, have been ridiculed till endurance is no longer possible, and they are slunk away from the sight and knowledge of their neighbors."[39] "The failure of those ill-starred phalanxes," they concluded, "prejudiced the public mind to an undue degree, and deferred the hope of our cause throughout Western New York."[40] The story was apparently similar in Wisconsin, where Warren Chase reported that local pundits had dubbed Associationists "Four-year-ites" because of the expected duration of their communities.[41]

Even the obtuse and ever optimistic Albert Brisbane recognized the writing on the wall. In 1847 he decided to retire temporarily from active propagation of Fourierism. "The failure of these little associations," he later wrote, "had led the public to suppose that fair trials had been made and the valuelessness of the system demonstrated." Feeling that "it was hopeless to begin anew," he returned to his studies with the hope of extending Fourier's theoretical schema to the natural sciences. He cut back drastically on his lecturing and writing: in April 1847 his last contribution to *The Harbinger* appeared, and the next month he declined reelection as an AUA officer. Although Brisbane appeared sporadically at Associationist functions that year, the AUA had lost the services of a tireless, if controversial, promoter of Association.[42]

By the summer of 1847, Fourierist hopes for a national network of phalanxes were effectively ended. But American Fourierism did not die; it evolved— in two main directions. In one direction it increasingly took on the characteristics of a sect; in the other it retreated into promoting gradual or partial schemes of reform, with the idea that these might serve as a transition to full Association.

From Movement to Sect: A Socialist Church

"Sect" as a generic term can refer to a group or school of persons devoted to a creed or doctrine set apart from the mainstream. Often used to disparage such a group, it connotes small size, a certain exclusiveness, rigid emphasis upon doctrine, and often distance from centers of prevailing opinion and power. As prospects for a broad-based Associative movement faded in the 1840s, the Fourierists increasingly fit this description. Intricate articles in *The Harbinger* on Fourier's arcane theories of analogy and cosmology, hostile responses to religious and secular critics, the relatively elite membership and clublike atmosphere of the affiliated unions, a growing interest in distinctive ceremony and ritual—all these testified that the Associationists were solidifying their position and postponing the anticipated mass conversion of Americans to their ideas. What was even more striking was the specifically *religious* dimension of sectarianism that became increasingly characteristic of the Associationist movement.[43]

This was not a unique trend. In Europe, utopian socialism of all varieties tended to adopt a sectarian religious mode, especially after each one's initial failure to convert large numbers had reduced adherents to a hopeful band of true believers. Devoted to a doctrine handed down by a prophetic "master," these movements often evolved into "churches" espousing a "new Christianity" that proposed to replace the old by actualizing it. After Robert Owen proclaimed his discovery of the "New Moral World," he became increasingly messianic, and his followers constituted a loosely organized "millennarian sect" that anticipated a Second Coming identified with the triumph of their doctrine. Etienne Cabet, the most politically astute of the utopian socialists and the one most directly involved in working-class agitation, also succumbed to the sectarian impulse. As economic conditions worsened in France and bourgeois democrats deserted his coalition, Cabet began to see himself as the prophet of "true Christianity" and eventually migrated to America with his closest followers to create a communist New Jerusalem in Texas. The most explicitly sectarian utopian socialists were the Saint-Simonians, whose religion of industrial progress and fraternity influenced early Fourierists and whose cultlike socialist church, with elaborate rituals, bizarre costumes, and monastic rules, signaled the movement's demise.[44]

The Fourierists were also prone to sectarian tendencies, though their case was more complicated because their movement was never reduced to a church. Fourier himself, as Jonathan Beecher has noted, was too much a product of the Enlightenment to consider his theory a religion and his followers a sect. Although he could refer to himself as "the Messiah of Reason" and sometimes compared his sufferings to Christ's, he dismissed Owenite and Saint-Simonian attempts to dress their theories in Christianity as a "religious masquerade" and called them "sects" derisively.[45] Yet Fourier's French followers set out after his death to Christianize the doctrine they inherited and to deify its inventor. In speeches, popular biographies of Fourier, and best-selling yearly almanacs, Victor Considerant and his colleagues portrayed themselves as devoted "apostles" and their master as "the man chosen by Christ" to bring the kingdom of God to earth.[46]

Such imagery and rhetoric abounded among American Associationists as well. Coming in the wake of the Transcendentalist revolt and the religious revivals of the 1830s, as we have seen, Associationism developed into a quasi-religious movement whose adherents freely blended utopian socialist teleology with Christian rhetoric. At public meetings and in private correspondence, they quoted scripture and styled themselves "apostles" proclaiming a "new gospel," "crusaders" restoring the Holy Land, or prophets envisioning a "New Jerusalem" of love and harmony.[47] Yet jeremiads, prophecies, and scriptural analogies were not enough to satisfy some Fourierists' desire to infuse their movement with a millennial aura. By the mid-1840s several Associationists were demanding visible representations of socialist piety in a distinctive "church of humanity" or "church of universal unity." "We have a *Religion* to announce to our fellows," proclaimed William Henry Channing, the leader of this group, and to promote it, a "Church" was a "necessary function."[48]

Officially, the movement styled itself a nonsectarian effort to rally the hopeful of all faiths to implement the "Divine Social Code." Associationists guaranteed freedom of religious expression, and most phalanxes had meeting halls where groups of any persuasion could gather. Fourierists proudly pointed out that their ranks included members of diverse sects, from Catholics to all varieties of Protestants to Jews. But there were always important qualifiers. The great majority came from liberal Protestant backgrounds, and their fierce polemics against Calvinist doctrines belied their supposed neutrality. According to Parke Godwin, Fourierists regarded all who denied human goodness and the promise of an earthly kingdom as "infidels, whatever may be their *professions* or *creeds*."[49] If Fourierism was "true" Christianity, then some existing varieties were "false" ones. The tension between holding beliefs hostile to contemporary religious groups and insisting that Associationists were devout Christians seemed to impel them irresistibly toward formalized religious expression.

For a time, it appeared that Swedenborgianism might become what Noyes called the "state-religion" of the Fourierists. The role of New Church ministers in founding phalanxes has already been noted, and Swedenborg's writings were the basis for Sabbath meetings in several communities. But the campaign to merge Swedenborgians and Fourierists quickly lost momentum. An alliance would have blatantly violated Associationists' professed neutrality toward existing churches, and too many Fourierists were committed Unitarians, Universalists, or other Protestant sectarians to make it feasible. For their part, Swedenborgians who turned to Fourier soon came under attack in the orthodox *New Jerusalem Magazine* and *New Church Repository* for the "horrible falsity" of their endeavor. Fourierists who were New Church ministers were forced to retreat to orthodoxy or face suspension; New Church laymen remaining in the movement learned to identify themselves merely as "Swedenborgians."[50]

The most visible form of religious sectarianism was not engrafted upon the movement but developed from within. The process by which it evolved and the forms it took were best demonstrated at Brook Farm, whose members and friends made it the religious center of the Associationist movement.

Largely because Brook Farm was born in a rebellion against religious formalism, most members left church ties behind when they entered the community.[51] Thus in Brook Farm's first two years a general consensus prohibited formal religious meetings or worship on the community's grounds. But conversion to Fourierism in 1844 stimulated the desire for religious expression. In part this desire derived from members' apprehension that Fourier's mechanistic plan might snuff out the community's idealism if not counterbalanced by organized spiritual forces. But it also reflected a new sense of mission gained from allegiance to Fourier's social science. Brook Farmers came to believe that Fourier was the "chosen messenger" whose blueprint for the earthly kingdom Christ had foretold, and their community the center of a providential movement to bring salvation to humanity. All these factors encouraged some Brook Farmers to experiment with new religious rituals investing utopian socialism with Christian overtones and "socializing" Christianity. On important Brook Farm occasions—such as weddings or gatherings of Fourierist leaders—members formed circles symbolic of "universal unity," took "vows" to the cause and one another, and gave toasts to the coming millennium.[52]

Gradually, the rituals became more elaborate and more insistent in blending Fourierist and religious motifs. As Charles Crowe has pointed out, at Brook Farm and other Associationist centers the annual celebration of Fourier's birthday became a kind of "socialist Christmas." On one such April 7 at Brook Farm, a plaster bust of the Frenchman faced the cruciform dining table, evergreen decorations suggested the immortality of Fourier's message, and decorated signs identified Fourier with "the Comforter . . . whom the Father will send in my name." To Brook Farmers, Fourier's dictum that "attractions are proportional to destinies" seemed to confirm God's promise of an earthly kingdom, and their banquet toasts suggested Fourier himself as "the Second Coming of Christ."[53]

Ironically, installation of Fourier among the deities came at a time when Associationists were otherwise dissociating themselves from his complete doctrinal system. The fact that they ignored or overrode this consideration as well as their opposition to sectarianism showed how deeply Associationists felt the need to "spiritualize" socialism and join in communal rituals. Annual celebrations did not satisfy a devout circle of Brook Farmers who wanted more frequent and private gatherings. In October 1845 William Henry Channing met with this group to plan weekly services in a chapel to be built in Brook Farm's new phalanstery. These arrangements were cut short by the fire of March 1846.[54]

At this point, Brook Farm's religious mission was taken up by Boston friends. With the phalanx gone, a utopian socialist church was especially needed to rally dispersed members. After discussions with Associationist leaders from New York, Philadelphia, and other cities, Brook Farmers and Bostonians officially formed the Religious Union of Associationists (RUA) in January 1847. With Channing as minister to this "Church of Humanity," the group adopted a general statement of beliefs and purposes which proclaimed "the will of God, by the ministry of man, to introduce . . . the Kingdom of Heaven upon Earth" and consecrated each member to fulfill this mission through Association.[55] Despite disclaimers that it had no sectarian plans, the RUA invited Fourierists to establish a "congregation" whose goal would be "the reconciliation of the Christian Church and Social Reform."[56]

With such a mission, the Church of Humanity quickly developed Christian socialist rituals parallel to the rituals of other churches. Weekly services imaginatively blended Fourierist and Christian symbolism. Busts of Fourier and Christ were placed in the chapel, an empty chair near the altar symbolized both the invisible presence of God and the absence of "Universal Unity." Channing himself effused warmly in sermons that described Christ as a reformer and compared Associationists to traditional religous orders. John Dwight composed Fourierist prayers to be sung with musical arrangements from Schubert and conducted selections from Mozart or Mendelssohn to accompany the day's "sentiments." One particularly striking ceremony was a utopian socialist version of communion in which a dozen goblets of water, recalling the twelve apostles and twelve Fourierist "passions," were passed around with bread and fruit and consumed silently after an interlude of music and prayer. At evening meetings closed to the public there were "confessional" sessions in which members shared accounts of their religious pilgrimage to Association, discussed spiritualism, antislavery, and other reform topics, or heard readings from Fourier or Swedenborg. A Sunday School was established to teach the Associationist brand of Christianity to young people.[57]

The formula was so successful that plans were hatched to establish congregations of the Church of Humanity elsewhere. Early in 1848 the group ordained John Allen as a "Minister of Universal Unity" and dispatched him to lecture in Pittsburgh and Cincinnati. Proposals were made for Channing to rotate his ministry among the parent group in Boston, the Philadelphia Union, and the North American Phalanx.[58] These branch "churches" met sporadically, but none lasted beyond a season. Instead, the Boston church became a Mecca for visiting Associationist leaders from Providence, Philadelphia, the NAP, and even abroad.

Like the AUA's affiliated unions, the Religious Union was a gathering of the Fourierist elite rather than a representative cross-section of the movement or society in general. Whereas Brook Farm had an artisan majority, the RUA was dominated by professionals and white-collar workers (see Appendix Table 12). The church enrolled forty men, thirty-seven of whose occupations can be identified; only nine were artisans or semiskilled workers, and six of these were former Brook Farmers. Roughly 80 percent of the non–Brook Farm communicants were professionals, proprietors, and clerks, a proportion nearly identical to that of the Boston Union, which shared many members with the church. Those who contributed to the Religious Union without formally joining were even better heeled: over half were merchants, ministers, doctors, and philanthropists.[59] This occupational profile supports the previous conclusion that middle- and upper-class Fourierists dominated local clubs, whereas working-class Fourierists preferred phalanxes and left the Associationist coalition after their collapse. When combined with a religious poll showing that RUA members came overwhelmingly from Unitarian or Universalist backgrounds, it also suggests that the Church of Humanity approached the social homogeneity usually identified with sects.[60]

In one sense the Religious Union was among the most successful of American Fourierist institutions. Its amalgam of Christianity and Associationism expressed a genuinely felt religious enthusiasm, plausibly bridged the gap between secular and religious ideas, and developed unique and apparently satisfying rituals. Regular meetings and a stream of visitors from around the country kept Fourierists in contact after the American Union and all but one of the phalanxes had disappeared. Despite the decline of general interest in Fourierism, the church continued in existence until 1853.[61] But the Religious Union was not simply another Fourierist institution. Its religious basis, elite composition, and distinctive rituals marked an important development. In the early 1840s the Associationist movement had begun as a spontaneous coalition of classes and religious groups bent upon transforming America through nonsectarian communities. By 1847 only a few phalanxes still existed, but rather than joining or supporting them, an important Fourierist remnant gathered in a utopian socialist church to keep their faith alive.

The Fourierist movement may not have *become* a church, but adherents who founded one and concentrated their remaining fervor upon it were admitting Associationism's defeat as a social movement and adopting the same sectarianism they had sworn to avoid.

Retreat to Gradualism: "Guarantist" Reforms

When the sudden leap to Harmony failed to materialize, many Associationists retreated to more limited and gradual reforms, hoping these would pave the way for full Association. Such institutions as mutual insurance plans and producer and consumer cooperatives demonstrated the benefits of Association on a small scale and gave utopians realistic goals to strive for while accruing funds for a trial phalanx. But admitting evolutionary thought into communitarianism had costs as well as advantages. Even as they endorsed it, Fourierists were seriously divided over the strategy of gradualism. Some were uncomfortable with abandoning the phalanx as an immediate goal; others embraced such practical measures so avidly that they lost sight of the movement's larger aims altogether; still others saw these reforms as a way to end their affiliation with Fourierism without forsaking social progress. In the end, fears that gradualist reforms might be co-opted or frustrate larger aims proved well founded. Associationists rightly claimed that their propaganda had inspired and encouraged these cooperative institutions, but the Fourierists were too weak and divided to guide the participants toward full Association or even to convince them that such a goal was desirable.

As we have seen, there had always been ambiguity within Fourierism about the length of the road to Harmony. In the early 1840s this caused few problems. Anticipating quick success, Associationist leaders pushed for model phalanx experiments and downplayed "partial" or transitional reforms with their narrow application of cooperative principles. Around 1847 the rash of phalanx failures caused some leaders to rethink the Fourierist strategy of founding a model community, especially as more limited crusades—including cooperative stores and access to public lands—were gaining ground. John Orvis reported from western New York that the only way for Associationists to get a hearing was to advertise lectures on consumer cooperatives and land reform; he urged *The Harbinger* to take up these causes in order to survive.[62] As if in response, Associationist writings began to present Fourierism as an evolutionary social science. Contemporary developments from the factory system to benevolent societies were used as evidence that Fourier's prediction of a transitional period of "Guarantism" was being fulfilled. Some Associationists began to assert that a sudden leap to "Compound Association" was, "in the nature of things, impossible." Instead, there would be a gradual transition consisting of various "preparatory measures" to relieve the sufferings of Civilization and prepare humanity for the novelties of Harmony. Reformist measures and schemes of "guarantyism" did not compete with Association but complemented it: they demonstrated cooperative principles, were immediately attainable, and attracted those unwilling or unable to join phalanxes. Adopting cooperative forms of organization inside the Fourierist movement might draw new members; encouraging outside groups to establish similar forms would win new allies and eventually steer them to communitarianism.[63]

The Harbinger urged affiliated unions to develop a range of mutual guarantees: cooperative purchasing arrangements, group insurance, subscription libraries, "club-houses," or even a "common hotel." In 1847 the annual convention of the American Union suggested that the unions join in purchasing agreements, and the next year the AUA advocated "a progressive system of Guarantees" for all unions.[64] Several unions responded with plans, and a few were able to implement them. The Albany group provided sickness and funeral benefits for dues-paying members and in 1848 opened its own cooperative store, as did the Ceresco Union at the Wisconsin Phalanx. The Boston Union discussed a wide range of projects, including a clubhouse, cooperative store, and mutual insurance. The Philadelphia Union established a "Group of Actuation," which offered sickness and death benefits.[65]

One group of projects, pioneering plans for "combined households" and "unitary dwellings," deserves fuller discussion. Though Fourier has been called an agrarian escapist, the phalanx had its roots in urban design; its blueprint derived not from agricultural villages but from the boulevards of Paris. The neoclassical design, urban amenities, and economies of scale of the Palais Royal, residential hotels, and large public buildings of Paris impressed Fourier indelibly and left their mark in the central courts, covered galleries, and other details of his phalanx plan. Several commentators noted the phalanstery's likeness to a great hotel.[66] Fourier's Parisian followers not only envisioned the phalanx as a kind of residential hotel but were instrumental in developing a new urban architectural form to match their vision: the apartment house. As explosive urban growth pushed up land values and fashionable residences became prohibitively expensive, Parisian architects of the 1830s developed designs for elaborate rental quarters for respectable middle-class dwellers. The Fourierist architect César Daly was one of the most influential champions of this movement. To Daly, the architecture of each age reflected the structure of the household and the nature of the society of its times. If the most appropriate architectural style of the historically conscious nineteenth century was eclecticism, Daly wrote, the most typical urban dwelling was similarly transitional. The varied flats of an apartment building expressed the tastes and classes of Civilization, but in attempting to reconcile community needs and individual privacy, such structures also prefigured the phalanstery of Harmonic society.[67]

In their guarantist phase, American Associationists found the idea of such hotellike residences especially attractive. Several Rochester, Boston, and New York Fourierists had already gathered in congenial boarding-houses where they shared reform talk and vegetarian fare. Now, they envisioned more comprehensive dwellings where Fourierists would share living arrangements or "domestic Association" while working in capitalist society. The Philadelphia Union developed the most elaborate plan: a sprawling, four-story, neoclassical building almost four hundred feet long to be located in the suburbs near a commuter railroad. Associationists would live in separate apartments with their own baths but share a library, dining hall, and swimming pool. A similar plan for a suburban "palace" came from the Cincinnati Union, while the Boston Union debated the construction of a "Combined House" based on French apartment house models. Although none of these projects ever reached the construction stage, they place the Associationists among the pioneer advocates of apartment living in America. Their plans were developed thirty years before the first large-scale apartment building appeared in New York City.[68]

A more modest but nonetheless important collective living arrangement eventually *was* established by the Bostonians. In the fall of 1848 seven Boston Union members moved into the home of their friend Anna Parsons in Boston and ran it as a cooperative. Each resident contributed rent and did housework; the group's meals were prepared by the women in exchange for a reduction in rent; the Boston Union held its meetings in the parlor. The arrangement survived at least until the 1850 census. Another group of nine ex–Brook Farmers—two couples and five unmarried men and women—was recorded in the same census as sharing a residence in Boston. Bringing the scaled-down phalanstery to the city, these "combined households" may well have been America's first urban communes.[69]

Although fledgling affiliated unions could adopt only a few such "guarantees," the Fourierists provided valuable support for gradualist reforms centered outside the movement. Two of these measures, "protective unions" (cooperative stores), and land reform, were important links to the working class (see Chapter 11), but several other transitional schemes were no less significant.

Associationists promoted mutual insurance, for example, as a widely applicable partial reform. The insurance industry in the United States lagged behind established practice in England, and only a few companies offered life policies before the 1840s. But the period 1843 to 1847 was the great founding era of American life insurance. Nearly a dozen firms were started, most being mutual rather than stockholding companies, run by the premiums and votes of policyholders rather than for the benefit of investor-owners. Mutual life insurance became increasingly safe and accessible to the common person.[70] Fourierists were doubly pleased by this development. Here was a collective guarantee akin to the "social insurance" of the phalanx world, and the mutual method of democratic control and profit-sharing through dividends exemplified Associative techniques. *The Harbinger* urged Associationists to promote and adopt mutual insurance. New Orleans Fourierist Thomas Durant introduced a bill in the state senate to establish mutual insurance in Louisiana. The American Union's 1847 annual meeting endorsed mutual insurance as an important guarantee reform—and to hasten the Fourierist millennium, its officers recommended that union members make the model phalanx fund the beneficiary of their policies.[71]

It was no coincidence that a prominent Associationist fellow traveler later became known as the "father of life insurance." The passionate antislaveryite and reform journalist Elizur Wright, Jr., defended Fourierism in his *Boston Daily Chronotype*, hired Charles Dana as an editor after the collapse of Brook Farm, and eventually sold space in his paper to Associationists. Though he never formally joined Fourierists' organizations, Wright attended their meetings and shared their interest in workingmen's causes and their belief in social reorganization through cooperative institutions.[72] In England in 1844, Wright examined insurance practices and was shocked to find systematic fleecing of the sick and aged by companies that would not buy back policies. When he returned to Boston, Wright set about promoting life insurance and attacking business abuses. In 1853 he published the first mathematically reliable valuation tables in the industry, and five years later he was appointed Commissioner of Life Insurance for Massachusetts, where he continued his reform crusade with such fervor that eventually the insurance companies had him fired.[73]

With a similar blend of idealism and pragmatism, Associationists imported "phonography," a system of phonetic shorthand invented by the Englishman Isaac Pitman. Stephen Pearl Andrews of the Boston Union was an eccentric reformer, born in Texas yet bred on antislavery and Transcendentalist beliefs. Andrews was introduced to phonography while he was in England pursuing an abortive scheme to end slavery in Texas; when he returned to Boston in 1844, he published a shorthand instruction book and opened a school that taught Pitman's system of hooks, lines, and dots.[74] To Andrews and other Associationists, phonography was not simply a faster way to write; it promised to become a universal writing system in which all the world's languages could be transcribed. In bringing "unity of language," such an instrument would prepare minds for social unity as well. (Later in his life Andrews invented a universal language called Alwato.)[75] Theron C. Leland, a veteran of several New York phalanxes, and Henry M. Parkhurst of the Boston Union joined Andrews in popularizing the shorthand. Lectures on phonography were given at Brook Farm, and classes were held at the Trumbull Phalanx school. Ohio Fourierist E. P. Grant corresponded with Brisbane, Dana, and other eastern leaders in phonographic shorthand.[76]

Eventually, phonography took hold as an indispensable tool for court reporters and newspapermen. In 1848 the U.S. Senate, influenced by Andrews's propaganda, contracted with two Washington newspapers to print verbatim reports of its proceedings from shorthand notes. Park-hurst was named chief official reporter of the Senate, a post he held until 1854. During the long and crucial session of 1849–50, Andrews temporarily joined Parkhurst's corps of reporters and took careful notes of speeches by Daniel Webster, Henry Clay, and Jefferson Davis.[77] Only because of phonography do we now have accurate transcripts of many of the great events of the Civil War era, from speeches on the Compro-mise of 1850 to the impeachment trial of Andrew Johnson. Still later, phonography became the standard shorthand for business before being replaced by John Robert Gregg's system at the turn of the twentieth century. Ironically, a system of shorthand introduced to speed communi-tarian socialism helped to grease the wheels of capitalist enterprise.

Like insurance and phonetic shorthand, savings banks were an innova-tion of the early nineteenth century which blurred the distinction be-tween the emerging capitalist order and the socialist world view. Espe-cially when organized as mutual institutions, savings banks appealed to Associationists as a pool of hard-earned capital free from predatory middlemen, capital that might also be available to fund cooperative ex-periments. Savings banks by themselves were linked to no larger system or program; only when placed in a radical theoretical context and joined to cooperative production and consumption were they truly socialist. This kind of "mutual bank" or "bank of exchange" was the form given the mutual savings idea in many Associationist writings, and it proved controversial.

The mutual bank was the invention of Pierre-Joseph Proudhon, the combative French anarchist and social thinker whose ideas on money and credit, labor and capital had a great influence on socialist debate in Europe in the 1840s and 1850s. It was Charles Dana who brought Proudhon's ideas to the American public. In Paris in 1848, he heard Proudhon speak in the National Assembly, and on his return to New York in 1849 Dana published a series of articles in the *Tribune* on Proudhon and his banking scheme. In the fall, he printed revised versions of these articles in *Spirit of the Age* (which had just been established as the Associa-tionists' new weekly journal). With obvious sympathy Dana presented Proudhon's idea that since capital is itself unproductive, interest and rent "violate the law of fraternity" and should be eliminated. The institution to replace them should be a mutual bank, managed by the community of producers, in which credit could be provided at cost. This would ensure equitable exchange, prevent capitalist accumulation, and stimu-late production. When the bank lent money to cooperative workshops and stores, full Association would be on the way. Mutual credit, Dana wrote, was "the great idea of modern economical science." He reported that Considerant, Jules Lechevalier, Hugh Doherty, and most French Fourierist leaders had repudiated the payment of interest, apparently in response to working-class opinion and as a means of grafting "Syndicates of Production and Consumption" onto Proudhon's bank. A pilot "Bank of the People" was being organized in Paris by Proudhon, the workers, and the Fourierists.[78]

In the long run the mutual credit idea served as a bridge to currency reform for several Fourierists, but at first the no-interest platform sparked controversy among utopians. Francis Shaw audaciously presented a mutual bank proposal in *Hunt's Merchant's Magazine;* Henry Parkhurst more appropriately recommended it for consumer cooperatives.[79] Brisbane, who had visited Proudhon in a Parisian prison and talked with him "by the hour," came out against interest; he attached mutual banking and labor exchanges to a proposed "Mutualist Township" with individually owned houses and farms. A similar plan was announced by Associationist and land reformer J. K. Ingalls, who reached the stage of drafting a constitution and scouting potential sites before the project foundered.[80] On the other side, Ripley, Godwin, and Lazarus attacked the denial of interest as destructive and heretical. According to Lazarus, to repudiate Fourier's guaranteed share to capital was to abandon social science, "the greatest revelation of God to the human mind." As the Associationist movement wound down in 1849, its journals were preoccupied with a long and acrimonious dispute over the merits of capital, Fourier's actual position on interest, and whether there was such a thing as Fourierist "orthodoxy."[81]

The debate over interest and mutual credit typified one set of problems that Associationists' faced in adopting gradualist reforms. The link between such "guarantee movements" and full Association was often tenuous. Surely most holders of insurance policies or depositors in savings banks were not Fourierists, nor were arrangements such as mutual banking completely consistent with Fourierist principles. Even when demonstrably cooperationist, such "fragmentary" reforms were hard for some Fourierists to get excited about. Orthodox Associationists had their hearts set on a model phalanx and found it nearly impossible to compromise. This reluctance virtually paralyzed the Boston Union as it scanned transitional movements for one to support. Unable to fund more than one venture and afraid of "lowering their standards" (as one put it), members ended by discussing them all to death. Guarantee movements were "all right for those no better enlightened," one Bostonian declared, "but *we* should aim at something higher." The Philadelphia Union guarded against compromise by incorporating the phalanx directly into the constitution of its "Group of Actuation." Its three-phase plan was to begin with mutual benefits, develop into a "commercial phalanx" housing a cooperative store, and culminate in a complete rural phalanx of two thousand persons. Needless to say, members failed to raise the half-million dollars required.[82]

Another problem was the direct opposite. Spokesmen for a fading Fourierist movement who presented themselves as the allies of flourishing transitional movements risked being absorbed by them. Some practical-minded Associationists embraced gradualist reforms so whole-heartedly that they ceased to be communitarians. Associationists with close ties to working-class constituencies joined the cooperative and land reform movements, hoping to guide them toward full Association, but soon tranferred allegiances completely when prospects for social reorganization diminished. This was true for Brook Farm's John Orvis, Lewis Ryckman, and Henry Trask, who pursued the cooperative cause into the 1850s and—in Orvis's case—beyond the Civil War.

A third group of Associationists made such a quick and easy transition to gradualist movements that it revealed how limited their specific commitment to Fourierism had been all along. Typified by Horace Greeley, these reformers portrayed Association not in opposition to Civilization but as a natural outgrowth of modern progress toward organization and brotherhood—in short, toward "association" without the capital letter. The notion that Fourierism was but one manifestation of the gradual, providential tendency toward cooperative enterprises of all sorts—from benevolent societies to corporations—allowed fuzzy idealists to switch to such causes without doubts or regrets. Since all reforms led in the same direction, why not adopt those most immediately beneficial and attainable?

Both the proliferation of such reforms and Associationist support for them, however compromised, suggest the remarkable fluidity of early industrial society. In the context of the 1840s, cooperative forms of organization such as joint-stock enterprises could plausibly be thought to represent the germ of the socialist future rather than the solidifying of capitalist control. The widespread antebellum belief in the plasticity of social institutions supported such an assumption. Transitional reform brought to the surface certain tensions within Fourierism and posed the problem of co-optation, but by remaining open to reform coalitions and compromises, Associationists tried to guide contemporaries' first steps toward Harmonic society. If the success of communal groups can be judged partly by their influence on outside society, "guaranty" movements were in fact a significant Fourierist achievement. Through their inspiration and support for mutual insurance and cooperative organizations, reform-minded Associationists extended practical benefits to thousands of men and women—far more than were reached by phalanxes. Cooperative households and stores were only "fractional phalanxes," but they were surely an improvement upon Civilization.[83]

The Demise of *The Harbinger* and the AUA

Transitional reforms and utopian socialist "churches" could be actively linked to Associationism only if Fourierists maintained a viable organizational network and a widely circulated movement journal. By 1848, however, both *The Harbinger* and the American Union of Associationists were in trouble. The move to New York did not resolve *The Harbinger's* financial problems: in May 1848 subscriptions remained at the pre-move average of one thousand, and the journal faced a deficit of nearly $1,500. George Ripley's letters to colleagues in Boston listed additional unanticipated problems encountered in the transition: publishing delays, countless typographical errors, and a less attractive format.[84] Once again, New Yorkers and Bostonians quarreled. Parke Godwin, now chief editor, complained of too little help from editors Channing and Dwight, whom he confined to the artistic and literary departments, reserving for himself the "discussion of current questions." Ripley reported that Godwin was selfish and "not inexhaustible," and that the New York Fourierists were "a good deal discouraged" by the "uphill work" the movement faced. Here was further proof that the New Yorkers were fair-weather friends who "feel, if they do not say, 'martyrdom be d——d.' "[85] An appeal for additional pledges sent to affiliated unions in August 1848 drew a meager response, and a few patrons barely kept *The Harbinger* afloat. At the end of 1848 the editors relinquished part of their salaries. In the issue of February 10, 1849, they announced that the journal would appear thereafter as a monthly or as a smaller weekly. It was never published again.[86]

In time, the vaccuum left by *The Harbinger* was filled by two successors. In July 1849 the AUA executive committee purchased space in Elizur Wright's *Boston Daily Chronotype*. Under the editorship of John Dwight, Fourierist columns first appeared there in August 1849 and were supposed to continue for three years. Attempting to present "a fair, industrious, kindly and intelligent account of the great Socialistic movement in all branches," the contributions reflected both Dwight's gentle personality and the eclecticism of the late Associationist movement. But the *Chronotype* was a slim reed to base the Fourierists' hopes upon, and when it was forced to suspend publication in January 1850 the Associationist column disappeared with it.[87]

The *Chronotype* columns, with a local circulation of about three thousand, were intended to be supplemented by a national Fourierist magazine offering longer and more theoretical articles. When *The Harbinger* expired, the AUA authorized Godwin to solicit contributions for a monthly magazine to be entitled *New Times* and coedited by Henry James. While this arrangement was being pursued (without success), William Henry Channing took control of a weekly reform and spiritualist paper. Rechristened *Spirit of the Age*, Channing's magazine began publication in July 1849 as the organ of the AUA and official successor to *The Harbinger*.[88] Ironically, though Channing championed the "all-reconciling" nature of Association, *Spirit of the Age* publicized the breakup of the movement into factions bickering over theory in the absence of tangible success. "The whole movement is becoming more and more ambiguous," Ripley complained to Dwight, "the theoretical, speculative . . . element has got too far ahead of the practical." A long exchange between Channing and Godwin over the Christianity of Fourier's system aired irreconcilable differences among Associationist leaders. It was accompanied by other disputes over the French "Red Republicans" of 1848, the mutual bank and the abolition of interest, and the alleged "pantheism" of Henry James. In April 1850 Channing announced that *Spirit of the Age* was being discontinued because he was "brain-sick" and out of money. His role as reconciler among the Associationists had proved exhausting and fruit-less.[89] Associationists now had to depend upon sympathetic publicity in Boston's *Protective Union*, a short-lived pro-Fourierist weekly, and periodic notices in Greeley's *Tribune*.

The death of *The Harbinger* and its successors sealed the doom of the American Union. Though Boston remained an active center of local Fourierist agitation and the North American Phalanx still survived, without a journal to sustain the AUA's educational mission and to organize regional and national meetings, the affiliated unions were reduced to perfunctory observances of Fourier's birthday—attended by fewer and fewer each year. The American Union confined itself to somber and largely symbolic annual meetings, the last of which was held in 1851.

11

Campaigns with Labor

While Fourierist leaders were attempting to sustain a journal and build a permanent national organization, they also sought to broaden their doctrine's appeal among the working class. When communal experimentation was at its peak and Brook Farm established as a propaganda center, Associationists set out to win over the antebellum labor movement. But Fourierism was only one of several ideas and plans vying for workers' support: at conventions and rallies throughout the 1840s, various labor activists called for political organizing, reduced work hours, access to public lands, and self-help cooperatives. In mid-decade the Fourierists succeeded in converting a small but active nucleus of artisans to the phalanx idea, but the ten-hour movement had far and away the greatest impact upon mechanics and factory operatives. Though disappointed, the Associationists cooperated with ten-hour advocates and land reformers in building the first relatively permanent workers' associations in New England.

Not until the failure of strikes and the ten-hour agitation turned workers' attention to mutual benefit cooperatives did the Fourierists gain center stage. Then the Associationist press sustained the new cooperative movement with publicity, and Fourierist leaders guided it with their ideas and organizational skills. Despite pressures on workers to adopt entrepreneurial attitudes or endorse accommodationist demands, Associationist agitation helped sustain opposition to wage labor under competitive capitalism and linked practical programs to this larger goal. At the end of the decade the Fourierists played a part in building a network of producers' associations and a huge chain of cooperative stores, experiments which, though short-lived, demonstrated the practical benefits of the cooperative idea to thousands of workers who had remained untouched by ten-hour legislation, land reform, or phalanxes.

Association and the Antebellum Labor Movement

The foregoing summary of Fourierist activity suggests that traditional interpretations of the 1840s labor movement and the Associationists' role in it need to be revised. Until recently, the dominant approach regarded workers' involvement with reform in the 1840s as an unfortunate diversion from the proper path of pragmatic trade unionism. According to Norman Ware, the "institutional" labor historian who analyzed the 1840s most closely, Associationists were patronizing middle-class intellectuals with little true knowledge of working conditions. Denying the reality of the Industrial Revolution, they promoted unrealizable, visionary schemes of phalanxes and large-scale cooperatives rather than unions and strikes to achieve higher wages and other practical demands. For a time they successfully imposed their reform ideas on the rudderless workers, but when phalanxes and cooperatives failed, the workers took up the narrower but more realistic strategy of trade unionism in the 1850s.[1]

This interpretation, though it highlights some of the trends and divisions of the antebellum labor movement, is badly flawed. Not only does it misread the Fourierist approach to industrialism and impose a highly debatable criterion of "realism" upon labor history, but at its heart lies a false dichotomy between "workers" and "reformers."[2] White-collar labor reformers, most only marginally middle class in a society they were pledged to overhaul, often found a ready hearing as "friends" of workingmen. More important, many Associationists—in fact, a majority in the eastern phalanxes and a significant minority in local affiliated unions— were themselves working class in origin. Some of these, far from being diverted from labor agitation by utopian socialism, brought Associationist ideas into the labor movement. The careers of Lewis Ryckman and Henry P. Trask of Brook Farm attest to the direct involvement of Fourierist artisans in promoting key labor organizations in the 1840s and 1850s.

Workers of the period were not uniformly or solely interested in bread-and-butter issues. Fourierism never attracted the kind of mass support among them that ten-hour agitation did, but it was widely influential. Ware claimed that the Associationists were not the "authentic voice" of the workers, yet the spokesman he proposed as a truer representative, labor editor William F. Young, has been portrayed by historian Jama Lazerow as a Fourierist sympathizer whose writings were "suffused" with Associationist rhetoric.[3] Like Young, many workers favored pragmatic labor measures but also listened readily to general reform schemes that put their plight in larger perspective and promised long-range benefits. Simultaneously with resolutions calling for decent wages and shorter work days, labor conventions of the 1840s endorsed the land reform platform and Fourierist plans for worker cooperatives. At least from some workers' point of view, hour and wage-conscious unionism and Fourierist cooperatives were complementary rather than conflicting aspirations, both rooted in a labor theory of value, both rejecting the growing power of employers and invoking the goal of economic independence.[4] Especially when strikes and legislation failed to improve conditions, workers turned naturally to self-help schemes and social reform.

For their part, though the Associationists pushed for phalanxes, most also supported less drastic proposals. In 1844 the Brook Farmers and their New York allies set out to "capture" the workingmen's movement, but within a year they changed their tone and strategy to one of coalition building and support for workers' gradualist projects. Throughout the decade the Associationists endorsed demands for the ten-hour day and political action, speaking against them only when such demands were pressed to the exclusion of reform ideas. Just as Greeley's *Tribune* sympathetically reported the whole spectrum of labor movement activities in New York and the Midwest, the *Voice of Industry* (1845–48), run by a series of Associationist editors, was the engine of the ten-hour movement in New England. When after 1845 workers adopted the strategy of cooperative production and consumption, the Associationists proclaimed it "Fourierism without the phalanx" and joined enthusiastically in this "partial" reform.

Perhaps the most misunderstood Associationist labor position was their opposition to strikes. Ware and others, focusing especially upon Horace Greeley, accuse Fourierists of pacifying workers and delaying the emergence of class-conscious unionism by opposing labor conflict and proclaiming a "harmony of interests" between capitalists and laborers.[5] With few exceptions, however, the Fourierists' opposition to strikes was based far less on middle-class idealism or timidity than on the conviction that strikes would accomplish little unless attached to some larger, constructive plan of action. Associationists emphasized that under competitive capitalism there could never be a "harmony of interests" but only increasing worker dependence upon employers and antagonism between classes.[6]

To be sure, in proposing phalanxes the Fourierists sought to bring opposing groups together in voluntary cooperation, and in promoting worker-based cooperatives they renounced class conflict for the more pacific and (they believed) Christian strategy of mutual protection. Fourierist labor reformers, Lazerow has noted, were caught in a dilemma. As radicals they called for sweeping changes in the organization of society, while as Christian and voluntarist reformers they disavowed conflict with that society's capitalist defenders and beneficiaries.[7] It was a paradox that I have argued was central to utopian socialism. Nevertheless, a few points mitigate this critique of Associationist ideology. First, in the context of the 1840s the Fourierists' idea of producer associations seemed a logical way to solve this dilemma. The strategy of simply bypassing class conflict by having workers pool their resources to control working conditions and profits made sense to many artisans who sought to preserve craft traditions yet still compete in an increasingly organized economy. Second, the Fourierists' call for warfare against a *system* that produced classes—rather than against the capitalists themselves—was still a position too radical for most workers, who sought modest gains or else ignored labor protest altogether. And third, while the Fourierists cast themselves as conciliators, their rhetoric often undeniably stimulated working-class consciousness. Most Fourierist labor reformers believed that heightened class feeling was a necessary precondition to voluntarist socialism. "Suppose our movement does produce the effect of which it is accused—i.e., set the employed against the employer," S. C. Hewitt responded to critics in 1844. "The agitation which is now going on, . . . instead of creating new prejudices and antagonisms, is only showing those more clearly, which have already too long slumbered and slept." Not until the conflicts of Civilization became obvious would the logic of Association prevail: "When the body is diseased, in order to expel the cause, the patient must sometimes be made to feel the greater disagreeable effects of medicine, for a short time."[8] The Fourierist message to antebellum workers was thus, like the labor movement itself, a mixture of attitudes and strategies that pointed in different directions at once: to immediate reforms as well as social reorganization, to class conflict as well as class cooperation.

It is a mistake to judge the labor movement of the 1840s by either the militant standards of Marxism or the expectations of conventional trade unionism. What has been viewed as an anachronistic, unfortunate decade of agitation was in fact a creative period of labor organization when, at the onset of industrial capitalism, intriguing alternatives to "wage slavery" were promoted in a broad agitation that gathered workers and reformers in productive alliances. Just as labor organizations and Fourierist circles had overlapping memberships, they both opposed the Europeanization of American working conditions. While they sometimes argued over strategy, they shared enough ideas, interests, and goals to cooperate in campaigns to consolidate worker resistance. Mechanics and operatives brought the Fourierists' attention to immediate problems in the factory and workshop; Fourierism offered workers a rhetoric and point of view linking their struggle to the larger trends of the Industrial Revolution and legitimating social reconstruction with the dissenting traditions of republicanism and social Christianity.

By the 1830s many workingmen had independently evolved a version of the traditional republican ideals of virtue, equality, independence, and commonwealth into a distinctive world view that helped shape their collective protest against capitalist encroachment on timeworn practices. As the Owenite and free-thought influence waned and workers were caught up in the evangelical awakenings of the 1830s, they increasingly adopted an activist version of Christianity arguing that labor protest as a religious endeavor would ultimately bring millennial harmony and brotherhood to social relations. Both these ideological strains converged in the labor movement of the 1840s. Both have been analyzed extensively in a fine series of "new" labor histories which, rather than confronting

Ware and John R. Commons directly, document the emergence of an artisan working class through detailed case studies of key antebellum cities.[9] The result is a complex story of working-class formation, with a rich interweaving of culture, social development, and politics. But like earlier histories, these studies still largely relegate Associationists to the periphery of the antebellum labor movement, whereas in fact, Fourierists spoke the same language as worker activists: condemning "anti-republican distinctions" of class, denouncing "wage slavery," urging workers to declare their independence, and presenting labor reform as "practical Christianity." Associationists promoted these themes in the labor movement of the 1840s and attached them to a specific program of social transformation which influenced workers' activities and organizations at crucial junctures. For significant numbers of workers, Fourierist institutions were a social equivalent of the republican and religious ideals nurtured in the preceding decades.

The New England Workingmen's Association

Until the end of the 1840s, Associationists in New York had few successful contacts with working-class organizations. New York mechanics attracted to Fourierism in effect took themselves out of the picture by establishing two phalanxes in Pennsylvania: Social Reform Unity, and Sylvania. Lewis Ryckman, a middle-aged cordwainer and Fourierist, left New York City early in 1843 to join Brook Farm, where he led the Associationists' foray into the New England labor movement. His departure meant that neither the North American Phalanx nor the New York Union became a base for regional labor agitation. Moreover, New York was the headquarters of George Henry Evans's National Reformers and had been a stronghold of land reform ideas since the rise of the Workingmen's Party of the late 1820s. Fourierism in New York was not simply a conduit for some workers and reformers into land reform, as Sean Wilentz claims, but it was usually overshadowed by its older and more popular rival.[10] Finally, there were the individualistic tendencies of New York Fourierist leaders. Preoccupied with their careers, newspapers, lecturing schedules, or political connections, neither Greeley, Godwin, nor Brisbane developed the New York Union of Associationists into an effective cross-class coalition.[11]

Without working-class recruits to penetrate labor circles, Greeley and Godwin attempted through journalism to sell the Fourierist program to local workers. Greeley's *Tribune* faithfully printed news of Associationist conventions and labor movement activities, and in speeches before lyceum audiences and mechanics' institutes, Greeley looked forward to the day when "Industrial Association" would banish the war between labor and capital. Godwin—who, unlike Greeley, did not disavow strikes—maintained contact with New York radicals from his old Locofoco days and his friendship with Evans. Largely through Evans's influence, the

New York Workingman's Association nominated Godwin for Congress from the Fifth District in September 1844. Though he lost the election, Godwin was optimistic about Associationist chances to win over the emerging labor movement. To Charles Dana he confided that "the working classes are ready for us—and absolutely ask for instruction and guidance." In speeches sponsored by Evans's National Reform Association, Godwin told New York workers that wage labor made them worse off than southern slaves, assured them that Association was not trying to turn them into abolitionists or temperance men, and predicted that "the organization of labor" into phalanxes would end their subjection to employers. In August 1845, however, Godwin reported to Dana that he had lost faith in the New York "Workies": despite his pleas, the land reformers had rejected the Fourierists' conciliatory call for a "union of reformers," and most rank-and-file workers were completely apathetic. Greeley, meanwhile, in a speech on the emancipation of labor, lamented that "those who most palpably need a true Social Reform seem most indifferent to its accomplishment." Though New York Fourierists continued to agitate for labor reform, they had little discernible influence on local workers' groups until the crisis at the end of the decade.[12]

In New England, ties between Fourierist leaders and labor organizations were closer. Brook Farm's dedicated corps of lecturers spread Associative ideas to nearby towns, while Ryckman, Trask, and Sarah Bagley served effectively as working-class intermediaries between the Fourierists and labor groups. Land reform had not preempted workers' attention as in New York, and the largely native Protestant workforce often shared middle-class enthusiasm for such reforms as temperance, abolitionism, and Association.[13] Relations between Associationists and New England labor activists were hardly free of tension: if utopians sometimes alienated pragmatic workers with visionary schemes and condecending smugness, most workers seemed to the Fourierists too myopic and fickle. By 1847, however, both groups had been chastened by the failure of their favorite panaceas and were able to cooperate in scaled-down self-help projects that promised practical gains for workers. The history of the New England Workingmen's Association (NEWA) illustrates the fluctuations, the frustrations, and the small triumphs of this on-again-off-again alliance.[14]

The initial push toward a regional labor organization came from the mechanics of Fall River, Massachusetts, who in 1844 issued a circular publicizing their grievances and calling for a general labor convention. From the outset, a mixture of the ten-hour idea with broader reform notions characterized the movement. The mechanics' primary goal was a workday shorter than the twelve- to fifteen-hour norm, but the influence of Fourierism was evident in their demand for alternatives to the "prevailing system of labor." As if to highlight this blend, the Fall River workers hired Fourierist S. C. Hewitt as a lecturer. During five weeks in July and August, Hewitt canvassed seventeen towns in Massachusetts, Rhode Island, and eastern Connecticut, advocating Fourierism and a ten-hour law, organizing local mechanics' associations, and urging workers to attend a Boston convention in the fall.[15]

When the organizing convention of the NEWA met in October, a Brook Farm delegation of George Ripley, Lewis Ryckman, and John Allen participated along with two hundred representatives of New England workers' organizations and land reform groups. Setting the pattern for the next three years, resolutions were passed favoring the ten-hour workday, the opening of public land to settlers, and two Fourierist measures: joint-stock associations in which workers could pool their capital and control production cooperatively, and "the introduction of a system of attractive industry" throughout society.[16]

Flushed with this initial success, Fourierist leaders professed themselves "highly gratified" by the New England workers' endorsement. Privately, Dana gloated that the workingmen's movement would soon be "in our hands": "We are in fact the only men who can really point out their course for them and they can hardly help looking to us for their advisers." At the January convention of the New England Fourier Society, delegates pointed out that Association was "the destined road" to everything the workingmen sought and, in the same paternalistic spirit, welcomed the establishment of the "Society of Inquiry of Fall River," a middle-class Fourier club whose object was to lend money to workers who wished to join phalanxes. Fourierists urged that similar societies be formed in every industrial town of New England.[17]

In the ensuing months Associationist leaders moderated this doctrinaire stance, realizing that preaching the phalanx divorced from more practical measures would alienate most workers. At the second organizing convention of the NEWA in March 1845, the Fourierists became true partners in the labor-reform coalition. Almost two thousand delegates attended, including land reformers and labor leaders from Lowell, Lynn, and other industrial towns. The Fourierists were able to achieve some key objectives, such as the adoption of an NEWA constitution with Fourierist overtones, the appointment of John Allen to the convention's steering committee, and, most important of all, the election of Ryckman as the NEWA's first president. But the Fourierists also joined with delegates in passing a wide range of practical resolutions endorsing free public education, labor representation in Congress, free public lands to settlers, and a campaign against chartered monopolies. Resolutions calling for political action to achieve the ten-hour workday were especially popular, and the Fourierists, who had previously called such a demand "a demeaning compromise" with wage-labor capitalism, now quietly added their support.[18]

Fourierists insisted, however, that delegates also make larger plans. Brisbane lectured the convention on Fourierism and reminded delegates that in addition to "secondary measures" such as ten-hour laws, more "fundamental" questions needed to be agitated. Ryckman proposed that workers set up an annual "industrial congress" like the prerevolutionary

Continental Congress to vote in a government that would recognize the rights of labor. Though Ryckman's advocacy of politics was unusual for Fourierists (it probably reflected his earlier involvement in western land reform and the workingmen's parties of the 1830s), the idea of an industrial congress fit the republican rhetoric and national scope of Fourierist organizing. But Brisbane and Ryckman's radical views doubtless scared many workers, and their emphasis away from immediate local concerns seemed counter-productive to advocates of the convention's most popular cause, the ten-hour day.[19]

Signs of an emerging rift between reform and pragmatic labor activists were already apparent when the NEWA held its first formal meeting in Boston at the end of May. Only thirty delegates attended, at least a third of them Brook Farmers and Associationist colleagues, so when Ryckman was officially installed as president and George Ripley was placed on the executive committee, it seemed a somewhat hollow victory. Though the customary resolutions favoring workers' organizations and the ten-hour workday were adopted, the focus of the meeting was on national publicity for reform. Greeley, Channing, Dana, and Brisbane spoke, as did the venerable Robert Owen, then on an American tour. Ryckman and Brisbane persuaded the delegates to endorse a joint industrial congress with the land reformers to be held in New York in October; an impressive slate of delegates—including abolitionists as well as Fourierists and ten-hour advocates—was elected to attend.[20]

Eventually, many members of the NEWA grew restless with expositions of communitarian doctrine and plans for national action. A group of South Boston workers captured the mood of these "practical laborers" when they complained that although pledged to "remove existing evils from the present state of society," they had neither "the means [n]or the inclination to withdraw from society." In June, Fitchburg mechanic and Fourierist sympathizer William Young warned in the *Voice of Industry* that an NEWA endorsement of "strong measures" such as industrial congresses and the phalanxes would turn away "many good and honest workingmen, who are willing to go with us as fast as they can see and understand." He and other workers might privately approve of Associationist doctrine but opposed its becoming official NEWA policy. Instead, Young wanted the NEWA to agitate for "various speedy and partial ameliorations" while the Brook Farmers served as a vanguard of more advanced "social science" for workers to learn from.[21]

At the September NEWA meeting the schism Young had forecast did materialize but from the opposite direction: it was the pragmatists who alienated the utopians with their piecemeal plans. Faced with competing resolutions, one advocating political action and the other consumer cooperatives as "the only practical and effectual measure which the Workingmen can at present adopt for the defense of their rights," the Associationists were unwilling to adopt either as the exclusive goal of the NEWA and thus to proclaim the irrelevance of phalansterian socialism. The convention ended in disarray as Ryckman desperately tried to steer delegates to a more "general plan of . . . reform." At the next month's meeting in Lowell, a compromise was reached in which *both* the ballot and cooperative stores were endorsed as useful methods to improve working conditions, and a clause on the "failure" of social reform "to unite the producing classes" was dropped. By that time, however, Ryckman and other Associationist leaders had abandoned the NEWA in disappointment and were instead placing their hopes in the New York Industrial Congress.[22]

When NEWA workers endorsed political action, they meant the ten-hour working day, not land reform or Ryckman's radical plan to set up an "Industrial Revolutionary Government." For nearly a year after the schism of September 1845, the NEWA concentrated its efforts on the ten-hour campaign. Two massive petition campaigns resulted in the Massachusetts legislature's appointment of committees to investigate factory conditions in the state. Despite the damaging testimony of workers, however, both committees rejected the ten-hour idea summarily.[23]

During this period of intense agitation the Associationists were conspicuously absent from NEWA conventions. It was not simply that they were impatient with the ten-hour movement as a palliative reform; the Brook Farmers were struggling to keep their own community alive, and after the fire of March 1846 they lost their main labor organizer when Ryckman returned to New York City. Beginning in May 1846 the New England leaders concentrated on forming local affiliated unions of the AUA as the Fourierists' independent base of support in New England towns; once these local clubs were established, national leaders urged them to make contact with local labor organizations. Particularly in Boston and Lowell, the pace of collaboration again picked up, thanks largely to former Brook Farmer John Allen, who emerged as Ryckman's successor in the role of Fourierist agent to the working classes. After a hiatus of nearly a year the Fourierists and the New England Workingmen's Association renewed their alliance in the fall of 1846. As they rebounded from the disappointments of the previous year, the two movements' ideas had converged. The Fourierists' disillusionment with the phalanx plan in the wake of community failures in the mid-1840s led them toward more gradualist measures. In October 1846 *The Harbinger* endorsed cooperative stores and other such systems of "mutual guarantees" as preliminary steps toward full Association.[24] Simultaneously, after the ten-hour movement failed to bring results, New England workers became more interested in self-help plans such as homesteads and cooperatives.

By the time the NEWA convened in Nashua in September 1846, utopian and pragmatist soul-searching had produced a new consensus. Under the leadership of Allen, who was elected business committee chairman, delegates decided to dissolve the NEWA and form a new organization, the Labor Reform League of New England (LRL). No striking difference was immediately apparent; the new league was no middle-class coup, as Norman Ware has suggested, but like its predecessor an unstable coalition of workers and middle-class sympathizers. The LRL also endorsed the ten-hour day: in conjunction with the convention a thousand Nashua operatives paraded for shorter hours, and members pledged to support only political candidates who accepted the ten-hour plank. After the disappointing fall elections, however, the LRL's distinctiveness emerged. Whereas the NEWA had been an omnibus coalition of workers' interest groups, the LRL's constitution explicitly committed members to "the principles of Industrial Reform," to be publicized through lectures and writings. As a reform coalition the league's appeal was necessarily limited, but members hoped that practical proposals would attract workers weary of ten-hour crusades. The constitution's preamble announced the two measures its leaders saw as bridges to larger reform: the "inalienable homestead" of the land reformers, and consumer cooperatives—"the establishment of guaranteeism in Protective Union."[25]

In LRL conventions the next year, land reform and protective unions shared the floor, both now supported by the Associationists as promising transitional reforms. For their part, after more than a year of carping, the land reformers endorsed cooperative stores at their June 1847 Industrial Congress. The mood of cooperation seemed infectious: auxiliary associations of the LRL were established in Lowell, Dover, and two other Massachusetts towns; and land reformers, Associationists, and independent worker-reformers like Young shared the LRL's major offices. Former Brook Farm artisans Charles Hosmer and Henry Trask spoke at league conventions to promote cooperative stores, and through their influence Protective Unionists were elected to the majority of LRL posts in 1848. By that time, however, the LRL had become a toothless coalition of labor reform leaders with few followers. Without a popular issue like the ten-hour workday, it proved unable to attract significant worker support. Labor reform leaders within the coalition began defecting to their parent organizations, the land reformers to the National Reform Association and the cooperativists to the Working Men's Protective Union. When the LRL convened in January 1848, the meeting was "sparsely attended"; in March nothing was done but to appoint delegates to the Industrial Congress, and the meeting adjourned sine die.[26]

Lowell and the Boundaries of Working-Class Fourierism

Among the local workers' associations that fed into the NEWA and the LRL, those in Lowell stood out for their vitality and especially their pioneering involvement of women in labor activism. Lowell organizations duplicated in miniature the development of the NEWA, centering their agitation on ten-hour petitions and eventually turning to mutual benefit schemes. More clearly than the shifting, multifaceted regional coalition, however, developments in Lowell revealed the extent to which industrial organizing depended upon ten-hour agitation and, by implication, demonstrated the limited appeal of Fourierism in a factory environment. Despite Fourierist leaders' efforts to promote Association in America's premier industrial setting, the vision of cooperative production in phalanxes or small-scale workshops made Fourierism more congenial to artisan radicalism than to the protest of factory operatives.

In response to the regional agitation of 1844, a group of fifteen female operatives led by Sarah Bagley and Huldah Stone formed the Lowell Female Labor Reform Association (LFLRA) in January 1845. Within six months it enrolled over four hundred members and became a vital force in the New England labor movement. Bagley, called the first woman labor leader in American history, had come to Lowell from New Hampshire in 1836 and worked in the mills as a weaver for eight years, during four of which she also conducted a free evening school for factory women. For most of 1845 she was a full-time labor organizer. Mature and outspoken, she defended the right of women to speak in public, exposed the "operatives' magazine" the *Lowell Offering* as a tool of the mill owners, and testified before the Massachusetts legislature on conditions in the mills.[27]

Under the leadership of Bagley and Stone the LFLRA became a mainstay of the misnamed New England Workingmen's Association. The Lowell women secured admission of female labor groups to the NEWA on an equal footing with male organizations; Bagley gave ringing speeches before NEWA gatherings; and Stone was repeatedly elected the group's secretary. Lowell women were always among the largest contingents at NEWA conventions, and the LFLRA was instrumental in forming kindred organizations in other factory towns, including Manchester, Nashua, and Dover, New Hampshire. Perhaps its most important contribution to the wider labor movement was its support for the *Voice of Industry*, the offical newspaper of the NEWA. Stone served as a correspondent and subscription agent; Bagley edited a "Female Department" with articles by women workers. When the paper moved to Lowell in October 1845, Bagley was named to the publishing committee. Early in 1846 the LFLRA purchased the press to help the struggling paper, and for a month that spring Bagley was editor-in-chief while William Young recuperated from illness.[28]

The central thrust of the LFLRA's activity, and the only issue that could claim massive support among Lowell workers, was the campaign for the ten-hour workday. Members testified before the state committee investigating the mills, rounded up over a thousand signatures to present to it, and led a successful campaign against its chairman's reelection to the legislature. In the second round of petitioning the LFLRA accumulated nearly half the statewide total of signatures. The *Voice* constantly printed ten-hour propaganda and sparked support for the movement in lesser mill towns.[29]

For Bagley and Stone, however, the labor question outgrew the ten-hour issue, and their search for larger answers to the dilemmas of industrialism led them and several dozen Lowell workers to join forces with the Associationists. Bagley had shared the NEWA speaker's platform with Brisbane in July 1845 and praised the Fourierists as heroes of labor's coming "revolution." For their part, because of Lowell's symbolic place as the entering wedge of the factory system, the Associationists were eager to gain a foothold there. Brook Farmers Orvis and Allen lectured in Lowell in the winter of 1845–46, and four Associationist speakers (Channing, Ripley, Greeley and William White) were featured the following March in the Industrial Reform Lyceum, an LFLRA-sponsored lecture series aimed at promoting social and economic discussion. Channing and John Allen returned to speak at a fund-raising party for the women's association in May 1846. The Fourierists considered Lowell so important that in June Brisbane and Dana opened the AUA's national lecture campaign there, and Allen remained in Lowell to take over the struggling *Voice of Industry*.[30]

These efforts began to pay off when a small Lowell Fourier Society was formed early in 1846, and they culminated the following July when Bagley and Stone joined Allen and local operatives, reformers, and artisans to form an affiliated union. The Lowell Union of Associationists reported to *The Harbinger* that it had sixty-one members, thirty-one of them female—an unusually high percentage for Fourierist unions. The union's leaders were only indirectly connected with the mills, however: Bagley was vice-president; Mary Emerson, who ran a variety store, served as secretary; and William Pierce, a harnessmaker, was treasurer. Other prominent members were James McCoy, a "writing master," Alfred Cory, another harnessmaker, and D. H. Jaques, a former medical student listed in the Lowell directory as a schoolteacher. Mary Emerson reported that the rest of the members were "mostly operatives and mechanics" but added that only a third of the entire group could "really be counted on," suggesting that the factory workers' support of Fourierism was lukewarm at best.[31]

Fourierism gave Bagley, Stone, and other labor reformers the sense of belonging to a larger movement of social change and the vision of an equitable labor system without factories or wages. Their reform horizons widened when Bagley attended the AUA convention in Boston in September 1846 and Stone accompanied Brisbane on the lecture circuit.[32] Meanwhile, in the hope of fueling local interest, the union discussed Fourierism at regular meetings and in April 1847 sponsored a series of "Lectures for the People" whose speakers included Greeley, Channing, and Brisbane. Members pledged to provide money to the AUA for its propaganda fund and a model phalanx. But the "rent fund" was slow in getting off the ground—it did not begin until mid-1847—and few factory workers were interested in phalanxes. Eventually, two Lowell operatives found their way to the North American Phalanx: Samuel Kennison in

1849 and Mary Paul in 1854.[33] But most factory employees, even those who were Fourierists, found it difficult to envision phalanx living as the solution to their problems.

The Lowell Union's most concrete achievement was to promote mutual benefit schemes and consumer cooperatives after the collapse of the ten-hour campaign. Associationists influential in the LFLRA convinced its remaining members that mutual aid was a useful partial reform and a practical benefit to boost workers' morale. As membership in the LFLRA plummeted after the petition failures, Mary Emerson and Huldah Stone, returned from organizing the New England Labor Reform League, transformed the local remnant into the Lowell Female Industrial Reform and Mutual Aid Society. Like the LRL, the new organization represented continuity in leadership but a shift in strategy to mutualism and reform propaganda. The society's mission was in part educational, dedicated to "the diffusion of correct principles and useful practical knowledge among its members." To attract recruits and promote mutual benefit schemes, it established two charitable committees and enrolled members in a sickness insurance fund. Workers who paid an initiation fee of 50 cents and weekly dues of 6 cents would become eligible for sick fund benefits of a full salary for up to a month.[34]

The second gradualist measure that Lowell Union members advocated was the cooperative store. Partly through the organizing efforts of the Associationists, Lowell quickly became a center of the Protective Union movement of the late 1840s, with eight stores and 984 members at its peak. Four of the local branches were organized among mill employees, and two of these consisted entirely of female operatives. Lewis Tebbets of the Lowell Union became a full-time store administrator, and Eliza Hemingway, an LFLRA member who had been a leader in ten-hour agitation, was president of one of the Protective Union locals.[35] Energies that had been directed toward political campaigns and social reorganization were now channeled into modest local institutions. The cooperative store movement was a resounding success numerically, but failed to help the union attract operatives to any larger reform program.

The Lowell Union itself was in trouble by mid-1847. To support her aged parents, Bagley took a job as supervisor of the telegraph office, first in Lowell and then in Springfield, and gradually withdrew from reform activities. Mary Emerson complained that the best remaining members were devoting their time to Protective Unions and not Fourierism. Increasingly, the group was held together by middle-class Fourierists such as Jaques, who took over the *Voice* in September 1847, rather than those with close ties to workers. The rank-and-file membership, especially the factory workers, proved too transient to ensure a stable organization. In August 1847 it was reported that one-third of the union's members had left Lowell in the past year, and the new workers hired at the mills were Irish women so desperate for jobs that they had little choice but to accept working conditions and dared not risk agitation or reform. In November

1847 a faithful remnant was still holding regular meetings, but the union and the Industrial Reform Society could no longer sustain the *Voice*. The next month Jaques and John Orvis moved the paper to Boston, where it was published intermittently until August 1848. Shorn of their publicity and without the ten-hour agitation to build upon, the Lowell Union and the Mutual Aid Society faded out of existence.[36]

The history of the Lowell Female Labor Reform Association and the Lowell Union of Associationists brings into clearer focus how dependent labor organizations in industrial towns of the 1840s were upon the ten-hour agitation. The drive to shorten the mechanics' and operatives' workday provided most of the energy and coherence of the LFLRA, and the spillover of enthusiasm into questions of larger reform sustained the Lowell Union during its brief life. As that excitement waned, the Lowell Union managed to institute mutual insurance and cooperative purchasing among local workers, but these pragmatic arrangements were not linked in workers' minds to any larger program of reform. Compared to the membership of the LFLRA, which reached six hundred at its peak, or the five thousand Lowell signatures on ten-hour petitions in 1846, the Lowell Union had always been a tiny organization. Some operatives and mechanics were receptive to Fourierist criticisms of competitive capitalism and utopian calls to reform, but the first choice of the factory workers who were the core of New England labor associations was clearly the ten-hour day.

In contrast to manufacturing centers like Lowell, Fourierism made its strongest impact upon workers in Boston and those small New England towns where industrialization lagged and older craft traditions still prevailed.[37] A glance at the most ardent adherents among New England workers demonstrates that working-class Fourierism was largely a movement of traditional craftsmen rather than of semiskilled factory workers or mill operatives. Brook Farm's working-class members, for example, were not laborers or factory operatives but skilled craftsmen. Of the thirty-three men whose prior occupations can be identified, there were eight shoemakers, six carpenters, five printers, two mechanics, two cabinetmakers, and a baker, a tallow chandler, a pewterer, a bricklayer, a carriagemaker, a butcher, a sawyer, a tailor, a gardener, and a domestic servant. Except for a few foreigners and two men from New York, they came from small New England towns or from Boston, to which several had migrated from outlying villages. None of the shoemakers had been based in Lynn, where factories were rapidly replacing the putting-out system of independent contractors; they came from smaller centers where, S. C. Hewitt noted on his 1844 tour, "shoemakers, for the most part, work by the job, and pretty much as they please, as respects the hours of labor" (not surprisingly, Hewitt found almost no support among these men for ten-hour legislation). And none of the others came from the expanding textile centers of Lowell and Fall River, where the factory system most drastically affected employment conditions. Working-class members of the Boston Union of Associationists fit the same mold. Of the ten who had not been Brook Farm members, two were unskilled workers (a waiter and a watchman); the others were two printers, a baker, a plasterer, a tailor, a ship carver, a harnessmaker, and a surveyor.[38]

For the Lynn, Lowell, and Fall River manufacturing workers among whom the NEWA and the LFLRA originated and who were the majority of its rank and file, interest in Fourierist proposals was secondary to the need for a strong employee organization to push for better wages and especially shorter hours. Fourierist artisans in Boston and the rural villages, however, were still enough removed from the grasp of manufacturing companies that preserving autonomy through small-scale workshops or even phalanxes could be their logical first priority. This socially based difference helps explain important features of the labor agitation of the 1840s: the constant tug within coalitions between ten-hour and reform advocates, the dependence of regional labor organizations in industrializing New England upon ten-hour agitation, the relatively superficial appeal of Fourierism in factory centers such as Lowell, and Fourierist workers' special interest in producer cooperatives.

Land Reform and Protective Union Cooperatives

When cross-class coalitions such as the Labor Reform League and the Lowell Union of Associationists dissolved, Fourierist leaders committed to labor were left to choose between land reform and consumer cooperatives, the two most vital workers' causes of the mid-1840s. Which of these gradualist measures Associationists worked for was largely a matter of geography and temperament. By 1846 New England was already established as the base of the cooperative store movement and New York City the home of the land reformers, so Fourierists in those places simply linked up with the most available cause. In the West the question of expansion made land reform prominent. Upstate New Yorkers, sharing both New England and western concerns, established local organizations of both kinds. New York City Associationists had always styled themselves reform spokesmen who favored grand causes and national agitation. Brisbane's aptitude for theory rather than practice, Greeley's almost religious faith in the homestead, Godwin's expansionist tendencies, and Ryckman's desire to involve workers in politics all led them in the direction of land reform. By contrast, New England Fourierists, with their larger working-class contingent and a greater commitment to practical action, got closely involved with cooperative stores, though as land reform became tinged with free-soil antislavery, several were attracted to it as a secondary cause.

Since early 1844 Associationist leaders had debated George Henry Evans and the land reformers and jockeyed with them for influence in the workingmen's movement. As codified by Evans's National Reform Association, the land reform platform had three planks: provision of free public lands to actual settlers, limitation of the quantity of land any one person could own, and exemption of the homestead from seizure for debt. What made land reform a labor measure was the surplus-labor argument, a variation of the popular idea of the frontier as a safety valve for eastern discontent. According to Evans, eastern workers could move west and take up farming in order to escape overcrowded cities, tyrannical employers, and depressed wages. Because "land monopoly" kept workers penned in urban areas, an oversupply of labor had forced wages down; an exodus to free land would not only benefit those who migrated but boost wages for artisans who stayed behind.[39] Many Associationists shared the land reformers' faith in the frontier but during the initial phalanx enthusiasm refused to settle for a partial approach. In *The Phalanx* and *The Harbinger* Fourierists pointed out that without a frontal assault on free-labor capitalism, western homesteads would only replicate the competitive individualism of eastern cities. To bring meaningful social change, land had to be "kept in the possession of communities or organized townships, not of individuals." When a delegate from the National Reform Association presented a land reform resolution to the New England Fourier Society in January 1845, Brisbane dismissed it by arguing that only Association could work the land equitably and efficiently.[40]

Within a few months, however, Associationists were reconsidering. As land reform became a national movement during the expansionist 1840s, and as phalanx fortunes declined, an alliance between reforms might help revive Association. There were in fact genuine convergences of viewpoint between the two movements. Fourier had warned that land monopoly was one of the vicious symptoms of Civilization's descent into a new feudalism. Without free land and some limitation on holdings, western lands could become huge tracts not unlike the giant corporate farms Fourier correctly foresaw. Another scenario put these lands into the hands of speculators who would make enormous fortunes from selling small subdivisions. If, on the other hand, the land reformers succeeded, cheap western lands could be used for phalanx attempts as migrating utopians pooled their homesteads to form Associations. Even the six-square-mile "rural republican township" that land reformers advocated asserted communal control over minerals, timberland, and water; other features could be added to evolve it toward Fourierist cooperation.[41]

Some disillusioned Associationists, moreover, came to blame land monopoly for the failure of the phalanxes, many of which had begun with heavy mortgages. Writing to the National Reformers' paper *Young America*, a veteran Fourierist noted that each phalanx "was crippled in the start . . . by being bound hand and foot to capitalists," mainly for their land. He and his Fourierist friends were now "unitedly" for land reform, believing it "an indispensable preliminary" to any communal experiments. A final rationale for alliance came when Brisbane, Godwin,

Ryckman, and other Associationists who had flirted with Democratic politics warmed to the land reformers' un-Fourierist idea that workers could use the ballot to press for social reorganization.[42]

By the spring of 1845, Brisbane and Godwin were cooperating with New York land reformers. At the March NEWA meeting Brisbane called "the right of labor" and "the right to the soil" "the two great fundamental rights of man." Ryckman, who had begun his public career as a land reform advocate, returned to the doctrine in 1845 in a series of lectures given at Hudson River towns in support of "Anti-Rent" protests against the lingering Dutch patroon system. John Allen even ran for lieutenant governor of Massachusetts on a land reform and anti–Mexican War platform in 1846. But the most important convert among Associationist "friends of labor" was Horace Greeley. Long a believer in the safety-valve idea, Greeley hesitated at first because of commitments to the Whigs' distribution scheme and to the phalanx, but by 1846 the editor was telling *Tribune* readers and lecture audiences that land reform was "the broad and sure basis whereon all other reforms may be safely erected."[43]

The centerpiece of the Fourierist–land reform alliance and the fulcrum of its leverage with workingmen was to be an annual Industrial Congress. First proposed by the National Reformers in May 1845, the idea of a yearly convention to adopt measures on which all labor reformers could unite was quickly endorsed by the NEWA and the Associationists. The Fourierists expected to be full partners in the three-way coalition, and *The Harbinger* claimed that Association could be the basis on which delegates' differences were reconciled.[44] The history of the congresses proved otherwise. At the preliminary meeting in October 1845 the Fourierists were well represented: among the roughly thirty delegates were Dana, Ryckman, Brisbane, Charles Sears, and James Warren of the North American Phalanx, E. P. Grant of Ohio, and James P. Decker of the New York Union. But the National Reform delegation outnumbered all others, and in the new constitution and the meeting's resolutions Association ran a distant third to land reform and the ten-hour law. At the first formal Industrial Congress in Boston in June 1846 and again in New York the following year, the story was the same, despite the dogged persistence of Brisbane and Ryckman. Fourierists continued to participate: at the 1848 Industrial Congress the Philadelphia Union of Associationists was represented by three delegates, who secured passage of a resolution recommending phalanxes to follow "freedom of the soil"; the next year William McDiarmid presented a pamphlet, "The Right to Labor," to the congress in Cincinnati. But the National Reformers easily outmaneuvered and outnumbered the Associationists and were able to dominate all these conventions.[45]

Among Fourierists attracted to land reform, Greeley continued to preach free homesteads in the *Tribune* and westerners H. H. Van Amringe of Pittsburgh and Lucius Hine of Cincinnati simply transferred allegiance to the new cause. But most Associationist spokesmen drifted away from the Industrial Congress, consoling themselves with the fact that few genuine worker organizations took part in this annual ritual orchestrated by Evans and the National Reformers.[46]

Cooperative stores, though less dramatic than a national campaign for free land, were closer to workers' actual needs, and here the Associationists were able to play an important role in inspiring successful worker projects. Whereas Robert Owen's brand of utopianism, filtered through the Rochdale pioneers of 1844, influenced the founding of working-class cooperatives in England, in the United States (as in France) Fourierism was the philosophy that underlay the movement.[47] As the most vocal and organized proponents of cooperation in America, the Fourierists helped make workers association-conscious through the press, on the platform, and by their community experiments. Taking advantage of their ties with artisans in Massachusetts, the center of the cooperative movement, they helped establish and run such ventures and tried to guide them to larger reform.

Pushed by stagnating wages and inspired by growing agitation among New England mechanics, during the winter of 1844–45 workers' groups in Boston and outlying towns privately discussed suggestions to cut their cost of living through buying clubs or grocers' associations. In October 1845 a splinter group from the Boston Mutual Benefit Association drew up a constitution for a "Protective Union," or cooperative store. Their leaders were working-class Fourierists: Henry P. Trask, who had joined Brook Farm in 1844 as a twenty-four-year-old carriagemaker from Cambridgeport and had set up his own shop when the community closed down; and an unlettered journeyman tailor from Boston named John G. Kaulback.[48]

The plan of the Working Men's Protective Union (WMPU) was simply to combine workers' funds in order to purchase "the necessaries of life" at wholesale and thus provide them to members at the lowest possible price. Membership was open to any person of good moral character (and who did not use intoxicating liquor) with visible means of support. An initiation fee of three dollars and a monthly assessment of 25 cents were meant to assure the organization liquid capital and to accumulate a benefit fund for the sick and aged. Any group of fifteen or more members could form a division (a purchasing group or store). Officers were elected democratically. Eventually a "Supreme Division" consisting of delegates from the local divisions was set up as a central agency to arrange for large-scale purchases and their distribution to the various stores. Here was a limited but practical reform that workers could readily support.[49]

From the outset there was a hidden agenda, however. Most of the Protective Union movement's early leaders conceived trade cooperatives, in Norman Ware's phrase, as "bait to entice the workers along the road to Association." John Allen and Brisbane had pressed this angle when they lectured before the Mutual Benefit Association while workers were forming their plans. Among the first leaders of the WMPU, Trask and

Peter I. Blacker were confirmed Associationists, and Kaulback, A. J. Wright, and William F. Young were sympathetic to Fourierist reform. Trask remained a faithful member of the Boston Union after Brook Farm closed and became the Fourierists' chief intermediary with local workers. Blacker, a journeyman chaise trimmer from Boston who had been attracted to Fourierist ideas in 1841 through Brisbane's New York *Future,* hoped that Protective Unions would "lead on to Association." Establishing cooperative trade arrangments, these leaders later recalled, was but "one-half of the object of our association"; the "organization of industry" was the other. They hoped that savings gained from patronizing the stores would win workers to the idea of complete cooperation; perhaps enough membership fees would accumulate to create a fund for cooperative workshops.[50]

None of this was mentioned in the WMPU's constitution or early publicity, which highlighted the plan's origins among "practical working men" rather than "mere theorists" and stressed the obvious advantage of bypassing commercial middlemen. And in fact, despite the involvement of Fourierists in the WMPU's founding, the initial response of Fourierist leaders was ambivalent. The New England Fourier Society convention of January 1845 approved the idea of replacing "our present expensive modes of distribution" with cooperative exchanges, but some Associationists were not yet ready to compromise the phalanx and "integral Association." When Kaulback presented the Boston workers' plan to the New England Workingmen's Association in September 1845, Lewis Ryckman objected that the NEWA was organized "upon a broader and nobler basis" and should aim for a reform "more fundamental in its character that shall not merely ameliorate the working classes, but disenthrall the laborer from the power of misused capital." A month after the WMPU appeared, *The Harbinger* gave the plan only qualified approval, labeling it "crude" and "incomplete."[51]

But as the workers' movement proved a success and cooperative stores sprang up throughout New England, Associationist leaders quickly warmed to the idea. Begun with a dozen members and capital of about forty dollars, the parent Boston organization had a hundred members by April 1846; by October, the WMPU's first anniversary, there were eleven more divisions. A year later the number of divisions had grown to forty; they blanketed towns in eastern Massachusetts, spread to more distant areas, and enrolled nearly three thousand subscribers. Members found that the stores could consistently offer groceries and dry goods at 20 percent less than conventional markets.[52] By this time the Associationists had come to appreciate practical gradualist measures. *The Harbinger* saw in the WMPU's success "a favorable omen" that the transitional period of "Guarantyism" or semi-Association was being fulfilled. The "pecuniary advantages" of the Protective Unions would push workers toward more complete systems of cooperation. Greeley's *Tribune* endorsed the WMPU and helped spread the movement beyond New England by publishing its constitutions, quarterly reports, and convention proceedings. The *Voice of Industry,* under the editorship of D. H. Jaques and John Orvis, carried weekly articles that informed workers about the arrangements of Protective Unions and linked them to wider "associative principles."[53]

Once won over to cooperative stores, the Fourierists promoted them inside their movement and out. In May 1847 an AUA convention suggested that the affiliated unions join in cooperative purchasing agreements. In response, the Albany Union and the Wisconsin Phalanx opened stores the following year.[54] Associationists helped establish a division on Nantucket Island; the Providence Benefit Union store was founded shortly after John Orvis lectured in that city, and local Associationists steered its charter through the state legislature. Though little information is available about them, Protective Union stores in Cleveland (1848) and Pittsburgh (1850) may also have been set up with local Fourierists' participation. One Associationist attempted to form a cooperative among New York City's blacks. In perhaps the most innovative link between the two groups, the North American Phalanx provided a huge supply of hominy, wheat, flour, and mustard on favorable terms to the WMPU's central division. By the time the AUA officially endorsed the New England Protective Union (the WMPU's successor) in 1850, some Fourierists had been actively enlisted in the movement for years.[55]

Boston Associationists were the most committed and successful in promoting cooperative stores. Henry Trask brought Protective Union officers to Boston Union meetings, where they sparked lively discussions and received legal and organizational advice. Though no formal alliance was completed, many area Fourierists participated in the movement.[56] John Dwight publicized it in the *Daily Chronotype;* he and John Orvis attended WMPU conventions; and Orvis and John Allen lectured on cooperative stores in New England and western New York. Calvin Brown, George H. Merriam, and William A. White, all middle-class officers of the Boston Union of Associationists, became officers of WMPU divisions. White, who edited the *New England Washingtonian,* was won to the cooperative store movement by its associative principles and its temperance pledge, and played a leading role in the WMPU's central division.[57]

Participation by middle-class as well as working-class Associationists suggests that the Protective Union movement quickly spread beyond its worker origins to become a broad gathering of employers, workers, and professionals. A cross-check of an 1849 list of division officers with city directories shows shopowners, overseers, and professionals as well as artisans and factory operatives among the movement's leaders. According to Kaulback, there were tensions between "those who wish[ed] to admit all classes [and] others who wish[ed] to exclude." Nevertheless, recognizing that the term "workingmen" had become too exclusive, in 1849 the WMPU officially changed its name to the New England Protective Union (NEPU).[58] The change represented a victory for the Associationist point of view, and doubtless helped quicken the organization's phenomenal growth to its peak of four hundred divisions and 15,000 members in 1852. Yet rapid expansion and then dilution of the Protective Union movement's original activist working-class constituency may also have contributed to the increasingly narrow orientation of members and an almost palpable sense of letdown among long-time leaders. After an exciting but brief phase of cooperation with workers' producer associations in Boston in 1849 and 1850, the NEPU settled down to a profitable but isolated existence. Pragmatic new leaders appeared from rural areas outside the reach of labor agitation. Mundane questions of organization and trade predominated at the conventions. Many divisions began to drop the mutual benefit provisions, over the protests of veteran officers such as A. J. Wright that worker solidarity had been one of the movement's chief aims. Some divisions reorganized in order to earn income for members by opening the stores to all shoppers, charging above cost for goods, and returning profits to members in the form of dividends. Wright complained that from its broad reform origins the NEPU had narrowed to "a mere trading operation accomplishing a saving of dollars and cents."[59] As the Associationist movement waned, so did the the reform impulse within its cooperativist offshoot.

In truth, there was always the question of how deeply the doctrines of Association had penetrated to the membership. Many leaders may have regarded cooperative stores as the first step to "integral Association," but most of the rank and file, according to the Union's own quarterly report, had "no motive . . . beyond their own personal economy." "Do they care about Socialism?" Albert Brisbane asked rhetorically; "No they don't; but they've found out that they get their goods at thirty percent less than they used to at the grocers, and they care about that."[60] For most members, Protective Unions were far closer to discount stores than to phalanxes. They took the capitalist bait—to continue Ware's metaphor—without being caught on the Associationists' hook.

Yet it would be unfair to dismiss cooperative stores as a trivial gain for workers. Against tremendous odds and far from the limelight, the Protective Union movement survived until after the Civil War. In 1853 a bitter dispute over the Supreme Division, apparently related more to personalities and power than to ideology, split the NEPU into two separate organizations: the majority, including Kaulback, became the American Protective Union; the splinter group, headed by Young and Wright, retained the old name. Both suffered from a lack of capital, struggled through the Panic of 1857, and faced constant hostility and competition from local merchants. After a long, slow decline the last of these purchasing agencies disappeared in 1867.[61] But the success of the movement had been remarkable. In two decades, over eight hundred Protective Unions had been organized, with more than 30,000 members. To many of them, cooperative stores had brought real material savings. To rural workers, the system meant relief from the tyranny of store credit; to industrial workers, it meant freedom from company-town prices. It preserved some sense of achievement and solidarity among labor activists in the period of disorganization after the ten-hour movement failed. Though the Protective Unions did not convert many members to wider social reform, they testified unmistakably to the benefits of cooperation. Disappointed Associationist leaders notwithstanding, the Protective Union movement was one of the finest achievements of American Fourierism.

Producers' Associations and the "Uprising" of 1850

The most direct and radical form of working-class Fourierism, and one that Associationists promoted without reservation, was the cooperative workshop. If workers were to pool their own labor and capital in a craft collective, they would not only mount a clear and direct assault on the wage system but would stand one short step away from combined living in Association. At the end of the 1840s artisans in northern cities, disillusioned with the failure of strikes, increasingly experimented with cooperative workshops as a guarantee of employment, an alternative to wage labor, and an expression of solidarity. These producers' associations, which historian Sean Wilentz calls "the most systematic attempts [of the period] to find a practical alternative to capitalist production," were inspired, supported, and in some cases organized by the American Fourierists.[62] Through their newspapers, Protective Unions, and local clubs, and especially through the efforts of working-class agitators such as Ryckman and Trask, the Associationists played an important (though largely unnoticed) role in the remarkable labor "uprising" of 1849–50, a regional outburst of organizing that reminded some observers of the worker-led agitation in contemporary Paris.

Discussion of producer cooperatives in New England began before the Protective Union movement, though its fruition came later. Associationists at the October 1844 organizing convention of the New England Workingmen's Association pushed through a resolution recommending "practical associations" where workers could "use their own capital, work their own stock, establish their own hours and have their own price." Led by John Allen, a committee of the Mechanics and Laborers Association of Boston reported in January 1845 an ambitious plan of self-employment through cooperative workshops. Declaring that "our Lowells must be owned by the artisans who build them and the operatives who run the machinery and do all the work," it proposed to form a joint-stock "Industrial Firm" in Boston, capitalized at one million dollars, with its huge "unitary edifice" housing a community store, a meeting hall, and cooperative workshops. Dividends were to be apportioned according to a Fourierist formula giving only one-fifth to capital. It would be an urban phalanx without apartments.[63]

Though obviously visionary, the Boston plan left a lasting impression on the founders of the Working Men's Protective Union. Trask, Blacker, and other leaders initially intended the WMPU to combine consumers' and producers' cooperatives, but from "want of means," according to Trask, they "could not . . . commence the organization of trade and industry at the same time." The cooperative workshop idea, submerged as Protective Union stores spread through New England, resurfaced in 1848 when a special WMPU committee investigated a plan to encourage producer cooperatives. The central division, citing lack of funds, could not approve the committee's recommendation for a "Franklin Institute" to provide seed money for cooperative shops, but it did pledge to market such workshops' goods through Protective Union stores. The new WMPU constitution of January 1849 declared the group's aim "to associate producers into an organization for their mutual benefit and improvement."[64]

Meanwhile, a New York City group influenced by the Fourierists undertook a joint producer-consumer scheme. The New York Protective Union (NYPU) organized in 1847, sought to unite all trades in a cooperative store and use the profits to start workshops. For an initiation fee of five dollars, workers were enrolled in a benefit fund, given purchasing rights at the cooperative store, and guaranteed employment in a cooperative shop. Lewis Ryckman was the first business agent. By the middle of 1850 the NYPU had enrolled four hundred members, and profits from its grocery and bakery were sustaining new blacksmith and wheelwright shops.[65]

The cooperative explosion at decade's end was triggered not by the Protective Unions, however, but by the convergence of two other forces: workers on strike in major northern cities looking for alternatives to the exploitation of wage labor; and the example of the French producers' associations of 1848, as promoted by Fourierists Greeley, Brisbane, Dana, Ryckman, and Trask.

At its heart the French revolution of 1848 was social as well as political, and while the French provisional government debated various plans for the "organization of labor," skilled Parisian workers took production into their own hands. Under the Second Republic nearly three hundred producers' associations were formed in 120 Parisian trades, enrolling some 50,000 members. These small, democratic workshops became powerful enough to win loan subsidies from the government, and until disbanded by Louis Napoleon after his *coup d'état* in 1851, they were a focal point of the republican and labor movement effort to transform the French economy into a form of cooperative socialism. French Fourierists were actively involved with these associations, publicizing their efforts, patronizing their shops, uniting with leaders in cooperative federations, and in a few cases establishing workshops themselves.[66]

Charles Dana and Albert Brisbane, who were in Paris at the height of the revolution, saw in the French cooperatives a constructive and practical plan of "partial association." Guided by a French Fourierist, Dana visited the Parisian saddlers' association in September and described it carefully

for *Boston Chronotype* readers. So rapid was the spread of worker cooperatives that Dana predicted, "In five years the greater part of the labor
done in Paris will be so done that the workman will be his own master,
and receive that full fruit of his toil." Brisbane was no less enthusiastic:
in March 1849 he inspected several Paris cooperatives, dined at the
Parisian cooks' association, and became a convert.[67] Horace Greeley recognized worker cooperatives as the perfect practical alternative to his
dreaded scenario of unemployment, strikes, and class warfare; throughout 1848 and 1849 the *Tribune* disseminated information about producers' associations and urged striking American workers to follow the
French example. Greeley also printed and distributed copies of Charles
Sully's *Associative Manual,* which collected the plans and constitutions of
French and British worker associations. When Brisbane got back from
Europe, he returned to the lecture circuit to proselytize for cooperative
workshops before worker audiences in Boston, New York, Pittsburgh,
and Cincinnati. Dana spoke before the Mechanics Institute and trade
societies in New York.[68] The Associationists' reports from Paris and
their lectures at home focused American workers' discontent on the
cooperative workshop plan. When these ideas coincided with the needs
of striking workers, a movement was born.

The pioneers were the iron-molders of Cincinnati, who in 1847 failed
to win a strike against wage cuts. As the workers considered their next
course of action during the winter slack season, John Allen arrived from
Boston to form an affiliated union of the AUA and give a series of
lectures on Association, and Cincinnati Fourierists sponsored a "reform
banquet" hailing the National Workshops and other achievements of
the French revolutionaries. After much discussion, about twenty iron-
molders incorporated themselves as the Journeyman Molders Union
Foundry. Fourierist landowners S. H. and I. Goodwin gave them "favorable terms" for building a new foundry eight miles downriver from the
city. The association began operations in August 1848 with $2,100 and
ten worker associates; by 1850 forty-seven workers were employed at its
foundry, and the molders had established a store in Cincinnati to sell
their stoves and castings.[69] Long considered a spontaneous workers' project, the Cincinnati cooperative was actually formed under Fourierist
sponsorship. Indeed, within a year the foundry became the inspiration
for an ambitious plan hatched by local Fourierists to build an entire city
of cooperative workshops outside Cincinnati. In the summer of 1849 a
few middle-class sponsors and fifty aspiring journeymen began building
"Home City," a workers' community intended eventually to house five
thousand persons. Factories and workshops were to be owned cooperatively and individual homes built with worker dividends. By the spring
of 1850 the town boasted its own cooperative foundry and shoe shops.
Houses were rising, a library was planned, and Cincinnati reporters
described the settlement as a successful venture.[70]

Outside Cincinnati, the full impact of the cooperative idea did not become apparent until the fall of 1849. The first large-scale agitation took place in Boston, with the Associationists directly involved. For fourteen grueling weeks in the summer of 1849, several hundred Boston journeyman tailors were on strike to have their price scale accepted by employers. When the large shops rejected their demands, workers began to discuss alternatives. At this point the Boston Associationists intervened decisively. In the *Chronotype* Brisbane provided a detailed history of the French producers' associations and a copy of the saddlers' constitution forwarded by Dana. At mass meetings cosponsored by the Fourierists, donations were collected to begin a cooperative venture. Greeley and fellow Associationists William F. Channing of Boston and Joseph Barker of Providence provided most of the $500 capital accumulated. In late September about seventy workers organized the Boston Tailors' Associative Union and opened a workshop. B. S. Treanor, an exiled Irish Chartist and a crusading Fourierist, drew up the group's constitution and became its secretary. Within a few months the tailors reported a modest expansion of membership to eighty and plans to open an additional store. The Boston Associationists congratulated them on their progress and urged continued devotion to associative principles.[71]

Immediately after the tailors' work stoppage came a strike of Boston's journeyman printers. Following extended discussion, three hundred workers formed the Boston Printers' Protective Union, with Fourierist printer William Manning among the officers. Its constitution adopted Dwight's idea of a dividend to labor and his safeguards against inequalities in shareholding. While it was being finalized, about two-thirds of the printers were rehired by their old employers; the union sought to provide work for the remainder by taking in book and job printing. Most important, the union published a weekly newspaper, the *Protective Union*, which became the chief organ of New England's producer and consumer cooperatives. The paper lasted eleven months, thanks in large part to Treanor, who assumed coproprietorship in April 1850.[72]

The cooperative idea spread rapidly: Treanor organized the Boston Seamstresses Cooperative Society in February 1850; in September, Trask, Treanor, and William Hibbard (a Boston Fourierist and civil engineer) aroused the South Boston machinists to create a Machinists and Pattern-Makers Association. Throughout the ferment, Associationist labor leaders not only organized producers' associations but publicized the idea to wider audiences. In November 1849 and April 1850, Boston Fourierists convened large meetings in Faneuil Hall, "composed almost exclusively of working men," to support the cooperative associations and to urge other trades to follow suit. The speakers included national Associationist leaders Brisbane and William Elder of Philadelphia. In April and again in August, Trask and Treanor lectured on cooperatives in Boston and outlying towns, urging working-class listeners to take up cooperation and all groups to patronize the new societies. Under their influence the annual convention of the AUA, meeting in Boston in May 1850, officially endorsed the producer association movement.[73]

Support for the printers, tailors and seamstresses also came from the New England Protective Union. In April 1849 the NEPU set up a Committee on the Organization of Industry whose members included reform-minded leaders Wright, Blacker, Kaulback, and chairman Henry Trask. In July the committee's report, citing the "noble precedent" of the Paris workers, reaffirmed the NEPU's wider mission to "proceed from combined stores to combined shops, from combined shops to combined houses, to joint ownership in God's earth," and asked members to help organize producers' associations. When the Boston workers set out to form cooperatives, the NEPU demonstrated solidarity by giving printers and tailors buying privileges and by purchasing goods from the tailors and seamstresses. Finally, the NEPU seemed to be fulfilling John Orvis's Fourierist dream that it be "a school in which the working classes are unconsciously fitting themselves for seats in other places now too exclusively filled by the myrmidons of a false, antagonistic industry."[74]

Inspired by developments in Cincinnati and Boston as well as Paris, tradesmen across the country rushed to organize cooperatives in the spring of 1850. There were cooperative glass works in Pittsburgh, a nail-cutters association in Wheeling, Virginia, and cooperative shoeshops in Montpelier, Vermont, and Randolph, Massachusetts.[75] The largest movement came in New York City, where cooperative organizing merged with general labor agitation in one of the most significant labor upheavals in America before the Civil War. The crisis began in March, when New York's cordwainers and carpenters went on strike to protest wage cuts and the subcontracting system. Shortly after Dana wrote an editorial urging cooperative production rather than strikes, the carpenters formed a short-lived Joint-Stock Building Association. Led by Lewis Ryckman, the cordwainers formed the Shoemakers Working Union in April, with Ryckman and Greeley on its board of trustees. From there the wave of strikes and cooperative organizing spread to the tailors (both native and German), cabinetmakers, upholsterers, confectioners, shipwrights, and other artisans. Brisbane attended a meeting of the house carpenters to promote Association. In the midst of the crisis, Greeley seemed to be everywhere, publicizing the movement at length in the *Tribune* (the only New York paper that sympathized with it) and leading a personal campaign "to get the unions off the picket lines and into cooperative workshops." To dramatize his support, Greeley announced that he was turning the *Tribune* into a joint-stock "association" owned partly by the workers. On April 10 the *Tribune* labeled the agitation a "general uprising," and many commentators compared the workers' mass rallies, marches to City Hall, and cooperative projects to the activities of the French revolutionaries of 1848.[76]

The New York agitation was a mélange of organizations and proposals pointing in different directions, with trade unions, land reformers, cooperativists, and benefit societies all taking part and advocating their favorite programs. Nor were the Fourierists alone in promoting cooperatives: Wilhelm Weitling, a German revolutionary exile who had sparred with Marx and Engels, was decisive in turning New York's German unions toward cooperative workshops. But through Greeley's constant publicity and the efforts of Ryckman, Brisbane, and others, Fourierist ideas and rhetoric were at the center of workers' discussions and spread widely among labor activists. Even the *Irish-American,* the newspaper voice of Irish labor, argued that cooperative plans and "the principles of association" were "the surest means to better the conditions of labor."[77] Producers' associations appealed as the most practical and systematic way for small masters and wage earners to unite in a system free of wage labor and capitalist control. At least for a few months, the separate lines of labor agitation of the 1840s seemed to be converging upon a Fourierist-inspired program of cooperative production.

Eventually, the cooperatives, benefit societies, and other labor organizations in each city undergoing the agitation sought to band together in citywide "congresses" (not to be confused with the land reformers' conventions of the same name). The Pittsburgh Workingmen's Congress first met in April 1850 to unite trade delegates in support of an ironworkers' strike. Among the organizers were Associationists James Thornburg and James Nichols, who reported resolutions on cooperatives. In Cincinnati, Brisbane and John Allen assisted in forming a "Laborer's League" combining various labor reform groups.[78] Other congresses were held in New York, Boston, Philadelphia, Baltimore, and Cleveland.

Those in Boston and New York were the largest and most active; their evolution demonstrated the dissipation of the remarkable labor campaign of 1850 when it moved its emphasis from cooperatives to politics. Early in May 1850 at the Boston Fourierists' meeting hall, a delegation from the Boston Union of Associationists met with representatives from the printers', tailors', seamstresses', and cabinetmakers' cooperatives along with Protective Union officers. After two other labor organizations joined the deliberations, the New England Industrial League was formed. Like the NEWA, the league accepted delegates from a variety of labor and reform groups, but its primary aim was to promote and sustain cooperative workshops. Members' dues paid for a strike fund to support labor protest and an "emancipation fund" to lend money to producers' associations. At the July 4 meeting, delegates declared their own "independence" by ratifying the league's constitution and electing a slate of officers led by Henry Trask as president. Almost immediately, however, the league became involved in politics. Interested in incorporating producers' associations, members began questioning candidates for governor on this issue and invited land reformers and ten-hour advocates to join them in a labor voting bloc. By October 1850 the New England Industrial

League had become a political coalition of labor and land reform groups supporting the ten-hour workday, free homesteads, and other measures. As politics came to dominate its meetings and cooperative experiments began to fail, the Associationists left the group, which evolved into the Massachusetts State Ten-Hour Convention.[79]

The New York City Industrial Congress also splintered on the rocks of politics. Far more than the Boston group, it was a broad coalition of labor and reform organizations, with the result that cooperativists had to share power with land reformers, benefit societies, and trade union delegates. The congress was huge and unwieldy. Formed in June 1850, it gathered eighty-three delegates representing fifty societies; by December more than ninety labor organizations were members. Such a diverse collection found unity only by endorsing a laundry list of labor reforms (including cooperative workshops) and by holding rallies in support of striking tailors at which trade unionists, land reformers, and Fourierists (including Brisbane) shared the rostrum. In the fall of 1850 its leaders, looking for new venues after the wave of strikes subsided, interviewed local candidates for political office on labor issues and recommended the ballot as the surest means to end workers' "oppressions and grievances." Gradually, the well-organized land reformers took control of the congress, leading it into a formal alliance with Tammany Hall in June 1851. When the land reformers' champion, Senator Isaac Walker, failed to win the Democratic nomination for U.S. president in 1852, the New York City Industrial Congress dissolved.[80]

The cooperative workshops themselves were short-lived. Brisbane, describing them for a British audience in 1851, complained that the associations were "just holding their own," and in fact most lasted less than two years. Plagued by the dearth of business experience among workers, many also ran up against wholesalers who refused to buy their goods. Cooperatives often lacked legal protection: unless they were incorporated by state legislatures, their members were individually liable for losses. At least one state, Massachusetts, refused to charter them; a legislator explained that encouraging cooperatives among journeymen tailors would "ruin the employers." Without enough capital to operate on a cash basis and guarantee paychecks, some cooperatives, among them the Cincinnati iron-molders, asked workers to take payment in stock. Others, such as the Boston printers, lost members when former employers matched their wage scale: not all workers were bent on "justice" to the extent of risking their living for it, as Brisbane noted. After surviving more than three years, the Cincinnati Union Foundry was driven out of business when the city's stove manufacturers launched a bitter price war. Socialist tradesmen learned that competing in a capitalist economy was difficult without endorsing ruthlessness and inequality; until cooperatives could trade with one another, as Fourierists envisioned, they were dependent upon the same market forces that capitalist employers faced.[81]

Their short lives and small size do not mean, however, that producers'

associations were doomed to failure simply because their practices ran
counter to the centralization of production and capital and other "long-
term industrial trends."[82] Such a conclusion takes into account neither
the numerous successes of cooperative organization in modern industries
nor the variety of options still open when early industrial capitalism was
contested terrain. The Fourierist phase of worker cooperatives ended
in 1850, but cooperative enterprises, like communitarian experiments,
would resurface when labor reformers again sought alternatives to wage-
labor capitalism after the Civil War.

12

The Last Communities

By mid-1850 the North American Phalanx was the only original Fourierist community still in existence. In many respects it was prospering. As the last surviving experiment, it attracted diehard veterans from other phalanxes, including more than a dozen Brook Farmers. And as the phalanx closest to New York City, it drew a steady stream of visitors and reporters, found a ready market for its produce in the metropolitan area, and gained the favor of wealthy local merchants sympathetic to Fourierism. NAP members had fended off the most prominent of these patrons, the Phalansterian Realization Fund Society, yet still managed to come away with substantial loans for their agricultural and building programs. With the help of PRFS funds, members began constructing their phalanstery in 1849, had added two wings by 1852, and completed a brick "seristery" to house fruit-preserving operations in 1850. All these improvements meant that the phalanx had begun to deliver the economic benefits promised by Association. In 1851 the community showed a profit for the first time and was soon able to supplement members' wages with a "labor dividend" declared at the year's end.[1]

Yet though the phalanx's situation seemed secure, problems arose that foreshadowed impending collapse. Despite active recruitment undertaken in the hope of evolving toward Fourierist specifications, the phalanx had in 1852 only some 120 members—about the same number of residents as four years earlier—and there was such continuous turnover in membership that it threatened the community's stability. A committee report complained that of an average fifty probationers a year, only half were productive, and no more than one-sixth eventually became members.[2] Conspicuously underrepresented among resident members were national Fourierist leaders, who were busy with their own careers and who nurtured expectations for communal living too exalted for the little phalanx to fulfill. Perhaps most distressing, the phalanx failed to attract and keep families; the NAP's minutes indicate that resident families found it difficult to cover food and clothing expenses for their children with standard phalanx "wages." Yet without children there would be no second generation to bequeath the community to. One could foresee, wrote a Fourierist leader well aware of the double meaning, that "the Association was likely to be childless."[3]

Whether they had families or not, artisans at the phalanx complained that their compensation lagged behind that of workers in the profitable agricultural series. A published report revealed that they earned little more than a dollar per working day in 1852, below the average for skilled workers in nearby New York City. Despite the low cost of living at the domain, few if any community artisans were able to end the year with a surplus. Since skilled workers owned fewer shares of community stock, the gap between working-class and middle-class members increased with each yearly dividend. Yet even middle-class members realized that they could do better in the outside world; those who made a profit at the phalanx invested it elsewhere. It was a foreboding vote of no-confidence in the community's economic future.[4]

These demographic and economic tensions were no doubt heightened by members' despondency over the decline of Fourierism and the community's sense of isolation as the sole surviving phalanx. Willingly or not, the NAP had become what John Humphrey Noyes called "the test-experiment upon which Fourierism practically staked its all in this country," and though this new status brought increased publicity, it also made the community a focus of doctrinal disputes and a whipping boy for the dashed hopes of national leaders and the Associationist rank and file.[5]

Marcus Spring and the Raritan Bay Union

When a religious dispute was added to existing divisions at the phalanx, complaints turned into arguments, and an overt split occurred. In the spring of 1853 about thirty members left the NAP to form a rival community, the Raritan Bay Union, just a few miles away. The secession, fed by ongoing disagreements in several areas of phalanx life, was precipitated by a controversy over religious worship and given direction by the plans of the wealthy benefactor Marcus Spring.[6]

Born into a Massachusetts Quaker family, Spring inherited his father's debt-ridden dry goods business and made it so profitable that he spent his middle age as a patron of the arts and reform. In 1836 he married Rebecca Buffum, daughter of the first president of the New England Antislavery Society, and the two moved to New York. Four years later the couple broke with the Garrisonians to join the antislavery Liberty Party, whose champions Theodore Weld and James G. Birney became the Springs' lifelong friends. The Springs also cultivated friendships with writers and artists: Emerson, Thoreau, Bronson Alcott, and especially

Margaret Fuller, whom they took along on a trip to Europe in 1846.[7] In the early 1840s the Springs absorbed Association through Brisbane and Parke Godwin and immediately became supporters. Marcus bought several hundred shares of stock in the North American Phalanx, and though he declined to move there, he attended stockholders' meetings and was a frequent visitor. His sisters and their husbands were prominent NAP residents.[8]

To Spring and his followers the phalanx lacked religious fervor. Like all Fourierist communities, the NAP professed religious tolerance, yet observers noted that there was little interest in religious discussion or ritual. Fredrika Bremer, visiting in 1849, deplored the phalanx's lack of public worship and doubted its ability to survive solely on "moral principle." Apparently, a faction in the community agreed. Encouraged by Spring, who believed the NAP needed a "spiritual leader" such as William Henry Channing and perhaps a religious test for membership, and led by Spring's brother-in-law George Arnold, a former Unitarian minister and the NAP's president in 1851, the group urged a mandatory fixed liturgy to be led by a minister supported from phalanx funds.[9] In Spring's mind, religious deficiencies were linked to cultural ones. Like Brisbane and other Associationists enthralled by Fourier's fantasies or by idyllic memories of Brook Farm, Spring lamented that the NAP "neglected the intellectual and aethetic element" and cautioned that community children were growing up without proper schooling.[10] No doubt such concerns were also undercover complaints about social class: always the patrician, Spring believed that phalansterians should recruit members used to "refined conditions" and provide more cultural amenities.[11]

A third source of friction was the degree of individual freedom in Association. Whereas the NAP apportioned profits among its members according to Fourier's formulas, the Springs believed that Americans were not ready to sacrifice individual economic independence to the group; the NAP rotated most jobs and expected members to live communally, but the Springs preferred privacy and abhorred manual labor. Perhaps to demonstrate this position, Spring had a private summer cottage built next to the phalanstery, remaining apart from the community during his visits except for meals in the common dining room.[12]

Spring's preference for "partial association" and greater individualism coincided with dissatisfactions expressed at the phalanx. Community craftsmen were open to suggestions that they could "do better" if allowed to operate independently. In 1852 the residents switched from family-style meals to a restaurant-type system whereby persons ordered and paid individually. One skilled worker told A. J. Macdonald that "he wanted to see the individual system carried out still further among them; for in proportion as they adopted that, they were made free and happy; but in proportion as they progressed toward Communism, the result was the reverse."[13]

Spring's cherished dream of building a magnificent Fourierist "unitary

edifice" coexisted uneasily with this individualism. He apparently believed that apartment-style living without communal work or property
was an appropriate "half-way means" to Association—at least for the
Fourierist rank and file.[14] As a leader of the Phalansterian Realization
Fund Society, he pressured NAP members to construct a phalanstery far
grander than their needs. For a few years his "edifice complex" was
placated by the modest expansion achieved with PRFS funds. But when
the religious controversy peaked in 1852, Spring seized the chance to
realize his pet project.

In November 1852 Spring purchased a 268-acre estate called Eagleswood, overlooking picturesque Raritan Bay, just west of Perth Amboy, New Jersey. The next month the Raritan Bay Union was organized
at a meeting in New York City. Within half a year over $40,000 in stock
was purchased by Spring, Channing, and business supporters from New
York and Philadelphia, and two dozen residents had moved to the estate.
Among the directors were Spring, his brother-in-law George Arnold,
and Clement Read of the Hopedale Community, whose wife Lydia was
Spring's sister-in-law. Far less democratic than the NAP, Raritan Bay was
controlled by a kinship network of successful business families.[15]

Community arrangements reflected Spring's idiosyncratic blend of
individualism and association. A. J. Macdonald characterized the Raritan
Bay Union as a joint-stock venture in "an intermediate position between
the North American Phalanx and ordinary society." Its provisional prospectus of November 1852 called the group "unpledged to any social
theory as yet presented" and carefuly avoided mentioning Fourier.[16]
Each branch of work was kept separate and intended to be self-sufficient.
Fields, mill, and workshops were leased to individuals or groups, who
then paid rent for their living quarters and separate fees for meals,
washing, and ironing. Outside laborers were hired for some tasks, and a
few families even brought servants with them.[17]

Raritan Bay's central building was a monumental unitary dwelling
begun in 1853 and completed two years later. Costing over $40,000 and
constructed largely by hired laborers, it was an imposing four-story brick
and brownstone block in Italianate revival style, flanked by extended two-
and-a-half-story wings that culminated in large pavilions. With a facade
254 feet long, it was the largest and most impressive American phalanstery. One wing housed the community's school, members' apartments
occupied the other, and dining and meeting rooms formed the center.
The building combined the formal solidity of civic architecture with the
festive air of a resort hotel. First- and second-floor porches along the
facade tempered the design's severity and stimulated spontaneous association à la Fourier. Though symmetrical and self-contained, the building
could be enlarged by adding perpendicular wings to create formal courtyards, as in Fourier's design. Spring had planned an enormous and
elegant phalanstery affording every family pleasant views of the bay.[18]

Every family in the phalanstery, that is. An unusual feature at Raritan

Bay was that families could build private houses on individually owned lots if they preferred to, while still using the communal laundry, bakery, and dining room; James G. Birney and a few others did purchase parcels. The Springs lived in the fine mansion left by the previous owner of the estate, located to the side of the phalanstery and facing its parade ground at a right angle. This "perfectly private residence," Henry Thoreau noted with amusement during a visit, stood "within twenty rods of the main building."[19] The juxtaposition of patrons' mansion and members' dormitory was a jarring sight, more appropriate to a capitalist mill town than a utopian socialist community.

Raritan Bay announced plans to attract "the best class of mechanics" from the NAP and elsewhere by building extensive shops. Hired masons erected at the river's edge a large stone building with a steam engine, which was soon occupied by carpenters, cabinetmakers, and millers. But few other industries were established; as Charles Sears complained, the Springs intended primarily "a select society of literary people, artists and people of means and leisure."[20] Befitting this genteel version of the good life, emphasis was placed on cultural and intellectual amenities. The core of the community was a coeducational boarding school that attracted students from around the country and the children of Fourierists on and off the domain. In 1853 the Springs convinced fellow abolitionists Theodore Weld, his feminist wife Angelina Grimké, and her sister Sarah to move to Eagleswood and take charge of the school. Arriving the following year, the three designed an educational program that attempted, true to the communitarian tradition, to integrate school with community life and educate the whole person. Students learned farming and household skills as well as the usual academic and classical subjects, and young men and women exercised in the community gymnasium. Weld and the Grimkés attracted a talented young faculty. Elizabeth Palmer Peabody, the Brook Farmers' friend who had taught at Bronson Alcott's progressive Temple School, attempted to start the first American kindergarten at Eagleswood but found the venture "premature." Steele MacKaye, who would become America's foremost Shakespearian actor, taught art and directed student plays. Together with Saturday evening lectures, lyceum courses, informal dramatic presentations, and Quaker-style religious meetings on Sundays, the school lent Raritan Bay the kind of moral and cultural refinement the Springs had enjoyed at Brook Farm and missed at the North American Phalanx.[21]

Nevertheless, the Raritan Bay Union lacked a communal focus. According to William Henry Channing, without allegiance to Fourier "no two of the originators were of the same way of feeling or thinking . . . [about] the method of working out the better life."[22] Channing himself was unwilling to move to Eagleswood to form a religious union. Benefactor Spring's vision of the community was too individualistic and perhaps too idiosyncratic to be compelling; in any event, he was often absent on business and pleasure trips to Paris and elsewhere and sought no involvement in his community's day-to-day affairs.[23] The school was a key activity but was unrelated to Raritan Bay's other economic functions.

One serious problem was social class. The odd mixture of wealthy families with servants, outside hired laborers, and struggling artisan families constituted the widest range of classes in any phalanx. Because each family was expected to pay its own way, class differences were embedded in the community's very structure. Without the Fourierist commitment to shared tasks and guaranteed subsistence, Raritan Bay became a two-tier community of grumblers. On one level, well-heeled families mingled reluctantly with workers and resisted doing manual labor. Sarah Grimké found most members "not at all to my taste" and felt that her sister Angelina was not "designed to serve tables any more than Theodore was designed to dig potatoes." On the other level, harried working-class members had little time for socializing or stockholders' gatherings and found it hard to make ends meet. One carpenter who had come from the NAP to work on the phalanstery tried two other trades once its construction was completed but left in disgust after sixteen months, his wife complaining that success at Raritan Bay was impossible for "people of small means."[24]

Spring himself admitted to Emerson that the experiment had fallen "far short of our hopes." With the community neither a cooperative nor a business success, he took steps to dissolve remaining communal ties: in 1856 he bought back most shares of the community's stock.[25] The next year he began selling lots to business associates for private houses and then issued a public circular offering to sell "villa and cottage sites" to any families "desiring quiet country homes."[26] Some members continued to live in the unitary building as teachers or service workers for the school, but when Weld and the Grimké sisters left in 1861, the school closed, and remaining communal features at Eagleswood were ended.

Breakup of the North American Phalanx

Losing prominent members to the Raritan Bay Union hurt the North American Phalanx. The thirty seceders included an accomplished horti-culturalist, the chief carpenter, and other major stockholders. Raritan Bay members and supporters now held more than one-sixth of the NAP's stock, a dangerous conflict of interest.[27] Charles Sears, president of the phalanx and its "leading mind," vowed to continue the Fourierist pattern of living and working. The NAP was bolstered by the addition of six French exiles, and its farm was so bountiful that members established a thriving depot in New York City to sell their produce. But the split with Spring and his followers had clearly damaged community morale. The debates that preceded it established a new atmosphere of contention, and the secession itself cast doubts on the community's Fourierist princi-ples. One index of growing disenchantment with Fourierism was the increasing individualization of community arrangements. As previously noted, by 1852 families were being permitted to have separate residences and meals; soon proposals were aired to abolish sickness and death benefits and allow private enterprise on the domain.[28]

The crushing blow came in September 1854 when a fire destroyed the community's gristmill, sawmill, business office, and some workshops. Two thousand bushels of wheat and corn were consumed, and the phalanx's insurance agent, unable to cover the $14,000 in damages, declared bankruptcy. Although Horace Greeley offered to lend the community $12,000 to rebuild, members could not agree on what to do next.[29] The fire revived an old debate on whether the community's mills should be on the landlocked domain or at Red Bank, five miles away at the mouth of the Navesink River. As the discussions dragged on for four months, it became evident that fundamental questions about the phalanx were at issue. One side, taken by many of the community's carpenters and mechanics, argued that the NAP could relieve its financial difficulties and give a boost to mechanical pursuits by locating the new mills at Red Bank. The other side, led by Sears, acknowledged the economic advantages of the move but clung to the Fourierist vision of a self-contained model community. Separating industrial operations from the farm would destroy the integrity of the experiment. Caught between communitarian ideals and economic necessity, members reached an impasse that was resolved only when the community's mounting debts made dissolution the inevitable choice.[30]

At the January 1855 stockholders' meeting, members began discussing proposals to liquidate. The New York Club of Associationists—NAP nonresident stockholders—suggested that the phalanx either issue new shares of stock or sell part of the domain to regain solvency.[31] Sears and other Fourierist leaders urged Victor Considerant, the leader of the French Fourierists, to purchase the phalanx as a staging point for his planned colony in Texas, but no such arrangement materialized.[32] In June 1855 the stockholders voted to dissolve the community, and in October the phalanx lands were divided and sold at auction, mostly to former members of the community (including, ironically, Marcus Spring). Arthur Young, the English philanthropist who had subsidized the French phalanx at Citeaux, attempted unsuccessfully to reorganize the community among the purchasers. By the end of 1855 the former phalansterians were either dispersed in Civilization or settled as family farmers on the domain. About a third continued to live in the phalanstery; although they were no longer Fourierists, they ran their own school and enjoyed a countercultural existence to the turn of the twentieth century.[33]

The NAP did have one direct Fourierist descendant. Alcander Longley, the Cincinnati printer who joined the NAP in 1853, attempted five years later to establish a "Fourier Phalanx" on a rented farm at Moore's Hill, Indiana. But the Panic of 1857 changed the plans of several Cincinnati supporters, and in February 1858 Longley found only twelve Fourierists ready to join. After a few months the small band gave up the farm and separated. This was the first of a lifetime of failed communities the persistent Longley formed after the Fourierist movement collapsed.[34]

La Réunion: Fourierism on the Texas Frontier

While the North American Phalanx struggled to stay alive and the Raritan Bay Union was getting established, a combined force of French and American Fourierists gathered in a colony on the Texas frontier for one last attempt to build a model phalanx.[35] The main impetus came from France, where Louis Napoleon's *coup d'état* of December 1851 effectively shut down the Ecole Sociétaire and ended Victor Considerant's hope of returning from exile in Belgium to resume propaganda. With European socialists in retreat, Albert Brisbane—once again in Europe—renewed his campaign for a French phalanx in America. In Paris he persuaded a few Fourierist notables to transfer their activities to America, and from there he traveled to Belgium in May 1852 to argue with Considerant.[36] Throughout the 1840s Considerant had been reluctant to endorse a Fourierist experiment without guarantees of success, but as prospects for a mass movement in France grew dim, his thoughts turned increasingly to the establishment of a communal "asylum" for faithful Fourierists, preferably somewhere in Europe. When his plan for a Swiss colony of socialist emigrés failed to win support, Considerant finally agreed to return with Brisbane to scout out opportunities in the New World.[37] Brisbane's appeals had won out after twenty years.

After arriving in New York in mid-December, Considerant spent six weeks at the North American Phalanx.[38] There he worked on his English and began to devise a plan, based on arrangements he saw at the NAP, for a joint French and American Fourierist community. In response to invitations from New England Fourierists, he visited Boston, Lawrence, and Lowell. Then in April 1853 Considerant joined Brisbane in upstate New York, and the two set out on a trip that took them down the Ohio Valley, across the Mississippi, and eventually on horseback through the Indian Territory. When they reached the Red River Valley at the Texas border, the landscape began to capture Considerant's imagination:

> Suddenly, on the fourth day, after four or five hours' march, the horizon enlarged, the forest opened and we came out into the head of a valley whose loveliness confounded all my previous notions of terrestial reality. It extended before us in its length. To the right and left, rich prairies rose in elegant undulations towards lines of wooded mountains, whose summits, ranging on different plains, all verdant and blue in the distance, enframed the landscape.[39]

Along the banks of the Trinity River in the present-day Dallas–Fort Worth area, Considerant discovered a land of suitable grandeur and fertility for the glorious phalanx he and Brisbane, and before them Fourier, had dreamed of. "I was expecting something wild and rude," he later wrote, "coarse grasses and weeds of enormous height." Instead, he claimed to have found a virgin land with soil of "superior richness," which could become "the garden of the world" within a few years. Such land was available for pennies per acre, allowing a vast domain to be purchased and virtually guaranteeing a hefty profit to those who held it. In a flush of enthusiasm, Considerant wrote home from Texas urging French Fourierists to organize a colonization society as soon as possible.[40]

The speed of his conversion was remarkable. When he yielded to Brisbane's entreaties at Brussels, Considerant had grudgingly acknowledged that a trip to America could "do no harm." But once in the New World the Frenchman quickly and effortlessly absorbed the wondrous rhetoric of American exceptionalism and the breathless exaggeration of frontier boosterism. His letters to his wife, Julie, and his more carefully composed public statements to French colleagues portrayed the United States as the utopians' "promised land," a "wild Eden" where abundance comes naturally, an asylum of liberty where new ideas could flourish, and the home of pragmatic optimists who could overcome any obstacles.[41] On one level the book Considerant wrote about his experience, *Au Texas* (1854), serves simply as a community prospectus, but on another it records the dramatic conversion of a French socialist to American mythology: "The appearance of this nature so manifestly friendly, this sweet and majestic invitation given to social man by the primitive land, these betrothals so magnificently prepared between it and free labor, combined and harmonious, acted on us like a sudden revelation of Destiny. . . . A horizon of new ideas, of new sentiments and hopes opened like magic before me. Brisbane was confirmed in his American faith; I, baptized."[42]

By September 1853 Considerant was back in Brussels promoting his plan, and the next spring copies of *Au Texas* circulated among French Fourierist leaders. In his prospectus Considerant envisioned a joint European and American colonization society, capitalized at a million dollars, which would purchase land, transport emigrants across the Atlantic, and prepare the domain for settlement. With encouragement from the American consul in Brussels, Considerant hoped for a generous land grant from the Texas legislature. On this tract an advance guard of 150 Americans would clear fields and begin farming and building before European emigrants arrived. Though he appealed primarily to Fourierists, Considerant believed that the main objective was to establish a flourishing and profitable colony before a full-scale phalanx could be organized; meanwhile, if enough colonists were interested, work arrangements could be modeled on the semi-Fourierist plan of the North American Phalanx.[43] A serious tension between speculative colony and Fourierist phalanx thus haunted the experiment from the beginning.

Nevertheless, the response from French Fourierists was immediate and positive. One year after Considerant returned, the Société de Coloni-

sation Européo-Américaine au Texas, or Colonization Society, was
formed as the organizational successor to the Ecole Sociétaire. Considerant as executive agent would lead the colonists while three other directors remained in Paris. By the end of 1854 over a quarter of a million
dollars had been subscribed, and 2,500 persons had declared their willingness to embark.[44] In February 1855 Considerant, architect César Daly,
and a few other French Fourierists arrived in New York, while two
thousand miles inland the society's agent François Cantagrel and the
American Fourierist John Allen purchased 2,400 acres on the south bank
of the Trinity River, about three miles west of the village of Dallas. Within
weeks an advance guard of about forty, including Allen and a dozen
Americans, began clearing fields and planting crops.

From the outset La Réunion, as the Fourierists named the colony, was
a fiasco.[45] The powerful Know-Nothing party, which had sprang up in
Texas during Considerant's absence, opposed the colony as an alien
foothold. Austin newspapers, noting that "the socialist is an *abolitionist*
everywhere," declared that they "would rather see the State a howling
desert than witness the spreading waves of Socialism stretch itself over
the Christian Churches and the Slave Institution of Texas." The mere
fact of Greeley's *Tribune* endorsement was enough to convince Texans
that the colony was a free-soil venture.[46] Considerant himself publicly
declared the colony neutral on slavery, but his pamphlet *European Colonization in Texas* contained remarks criticizing the institution, and rumors
circulated even among American Fourierists that the colony would undertake an emancipation experiment.[47] With so much local opposition
the Texas legislature failed to provide a land grant, despite Considerant's
personal appeals to the state's congressmen in Washington. To make
matters worse, in the interim following Considerant's trip with Brisbane
the Texas government had terminated homestead privileges, and land
prices had climbed to $7 per acre—many times the society's initial esti-
mate. Even at that price, the colonists could purchase from speculators
only tracts in scattered sections—a standard practice of frontier land
sharks to raise the value of the holdings they retained—so Considerant's
plans for a three-square-mile city were thwarted.[48]

With its white cliffs overlooking the river, the colony's original site was
picturesque, but the soil proved sandy and unproductive and the climate
too harsh for European immigrants used to temperate conditions. The
water supply dried up in a few months. Despite Considerant's warnings,
emigrants continued to arrive before adequate food and shelter were
available; by the torrid summer of 1855 more than two hundred were
huddling in the ramshackle dormitories.

A further problem was the composition of the colonists. Like most
Fourierists, Réunion residents were artisans and professionals, ill suited
to life on the prairie frontier. The colony had more than its share of
musicians, artists, lawyers, and journalists, but there were never more
than ten farmers in residence.[49] And because the overwhelming majority

of colonists came from France, few spoke enough English to conduct business with local Texans.

In fact, the inadequacy of American participation in Réunion was a major disappointment. Both Brisbane and Considerant hoped that American Fourierists would invest in the colony and migrate there to lend the venture their practical experience—and some did help. To attract support, Brisbane published *The Great West* (1854), an abridged translation of *Au Texas,* and Greeley's *Tribune* carried favorable notices of the project. Throughout Considerant's first trip to the west in 1853 and in his dealings with state governments, banks, and land offices, American Fourierists acted as intermediaries and agents. James T. Fisher of Boston and Benjamin Urner of Cincinnati raised money by selling Fourierist tracts; Brisbane, Urner, Lazarus, and Thomas Durant bought stock in the venture.[50] Nicholas P. Trist, Polk's negotiator of the Mexican War treaty, whom Brisbane had been badgering for years, contributed over $1,000 and gave the colonists legal advice.[51] And in August 1855 sympathetic American Fourierists formed the Texas Emigration Union, which publicized the colony and recruited American members. Through these various propaganda efforts several Associationist veterans, including half a dozen former residents of the North American Phalanx, were persuaded to join La Réunion.[52]

Yet in the end the level of American support was dismal. Probably no more than two dozen of Réunion's approximately 350 colonists were Americans, and Allen was the only prominent Associationist among them.[53] Even Brisbane, who disliked the site chosen by the advance party and feared the colony's failure, contributed only $7,000 of the $20,000 he had promised—and meanwhile, with characteristic irresponsibility, he privately circulated plans for a rival Fourierist colony in the west, composed of Americans and better funded than Réunion.[54] There is no doubt that lack of sufficient American backing was a key factor in Réunion's demise. French utopians discovered America too late for full-scale transatlantic cooperation. Over two dozen previous community launchings had drained the Associationists' resources and morale; by 1854 there simply was no American movement left to mobilize for one last phalanx attempt. Indeed, La Réunion only further divided the supporters who were left. Its establishment diverted Associationists' attention from the North American Phalanx's problems, and together with the Raritan Bay Union it drew over three dozen of the New Jersey community's 115 members, thus sealing the doom of the only viable phalanx left in the United States.

Considerant himself proved incapable of guiding the colony to survival. Arriving at Réunion in May 1855, he found its gardens and crops ruined by the severe Texas weather, its grounds infested with rattlesnakes, and the colonists fiercely debating whether to live cooperatively or on individual homesteads. Most were committed Fourierists aspiring to live in a phalanx, but few agreed upon an exact transitional plan.

Despite his hope that a "phalansterian society" would evolve at Réunion, Considerant strongly believed it was more important to establish a successful colony than another Fourierist failure. Not only did this opinion alienate ideologically committed colonists, but Considerant had no clear and workable substitute for Fourierism to make the project economically viable. Caught between his two roles as promoter of a profit-seeking colonization scheme and leader of a Fourierist experiment, Considerant fell into a deep depression that confined him to bed, isolated him from the settlers, and paralyzed his leadership; at one point he even contemplated suicide.[55]

When he finally recovered, Considerant decided that his primary obligation was to French shareholders. Convinced that Réunion could not be salvaged, he began extracting the Colonization Society from it, offering settlers an exchange of Réunion's land for their shares in the society. Meanwhile, he bought more than 32,000 acres in Uvalde County, eighty miles west of San Antonio, in the hope of starting over with funds and migrants from the Colonization Society, now finally incorporated by the Texas government. Accused of mismanagement at La Réunion and of discouraging French emigrants from joining the colony, Considerant resigned the presidency in July 1856 and left the domain. When reports reached Paris of the disastrous situation, the directors of the Colonization Society officially dissolved the Réunion experiment and began settling individual claims. But Considerant was not through: he wrote a long and elaborate defense of his actions, urged the directors and shareholders to undertake a new colonization at Uvalde, and even went to Paris to plead his case.[56] Understandably, French Fourierists were reluctant to risk another "shipwreck in Texas," as one disillusioned colonist called the experience, and lacked confidence in Considerant's leadership.[57] The directors refused to support a new venture, and in 1859 began the long process of selling the lands Considerant had purchased. Considerant himself returned to Texas, bought a farm near San Antonio for his family, and settled down to ten years on the Texas prairie. It was a bizarre end to a quarter-century of French Fourierism.

At Réunion many shortcomings of the phalanx movement of the 1840s reached their disastrous climax: grandiose and unrealistic visions of community prospects, the damaging tension between capitalist venture and communal experiment, the lack of coordination between French and American efforts, the practical incompetence of Fourierist leaders and their inability to stick with a single experiment. Following the breakup of Raritan Bay and the North American Phalanx, the collapse of the Texas venture brought to a formal close the Fourierist phase of American communitarianism.

IV

The Decline
and Evolution
of Utopia

Most of these writers were in the prime of youth, and Socialism
was their first love. It would be interesting to trace their several
careers in after time, when acquaintance with "stern reality"
put another face on their early dream, and turned them aside
to other pursuits. Certain it is, that the socialistic revival, barren
as it was in direct fruit, fertilized in many ways the genius of
these men, and through them the intellect of the nation.

—John Humphrey Noyes, *History of American Socialisms*

The Fading of the Utopian Dream

Since American Fourierism was an intellectual as well as a social movement, even after the failure of communities and cooperatives its ideas continued to evolve and influence northern reform circles. This chapter and the two that follow trace the intellectual paths of key Associationists after 1848, seeing them as emblematic not just of Fourierism's fate but of general trends in antebellum culture. The Fourierists' gradual abandonment of utopian socialism, their accommodation to northern capitalism, their drift into journalistic careers, and their connection with antislavery and new crusades for personal liberation were important events of the 1850s, barometers of a changing American intellectual climate. As the economic woes of the 1840s abated, reform crusades lost adherents to commercial and national expansion. And as the sectional debate rallied northerners in defense of their society, increasing numbers of reform spokesmen evolved from the boundless optimism of the 1830s and 1840s to a new, more conservative orientation toward American life and institutions. The fading of the Fourierist dream was part of this larger story.[1]

The God That Failed: The Revolutions of 1848

The seeds of Associationist failure were sown on European as well as American soil. When the French revolution of 1848 broke out, American Fourierists immediately hailed it and avidly followed its progress. The abdication of the "Citizen King" Louis Philippe in February and the formation of the Second Republic precipitated nationalist and republican revolts throughout continental Europe. This "springtime of peoples" was one of the century's great events; in France it was the denouement of utopian socialism. Three Associationist leaders who went to Europe for

335

a firsthand look at the revolutions not only revived contacts with French Fourierists but learned important lessons about the doctrine they shared. From their standpoint the revolutions demonstrated the vitality of Fourierist ideas, but as popular agitation was brutally repressed, the failure of these ideas shook the Americans' faith in communitarian reform. When the smoke cleared and the excitement was over, Fourierist theory had suffered a fatal blow.

When news of the February revolution reached America late in March 1848, Fourierists in Boston and New York held mass meetings to express support. In public speeches and *Harbinger* articles, Dana, Ripley, Dwight, Godwin, and Brisbane proclaimed the revolution a triumph for Association. Here was "the greatest political event of modern times," a peaceful transition from absolutism to democracy; more important to utopians, it was a social rather than just a political revolution. Unlike the 1789 revolution, when philosophers led the way, or 1830, when the bourgeoisie gained control, the 1848 uprising was apparently initiated by the working classes, who knew that republican institutions alone could not guarantee economic justice. Although middle-class politicians were in control of the Provisional Government, they championed "fraternity" and endorsed the "organization of labor" as a key objective.[2]

American utopians claimed an important role for Fourierism in the revolution. French Fourierists' agitation had prepared the public mind for the "social republic," and their moderation helped to keep the revolt orderly. Circulation of the *Démocratie Pacifique* jumped from 3,000 to 15,000 within a month. Victor Considerant was elected to the National Assembly; the English Fourierist Hugh Doherty broke into the royal palace at the Tuileries with the revolutionary mob. Other reports claimed that the poet Lamartine, a key minister in the Provisional Government, was "on intimate and friendly terms" with Associationist leaders. The government itself adopted socialistic rhetoric and goals: under pressure from workers and political clubs the deputies established National Workshops to provide public works employment, guaranteed workers the right to organize cooperatives, and appointed a commission of labor (the Luxembourg Commission, on which Considerant served) to study working conditions and propose reforms. "For the first time in the history of the world," rejoiced Godwin, "LABOR, . . . its interest and its organization, has been proclaimed as a leading object of the State." If the revolution in France kept to its social reform agenda, it would be the model for the world.[3] Closer to home, Associationists rejoiced that the French outbreak gave them a "new mission" and "new claims on the public" for their ideas. *Harbinger* editor Parke Godwin reported that subscriptions had increased and exulted that socialist ideas were being widely discussed by the American press.[4]

Three Associationists managed to steam across the Atlantic to witness the events themselves. Brisbane came out of semi-retirement to speak to American rallies, then left for France by way of London. Charles Dana,

now writing for Greeley's *Tribune*, arranged to become a foreign correspondent for the New York daily and four other papers. (Although his
letters to the various papers were not always identical, his was the first
syndicated correspondence in American journalism.)[5] James T. Fisher
was sent by Boston Associationists to report on conditions in England
and France and to establish better ties with French colleagues. All three
expected excitement—it was Dana and Fisher's first trip to the Old
World—but not as much as they were to encounter.

Forty years later Brisbane remembered the events of June 23–25 more
vividly than any of his life. By coincidence he arrived in Paris at the
height of the bloody June insurrection, during which Parisian workers
battled the increasingly conservative Provisional Government over the
closing of the National Workshops. While his British Fourierist companions Garth Wilkinson and Lord Wallscourt took a safe but circuitous
route into the city, Brisbane befriended a militant weaver who guided
him through the streets of the working-class suburbs, then entered the
city by the Porte St. Denis, coursing up and down streets to avoid barricades. When one final barricade remained, Brisbane carried his rifle and
luggage over the top while armed workers awaited the attack of the
National Guard.[6]

Dana, who also arrived during the June Days, roamed the streets for
more than a week, providing graphic accounts for American readers of
the government's brutal suppression of the insurrection. Once the violence subsided, he met and sketched sharp journalistic portraits of the
French Fourierists: the ever busy Considerant buried in his dual role as
head of the Fourierist school and member of the National Assembly; the
eclectic Lechevalier, who criticized the others as "too Fourieristic"; and
Baudet-Dulary, the wealthy patron of the phalanx at Condé-sur-Vesgre,
by then a profit-sharing farm.[7] But Dana ranged widely beyond utopian
socialist circles. Attending sessions of the National Assembly, he reported
on speeches by Victor Hugo, General Cavaignac, Adophe Thiers, and
Alexis de Tocqueville. He gave the American public firsthand impressions of Etienne Cabet, Louis Blanc, Lamennais, and Proudhon. Leaving
Paris in early October, Dana headed for Germany. In Cologne either
Brisbane or the poet Ferdinand Freiligrath introduced him to Karl Marx,
whom Brisbane described as "a man of some thirty years, short and
solidly built, with a fine face and bushy black hair." Impressed by this
intense Communist with "the strongest . . . intellect which . . . ever ap-
proached the labor problem from a workman's point of view," Dana
hired Marx in 1851 to contribute articles on European affairs to the
Tribune, and their association continued for eleven years.[8] From Cologne,
Dana went on to Berlin, where he met Marx's friend Bruno Bauer and
rejoined Brisbane. Together the Americans visited Dresden, Prague, and
Vienna, the last under siege by counterrevolutionary Austrian forces.
Back in Paris early in December, Dana reported on the election of Louis
Napoleon as president of the Republic. The next month he returned to

the United States, having seen "plenty of revolutions," compiled a "who's who" of the European left, and filed forceful and penetrating reports on events in France and Germany.[9]

Fisher traveled less widely than Brisbane and Dana, spoke no French, and arrived after the June revolt. Still, he relayed valuable comments on leading French Fourierists and marveled at shopping arcades in Paris and magnificent public buildings in which he saw "the originals" of Fourier's phalanstery. His most memorable experience came when in a gesture of transatlantic solidarity he joined Parisian Fourierists on the anniversary of Fourier's death (October 10) in a circle of unity around their master's grave. A few days later he returned to America.[10]

The three Americans were afire with revolutionary enthusiasm, but gradually a more realistic mood began to set in. Fisher had to report failure in his mission to establish stronger connections with the French. Transatlantic mail was unreliable, and French socialists were so preoccupied with domestic affairs that efforts to unite with them in propaganda or phalanxes were "futile."[11] More important, the Americans discovered that contrary to impressions at home, French Fourierists were not central players on the revolutionary stage. Until mid-1847 Considerant had defended the constitutional monarchy of Louis Philippe; in February 1848 the French school had "accepted" the revolution rather than engineered it; and although Considerant took his place among the democratic faction in the National Assembly ("the Mountain") he and the *Démocratie Pacifique* seemed to react to events rather than make them. Considerant rarely spoke in the assembly and waited until April 1849 to ask it to underwrite a trial phalanx. By contrast Alexandre Lédru-Rollin, Louis Blanc, and Pierre Proudhon were dynamic leaders with a strong popular following. According to Dana, it was the radical clubs of agitators such as Auguste Blanqui and Armand Barbès rather than the utopian socialist sects who held the workers' attention, and the Associative school was "even more remote than other Socialists from any participation in the whole [popular] movement."[12]

Worse still, this aloofness was not simply a matter of personality; it was based on Fourierist theory. Although some French Fourierists agitated for immediate social measures, most urged "consolidating" the republic and educating political moderates in the mysteries of the phalanx. Time was running out, however. As nationwide elections returned a reactionary plurality to the National Assembly and the government reneged on economic reform, the French Fourierists seemed strangely paralyzed. In the heat of the crisis Brisbane found the Fourierists full of "speculations and theorizing, which seemed very tame and inadequate"; Dana complained that they clung to "the mistaken idea derived from Fourier that the delights and glories of the Phalanstery were going to induce . . . some half dozen capitalists" to pay for an experiment. Both Americans favored Proudhon's no-rent, no-interest scheme and worker cooperatives as immediate practical reforms that expressed working-class needs. But only

Lechevalier and a few French Fourierists agreed; the rest were frozen between the workers' immediate, militant demands and the bourgeois government's intransigence, and their Fourierism perished in the crossfire.[13]

More than any other event, the June insurrection exposed the inadequacy of the Fourierists' conciliatory approach toward the Provisional Government and the bourgeoisie. Here was precisely the kind of event Fourierism was supposed to prevent. Doherty wrote that utopian socialism was "crucified" in 1848; the voice of reason went unheeded by desperate workers on one side and a frightened bourgeoisie on the other.[14] It is more accurate to say that Fourierism was bypassed. Formulated to avert a social cataclysm, it proved virtually irrelevant once a revolutionary situation had already developed. In the face of bitter class antagonism the Fourierists could only call for a ceasefire, side with the party of order, and scold both participants for their ignorance in not adopting the peaceful reconcilation of the phalanx. If one scene of June 1848 best captured this impotence, it was Garth Wilkinson sitting in bed one night plodding through an abstruse exposition of Fourier's law of the series while fighting raged between Parisian insurgents and the National Guard in the streets below.[15] Fourierism remained vital only as long as class tensions and political positions could be bridged by a compromise that blended socialist and capitalist forms in roughly equal parts. This proved impossible in 1848, and though few realized it, the utopian socialist moment in France had been irretrievably lost.

At the time, however, the American Associationists took more immediate lessons from the June Days. When news of the June revolt reached the United States, George Ripley denounced it vehemently as the work of the "foam and scum" of the Parisian population inflamed by ultrademocrats and bribed by *provocateurs*. Godwin confessed that Associationists were "disappointed" by the outbreak, which had to be put down because "despotism" and "pillage" would have been the result. Publicly, they hoped that the insurrection would spur the National Assembly to meaningful action; privately, they heard Fisher report that more bloodshed was inevitable.[16] Moreover, the insurrection gave the Americans a sticky public relations problem: having labored for four months to identify Fourierism with the revolution, they now had to deny that it lay behind the latest outbreak.[17]

The problem intensified as reports crossed the Atlantic that Considerant had joined Lédru-Rollin in June 1849 to protest the French army's expedition to restore the Papal States; the two had called for a new republican constitution. When this nonviolent coup attempt failed, the Fourierist leader was charged with treason and fled to Belgium to avoid arrest. Channing wrote that the Fourierist movement had been "compromised by its friends" and lamented that socialists had given up their "mediating" role. Dwight explained uneasily that Fourierists "are the party of Peace. . . . We are not Red Republicans. We have no sympathy with the red banner. Nor . . . do we believe that the spirit and tendency of Socialism, even in revolutionary France, has been any thing but peaceful. . . . [Yet French socialists] are to be forgiven, that once or twice they have been provoked, entrapped, almost necessitated to rebellion . . . in order that by force (the only argument of those in power . . .) they might be put down."[18] It was a contradiction the Associationists could not resolve.

The most enduring lessons of the revolutions were personal; Brisbane and Dana felt them most keenly, albeit in different ways. Disheartened by the utopians' distance from "questions which were real and fundamental," Brisbane left Paris in September to tour the Continent. He interviewed Robert Blum, leader of the radicals in the Frankfort Assembly, visited Berlin and Vienna with Dana, then went to Rome, where a few weeks earlier a revolution had sent Pope Pius X into exile. Summarizing his tour, Brisbane lamented that although a few leading thinkers were socialists, the revolutions were as yet "essentially political," based upon the desire for national republics or constitutional monarchies rather than for sweeping social reforms. Even popular freedom remained a "dream of the educated classes" which inspired few workers and peasants.[19]

When he returned to Paris in January 1849, Brisbane grew even more pessimistic, for in his absence the counterrevolution had won out. Lamartine and Lédru-Rollin were no longer ministers; Proudhon had been jailed for slandering the government; and the National Assembly had repudiated social reform. The French Fourierists were still permitted to propagandize—a measure of their harmlessness—but most socialists were reduced once again to publicizing reform at banquets. On one such occasion, commemorating the first anniversary of the 1848 revolution, "Citizen Brisbane" was called upon to speak. After a brief account of socialism in the countries he had toured, he proclaimed that Europe's salvation hinged upon the French and called for a second peaceful takeover of the government by those committed to organizing labor. Brisbane later characterized it as a "conservative" speech, but it was enough to get him expelled from France by the government the next month, after which he returned directly to America.[20]

The socialist fiasco of 1848–49 caused Brisbane to rethink his position. If socialism had been especially advanced and deep-rooted in France— far more popular than all the reform movements put together in America, he had reported—and still failed, what were the prospects at home?[21] His European experience meant a trip back to the drawing board to revise Fourierism along more gradualist lines that would meet "the real wants and interests . . . of the people." For the first time, Brisbane recognized the need for a transitional phase preceding social reorganization through phalanxes. Reversing his doctrinaire opposition to cooperatives and adopting Proudhon's idea of mutual credit, he returned to America chastened by events, clinging to the conviction that socialism would evolve in the long run from progressive reforms in American life.[22]

Dana's reaction was more complex but in the long run more decisive. Responding pragmatically to revolutionary situations and personalities, Dana began to turn away not simply from Fourierism but from the radical idealism of his youth. Though the change was not yet obvious, it was his European experience that initiated Dana's evolution into the conservative, hard-boiled newspaper editor that he became in his later career.[23] His assessments of French leaders and movements punctured "the illusions and halos of distance." General Louis Cavaignac, named president after he put down the June insurrection, was "a skillful soldier, but politically a cipher." Louis Napoleon was not "a man of sufficient intellect and character to be capable of genuine sincerity"; with shrewd foresight, Dana saw that he would "rather be Emperor than President." The bourgeoisie, which Fourierist theory predicted would be converted to social justice, actually caused the June insurrection, according to Dana, by closing the National Workshops and guarding its economic privileges. Moderates and leftists were not spared sharp criticism, either: Lamartine could utter nothing but glittering generalities; Louis Blanc proved an indecisive exponent of labor's interests; and the Fourierists cared more about maintaining doctrinal purity than helping the masses. In short, there were "all sorts of intrigue and stupidity" at work among the leading actors on all sides.[24]

Not surprisingly, Dana returned dissociated from Fourier. Impressed by the no-nonsense Proudhon, Dana believed that mutual banking could be a useful alternative to the phalanx; in the same pragmatic spirit he supported cooperative stores and workshops. Yet even from these causes Dana kept his distance; he had come back "freed from all exclusive devotion to any special method of helping the world into a better case." He was "no longer a Fourierist" but thought that "a sincere blow struck anywhere" would help the cause of reform.[25] Unfettered by doctrine, Dana argued with old Associationist colleagues over the revolutions. When Channing called violence a "mistake" and blamed socialist impatience for the failure of the 1848 revolution, Dana responded angrily. The February Revolution and perhaps the June insurrection were necessary because "war and destruction" were preferable to a peace dominated by reactionaries: "The privileged and powerful, by whatever name they are called, do not yield their privileges except as they are compelled." Class antagonism rendered Fourierist pleas for reconciliation a utopian delusion. As Dana wrote to Karl Marx, "To conquer is better than to be conquered."[26]

Yet Dana was no Marxist. Revolutionary violence was legitimate only to topple kings and establish republics; after that, the ballot would eliminate monopolies or enact economic reforms. Like French utopians, he had learned that "Socialism presupposes Republicanism" and could not be realized without it.[27] The immense difficulty of establishing republics in Europe led Dana to a greater appreciation of the American political system. Before leaving for Europe, he had warned that republican governments were inadequate to solve social problems; when he returned, the failure of European republicans made him count "the blessings of even comparative Freedom, as evinced in the condition and progress of these United States."[28] Even American economic conditions looked better to him: to one who had seen the real thing in Europe, New World poverty and class tensions seemed imaginary. By 1852 Dana was calling the idea that Civilization forged labor and capital into two opposed and hardened classes "untrue and pernicious." Only land monopoly and high interest rates were serious obstacles to American enterprise. When Dana told Elizur Wright that free land and free credit were the most vital reforms, he was hoping to open up opportunities within capitalism rather than overturn it.[29]

And what of Fourierism? Praising the advantages of large commercial enterprises, the new Dana argued that Association was the extension of, not an alternative to, free enterprise; "not the patent remedy for a disease but the more thorough application of its most vital principle," voluntary combination. Interpreted as benevolent corporate capitalism, Association spread profits equitably and helped to prevent unscrupulous monopolies. Yet even this diluted Fourierism failed the test of reality. As the North American Phalanx disbanded, Dana decided that the equitable wages and social guarantees of Association required more wealth as a starting premise than did individualist enterprise and thus had to await the time when "the progress of science, invention and industry" eliminated material necessity altogether.[30] Until then—and without much lingering regret—Dana made his peace with American capitalism.

Prosperity and Co-optation in the Gold Rush Era

In a very different way from the revolutionary upheavals of 1848 in Europe, the booming prosperity of the 1850s and especially the gold rush eptomized America's transition from the "age of revolution" to the "age of capital."[31] By 1850 the nation's recovery from the depression of the early 1840s was complete, and the economy was in high gear. National expansion, apparently safeguarded from division over slavery by the Compromise of 1850, promised continued prosperity. The discovery of gold in California beckoned hundreds of thousands of ambitious men, women, and families and pumped millions of dollars into the economy. These developments belied the Associationists' gloomy predictions of an "industrial feudalism" and the progressive Europeanization of American social relations. Especially when compared with an Old World that had sunk back into despotism and social stratification after its revolutions failed, the United States seemed a political and economic miracle, even to those who had been its severest critics five years earlier.

Parke Godwin, who traveled to Europe in 1852, found that restoration of the monarchies had resulted in "the depression of enterprise, the discouragement of social ambition, the aggrandizement of the ruling classes, and the generation on the part of the people of a feeling of utter dependence and subserviency." By contrast, the United States of the 1850s was an open and enterprising society renewed once again, Godwin believed, by westward expansion, which multiplied economic opportunities and spread free institutions. In "The Future Republic," a popular lyceum lecture of the early 1850s, Godwin publicly retracted his earlier Fourierist critique of free competition: "It is a prevalent opinion vociferously enforced by certain Socialists . . . that the tendency of all social growth is to make the rich richer, and the poor poorer, . . . but in democratic states, where the field of exertion is open, where the laws are made for all, where property and the rights of labor are secured, it is not so . . . while the rich grow richer, the poor grow richer too, only at a greater rate of rapidity. What a consoling, beneficent, beautiful economy it is!"[32]

The most spectacular demonstration of free enterprise was the free-for-all of the gold rush. One thoughtful commentator in *The Harbinger* hoped that reaching the Pacific would exhaust expansionist energies and finally turn Americans from rugged individualists into high-minded cooperators.[33] But most Associationists greeted the discovery of gold in California enthusiastically: they cheered the extension of American institutions to the Pacific and put aside qualms about its materialism. Rather than being a symptom of national debasement or "life without principle," as Henry Thoreau saw it, California gold prefigured the wealth and splendor of Association. Some Fourierists even conceived schemes to use gold diggings to promote Association. The Trumbull Phalanx, reorganized in 1849, sent a member to find money for the community in the goldfields, but the plan backfired when he lured three phalanx leaders west upon his return.[34] In July 1849 the North American Phalanx appointed a committee to consider the plan of a "Phalansterian Company" that would draft Fourierists into a "California Legion" whose booty would convert the NAP into an "Experimental Model Phalanx" accommodating over five hundred persons. This and other such propositions were "respectfully declined," but for several unattached members of the NAP and the Wisconsin Phalanx, the prospect of easy money proved far more enticing than the difficult process of establishing communal life.[35] Rather than saving the Fourierist movement, gold fever helped kill off the last phalanxes. Remaining communitarians, Warren Chase among them, turned to poetry to express their disillusionment:

> Behold the struggle! the mad, selfish rush
> For shining baubles or a beggar's crust! . . .
> Shut up the book; talk not of brotherhood;
> Man lives for self, not for the common good.[36]

The rush to California became such a dominant symbol of an era of expansion and enterprise that we forget how many other events of the period fed Americans' faith in material progress. The 1850s witnessed the Crystal Palace exhibitions, the laying of the Atlantic cable, the tremendous expansion of railroads, the linkage of eastern and western states by telegraph, and the introduction of oceangoing steamships. Like many commentators, the Associationists welcomed these technological developments, seeing in them greater knowledge of natural laws and harbingers of world unity. With a similarly fuzzy optimism, they interpreted new institutions as disparate as common schools, factories, lyceums, insurance companies, and urban fire and police departments as part of a growing impulse toward collective organization, an impulse that promised greater enlightenment and abundance to all. In an era of organizational growth and material prosperity, the concept of "Association" gradually became dislodged from the phalanx or workshop and increasingly was interpreted simply as voluntary "association" or, as Horace Greeley put it, "the combination of many heads and hands to achieve a beneficent result, which is beyond the means of one or a few."[37]

The dilution of Association into association and the Fourierists' accommodation with capitalism in the 1850s was especially easy because two elements of American Fourierism made it ripe for co-optation: its acceptance of the pursuit of wealth, and its openness to gradualism. Starting with Brisbane—the most extreme example—many Fourierist leaders were attracted to speculation and moneymaking, and all acknowledged the rights of capital and promoted the "pecuniary advantages" of Association. Such tendencies had been balanced during the movement's heyday by denunciations of capitalist greed and calls to self-sacrifice in a sacred cause. But with the movement in disarray, qualms about individual self-advancement seemed to disappear. Pragmatic Wisconsin Phalanx members dissolved their association and used the profits to establish themselves as farmers and businessmen. According to A. J. Macdonald, the cause of their breakup was "speculation; the love of money and the want of love for Association. Their property becoming valuable, they sold it for the purpose of making money out of it." North American Phalanx members invested dividends not in their own community but in more profitable enterprises, a strategy that enabled them to purchase their own lots on the domain when the group disbanded.[38]

By seeming coincidence, a national era of confident prosperity matched the need of former communitarians to find a living and legitimated their less altruistic instincts. Dozens of ex-Fourierists returned to the outside economy, found new outlets for talents honed in Association, made good money, and put aside communitarian ideals. Friends began to worry about George Ripley's "pride of wealth" as he became a successful man of letters. Charles Sears of the North American Phalanx went into railroad promotion in Kansas. John Kaulback of the New England Protective Union became an independent wholesale grocer. And John

Orvis, the Fourierist labor organizer who had cursed mechanization under capitalism as the bane of seamstresses and weavers, was for a time part owner of a sewing machine company.[39] Radicals of a later era would say they had "sold out."

Gradualism, a less obvious capitulation, reflected the dilemma of admitting evolutionary thought into communitarian reform. When the Associationists retreated to gradualist reform in the late 1840s, they set realistic goals but also risked making their position indistinguishable from that of contemporaries. Joint-stock organization, mutual insurance, mutual banking, and apartment living could serve the prevailing competitive system rather than challenge it; in fact, they proved to be easily compatible with private property and corporations. By the 1850s Godwin and Dana had watered down communitarianism to joint-stock organization and profit sharing and were advocating a more humane version of corporate capitalism rather than a transformed socioeconomic system. Eternal optimists Greeley and Channing, who believed that the "spirit of the age" and improvements in organization and technology must inevitably lead Americans toward Association, went even further down the accommodationist road. The return of prosperity and the consolation that progress was occurring without phalanxes produced a mood of misty quiescence that saw Association advance with "every effort to achieve . . . a less sordid and fettered . . . life." John Gray of the North American Phalanx told a visitor in 1851 that "society was progressing 'first-rate' by means of Odd-Fellowship, Freemasonry, benevolent associations, railroads, steamboats, and especially . . . large manufactories, without such little attempts as these [phalanxes] to regenerate mankind."[40] By the 1850s the Fourierists' acceptance of key capitalist features and support for gradualism had undermined their movement's challenge to American ways.

From Utopia to Journalism

Like Charles Dana, several Associationist leaders landed in journalistic careers when the movement collapsed. As publicists for Fourierism and frequent contributors to *The Harbinger*, Ripley, Godwin, Dwight, and Dana had tackled an amazing variety of subjects, developed a crisp writing style, and learned the mechanics of publishing—skills and experiences that enabled them to find editorial jobs. But connections also helped. Before joining the Associationists, Godwin had worked for the *New York Evening Post*, edited by his father-in-law William Cullen Bryant; when *The Harbinger* failed, Godwin simply returned to the *Post*. Meanwhile, Horace Greeley, friend of Ripley and Dana through many visits to Brook Farm, improved the *Tribune* by taking them on after the Roxbury community closed. Both joined Greeley's staff in 1847, Ripley as a book reviewer and rewrite man, Dana as city editor after a brief apprenticeship on the *Boston Daily Chronotype*. Greeley also hired N. C. Meeker of the Trumbull Phalanx as agricultural editor and Fourierist William Henry

Fry as music critic. Their journalistic connections served Associationists well.

At least three became pioneers in their fields. Ripley worked his way up the *Tribune* ladder to become the first full-time book reviewer for an American newspaper, a position he held until his death in 1880. Dwight, freed by Fourierism's demise to pursue his amateur's interest in music, founded his *Journal of Music* in 1852—the first American magazine devoted exclusively to the subject—and presided over it until 1881 as the arbiter of American musical taste.[41] Dana's 1848 correspondence together with Margaret Fuller's letters from Italy gave the *Tribune* the most thoughtful and colorful coverage of the European uprisings among American newspapers. When Dana returned, Greeley promoted him to second-in-command. Dispatching reporters and editing the news with succinct orders, Dana became the first managing editor of an American daily. His "power . . . of deciding with despatch and . . . announcing his decision with civil brevity" defined the position for generations to come.[42]

Journalism had its own imperatives, however, and in many cases transformed its practitioners as much as they revolutionized it. In the middle decades of the nineteenth century, a dramatic series of changes in the production, content, and format of American newspapers created a mass medium that appealed to urban audiences looking for "the facts" interestingly presented and easily digested.[43] With his terse, direct style and his nose for news, Dana came to personify the new journalism. At the *Tribune* he broke away from Greeley's tutelage and emphasized colorful news over editorials, as when he urged Washington editor James Pike to "kick up a row of some sort, fight a duel, . . . get Black Dan [Webster] drunk, or commit some other excess, that will make a stir." When he became editor of the *New York Sun* in 1868, Dana announced the paper's new spirit in a single sentence: "It will study condensation, clearness, point and will endeavor to present its daily photography of the whole world's doings in the most luminous and lively manner."[44] The formula was so successful it gave the *Sun* the city's largest daily circulation. Dana cast his editorial lot unapologetically with the average person, leaving his readers informed, entertained, and opinionated if not reflective or refined. As a newsman, he deliberately renounced utopia for life as it was.

In the later years of Dwight and Ripley, we see a very different trajectory: these reform editors abandoned agitation for careers as men of letters catering to the literate public. As Ripley's financial situation became less precarious, he settled comfortably into his position on the *Tribune* as the dean of American reviewers. He was, as James Parton noted, "a gentleman of sound digestion and indomitable good humor" who believed that "anger and hatred are seldom proper, and never 'pay.' " Tasteful, decorous, generous, and a bit stodgy, Ripley left reform behind for the life of a genteel man of letters. Dwight, the gentle lover of flowers and music, moved even further in this direction as he addressed an elite audience with his musical editorials and joined Boston's polite society in his middle age.[45]

In their Brook Farm days, Dana, Ripley, and Dwight had worked side by side for Ripley's vision of "a more natural union between manual and intellectual labor" in a society combining thinker and doer in the same cultural nexus, even in the same person. Well before the Civil War, this utopian mission had failed, and the three became in a sense its spiritual victims. The sharp divergence of their later careers was certainly influenced by temperamental differences, yet in its largest meaning the estrangement of the elderly Ripley and Dwight from Dana exemplified the problem that Walt Whitman feared in his essay "Democratic Vistas" and that George Santayana later called the "genteel tradition." In the absence of a socialist or truly democratic culture in late nineteenth-century America, the vital material concerns of everyday existence became severed from an increasingly refined and irrelevant American intellectual life.[46] It was left to twentieth-century radicals to revive the Fourierists' dream of a culture integrating ideals and reality in a more satisfying way than Emerson and his imitators had achieved.

14

New Directions of the 1850s

In 1855, Thomas Low Nichols and Mary Gove Nichols announced plans to form a "Progressive Union," an association of "Harmonic Homes" in different sections of the country. In each home a "family" of believers would constitute a miniature society in which no one ate meat, took medicine, owned property, or pursued personal gain; all would be free to work, play, or choose sexual partners at will. The plan was guaranteed to work, having been dictated to the Nicholses by "Heavenly Intelligences" seeking to replicate upon the earth the spirits' own harmonic existence above.[1] This strange hodgepodge of anarchism, free love, and spiritualism, which enlisted as many as five hundred supporters, was the product of radicals who proudly identified themselves as "socialists of the school of Fourier."[2]

Despite the phalanxes' failure, Fourierism lingered in radical circles during the 1850s and inspired new plans and organizations. In fact, as the Associative movement withered away, the potential for innovation multiplied: those still moved by communitarian ideals were now free to develop Fourierist theory beyond the constraints of official Associationist propaganda. The Progressive Union plan compressed into one blueprint three major excitements that became popular outlets for these Fourierists. The outburst over spiritualism, following reports late in 1848 that two young sisters named Margaret and Kate Fox had successfully communicated with spirits at a public exhibition in Rochester, New York, attracted several Fourierists, from veteran spokesmen to ordinary phalanx members. Meanwhile, a raging public controversy over free love involved several influential Associationists, mainly those bred in late Fourierism and still evolving definitive reform positions. Some, including the Nicholses, eventually affiliated with Modern Times and other small communi-

348

ties of the 1850s that were attempting to live out the anarchist ideal of "individual sovereignty."

All three causes—spiritualism, free love, and anarchism—not only demonstrated the long, slow erosion of Fourierist doctrine but registered a crucial shift in the goals and strategies of communitarian reform after 1848. In much the same way that the "Me Decade" succeeded the turbulent 1960s, utopians during the prosperous 1850s turned from advocating broad structural reform to preaching changes in personal lifestyle. Spiritualists, sex radicals, and anarchists shared a scaled-down vision of the millennial future, one that centered on select circles of liberated middle-class individuals rather than cross-class utopian experiments. This strategy of retreat and its promise of fulfillment for the enlightened few fit well with the prevailing mood in the waning days of utopian excitement and offered an attractive outlet for radicals' energies. Yet as communitarians turned from socioeconomic to personal issues and from collectivistic to individualistic solutions, their ideology lost much of its distinctive and radical edge, even as their existence became marginalized.

Spiritualist Connections

Several Associationist leaders expressed interest in spirit revelations and the public discussion of mesmerism that foreshadowed them. Horace Greeley, who believed many spirit communications authentic, played an important part in popularizing spiritualism and making it respectable. Favorable notices in the *Tribune* brought the Fox sisters to prominence, and Greeley himself was a member of spiritualist Thomas Lake Harris's Washington Square congregation in the 1850s. Albert Brisbane, interested in mesmerism since his 1844 trip to France, attended trance sessions in New York in 1847, during which the remarkable A. J. Davis dictated his *Revelations*. By his own admission, Brisbane was a party to other séances, met "many" mediums, and felt that spiritual manifestations "contained a reality."[3] George Ripley and Parke Godwin were so impressed by Davis that they endorsed his book in *The Harbinger;* Ripley called the young seer "the most surpassing prodigy of literary history." Three years later Ripley participated, along with Greeley, George Bancroft, William Cullen Bryant, and James Fenimore Cooper, in a séance of notables at the home of literary critic Rufus Griswold.[4] William Henry Channing, who lived in Rochester for two years at the height of the spiritualist excitement, experimented frequently with otherworldly communication, at one point sensing himself "sitting amidst a circle of the most beautifully harmonized spirits." Lindsay Swift said that Channing came "dangerously close" to preaching spiritualism.[5]

Fourierist phalanxes sometimes served as incubators of spiritualism. Visitors found practicing spiritualists at the North American Phalanx in 1852, and at the Raritan Bay Union, Lydia Read held regular séances whose table rapping disturbed residents in rooms below. Anna Parsons delighted Brook Farm friends with mesmeric "readings" in which she divined the writer's character by pressing a letter to her forehead. Interest was probably most intense at the Wisconsin Phalanx. During the Fourierist excitement in the area, Warren Chase began reading Swedenborg and studying mesmerism; once the phalanx was established, Chase promptly formed a spiritualist circle there, more than a year before Davis's revelations and several years before the Rochester rappings. When the phalanx's dissolution coincided with the Rochester craze, Chase became an itinerant spiritualist lecturer.[6]

Like other contemporaries, some Associationists went to séances to contact a recently deceased relative or friend, or at least to establish the fact of an afterlife to console themselves. In 1850 Greeley and his wife tried to communicate with their son "Pickie," whose death the editor lamented movingly. Chase, who began mesmeric researches after an infant son died, claimed to be in frequent contact with the child's spirit. During Channing's first recorded spiritual communication, he prayed for his recently drowned friend Margaret Fuller. As a comforter for troubled survivors, spiritualism both reflected and encouraged the increasing romanticization of childhood and death in nineteenth-century European-American culture.[7]

Such intensely private needs were only part of spiritualism's appeal to Associationists. Shared ideological orientations and emotional affinities were also responsible. Underlying both causes was the liberal theology view that humans were perfectible and nature benign. Their common interest in Swedenborg's writings reflected not simply their fascination with a Protestant version of Dante's paradise but a deep conviction that there were demonstrable "correspondences" between spiritual and material worlds. The harmony in the spiritualists' "Harmonial Philosophy" meant the basic identity of science and theology. Like Fourierists, philosophical spiritualists viewed the world as a divine machine whose material and spiritual parts operated according to the same principles of natural law. Spiritualists argued that these laws could be glimpsed by internal senses, whereas Fourierists stressed instead the logic of "analogy" and deductive investigation, but each group complemented the other in explicating "universal unity" through the progress of "science."[8]

More practically, mediums and spirit rappers displayed a penchant for reform theories and measures that Fourierists could approve. Before the Civil War, spiritualist believers involved themselves in temperance, antislavery, and health reform and professed—like Fourierists—a limited degree of feminism. More important, several spiritualist personalities turned to communitarian reform to pursue collective contact with the other world and allow spiritual "affinities" full play in this one. In his trance sessions of 1847, A. J. Davis spouted large amounts of Fourierist theory, much to Brisbane's delight. Davis's "Harmonial Philosophy" as outlined in his *Principles of Nature* (1847) judged Fourier an important spiritual leader, praised attractive "industry," and culminated in an extensive description of a Fourierism-tinged utopia.[9]

The experiences of Davis, the Nicholses, and several reform clairvoyants suggest that contact with Fourierism pushed mesmeric seers and spiritualist lecturers toward communal experimentation. Thomas Lake Harris perhaps best exemplifies this trend. A classic mystical type with flowing beard and dark, deep-set eyes, Harris moved from Calvinism to Universalism before he followed Davis's writings into a lifelong belief in communication with the dead. En route he joined the Fourierists, serving as a delegate to the 1847 convention of the American Union of Associationists. Fourierist concepts imbibed from *The Harbinger*, Davis, and Greeley emerge frequently and explicitly in Harris's visionary writings. And there were strong echoes of Associationism at Mountain Cove, Brocton, and Fountain Grove, the three colonies Harris later established for his "Brotherhood of the New Life." Like the phalanxes, these searched for an alternative to "communism" that would incorporate individual incentives and aim at what Harris called "the reorganization of the industrial world" through socialized "municipalities." If, as John Humphrey Noyes contended, Fourierism "sent streams" into the spiritualist movement, the communitarian idea was perhaps the most important.[10]

There were other, more emotional connections between the two movements. A sense of being outsiders or martyrs attracted certain Associationists toward other equally unorthodox movements; by linking with a network of quirky clairvoyants, they found further justification for estrangement from society and an even more colorful way of advertising it. Warren Chase's career, portrayed in two autobiographies alternately bristling with defensiveness and wallowing in self-pity, is a revealing example. Born an illegitimate child in New Hampshire in 1813, Chase was orphaned at five ("fatherless, motherless, penniless, friendless, worthless, useless"), then apprenticed to a "cruel and cold-hearted" farmer for the next ten years. A family of Universalists kindly took him in; after absorbing their freethinking tendencies, he headed west. Yet he fared no better on the frontier: abject poverty, setbacks in his political career, the naggings of his practical wife, and finally the dissolution of his beloved Wisconsin Phalanx confirmed his status as a despised "Lone One." When the spiritualist craze caught fire, Chase immediately hailed its truth. Through it his martyrdom found justification: a "society of spirit-teachers" told him that worldly failure had been ordained to prepare him for preaching the "glorious gospel of good news." As he "took his staff and travelled on, lecturing" and was "crucified" by slanderers, Chase could take comfort in the "marked correspondences" between himself and Jesus. As well as a religion to satisfy his defiant freethinking, Chase found in spiritualism consolation for his rocky life and a much needed boost for his identity as a reform crusader.[11]

Few Associationists shared Chase's extreme alienation, but the path several followed supports R. Laurence Moore's suggestion that spiritualism "fed on the discouragement" of antebellum reformers.[12] After Brook Farm broke up, John Allen joined a circle of Swedenborgian and mesmerist investigators in Cincinnati; in 1847 this "Brotherhood," led by John O. Wattles and Fourierist supporter J. P. Cornell, formed a short-lived cooperative association on the main property of the recently defunct Clermont Phalanx.[13] Allen's Fourierist lecturing partner John Orvis was an officer in the bizarre spiritualist Harmonia Community led by John Murray Spear in the 1850s. A few years later William McDiarmid of the Wheeling Fourierists could be found in the Arkansas Ozarks at the spiritualist Harmonial Vegetarian Society.[14] Fittingly, remnants of a dying communitarian movement found consolation in a creed affirming life after death, preaching gradual but inevitable progress, and sometimes experimenting with communal forms.

Still, spiritualism's impact on Fourierists was never profound. The two groups exchanged subscription lists, communal properties, and even some members, but among major Fourierist figures only Chase made the transition to spiritualist preaching. The odor of disreputability that hovered around spiritualism grew stronger as the movement became commercialized, attracted sharpers and quacks, and strengthened its connections with free love and free thought. By the mid-1850s spiritualism had alienated many writers and professionals previously drawn to it, and the pattern of ex-Fourierists' involvement followed a similar downward course. After 1853 nothing favorable to the movement was heard from Ripley, Godwin, Channing, and Henry James, and even Greeley became wary of defending mediums.[15] For their part, spiritualists showed little interest in a formal alliance with a waning utopian movement. Their confidence that the next wave of reform would be guided by divine communication rather than social engineering prevented such an alliance, as did a serene individualism that led many to dismiss "all combinations, societies, churches, sects, associations, phalanxes, etc." and instead favor small circles of congenial souls drawn together by subtle "affinities." *The Harbinger* smoothed over these differences by stressing Fourier's provision for gradual reform, but few spiritualists were proper partners for the community movement Fourierists hoped to rebuild.[16]

Yet spiritualism's indirect impact upon Fourierism far exceeded actual contacts. Similarities between the two creeds were obvious and personal ties substantial enough that almost from the appearance of Davis's *Revelations,* Fourierism and spiritualism were pegged as close relatives by the reading public. Identification with spiritualism was just what a failing communitarian movement did not need. Especially after 1850, when a new wave of anti-reform sentiment focused on spiritualism, the connection hurt the already damaged reputation of Fourierist ideas. One index of this hostility was an outburst of satirical novels and sensationalized exposés in which writers condemned spiritualism and social reform as pernicious allies. Nathaniel Hawthorne's *Blithedale Romance* (1851) was a complex and ambiguous meditation on the emotional affinities of social science and pseudoscience. Less artful and far more strident was *The Spirit Rapper* (1854), in which the Associationists' old enemy Orestes Brownson contended that the Devil himself had instigated spiritualism, Fourierism, the women's rights movement, and the European revolutions of 1848, all as part of a grand conspiracy to overthrow Christianity and social order. Charges that a marriage of Fourierism and spiritualism produced free love were especially frequent. Midcentury mediums and ex-Fourierists often opposed marital "slavery" and showed an undeniable "affinity" for more experimental relationships. Husbands smarting from separation or divorce, newspaper editors hoping to boost circulation, novelists looking for a titillating subject, and conservatives fearing a new threat to the traditional family all took to detailing reformers' alleged immoralities. Books such as T. S. Arthur's novel *The Angel and the Demon* (1858) and Benjamin Hatch's exposé *Spiritualists' Iniquities Unmasked* (1859) uncovered spiritualist liasons, while the *New York Times* assailed free love as "the bolder and more immodest phase of the Fourierist philosophy."[17]

When anti-reform writers indicted Fourierism as the parent of both spiritualist and free-love "delusions," they promoted a plausible half-truth. Rather than importing or inventing spiritualism, the Fourierists merely helped publicize it. But Associationists were more directly involved in instigating an important controversy over free love and marital reform in the late 1840s.

Fourierism and the Free-Love Controversy

At the height of their movement Associationists walked a tightrope on issues of love, marriage, and the family, balanced nervously between the radical principles of "passional attraction" and the desire for respectability. In the late 1840s that fragile balance broke down. When the official strategy of revealing only hints of Fourier's ideas about bourgeois familism and future sexuality—and then repudiating these or putting them off into the indefinite future—proved impossible to maintain, a small but influential group of Fourierists and former Associationists led a new movement to promote sexual liberation.

These promoters were influenced by the extraordinary publicity given to marital and sexual reform issues in the late 1840s. Under pressure from a strange coalition of liberals and conservatives, several northern states debated liberalizing their divorce laws, adopted punitive legislation against seducers and adulterers, and considered laws extending married women's right to property. The first Woman's Rights Convention, meeting at Seneca Falls in 1848, issued a "Declaration of Sentiments" claiming that contemporary marriage laws enforced wives' dependence upon husbands and urging equity in divorce and custodianship. At nearby Oneida, John Humphrey Noyes and the Perfectionists adopted a form of controlled and contraceptive free love labeled "complex marriage"; the community's first annual report (1849) proclaimed its success to the public. Reports filtering eastward in 1852 that the Mormons of Utah officially endorsed plural marriage confirmed what rumors had intimated for nearly a decade. Newspaper accounts brought a storm of protest that eventually led to the outlawing of polygamy in the territories. In addition to sensationalized exposés of spiritualist mediums searching for female "counterparts," the establishment of Modern Times and kindred anarchist free-love circles in northern states gained the attention of journalists and ministers. Such activities fed on one another's publicity, and together they impressed commentators as an important trend or even a movement.[18]

Yet Fourierists and ex-Fourierists were not simply jumping on someone else's bandwagon; they were instrumental in formulating the free-love philosophy, stimulating debate over marriage and divorce, and putting sexual freedom into practice. Fourierism bequeathed to free love the vocabulary of passional attraction, a reform network in which it could circulate, and leaders who had served apprenticeships as utopian publicists. Until recently, the Fourierist roots of antebellum free-love agitation have not been fully appreciated.[19] As the communitarian movement of the 1840s faded, the dynamic of Fourierist ideas led directly toward free-love anarchism.

If "equity in commercial relations" had been "one half of Socialism," "*justice to the human passions*" was the other.[20] As long as Fourierism remained a viable communitarian movement, economic cooperation took precedence over the creation of a liberated culture, and elaborating the "passional" benefits of Association might have jeopardized the movement's success. But the collapse of the phalanxes and the return of prosperity in the late 1840s discredited the economic side of Fourierist ideology and favored the psychological. Most Associationists chose to retreat and await a better day, but for those attracted to Fourier's more controversial theories, the death of the Fourierist movement meant new life. No longer limited to "Industrial Association," they could "come out" on issues such as sex and marriage; they were free to speculate, to announce personal positions, and to implement among themselves advanced ideas of liberation. By and large, the free-love advocates were not the Associationist movement's founding fathers or even its prominent officers. Unlike spiritualism, sexual liberation had little attraction for Ripley, Channing, Godwin, and Greeley.[21] Even Brisbane, far bolder in criticizing the "isolated household" and privately sympathetic to sexual reform, avoided publicly endorsing it. Utopians who carried Fourierism toward toward free love were instead independent, generally younger spirits more interested in personal liberation than in community. They joined the Associationist movement late in its course, had little practical stake in it, and were impatient with official timidity. Unlike Fourierist diehards like Brisbane, free-love advocates were still developing their views and eventually moved beyond Fourierism to their definitive reform stances.

Agitation fell roughly into two overlapping phases. In the first, Associationists revealed and endorsed Fourier's views on sex and marriage, sparking a widespread public discussion. In the second, several ex-Fourierists announced that sexual freedom was to begin immediately, and some even experimented with it in communal settings. In *The True Organization of the New Church* (1848), C. J. Hempel became the first Associationist to defend in print Fourier's view of freer love relations in Harmony. This Swedenborgian physician mentioned the four "corporations of love" that Fourier had envisioned in future society, ranging from the faithfully married "Vestals" to the "Bayadères," the free-lovers of the phalanx. Rather than disavowing such practices, Hempel proclaimed them necessary to satisfy the variety of temperaments in humans, though he assured readers that "very few women" would enlist in groups favoring sexual variety.[22]

Hempel's endorsement, inserted in a long-winded book on the religious bearings of Fourierism, went virtually unnoticed. Later in 1848 there appeared the first Associationist tract concentrating solely upon Fourier's sexual theories, an anonymous translation of Victor Hennequin's *Love in the Phalanstery*. An article in *The Harbinger* revealed that the pamphlet's translator was another Swedenborgian Fourierist, Henry James, Sr.[23] In his preface James explained that he translated Hennequin's exposition to replace innuendo about Fourierism with facts and to "provoke the attention of honest minds to the truths involved in these views." There followed a sketchy outline of graded sexual series in the phalanx (vestalate, damoisellate, féate, faquirate, and pivotate), each with progressively greater freedom. In follow-up articles in *The Harbinger* James made clear that he hoped these freer practices would replace Civilization's coerced monogamy. Although the sexually liberated future must await a "superior social order," and although he himself had no desire for free love, he looked forward to the day when "the private will of the parties" would be the sole sanction for sexual contact. At that point, the law would approve either an "exclusive" or a "varied alliance," depending upon the subjects' wishes.[24]

Reaction came swiftly from the conservative evangelical *New York Observer*, which attacked the book's Fourierist morals as "abominable." A. E. Ford, a New Church minister and also an Associationist, engaged James in a lengthy dispute on love, marriage, and the family which continued in *The Harbinger* until the paper folded in February 1849.[25] Begun with a proclamation of universal unity, Association's official journal ceased publication in the midst of wrangling over sexual reform.

Soon thereafter, a second Fourierist-inspired tract on marriage appeared: Thomas Low Nichols's *Woman in All Ages and Nations*. Nichols and his wife, Mary Gove Nichols, were two of the busiest and most colorful cultural radicals of the century; one biographer calls them the Marx and Engels of the free-love movement.[26] Thomas Nichols left Dartmouth medical school for reform journalism after hearing Sylvester Graham denounce contemporary methods of healing. A forceful writer attuned to several reform enthusiasms, he had been active as a Democratic editor, a novelist, and a student of phrenology and mesmerism when he met Mary Gove at the end of 1847. By then Gove was an established reformer with a flair for the unorthodox and the sensational. As early as 1838 she had begun lecturing on physiology, health, and dress reform in Massachusetts, feeling called to educate women about their bodies and to fight for their rights. Opposed by her first husband, she left for a romantic interlude with an English reformer who introduced her to water cure and sexual freedom. Late in 1845 Mary Gove and her daughter left for New York City, where she lectured on water cure and phrenology and wrote stories for *Godey's Ladies Book* and other magazines. Edgar Allan Poe included Gove among the New York literati he sketched for *Godey's*. Poe described her as below medium height, "somewhat thin, with dark hair and keen intelligent black eyes," and (in a rare understatement for Poe) "a very interesting woman."[27] Fourierism was an integral part of Gove's reform repertoire. As early as 1841 she had endorsed Brisbane's writings; four years later she visited the Columbian Phalanx in Ohio; and when she moved to New York, she joined the Fourierist circle there. Her Grahamite boardinghouse featured Associationist lectures at regular Saturday evening gatherings. Gove herself contributed to *The Phalanx* and lectured locally on Association.[28]

Although it never mentions Fourier by name, *Woman in All Ages and Nations* reflects the Fourierist-tinted view of love and marriage that Nichols absorbed in New York on his own or through Mary Gove, whom he married in 1848. Starting out as a straightforward history of women, covering such areas as costume, education, and courtship, the dry text gives way to its author's editorializing. Adopting the language shared by Fourierists, feminists, and marital reformers, Nichols distinguished between legal marriage and "true" unions of mutual love; argued that woman should be "an independent, self-relying, self-sustaining being"; and condemned indissoluble marriage as "legal prostitution." His final chapter predicted that after Civilization, the human family would gather in Fourieristic "harmonious association," where attractions would realize their destinies without social or legal interference.[29]

The James and Nichols books broke new ground, but it was left to Marx Edgeworth Lazarus's *Love vs. Marriage* (1852) to touch off the fullest discussion of sexual reform to appear in the mid-nineteenth century. A sensitive dreamer who practiced homeopathy, vegetarianism, and water cure, Lazarus lived at both Brook Farm and the North American Phalanx and contributed dozens of articles to *The Harbinger* on esoteric subjects. To A. J. Macdonald, "the Doctor" spouted many theories "which the world would deem crazy nonsense"; but Mary Gove, whom Lazarus met in New York's Fourierist circle, found this "inveterate mystic" a congenial soul. Lazarus financed Gove's New York boardinghouse and resided there himself in 1847.[30] Their friendship probably strengthened Lazarus's declared preference for natural and spontaneous ways of life over the repressive artificiality of Civilization; in any case, by 1852 Lazarus was ready to cast caution to the winds and proclaim the blessings of Fourierist "passional liberty." According to his analysis, contemporary marriage—or "permanent exclusive possession of the person"—stifled the God-given passions, converted love into property, and institutionalized woman's inferiority. By contrast, the phalanx would leave members "free at any time to dissolve their relation and to form others." Once they were guaranteed financial independence and child care in a "unitary nursery," Associationists would follow their inclinations toward constancy or, more likely, "numerous and varied love relations." Freed from legal chains and the isolated household, women would enjoy "an equality, though not an identity with man, in civil and political privileges."[31]

Marriage as conventional society understood it was, Lazarus declared, "totally incompatible with social harmony" and had to be "excluded from any successful phalansterian institution." The Shakers might read Christ's statement that "in heaven they neither marry nor are given in marriage" and adopt celibacy; the Mormons might see it as a warning to marry more often on earth; and the Oneidans could use it to justify their regulated system of "complex marriage." But the "interior sense" of Christ's words was Fourierist, condemning the "isolated household" and blessing complete "liberty in love" under Association. If Associationists had not yet acknowledged this, Lazarus asserted, they were either hypocritical or inconsistent. He boldly claimed that such Fourierists as James and Brisbane shared his views, "although considerations entirely personal may prevent them from taking openly the same ground."[32]

Lazarus's book was important not just because it named names and broke Fourierist constraints on sexual reform. *Love Vs. Marriage* illustrates three distinctive contributions that the Fourierist approach made to contemporary free-love discussion. Unlike most feminists and other reformers, Associationists had an economic angle of criticism which broadened the problem of gender relations into a crisis of social structure. Instead of tracing marital "slavery" to male supremacy or an anachronistic legal system, Fourierists proclaimed it the necessary result of individualistic, competitive Civilization. The "isolated household" trapped women and made them economically dependent upon men, and Civilized selfishness made affections a commodity to be bought and sold. Marriage between equals was possible only in a reorganized society. Further, the Fourierists' theory of the passions extended dissatisfactions with marriage to wider social reform. Fourierist psychology provided a vocabulary of "passions," "attractions," and "harmony" to legitimate sexual reform, but it also linked free love to a general program of personal fulfillment in a transformed society. Finally, Fourierism helped inject communitarian ideas into the free-love program. Rather than attempt new relations in private trysts or traditional nuclear households, free love between the sexes could be worked out in a communal experiment providing a full support structure: as Lazarus wrote, "a colony with a soil, a government, and social institutions all its own."[33]

Lazarus's arguments against legal marriage and for passional freedom came to dominate the free-love movement in the next two decades, but its experiments did not adopt his Fourierist program. Free-lovers were attracted more to individualist anarchism than to community blueprints; they appealed almost exclusively to middle-class audiences; and their preference for informal networks made them a countercultural avant-garde rather than a reform movement.[34] As class lines hardened and prospects for reform dimmed after 1850, cultural rebellion in small bohemian enclaves had a more persuasive appeal to sexual reformers than a broad-based communitarian movement.

Love vs. Marriage ignited a long debate in the New York Tribune over marriage and free love, one that involved women's rights advocates and spiritualist spokesmen such as A. J. Davis but was especially tense and interesting because all its principals were ex-Fourierists. The main part of the debate was a three-way joust involving James, Greeley, and Stephen Pearl Andrews. Though his preface to Love in the Phalanstery had sounded Fourierist arguments similar to Lazarus's, James now spoke the idealized language of Swedenborg's "conjugal love." Present marriage was often a failure, but "divine marriage" was monogamous and eternal, wrote James, and Lazarus had allied himself with the "insatiate ape" by attacking it. James argued for liberalized divorce laws so that marriage could rest upon the heart rather than legal restraint. Greeley's position was traditional and conservative, defending indissoluble marriage with conventional religious and moral sanctions such as the seventh commandment and "the express words of Christ." Like many contemporaries, Greeley used the economic analogies of "saving" and "spending" in thinking about sex; in true Whig fashion, he portrayed strict marital laws as a protective tariff encouraging home industry rather than "free trade." As an advocate of Association, Greeley criticized the "isolated household" for its inefficiency and endorsed communal kitchens and laborsaving devices to take the drudgery out of housework, but he would leave the legalized nuclear family intact. Once again Greeley proved himself only "a sort of Fourierist," as the Nicholses charged, one ignorant of passional psychology and afraid of true social change. His Fourierism renovated the workshop and kitchen but stopped at the bedroom door.[35]

Stephen Pearl Andrews entered the controversy not so much to defend Lazarus as to champion a new, more extreme position. From Fourierist beginnings, his thinking had evolved to free-love anarchism. When in the late 1840s he moved from Boston to New York to open another "phonographic institute," he joined the Fourierist circle of Lazarus and the Nicholses. Through their influence he absorbed free-love ideas, but rather than using a Fourierist framework, Andrews grafted sexual freedom onto a new cluster of ideas picked up from Josiah Warren, the father of American anarchism. "Individual sovereignty," "cost the limit of price," and "equitable commerce" formed the intensely individualistic core of Andrews's new credo.[36] Sexual permissiveness seemed a natural addition to this anarchist program of extreme laissez faire. In response to Greeley's prudishness and James's hedging, Andrews claimed "an inalienable God-given right" for all men and women "to judge for themselves what is moral and proper for them to do or abstain from doing." This "sovereignty of the individual" denied the state's right to interfere in marriage, divorce, or any other private transaction. Whatever the variety of sexual relations that resulted, they were preferable to the legally enforced "slavery" of conventional marriage.[37]

Begun in September, the *Tribune* symposium lasted until the end of 1852, when Greeley refused to publish a sensational statement from Mary Gove Nichols and terminated the debate. By this time The Modern Times community was practicing what Andrews was preaching and attracting publicity in the *Tribune* and elsewhere. On a sandy Long Island plot forty-three miles east of New York City, Warren and Andrews had set up in 1851 an anarchist "equitable village" of a few score cottages. Business at Modern Times was conducted as much as possible through "labor notes" promising work in exchange for services. The village store sold goods at cost plus a time charge for waiting on the customer. There were no churches, no police, no town government; the mail and utilities were provided by individual residents who contracted with others. Marriage, abolished in the legal sense, was reduced at Modern Times to a private and sometimes temporary relationship between mutually agreeing parties. As Thomas Nichols later remembered, "Those lived together who chose to do so, and people parted without giving any trouble to the courts of common pleas. The right of the law either to united or separate was denied, and free love was placed in the same category with all other freedom." Moncure Conway, who visited the village in 1857, reported that "it was not considered polite to inquire . . . who the husband or wife of any individual might be." While the community's professed indifference to private lives was not the same as endorsing promiscuity—in fact, the sexual practices of Modern Times members were greatly exaggerated by contemporary journalists—the presence of the Nicholses and the community's association with Andrews were enough to stoke the fires of notoriety.[38]

The *Tribune* symposium and the establishment of Modern Times publicly proclaimed that a movement to revolutionize domestic relations was under way. Within a few years free-love advocates had held lecture series in northern cities, established their own journals, created informal networks of like-minded radicals, and started communal experiments. The *New York Times* saw Fourierism as the key to this "anti-marriage movement": "It is to Fourierism . . . and its introduction and promulgation, that we attribute the disgusting and destestable *Free Love* system . . . which is obtaining a wide and alarming currency throughout the country. The seed thus planted by the Fourierists, has taken root and attained rapid growth, under the united efforts of a great many persons who have watched and watered it, in various ways."[39]

Certainly the movement was built on Fourierist foundations, both ideological and organizational. Fourier's former disciples broadcast the Frenchman's free-love ideas; the New York circle of Brisbane, Lazarus, Andrews, and Thomas and Mary Nichols became the first center of agitation; and Fourierist veterans carried the new gospel to friends in Ohio and Wisconsin. "Those who had come to despise the isolated household" under Brisbane's tutelage, writes historian John Spurlock, "were most likely to call for its destruction when the Fourier movement no longer provided a less harsh alternative."[40]

As agitation drew out opinions, and free-love institutions multiplied, it became clear that the ex-Fourierists' positions covered a wide spectrum, ranging from Greeley's conventional proprieties to Henry James's and Warren Chase's support for more liberal divorce laws to Andrews's and the Nicholses' libertarian radicalism.[41] Among those involved in sexual reform, it is hard to separate those who merely prophesied free love from those who preached it and the latter from those who practiced it. Like their contemporaries, most free-love radicals were reticent to speak openly about their own sexual experience. Even more important, free-love publicists stressed that their intent was to purify marital relations, not to sanction immorality: "free love" implied the freedom to withhold sex, even in marriage, unless true love was involved. The hyperbole of sexual reformers' rhetoric often led audiences to exaggerate their deviance. Recent studies showing that antebellum sexual reform advocates were as obsessed with privacy, self-control, and romantic love as their Victorian contemporaries are necessary correctives to the traditional "lunatic fringe" approach. With its bourgeois constituency, exclusively cultural concerns, and uncompromising middle-class values, free love was a decidedly middle-class movement.[42] Still, the diversity and often the unconventionality of the ex-Fourierist free-lovers' lives and views ought to be appreciated.

Some Fourierists led conventional private lives despite looking forward to Harmonic freedom. Henry James depicted love in the future phalanstery but professed himself "unconscious . . . of any desire after greater passional liberty in any sphere, than the present constitution of society affords."[43] Marx Lazarus dedicated *Love vs. Marriage* "to all true lovers . . . who believe that God reveals to the instinct of each heart the laws which he destines it to obey, [and] who . . . defy the interference of all foreign powers." Yet Lazarus put off free love to the phalansterian future and meanwhile urged "full and unreserved acquiescence in the established laws and customs so long as they shall continue." Shortly after publishing his book, Lazarus legally married a young woman from

Indiana, was twitted by sexual radicals for this concession, and dropped out of the free-love network.[44]

Albert Brisbane was the converse of James and Lazarus, an Associationist who edited out Fourier's sexual future yet tried to live it. Brisbane's few public statements on marriage relegated radical sexual change to the distant future, but his private life suggested little postponement. When his wife, Adèle, returned to her native Europe in 1838, Brisbane never obtained a divorce. Shortly thereafter, he enjoyed an affair with Lodoiska Durand, the married daughter of his tutor Jean Manesca; after Mrs. Durand's divorce the two lived in common-law marriage from 1849 until 1857. Meanwhile, Brisbane became embroiled in an embarrassing free-love incident. In the fall of 1855 Stephen Andrews's "Club" or "Grand Order of Recreation," evidently an innocent semiweekly soiree of free-thinking men and women, was "exposed" in the New York City press as a "Free-Love League." In an ensuing raid Brisbane was arrested for giving an "incendiary speech" and was detained overnight before Mayor Fernando Wood intervened to have the disorderly conduct charges dismissed.[45] After separating from Mrs. Durand, Brisbane married Sarah White of Buffalo in 1860; when she died in 1866 after bearing five children, Brisbane invited Mrs. Durand back into his house. They lived together until 1872, when Brisbane once again abandoned her to marry a younger woman, the adoring Redelia Bates. (Not until 1883 did this information surface, during a long and sensational divorce suit by Mrs. Durand.) Though he denied advocating free love, Brisbane went through four marriages (of sorts), enjoyed several affairs, and fathered three illegitimate children. No doubt Lazarus had Brisbane in mind in the 1850s when he warned that Fourierist theory did not excuse the socialist "from the consequences of his private misdeeds" and urged Associationists to tidy up their private lives.[46]

With Brisbane on the night of his arrest at the "Free-Love League" was Henry Clapp, Jr., who was more forthright in his public pronouncements on free love. After a controversial early career as an abolitionist and reform editor in Massachusetts, Clapp moved to New York City, where he translated Fourier's major works for Brisbane and helped Andrews promote his free-thinkers' "Club." Clapp lambasted conventional marriage in his long poem *Husband vs. Wife* (1858) and praised Fourier's sexually free phalansterians. His private relations remain obscure, but Clapp's antibourgeois habits were unconventional enough to have him crowned the first American "King of Bohemia." After sampling the sidewalk cafes of Paris in 1857, Clapp returned to preside over his own circle of bohemian writers and artists, dispensing bon mots and mocking respectable morality from his headquarters in Pfaff's beer cellar on Broadway in New York. Among his closest friends and admirers was Walt Whitman, whose works Clapp hailed for their sensual candor.[47]

There is no doubt that Stephen Pearl Andrews endorsed immediate free love, yet his private life seems to have been fairly conventional: he described himself as a happily married father of three children. Mary Gove Nichols claimed that Andrews's wife came to her water-cure house for sexual advice and was urged to let her husband express his large "amative propensity" by sleeping with others. There is no firm evidence of an affair, however.[48] Andrews and his second wife—married in 1856 after the death of his first—were founders of the Unitary Household (1858–60), a cooperative brownstone ménage in New York City; this experiment was a haven for sexual reform publicists (the Fourierist E. F. Underhill was house manager), but it was not run on free-love principles.[49]

Furthest out on the libertarian edge—at least philosophically—were ex-Fourierists such as Thomas and Mary Nichols, who publicized sexual laissez faire as championed by Andrews and put it into practice at Modern Times. In Thomas Nichols's *Esoteric Anthropology* (1853), his wife's sensational autobiography *Mary Lyndon* (1855), and their joint compendium *Marriage* (1854), the Nicholses extended their earlier critique of legalized marriage and came out in favor of the "right to love" whomever and whenever one wanted. Despite their own "blessed" (and apparently faithful) match, the Nicholses expected most sexual relationships to be neither permanent nor exclusive, and they counseled impatient free-lovers to join or form colonies.[50]

In the summer of 1853 the Nicholses secured from Andrews a hundred acres at Modern Times to establish a "School of Life" for education in health, diet, industry, and art. Elaborate plans for this "Institute of Desarollo" were announced—including lecture rooms, dormitories, an art gallery, and a social parlor—and a building to accommodate two hundred persons was begun. The Nicholses moved to Modern Times and invited all those "willing to be considered licentious by the world" to join them. They ran into two major obstacles, however: monetary contributions quickly ran out; just as serious, Josiah Warren, the anarchist godfather of Modern Times, opposed the plan to saddle the community with free-love doctrines. Anarchism, wrote Warren, was "as valid a warrant *for retaining the present relations,* as for changing them"; although members were free to do as they pleased, he himself was against free love. The rank and file at Modern Times found free love "a favorite text for many an argument," according to one resident, but only a handful were apparently involved in cohabitation, promiscuity, or other unconventional relations. Discouraged by their less than triumphant reception, Thomas and Mary Nichols left within two years for Ohio, there promoting free-love ideas through another communal experiment and the Progressive Union before beginning their retreat from sexual radicalism. In 1857 they announced their conversion to legalized monogamy and Roman Catholicism.[51]

Several ex-Fourierists besides Andrews and the Nicholses were associated with Modern Times. James H. Cook, who had visited Brook Farm and the Bloomfield Association in the 1840s, spent six months in 1852 at Modern Times, where sexual reform discussions convinced him that legal marriage was "the TRUNK of the tree of Social Evil." The community was in fact less a den of promiscuity than a haven where widows or refugees from disastrous marriages could settle in peace or take on a new partner without formally getting married. Marx Lazarus's sister Ellen moved there after her husband, Brook Farmer John Allen, died. Theron C. Leland, the Fourierist veteran connected with three New York phalanxes and Andrews's assistant in phonography, lived at the village with Mary Chilton, a southern woman who had run away from her husband to reconstruct her life.[52] Henry Edger, an English immigrant who later became the foremost American disciple of Auguste Comte, joined Modern Times in 1854 after five months at the North American Phalanx. While Edger weighed settling permanently at Modern Times, he was also evolving Fourierist passional theory toward "anti-domestic notions"—at least until converting to the complete chastity sanctioned by the Positivist Church.[53]

Free-love communitarianism spread to other ex-Fourierists. Some remaining members of the Wisconsin Phalanx formed the Ceresco Union in 1855, a combination study group and living cooperative. James Cook moved there; Warren Chase returned to lecture; and residents planned a "Unitary Edifice" where religious, economic, and affectional impulses could be given full rein. When outraged neighbors attacked the Ceresco community one night, breaking windows and doors, several members fled, and the experiment apparently disbanded. Cook and Thomas Wright joined a growing free-love enclave in Berlin Heights, Ohio.[54]

By the mid-1850s, Fourierist-inspired agitation on sex and marriage had completed its two phases: the first opened up discussion of marriage, divorce, and the sexual future; the second expounded the doctrine of free love and experimented with it in households and communal settings. As antimarriage sentiment became free-love agitation, it went beyond Fourierism. Gone was the Fourierists' proviso that sexual freedom had to await a changed environment and proceed by consensus. Free-lovers no longer endorsed the specifics of Fourier's phalanx, preferring instead to let passional affinities work themselves out without plans or predictions. "Equity in commercial relations" was still an avowed goal, but free-lovers spoke of it in terms foreign to the phalanx. Modern Times residents emphatically declared: "We are not Fourierites. . . . We do not believe in Association"; they proclaimed instead "the SOVEREIGNTY OF THE INDIVIDUAL."[55]

From Association to Individual Sovereignty

That slogan, Andrews's *Tribune* letters, and the Modern Times community's cluster of "free" practices indicate that in the 1850s free love became part of a generalized anarchistic creed. On the surface, "Individual Sovereignty" seemed a pragmatic accommodation to the motley

crowd of reform cranks assembled at Modern Times, a principle max-
imizing breathing room and the only platform upon which all could
unite. But in fact it represented an integrated program of social noninterference and economic individualism carefully thought out by the Modern
Times founders—a program which, like free love, had developed logically from utopian socialist roots.

Josiah Warren, the intellectual founder of Modern Times, formulated
his anarchist theory in direct response to the failure of "community"
systems. This ingenious little Yankee printer and inventor had moved
his family in 1825 from Cincinnati to New Harmony. When Owen's
experiment collapsed, Warren concluded that "community of goods"
and "combined interests" suppressed "individuality" and discouraged
personal responsibility: "What was everyone's interest was no one's business." New Harmony's various constitutions tried to coerce cooperation
through majority rule or Owen's personal despotism, but both proved
futile. As he left Indiana, Warren came to believe that a perfect society
would be one without government or laws, where persons could do as
they pleased but at their own cost.[56] Upon this basic commitment to
individual sovereignty Warren superimposed a theory of "equitable commerce," according to which business was to be conducted by individual
producers exchanging "labor notes" measured in units of time rather
than market values. To apply his principles, Warren founded three
short-lived "Time Stores" (in Cincinnati, New Harmony, and Evansville,
Indiana) and set up the Ohio villages of Equity (1835–37) and Utopia
(1847–51). The latter suggested the appeal Warren's individualistic principles had for disillusioned Fourierists. A few months after the Clermont
Phalanx disbanded, Warren appeared at the domain to interest its former
members in his own plan. In July 1847 he gathered several converts on
a tract at the eastern edge of the former phalanx and established his
"equitable village."[57]

When Warren moved to New York City around 1849 and converted
Andrews from Fourierism to Individual Sovereignty, the bridge from
Association to anarchism was completed. Andrews's energy and talent
for publicity made him a well-known apostle of the new individualism;
his Fourierist background, genteel bearing, and philosophical breadth
enabled him to make headway in reform circles where the unlettered
Warren could not. It was Andrews who won over Thomas Nichols, and
the two publicly repudiated their Fourierist past, finding "a lamentable
want of spontaneity" and stunted "passional development" in Fourier's
blueprint. Citing the recent phalanx failures, they argued that Fourier's
machinery was too complex and that the "combined interests" of
shareholding left phalansterians subject to majority tyranny or the whims
of large investors. Communal meals and dwellings violated privacy; work
in groups and series enforced "attractive industry" rather than letting it
occur. Fourierists might protest that their scheme was "expressly intended to end by achieving . . . entire individual freedom," wrote An-

drews, but since "individualities have to be crushed . . . in order that the scheme may *begin* to be carried out," their promise was "self-defeating."[58]

To confirmed "Individual Sovereigns" the "essential condition of freedom" was the "disintegration" of interests. Eliminating forms of group property would destroy the main source of tyranny and eventually do away with government itself. Individualized production would stimulate initiative, and equitable commerce through labor notes would ensure a just reward to labor. With economic individualism complemented by perfect freedom in social matters, the potential for personal growth was unlimited. The surest route to utopian self-fulfillment, in short, was to accommodate the individual "at *every step*" of social reorganization.[59]

Free love joined the anarchist list of freedoms by a process that radicals would call natural attraction. A shared background in Fourierism gave adherents a common vocabulary and an overlapping network of friends. In striving to release individuals from convention and constraint, the two ideas were strategic allies. Thus, while the Nicholses helped inject sexual liberation into Andrews's new anarchist program, Individual Sovereignty gave them a coherent rationale for the free-love immediatism toward which their experience was leading but at which Fourierist doctrine stopped short. Soon after meeting Andrews the Nicholses came out in anarchist terms for immediate "Freedom of Love" without social or legal interference, as long as others' rights were not violated.[60] Individual Sovereignty as worked out at Modern Times thus represented the convergence of two doctrines of personal liberation rising from the ashes of the phalanxes.

Anarchists who preached free-love immediatism departed from Fourier's belief in large-scale social change, his postponement of sexual freedom until Harmony, and his precise blueprint for the perfect society. But perhaps the most important disagreement between the two systems centered on the idea of community. For all their cultural radicalism, anarchists made crucial accommodations to the prevailing individualism of American society. And since theirs was the most vital form of dissent in the 1850s, these concessions had conservative implications for American intellectual life.

Marx Lazarus saw the anarchist program as a necessary first step toward a future that was still essentially Fourierist. His support stemmed from the same gradualist impulse that led Associationists in the late 1840s toward cooperatives and the no-interest schemes of Proudhon.[61] But few other anarchist converts envisioned the future in Fourierist terms. Andrews and Warren stretched individualism to the point where the only acceptable cooperative activities were "constructive competition" (temporary alliances between workers or consumers) and "beneficent despotism" (philanthropic projects run by generous patrons). The large-scale community operations proposed by Fourierists—nurseries, unitary dwellings, workshops—would be individually owned in the anarchist utopia, not controlled by workers or shareholders. Professing faith in competition and insisting upon personal ownership, anarchists of the 1850s believed that Fourierist communitarianism was an infringement on individual rights.[62]

To Andrews the assertion of the "rights of the individual over social institutions" was the mainspring of human progress and the "central idea and vital principle" of socialism itself. In *The Science of Society* he argued that Protestantism, democracy, and socialism were parallel developments, allowing progressively greater personal freedom in religion, government, and society. The Fourierists, he charged, had misled a generation of radicals by blaming Civilization's problems on competitive individualism, for it actually was responsible for "nearly all that there is good in existing society."[63] In redefining socialism as Individual Sovereignty, ex-Fourierists such as Andrews and the Nicholses reversed a decade of Associationist agitation, attempting a Copernican revolution that placed the self rather than the group at the center of renovated social life. Their program of middle-class villages, "disconnected interests," and unfettered self-expression rejected not just excessive organization but the communal goals that underlay utopian socialism. Theirs was a new kind of communitarian program, one without community values.

At bottom, Individual Sovereignty rested on the conventional liberal faith that if left completely to themselves, individuals would prosper and the whole society benefit. Andrews insisted that the wage system deplored by Fourierists was "essentially proper and right," needing only a lower profit margin to make it perfect. Unlike utopian socialist plans, equitable commerce gave "no guarantees whatever" to workers, denying any "right" to communal support and declaring sickness and death calculated "risks." Where Fourierists brought competition under communal control, Individual Sovereigns made it the basis of their utopia. They believed the Andrews-Warren plan of minimal government and social noninterference was the "natural order of society" that liberals everywhere had been seeking.[64]

Thus the anarchism of the 1850s was at once more radical and more conservative than the Fourierism from which it evolved. Anarchists brought the quest for liberation directly to the individual, the family, and the present, rejecting—at least in theory—obedience to government and social conventions. On the other hand, in reacting against Fourierist "combinations" and renouncing economic cooperation, they proposed a solution in tune with (and more consistent than) the laissez-faire individualism of mainstream middle-class contemporaries. By the mid-1850s Fourierist communitarians who had become anarchists no longer represented a distinctive dissenting voice. Together with northern liberals they praised the virtues of American "free society," and when the Civil War came, most swallowed their no-government principles and became ardent defenders of the Union.[65] Historians have detected a major cultural reorientation in the decade preceding the Civil War, a new mood of impatience with utopian reform and satisfaction with American free institutions.[66] The anarchists participated in this changed climate by sharing with many former Associationists a new respect for individualism. In a way that paralleled the conservative shift of Fourierists Dana and Godwin, Individual Sovereigns failed to keep alive a community-oriented critique of northern society and a truly alternative vision of its future.

15

Fourierism and the Coming of the Civil War

Reflecting on the antebellum communitarians fifty years later, Edward Bellamy concluded that the Fourierists of the 1840s—"precursors" of his own Nationalist movement—had been denied their full potential by the coming of the Civil War: "Horace Greeley would very possibly have devoted himself to some line of socialistic agitation, had not the slavery struggle come on, . . . and in this respect he was representative of a large group of strong and earnest spirits. But slavery had to be done away with before talk of a closer, kinder brotherhood was in order or, indeed, anything but a mockery. So it was that presently these humane enthusiasts . . . were drawn into the overmastering current of the antislavery agitation."[1]

Bellamy's history was not quite straight. Greeley did agitate for Fourierism in the 1840s and invest substantial sums in communitarian experiments. Also, the belief that slavery "had to be done away with" before social reform could make headway in the North was one that many Associationists at first resisted. But Bellamy's essential point—that antislavery played a key role in diverting utopian socialists from their mission against northern society—was sound. By the late 1840s the Associationist movement had been seriously weakened by phalanx failures, and Fourierism was struggling to remain an intellectual force in labor and reform circles. By siphoning off the last energies of utopian socialists and rallying them in defense of northern society, the dramatic rise of antislavery delivered Fourierism's deathblow. As it grew powerful, the antislavery movement virtually silenced criticism of northern capitalism and engineered a potent political coalition dedicated to the expansion of free labor. The denouement of the utopian socialist response to slavery thus has ramifications that go far beyond Fourierism. It illuminates the successful consolidation of northern opinion before the Civil War and provides a new perspective on the historical connection between capitalism and antislavery.

One of the most interesting and complex developments of the nineteenth-century Atlantic world was the simultaneous expansion of capitalist wage labor and the spread of abolitionist ideas. The relationship between the two has provoked considerable debate among historians, beginning with Eric Williams's *Capitalism and Slavery* almost fifty years ago and given focus more recently by David Brion Davis's brilliant volume *The Problem of Slavery in the Age of Revolution.* Though few now accept William's bold but reductionist thesis that British emancipation measures were (in Davis's paraphrase) "economically determined acts of national self-interest, cynically disguised as humanitarian triumphs," many scholars agree with Davis's more subtle and complex argument that on balance, abolitionism helped reinforce the hegemony of capitalist values during a critical period in the evolution of Western industrial society.[2]

The decade-long encounter between American Associationists and abolitionists, coming at the height of this critical period, was in fact a struggle over those very capitalist values. The Fourierists, like land and labor reformers, concentrated their energies on the "wage slavery" of the North rather than the chattel slavery of the South. In the 1840s they debated abolitionists over the uniqueness of the South's "peculiar institution" and the merits of the free-labor capitalism into which slaves were to be liberated. The Fourierists' analysis was a plausible, even prescient critique of liberal capitalism. But as the abolitionist minority gave way to a popular crusade against the expansion of slavery and as Fourierist arguments became part of a heated sectional debate over comparative labor systems, events favored those who defended the northern "free labor" system. By the mid-1850s many northerners had come to believe in an absolute dichotomy between their section's "free society" and the South's slave system, and even Fourierists who had been among the severest critics of northern "free labor" became its vocal champions as Republican party spokesmen. The process by which utopian socialism dissolved into the free-labor consensus was especially significant because the issue at stake was not simply reform priorities of the 1840s but the fate of radical criticism of northern society. By effectively co-opting Associationists and labor reformers, the antislavery crusade helped close discussion of meaningful alternatives to free-labor capitalism at the very point of that system's takeoff.

Free Soil, Free Labor, Free Men

Although the Mexican War divided Associationist leaders and emancipation schemes failed to rally the rank-and-file, after 1847 the issue of territorial slavery increasingly reunited the Fourierists. Once the war was over, both confirmed antislaveryites such as William Henry Channing and "orthodox" Fourierists such as Parke Godwin and Osborne Macdaniel could agree upon a formula that acquiesced in the nation's gain of territories but insisted that they be closed to slavery. Allowing slave-holders to bring human property into new territories would be to turn the social clock back to Barbarism rather than to continue the march to Harmony. If the slave system expanded, what would become of Associationist hopes for the West? Soaring land prices would make it impossible for eastern Fourierists to acquire tracts for "mutual townships" and other cooperative experiments leading to the phalanx. The mere presence of slavery would discourage laborers from going west for fear of contact or competition with black bondsmen.

Control of western lands by a planter oligarchy was a particularly vivid Associationist nightmare. Fourier himself predicted that "subversive" associations of farmer-capitalists would gradually take over agriculture and listed land monopoly as a vicious tendency of Civilization.[3] Plantations required huge tracts, which would be inaccessible to free labor; it would be far better to divide these lands and distribute them to worthy free settlers. By 1847 Greeley, Godwin, Van Amringe, and other Fourierists, entering Associationism's gradualist phase, embraced the National Reform program of free land, limitation on acreage privately held, and inalienable homesteads, seeing it as a step to the cooperative future. Because slavery's westward course threatened this agenda, land reform became for many a bridge to free-soil antislavery.

Fourierists realized that on the territorial issue there was in fact little choice for reformers. Lewis Cass and Stephen Douglas's "popular sovereignty" was unacceptable because it admitted the possibility of slavery in the West. The only guarantee, one Associationist wrote, was to "ask Congress to declare that while the territory is under its jurisdiction slavery shall not exist in it." With the increasing polarization of free-soil and proslavery positions, Associationists saw their duty clearly: "When freedom is on one side and slavery on the other," declared Godwin, "we will not hesitate."[4] Godwin's and other Fourierists' distaste for abolitionists and their fear of immediate emancipation no longer stood in the way. As opposition to the extension of slavery became the central political question of the 1840s, abolitionism and emancipation were pushed from the limelight. Through free-soil advocacy, antislavery became simultaneously a more moderate cause and a mass movement. In joining it, the Associationists were endorsing a positive rather than a "destructive" reform.

All these themes were sounded in *The Harbinger* as Fourierists confronted the territorial slavery question in the crucial period between the Mexican War and the Compromise of 1850. Ironically, it was Parke Godwin who led Associationist readers into the free-soil coalition. As editor-in-chief after *The Harbinger* returned to New York in November 1847, Godwin wrote most of the political articles. That same month saw the first local elections following the introduction of the Wilmot Proviso. Immediately, Godwin professed his "strongest sympathies" with the proponents of free soil, rejoicing that the slavery issue had jolted a moribund party system. By the summer of 1848 *The Harbinger* was completely caught up in free-soil agitation. For the first time the editors reported political news on a regular basis and abandoned the attempt to sound neutral. In June, Godwin rejected the nominations of Cass and Taylor and called upon antislavery Whigs and Democrats to join with National Reformers, Liberty Leaguers, and Fourierists in a new "universal and progressive" party. Antislavery, land reform, and Association could unite "without the sacrifice of fundamental convictions on the part of any." When the Free-Soil party made its debut that fall, Godwin accepted it as the next-best thing.[5] By the time *The Harbinger* expired in February 1849, its editors were squarely in the free-soil camp. John Dwight's column in the *Boston Daily Chronotype* picked up where *The Harbinger* left off, heartily endorsing the Free-Soil party in the elections of November 1849.[6]

Not surprisingly, the most aggressive Associationist free-soil positions were taken by two New Englanders named Channing. As he had during the Mexican War, William Henry Channing preached disunion. A successful attempt to extend slavery to the territories, he declared, should be treated as a "VIRTUAL DISSOLUTION OF THE UNION." If, on the other hand, southern states should secede because they failed to spread slavery, northerners should let them go in peace. Either way, Channing in true Garrisonian fashion hoped that by refusing to compromise with slaveholders and by calling their secession bluff, the northern public would stop "the Slave-Power" in its tracks. Declaring in his best jeremiad fashion that "the Crisis has come, the Judgment-Day of this Nation is opened," he called upon Fourierists to "repent and atone for . . . our past sins of omission and commission" by rallying to the free-soil cause.[7]

His cousin William Francis Channing was a medical doctor, a Fourierist, and an ardent abolitionist who sheltered Boston friends assisting runaway slaves. Always interested in labor reform, Channing warned workers against a political and commercial alliance of the "Lords of the Loom" and the "Lords of the Lash." Northern manufacturers and merchants, he said, had joined with southern planters to form "a gigantic feudal interest" that controlled the federal government and conspired against the rights of labor north and south. The southern aristocracy opposed the limitation of slavery for obvious reasons, but their northern counterparts joined them out of "an instinctive fear of succeeding steps for the elevation of free labor" such as land reform and cooperative workshops. The limitation—and, Channing believed, the consequent destruction—of slavery was the first step to removing the barriers to reform and improving workingmen's conditions. In arguing that free soil was "the first political measure of the Socialist," Channing tried to resolve the longstanding ideological debate between abolition and labor.[8]

Like the Channings, many Fourierists hoped that the free-soil movement would be a wedge for Associative reform. The movement against the extension of slavery, wrote Dwight, was "clearing the ground of weeds, to give us the more room to put in the better seeds, which springing up unchoked shall occupy it wholly." At the same time, Associationist writers urged free-soilers to progress toward Fourierist goals. In response to the new party's motto of "free soil, . . . free labor, and free men," Godwin cautioned that "free soil" ought to mean not simply the absence of slavery but the full adoption of land reform; he reminded politicians that labor would be truly "free" only when organized in Association. While endorsing the Free-Soil party, the Associationists hoped to "infuse the quickening life-blood of our Socialism" into it.[9]

As the debate over territorial slavery intensified, however, it was easy for Fourierists to lose sight of the distant goal in the struggle for the near one. Many gradually dropped the rhetoric of Association and the requirement that free-soilers endorse social reform. Hoping to influence the antislavery movement, most Associationists were instead increasingly absorbed by it. With questions of principle re-entering the political arena, many found their interest in parties revived at the expense of social reform. As they watched the national economy rebound from the slump of the early 1840s, Associationists began to drop the phrase "so-called" from "free labor" and to echo antislaveryites' defense of northern society. Perhaps with their own movement in disarray, many also felt, with Dwight, the need to join in a new cause, to "keep active upon *something good*."[10]

For Parke Godwin there was an additional motive. The case for antislavery was made especially compelling by lessons learned from the 1848 revolutions. Just as he had applauded the annexation of Texas and the Mexican War for their role in spreading free republican institutions, Godwin had looked to the European nationalist uprisings to democratize political life on the Continent and herald social reforms. Louis Kossuth and the Hungarian nationalist movement, frankly imitative of American democracy, enlisted Godwin's vocal support: here was the kind of republican idealism aspiring toward social justice which had been lacking in American politics since Andrew Jackson.[11] When Kossuth's army was defeated by Russian troops and he came to America in December 1851 to enlist support for a new revolution, Godwin helped drum up a hero's welcome. But Kossuth's tour, though a rousing spectacle, netted little practical aid, and shortly after his arrival the *coup d'état* of Louis Napoleon marked the end of the European revolutionary movement. Godwin, with Kossuth at a dinner in New York when reports of the coup arrived, realized its sobering import.[12]

Faced with the European liberals' failure, Godwin redoubled his call for aggressive promotion of American republicanism abroad. In the early 1850s he wrote an impressive series of essays for the new *Putnam's Magazine* which were widely read and later published in book form. In them Godwin advocated an activist foreign policy that would quickly recognize newly established foreign republics and even intervene in foreign revolutions when the cause of democracy was at stake. He repeated these sentiments in "Manifest Destiny," one of the most popular of all Lyceum lectures in the mid-1850s.[13] At the same time, he lamented that America's influence had not been greater; its image abroad needed to be systematically promoted and drastically improved. Domestic institutions had to be scrutinized for moral flaws tarnishing the nation's reputation. Godwin's conclusion was inevitable: slavery, he believed, prevented the United States from projecting an unstained image of republicanism to the world and from being truly free and democratic at home.[14]

In later years Godwin claimed that Kossuth himself had been partly responsible for the Americans' recognition that they had a despotism of their own. Though Kossuth avoided explicit references to slavery (much to the abolitionists' chagrin), his depiction of the Hungarians' plight reminded some Americans of oppressed Africans in the South. American sympathies were on Kossuth's side against tyranny, but a slaveholding republic was "living in an enormous glass-house" and thus "could not approve of an indiscriminate throwing of stones." The accuracy of Godwin's memory can be questioned, but clearly by 1854 he was convinced, like William Seward, that in slavery America had its own form of tyranny and the most damaging blot on its international image. In *Putnam's Magazine* Godwin showed how European monarchs used southern slavery to vilify the United States and labeled the South a despotic state comparable to any European regime. Southern elements usurping elections in Kansas were no different from the French army taking over the streets of Rome in 1849. Slavery, a blight on the nation's influence abroad, had become in Godwin's eyes the chief obstacle to progress at home and a threat to the Republic itself.[15]

Godwin's about-face on the slavery issue was dramatic, but probably the most important Associationist convert to antislavery—as Edward Bellamy later sensed—was Horace Greeley.[16] The editor of the *Tribune* had gone on record opposing the extension of slavery even before the Wilmot Proviso. To Greeley, slavery was not only against moral law; it threatened his entire Whig-Fourierist program of protective tariffs, internal improvements, and promotion of land and labor reform. Yet despite the *Tribune's* opposition to the Mexican War, Greeley was reluctant in the late 1840s to press the slavery issue, and in reacting to daily events his course was not always clear or consistent. While adamantly against expanding slavery, he remained loyal to the Whigs, especially to his hero Henry Clay, even when the party waffled on the territorial issue. His own ambition for office made Greeley hew a cautious line: he was proud that during his ninety days as a congressman in the winter of 1848–49, he "shunned and deplored any needless agitation respecting slavery."[17] Greeley preferred to stimulate discussion of constructive social and economic reforms. He balked at supporting the free-soilers because they did not endorse land reform or the tariff. At antislavery conventions in New York and London in the early 1850s, he told audiences that the surest way to free the slaves was to elevate the northern working class and restore the dignity of honest labor.[18] For a while, Greeley even tolerated the Compromise of 1850 in the hope that the slavery issue had been settled and politicians could address other much-needed reforms.

All this changed in the conflict-ridden years that followed. Greeley's beloved party split into warring factions after the Compromise of 1850: "Cotton" and "Conscience" Whigs battled for control. With "Cotton" Whigs supporting the compromise and also opposing Clay's American system, Greeley was driven closer to the antislavery position. The harsh features of the new Fugitive Slave Law repelled him, and southern agitation for slavery in New Mexico and Cuba kept the issue in the public eye. Perhaps most important to Greeley, if slavery were established in new territories or colonies, not only would free labor be shut out, but the sectional imbalance would allow southerners and northern Democrats to block progressive economic legislation indefinitely. By 1853 Greeley had turned against any compromise with slaveholders. There was no way, he came to believe, that the "Slave Power" could be appeased; it was bent upon a vast extension of slave territory and constantly increasing its control over national politics. The southern threat to America's economic destiny had to be met decisively.

By the early 1850s ex-Fourierists like Greeley, Godwin, and the Channings had fixed upon slavery as the overriding obstacle to their long-cherished programs to regenerate the nation, whether land reform, expansionist democracy, the promotion of labor, or moral uplift. As they felt increasingly threatened by the southerners' attempt to extend slavery, they accommodated themselves to the political system they had denounced in the 1840s, put aside agitation for other reforms, and joined the antislavery crusade. Most found a welcome home in the new Republican party, and at least two were instrumental in shaping that party's ideology. Parke Godwin broke with the Democrats after the Kansas-Nebraska Act. His essays in *Putnam's* had an "enormous impact" on Republican leaders, and in 1856 this former Associationist substantially wrote the Republicans' first national platform, basing it largely on those articles.[19] Horace Greeley was also convinced by the Kansas-Nebraska Act of the need for a staunch antislavery "fusion" party. When he joined the Republicans at the end of 1854, he not only took thousands of *Tribune* readers—many of them former Associationists—with him; he also set about broadening the Republican agenda to include free homesteads, the tariff, and internal improvements. In 1860 the former Fourierist personally worded and pushed through a series of economic planks at the Republican national convention, including one supporting free public lands in the West. When the Republicans finally passed the Homestead Law in 1863, it was—according to Jeter Allen Isely, the most careful historian of Greeley's Republican years—"his greatest public achievement."[20]

The ease with which Fourierists transferred their allegiance to the

Republican party demonstrated how effortlessly utopian socialism could be co-opted after its communitarian focus disappeared and its critique of competition faded. The affinity between Associationists and Republicans grew as Fourierism dwindled into gradualist measures and the Republicans widened their antislavery focus to include a compelling vision of a northern society of small-scale independent producers. The Republicans' conception of labor as the source of all social value and their association of freedom with economic independence had much in common with Fourierist themes. Republicans also attracted Fourierists when they came to adopt the homestead idea as a way to keep open the safety valve for eastern workers. In the Republican free-labor ideology Fourierists heard the same promise of a harmonious, classless, and progressive society that their utopian socialism had voiced. The Republicans, of course, were championing individual capitalism and blaming the expansion of slavery, not the wage system, for choking off the independence of northern workers. In identifying themselves with the ideals of utopians and labor reformers, as Eric Foner has noted, they "helped turn those aspirations into a critique of the South, not an attack on the northern social order."[21]

But by this time, Fourierists were ready to capitulate. In their zeal to contain slavery they seemed to forget the defects that had earlier disenchanted them with American political and social life; they had convinced themselves that northern institutions were fundamentally sound. With few exceptions, Associationist spokesmen gravitated to the Republican ranks. Once there, they infused its ideology with the same millennial and nationalist fervor that had animated their communitarianism. For William Henry Channing and others, the Republican crusade culminated "all the theories, plans, principles, projects of 1842–45" and promised to bring Christ's second coming, "the Easter morn of the Republic." To Henry James the antislavery victory signaled nothing less than "the beginning of a universal and effectual putting of the Lord's house on earth in order, that He may enter and reign."[22]

Proslavery Theory and the "Free Society" Consensus

There was one other force pushing Associationists into the Republican coalition and its positive view of northern society. As the sections polarized on the question of territorial slavery, northern and southern spokesmen entered into a full-fledged debate over the comparative benefits of their labor systems. To be more precise, the debate with abolitionists over "wage slavery" which had been opened by Fourierists and labor reformers in the 1840s was joined in the next decade by a group of southern ideologues who developed a startling critique of northern "free society." But the entrance of proslavery theorists into the discussion of wage slavery and free labor transformed the character of the debate. No longer an intramural squabble among northern reformers over priorities, it became an emotionally charged sectional dispute about the relative worth of "slave" and "free" societies. In an atmosphere akin to sectional Cold War, the utopians' position became ammunition for the cannons of the wrong section—the South—and lost all credibility as a "loyal" form of dissent in the North.

As early as 1838, in declaring slavery a "positive good," John C. Calhoun had asserted on the Senate floor that the chronic conflict between labor and capital which haunted northern capitalism could never take place in the South. There, masters were benevolent rulers and plantations little communities where interests were "perfectly harmonized." On the basis of such sentiments, Richard Hofstadter labeled Calhoun "the Marx of the Master Class"; in reality, Calhoun knew nothing of Marx, but his ideas had a striking affinity with aspects of American Fourierism.[23] Parke Godwin, like many members of the left-wing or Locofoco faction of the northern Democrats, was attracted to Calhoun's presidential bid in the early 1840s. Calhoun's defense of local rights, Godwin believed, could be a step to communal townships, and his depiction of the North as a battleground between capital and labor was a prediction similar to Fourier's. At least in these regards the southerner's theories were "a thousand times to be preferred" to the entrepreneurial and majoritarian beliefs of party liberals. In a remarkable series of discussions at Calhoun's Washington residence in 1842, Albert Brisbane introduced the senator to Fourier's theories. Though the two could not see eye to eye on the imperfection of human nature or the beneficence of slavery, they did agree on "the free competitive anarchical labor of the North," where, Calhoun told Brisbane, "the capitalist owns the instruments of labor, and he seeks to draw out of labor all the profits, leaving the laborer to shift for himself in age and disease."[24]

Not until the end of the 1840s, however, did the full-fledged proslavery critique of northern capitalism emerge. Led by George Frederick Holmes, Henry Hughes, Senator James H. Hammond of South Carolina, and George Fitzhugh, a younger generation of intellectuals followed Calhoun's example in defending southern interests. In *DeBow's Review* and the *Southern Literary Messenger,* in books and newspaper articles, these proslavery writers not only upheld the slave system but went on the offensive against the North, declaring boldly that its "free society" was a failure. Their no-holds-barred attack on northern capitalism revealed the close affinity between the feudal values of the slaveholding elite and the theories of utopian socialism.

Fitzhugh's books and articles presented the most fully developed and penetrating critique. In *Sociology for the South* (1854), *Cannibals All!* (1857), and other polemical writings, he compared the fortunate lot of the slave with the poverty and insecurity of the northern wage-earner. Under free competition capitalist employers held all the power and skimmed profits from labor; without guaranteed employment or fair wages, workers were forced to sell their labor at subsistence value or face starvation. If they

were not physically owned by capitalists, northern workers were nevertheless "slaves without masters." The wretched industrial slums of English cities, the anarchic free-for-all of northern politics, and the rise of
socialist sects throughout the industrial West testified to the failure of
free society. At bottom, Fitzhugh declared, it was a philosophical failure.
In accepting the Enlightenment ideals of natural equality and in grafting
Adam Smith's laissez-faire policy onto it, the North had opened the way
to an anarchic and uncaring future. By contrast, even without reading
Aristotle, southerners had recognized that man was a social being comfortable only in a stable, hierarchical network of duties and obligations.
Slavery, Fitzhugh claimed, symbolized this organic ideal. Protected by
their masters and treated as family members, "the negro slaves of the
South are the happiest, and, in some sense, the freest people in the
world." The master provided food, clothing, and shelter even for the
young, the aged, or the infirm, whatever the rates of production or the
price of cotton. Here, and not in the dreams and fantasies of utopians,
was the world socialists were striving for, a community of interests and
talents in which each member received a share of the profits according
to his or her needs. "Slavery," Fitzhugh concluded with typical perversity,
was "the very best form of Socialism," and only its system of ownership
and responsibilities could save civilization from the class war into which
it was heading.[25]

In gathering evidence for his polemic, Fitzhugh ranged widely, if not
deeply, in classical and contemporary writings from Aristotle to Robert
Filmer, from Dickens and Carlyle to British Parliamentary reports. Yet
especially in his attack on northern commercial capitalism, Fitzhugh drew
heavily on the Fourierists' arsenal. By his own admission he kept "whole
files" of the New York Tribune, which he considered the most influential
of the "infidel and abolition papers" and whose famous editor, he
claimed, was the first man in America to assert the inadequacy and
injustice of northern society. In the Tribune Fitzhugh followed the Greeley-Raymond debate of 1846–47, reports of the North American Phalanx, and the various free-love episodes of the 1850s. As a result Cannibals
All! is peppered with over two dozen references to Fourier and "Mr.
Greeley's Phalansteries," most often presented favorably.[26] When the
Virginian accused the North's "continual war of competition" of debasing
"the sentiments, principles, feelings and affections of high and low, rich
and poor," or when he argued that selfishness was the law of capitalism,
he could have been speaking at an Associationist convention. Likewise,
in declaring the northern wage earner worse off than the southern
slave and predicting the gradual "Europeanization" of northern social
relations, he appropriated key segments of the Fourierist critique. Fitzhugh's vision of the ideal society, however distorted by his attachment to
slavery, also reflected Fourierist principles. A community of guaranteed
employment, "associated labor," and harmony of interests would be not
only more efficient than free labor, as Fourierists argued; as run by a

benevolent master, it would be orderly and caring as well. "Add a Virginia overseer to Mr. Greeley's Phalansteries," suggested Fitzhugh slyly, "and Mr. Greeley and we would have little to quarrel about." Moreover, "a well-conducted farm in the South" was "a model of associated labor that Fourier might envy."[27]

Fitzhugh's assertion that slave society stood closer to socialist than to capitalist ideals was deliberately provocative. The degree to which the antebellum South remained outside the emerging capitalist society of the North is still controversial among historians, some of whom dismiss the southerners' "Reactionary Enlightenment" as a "fraud," while others argue that proslavery writers spoke for a genuine precapitalist society. Fitzhugh himself was typically ambivalent on the issue of capitalism. Despite his indictment of free society, he found it difficult to conceal his admiration for northern productivity, and scarcely a breath after excoriating capitalist plunder, he urged Virginians to manufacture goods for the far South and thus "become exploitators, instead of being exploitated [sic]."[28]

His view of socialism was similarly contradictory. Much of it was second-hand, gleaned from British reviews and used polemically to bolster any argument where it might be effective. Professing that he "would rather be right than consistent," often Fitzhugh was neither. His version of socialism was an illogical combination of anarchy and collectivism which aimed to destroy "religion, family ties, property, and the restraints of justice" yet also professed communitarian ideals that were realized by southern plantations. As Eugene Genovese has pointed out, Fitzhugh lumped socialistic creeds of different kinds—from Fourierism to Stephen Pearl Andrews' anarchism to agrarian agitation to Carlyle's Tory socialism—in an undifferentiated whole.[29] Still, Fitzhugh saw clearly that despite different panaceas and varying degrees of radicalism, all brands of contemporary socialism converged in their critique of individualist capitalism and its values. Southerners were thus presented with a golden opportunity to have the North hoist with its own petard, to turn the damaging socialist critique against the society from which it sprang.

Fitzhugh was by no means the only one to take advantage of it. Notwithstanding C. Vann Woodward's insistence that Fitzhugh was *sui generis,* the Virginian's arguments were seconded by several important proslavery thinkers.[30] George Frederick Holmes, Edmund Ruffin, William Grayson, James Hammond, and Henry Hughes all adapted elements of the utopian socialist critique to the defense of slavery. Holmes reviewed Fitzhugh's *Sociology for the South* favorably in southern periodicals and, like its author, turned Horace Greeley's Fourierism against the North. Ruffin, the Virginia agriculturalist and fire-eater, praised Fitzhugh's "novel and profound views on the comparison of slavery with what is miscalled 'free society.' " In his *Political Economy of Slavery* (1853), Ruffin voiced Fourierist criticism of the "isolated family" and repeated Fitzhugh's claim that the slave system of "associated labor" realized "all that is sound and valuable in the socialists' theories and doctrines." Grayson's popular but interminable poem "The Hireling and the Slave" echoed the socialist and labor reform attack on wage slavery. Hammond, in his famous "mud-sill" speech on the Senate floor in 1858, told northern politicians, "Your whole hireling class of manual laborers and 'operatives,' as you call them, are essentially slaves." And Hughes, who coined new social-science jargon to classify free and slave societies in his *Treatise on Sociology* (1854), borrowed the Fourierist phrases "association" and "mutualism" and insisted upon labeling the Southern order not slavery but "warranteeism," a modification of the Fourierists' "guaranteeism."[31]

Recent commentators point out that this anticapitalist line of attack was aimed partly at the home front: the proslavery argument was intended to rally southerners to a sense of their own distinctiveness and stimulate economic reform in the region.[32] But in the main, as the direct address of the proslavery arguments (for example, "A Warning to the North"), Fitzhugh's badgering correspondence with northerners, the repetition of these ideas by southern congressmen, and many other pieces of evidence clearly attest, the proslavery attack was meant to sting northern reformers and politicians and to score points in a growing sectional debate. At least in the first object they succeeded: proslavery tracts were reviewed and liberally quoted in the abolitionist and antislavery press. Greeley opened an exchange with Fitzhugh in the columns of the *Tribune,* and the Virginian was invited to New Haven to debate Wendell Phillips on the subject "The Failure of Free Society." Garrison printed long extracts of *Cannibals All!* in *The Liberator* as examples of the "gospel according to Beelzebub that is preached at the South," and Lydia Maria Child quoted Fitzhugh and other proslavery theorists in a popular antislavery tract. By 1858, as Harvey Wish has shown, Fitzhugh's theories had "attained wide notoriety in the North" and were being quoted in Congress by Republican stalwarts, including William Seward and Charles Sumner, as proof of southerners' intention to overturn the whole of northern civilization.[33]

One effect of such a wholesale entry of proslavery theorists into the discussion of "wage slavery" and northern society was to close abolitionists' ears to utopian socialist ideas. As early as 1846 the Garrisonians had decided that *The Harbinger* and its critique of free labor were essentially proslavery, and now the southerners' use of the socialist critique seemed to realize their fears of a sinister alliance between hypocritical slaveholders and northerners more interested in economic reform than in moral purity. Had not the Fourierists sparred with Phillips over "wage slavery" in 1847 just as Fitzhugh was doing in 1855? Even abolitionists sympathetic to communitarianism, such as Adin Ballou and Theodore Weld, backed away in the 1850s. Disheartened by the collapse of their favorite projects, they were already questioning whether utopia was possible with human materials when the southerners' attack on conventional free society drove them fully into the free-labor camp.[34]

The more proslavery writers adopted socialist arguments, the more discredited Fourierist ideas became in northern reform circles, abolitionist or otherwise. By the 1850s, talk of "wage slavery" was widely identified with the apology for chattel slavery in the the South and hence was becoming anathema among northern intellectuals. A case in point was the change in the views of Frederick Law Olmsted, the thoughtful young New Yorker who later became America's premier landscape architect. A close friend of Godwin and Dana, Olmsted at the beginning of the 1850s shared the Fourierists' belief that slavery, though unquestionably morally wrong, was no worse than the lot of northern slum dwellers and "wage slaves." In July 1852 Olmsted visited the North American Phalanx and found it "a most blessed advance" upon free labor. In contrast to both slavery and the drudgery of competitive society, cooperative arrangements at the phalanx had made labor efficient and "honorable." "The long and short of it," he confided to a friend, "is that I am *more of a Fourierist* than before I visited the experiment." Six months later Olmsted was sent to the slave states by the *New York Times* to provide a firsthand description of southern life. In summarizing his reports to the *Times* in 1854, Olmsted concluded that slavery was in fact economically ruinous to the South, but he surprised readers by urging the North to correct the injustices of its own labor system rather than attack the South's. Yet when the letters were published two years later as *A Journey in the Seabord Slave States,* Olmsted left out his call for northern labor reform, rounding off his discussion with a point-by-point refutation of the proslavery theory and a ringing defense of free labor. In the interim he had read the full proslavery argument of Fitzhugh, made the wage slavery question "the subject of careful inquiry," and put aside his Fourierist reservations about capitalism.[35]

Confronted with their new proslavery "allies," even committed Associationists began to drop their criticism of free labor. According to a Fourierist contributor to the *Boston Chronotype,* "the practice of Socialists, placing Wages Slavery and Chattel Slavery side by side, as though there was no choice between them," was wrongheaded. Talk of "White Slavery" played into proslavery hands. Another Fourierist declared that utopians should not spend their time "apologizing for Slavery in true Calhoun style, by deprecating liberty" but should join antislaveryites in defending free society.[36]

When labor reformers, Fourierist sympathizers like Olmsted, and Associationists themselves dropped their militant rhetoric and enlisted as Republicans, they paid a significant price. "The growing ideological conflict between the sections," Eric Foner has written, "had the effect of undermining a tradition of radical criticism within northern society." As the debate polarized, "the choices for America came to be defined as free society versus slave society—the idea of alternatives within free society was increasingly lost sight of." Impressed with the need to defend the North against southerners' assaults, social reformers and antislaveryites closed ranks around the banner of free labor.[37]

But what exactly *was* free labor? When southerners used socialist concepts to indict "free society," they prodded northern politicians, reformers, and intellectuals to define *for themselves* exactly what "free society" stood for. Ten years earlier, at the peak of Fourierist agitation, Association's spokesmen had spurred intellectuals and reformers to consider the philosophical basis of the northern social system. Yehoshua Arieli has shown that the word "individualism," coined by French socialists and used by American Associationists to condemn the selfish ethos of competitive capitalism, was adopted by Emerson and others as a positive term. As an expression of philosophical and economic self-reliance, "individualism" came to encapsulate for many northerners the distinctive virtues of their way of life.[38]

In much the same way and with even greater irony, the utopian socialist challenge, weirdly reincarnated in the writings of Fitzhugh and his colleagues, caused northern intellectuals in the 1850s to examine their institutions and attitudes, made them aware of their common ground, and evoked positive new meanings for "free labor" and "free society." By concentrating upon northern society rather than national political institutions, the proslaveryites' attack placed social and economic questions at the forefront of the sectional debate. At the same time, as abolitionism evolved into antislavery, northern reformers and politicians were more inclined to adopt the Fourierist and labor-reform view that slavery was primarily a labor system, and they stressed the necessity of keeping the territories open to free rather than slave labor. As a result, the concept of free labor was put at the very center of Republican ideology. In it, Republicans blended devotion to small-scale capitalism with their belief in self-help, social mobility, and westward expansion to create a rosy picture of the nature and prospects of northern society. Through this vision of a free-labor society, and especially its contrast with the world of the slaveholders, increasing numbers of northerners affirmed the superiority of their dynamic capitalist society.[39]

Abraham Lincoln's great formulation of "free labor" is widely recognized as the culmination of Republican ideology and hence the basis for a northern liberal consensus before the Civil War. It is well known that Fitzhugh's writings were the chief source of Lincoln's "house divided" notion and his fear that southern planters wanted to nationalize slavery.[40] But Lincoln also had southern polemics in mind when he developed and articulated his concept of free labor. Citing an article by Fitzhugh in the *Richmond Enquirer,* Lincoln told an audience in Kalamazoo in 1856 that southerners "insist that their slaves are far better off than Northern freemen. What a mistaken view do these men have of Northern laborers! They think that men are always to remain laborers here—but there is no such class. The man who labored for another last year, this year labors for himself, and next year he will hire others to labor for him. These men don't understand when they think in this manner of Northern free labor." The southern and socialist indictment was, as Hofstadter pointed

out, "the antithesis of everything that Lincoln had been taught to believe—the equality of man, the dignity of labor, and the right to move
upward in the social scale." Conceiving the northern social ideal as a
western small town writ large, Lincoln was confident that free labor
"open[ed] the way for all" to become capitalists and hence tended toward
equality. During the 1858 campaign he pasted in his scrapbook an editorial from a southern newspaper which mocked the northern social order:
"Free society! We sicken of the name! What is it but a conglomeration of
greasy mechanics, filthy operatives, small fisted farmers, and moon-
struck theorists?" When Lincoln debated Douglas at Galesburg, his
Republican supporters arrived with a banner declaring in defiance:
"Small Fisted Farmers, Mud-sills of Society, Greasy Mechanics for A.
Lincoln."[41]

It is significant that "moon-struck theorists" disappeared. Back in the
1840s Fourierists had entered the growing national debate over America's future as a "third voice" opposed to both the free-labor system of
northern capitalists and the slave-labor system of the South. They exerted
important influence over the terms of that debate, but they utterly failed
to control its outcome. In the movement's heyday its spokesmen, rather
than converting northern opponents, inspired Emerson and other writers to develop a coherent philosophy of individualism. During its demise
its ideas, filtered through the polemical writings of proslavery apologists,
spurred Lincoln and other Republicans to coalesce in defense of free
labor and "free society." In the strange dialectic that constituted national
discourse in the antebellum years, Fourierist ideas became pawns in the
sectional controversy and helped give birth to a northern consensus that
Associationists had never envisioned.

Given the changes that had taken place by the late 1850s, former
Associationists readily joined the free-society bandwagon. At Raritan Bay
Union, the last remaining Fourierist experiment in the North, antislavery
agitation overshadowed social reform in the community's final years.
Theodore Weld's students raised money in nearby towns to support the
Free-Staters in Kansas. The community's founders, Marcus and Rebecca
Spring, had met John Brown at an abolitionist meeting, and after his
raid and imprisonment Rebecca Spring visited him in jail. Brown's wife
and sister were welcomed at the community and for a time supported by
the Springs, and two of Brown's coconspirators were secretly buried at
Raritan Bay.[42]

When the "irrepressible conflict" erupted into war, ex-Fourierists with
few exceptions closed ranks in support of the Union. Many former
phalanx members became Union soldiers. The son of Brook Farm patron
Francis G. Shaw heroically led black troops in the attack on Fort Wagner,
and Charles Dana distinguished himself as an assistant secretary of war
under Edwin Stanton. Perhaps the greatest of the many ironies of American Fourierism was that two of its phalanxes ended their history as
military enclaves: Brook Farm became a Union camp during the war,

and at Raritan Bay the most impressive "unitary dwelling" the Fourierists ever erected was rented to the Eagleswood Military Academy.[43] On the same grounds where reformers had gathered to revolutionize northern social relations, soldiers were trained to defend free labor against its enemies in a bloody civil war.

16

The Fourierist Legacy

Stephen Pearl Andrews bravely announced in 1871 that Fourierism was "not dead, merely sleeping."[1] As the era of the Civil War closed, however, Fourierist phalanxes had ceased to be a vital option for American society. It was not just that such communities had failed or that northerners had rallied with confidence around their free-labor capitalist society, though these were immediate causes of Fourierism's demise. In the longer run the communitarian idea lost its salience when the fact became clear that urban-industrialism in its competitive capitalist form was here to stay. By the 1860s the institutions of individualism had become (according to J. F. C. Harrison) "so firmly based as to make efforts at challenging them appear quite impracticable," and the scale of urban settlements and manufacturing establishments had passed beyond the Fourierists' claim that a community of 1,620 persons could accommodate modern forms of production, consumption, and leisure. Communitarian projects appeared increasingly anachronistic. Organized as isolated colonies of true believers rather than "experiments carried out by interested citizens in the neighborhood where they already lived," they were denounced as escapist, tolerated as oddities, or else ignored completely. Communitarians themselves changed the meaning of their experiments by promoting them as mechanisms for settling the frontier, as islands of social justice in a hostile society, or as demonstrations of cooperative principles to be introduced into the larger society. As the century progressed, communitarianism became a "minor eddy" in a socialist stream whose "main channel" had once been Fourierist. In retrospect, the Fourierist movement appeared the last credible attempt to redirect American society into a communitarian path; its failure proved to be a crucial turningpoint in the nation's social history.[2]

Yet if the miniature phalanxes of the 1840s were not the germs of a new social world, they did serve in subtle and gradual ways as agents of change. The experience of communal life, however short-lived, was not easily forgotten by committed members. As Paul Goodman once observed about such fragile experiments:

> Perhaps the very transitoriness of such intensely motivated intentional communities is part of their perfection. Disintegrating, they irradiate society with people who have been profoundly touched by the excitement of community life, who do not forget the advantages but try to realize them in new ways. . . . Perhaps these communities are like those "little magazines" and "little theatres" that do not outlive their first few performances, yet from them comes all the vitality of the next generation of everybody's literature.[3]

To carry the Fourierists' case this far would exaggerate their later influence. Yet beginning in 1868 there occurred what Edward Spann calls "a modest revival" of Fourierism, sparked by publicity from their old critic John Humphrey Noyes, dislocations of the postwar recession and the Panic of 1873, and a general reawakening of northern radicalism during Reconstruction.[4] Fourierist ideals helped inspire the next generation of dissenters, and alumni of the Associative "school" kept its vision alive in new contexts. Communitarianism remained an option for a few, but most postbellum Fourierists pressed the kind of transitional forms the movement had turned to in the late 1840s. Worker cooperatives, new currency schemes, model factories, cooperative apartment houses, and municipal parks seemed more appropriate than the phalanx to the scale and complexity of urban life in the later nineteenth century. These projects were a tacit rebuke to Fourier's theory of instant social reorganization through phalanxes, but they also demonstrated the enduring appeal of communitarian values. Promoting such schemes and attempting to attach a radical dimension to them was the Fourierists' chief legacy to the Gilded Age.

Not surprisingly, Fourier's first American apostle was also his last. The doggedly persistent Albert Brisbane remained active as an advocate of Fourierism long after the Civil War. Much of his time was taken up with promoting the host of inventions he conceived in the 1860s, including a greenhouse heater and a system of transport through pneumatic tubes. His continued study of Fourier often verged upon obscurity as he tried to formulate a "science of laws" or a "method of study" to bequeath to the next generation of social theorists. Yet Brisbane remained a committed Fourierist reformer, pledging the profits from his patents toward Fourierist propaganda or a new communal experiment and reaffirming in 1875 that he "acknowledge[d] but one Mind on this earth—the great Fourier." In private letters, manuscripts circulated among friends, two sociological treatises, and several publications he continued to preach the master's theory, searching for a new way to restate it which would compel readers as he had been compelled by Fourier's writings in 1832. For three decades Brisbane churned out new communitarian proposals for frontier farms or eastern enclaves. Meanwhile, he hung around any reform movement which seemed to be gaining public support—free love, greenbackism, social science, worker cooperatives, Bellamyite Nationalism—trying to inject Fourierist influence into it. However compromised by his previous failures and his controversial private life, Brisbane's advocacy of Fourierism in the new era was a spur to other Associationist veterans almost to the time of his retirement to France in 1887, where he and Victor Considerant a decade earlier had enjoyed a tearful reunion among aging Fourierist associates.[5]

The Persistence of Communitarianism

Communitarianism did not suddenly end with the coming of the Civil War or the arrival of full-fledged urban industrialism. On the east coast, to be sure, social and economic institutions were entrenched, and villages of 1,600 persons had long since been outcompeted by nearby cities. In the West, however, cheap land was still available, and the communitarian promise to shape the future remained alluring. If each major northern city could no longer spawn a nearby phalanx, perhaps western colonies could gather the faithful in successful communitarian ventures. No new generation of leaders emerged to pick up the Fourierist banner, but more than a few diehards of the 1840s and 1850s believed that Fourierist communitarianism, properly modified and presented, could again take hold of the nation's imagination. Several became involved in new nonsectarian communities that showed traces of Fourierist influence: William H. Muller and Stephen Young in the Topolobampo colony in Mexico, Thomas Lake Harris at Fountain Grove in California, Earl Joslin and Theron C. Leland in various projects, and Osborne Macdaniel in an attempt to replicate Brook Farm in the Adirondacks.[6] Thomas J. Durant was president of the Cooperative Industrial Association of Virginia, which sponsored a short-lived semi-Fourierist community on the Potomac twenty miles from Washington in 1877.[7] There were, however, only three significant Fourierist-tinged experiments after the Civil War, all established and directed by antebellum veterans. Each reflected lessons its founders purported to have learned from early phalanx failures.

The Kansas Co-operative Farm, or Silkville (1869–92), was founded by the French Fourierist and philanthropist Ernest Valenton de Boissiere, who left home following Louis Napoleon's coup and eventually became a successful shipping magnate in New Orleans. A member of the French Associative school and apparently an investor in the North American Phalanx, de Boissiere had a long-standing commitment to utopian socialism; by the late 1860s he was ready to devote his wealth to a communitarian project. This brought him into renewed contact with Brisbane, whom he had met fifteen years earlier and who now was circulating plans for a "great joint-stock farm in the West" to be heavily capitalized by "men of means" and run by "a just and wise authority, which may be absolute, when necessary." The third key figure involved was E. P. Grant, whose directorship of the contentious and capital-starved Ohio Phalanx in the early 1840s had left him with "little faith in any associative experiment which is not directed by a single mind, and controlled substantially by a single will." For the Americans, a paternalistic, authoritarian, and disciplined form of Fourierism was a necessary corrective to the uncontrolled fiasco of the 1840s; for the Frenchman, it was a simple expression of utopian socialism as philanthropy.[8]

In September 1868 Brisbane toured the Great Plains looking for desirable land, and at the end of the year he returned with de Boissiere to Missouri and Kansas. Early in 1869 they completed the purchase of 3,200 acres of prairie land in Franklin County of eastern Kansas and published *Articles of Association of the Kansas Co-operative Farm*. Brisbane subscribed $5,000 to the venture, Grant $1,200. De Boissiere initially put in $22,000 and eventually invested a great deal more.[9] Almost immediately, de Boissiere and Grant squeezed the unreliable Brisbane out of a position of prominence. When the two deliberately left his name off the community's prospectus, a petulant Brisbane withdrew his claim to a guiding role, though not his investment.[10] Grant returned to Ohio in the spring of 1869 to act as an absentee adviser and publicist, leaving de Boissiere in charge of the community.[11]

As the sole landowner and prime shareholder, de Boissiere was, in Brisbane's words, "absolute master" of the Kansas community, which came to reflect his benevolent paternalism. He hoped eventually to make it a fully cooperative society with "equitable distribution of profits, mutual guarantees, association of families, integral education, and unity of interests."[12] Until then, his chief concern was to keep it economically viable without expoiting labor or creating an unpleasant group atmosphere. The result was that Silkville was run much like a model farm or factory: its enlightened owner provided fine facilities for his "hands" or operatives and rewarded supervisors handsomely. Revolving around its founder and relying mainly on hired labor, the community never progressed beyond the status of capitalist enterprise made more attractive by a few cooperative working and living arrangments.

De Boissiere was convinced that establishing stable industries was a necessary prelude to attracting committed communitarians or inaugurating real Fourierist reforms. He expected to set up silk culture and manufacturing in Kansas, believing the climate appropriate and the work fit for Fourierist groups. In the first few years more than forty French immigrants came to the community, most of them skilled in the production of silk. These were joined by several American families as well as the local hired laborers. For an experienced manager de Boissiere recruited Charles Sears, whom he had met at the North American Phalanx. In 1870 Sears obtained work as a railroad land agent, which enabled him to stay at Silkville for a year and visit frequently; in 1875 he moved there permanently to supervise the expanding silk industry.[13] Silk weaving began in 1869, silk culture a few years later when the colony's mulberry trees matured and silkworms were imported. Within a decade the colony became known as the center of silk culture in America. Other community industries included fruit orchards, a dairy and cheese operation, and wine production.

Until the farm and industrial operations succeeded completely, all arrangements at Silkville were to be transitional to the far-distant phalanx. When de Boissiere issued a second prospectus in 1873 for Silkville's "Prairie Home Colony," Fourierist ideas were evident in its projected "combined household," its emphasis on attractive labor, its promised freedom to organize industries and work groups, and its faith that Silkville would be a model for other communities. But de Boissiere introduced gradualist amendments and conservative additions: in the beginning, members' remuneration was to apportioned directly to their productive output rather than their hours worked; those preferring simple wages were accommodated; a deposit of $100 was required of all residents; and rent was to be paid every two months in advance.[14]

Actual arrangements at Silkville are difficult to reconstruct. It appears that the silk and cheese operations were run cooperatively as profit-sharing enterprises, at least for a time, but no other evidence of Fourierist economic ideas has survived. By and large, de Boissiere paid for his labor in straight wages, and those who lived on the domain paid in turn for room and board. The community's stone phalanstery, completed in 1874, housed fifty residents who took their meals in a common dining hall, were entertained in the assembly hall, and lounged in the large library and communal parlors, but they were never full-fledged members of a truly cooperative community. Instead, because Silkville never progressed toward becoming a phalanx, they continued to be de Boissiere's employees. Each day visitors could see the aging patriarch with the flowing beard rambling around the grounds hunched over his cane, exhorting his workers and personally supervising every aspect of production.[15]

In the 1880s de Boissiere found that the community could not compete with the importation of cheap raw silk from China, Japan, and France. The colony's silk industry had to be replaced by dairy farming and cattle raising. Other problems plagued Silkville in its later years. Without a variety of industries the work was monotonous and turnover frequent. The phalanstery, built to house a hundred residents, never held more than half that number. Many colonists, especially the mechanics and operatives de Boissiere recruited from France, were attracted elsewhere by cheap land or better pay. In 1884, with the community in decline, de Boissiere returned to France to set up a model industrial school on his estate near Bordeaux, leaving Sears's son in charge at Silkville. Eight years later the old man donated the property to the Odd Fellows, and the last, longest-lived, and certainly the most paternalistic Fourier-inspired community in the United States joined its predecessors as a dim memory in the minds of later utopians.

The second important example of Gilded Age communitarianism was actually a handful of experiments founded by the remarkable printer Alcander Longley. At the North American Phalanx in 1853–54 he had been disillusioned by the individualism of Fourier's system: capitalist investment, private property in shares, and allocation of community profits to individuals separated members' "pecuniary interests" and doomed the phalanxes to endless conflict. Association, as Skaneateles community founder John Collins wrote, had been "a great school for communism."[16]

Communism avoided the pitfalls of Association by having members' property and labor owned by the community and used for the general good. In 1867 Longley became a probationer at Etienne Cabet's Icaria experiment in Iowa; though his stay was brief, it apparently solidified his commitment to communistic organization. After Icaria, Longley moved to St. Louis, published *The Communist*, a journal that lasted into the second decade of the twentieth century, and began organizing his own colony on the basis of "mutual assistance, cooperative labor, and common property." At his Reunion Community (1868–70) a handful of members settled into a house on a quarter-section of rich Missouri farmland, then wrangled over marital theories and financial problems before breaking up. Undeterred by this failure, the indefatigible Longley proceeded to found a string of ill-fated Missouri colonies—Friendship (1872–77), Principia (1881?), Mutual Aid (1883–87), and the Altruist Community (1907–10?)—each based on his idea of common property and a "common home," and each plagued by shortages of members and capital. Longley's requirement that entrants surrender claims to present and future property—his alternative to what he saw as Fourier's capitalist bias—alienated middle-class supporters of communitarianism and attracted few prospects. His colonies and newspaper were testimony, however, to the amazing persistence not just of one man but of the communitarian idea.[17]

The Union Colony (1870–72), the third postbellum attempt, modified Fourierist arrangements in the opposite direction from Longley's projects, toward private households and economic individualism. On the dry plains of eastern Colorado hundreds of colonists came in a span of two years to build the town of Greeley, which eventually became a thriving farming, cattle-raising, and university center. At Greeley the key problem was not to recruit enough members but rather to maintain a measure of communitarian distinctiveness from nearby settlements and indeed from American society generally. Because the colony made even greater concessions to individualism than had the phalanxes of the 1840s, its dispersal and absorption into the surrounding society was even more rapid.[18]

Greeley was the brainchild of Nathan C. Meeker, a former Fourierist teacher and journalist who had joined the Trumbull Phalanx with his new bride in 1844. After the Associative movement waned, he became a correspondent for the *New York Tribune*. In 1866 he wrote for the *Tribune* a revealing "postmortem and requiem" for Fourierism based on a visit to the North American Phalanx as well as his Trumbull experience. At both places unhappy colonists had learned how annoying communal housing could be, how disruptive lazy or dishonest members were, and how little the individual under communalism gained from hard work. All these were "things which Fourier had not set down." Meeker decided that to be successful, communities had to avoid extensive "guaranty" provisions, encourage individual initiative, and provide private residences for married couples: "Disaster will attend any attempt at social reform, if the marriage relation is even suspected to be rendered less happy." The Union Colony would follow social and economic conventions yet still encourage cooperation.[19]

On a trip to Utah in 1869 to describe Mormon settlements for *Tribune* readers, Meeker toured Colorado with two land agents and returned with the idea of founding a communitarian settlement there. "A Western Colony," published in the *Tribune* at the year's end, drew an immediate response; within a few months five hundred colonists were pitching tents and building houses at the site chosen by their committee. The settlement, named after Meeker's mentor and enthusiastic backer, was based on an individualist version of Fourierism that resembled Mormon society without its religious bond. Like the Mormons, Greeley residents were required to sign a temperance pledge; they purchased the site collectively (funds were accrued through a colony membership fee) and undertook impressive irrigation, fencing, and tree-planting projects. Money from the sale of town lots supported schools and a public library.[20] In other respects, however, Greeley was closer to typical Great Plains settlements. It was laid out in the familiar speculative grid plan with a parklike central square; members bought individual lots and erected private homes; and community leaders advertised for hotels, businesses, and churches.

The most serious problem with this mixture of individualism and community was Meeker's belief that cooperative institutions should evolve naturally among the colonists. While luring private businesses through subsidies, he and the community's leaders did nothing to foster or support such efforts as the Lyceum, the Farmers' Club, and the Cooperative Stock and Dairy Association, which quickly withered away. In reaction to his phalanx experience, Meeker had become obsessed with the single-family home as the colonists' "highest ambition" and constructed his own substantial adobe house as a conspicuous model near the town square. His insistence on returning to the "isolated household" and his support for private enterprise undermined his colonists' fragile cooperative efforts. Once the fencing and irrigation projects proved too costly for the colony's resources and were abandoned, Greeley quickly lost its communal flavor. In July 1871 land sales were opened to the general public, and the ensuing population growth rapidly turned an intentional community into a frontier boomtown.[21] Thus, cooperative institutions became simply an instrument to expedite frontier settlement.

Meeker and Horace Greeley had hoped the colony would be a model for other cooperative towns (its official name was "Union Colony No. 1") and railroad land agents did in fact hire some Union colonists to launch new settlements. But only a few of these had cooperative features, and within a few years Greeley's own diluted version of Fourierism disappeared, leaving it "an average American town with a single idealistic episode in its early history."[22] Insofar as the Union Colony was an exaggerated version of the phalanxes' compromise with American individualism, its "success" was an ironic but all-too-appropriate postscript to the failure of Fourierist communitarianism.

Associationists and the Post–Civil War Labor Movement

By the end of the Civil War the workingmen's movement of the northeastern states was once again a formidable force. The critique of wage slavery, muted during the sectional controversy, resurfaced as craftsmen and factory workers linked protests against their conditions with the Radical Republican movement to eliminate oppression in the South. Associationist predictions that the bloody extinction of chattel slavery was simply "clearing the ground" for the peaceful destruction of the wage system suddenly appeared prescient. Prewar agitators such as Wendell Phillips, who had denounced the subordination of slaves and championed the cause of "honest industry," made an easy transition into labor reform.[23] For the Fourierists it was a case of renewing the old struggle. Once again utopian socialists, some of them veterans of antebellum labor campaigns, allied themselves with labor-reform associations, trade unions, and labor parties and came together in omnibus conventions akin to the National Industrial Congresses of the 1840s. For three decades after the war the course of the labor movement remained unsettled, with various voices advocating collective bargaining, legislative action to shorten the workday, financial reform, producers' cooperatives, free homesteads, or even revolutionary violence. Amid the confusion several former Fourierists remained active, their efforts usually aimed at steering labor organizations not toward the phalanx but into cooperative schemes to combat industrial capitalism with ever widening circles of associated workers.

Though cooperatives were their ultimate goal, the exact form of Fourierist agitation varied with the waxing and waning of worker interest in different panaceas. When greenbacks were the talk of labor conventions and parties, the Fourierists promoted their interests through currency reform. Associationist discussion of the issue had arisen in the late 1840s and centered on mutual banking schemes, government funding of worker cooperatives, and the gradual elimination of the interest due to capitalists. Not until the Civil War had drained the Union's coffers did the currency issue become a vital national issue, however. For more than a decade after the war the national currency was a hotly contested political topic, and the greenback crusade became an important plank in the labor movement's platform. Responding to recession and the failure of strikes, union leaders and labor reformers turned increasingly to the idea of interest-free greenbacks issued by the government and convertible to Treasury bonds. Many believed that high interest caused low wages and concentrated wealth in the hands of money lenders and bondholders. Greenbacks had the potential to remove financial middlemen and create a fairer bargain between employer and employee. In 1867 the National Labor Union endorsed interest-free greenbacks, leader William Sylvis declaring that successful greenback reform could "do away with the necessity of trades-unions entirely." In the emotional climate of Gilded Age politics, labor greenbackism, with its promise to resolve class tensions peacefully, took on the utopian flavor of a panacea.[24]

Thus, it was hardly surprising that ex-Fourierists became involved. Brisbane wrote a currency reform pamphlet at the outset of the Civil War and discussed it with E. G. Spaulding, the Buffalo banker-congressman who later sponsored the Legal Tender Act making greenbacks legitimate currency. Even Victor Considerant, before returning to Paris from his Texas ranch, drew up a currency proposal which he sent to President-elect Ulysses S. Grant at the end of 1868 and which Brisbane published and distributed in New York. In the late 1860s and 1870s Brisbane continued to publish his currency ideas in newspaper articles, eventually endorsing the greenback laborites' call for a convertible, interest-free fiat currency. On this same basis Fourierist veterans Charles Sears and John Drew of the North American Phalanx and Thomas Durant (by this time a prominent lawyer in Washington) played enthusiastic supporting roles in the Greenback party's campaigns of the late 1870s.[25]

Most Fourierist versions of currency schemes reflected the Associationist program of overturning wage slavery and replacing it with cooperative production. They updated Proudhon's idea that the government should lend money directly to workers' enterprises at negligible interest rates, and included schemes for government warehousing or other ways for farmers and workers to exchange products without depending on capitalist merchants or financial middlemen.[26] But the Fourierists' concern to link currency reform to more fundamental causes than antimonopoly and higher wages never became the central thrust of the Gilded Age greenback movement.

In the early 1870s, during a period of exceptional fluidity among worker organizations caused by a lull in the greenback crusade, the demise of the National Labor Union, the Liberal Republican insurgency, and finally the Panic of 1873, Fourierist influence in the labor-movement peaked with the formation of several omnibus labor-reform associations.

Ex-Fourierists were active in the Eight-Hour Leagues, which brought craftsmen, legislators, and reformers together in suppport of a shorter workday.[27] A less focused group, the New England Labor Reform League—which gathered trade unions, eight-hour advocates, the Knights of St. Crispin, and reform associations into an uneasy coalition—numbered Brisbane, Durant, William Henry Channing and Brook Farm's John Orvis among its guiding spirits. Brisbane and Orvis were vice-presidents of its national federation, the American Labor Reform League, formed in 1871.[28] For a time it even appeared that Karl Marx's "First International," the International Workingmen's Association (1864–76), might become a platform from which Fourierists could influence the labor movement. In the early 1870s Stephen Pearl Andrews became a prominent voice, along with flamboyant feminists Victoria Woodhull and Tennessee Claflin, in the infamous American Section 12 of the IWA. At its conventions and in *Woodhull and Claflin's Weekly*, the only American journal attached to the International, these sensation-mongering radicals publicized such causes as free love, woman suffrage, labor cooperatives, and language reform side by side with IWA news before being expelled by orthodox factions in 1872. Quite apart from Woodhull and Claflin, however, former Fourierists Orvis and Durant used American sections of the International to push for currency reform and worker cooperatives.[29]

It was the promotion of cooperatives, not greenbacks or broad labor coalitions, that proved to be Fourierism's most important role in the Gilded Age labor movement. John Orvis's long and dedicated career shows how Fourierists kept alive the vision of a network of producer and consumer cooperatives for the next generation.[30] His involvement was a direct extension of his support for Protective Unions in the late 1840s. After the collapse of communal experiments, he recalled in 1890, "socialism went down among the working classes, to whom it was a necessity; and has from that time been educating them into methods for its gradual application to the exigencies of their conditions."[31] During the Civil War Orvis studied the Rochdale system and other cooperatives at first hand in England and on his return resumed his agitation for Protective Unions. In the 1870s he championed consumer and producer cooperatives simultaneously, meeting some success when the depression of the mid-1870s once again turned workers toward self-help schemes. In 1874 Orvis helped found the Sovereigns of Industry, recruiting the Brook Farm printer Jonathan Butterfield as a fellow officer. For two years Orvis was employed as the society's national lecturer, inspiring the establishment of nearly fifty cooperative stores among members of the order, mainly in New England. In his effort to outflank the wage system with cooperative workshops, Orvis became president of the New England Reform League in 1873; a decade later he was an officer of District Assembly 30 of the Knights of Labor. There, he and other labor reformers enrolled over five thousand shoe workers, printers, and other "honest producers" under the banner of the eight-hour day and producer cooperatives—until Haymarket, the railroad strikes, and mayoral defeats in 1886 permanently wrecked the Knights' organization. Orvis's last years were spent as a member of Boston's Bellamyite Nationalist Club.[32] His plan to replace wage slavery with worker-owned cooperatives, not the phalanx, was the Fourierists' most important legacy to the labor movement.

The communitarian idea died a very slow death, however. In the non-Fourierist forms of the "cooperative commonwealth" and socialist worker colonies, the notion of building frontier enclaves based on true social relations contined to entice worker organizations to the end of the century, especially after strikes failed, unions were broken, or political action proved fruitless. Coalitions of radical workers, socialists, and Social Gospel advocates undertook at least a dozen community experiments in California, Washington, and the Appalachian South in the 1880s and 1890s. The main inspiration for such worker colonization came from Laurence Gronlund's *Cooperative Commonwealth* (1885) and Edward Bellamy's *Looking Backward* (1888).[33] But the link between antebellum Fourierism and later socialist communitarianism is suggested by the career of William H. Muller of Pennsylvania, a Fourierist writer of the 1840s who joined Julius Wayland's socialist colony at Ruskin, Tennessee, in the 1890s; and by the work of Richard J. Hinton, a Fourierist-tinged advocate of cooperatives who became chief of the colonization commission for Eugene Debs's Social Democracy of America.[34] Not until Debs and Victor Berger led their faction out of the colonizer-dominated Social Democracy in 1898 to form the purely political Social Democratic Party did the communitarian tradition effectively disappear from American socialism.[35]

Feminism and the "Grand Domestic Revolution"

Before it expired, Fourierism also played a significant role in the development of American feminism. The Associationist agitation of the 1840s highlighted two feminist issues: economic independence and sexual freedom. The first was the special mission of the phalanx, which was meant to liberate women from the domestic drudgery and financial bondage of the "isolated household." The second was raised without official sanction by sexual radicals such as the Nicholses and Marx Lazarus, who sought to replace legalized monogamy with woman's freedom to choose—or reject—amorous partners at will. Though neither goal was realized, these two strands of Fourierism helped give birth to American feminism in the 1850s and continued to influence woman's rights advocates in the second half of the century.

The association of Fourierist free love with radical feminism, initiated by Mary Nichols and Stephen Pearl Andrews in the 1850s, persisted into the Gilded Age. In 1870 Andrews teamed with Victoria Woodhull and her sister Tennessee Claflin to promote a wide platform of radical mea-

sures, the most notorious making free love a feminist issue. With Andrews's backing, the sensation-mongering Woodhull argued before the
U.S. Senate that women already had the vote, launched her bold campaign for president, and proclaimed the "inalienable constitutional right
to love whom I may, to love as long or as short a period as I can, to
change that love every day if I please!"[36] Thanks to their agitation, not
until the 1880s were the socialist movement on the one hand and the
woman suffrage campaign on the other able to dissociate themselves
plausibly from Fourierist-tinged free love.

As early as 1850, however, the Associationist movement sent more
conventional adherents into the mainstream women's rights movement.
Their involvement suggests the ways in which the communitarian experience had promoted feminist sentiments. Among the signers of the "call"
to the Woman's Rights Convention of 1850 at Worcester, Massachusetts,
were fourteen Fourierist veterans, including Brook Farm associates Mary
Bullard, Mary Lincoln Cabot, William Henry Channing, and Anna Parsons; most of the fourteen attended, and Channing and Parsons served
on committees.[37] Channing gave a major speech at the 1851 convention
in which he advocated liberalized divorce laws and Associative clubs for
young women migrating to the cities. To publicize the convention, in
September 1851 he and twenty women of the North American Phalanx
organized a communitywide discussion of "the social position of
woman."[38]

Conversely, without in any way endorsing free love, women's rights
advocates were drawn to Fourier's critique of the isolated household
and his vision of an enlarged sphere for women. Paulina Wright Davis,
feminist editor of *The Una,* promoted "the Science of Association" in the
mid-1850s. Davis and her husband signed the prospectus of the Raritan
Bay Union, though they apparently did not join.[39] The abolitionist and
feminist Grimké sisters, who hoped to relieve their "burdens of farming
and housekeeping" while agitating for reform, took a suite of six rooms
at the Raritan Bay phalanstery for the Weld-Grimké family. After a year
they were divided over Association. "If there are any blessings in Unitary
Life," the stern Sarah wrote to a friend, "I have thus far failed to realize
them." Expenses were higher than anticipated; she missed private family
meals; and the less cultured members offended her sensibilities. The
spunkier and more egalitarian Angelina, on the other hand, believed
that they were building a better future.[40]

The founder of the Woman's Rights Conventions was herself attracted
by the Fourierists' program of freeing women from the isolated household. Elizabeth Cady Stanton spent two days at Brook Farm in 1843,
finding it "a charming family" where men and women lived on a basis of
relative equality. Five years later, as she struggled with the burdens of
child rearing, house keeping, and loneliness in upstate New York, Stanton claimed she "now fully understood the practical difficulties that
women had to contend with in the isolated household. . . . Fourier's

phalansterie community life and co-operative households had a new significance for me."[41] Fourierism helped crystallize her discontent and led directly to her calling the first Woman's Rights Convention at Seneca Falls that year. Its famous "Declaration of Sentiments" was grounded far more in the desire to broaden woman's social sphere and extend her economic rights—aims the Fourierist movement had sought—than in the demand for the ballot, and for a time the Fourierist idea of "associated families" seemed to Stanton an attractive remedy for both her personal hardships and women's plight in general. Along with Lucy Stone, Stanton visited the North American Phalanx, and in 1852 she came very close to joining the Raritan Bay Union. "All our talk about woman's rights is mere moonshine," she told Paulina Davis, "so long as we are bound by the present social system. . . . Woman must ever be sacrificed in the isolated household." She looked longingly upon Association as "a truer mode of life" and was "resolved" to join the Raritan Bay community. Only the inability to buy enough shares of community stock and the opposition of her husband, who had "a horror of all associations of the kind proposed," prevented her from going, though she enrolled two sons in the school there.[42]

In her old age Stanton published a volume of memoirs that featured a Fourierist epigraph on the title page: "Social science affirms that woman's place in society marks the level of civilization."[43] By that time she had narrowed her feminist efforts primarily to legal rights and the campaign for suffrage, but other feminists brought the Fourierists' crusade against the isolated household into the second half of the century. The two lingering carriers of Fourierist influence—the free-love feminists and the more conservative but still independent-minded women's rights advocates—found common ground in the promotion of households grouped together to free women for nondomestic activities. The idea of creating group living arrangements that would socialize domestic work became the Associationists' most important legacy to the feminists.

In 1858 Stephen Pearl Andrews formed his Unitary Household in a Stuyvesant Street brownstone in New York City. About twenty members initially joined this nonprofit cooperative boarding-house, which lasted two years and eventually encompassed a hundred residents in three buildings. The Unitary Household was a scaled-down, semi-Fourierist, urban version of the phalanstery depicted in the huge painting in its dining hall. Families and individuals paid rent for private suites plus a share of the costs of common parlors, dining rooms, nurseries, and other group facilities. Reform lectures and refined "dance-receptions" enlivened evenings for young professional residents, who included Marx Edgeworth Lazarus and the poet Edmund Clarence Stedman. With cooking and domestic work performed by a crew of hired workers rather than the members, the experiment functioned as a transitional organization between the Fourierist "Combined Household" of the 1840s and the many apartment hotels built in the last quarter of the century. Living inexpensively yet enjoying the pleasures of Association, Andrews's Fourierist circle, according to a sympathetic *New York Times* reporter, had introduced into the "heart of New York, without noise or bluster, a successful enterprise based on Practical Socialism."[44]

When Andrews joined forces with Victoria Woodhull in the 1870s, the two vigorously promoted the idea of urban residential hotels with common dining and social rooms and cooperative nurseries. Woodhull tied women's sexual and economic freedom to "the establishment of cooperative homes" in suburban settings, and "for our cities, the conversion of innumerable huts into immense hotels, as residences." Andrews's tract *The Baby World*, reprinted in *Woodhull and Claflin's Weekly* in 1871, predicted a "grand Domestic Revolution" to be ushered in by cooperative apartment hotels housing two hundred residents and offering scientific day care for children.[45]

Another free-love feminist who proposed cooperative living was directly influenced by Fourierism. Marie Howland, born Marie Stevens, found in Fourierist ideas and experiments the inspiration for a lifetime devoted to feminism and communitarianism. A bright and unconventional young teacher in New York City in the 1850s, she became a friend of Brisbane, a frequent visitor to Andrews's free-thinkers' "Club," and a boarder at the Unitary Household, where she met her second husband, Edward Howland. During their frequent European travels in the 1860s, the Howlands visited Jean-Baptiste-André Godin's Familistère at Guise, the most elaborate and successful Fourierist attempt to develop a cooperative industrial community. Begun in 1859, the Familistère centered on a flourishing ironworks operation employing approximately 350 workers whose families lived in private apartments in a huge "social palace" modeled on Fourier's phalanstery. Residents shopped at cooperative stores, ate in cooperative restaurants and cafes, kept their children in carefully designed day nurseries, and shared the community's profits. Marie, who as a young woman had worked in the Lowell mills, was entranced by this Fourierist alternative to the capitalist factory town. After her return to the United States in the late 1860s, she and Edward spent the next two decades promoting Godin's ideas. In 1872 Edward described the Familistère for *Harper's Monthly* as a model Fourierist plan for joining labor and capital harmoniously and profitably. Two years later Marie published the only widely discussed Fourierist novel of the century. The hero of *Papa's Own Girl* establishes a Social Palace in New England where ample apartments satisfy male desires for a private home, while communal kitchens, nurseries, and schools liberate women from domestic drudgery. Both Howlands tried to promote this dream—specifically its communal dwellings, cooperative facilities, and the Fourierist organization of labor in series—in Albert K. Owen's ill-fated colony of Topolobampo in Mexico during the 1880s. After Edward died in 1890, Marie moved to the single-tax community of Fairhope in Alabama; her crusade for feminism, communal work, and cooperative households eventually spanned sixty years and four experiments. Charismatic, un-Victorian, and fiercely committed to women's independence through cooperative communities, Marie Howland came closer than any other Associationist woman to Fourier's ideal.[46]

It was not just sexual reformers such as Andrews and Howland who promoted cooperative living as an alternative to the isolated household; more conventional feminists also endorsed such projects, though detaching them from free-love connotations. Among these women too there were connections to the antebellum communitarians. Melusina Fay Peirce was a respectable Harvard faculty wife who attached the label "cooperative housekeeping" to groups of women who performed all their domestic work collectively—and charged their husbands for it. Peirce's Cambridge Cooperative Housing Society (1869–71) attracted families that had been connected to Brook Farm and Oneida, and her plan was publicized in Greeley's *Tribune* by Nathan Meeker. Charles Codman, who had been a teenager at Brook Farm, proposed cooperative kitchens as a worthy cause to the New England Women's Suffrage Association.[47] Elizabeth Cady Stanton published several articles praising such experiments in 1868–69, and thirty years later she tried to put cooperative housekeeping on the agenda of the National American Woman Suffrage Association convention. Even the late nineteenth-century social settlement movement, whose houses combined resident quarters with common rooms, nurseries, and collective cooking and cleaning facilities, reflected the Fourieristic ideal of cooperative living. It was no coincidence that at the first and most famous American settlement, Jane Addams's Hull House, the very first resident was the elderly Ora Gannett Sedgwick, who had been a student at Brook Farm, and that the men's boarding cooperative was named the Phalanx Club.[48]

Outside the context of feminism, the idea of cooperative residences appealed to many as a practical solution to the shortage of affordable housing for urban families. In the 1880s the New York architect Philip G. Hubert combined the apartment hotel concept with the idea of cooperative ownership through a joint-stock scheme. Called "Hubert Home Clubs," his projects featured large duplex units housing middle-class families and their servants, all using a central parlor and cleaning facilities. At least eight such clubs were successfully built and occupied in New York City. Hubert's ties to Fourierism were direct and familial, since his father, Colombe Gengembre, had been the architect at the French phalanstery of Condé-sur-Vesgre in 1832 and, after migrating to Ohio, a supporter of the American movement in the early 1850s.[49] But in Hubert's work the phalanstery had evolved almost to the point of disappearing. As Fourier's plan became transmuted into a group residence for the urban middle class, the crucial goals of sharing household work and uniting all social classes were left aside. Apartment hotels and housing co-ops inspired late nineteenth-century feminists and utopian novelists with the revolutionary potential of apartment dwellings. Like Fourier, they tended to believe that urban multifamily residences represented the next stage of social evolution toward "Guarantism" or increased cooperation.[50] But the "grand domestic revolution" never materialized. Utopian visionaries not only ignored the fact that many such projects involved no radical domestic reform and housed only the well-to-do; they also badly underestimated the hold of individualism on the capitalist economy and American cultural ideals. In the next eighty years the cooperative household idea was overwhelmed by the promotion of suburbs, the miniaturization of laborsaving devices, and the persistence of the single-family ideal. Only in the 1970s would feminists revive these plans—indeed, unearth a whole tradition of "material feminism," as Dolores Hayden has labeled it—and argue for a new domestic economy and architecture more reflective of women's aspirations than the typical family residence.[51]

Looking Forward: Olmsted, the ASSA, and Bellamy

Among the most influential aspects of Fourierism for succeeding generations of reformers was its emphasis upon planning and design. Fourier's unitary dwelling showed the way toward an architecture that would take full advantage of technological advances as well as economies of scale, yet still express social values. Especially important was the way the phalanstery was intended to preserve individual and family privacy while also promoting free socializing of a diverse population. Without embracing the phalanstery itself, later architects reflected Fourierist design principles in their work. From model farms in Europe to collective workers' housing in the Familistère at Guise, from the Oneida Community's Mansion House to Le Corbusier's Unité d'Habitation in this century, architectural visionaries and social reformers adopted Fourierist conceptions to shape group living and working environments.[52] In a less specific way, the phalanx's orderly blending of urban and rural forms and its provision for generous public spaces left an imprint upon urban planning in Europe and America.

The work of America's premier landscape architect and park designer, Frederick Law Olmsted, shows Fourierism's subtle influence on later shapers of the urban environment. As a gentleman farmer outside New York City, Olmsted became acquainted with Fourierist ideas in the 1840s through his friends Greeley, Godwin, and Marcus Spring. On his tour of English farms and cities in 1850, he met the British Fourierist Hugh Doherty, and after his return he stepped up contacts with the Associationist movement. In 1852 he penned a series of appreciative articles on the North American Phalanx, based on visits there, praising its "advantages of cooperation of labor," "united household of families," and diffusion of "moral . . . and aesthetic culture." Olmsted was a frequent guest at Spring's Raritan Bay Union and advised Victor Considerant on the location of his Texas colony. Though he never joined a phalanx or

Fourierist club, Olmsted provided warm public testimonials to the Associationist movement.[53]

Long after Fourierism disappeared as a distinguishable movement,
Olmsted translated some of its key ideals into the design of America's
largest and most important public parks.[54] In New York's Central Park
and elsewhere, Olmsted's plans reflected the Fourierist ideal of a harmonious counterpoint of city and country environments; the Fourierists'
belief in varied group recreation as a basic human need; and their conviction that society had a duty to provide public facilities for communal
activities. As an outdoor analogue to the phalanstery, the municipal
park was a public meeting ground where social classes mingled and a
communal spirit replaced selfish individualism. In 1870, in his most
concise statement of the social ideal of city planning, Olmsted described
New York's Central Park and Brooklyn's Prospect Park as "the only
places in those . . . cities where . . . you will find a body of Christians
coming together, . . . all classes largely represented, with a common
purpose, not at all intellectual, competitive with none, disposing to jealousy or spiritual or intellectual pride toward none, each individual adding
by his mere presence to the pleasure of all others, all helping to the
greater happiness of each." Like public transit, sewers, and gas and water
works, municipal parks demonstrated that city life was evolving from
wasteful individualism toward efficient collective control of resources
and technology.[55] Olmsted found in antebellum Fourierism an ideal of
social interdependence and a theory of historical development to give
landscape architecture its largest meaning. Yet because his parks were
meant to mitigate the effects of urban fragmentation and competition
rather than overturn the society that produced them, they exemplified
the evolution of utopian ideals into institutional reform in the late nineteenth century.

In this respect Olmsted's projects paralleled the civil service crusade
championed by ex–Brook Farmer George W. Curtis and especially the
reformist social science promoted by the American Social Science Association.[56] Founded in 1865 by the Massachusetts humanitarian reformer
Frank Sanborn, the ASSA was frankly philanthropic, intended to guide
social development scientifically to harmony and equilibrium. Its leadership was composed mainly of influential New England educators, writers,
and businessmen who believed that social questions were solvable
through scientific inquiry; they organized investigations in four areas—
education, health, economy, and jurisprudence—and made recommen-
dations to policymakers. Behind their promotion of social science lay the
urge to establish an impartial guide to "uplifting" the working classes
and managing a conflict-free capitalist society. For a brief time Albert
Brisbane was active in the New York City branch of the ASSA, into which
he and Osborne Macdaniel, E. P. Grant, and John Orvis attempted to
inject Fourierist social science. But their efforts failed, and the New York
branch quickly evaporated.[57]

The ASSA's brand of social science owed more to Herbert Spencer and Auguste Comte than to Fourier, and its policy efforts were directed at the un-Fourierist causes of free trade, civil service reform, and hard money. Nevertheless, its program struck a responsive chord among gentlemen reformers who had been touched by antebellum utopianism. Curtis was president of the organization for a time; Olmsted presented his planning philosophy before it; and ex-Associationist Walter Channing was active in its Health Department.[58] The ASSA played an important transitional role in the professionalization of social science and the evolution of the concept from utopian blueprints to a reformist human engineering that stressed social interdependence and cooperation. Through men like Olmsted, Curtis, and Channing, faint echoes of Fourierism passed into "Mugwump" reform and were eventually transmitted, albeit in forms antebellum Fourierists would hardly have recognized, into the Progressive movement of the next generation.

Before this evolution was complete, there was one final revival of Fourierist ideals. The apex of utopian planning—and the endpoint of direct Fourierist influence upon later visionaries—came with the publication in 1888 of Edward Bellamy's novel *Looking Backward*. With his fictional solution to the crisis of American industrial capitalism, Bellamy achieved a level of popularity surpassing the Fourierist craze of the 1840s.[59] When the book's hero, Julian West, wakes up in Boston in the year 2000 after sleeping for more than a century, he encounters a city peacefully transformed into a brave new socialist world of efficiency, abundance, and equality but otherwise reassuringly familiar. In *Looking Backward's* odd mixture of technological advance and cultural conservatism, Fourierist elements were absorbed into a new synthesis, one that decisively superseded communitarianism and framed American dissenters' discussions for the next generation.

As a young man, Bellamy had been quite familiar with Fourierism. For eight months in 1871 and 1872—the height of the postbellum Fourierist revival—he began a journalistic career in New York City. At the *Evening Post*, where he did a brief stint, he probably met Parke Godwin, still intermittently on the editorial staff. It *is* known that Bellamy was introduced by his brother Frederick to Albert Brisbane, whose theories, according to Frederick, "interested him deeply." Brisbane's son reported that the aging Fourierist "closeted himself for long sessions" with the budding socialist.[60] Later, Bellamy studied the history of antebellum communitarianism, which he considered "one of the most significant as well as most picturesque chapters of American history." He called his Nationalist program the heir of "the Brook Farm Colony and a score of phalansteries" that were *Looking Backward's* "precursors" in spirit if not in exact form.[61]

Several material features of Bellamy's Boston of 2000 were clear adaptations of Fourierist ideas and experiences. Probably the most obvious was the "industrial army," which Fourier had conceived as a vast mobile assemblage of workers committed to projects of construction rather than destruction. Bellamy, inspired by the Civil War and Prussian militarism, expanded the army to include the entire workforce, into which all citizens were drafted. His use of Fourier's term; the conviction that military organization could be harnessed for constructive purposes; the fascination with ceremony and parades; the belief that a proper job could be found for all human aptitudes; the idea of establishing an equilibrium between jobs and job seekers by adjusting work conditions to equalize "attractions"; reliance upon rivalry or "emulation" as a work incentive— all these reflect the influence of Fourier's "army" on Bellamy's utopia. Other borrowings worked their way down to architectural and technological details, such as Fourier's glass-covered street galleries and Brisbane's system of transport through pneumatic tubes.[62]

Even more important, the overall conception of Bellamy's socialism as expressed in *Looking Backward* bore the unmistakable mark of Fourierism. Like the Fourierists, Bellamy planned social reconstruction as the peaceful and voluntary culmination of historical change. In Fourier's communitarian scenario the phalanx provided an abrupt leap to Harmony; yet in developing a historical theory to validate the phalanx, Fourier depicted the gradual evolution of society through stages that prefigure Bellamy's. His competitive Civilization corresponds to Bellamy's era before "the concentration of capital into greater masses." Then, just as Fourier foresaw a new feudalism emerging in the expansion of corporations, banks, and other "subversive" associations, Bellamy described his America as a time of growing popular "servitude" to pools and trusts. The socialist utopia was only one evolutionary step away, for by taking over the machinery of such combinations, the people eliminated oppression while reaping the rewards of technology and association.[63] Following logically and inevitably from preceding social developments, Nationalism corresponded to the evolutionary version of Fourierism. Other aspects of Bellamy's vision that echoed Fourierist conceptions were his fascination with the practical economies of communal organization and his attempt to blend privacy and collectivism in socialist living arrangements.

The influence of the Fourierists penetrated even to the soul of Bellamy's socialism, as evidenced in his seminal essay "The Religion of Solidarity" (1874), which John L. Thomas has called "the psychological substructure" upon which *Looking Backward* was built.[64] Parallels between this essay and the philosophy of Pierre Leroux, who introduced the word "solidarity" to the socialist vocabulary and whose metaphysics was championed by the antebellum Fourierists, seem too close to be accidental.[65] Both Bellamy and Leroux began with human nature's split between individualistic and universal impulses. Both condemned individualism as the root cause of human problems, insisting that the key to human happiness lay in a mystical bond of fraternal love linking the individual with the species. So long as the individual was hindered from attaining "communion" (Leroux) or "merging" with humanity (Bellamy), his or her life would be one of tragic solitude, a condition both writers described through the metaphor of a prison. Heightened consciousness of our link to the universal could be glimpsed in fleeting, near-mystical experiences such as spiritual affinities (Bellamy) or intimations of immortality through reincarnation (Leroux), but future society would embody solidarity in daily relations animated by selflessness and sympathy. Though Bellamy's perspective is less theological than Leroux's, parallel arguments and the mutual use of "solidarity" to describe that quasi-religious unity between individual and humanity which prefigures and inspires the socialistic ideal, mark a strong connection between two generations of romantic socialist idealism. Here again Albert Brisbane may have been the main link between antebellum and postbellum utopians, for his own writings of the period 1870–72 centered on human longings for unity with "the Cosmic universe" and proclaimed that in the future "the whole life of Man will become religious." At the very time he met Bellamy, Brisbane was recommending Leroux's theories to his Fourierist associates.[66]

There were, of course, major differences between Bellamy's utopia and the Fourierists'. Two are particularly important for the light they shed on the popularity of *Looking Backward* and the fading relevance of Fourierism in the Victorian era. Fourier's utopia, with its passional psychology and its attack on bourgeois mores, was as much a program of cultural radicalism as of economic reform. In their ever changing rounds of work, play, and love, Harmonians would develop erotic and sociable impulses to a degree unimaginable under the repressions of Civilization. Though the official Associationist movement repudiated Fourier's free-love theories, there remained an air of spontaneity, experiment, even disreputability about the phalanxes; especially to younger antebellum radicals, utopian socialism implied a new lifestyle as well as a revamped economy. *Looking Backward* divorces socialism from this kind of cultural radicalism. Compared with the rich social life of Harmony, the world of Boston in the year 2000 is conservative, even insipid. Despite his intention to demonstrate solidarity, Bellamy retained much of the older ethic of individualism. If his Dr. Leete is representative, Bellamy's typical utopian citizen is remote and self-contained. Neighborhood clubhouses are hinted at and dining halls glimpsed in the novel, yet no social relationships—or any other interchanges—are depicted outside the small family circle. Antebellum communitarians envisoned utopians gathered almost daily in festive operas, parades, theatrical and religious rituals; Bellamy's Bostonians have radio concerts and church services piped into individual homes. Just as culture becomes connoisseurship, so too *Looking Backward* divorces production (in the industrial army) from consumption (through catalogue stores) and separates years of conscripted work from the freedom of leisure after age forty five. This impersonal and compartmentalized existence embodies Victorian middle-class privatism and consumerism far more than it reflects the antebellum communitarians' dream of a vital and integrated way of life.[67]

Bellamy's version of home life in the year 2000 is an extreme version of what sociologists later called cultural lag. Somehow, a century of drastic political, economic, and technological evolution has left conventional middle-class mores intact. Despite abolishing individual housework, the new society retains Victorian ideals of familism and domesticity. Family members have the alternative of domestic servants and the private table, spend nearly all their time in their quarters, and move about discreetly and converse politely without intense emotions, whether of sorrow or joy. The genteel Dr. Leete, his admirably domestic daughter Edith, and their curiously dispassionate world provide a diametric opposite to the "passional attraction" of the Fourierists' "combined household." Bellamy deliberately set out to make socialism respectable in America and to separate it from subversive cultural ideas, including foreign theories and "all manner of sexual novelties."[68] The popular success of his utopian vision was a measure of his achievement, but his depiction also indicated the distance he had traveled from the counterculture of his Fourierist predecessors.

Bellamy's Bostonians are calm and detached in part because a huge and impersonal bureaucracy has taken over their lives. Bellamy's second key divergence from Fourierists was his conviction that socialism was a matter of government ownership and the centralized direction of economic life, a condition to be achieved through political action. Its national focus and reliance upon legislation set Bellamy's brand of utopianism dramatically apart from the communitarian point of view. To be sure, a few aging ex-Fourierists showed up at Nationalist meetings, and Nationalist clubs in California and elsewhere incubated short-lived cooperative colonies.[69] But the utopia of Looking Backward arrived through a political takeover of national business and financial institutions. The collective ownership of industrial enterprises through government, not their replacement by novel voluntary associations, was the socialist strategy appropriate to the industrial age. Bellamy explicitly repudiated the communitarian approach as obsolete. In the context of an entrenched large-scale, urban-industrial society, utopian colonies seemed escape hatches for true believers rather than plausible models for a chain-reaction overhaul of social relations: "We nationalists are not trying to work out our individual salvation, but the weal of all. . . . A slight amendment in the condition of the mass of men is preferable to elysium attained by the few."[70]

Bellamy's centralized, bureaucratic polity—the state as "the Great Trust"—would have horrified antebellum communitarians, but it appeared reasonable in the late nineteenth century. To those who survived the nationalizing experience of the Civil War and witnessed the concentration of capitalists and laborers into contending national organizations, it seemed logical that popular government would expand to a corresponding dimension to save the republic from the specter of "plutocracy" or anarchy. It was Bellamy's call for action on a national scale rather than the Fourierists' decentralized communitarianism which set the agenda for the next generations of American radicals. As the legislative program implied in *Looking Backward* inspired the varied proposals of Populists, Progressives, and Socialists, the Fourierists' communitarian legacy finally passed into oblivion.

Appendix: Tables, Figures, Maps

Table 1. Fourierist phalanxes in the United States

Name and location	Acreage	Members*	Dates
1. Brook Farm, West Roxbury, Mass.	208	90	1841–47
2. Social Reform Unity, Pike Co., Pa.	2,000	20–30	1842–43
3. Jefferson County Industrial Association, Cold Creek, Jefferson Co., N.Y.	600	400	1843–44
4. Sylvania Association, Darlingville (now Greeley), Pike Co., Pa.	2,394	145	1843–44
5. Morehouse Union, Piseco, Hamilton Co., N.Y.	300	?	1843–44
6. North American Phalanx, Monmouth Co., N.J.	673	120	1843–55
7. LaGrange Phalanx, LaGrange Co., Ind.	1,045	150	1843–47
8. Clarkson Association (orig. Western New York Industrial Association; reorg., Port Richmond Phalanx), Clarkson Township, Monroe Co., N.Y.	1,460	420	1844–45
9. Bloomfield Union Association, North Bloomfield, N.Y.	750	148	1844–46
10. Ohio Phalanx, Belmont Co., Ohio	2,200	100	1844–45
11. Leraysville Phalanx, Le Raysville, Bradford Co., Pa.	600	40	1844–45
12. Alphadelphia Association, Kalamazoo Co., Mich.	2,814	225	1844–47
13. Sodus Bay Phalanx, Wayne Co., N.Y.	1,400	260	1844–46
14. Mixville Association, Mixville, Allegany County, N.Y.	?	?	1844–45
15. Trumbull Phalanx, Trumbull Co., Ohio	1,237	250	1844–48, 1849–52
16. Ontario (or Manchester) Union, Ontario Co., N.Y.	284	150	1844–45
17. Clermont Phalanx, Clermont Co., Ohio	1,140	120	1844–46

Table 1. (Continued)

Name and location	Acreage	Members*	Dates
18. Wisconsin Phalanx, Ceresco, Fond du Lac Co., Wis.	1,793	180	1844–50
19. Iowa Pioneer Phalanx, Mahaska Co., Iowa	320	50	1844–45
20. Philadelphia Industrial Association, St. Joseph Co., Ind.	?	70	1845–47
21. Integral Phalanx, Sangamon Co., Ill. (merged with Sangamon Association)	555	95	1845–47
22. Columbian Phalanx, Muskingum Co., Ohio	2,700	150	1845–45
23. Canton Phalanx, Canton Township, Fulton Co., Ill.	c.400	75	1845–45
24. Spring Farm Phalanx, Sheboygan Co., Wis.	c.100	30	1846–49
25. Pigeon River Fourier Colony, Sheboygan Co., Wis.	?	20	1846–47
26. Raritan Bay Union, Middlesex Co., N.J.	268	90	1853–57
27. La Réunion, Dallas Co., Tex.	2,240	350	1855–59
28. Fourier Phalanx, Dearborn Co., Ind.	220	13	1858–58
29. Kansas Co-operative Farm (also called Silkville or Prairie Home Colony), Franklin Co., Kan.	3,200	50	1869–92

Sources: Otohiko Okugawa, "Annotated List of Communal and Utopian Societies," *Dictionary of American Communal and Utopian History,* ed. Robert S. Fogarty (Westport, Conn.: Greenwood Press, 1980), app. A., 173–233; Arthur Bestor, "Checklist of Communitarian Experiments," *Backwoods Utopias: The Sectarian Origins and the Owenite Phase of Communitarian Socialism in America, 1663–1829,* 2d ed. (Philadelphia: University of Pennsylvania Press, 1970), 280–82; A. J. Macdonald Collection, Beinecke Library, Yale University; William A. Hinds *American Communities* Collection, George Arents Research Library, Syracuse University; Arthur Bestor Papers, Illinois Historical Survey, University of Illinois; surviving community records, letters to *The Phalanx* (1843–45) and *The Harbinger* (1845–49), and various secondary sources.

*Maximum in residence at one time.

Table 2. Other phalanx projects

Name and location	Date	Result
Bureau County Phalanx, Bureau County, Ill.	1843	issued prospectus and was granted state charter but apparently never began operations
Ontario Phalanx, Rochester, N.Y.	1843	split into Sodus Bay Phalanx and Clarkson Association
Rochester Industrial Association, Rochester, N.Y.	1844	absorbed into Ontario Union
Rush Industrial Association, Rush, N.Y.	1844	sent delegates to American Industrial Union but never began communal life
Washtenaw Phalanx, Ann Arbor, Mich.	1844	absorbed into Alphadelphia Association
Sangamon Association, Sangamon Co., Ill.	1845	began buildings, then merged with Integral Phalanx
Athens Union, Crawford Co., Pa.	1845	phalanx never materialized
Beverly Association, Beverly, Ohio	1845	absorbed into Columbian Phalanx
Industrial Association of Cleveland, Cleveland, Ohio	1845	phalanx never materialized
Virginia (or Eclectic) Phalanx, Gilmer Co., Va.	1845	issued constitution but never began operations

Sources: See Table 1.

Table 3. Fourier clubs and societies before May 1846

Location and name	Founding date
Maine	
Bangor Fourier Club	1844
Hallowell Fourier Club	1844
Massachusetts	
Fall River Society of Inquiry into the Science of Association	1844
Lowell Fourier Society	1846
New England Fourier Society (Boston)	1844
New York	
Fourienne Society of New York (N.Y.C.)	1838
Fourier Association of the City of New York	1842
Hamilton Fourier Association	1843
Rochester Fourier Society	1843
Seneca Falls Fourier Club	1844
Society of Social Reform and Human Progress (Poughkeepsie)	1843
Syracuse Fourier Club	1843
Pennsylvania	
Philadelphia Social Reform Society	1845
Pittsburgh Fourier Club	1844
Ohio	
Cincinnati Fourier Association	1843
Western Reserve Fourier Society (Cleveland)	1843
Wisconsin	
Southport Fourier Club	1843

Sources: New York Tribune, 1842–43; *The Phalanx;* Arthur Bestor Papers, Illinois Historical Survey, University of Illinois.

Table 4. Affiliated unions of the American Union of Associationists

Location	Dates	Members
Maine		
Bangor	1847–	
New Hampshire		
Manchester	1847–	
Vermont		
Brandon	1846–	20–30
Clarendon	1846–	20–30
Middlebury	1846–	20–30
Pittsford	1846–	20–30
Massachusetts		
Amesbury	1847–	
Boston	1846–53	112
Lowell	1846–48	61
Mattapoisett	1847–	
Nantucket	1847–	
New Bedford	1847–	
Newburyport	1847–	
Springfield	1847–	
Rhode Island		
Providence	1847–50	49
Connecticut		
Waterbury	1848–	
New York		
Albany	1847–	
King's Ferry	1848–	
New York City	1846–50	33
Oneida	1847–	
Utica	1847–	28
Westmoreland	1847–	
Pennsylvania		
Philadelphia	1847–54	84
Pittsburgh	1848–	
District of Columbia		
Washington	1848–	
Virginia		
Wheeling	1846–	
Ohio		
Cincinnati	1847–49	20
Wisconsin		
Ceresco	1847–	

Sources: The Harbinger 3 (30 Oct. 1846): 271; 7 (13 May 1848); 12–14; 8 (14 Dec. 1848): 54; 8 (10 Feb. 1849): 112; Records of the Boston Union of Associationists, Houghton Library, Harvard University; Philadelphia Union of Associationists Records, Harriet Sartain Collection, Historical Society of Pennsylvania; Marianne Dwight Orvis to Anna Q. T. Parsons, 1 July 1847, Brook Farm Papers, Massachusetts Historical Society; Abernethy Library Manuscripts, Middlebury College; and Charles R. Crowe, "Utopian Socialism in Rhode Island, 1845–1850," *Rhode Island History* 18 (Jan. 1959): 20–26.

Table 5. Resident members of phalanxes

Phalanx	Date	Men	Women	Children
Ohio Phalanx	Jan. 1844	30	17	26
LaGrange Phalanx	Feb. 1844	40	35	75
Leraysville Phalanx	1844	c.20	c.20	
Sylvania Association	Aug. 1844	52	33	51
Trumbull Phalanx	June 1844	43		97
Ontario Union	Fall 1844	50	c.35	c.65
Clermont Phalanx	—		80	40
Alphadelphia Association	Mar. 1845	78	47	100*
Wisconsin Phalanx	Dec. 1846	56	42	78**
North American Phalanx	1850	40	26	33
North American Phalanx	Dec. 1852	48	37	27
Fourier Phalanx	1858	8		5

Sources: John Humphrey Noyes, *History of American Socialisms* (Philadelphia: Lippincott, 1870), 243, 263, 298, 329, 373, 398, 423, 462; Census of March 1845, Alphadelphia Association Papers, Bentley Historical Library, University of Michigan; United States Census of 1850 [North American Phalanx]; E. P. Grant Papers, University of Chicago Library [Ohio Phalanx]; *Phalansterian Record* 1 (January–December 1858): 19, 28 [Fourier Phalanx].
  * Under age 15.
  **Under age 21.

Table 6. Population characteristics of Fourierist communities

	Maximum resident population	Total members identified	Men	Women	Children
Brook Farm (1844–47)	90	129	61	40	28
North American Phalanx (1843–55)	120	194	91	55	48
Wisconsin Phalanx (1844–50)	180	259	90	53	116

Sources: For Brook Farm, Constitution of 11 February 1844; minutes of meetings, 1841–45; and Journal B, 1844–46, in Brook Farm Papers, Massachusetts Historical Society. For North American Phalanx, John Humphrey Noyes, *History of American Socialisms* (Philadelphia: Lippincott, 1870), 467; the 1850 U.S. Census; and records in the North American Phalanx Manuscript Collection, Monmouth County (N.J.) Historical Association. For Wisconsin Phalanx, records in Wisconsin Phalanx Papers and Ceresco Community Microfilms, State Historical Society of Wisconsin, especially lists prepared by a research assistant for F. Gerald Ham, State Archivist of Wisconsin.

Table 7. Age and marital status of phalanx adults

	Males		Females	
	Median age at entry	% married	Median age at entry	% married
Total membership				
Brook Farm (1844–47)	26	34*	25.5	58*
North American Phalanx (1843–55)	28.5	34*	30.5	55*
Wisconsin Phalanx (1844–50)	31	41*	29	62*
Membership at one time				
Ohio Phalanx (Jan. 1844)	—	47	—	82
Alphadelphia Association (March 1845)	—	63	—	85
Sylvania Association (Aug. 1844)	—	54	—	82
North American Phalanx (1850)	—	40	—	62
Wisconsin Phalanx (Dec. 1846)	—	54	—	86

Sources: John Humphrey Noyes, *History of American Socialisms* (Philadelphia: Lippincott, 1870), 243, 329, 423; Elijah P. Grant Papers, University of Chicago Library; Alphadelphia Association Papers, Bentley Historical Library, University of Michigan; U.S. Census, 1850. For sources of total membership lists, see Table 6.
*At entry.

Table 8. Family, children, and fertility in the phalanxes

	North American (1850)	Alphadelphia (March 1845)	Wisconsin (Dec. 1846)	U.S. Census (1850)
Number of families	16	40	36	—
% adults married	49	71	73	—
Children under age 15 per family	1.8	2.4	1.9	2.7*
Ratio of children ages 0–14 to women ages 15–49	0.42	1.04	.76	.62
% population ages 0–14	29.3	44.4	38.6	41.3

Sources: U.S. Census, Manuscript Population Schedules of the Seventh Census (NAP); Census of March 1845, Alphadelphia Association Papers, Bentley Historical Library, University of Michigan; Wisconsin Phalanx Collection, State Historical Society of Wisconsin; Bureau of the Census, *Historical Statistics of the United States: Colonial Times to 1970* (Washington, D.C.: Government Printing Office, 1975), pt. 1, ser. A119–134, A288–319.
*Per household.

Table 9. Patterns of phalanx shareholding

	Alphadelphia (March 1845)	Wisconsin (Dec. 1847)	North American (Aug. 1850)
Value of shares outstanding	$36,805	$29,125	$35,580
Shareholders	80	96	87
Male	71	83	66
Female*	9	13	21
Resident	62	62	69
Nonresident	18	34	18
Average investment	$460	$303	$450
Male	510	326	477
Female	70	158	196
Resident	424	357	322
Nonresident	585	205	741
% shares held by males	98.3	93.0	88.4
% shares held by nonresidents**	28.5	23.9	37.5

Sources: "List of Certificates of the Capital Stock of the Alphadelphia Association," in Stock Ledger, Alphadelphia Association Papers, Bentley Historical Library, University of Michigan; "List of Stockholders of the North American Phalanx . . . August 5th, 1850," North American Phalanx Manuscript Collection, Monmouth County (N.J.) Historical Society; Stock Ledger, Wisconsin Phalanx Collection, State Historical Society of Wisconsin. Shareholding data were coordinated with information on resident membership compiled from each collection.

*Almost all female stockholders were wives or dependents of male residents.

**Most nonresident shares were owned by former residents, but 91.5% of the NAP's nonresident shares were held by outside investors, including 39.5% (or 14.8% of total stock) by the Phalansterian Realization Fund Society.

Table 10. Distribution of shareholding in phalanxes

Dollar value of shares*	Alphadelphia (March 1845)			Wisconsin (Dec. 1847)			North American (Aug. 1850)		
	Residents	Nonresidents	Total	Residents	Nonresidents	Total	Residents	Nonresidents	Total
Over 5,000								1	1
4,000–4,999	1		1						
3,000–3,999	1	1	2						
2,500–2,999								1	1
2,000–2,499	1	2	3	1	1	2	1		1
1,500–1,999	1		1					2	2
1,000–1,499	2	1	3				6		6
700–999	4		4	6	2	8	3		3
400–699	9	1	10	13		13	8		8
200–399	5	1	6	21	7	28	12	3	15
100–199	12	2	14	12	4	16	17	5	22
1–99	26	10	36	9	20	29	22	6	28
Total	62	18	80	62	34	96	69	18	87
Shares owned by ten largest shareholders (%)			62.2			36.3			54.7

Sources: See Table 9.
*Par values per share: Alphadelphia Association, $50; Wisconsin Phalanx, $25; North American Phalanx, $10.

Table 11. Prior occupations of phalanx men

	Brook Farm	North American	Wisconsin	Alphadelphia*
Professionals, major proprietors	5	9	6	5
Clerks, semiprofessionals	5	16	8	7
Farmers	4	7	4	99
Skilled artisans	33	27	15	116
Semiskilled and service workers	2	3	—	4
Unskilled workers	—	—	—	5
Unclassifiable or unknown	12	31	57	—
Total	61	91	90	236

Sources: Alphadelphia: Report of the Board of Directors, 2 May 1844, Alphadelphia Association Papers, Bentley Historical Library, University of Michigan. NAP: North American Phalanx Manuscript Collection, Monmouth County (N.J.) Historical Society; U.S. Census, 1850; and city directories. Wisconsin: Wisconsin Phalanx Collection and Samuel M. Pedrick Collection, State Historical Society of Wisconsin; U.S. Census, 1850; *The History of Fond du Lac County, Wisconsin* (Chicago: Western Historical Company, 1880), 881–912; and Joan Elias, "The Wisconsin Phalanx: An Experiment in Association" (M.A. thesis, University of Wisconsin, 1968), 211. Brook Farm: Constitution of 11 February 1844, and memoirs, community histories, and other records in Brook Farm Papers, Massachusetts Historical Society.

Note: Occupational categories follow Michael B. Katz, *The People of Canada West: Family and Class in a Mid-Nineteenth-Century City* (Cambridge, Mass.: Harvard University Press, 1975), 343–48, with a separate classification added for farmers.

*Includes nonresident stockholders.

Table 12. Occupations of men in Fourierist affiliated unions

				Religious Union	
	Boston	New York	Philadelphia	Members	Subscribers
Professionals, major proprietors	11	5	12	7	23
Clerks, semiprofessionals	36	12	20	22	10
Skilled artisans	17	2	7	8	5
Semiskilled and service workers	2	—	—	1	1
Unskilled workers	—	—	1	—	—
Unclassifiable or unknown	7	9	13	4	3
Total	73	28	53	42	42

Sources: Records of the Boston Union of Associationists, Houghton Library, Harvard University; Records of the Boston Religious Union of Associationists, Massachusetts Historical Society (for members); Treasurer's Account Book, Records of the Religious Union of Associationists, Houghton Library (for subscribers); Harriet Sartain Collection, Historical Society of Pennsylvania (for Philadelphia); *The Harbinger* 7 (13 May 1848): 12 (for New York); U.S. Census, 1850; and city directories.

Figure 1. Migration among phalanxes and other communities

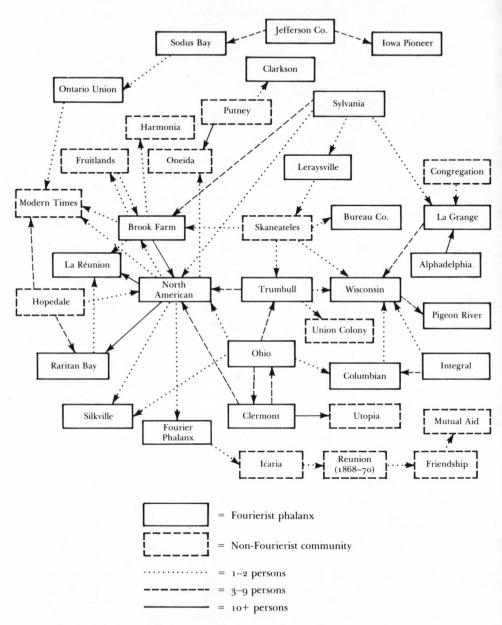

= Fourierist phalanx

= Non-Fourierist community

·············· = 1–2 persons

- - - - - - - = 3–9 persons

———————— = 10+ persons

Note: This figure does not include two communitarians who came to phalanxes (North American and Alphadelphia) from unnamed Shaker communities.

Source: Otohiko Okugawa, "Intercommunal Relationships among Nineteenth-Century Communal Societies in America," *Communal Societies* 3 (1983): 78, amended by subsequent research.

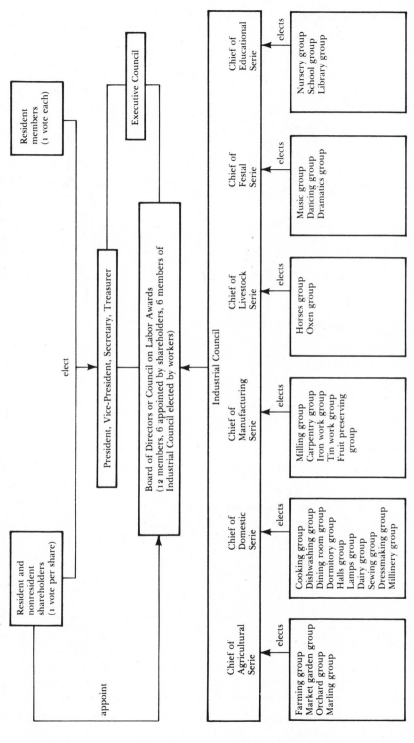

Figure 2. Organization of the North American Phalanx, 1849

Map 1. Location of Fourierist phalanxes

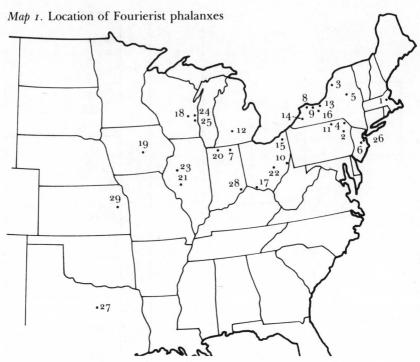

Note: Numbers correspond to phalanxes listed in Table 1

Map 2. Fourierism in western New York

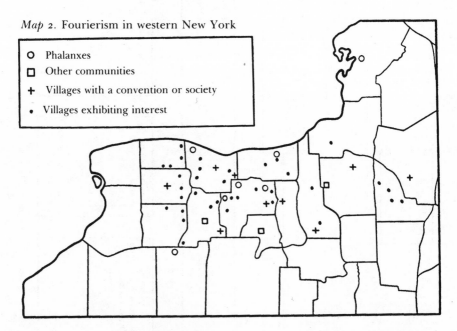

○ Phalanxes
□ Other communities
+ Villages with a convention or society
• Villages exhibiting interest

Source: Whitney R. Cross, *The Burned-Over District: The Social and Intellectual History of Enthusiastic Religion in Western New York, 1800–1850* (1950; New York: Harper & Row, 1965), 330. Copyright © by Cornell University. Used by permission of Cornell University Press.

Abbreviations and Short Forms Used in Notes

AA Papers	Alphadelphia Association Papers, Bentley Historical Library, University of Michigan.
ABS-IHS	Albert Brisbane Papers, Illinois Historical Survey, University of Illinois.
AB-Syr	Albert Brisbane Papers, George Arents Research Library, Syracuse University.
B-G Collection	Bryant-Godwin Collection, New York Public Library.
Brisbane, *Mental Biography*	*Albert Brisbane: A Mental Biography; with a Character Study by his Wife Redelia Brisbane.* Boston: Arena, 1893.
Brisbane, *Social Destiny*	Albert Brisbane, *Social Destiny of Man; or, Assocation and Reorganization of Industry.* Philadelphia: C. F. Stollmeyer, 1840.
BRUA Records	Boston Religious Union of Associationists Records, Massachusetts Historical Society.
BUA Records	Boston Union of Associationists Records, Houghton Library, Harvard University.
Diary I	Albert Brisbane Diary, 14 October 1830–5 January 1831, Albert Brisbane Papers, George Arents Research Library, Syracuse University.
Diary II	Albert Brisbane Diary, 26 September 1831–29 January 1832, Albert Brisbane Papers, George Arents Research Library, Syracuse University.
DocHist	John R. Commons et al., eds. *A Documentary History of American Industrial Society*, Vols. 7–8, *Labor Movement, 1840–1860.* New York: Russell & Russell, 1958.
EPG Papers	Elijah P. Grant Papers, University of Chicago Library.
FNA	Archives Sociétaires, Fonds Fourier et Considerant, French National Archives.
Greeley-LC	Horace Greeley Papers, Library of Congress.
Greeley-NYHS	Horace Greeley Manuscripts, New York Historical Society.

419

Greeley-NYPL	Horace Greeley Papers, New York Public Library.
HL	Houghton Library Miscellaneous Manuscripts and Autograph File, Harvard University.
JSD Collection	John S. Dwight Collection, Boston Public Library.
JTF Papers	James T. Fisher Papers, Massachusetts Historical Society.
LC	Library of Congress.
MHS Broadsides	Massachusetts Historical Society Broadside Collection.
NAP Collection	North American Phalanx Manuscript Collection, Monmouth County (New Jersey) Historical Association.
NAP-HL	North American Phalanx Records and Miscellaneous Papers, Houghton Library, Harvard University.
Noyes, *American Socialisms*	John Humphrey Noyes, *History of American Socialisms*. Philadelphia: Lippincott, 1870.
OC	*Oeuvres complètes de Charles Fourier*, 12 vols. Paris: Editions Anthropos, 1966–68.
PRFS Records	Phalansterian Realization Fund Society Records, Houghton Library, Harvard University.
RBU Collection	Raritan Bay Union Collection, New Jersey Historical Society.
RUA Records	Religious Union of Associationists Records, Houghton Library, Harvard University.
W-CC Collection	Wisconsin Phalanx Collection, Ceresco Community Papers and Microfilms, State Historical Society of Wisconsin.

Additional manuscript collections are cited in notes by the surname or repository under which each one appears in the alphabetical bibliography listing.

Notes

INTRODUCTION

1. Friedrich Engels, *Socialism: Utopian and Scientific*, trans. Edward Aveling (1892; New York: International Publishers, 1975), 36.

2. A rather heavy contemporary satire is [Orestes Brownson], *The Spirit Rapper: An Autobiography* (Boston: Little, Brown, 1854); more bemused reactions can be found in Ralph Waldo Emerson's lectures and essays, such as "New England Reformers" and "Historic Notes of Life and Letters in New England." A similar approach later surfaces in such histories as Grace Adams and Edward Hutter, *The Mad Forties* (New York: Harper, 1942).

3. Exceptions should be made for two fine studies of utopianism. T. D. Seymour Bassett, "The Secular Utopian Socialists," in *Socialism and American Life*, ed. Donald D. Egbert and Stow Persons (Princeton, N.J.: Princeton University Press, 1952), 1:155–211, respects the integrity of Fourierism and by concentrating on its Americanization lays the groundwork for my own approach. John F. C. Harrison, *Quest for the New Moral World: Robert Owen and the Owenites in Britain and America* (New York: Scribner, 1969), provides a model for viewing utopian socialism as a generalized response to nineteenth-century social change rather than in relation to "partial interpretations" (p. 3) or presentist concerns.

4. Noyes, *American Socialisms*; Arthur Bestor, *Backwoods Utopias: The Sectarian Origins and the Owenite Phase of Communitarian Socialism in America, 1663–1829*, 2d ed. (Philadelphia: University of Pennsylvania Press, 1970), 1–59, 230–52; John L. Thomas, "Romantic Reform in America," *American Quarterly* 17 (Winter 1965): 656–81. For a focus on secular experiments, see Edward K. Spann, *Brotherly Tomorrows: Movements for a Cooperative Society in America, 1820–1920* (New York: New York University Press, 1989). For a socialist account, see Morris Hillquit, *History of Socialism in the United States* (New York: Funk & Wagnalls, 1903), 15–25, 77–117. For an institutional labor history point of view, see Norman F. Ware, *The Industrial Worker, 1840–1860* (Boston: Houghton Mifflin, 1924), 163–79. An approach using modernization theory to "situate" Fourierism in American culture is Daniel Walker Howe, *The Political Culture of the American Whigs* (Chicago: University of Chicago Press, 1979).

5. Bestor, *Backwoods Utopias*, 1–19.

6. Karl Marx and Friedrich Engels, "Manifesto of the Communist Party," in

Basic Writings on Politics and Philosophy, ed. Lewis Feuer (Garden City, N.Y.: Doubleday, 1959), 37. The literature on utopias is vast, but the best introduction remains Frank E. Manuel, ed., *Utopias and Utopian Thought* (Boston: Beacon Press, 1966). For Fourier's place in the utopian tradition, see Frank E. Manuel and Fritzie P. Manuel, *Utopian Thought in the Western World* (Cambridge, Mass.: Belknap Press of Harvard University Press, 1979), 12–21, 25–29, 581–89, 641–75.

7. Cf. the interpretations of utopian communities in John R. Commons et al., *History of Labour in the United States* (New York: Macmillan, 1918–35), 1: 496–506; Gerald R. Grob, *Workers and Utopia* (Evanston, Ill.: Northwestern University Press, 1961); and Ware, *Industrial Worker,* xvi–xvii; with the socialist point of view of Hillquit, *History of Socialism,* 15–25.

8. Marx and Engels, "Manifesto," 38.

9. Eric Hobsbawm, *The Age of Revolution, 1789–1848* (New York: New American Library, 1962), 357.

10. William Jenkins, *Pro-slavery Thought in the Old South* (Chapel Hill: University of North Carolina Press, 1935); Louis Hartz, *The Liberal Tradition in America* (New York: Harcourt, Brace & World, 1955), 145–200; and Drew Gilpin Faust, *A Sacred Circle: The Dilemma of the Intellectual in the Old South* (Philadelphia: University of Pennsylvania Press, 1977), offer interpretations of proslavery ideology. For its impact on Republicans, see Eric Foner, *Free Soil, Free Labor, Free Men* (New York: Oxford University Press, 1970), 66–67; and Yehoshua Arieli, *Individualism and Nationalism in American Ideology* (Baltimore, Md.: Penguin Books, 1966), 301–5.

11. John Ashworth, *"Agrarians" and "Aristocrats": Party Ideology in the United States, 1836–1847* (New York: Cambridge University Press, 1987); Sean Wilentz, *Chants Democratic: New York City and the Rise of the American Working Class, 1788–1850* (New York: Oxford University Press, 1984); Anthony F. C. Wallace, *Rockdale: The Growth of an American Village in the Early Industrial Revolution* (New York: Knopf, 1978).

12. Bestor, *Backwoods Utopias,* 270. Although the literature on individual communities and sects is vast, the most inclusive and colorful overview of antebellum communities is still Alice Felt Tyler, *Freedom's Ferment: Phases of American Social History from the Colonial Period to the Outbreak of the Civil War* (Minneapolis: University of Minnesota Press, 1944). Bestor, *Backwoods Utopias,* 279–84, contains a checklist of ninety-five experiments founded between 1825 and 1860.

13. For interpretations of Fourierism as escapism, see Arthur Schlesinger, Jr., *The Age of Jackson* (Boston: Little, Brown, 1945), 361; L. L. Bernard, "Early Utopian Social Theory in the United States (1840–1860)," *Northwest Missouri Teachers College Studies* 2 (1938): 79; and James Macgregor Burns, *The Vineyard of Liberty* (New York: Knopf, 1981), 442–44.

14. F. O. Matthiessen, *American Renaissance: Art and Expression in the Age of Emerson and Whitman* (New York: Oxford University Press, 1941), viii.

15. Bestor, *Backwoods Utopias,* 248, 266.

CHAPTER 1. FOURIERISM CROSSES THE ATLANTIC

1. An interpretation that emphasizes American Fourierism as an indigenous product is Arthur Bestor, "The Transit of Communitarian Socialism to America," in *Backwoods Utopias: The Sectarian Origins and the Owenite Phase of Communitarian Socialism in America, 1663–1829,* 2d ed. (Philadelphia: University of Pennsylvania Press, 1970), 253–71, esp. 265–66. Bestor's label "strictly American" is quoted in Henri Desroche, *La Société festive: Du Fouriérisme écrit aux Fouriérismes pratiqués* (Paris: Editions du Seuil, 1975), 215.

2. The apple story is such a good one that two excellent commentaries on

Fourier open with it. See Frank Manuel, *The Prophets of Paris* (Cambridge, Mass.: Harvard University Press, 1962), 197; and the introduction to *The Utopian Vision of Charles Fourier*, ed. and trans. Jonathan Beecher and Richard Bienvenu, (Boston: Beacon Press, 1971), 1. The quotations are from *OC*, 10:17, 53; these and other translations are the author's unless otherwise noted.

3. The definitive biography of Fourier, and a superb analysis of his thought in the context of his times, is Jonathan Beecher, *Charles Fourier: The Visionary and His World* (Berkeley: University of California Press, 1986). Charles Pellarin, *Life of Charles Fourier*, 2d ed., trans. Francis G. Shaw (New York: W. H. Graham, 1848), written by a French disciple, remains a valuable source. See also Hubert Bourgin, *Fourier: Contribution à l'étude du socialisme français* (Paris: Société Nouvelle de Librairie et d'Edition, 1904); and Emile Lehouck, *Vie de Charles Fourier* (Paris: Gonthier, 1978).

4. Fourier, "Universal Harmony," *OC*, 10:52.

5. For a psychological portrait that seeks to understand these "sublimations of ungratified desires" and penetrate Fourier's "mask of harlequin," see Manuel, *Prophets of Paris*, 243–48.

6. Fourier's complete works have been published in French; the heart of his theory is available in English translation through Beecher and Bienvenu, *Utopian Vision; Harmonian Man*, ed. and trans. Mark Poster (Garden City, N.Y.: Doubleday, 1971); and *Design for Utopia*, ed. Charles Gide, trans. Julia Franklin (New York: Schocken Books, 1971). Among the many studies of Fourier's thought, the most useful and important are Bourgin, *Fourier*, bks. 1–2; Manuel, *Prophets of Paris*, 195–248; Nicholas V. Riasnovsky, *The Teaching of Charles Fourier* (Berkeley: University of California Press, 1969); Roland Barthes, *Sade, Fourier, Loyola*, trans. Richard Miller (New York: Hill & Wang, 1976), 76–120; Jean Goret, *La pensée de Fourier* (Paris: Presses Universitaires de France, 1974); Desroche, *La société festive*; Simone Debout-Oleskiewicz, *L'utopie de Charles Fourier* (Paris: Payot, 1978); and Beecher, *Charles Fourier*, 193–352.

7. Beecher, *Charles Fourier*, 197; *OC*, 2:78.

8. Riasnovsky, *Teaching of Fourier*, 163, 176.

9. *OC*, 6:47.

10. For discussions of Fourier's relation to Newton, see Riasnovsky, *Teaching of Fourier*, 38–39; and Beecher, *Charles Fourier*, 66, 224–25, 334–35.

11. *OC*, 1:79.

12. *Le nouveau monde amoureux*, ed. Simone Debout-Oleskiewicz, was published as *OC*, vol. 7.

13. Quoted in Beecher, *Charles Fourier*, 341. For the full description of the *archibras* or tail, see Beecher, "L'archibras de Fourier: Un manuscrit censuré," *La Brèche: Action Surréaliste* 7 (1964): 66–71.

14. Fourier, "Letter to the High Judge" (1803), in Beecher and Bienvenu, *Utopian Vision*, 84.

15. Beecher, *Charles Fourier*, 356.

16. On Fourier's early converts, see Beecher, *Charles Fourier*, 161–75, 387–90; and Bourgin, *Fourier*, 426–35. The best biography of Considerant is Rondel Van Davidson, *Did We Think Victory Great? The Life and Ideas of Victor Considerant* (Lanham, Md.: University Press of America, 1988). My discussion of the French Fourierist movement prior to 1833 is especially indebted to Beecher, *Charles Fourier*, 355–495.

17. The best discussion of the life and thought of Saint-Simon is Frank E. Manuel, *The New World of Henri Saint-Simon* (Cambridge, Mass.: Harvard University Press, 1956). Manuel distilled his portrait into a brilliant sketch in *Prophets of Paris*, 103–48; and again in Frank E. Manuel and Fritzie P. Manuel, *Utopian*

Thought in the Western World (Cambridge, Mass.: Belknap Press of Harvard University Press, 1979), 590–614.

18. The most complete work on the Saint-Simonians remains Sebastien Charléty, *Histoire du Saint-Simonisme (1825–1864)* (Paris: Paul Hartmann, 1931). But see also Henry-René d'Allemagne, *Les Saint-Simoniens, 1827–1837* (Paris: Grund, 1930); J. L. Talmon, *Political Messianism: The Romantic Phase* (New York: Praeger, 1960), 35–124; Manuel, *Prophets of Paris,* 149–93; and, most recently, Robert B. Carlisle, *The Proffered Crown: Saint-Simonianism and the Doctrine of Hope* (Baltimore, Md.: Johns Hopkins University Press, 1987). For one aspect of Saint-Simonian ritual, see Ralph P. Locke, *Music, Musicians, and the Saint-Simonians* (Chicago: University of Chicago Press, 1986).

19. See, e.g., E. M. Butler, *The Saint-Simonian Religion in Germany* (Cambridge: Cambridge University Press, 1926); and for England, Richard K. P. Pankhurst, *The Saint-Simonians, Mill, and Carlyle* (London: Sidgwick & Jackson, 1957).

20. *Correspondance: articles extraits du Globe* (1831), quoted in Manuel and Manuel, *Utopian Thought,* 620. For Brownson's adoption of the Saint-Simonian doctrine of "solidarity," see below, Chapter 2.

21. Charléty, *Saint-Simonisme,* 120–85; Carlisle, *Proferred Crown,* 159–94, 214–21.

22. Charles Fourier, *Pièges et charlatanisme des deux sectes Saint-Simon et Owen* (Paris: Bossange, 1831). For Fourier's relations with the Saint-Simonians, see Henri Louvancour, *De Henri Saint-Simon à Charles Fourier* (Chartres: Durand, 1931), 91–213; and Beecher, *Charles Fourier,* 413–21.

23. On Fourierism's appeal to Saint-Simonian dissidents, as well as the conversion of Lechevalier and others, see Louvancour, *De Saint-Simon à Fourier,* 214–310. Jules Lechevalier recounted his transition to Fourierism in *Etudes sur la science sociale* (Paris: E. Renduel, 1834), 18–24; for his later career as an independent socialist in France and England, see Torben Christensen, *Origin and History of Christian Socialism, 1848–1854* (Aarhus: Universitetsforlaget, 1962), esp. 109–18, 163–67.

24. Beecher, *Charles Fourier,* 431–53, recounts the first year of Fourierist movement propaganda and is especially perceptive on the ideological and personality clashes between Fourier and his disciples (quotations, pp. 433, 448). For a fascinating fictional portrayal of the shift from Enlightenment to Romantic sensibilities—with Fourier himself introduced as a transitional character—see Richard Sennett, *Palais-Royal* (New York: Knopf, 1983). There is no complete history of the French Fourierist movement. Its outlines can be pieced together from many accounts, the fullest of which are Alphonse Alhaiza, *Historique de l'école sociétaire fondée par Charles Fourier* (Paris: La Rénovation, 1894), 19–59; Bourgin, *Fourier,* 409–508; Desroche, *La Société festive,* 159–77, 217–72; Beecher, *Charles Fourier,* 431–95; and, among biographies of Considerant, Maurice Dommanget, *Victor Considerant, sa vie, son oeuvre* (Paris: Editions Sociales Internationales, 1929); and Davidson, *Did We Think Victory Great?*

25. For the Condé experiment, see Beecher, *Charles Fourier,* 454–71; Alhaiza, *Historique,* 25–27; Jules Prudhommeaux's manuscript on the Colonie Sociétaire (1913) published in Desroche, *La société festive,* 220–35; and Gabriel Vauthier, "Un essai de Phalanstère à Condé-sur-Vesgre," *La Révolution de 1848* 21 (February 1925): 327–44.

26. For the split among French Fourierists, which had regional, class and ideological dimensions, see Bourgin, *Fourier,* 468–70, 477–78; Emile Poulat, *Les cahiers manuscrits de Fourier* (Paris: Editions de Minuit, 1957), 42–44; Desroche, *La société festive,* 164–77, 248–54; and Davidson, *Did We Think Victory Great?* 51–55. Fourier's endorsement of Considerant is discussed in Poulat, "Sur deux textes

manuscrits de Fourier," in Desroche et al., *Etudes sur la tradition française de l'association ouvrière* (Paris: Editions de Minuit, 1956), 5–19. *Correspondance Harmonienne* (1837–41) and later *Le Nouveau Monde* (1839–43) were the chief organs of dissident Fourierists.

27. Gabriel Vauthier, "Arthur Young et la colonie sociétaire de Citeaux (1841–1844)," *La Révolution de 1848* 22 (April 1926): 771–80.

28. For the Brazilian colony at Palmetar, the Union Industrielle du Sahy, see Bourgin, *Fourier*, 502; for the Algerian venture, see Fernand Rudé, "Les Fouriéristes lyonnais et la colonisation de l'Algerie," *Cahiers d'Histoire* (published by the Universities of Clermont-Ferrand, Lyons, and Grenoble) 1 (1956): 41–63. The most successful French phalansterian project, Jean-Baptiste Godin's semi-Fourierist "Familistère" at Guise (1859–78), was founded long after Fourierism was a vital communitarian movement and lies outside the time frame of this chapter (see Chapter 16).

29. Charles Fourier, *Traité de l'association domestique-agricole*, 2 vols. (Paris: Bossange and Mongie, 1822); Fourier to John Barnet, 30 December 1823, with note by Barnet, quoted in Victor Considerant, *Au Texas* (Paris: Librairie Phalanstérienne, 1854), 175–76; Fourier, *La fausse industrie* (1835–36), *OC*, 9:782. For Fourier's campaign of 1822–23 to publicize the treatise and find a "candidate," see Beecher, *Charles Fourier*, 355–71.

30. Among appeals to Fourier to supervise a phalanx attempt in America, see Jean Manesca to Fourier, February 1835 and 30 January 1836, FNA (10 AS 36, doss. 11); and Albert Brisbane to Fourier [1836], quoted in Desroche, *La société festive*, 352. Fourier admitted that America had "a good chance" to precede France in organizing a successful phalanx, primarily because of cheap land; see Fourier to Brisbane, 22 May 1834, HL. For more optimistic assessments of America as the field for utopian experimentation, see Hugh Honour, *The New Golden Land: European Images of America from the Discoveries to the Present Time* (New York: Pantheon Books, 1975); and R. Laurence Moore, *European Socialists and the American Promised Land* (New York: Oxford University Press, 1970), 22–23.

31. Bestor, "Transit," 266. For the French movement's attitude toward the United States, see below, Chapter 8.

32. Walt Whitman, "New York Dissected, V. Street Yarn," *Life Illustrated*, 16 August 1856, reprinted in *New York Dissected*, ed. Emory Holloway and Ralph Adimari (New York: R. R. Wilson, 1936), 129.

33. Brisbane, *Mental Biography*. For an able discussion of the book's reliability, see Arthur Bestor, "Albert Brisbane—Propagandist for Socialism in the 1840's," *New York History* 28 (April 1947): 153–58. Because he lacked access to manuscript sources of the 1830s, Bestor's otherwise excellent biographical sketch (pp. 128–50) repeated some of the aged Brisbane's improbable schemas and errors of hindsight. Other studies include Oliver Carlson, *Brisbane: A Candid Biography* (New York: Stackpole, 1937), 15–66; Michael Fellman, *The Unbounded Frame: Freedom and Community in Nineteenth Century American Utopianism* (Westport, Conn.: Greenwood Press, 1973), 3–19; and Lloyd Rohler Earl, Jr., "The Utopian Persuasion of Albert Brisbane, First Apostle of Fourierism" (Ph.D. diss., Indiana University, 1977). The account that follows is the first published one to make full use of the Brisbane Papers at Syracuse University and correspondence from the French National Archives.

34. Brisbane, *Mental Biography*, 49–57; *New York Times*, 8 May 1883; Quotation from T. D. Seymour Bassett, "The Secular Utopian Socialists," in *Socialism and American Life*, ed. Donald Drew Egbert and Stow Persons (Princeton, N.J.: Princeton University Press, 1952), 1:179. For Brisbane's ancestors, see the genealogical chart in the typescript biography of Brisbane by his grandson, Michael

McCrary, AB-Syr. Brisbane's financial records from the 1850s detail the property left by James Brisbane to his sons Albert and George; see Financial Notebook (n.d.), AB-IHS. For James Brisbane's role in the Holland Land Company and Batavia, see William Wyckoff, *The Developer's Frontier: The Making of the Western New York Landscape* (New Haven, Conn.: Yale University Press, 1988), 85, 127–28.

35. Brisbane, *Mental Biography*, 62–64.

36. See, e.g., Charles F. Thwing, *The American and the German University* (New York: Macmillan, 1928), 15–22, 42, cited in Bestor, "Brisbane," 132 n.6.

37. Horatio Greenough to Samuel F. B. Morse, 3 June 1832, in *Letters of Horatio Greenough, American Sculptor*, ed. Nathalia Wright (Madison: University of Wisconsin Press, 1972), 131.

38. David O. Evans, *Social Romanticism in France, 1830–1848* (Oxford: Clarendon Press, 1951), uses the term to cover liberal and socialist thought stemming from the Romantic idealism of the early nineteenth century; it could apply equally to Transcendentalism and American reform.

39. Brisbane, *Mental Biography*, 71, 73. For Cousin and American Transcendentalists, see Walter L. Leighton, *French Philosophers and New England Transcendentalism* (1908; rpt. New York: Greenwood Press, 1968); and Charles Crowe, *George Ripley, Transcendentalist and Utopian Socialist* (Athens: University of Georgia Press, 1967), 69–70.

40. Brisbane, *Mental Biography*, 96–97; Diary I, 142, 21; Diary II, 59.

41. Diary I, 143, 150; Brisbane, *Mental Biography*, 118. Brisbane's later recollection that his Mediterranean tour destroyed his faith in republicanism (pp. 113–15, 118) is belied by his pro-American and republican remarks in Diary I, 13. He described this trip also in a letter to Samuel F. B. Morse, 3 May 1831, Morse Papers, LC.

42. Diary I, 45, 192, 206, 100, 48; Diary II, 231.

43. The most notable example was Brisbane's on-again-off-again relationship with Lodoiska Durand, Jean Manesca's daughter. When she sued for divorce in 1883, testimony at the sensational trial revealed that Brisbane had had an affair with Lodoiska in 1839 or 1840, lived with her at three different times, and fathered three children before breaking off the relationship; he claimed that their marriage was invalid because he had never been divorced from his first wife, Adèle le Brun. The court ordered him to pay alimony of $25 per week. As late as 1889 Brisbane asked his son in Paris to check on Lodoiska's health, for "were she to die, they might keep her death secret and [continue to] draw alimony"; see Brisbane to Arthur Brisbane, 10 April 1889, Arthur Brisbane Papers, George Arents Research Library, Syracuse University. The story can be pieced together from accounts in the *New York Tribune*, 6, 30 May 1883 and 8 July 1883; and the *New York Times*, 6, 8, 13, 30, 31 May 1883, and 13 June 1883.

44. Diary II, 95, 193, 82, 43. Cf. Bestor, "Brisbane," 135.

45. Diary II, 117–18, 194; Brisbane, *Mental Biography*, 131–32.

46. Diary II, 55–56, 215–216.

47. Brisbane, *Mental Biography*, 173–74; Diary II, 203, 228; Butler, *Saint-Simonian Religion*, 71–72. and Rahel Varnhagen von Ense to Heinrich Heine, 5 June 1832, in Heine, *Briefswechsel*, ed. Friedrich Hirth (Munich: G. Muller, 1914–20), 2:23. On Varnhagen (the former Rahel Levin) and her circle, see Hannah Arendt, *Rahel Varnhagen: The Life of a Jewish Woman*, trans. Richard Winston and Clara Winston (New York: Harcourt Brace Jovanovich, 1974); and Deborah Hertz, *Jewish High Society in Old Regime Berlin* (New Haven, Conn.: Yale University Press, 1987), esp. 100–103. Chevalier's letter of 20 May 1832 to Brisbane is

reprinted in *Oeuvres de Saint-Simon et d'Enfantin* (Paris: Librairie de la Société des Gens de Lettres, 1866), 7:33–40.

48. Diary II, 235, 146. For Brisbane's misgivings about the Saint-Simonian movement, see Diary II, 145, 154, 213; and Brisbane, *Mental Biography*, 153.

49. Lechevalier's statement of withdrawal is reprinted in *Oeuvres de Saint-Simon et d'Enfantin*, 4:160–76.

50. Brisbane, *Mental Biography*, 170–71.

51. This chronology, blurred by Brisbane in his autobiography, is clarified in his earlier reminiscences, "Brisbane and Fourier," *Oneida Circular* 5 (26 October 1868): 254.

52. Brisbane to Jules Lechevalier, June 1832, FNA (10 AS 36, doss. 11).

53. Brisbane to K. A. Varnhagen von Ense, 19 February 1833, in *Letters of the American Socialist Albert Brisbane to K. A. Varnhagen von Ense*, ed. Terry H. Pickett and Françoise deRocher (Heidelberg: Carl Winter Universitätsverlag, 1986), 32; Brisbane, *Mental Biography*, 186, 190, 187.

54. Ibid., 177–84.

55. Brisbane, quoted in Manesca to Charles Fourier, 30 January 1836, FNA (10 AS 36, doss. 11).

56. Brisbane to Fourier, 1 April 1834, in ibid.; Brisbane, *Mental Biography*, 197–200. In 1844, Brisbane explained that a "nervous condition" had prevented his studying and writing; see Brisbane to K. A. Varnhagen von Ense, 16 August 1844, in Pickett and Rocher, *Letters*, 50.

57. *New York Tribune*, 30 May 1883. For the family's opposition to Adèle, see McCrary, typescript biography of Brisbane, 15.

58. Brisbane to Fourier, 14 April 1836, quoted in Bourgin, *Fourier*, 474 n.1; Brisbane to Considerant, 20 November 1836, FNA (10 AS 36, doss. 11).

59. See Riasnovsky, *Teaching of Fourier*, 117–31.

60. Brisbane to Victor Considerant, 1 May 1840, FNA (10 AS 36, doss. 11). Brisbane's investments of the 1850s and 1860s are listed in Financial Notebook, AB-IHS. Despite his incurable optimism, his investments rarely met his expectations but instead tied up his money so much that he relied on friends for small cash loans. An R. G. Dun and Company agent accurately reported in 1860 that Brisbane and his brother George, though worth about $400,000, were "not good business men and . . . put off [their obligations] as long as possible"; see R. G. Dun and Company Collection, vol. 103 (N.Y.), p. 16, Baker Library, Harvard University Business School.

` 61. Manesca to Fourier, 4 April 1833, quoted in Desroche, *La Société festive*, 350; Manesca to Fourier, February 1835 and 30 January 1836, FNA (10 AS 36, doss. 11).

62. Manesca to Monsieur Bécour, 14 October 1837, FNA (10 AS 40, doss. 1); *La Phalange* 2 (1 November 1838): 322–23. The pamphlet's full title was *Two Essays on the Social System of Charles Fourier, Being an Introduction to the Constitution of the Fourienne Society of New York* (New York: H. D. Robinson, 1838). Around the same time, a French-American named L.-A. Tarasçon circulated a tract, *Raisonie; ou Douce demeure* (New York, 1839), which acknowledged Fourier's influence (among others) and proposed to establish a model farm for orphans somewhere in the Middle Atlantic states. Nothing seems to have come of this plan.

63. See Brisbane to Considerant, 20 November 1836, for comments on America's destiny to realize Fourierism; and Brisbane to Considerant, 1 May 1840, for his characterization of the book. Both are in FNA (10 AS 36, doss. 11).

64. See Emerson to Lidian Emerson, 3 March 1842, in *The Letters of Ralph*

Waldo Emerson, ed. Ralph L. Rusk (New York: Columbia University Press, 1939), 2:21; Brisbane to Emerson, 26 May 1842, Emerson Papers; Brisbane to Nicholas Biddle, 16 November 1840, AB-IHS; Brisbane to Brownson, 21 February 1844, Brownson Papers; Brisbane, *Mental Biography,* 219–23.

65. See Brisbane's articles in *United States Magazine and Democratic Review* 10 (January–June 1842): 30–44, 167–81, 321–36, 560–80; "Letter from Mr. Brisbane," *Boston Quarterly Review* 4 (October 1841): 501–12; and [Brisbane and Ralph Waldo Emerson], "Fourier and the Socialists," *Dial* 3 (July 1842): 86–96.

66. *La Phalange* 2 (1 July 1839): 625–27; Bestor, "Brisbane," 143.

67. Bestor's, "Brisbane," 144–45, relates the origins of the Greeley-Brisbane collaboration, and his "Supplementary Note," (pp. 150–51) carefully sorts out conflicting accounts of Brisbane's first acquaintance with Greeley. *The Future* first appeared on 30 January 1841 with an introduction by Greeley, "To the Thinking Public." The next issue was not printed until 29 May, after which the paper became a weekly. For the Fourier Association, see *Future* 4 (12 June 1841).

68. Bestor's "Supplementary Note" in "Brisbane," 150–54 untangles the details of the *Tribune* column arrangement; and his excellent analysis (pp. 145–48) highlights Brisbane's skill as a propagandist (quotations, p. 145). The column in the *Weekly Tribune* of 15 October 1842 reported the figure of forty sympathetic papers. For a complete list of Brisbane's *Tribune* columns, see Arthur Bestor, "American Phalanxes: A Study of Fourierist Socialism in the United States (With Special Reference to the Movement in Western New York)" (Ph.D. diss., Yale University, 1938), 2:28–43. Attempting to gain support from Democrats as well as Greeley's Whigs, Brisbane made a similar arrangement with the staunchly Democratic *New York Daily Plebian,* where his separately edited column "Association; Or, Social Reform" began appearing twice a week at the end of June 1842. The *Plebian* never approached the influence of Greeley's *Tribune.* See Brisbane, *Mental Biography,* 208; and the notice in the *New York Daily Plebian,* 2 July 1842.

69. Brisbane, *Association; or, A Concise Exposition of the Practical Part of Fourier's Social Science* (New York: Greeley & McElrath, 1843). Subsequent editions used the subtitle alone. For the total printing, see Bestor, "Brisbane," 148.

CHAPTER 2. APOSTLES OF ASSOCIATION

1. George Ripley, quoted in Marianne Dwight, *Letters from Brook Farm, 1844–1847,* ed. Amy L. Reed (Poughkeepsie, N.Y.: Vassar College, 1928), 73.

2. Glyndon G. Van Deusen, *Horace Greeley: Nineteenth-Century Crusader* (Philadelphia: University of Pennsylvania Press, 1953), 79–81, mixes most of these interpretations with the truer insight that Greeley's Fourierism was "both humanitarian and conservative" (p. 79).

3. Brisbane, quoted in *Phalanx* 1 (20 April 1844): 116. Greeley's support for Fourierism is well documented in Cecelia Koretsky, "Horace Greeley and Fourierism in the United States" (M.A. thesis, University of Rochester, 1952); but for his investment in the Clermont Phalanx, which Koretsky overlooks, see Greeley to A. L. Child, 12 October 1846, Greeley-NYPL.

4. Daniel Walker Howe, *The Political Culture of the American Whigs* (Chicago: University of Chicago Press, 1979), 300. My analysis throughout this section is indebted to Howe's shrewd but sympathetic discussion of Greeley (pp. 184–97).

5. See, e.g., Louis Hartz, *The Liberal Tradition in America* (New York: Harcourt, Brace & World, 1955), 110–12; Rush Welter, *The Mind of America, 1820–1860* (New York: Columbia University Press, 1975), 105–62; and John Ashworth, *"Agrarians" and "Aristocrats": Party Ideology in the United States, 1836–1847* (New York: Cambridge University Press, 1987), 147–70.

6. Horace Greeley, "Glimpses of a Better Life," in *Hints toward Reforms* (New York: Harper, 1850), 369. For suggestions of the religious aspect of Whig thought, see Howe, *Political Culture*, 9–10, 18; and David Grimsted, ed., *Notions of the Americans, 1820–1860* (New York: Braziller, 1970), 11–14.

7. Van Deusen, *Horace Greeley*, 76–77. For similar views of Lowell, see John F. Kasson, *Civilizing the Machine: Technology and Republican Values in America, 1776–1900* (New York: Grossman, 1976), 79–86.

8. Horace Greeley, *Recollections of a Busy Life* (New York: J. B. Ford, 1868), 122, 144–45.

9. Van Deusen, *Horace Greeley*, 61; Greeley, "The Organization of Labor," and "What Free Trade Is Doing," in *Hints toward Reforms*, 181, 348–51.

10. See Greeley "Strikes and Their Remedy," in *Hints toward Reforms*, 364–366; Van Deusen, *Horace Greeley*, 146–47.

11. Greeley, "The Social Architects—Fourier," in *Hints toward Reforms*, 272–99; Howe, *Political Culture*, 193.

12. *New York Daily Tribune*, 20 April 1842; Greeley, quoted in Van Deusen, *Horace Greeley*, 70; Greeley, "The Relations of Learning to Labor," in *Hints toward Reforms*, 134.

13. Greeley, "The Right to Labor," in *Hints toward Reforms*, 318–22.

14. Howe, *Political Culture*, 193.

15. For Greeley's defense of Fourierism as "Industrial Association" rather than sweeping social reform, see Greeley and H. J. Raymond, *Association Discussed; or, The Socialism of the Tribune Examined* (New York: Harper, 1847); and *Love, Marriage, and Divorce, and the Sovereignty of the Individual: A Discussion by Henry James, Horace Greeley, and Stephen Pearl Andrews*, ed. Stephen Pearl Andrews (New York: Stringer & Townsend, 1853). For Greeley's grilling of one phalanx, see *Exposé of the Condition and Progress of the North American Phalanx, in Reply to Horace Greeley* (New York: DeWitt & Davenport, 1853).

16. [Parke Godwin], "Democracy," *United States Magazine and Democratic Review* 7 (March 1840): 227, 225, 216. For an able account of Godwin's career and thought, see Edward K. Spann, "Dissent from the Left: Parke Godwin," in *Ideals and Politics: New York Intellectuals and Liberal Democracy, 1820–1880* (Albany: State University of New York Press, 1972), 142–54. John Raymond Wennersten, "A Reformer's Odyssey: The Public Career of Parke Godwin of the New York *Evening Post*" (Ph.D. diss., University of Maryland, 1970), is more thorough but less interpretive.

17. [Parke Godwin], "Dr. Channing's Recent Writings," *Democratic Review* 9 (October 1841): 319, and "Democracy and Literature," 11 (August 1842): 197. On O'Sullivan and "Progressive Democracy," see Welter, *Mind of America*, 45–74, 129–35. For the literary side of "Young America," see Perry Miller, *The Raven and the Whale: The War of Words and Wits in the Era of Poe and Melville* (New York: Harcourt, Brace & World, 1956), 69–117.

18. [Parke Godwin], "Journalism," *Democratic Review* 10 (January 1842): 52.

19. [Godwin], Channing's Recent Writings"; [Parke Godwin], "The Christian Union," *Democratic Review* 12 (June 1843): 563–67 (quotation, p. 564).

20. Godwin paid tribute to Carlyle several times before losing patience with the Scot's opposition to utopian reform. See "Carlyle's Chartism," *New York Evening Post*, 2 May 1840; Godwin, *Democracy, Constructive and Pacific* (New York: J. Winchester, 1844), 12, 44–45; and Godwin, *A Popular View of the Doctrines of Charles Fourier* (New York: J. S. Redfield, 1844), title page.

21. [Parke Godwin], "On the Elevation of the Laboring Portion of the Community," *Democratic Review* 8 (July 1840): 59–61. Godwin learned of Saint-Simon's philosophy from articles in Orestes Brownson's *Boston Quarterly Review* in 1840

and 1842. Brisbane's *Social Destiny* was reviewed in *Democratic Review* 8 (November 1840): 431–74; and his *Tribune* column of 1842–43 was familiar to Godwin, who was writing for a rival New York daily. In March 1843 Godwin testified that he had read "the greater part" of Fourier's *Oeuvres complètes* (a four-volume edition). See *Pathfinder*, 18 March 1843, p. 52.

22. [Godwin], "Channing's Recent Writings," 320; [Parke Godwin], "The History and Moral Relations of Political Economy," *Democratic Review* 8 (October 1840): 307.

23. Wennersten, "Reformer's Odyssey," 15; Godwin to W. H. Channing, 19 May 1840, B-G Collection; Parke Godwin, "The Late City Election," *Pathfinder*, 22 April 1843, p. 129.

24. Godwin, *Democracy*, 9–10; 11–12, 21–22. For Godwin's sources among political economists, see *Phalanx* 1 (13 July 1844): 202, and 1 (24 August 1844): 250.

25. Godwin, *Democracy*, 18.

26. [Parke Godwin], "Address to the People of the United States," *Phalanx* 1 (20 April 1844): 107.

27. Godwin, *Democracy*, 41; Godwin, *Popular View*, 50.

28. See Noyes, *American Socialisms* 23; Arthur Schlesinger, Jr., *The Age of Jackson* (Boston: Little, Brown, 1945), 363–65; and T. D. Seymour Bassett, "The Secular Utopian Socialists," in *Socialism and American Life*, ed. Donald Drew Egbert and Stow Persons (Princeton, N.J.: Princeton University Press, 1952), 1:177.

29. Marvin Meyers, *The Jacksonian Persuasion: Politics and Belief* (Stanford, Calif.: Stanford University Press, 1957), 13.

30. Greeley, *Hints toward Reforms*, 8; Greeley, quoted in Van Deusen, *Horace Greeley*, 80. See Godwin, *Popular View*, 27, 110.

31. Charles R. Crowe, "Transcendentalist Support of Brook Farm: A Paradox?" *Historian* 21 (May 1959): 281, raised the question explicitly; Crowe, "This Unnatural Union of Phalansteries and Transcendentalists," *Journal of the History of Ideas* 20 (October–December 1959): 495–502, answered it by portraying Brook Farm as a cooperative means to individualist ends. Similar interpretations can be found in Herbert W. Schneider, "Transcendentalism," *Encyclopedia of the Social Sciences* (New York: Macmillan, 1935), 15:76; Stanley Elkins, *Slavery: A Problem in American Institutional and Intellectual Life* (Chicago: University of Chicago Press, 1959), 153; and John L. Thomas, "Romantic Reform in America, 1815–1865," *American Quarterly* 17 (Winter 1965): 671–79.

32. For Emerson's designation, see George M. Frederickson, *The Inner Civil War: Northern Intellectuals and the Crisis of the Union* (New York: Harper & Row, 1965), 14. Though no history of this group exists, the emergence of its key figures can be traced in Perry Miller, ed., *The Transcendentalists: An Anthology* (Cambridge, Mass.: Harvard University Press, 1950); and (with the curious omission of Theodore Parker) Anne C. Rose, *Transcendentalism as a Social Movement, 1830–1850* (New Haven, Conn.: Yale University Press, 1981).

33. George Ripley, *"The Latest Form of Infidelity" Examined* (Boston: Munroe, 1839), 7; and Ripley, *Philosophical Miscellanies, Translated from the French of Cousin, Jouffroy, and Benjamin Constant* (Boston: Hilliard, Gray, 1838), 1:32. For the fullest biography of Ripley, with a complete account of the controversy with Norton, see Charles Crowe, *George Ripley, Transcendentalist and Utopian Socialist* (Athens: University of Georgia Press, 1967).

34. Orestes Brownson, *New Views of Christianity, Society, and the Church* (Boston: J. Munroe, 1836); Ripley, quoted in Henry Golemba, *George Ripley* (Boston: Twayne, 1977), 46. In 1842 Ripley said that had he not known Brownson, he

would "never have been engaged" in establishing Brook Farm; see Ripley to Brownson, 18 December 1842, Brownson Papers.

35. Ripley, quoted in Octavius Brooks Frothingham, *George Ripley* (Boston: Houghton Mifflin, 1882), 86, 74; Ripley to Carlyle, 29 December 1836, reprinted in Joseph Slater, "George Ripley and Thomas Carlyle," *Proceedings of the Modern Language Association* 67 (June 1952): 344–46.

36. George Ripley, "The Claims of the Age on the Work of the Evangelist," *Western Messenger* 8 (September 1840): 236; Ripley, *A Farewell Discourse* (1841), in Miller, *The Transcendentalists*, 259.

37. [Orestes Brownson], "Introductory Statement," *Boston Quarterly Review* 3 (January 1840): 17; Octavius Brooks Frothingham, *Memoir of William Henry Channing* (Boston: Houghton Mifflin, 1886), 202–3; [George Ripley], Review of *Social Destiny*, *Dial* 1 (October 1840): 265–66.

38. Orestes Brownson, "Church of the Future," *Boston Quarterly Review* 5 (January 1842): 2–3. See David O. Evans, *Social Romanticism in France, 1830–1848* (Oxford: Clarendon Press, 1951).

39. Frothingham, *Memoir of Channing*, 202–3.

40. Ripley quoted in Frothingham, *George Ripley*, 87.

41. [W. H. Channing], "Emerson's Phi Beta Kappa Oration," *Boston Quarterly Review* 1 (January 1838): 116–17.

42. *Journals and Miscellaneous Notebooks of Ralph Waldo Emerson*, ed. William H. Gilman et al. (Cambridge, Mass.: Harvard University Press, 1960–82), 7:407–8, 9:381.

43. Crowe, "Transcendentalist Support of Brook Farm," 286–88; Rose, *Transcendentalism*, 93–94. For a sensitive portrayal of Emerson's emotional boundaries, see Henry James, *Partial Portraits* (1888; rpt. Ann Arbor: University of Michigan Press, 1970), 1–33.

44. Ripley to Emerson, 9 November 1840, and Ripley to congregation, both quoted in Frothingham, *George Ripley*, 311, 87.

45. Ripley to Emerson, 9 November 1840, in Frothingham, *George Ripley*, 307–8.

46. Emerson to Ripley, 15 December 1840, in *The Letters of Ralph Waldo Emerson*, ed. Ralph L. Rusk (New York: Columbia University Press, 1939), 2:369.

47. Emerson, *Journals*, 7:407–8. Rose, *Transcendentalism*, 106, 114–17, assesses Emerson's decision against joining Brook Farm in light of his attitude toward Concord and his interest in reforming labor.

48. Emerson, "Self-Reliance," and "New England Reformers," in *The Complete Works of Ralph Waldo Emerson*, ed. Edward Waldo Emerson (Boston: Houghton Mifflin, 1903–4), 2:49–50, 3:267.

49. Hawthorne to Sophia Peabody, 1 June 1841, in *Autobiography of Brook Farm*, ed. Henry W. Sams (Englewood Cliffs, N.J.: Prentice-Hall, 1958), 21.

50. John Van Der Zee Sears, *My Friends at Brook Farm* (New York: Desmond Fitzgerald, 1912), 141–42. The best account of life during the community's early years remains Lindsay Swift, *Brook Farm: Its Members, Scholars, and Visitors* (New York: Macmillan, 1900).

51. Crowe, "Transcendentalist Support of Brook Farm," 282–85; Rose, *Transcendentalism*, 133.

52. Ripley, quoted in Frothingham, *George Ripley*, 147.

53. Rose, *Transcendentalism*, 138.

54. Elizabeth Peabody, "Plan of the West Roxbury Community," *Dial* 2 (January 1842): 364; Frothingham, *George Ripley*, 310. The Articles of Association are reprinted in Frothingham, pp. 112–17.

55. Swift, *Brook Farm*, 155. For Dwight's biography, see George Willis Cooke, *John Sullivan Dwight: Brook Farmer, Editor, and Critic of Music* (Boston: Small, Maynard, 1898).

56. J. S. Dwight, "Another 'Latest Form of Infidelity,' " *Boston Daily Chronotype*, 4 September 1849; Emerson to Carlyle, 19 March 1839, in *The Correspondence of Emerson and Carlyle*, ed. Joseph L. Slater (New York: Columbia University Press, 1964), 220; Dwight, "Mozart," *Democratic Review* 13 (November 1843): 470.

57. James Harrison Wilson, *The Life of Charles A. Dana* (New York: Harper, 1907), 19–59.

58. James Kay, Jr., to John Sullivan Dwight, 2 March 1846, JSD Collection; Swift, *Brook Farm*, 135, 281; Miller, *The Transcendentalists*, 469. For echoes in popular history of Swift's judgment regarding Fourierism's role at Brook Farm, see V. F. Calverton, *Where Angels Dared to Tread* (Indianapolis, Ind.: Bobbs-Merrill, 1941), 197–227; and Mark Holloway, *Heavens on Earth: Utopian Communities in America, 1680–1880*, 2d ed. (New York: Dover, 1966), 128–31, 152–54.

59. John Thomas Codman, *Brook Farm: Historic and Personal Memoirs* (Boston: Arena, 1894), 25–45; Charles R. Crowe, "Fourierism and the Founding of Brook Farm," *Boston Public Library Quarterly* 12 (April 1960): 87. Three recent accounts have portrayed Fourierism as a logical choice for the Brook Farmers, two mainly on practical and one on intellectual grounds: Rose, *Transcendentalism*, 144–50; Golemba, *Ripley*, 88–94; and Richard Francis, "The Ideology of Brook Farm," in *Studies in the American Renaissance 1977*, ed. Joel Myerson (Boston: Twayne, 1978), 1–48.

60. Charles Dana to Isaac Hecker, [August 1843], and Orestes Brownson to Hecker, 2 September 1843, Hecker Papers. "I am reading Brisbane's book on the reorganization of Society," the Brook Farmers' friend Samuel Osgood wrote in 1840. "I understand, however, that our new light Socialists eschew Brisbane's dictum." See Osgood to J. S. Dwight, 21 November 1840, JSD Collection. For evidence that Ripley read Brisbane's book at that time, see note 37 above.

61. Greeley to Dana, 29 August 1842, quoted in Wilson, *Dana*, 41.

62. Godwin to Dana, 17 May 1844, B-G Collection.

63. Rose, *Transcendentalism*, 139.

64. See Francis, "Ideology of Brook Farm," 15–29; Crowe, "Fourierism and Brook Farm," 83–84; Carl J. Guarneri, "Utopian Socialism and American Ideas: The Origins and Doctrine of American Fourierism, 1832–1848" (Ph.D. diss., Johns Hopkins University, 1979), 81–84.

65. Dwight, "Another 'Latest Form of Infidelity' "; Codman, *Brook Farm*, 39.

66. Francis to Theodore Parker, 22 June 1844, Abernethy Library; Ralph Waldo Emerson, "Fourier and the Socialists," *Dial* 3 (July 1842): 88–89; Ripley to *New York Tribune*, 13 August 1842.

67. Ripley to Minot Pratt, 22 July 1843, Fruitlands Museum.

68. Rose, *Transcendentalism*, 137; Frothingham, *George Ripley*, 163.

69. Rose, *Transcendentalism*, 139–40.

70. Frothingham, *George Ripley*, 161–62; Codman, *Brook Farm*, 115.

71. Ripley to Minot Pratt, 22 July 1843, Fruitlands Museum; Ripley to Isaac Hecker, 18 September 1843, Hecker Papers; Sophia Ripley to Margaret Fuller, [December 1843], quoted in Edith Roelker Curtis, *A Season in Utopia: The Story of Brook Farm* (New York: Thomas Nelson, 1961), 159–60.

72. See Frothingham, *Memoir of Channing*, for a character sketch (p. 44) and biographical details. A recent analysis is David Robinson, "The Political Odyssey of William Henry Channing," *American Quarterly* 34 (Summer 1982): 165–84.

73. Codman, *Brook Farm*, 71.

74. [Channing], "Emerson's Phi Beta Kappa Oration," 115.

75. Channing to Parker, 9 June 1842, in Frothingham, *Memoir of Channing*, 174–75.

76. See Pierre Leroux, *De l'humanité* (Paris: Perrotin, 1840); and Brownson, "Leroux on Humanity," *Boston Quarterly Review* 5 (July 1842): 257–322. For Leroux's impact on Godwin, see Godwin, *Popular View*, 27n; and *Pathfinder*, 20 May 1843, p. 194: "All we know of the doctrine of Life ('solidarity') we derive from the writings of Leroux." Arthur Bestor, "The Evolution of the Socialist Vocabulary," *Journal of the History of Ideas* 9 (June 1948): 259–302, traces the origin of the word "socialism."

77. J. S. Dwight, "The Idea of a Divine Social Order," *Harbinger* 6 (April 1848): 170; Codman, *Brook Farm*, 227. For Brownson, who came to envision the Catholic Church as "the realm of true solidarity" through which all humans shared divine grace, see A. Robert Caponigri, "European Influences on the Thought of Orestes Brownson: Pierre Leroux and Vincenzo Gioberti," in *No Divided Allegiance: Essays in Brownson's Thought*, ed. Leonard Gilhooley (New York: Fordham University Press, 1980), 108.

78. Parke Godwin, "A Letter to Joseph Mazzini on the Doctrines of Fourier," *Harbinger* 4 (15 May 1847): 364; W. H. Channing, "To Our Friends," *Western Messenger* 8 (May 1840): 1.

79. W. H. Channing, "Social Reform Convention at Boston," *Present* 1 (15 January 1844): 283. See also Channing, "Call of Present—No.2.—Science of Unity," *Present* 1 (15 November 1843): 73–80. For Brownson's skepticism, see "The Community System," *Democratic Review* 12 (February 1843): 134–35.

80. James Freeman Clarke, "Fourierism," *Christian Examiner* 37 (July 1844): 76–78; Elizabeth Peabody, "Fourierism," *Dial* 4 (April 1844): 481–82.

81. Francis, "Ideology of Brook Farm," 5, 36–41; Robinson, "Political Odyssey," 177.

82. Zoltan Haraszti, *The Idyll of Brook Farm* (Boston: Trustees of the Public Library, 1937), 27.

83. "Call to the Friends of Social Reform," *Phalanx* 1 (5 December 1843): 44; "Social Reform Convention at Boston," *Phalanx* 1 (5 January 1844): 46–47.

84. Channing, "Social Reform Convention," 277; *Present* 1 (1 April 1844): 432.

85. *Constitution of the Brook Farm Association for Industry and Education* (Boston: I. R. Butts, 1844), 6–7.

86. Curtis to Dwight, 3 March 1844, in *Early Letters of George William Curtis to John S. Dwight*, ed. George W. Cooke (New York: Harper, 1898), 157. For indications that only a few Brook Farmers defected specifically because of the transition to Fourierism, see Codman, *Brook Farm*, 41; and Rose, *Transcendentalism*, 153.

87. Dwight, *Letters From Brook Farm*, 140; Georgianna Bruce Kirby, *Years of Experience: An Autobiographical Narrative* (New York: Putnam, 1887), 183ff.

88. *Phalanx* 1 (1 March 1844): 81; Rose, *Transcendentalism*, 152–53.

89. Codman, *Brook Farm*, 74.

Chapter 3. Roots of Popular Participation

1. Albert Brisbane, "Spread of the Doctrine of Association," *Phalanx* 1 (5 December 1843): 34; Arthur Bestor, "American Phalanxes: A Study of Fourierist Socialism in the United States (with Special Reference to the Movement in Western New York)" (Ph.D. diss., Yale University, 1938), 1:263.

2. Arthur Bestor, "The Transit of Communitarian Socialism to America," in *Backwoods Utopias: The Sectarian Origins and the Owenite Phase of Communitarian Socialism in America, 1663–1829*, 2d ed. (Philadelphia: University of Pennsylvania Press, 1970), 266–68.

3. Bestor, *Backwoods Utopias,* 59.

4. See especially Bestor, "Patent-Office Models of the Good Society: Some Relationships between Social Reform and Westward Expansion," *American Historical Review* 58 (1953), reprinted in *Backwoods Utopias,* 230–52.

5. For summaries of these trends, see George R. Taylor, *The Transportation Revolution, 1815–1860* (New York: Holt, Rinehart & Winston, 1951); and Douglass C. North, *The Economic Growth of the United States, 1790–1860* (Englewood Cliffs, N.J.: Prentice-Hall, 1961).

6. Urbanization and the rise of industrialism are the organizing concepts of most textbooks and economic histories covering the antebellum North. The fullest attempt to apply the concept of modernization to the period is Richard D. Brown, *Modernization: The Transformation of American Life, 1600–1865* (New York: Hill & Wang, 1976).

7. The classic account of the extension of the market economy in antebellum America is Taylor, *Transportation Revolution.* On the crash, see Reginald McGrane, *The Panic of 1837* (1924; rpt. New York: Russell & Russell, 1965). J. R. T. Hughes and Nathan Rosenberg, "The United States Business Cycle before 1860: Some Problems of Interpretation," *Economic History Review,* 2d ser., 15 (April 1963): 476–93, documents the economy's peaks and troughs but questions traditional interpretations based on trade and credit.

8. Jeffrey G. Williamson, "American Prices and Urban Inequality since 1820," *Journal of Economic History* 36 (June 1976): 303–33; Edward Pessen, "The Egalitarian Myth and the American Social Reality: Wealth, Mobility, and Equality in the 'Era of the Common Man,' " *American Historical Review* 79 (1971): 989–1034; Pessen, *Riches, Class, and Power before the Civil War* (Lexington, Mass.: D.C. Heath, 1973); Lee Soltow, "Economic Inequality in the United States in the Period from 1790 to 1860," *Journal of Economic History* 31 (1971): 822–39; and Douglas T. Miller, *Jacksonian Aristocracy: Class and Democracy in New York, 1830–1860* (New York: Oxford University Press, 1967), 106–54. For the estimate of wage earners, see David Montgomery, *Beyond Equality: Labor and the Radical Republicans, 1862–1872* (New York: Random House, 1967), 26–30.

9. The impact of reorganized production upon artisans is traced in several recent studies, the best of which are Alan Dawley, *Class and Community: The Industrial Revolution in Lynn* (Cambridge, Mass.: Harvard University Press, 1976); and Sean Wilentz, *Chants Democratic: New York City and the Rise of the American Working Class, 1788–1850* (New York: Oxford University Press, 1984). For the effect of the factory system, see Thomas Dublin, *Women at Work: The Transformation of Work and Community in Lowell, Massachusetts, 1826–1860* (New York: Columbia University Press, 1979).

10. Mary P. Ryan, *Cradle of the Middle Class: The Family in Oneida County, New York, 1790–1865* (Cambridge: Cambridge University Press, 1981), esp. 18–59. My description of family and household change relies on Ryan and on recent family history literature, much of which is represented in *The American Family in Social-Historical Perspective,* ed. Michael F. Gordon, 3d ed. (New York: St. Martin's Press, 1983).

11. The standard account, Whitney R. Cross, *The Burned-Over District: The Social and Intellectual History of Enthusiastic Religion in Western New York, 1800–1850* (Ithaca: Cornell University Press, 1950), may be supplemented with more recent specialized studies such as Paul E. Johnson, *A Shopkeeper's Millennium: Society and Revivals in Rochester, New York, 1815–1837* (New York: Hill & Wang, 1978); and (for the Millerites and utopians) Michael Barkun, *Crucible of the Millennium: The Burned-Over District of New York in the 1840s* (Syracuse, N.Y.: Syracuse University Press, 1986).

12. Brisbane, *Social Destiny*, 133; Noyes, *American Socialisms*, 23.

13. See below, Chapters 6 and 11.

14. The origins of the Panic of 1837 remain in dispute. Traditional accounts stress domestic overspeculation, first stimulated then disastrously halted by Andrew Jackson's fiscal policies. More recently, Peter Temin, *The Jacksonian Economy* (New York: Norton, 1969), has pointed to foreign influences in slowing American growth, particularly declining British investment and decreased British demand for cotton. For the impact of the depression, see Samuel Rezneck, "The Social History of an American Depression, 1837–1843," *American Historical Review* 40 (1935): 662–687.

15. Brisbane, *Mental Biography*, 246; Barkun, *Crucible of the Millennium*, 115; Norman F. Ware, *The Industrial Worker, 1840–1860* (Boston: Houghton Mifflin, 1924), 112, 26, 31–32.

16. A. J. Macdonald, quoted in Noyes, *American Socialisms*, 256; Joan Elias, "The Wisconsin Phalanx: An Experiment in Association," (M.A. thesis, University of Wisconsin, 1968), 28–45.

17. Brisbane, *Mental Biography*, 206.

18. Bestor, "American Phalanxes," 1:54, 217–18; Noyes, *American Socialisms*, 259–62 (for Pennsylvania); H. U. Johnson, "History of the Trumbull Phalanx" (Ohio), *Western Reserve Chronicle*, 5 May 1897. For the Wisconsin Phalanx and the Alphadelphia Association in Michigan, see Stock Ledger, Records of 4 December 1848, W-CC Papers; and appraisals of members' property upon joining, AA Papers.

19. Anne C. Rose, *Transcendentalism as a Social Movement, 1830–1850* (New Haven, Conn.: Yale University Press, 1981), 73 n.5.

20. See William Charvat, "American Romanticism and the Depression of 1837," *Science and Society* 2 (1937): 67–82; Michael T. Gilmore, *American Romanticism and the Marketplace* (Chicago: University of Chicago Press, 1986); John R. Bodo, *The Protestant Clergy and Public Issues, 1812–1848* (Princeton, N.J.: Princeton University Press, 1954); and Charles C. Cole, Jr., *The Social Ideas of the Northern Evangelists, 1826–1860* (New York: Octagon Books, 1977).

21. "On the Elevation of the Laboring Classes," in *The Works of William Ellery Channing* (Boston: American Unitarian Association, 1875), 58.

22. William Henry Channing, "Social Reform Convention at Boston," *Present* 1 (15 January 1844): 283.

23. Noyes, *American Socialisms*, 228–29 (quotation), 21–29; Cross, *Burned-Over District*, 328.

24. Johnson, *Shopkeeper's Millennium;* Anthony F. C. Wallace, *Rockdale: The Growth of an American Village in the Early Industrial Revolution* (New York: Knopf, 1978).

25. John L. Thomas, "Romantic Reform in America, 1815–1865," *American Quarterly* 17 (Winter 1965): 656–81.

26. [Henry James, Sr.], *Tracts for the New Times, No. 1: Letter to a Swedenborgian* (New York: John Allen, 1847), 3, 11–12; Noyes, *American Socialisms*, 27.

27. Cross, *Burned-Over District*, 332; James L. McElroy, "Social Reform in the Burned-Over District: Rochester, New York as a Test Case, 1830–1854" (Ph.D. diss., State University of New York, Binghampton, 1974), 195.

28. H. R. Schetterly to George Sanderson, [1838], Nathaniel Stacy Papers, William L. Clements Library, University of Michigan.

29. Cross, *Burned-Over District*, 280.

30. For Noyes's career, see Robert A. Parker, *A Yankee Saint: John Humphrey Noyes and the Oneida Community* (New York: Putnam, 1935); and Robert David Thomas, *The Man Who Would Be Perfect: John Humphrey Noyes and the Utopian*

Impulse (Philadelphia: University of Pennsylvania Press, 1977). For Stillman, see Noyes, *American Socialisms*, 277; and Bestor, "American Phalanxes," 36–37.

31. Joseph Cooke, "A Personal Experience," *Harbinger* 5 (10 July 1847): 65–67; reprinted in Charles Crowe, "The Religious History of a Christian Socialist," *Rhode Island History* 23 (1964): 81–89.

32. Ronald G. Walters, *The Antislavery Appeal: American Abolitionism after 1830* (Baltimore, Md.: Johns Hopkins University Press, 1976), 39, confirms such a trajectory among antislaveryites.

33. William Henry Channing, *The Gospel of To-day* (Boston: Crosby & Nichols, 1847), 8.

34. H. H. Van Amringe, *Nature and Revelation* (New York: R. P. Bixby, 1843); and Van Amringe, *Association and Christianity* (Pittsburgh, Pa.: J. W. Cooke, 1845), 67–119. For Van Amringe's Fourierist activity, see Noyes, *American Socialisms*, 336, 345, 358, 364, 437–38.

35. For Smolnikar, see "Great Movements in Limestone County, Penn.," *Present* 1 (1 March 1844): 353–54; "Peace-Union Settlement," *Phalanx* 1 (1 April 1844): 100, and 1 (20 April 1844): 103.

36. Cross, *Burned-Over District*, 332; T. D. Seymour Bassett, "The Secular Utopian Socialists," in *Socialism and American Life*, ed. Donald Drew Egbert and Stow Persons (Princeton, N.J.: Princeton University Press, 1952), 1:194; John Caroll Power and S. A. Power, *History of the Early Settlers of Sangamon County, Illinois* (Springfield, Ill.: E. A. Wilson, 1876), 699; *DocHist* 7:281; *Harbinger* 1 (26 July 1845): 98.

37. Noyes, *American Socialisms*, 550. For Swedenborgians among the Owenites, see John F. C. Harrison, *Quest for the New Moral World: Robert Owen and the Owenites in Britain and America* (New York: Scribner, 1969), 107. The best history of the New Church is Marguerite Beck Block, *The New Church in the New World: A Study of Swedenborgianism in America* (New York: Holt, Rinehart & Winston, 1932).

38. Ophia D. Smith, "The Rise of the New Jerusalem Church in Ohio," *Ohio State Archaeological and Historical Quarterly* 61 (October 1952): 404. For the phalanxes, see "Leraysville Phalanx," *Phalanx* 1 (5 February 1844): 69, and 1 (7 September 1844): 276; Noyes, *American Socialisms*, 262–64; Block, *New Church*, 153–54. In September 1843 Brisbane recruited the Rev. B. F. Barrett of the New York City New Church to testify that Fourierism was in "perfect harmony" with Christianity. The Swedenborgian ministers James P. Stuart of Ohio and A. E. Ford of Philadelphia were active in the Fourierist movement. See "Opinion of a Clergyman in Regard to Association," *Phalanx* 1 (5 October 1843): 13–14, and 1 (4 November 1843): 20; and "Letter from Philadelphia," *Harbinger* 6 (15 April 1848): 189. Barrett and Stuart eventually retracted their support for Association under pressure from orthodox New Churchmen.

39. Austin Warren, *The Elder Henry James* (New York: Macmillan, 1934), 55–86.

40. John L. Thomas, "Antislavery and Utopia," in *The Antislavery Vanguard: New Essays on the Abolitionists*, ed. Martin Duberman (Princeton, N.J.: Princeton University Press, 1965), 249–62. John Orvis came to Brook Farm in 1844 from Collins's Skaneateles community. See Marianne Dwight, *Letters from Brook Farm, 1844–1847*, ed. Amy L. Reed (Poughkeepsie, N.Y.: Vassar College, 1928), 14.

41. George Throop to DeWitt Throop, 4 October 1843, in Cross, *Burned-Over District*, 329. For Clapp, see Lewis Perry, *Radical Abolitionism: Anarchy and the Government of God in Antislavery Thought* (Ithaca: Cornell University Press, 1973), 114–17; for Allen, John Thomas Codman, *Brook Farm: Historic and Personal Memoirs* (Boston: Arena, 1894), 123.

42. Among overviews of the huge literature on millennialism and nineteenth-

century American culture are *The Rise of Adventism: Religion and Society in Mid-Nineteenth Century America,* ed. Edwin S. Gaustad (New York: Harper & Row, 1974); and David E. Smith, "Millenarian Scholarship in America," *American Quarterly* 17 (Summer 1965): 163–86.

43. *Phalanx* 1 (20 April 1844): 104, 113; W. H. Channing, "Association in the United States," *Harbinger* 1 (20 September 1845): 237. For a fuller analysis of Fourierist millennialism, see Chapter 4, below.

44. W. H. Channing, "Objections to Association—No. III," *Harbinger* 3 (1 August 1846): 126.

45. "Man the Reformer," in *The Complete Works of Ralph Waldo Emerson,* ed. Edward Waldo Emerson (Boston: Houghton Mifflin, 1903–4), 1:228. An excellent survey is Ronald G. Walters, *American Reformers, 1815–1860* (New York: Hill & Wang, 1978).

46. On reform organizations and techniques and their roots in the "benevolent empire," see Charles I. Foster, *An Errand of Mercy: The Evangelical United Front, 1790–1837* (Chapel Hill: University of North Carolina Press, 1960); and C. S. Griffin, *Their Brother's Keepers: Moral Stewardship in the United States, 1800–1860* (New Brunswick, N.J.: Rutgers University Press, 1965). For the social role of the reformer, see Walters, *Antislavery Appeal,* 19–25.

47. For summaries of these developments, see Gunther Barth, "The Metropolitan Press," in *City People: The Rise of Modern City Culture in Nineteenth-Century America* (New York: Oxford University Press, 1980), 58–109; Carl Bode, *Antebellum Culture* (Berkeley: University of California Press, 1959), 109–32; and Taylor, *Transportation Revolution.*

48. Horace Greeley, *Hints toward Reforms* (New York: Harper, 1850). For Associationists on the lyceum circuit, see Carl Bode, *The American Lyceum: Town Meeting of the Mind* (New York: Oxford University Press, 1956), 144–45, 176, 194, 208–9; and Carl David Mead, *Yankee Eloquence in the Middle West: The Ohio Lyceum, 1850–1870* (East Lansing: Michigan State College Press, 1951), 96–97, 254. By 1852, Greeley claimed, he was on the road lecturing "a full third of the time"; see Greeley to Schuyler Colfax, 20 January 1852, quoted in Glyndon G. Van Deusen, *Horace Greeley, Nineteenth-Century Crusader* (Philadelphia: University of Pennsylvania Press, 1953), 154–55.

49. Considerant to Julie Considerant, 9 March 1853, FNA (10 AS 28, doss. 9).

50. Emerson, "Man the Reformer," 1:230. For suggestive comments on reform as a career, see Walters, *Antislavery Appeal,* 22–23; and *American Reformers,* 13–14.

51. "Progress at the West," *Harbinger* 1 (16 August 1845): 160.

52. Bestor, *Backwoods Utopias,* 56–57.

53. Noyes, *American Socialisms,* 26, 28. For a review of the literature distinguishing between "moral" and "social" reform, and a persuasive argument against the distinction, see C. S. Griffin, *The Ferment of Reform, 1830–1860* (New York: T. Y. Crowell, 1967), 51–55.

54. Walters, *American Reformers,* is especially sensitive to the ways antebellum reformers were anchored in the prevailing culture. But this emphasis should be counterbalanced by an appreciation of how reformers contested the meaning of the republican and Christian heritage. The notion that language and rhetoric have the power not only to impose cultural hegemony but also to resist it lies behind the recent "linguistic turn" of intellectual and cultural history. See esp. Dominick La Capra, *Rethinking Intellectual History: Texts, Contexts, Language* (Ithaca: Cornell University Press, 1983); and T. J. Jackson Lears, "The Concept of Cultural Hegemony: Problems and Possibilities," *American Historical Review* 90 (June 1985): 567–93.

55. David Brion Davis, "The Emergence of Immediatism in British and American Antislavery Thought," *Mississippi Valley Historical Review* 49 (September 1962): 209–30.

56. Among the first to make this point was David M. Ludlum, *Social Ferment in Vermont, 1791–1850* (New York: Columbia University Press, 1939), 260–62.

57. William Throop to DeWitt Throop, 7 January 1844, Throop Papers, quoted in Cross, *Burned-Over District*, 329; Charles Crowe, "Utopian Socialism in Rhode Island, 1845–1850," *Rhode Island History* 18 (January 1959): 23–24.

58. T.C.P. [Thomas C. Palmer], *A Plain Lecture on Association* (Boston: Crosby & Nichols, 1847), 15–20; [Parke Godwin], "Address to the People of the United States," *Phalanx* 1 (20 April 1844): 111; Channing, *Gospel of To-day*, 11–16; Channing, "Anniversary Week," *Harbinger* 1 (21 June 1845): 29.

59. Albert Brisbane, *Association; or, A Concise Exposition of the Practical Part of Fourier's Social Science* (New York: Greeley & McElrath, 1843), 73–74.

60. Bestor, *Backwoods Utopias*, 1–19.

61. See Mark Holloway, *Heavens on Earth: Utopian Communities in America, 1680–1880*, 2d ed. (New York: Dover, 1966), 31–100. For a checklist of sectarian communities, see Bestor, *Backwoods Utopias*, 277–84.

62. Brisbane, *Social Destiny*, 29; [Sophia Ripley], "Letter from Zoar" (dated 9 August 1838), *Dial* 2 (July 1841): 122–29; Horace Greeley, "A Sabbath with the Shakers," *Knickerbocker, or New-York Monthly Magazine* 11 (June 1838): 532–37; [Elizabeth P. Peabody], "A Glimpse of Christ's Idea of Society," *Dial* 2 (October 1841): 222; Bestor, *Backwoods Utopias*, 58–59.

63. Noyes, quoted in Bestor, *Backwoods Utopias*, 53–54; Dolores Hayden, *Seven American Utopias: The Architecture of Communitarian Socialism, 1790–1975* (Cambridge, Mass.: MIT Press, 1976), 18. According to a memoir of a Shaker sister at the same community, Charles Sears of the North American Phalanx, John Orvis of Brook Farm, and Marcus Spring of the Raritan Bay Union—all Fourierist leaders—either visited or wrote letters to the New York Shakers in the 1840s. See Bestor, *Backwoods Utopias*, 50.

64. Bestor, *Backwoods Utopias*, 55.

65. Otohiko Okugawa, "Intercommunal Relationships among Nineteenth-Century Communal Societies in America," *Communal Societies* 3 (1983): 71–82.

66. Lloyd Easton, *Hegel's First American Followers* (Athens: Ohio University Press, 1966), 108–10; A. D. P. Van Buren, "The Alphadelphia Association," *Michigan Pioneer and Historical Collections* 5 (1884): 412; Noyes, *American Socialisms*, 478–79, 484.

67. [Peabody], "Glimpse," 222; J. S. Dwight, "The Shakers at New Lebanon" (pt. 2), *Harbinger* 5 (21 August 1847): 175–76. For Engels, see Lewis S. Feuer, "The Influence of the American Communist Colonies on Engels and Marx," *Western Political Quarterly* 19 (September 1966): 456–65.

68. Bestor, *Backwoods Utopias*, 47, 57; Noyes, *American Socialisms*, 670.

69. Noyes, *American Socialisms*, 192.

70. J. S. Dwight, "The Shakers at New Lebanon" (pt. 1), *Harbinger* 5 (14 August 1847): 157–58.

71. Bestor, *Backwoods Utopias*, 58; Parke Godwin, *A Popular View of the Doctrines of Charles Fourier* (New York: J. S. Redfield, 1844), 11–13. Godwin's conclusion echoed the British liberal Harriet Martineau's opinion of the Shakers; see her *Society in America* (London: Saunders & Otley, 1837), 2:57.

72. Brisbane, Godwin, Greeley, and other New York Associationists met Owen during his American tour; Owen himself visited Brook Farm in May 1845; and Brisbane and Lewis Ryckman attended Owen's World Reform Convention in New York City on October 1, 1845. See Godwin to Charles Dana, 17 September

1844, B-G Collection; Marianne Dwight to A. Q. T. Parsons, May [1845], in Dwight, *Letters from Brook Farm*, 94–95; and Ware, *Industrial Worker*, 215–16.

73. George Ripley, Review of *Social Destiny of Man, Dial* 1 (October 1840): 266; Samuel Osgood to John S. Dwight, 21 November 1840, JSD Collection.

74. Ripley, Review of *Social Destiny*, 265–66; Ripley to Ralph Waldo Emerson, 9 November 1840, quoted in Octavius Brooks Frothingham, *George Ripley* (Boston: Houghton Mifflin, 1882), 311. See Charles Crowe, "Fourierism and the Founding of Brook Farm," *Boston Public Library Quarterly* 11 (April 1960): 79–88. Writing in the summer of 1841, the Brook Farmers' friend Christopher P. Cranch referred to the community as "the Phalanx." See Cranch to Dwight, 22 July 1841, Cranch Papers.

75. This and the following paragraph are indebted to Arthur Bestor's fine discussion in *Backwoods Utopias*, 16–19, of the correspondences between communitarianism and the American experience.

76. Thomas, "Romantic Reform," 676–77.

77. See [Godwin], "Address," 109; and Godwin, *Democracy, Constructive and Pacific* (New York: J. Winchester, 1844), 35–38.

78. Readers familiar with Bestor's "Patent-Office Models," 230–52 (quotation, p. 248), will note that I have condensed and paraphrased his argument in this paragraph.

79. See Georg G. Iggers, "Further Remarks about Early Uses of the Term 'Social Science,' " *Journal of the History of Ideas* 20 (June–September 1959): 433–36; and, on the Owenites, Harrison, *Quest for the New Moral World*, 74, 78, 83–84.

80. Orestes Brownson, "The Laboring Classes," *Boston Quarterly Review* 4 (October 1840): 476; Brisbane, *Social Destiny*, 453; Brisbane, "Association and a Social Reform," *Boston Quarterly Review* 5 (April 1842): 183; Codman, *Brook Farm*, 41.

81. "Letter from Mr. Brisbane. . .," *Boston Quarterly Review* 4 (October 1841): 495.

82. See, e.g., Orestes Brownson's *New Views of Christianity, Society, and the Church* (Boston: J. Munroe, 1836).

83. Dwight, quoted in *Harbinger* 1 (6 September 1845): 206; W.H.M. [William H. Muller], *There Exists a Social Law; or, A Divine Order of Human Society* (Pittsburgh, Pa.: Johnston & Stockton, 1849); W. H. Channing, "Call of the Present—No. 2—Science of Unity," *Present* 1 (15 November 1843): 73–80.

84. On antebellum pseudosciences and their philosophical claims, see Arthur Wrobel, ed., *Pseudo-Science and Society in Nineteenth-Century America* (Lexington: University Press of Kentucky, 1986); John D. Davies, *Phrenology, Fad and Science: A Nineteenth Century American Crusade* (New Haven, Conn.: Yale University Press, 1955); R. Laurence Moore, *In Search of White Crows: Spiritualism, Parapsychology and American Culture* (New York: Oxford University Press, 1977); Martin Kaufman, *Homeopathy in America: The Rise and Fall of a Medical Heresy* (Baltimore, Md.: Johns Hopkins University Press, 1971); and Robert C. Fuller, *Mesmerism and the American Cure of Souls* (Philadelphia: University of Pennsylvania Press, 1982).

85. Wrobel, introduction to *Pseudo-Science and Society*, 7–8; Hugh M. Ayer, "Joseph Rodes Buchanan and 'The Science of Man,' " *Filson Club Historical Quarterly* 36 (January 1962): 32–42; Madeleine B. Stern, *Heads and Headlines: The Phrenological Fowlers* (Norman: University of Oklahoma Press, 1971), 79. For Buchanan's endorsement of Fourierism, see "The Seventh of April in Cincinnati," *Harbinger* 6 (6 May 1848): 4–6. Fourierists were also interested in "physiognomy," an offshoot of phrenology popularized by their friend J. S. Redfield, which claimed to read character traits in facial structure. See Marx Edgeworth Lazarus, "Physiognomy—The Science of Incarnation—Dr. Redfield's Discoveries," *Har-*

binger 6 (12 February 1848): 113–14. Fowlers and Wells published several Fourierist tracts by Lazarus.

86. Ripley, "Association and Medical Reform," *Harbinger* 4 (13 February 1847): 158–59. For the individuals listed, see Bertha-Monica Stearns, "Two Forgotten New England Reformers," *New England Quarterly* 6 (March 1933): 59–84; John B. Blake, "Mary Gove Nichols, Prophetess of Health," *Proceedings of the American Philosophical Society* 106 (June 1962): 219–34; Grace Adams and Edward Hutter, *The Mad Forties* (New York: Harper, 1942), 72, 102 (Calvert); and *Dictionary of American Biography*, s.v. "Hempel, Charles Julius," and "Neidhard, Charles."

87. Marx Edgeworth Lazarus, *Comparative Psychology and Universal Analogy* (New York: Fowlers & Wells, 1851), 260–62; [Charles J. Hempel], *The True Organization of the New Church* (New York: Wm. Radde, 1848). Block, *New Church*, 161–65, documents the close relationship between homeopathy and American Swedenborgians. Several French Fourierists were also homeopathic physicians, including Fourier's biographer Charles Pellarin and the internationally renowned Edouard Brown-Séquard.

88. For "Christian capitalism," see Wallace, *Rockdale*, 350–97. That the Fourierists attracted merchants and propertied professionals rather than manufacturers was most apparent in the Boston area, where no industrialists could be found among some three dozen wealthy contributors to local Associationist clubs and churches.

89. For the French experiments at Condé-sur-Vesgre and Citeaux, see Chapter 1, notes 25 and 27.

90. In Boston, for example, James T. Fisher—a partner of Fishers and Chapin, dealers in wholesale salt provisions—was a frequent contributor to the Boston Union of Associationists, the Religious Union of Associationists, and the parent society, the American Union of Associationists. Fisher also invested in Brook Farm and owned $1,550 worth of capital stock in the North American Phalanx. See the correspondence and receipts in the JTF Papers.

91. See Hayden, *Seven American Utopias*, 164, 172.

92. Garrett R. Carpenter, *Silkville: A Kansas Attempt in the History of the Fourierist Utopias, 1869–1882* (Emporia: Kansas State Teachers College, 1954). For more on Silkville, see Chapter 16.

93. David J. Rothman, *The Discovery of the Asylum: Social Order and Disorder in the New Republic* (Boston: Little, Brown, 1971), assesses the antebellum reform of penal institutions; revisionist historians of education such as Michael Katz, David Tyack, and Carl Kaestle emphasize the impulse to order and discipline among common school advocates. A synthetic look at conservative institutional reform in the nineteenth century is Paul S. Boyer, *Urban Masses and Moral Order in America, 1820–1920* (Cambridge, Mass.: Harvard University Press, 1978).

94. Ludlum, *Social Ferment in Vermont*, 229–232, 265.

95. W. H. Channing, "Call of the Present—No.1.—Social Reorganization," *Present* 1 (15 October 1843): 43; Channing, "Social Reform Convention," 283.

96. Ripley, Reply to Skaneateles Convention Call [1844], in Frothingham, *George Ripley*, 147; Dwight, "Shakers," 157–58.

97. Bestor, "Patent-Office Models"; Thomas, "Romantic Reform," 678.

CHAPTER 4. ASSOCIATION AND AMERICAN SOCIETY

1. The clearest and fullest survey of Fourier's thought in English is Nicholas V. Riasnovsky, *The Teaching of Charles Fourier* (Berkeley: University of California Press, 1969). For other sources, see Chapter 1, note 6.

2. Arthur Bestor, "Albert Brisbane—Propagandist for Socialism in the 1840's," *New York History* 28 (April 1947): 128–58, esp. 146–48.

3. Brisbane traveled to France in 1844 and 1848, Dana and Fisher in 1848. The Americans published seven complete French Fourierist tracts in translation and excerpted several more in their periodicals. *Harbinger* 4 (29 May 1847): 400, listed French Fourierist books and pamphlets available for sale in the United States.

4. *Phalanx* 1 (15 June 1844): 180, named *Destinée sociale*, the volumes by Paget and Lechevalier, and several other French Fourierist tracts in Brisbane's possession. For his borrowings from Considerant, see Brisbane, *Social Destiny*, 239, 295, 364.

5. Brisbane, *Social Destiny*, 219. For early criticisms of Fourier's theory, see "The Assaults of the New York Express," *Harbinger* 1 (30 August 1845): 189–191; Orestes Brownson, "Church Unity and Social Amelioration," *Brownson's Quarterly Review* 1 (July 1844): 310–27; and Donald C. M'Laren, *Boa-Constrictor; or, Fourier Association Self-Exposed as to Its Principles and Aims* (Rochester: Canfield & Warren, 1844). For Brisbane's account of these, see Brisbane, *Mental Biography*, 210–11.

6. Parke Godwin, *A Popular View of the Doctrines of Charles Fourier* (New York: J. S. Redfield, 1844), 84; "General Convention of the Friends of Association in the United States," *Phalanx* 1 (20 April 1844): 106, 109.

7. Although Americans had previously used the term "Association," the label "Associationist" was apparently coined just before the April 1844 New York convention, simultaneously with the first use of "Association" that explicitly distinguished it from "Fourierism"; see *Phalanx* 1 (1 April 1844): 87. Throughout this book, however, for the sake of variety I use "Fourierists" and "Associationists" interchangeably to denote the Americans, and the corresponding "isms" for their thought, as long as the limited nature of their doctrine is clear. I choose "Fourier*ists*" rather than "Fourier*ites*," another common usage, because this was the Associationists' own preference. See Charles Dana in *Harbinger* 1 (5 July 1845): 58.

8. *Phalanx* 1 (10 August 1844): 239n.

9. Albert Brisbane, *Association; or a Concise Exposition of the Practical Part of Fourier's Social Science* (New York: Greeley & McElrath, 1843). See also Bestor, "Brisbane," 148.

10. Victor Considerant, *Exposition abrégée du système phalanstérien du Fourier* (Paris, 1841). Considerant's pronouncement on realization is in the 3d ed. (Paris: Librairie Sociétaire, 1846), 65. For French movement strategy, see Hubert Bourgin, *Fourier: Contribution à l'étude du socialisme français* (Paris: Société Nouvelle de Librairie et d'Edition, 1905), 463, 502.

11. [Albert Brisbane and Osborne Macdaniel], "What Is Association?" *Phalanx* 1 (5 January, 4 May 1844): 56–58, 131–32.

12. Charles Fourier, *The Social Destiny of Man; or, Theory of the Four Movements*, trans. Henry Clapp, Jr. (New York: Dewitt, 1857).

13. Godwin, *Popular View*, 98, 105–6, 88–89, 90; cf. Hippolyte Renaud, *Solidarité: Vue synthétique sur la doctrine de Ch. Fourier* (Paris: Librairie de l'Ecole Sociétaire, 1842), 194, 144–45.

14. Charles Dana, *A Lecture on Association, in Its Connection with Religion* (Boston: B. H. Greene, 1844), 27; H. H. Van Amringe, *Association and Christianity* (Pittsburgh, Pa.: J. W. Cook, 1845), 50–51; J. S. Dwight, *Harbinger* 3 (8 August 1846): 138.

15. E. P. Grant to Charles Dana (in phonographic shorthand), 8 December

1846, EPG Papers. For Fourierism and the free-love controversy after 1848, see Chapter 14.

16. Jules Prudhommeaux, quoted in Henri Desroche, *La société festive: Du Fouriérisme écrit aux Fouriérismes pratiqués* (Paris: Editions du Seuil, 1975), 357. Contrast the seventy-odd Associationist book and pamphlet titles of the 1840s with the nearly five hundred French tracts listed in the most complete bibliography available: I. I. Zilberfarb, *The Social Philosophy of Charles Fourier* (in Russian) (Moscow: Izdatel'stvo Nauka, 1964), 473–85.

17. For the laissez-faire current in American radicalism, see David DeLeon, *The American as Anarchist* (Baltimore, Md.: Johns Hopkins University Press, 1978).

18. See Raymond Williams, *Culture and Society, 1780–1950* (New York: Harper & Row, 1966), xi–xvi; Arthur Bestor, "The Evolution of the Socialist Vocabulary," *Journal of the History of Ideas* 9 (June 1948): 259–302; and Yehoshua Arieli, *Individualism and Nationalism in American Ideology* (Cambridge, Mass.: Harvard University Press, 1964), 179–230.

19. Albert Brisbane and Osborne Macdaniel, "Exposition of Views and Principles," *Phalanx* 1 (5 October 1843): 4.

20. Van Amringe, *Association and Christianity*, 9–10; Brisbane, *Social Destiny*, 75–78.

21. Albert Brisbane and Osborne Macdaniel, "Gradual Abasement of the Producing Classes," *Phalanx* 1 (1 March 1844): 73; W. H. Channing, "Labor for Wages," *Harbinger* 2 (30 May 1846): 396; and Parke Godwin, "Wages Slavery," *Harbinger* 6 (25 March 1848): 164.

22. Charles Dana, "Commerce," *Harbinger* 1 (21 June 1845): 31; [American Union of Associationists], *Industrial Association: An Address to the People of the United States* (Boston: AUA, [1850], 4. See Marvin Meyers, *The Jacksonian Persuasion: Politics and Belief* (Stanford, Calif.: Stanford University Press, 1957), 21–24; and J. G. A. Pocock, "Virtue and Commerce in the Eighteenth Century," *Journal of Interdisciplinary History* 3 (Summer 1972): 119–34.

23. Brisbane, *Social Destiny*, 274; Parke Godwin, *Democracy, Constructive and Pacific* (New York: J. Winchester, 1844), 9–10. For a brief but brilliant discussion of how early European socialists turned "the very arguments of classical liberalism . . . against the capitalist society which they had helped to build," see E. J. Hobsbawm, *The Age of Revolution, 1789–1848* (New York: New American Library, 1962), 285–89 (quotation p. 286).

24. Brisbane and Macdaniel, "Exposition," 5; Godwin, "Wages Slavery," 164; Brisbane and Macdaniel, "Gradual Abasement," 73. The political economists whom Associationists cited most often on the effects of competition were Ricardo, Jean-Baptiste Say, Thomas Malthus, J. R. McCulloch and Jean Charles Sismondi. See especially Godwin, *Democracy*, 13–15.

25. Horace Greeley, "Land Reform," in *Hints toward Reforms* (New York: Harper, 1850), 316–17; Brisbane, *Social Destiny*, 296.

26. Brisbane, *Association*, 9.

27. See Riasnovsky, *Teaching of Fourier*, 155–56.

28. Greeley, "Human Life," in *Hints toward Reforms*, 173–74.

29. "Influence of the Trading Spirit upon the Social and Moral Life of America," *American Whig Review* 1 (January 1845): 95ff. For Hale and other northerners' second thoughts about American acquisitiveness, see William R. Taylor, *Cavalier and Yankee: The Old South and American National Character* (New York: Braziller, 1961): 115–41. Tocqueville's *Democracy in America*, translated in 1838 by Henry Reeve, played an important part in stimulating this literature. Associationists never seemed to realize that their view of Americans as particularly materialistic contradicted Fourier's notion that selfishness originated in scarcity.

30. Rochester Fourier Society, *Labor's Wrongs and Labor's Remedy* (Rochester, N.Y., 1843); George Ripley, "The Infidelity of Modern Society," *Harbinger* 1 (14 June 1845): 13–14; Dana, "Commerce," 31.

31. H. R. Schetterly, quoted in Noyes, *American Socialisms*, 392; Brisbane, *Social Destiny*, 133. See also Charles Dana, "Civilization: The Isolated Family," *Harbinger* 1 (27 September 1845): 251–53. For a fuller discussion of the Associationists' relation to domesticity, see Chapter 7.

32. Parke Godwin, "Political Economy," *Harbinger* 6 (1 April 1848): 173.

33. Arieli, *Individualism and Nationalism*, 179–230; Brisbane, *Social Destiny*, esp. 210.

34. George Ripley, "Life in Association," *Harbinger* 2 (20 December 1845): 32; J. S. Dwight, "Individuality in Association," *Harbinger* 1 (4 October 1845): 264.

35. Ripley, quoted in *Phalanx* 1 (20 April 1844): 102; Osborne Macdaniel, "George and John Evans," *Phalanx* I (12 December 1843): 40; [American Union of Associationists], *Industrial Association*, 14.

36. Charles Dana, "The Other Side of the Picture," *Harbinger* 3 (8 August 1846): 142. See also Albert Brisbane and Osborne Macdaniel, "Tendency of the Age to a Commercial Feudalism," *Phalanx* 1 (5 December 1843): 31–34.

37. Parke Godwin, "Pauperism," *Harbinger* 6 (4 December 1847): 36; Godwin, "Is It Needed?" *Harbinger* 6 (11 December 1847): 44. George Foster's "Letters from Broadway" appeared in *Harbinger* 1 (1845): 72–73, 104, 134, and 2 (1846): 73, 327–28. On Lippard and Foster, see David S. Reynolds, *George Lippard* (Boston: Twayne, 1982); and George Rogers Taylor, "Gaslight Foster: A New York 'Journeyman Journalist' at Mid-Century," *New York History* 58 (July 1971): 297–312. For a virtual catalogue of Jeffersonian fears of "Europeanization," see Morton and Lucia White, *The Intellectual versus the City, from Thomas Jefferson to Frank Lloyd Wright* (Cambridge, Mass.: Harvard University Press, 1962).

38. Albert Brisbane, "False Association . . . Contrasted with True Association," *Harbinger* 3 (14 November 1846): 365–68; J. S. Dwight, "Meeting of the American Union of Associationists in Boston," *Harbinger* 3 (27 June 1846): 46–47; and "Lectures in Cincinnati," *Harbinger* 6 (4 March 1848): 141–42. On the cultural background of Lowell's founding, see John F. Kasson, *Civilizing the Machine: Technology and Republican Values in America, 1776–1900* (New York: Grossman, 1976), 55–106; and Thomas Bender, *Toward an Urban Vision: Ideas and Institutions in Nineteenth-Century America* (Lexington: University Press of Kentucky, 1977), 71–94.

39. Charles Dana, "Has It Come to This?" *Harbinger* 3 (19 September 1846): 238.

40. Godwin, *Democracy*, 18–20; Charles Dana, "Industrial Feudalism," *Harbinger* 3 (19 September 1846): 238; Brisbane, *Social Destiny*, 303.

41. Dana, "Other Side of the Picture," 142; Brisbane and Macdaniel, "Exposition," 5; Van Amringe, *Association and Christianity*, 40. On Dana's point, see also Godwin, *Popular View*, 69; Greeley, *Hints toward Reforms*, 180–81; and Van Amringe, *Association and Christianity*, 17–20. Fourier's attitude toward industrialism is best described in Riasnovsky, *Teaching of Fourier*, 196–202.

42. Arthur Schlesinger, Jr., *The Age of Jackson* (Boston: Little, Brown, 1945), 361; Norman F. Ware, *The Industrial Worker, 1840–1860* (Boston: Houghton Mifflin, 1924), 163; James MacGregor Burns, *The Vineyard of Liberty* (New York: Knopf, 1982), 442–44.

43. Godwin, *Popular View*, 40; Dana, "Other Side of the Picture," 142. For a similar point about the Owenites, see J. F. C. Harrison, *Quest for the New Moral World: Robert Owen and the Owenites in Britain and America* (New York: Scribner, 1969), 69–70.

44. Dwight, *Harbinger* 3 (1 August 1846): 123. "The Prophetic Pictures" is from Hawthorne's *Twice-Told Tales* (1837).

45. [John S. Williams], *The Detriments of Civilization* (Cincinnati, Ohio: Integral Phalanx, 1844), 5; Brisbane, *Social Destiny*, 88; Brisbane, *Association*, 7; George Ripley, "Tendencies of Modern Civilization," *Harbinger* 1 (28 June 1845): 35.

46. Van Amringe, *Association and Christianity*, 18–19, 34; Greeley, "Land Reform," 311–17; Brisbane and Macdaniel, "Tendencies," 31–33; and Ripley, "Agricultural Feudalism," *Harbinger* 5 (10 July 1847): 80. See Orestes Brownson, "The Laboring Classes," *Boston Quarterly Review* 3 (October 1840): 473–74.

47. Godwin, *Democracy*, 21.

48. Channing, quoted in *Spirit of the Age* 1 (7 August 1849): 35; Horace Greeley, "Duty of Associationists to the Cause," *Harbinger* 1 (25 October 1845): 315.

49. George Ripley, "Association and Science," *Harbinger* 6 (18 December 1847): 52. David Brion Davis, "The Emergence of Immediatism in British and American Antislavery Thought," *Mississippi Valley Historical Review* 49 (September 1962): 209–30; John L. Thomas, "Romantic Reform in America, 1815–1865," *American Quarterly* 17 (Winter 1965): 656–81; and Lewis Perry, *Radical Abolitionism: Anarchy and the Government of God in Antislavery Thought* (Ithaca: Cornell University Press, 1973, all stress the millennial urgency of antebellum reform.

50. Arthur Bestor, "Patent-Office Models of the Good Society: Some Relationships between Social Reform and Westward Expansion," in *Backwoods Utopias: The Sectarian Origins and the Owenite Phase of Communitarian Socialism in America, 1663–1829*, 2d ed. (Philadelphia: University of Pennsylvania Press, 1970), 230–52 (quotation, p. 247).

51. For diverse fears of "Europeanization," see Eric Foner, "Abolitionism and the Labor Movement in Ante-bellum America," in *Politics and Ideology in the Age of the Civil War* (New York: Oxford University Press, 1980), 71; Perry Miller, "The Romantic Dilemma in American Nationalism and the Concept of Nature," in *Nature's Nation* (Cambridge, Mass.: Harvard University Press, 1967), 197–207; and Thomas R. Hietala, *Manifest Design: Anxious Aggrandizement in Late Jacksonian America* (Ithaca: Cornell University Press, 1985), 95–131.

52. Brisbane, *Social Destiny*, 112, title page, 98, 331.

53. [American Union of Associationists], *Industrial Association*, 7.

54. See Daniel Walker Howe, *The Political Culture of the American Whigs* (Chicago: University of Chicago Press, 1979), 8, 52–53.

55. Brisbane, *Mental Biography*, 219–26; and letters to Nicholas Trist in Trist Papers.

56. French Fourierists, by contrast, both participated in the reform politics of the 1840s and looked to the state to finance a phalanx experiment. In 1848 Victor Considerant was elected to the National Assembly, where he promoted legal reform and female suffrage as well as Fourierism. He was also appointed to the Provisional Government's Luxembourg Commission, studying the question of labor and unemployment; later he presented the phalanx plan before the National Assembly. For Considerant's political career, see Rondel Van Davidson, *Did We Think Victory Great? The Life and Ideas of Victor Considerant* (Lanham, Md.: University Press of America, 1988), 129–215.

57. Brisbane, *Association*, 8–9.

58. This focus on the civic duties and political representation of groups is implicit throughout Gordon S. Wood, *The Creation of the American Republic, 1776–1787* (Chapel Hill: University of North Carolina Press, 1969). Meyers, *Jacksonian Persuasion*, and Rush Welter, *The Mind of America, 1820–1860* (New York: Columbia University Press, 1975), 75–104, indicate clearly that such Jacksonian concepts

as "aristocracy" were "at bottom . . . political rather than . . . social or economic" (Welter, p. 78)

59. J. S. Dwight, "Democracy *versus* Social Reform," *Harbinger* 5 (16 October 1847): 301, 300; Brisbane, *Social Destiny*, 109, 112.

60. Godwin, *Democracy*, 9, 18; Godwin, "Political Economy," 172; Dana, review of the *Democratic Review*, *Harbinger* 2 (28 March 1846): 249–50.

61. See Howe, *Political Culture*, esp. pp. 192–94, comments on Horace Greeley's version of Fourierism.

62. Parke Godwin, "The Power of Concentration," *Harbinger* 6 (29 January 1848): 100; Charles Dana, "Daniel Webster on Labor," *Harbinger* 3 (12 September 1846): 220–21.

63. T. D. Seymour Bassett, "The Secular Utopian Socialists," in *Socialism and American Life*, ed. Donald Drew Egbert and Stow Persons (Princeton, N.J.: Princeton University Press, 1952), 1:177. For similar assertions, see Noyes, *American Socialisms*, 23, Schlesinger, *Age of Jackson*, 363–65; and Ware, *Industrial Worker*, 169.

64. "Introductory Notice," *Harbinger* 1 (14 June, 1845): 9. My research has yielded seven Democratic sympathizers, seven Whig sympathizers, and seven whose preference is undetermined among twenty-one nationally prominent Associationist leaders. For Chase's report, see "Correspondence," *Harbinger* 1 (6 September 1845): 208.

65. Charles Dana, "Social and Political Science," *Harbinger* 1 (26 July 1845): 109–10; "Statement of the American Union of Associationists, with Reference to Recent Attacks," *Harbinger* 3 (15 August 1846): 154; Parke Godwin, "Social Progress," *People's Journal* 4 (1847): 83.

66. Brisbane, *Association*, 7; Brisbane, "The Question of Slavery," *Harbinger* 1 (21 June 1845): 31. For a contrasting conception among Marxists, see R. Laurence Moore, *European Socialists and the American Promised Land* (New York: Oxford University Press, 1970).

67. George Ripley, "Model Phalanx," *Harbinger* 4 (16 January 1847): 94; "Documens Phalanstériens," *La Phalange* 1 (January–February 1845): 133; Parke Godwin, "Address to the People of the United States," *Phalanx* 1 (20 April 1844): 113; Channing, quoted in *Present* 1 (15 December 1843): 209.

68. "Convention in Boston," *Harbinger* 2 (6 June 1846): 410.

69. Brisbane and Macdaniel, "Exposition," 5; Godwin, *Democracy*, 41; Channing, "Many United in One," *Harbinger* 1 (26 July 1845): 111.

70. "Convention of the New England Fourier Society," *Phalanx* 1 (8 February 1845): 310; W. H. Channing, "The Philadelphia Riots," *Phalanx* 1 (18 May 1844): 133, 135; Channing, "A Confession of Faith," *Present* 1 (September 1843): 9.

71. Quoted in Charles Crowe, *George Ripley, Transcendentalist and Utopian Socialist* (Athens: University of Georgia Press, 1967), 190.

72. Perry Miller, *The Life of the Mind in America, from the Revolution to the Civil War* (New York: Harcourt, Brace & World, 1965), 3–95; Sacvan Bercovitch, *The American Jeremiad* (Madison: University of Wisconsin Press, 1978), xiii, 176–203.

73. On Fourier's relation to Christianity, see Riasnovsky, *Teaching of Fourier*, 100–105. The distinction between Fourier as child of the Enlightenment and his disciples as Romantic crusaders pervades Jonathan Beecher, *Charles Fourier: The Visionary and His World* (Berkeley: University of California Press, 1986).

74. See Davidson, *Did We Think Victory Great?* 46–48, 118–19. Beecher, *Charles Fourier*, fig. 29 (following p. 258) reproduces an engraving of Fourier flanking Christ along with chosen artists, scientists, and saints, from *L'Almanach Phalanstérien pour 1845*.

75. See, e.g., Bassett, "Secular Utopian Socialists"; and Bestor, *Backwoods Utopias*, 37–38.

76. Bestor, *Backwoods Utopias*, 131, 222. Harrison, *Quest for the New Moral World*, 106–8, on the other hand, notes the use of millennial rhetoric by Owen and a few of his American followers.

77. Bestor, "Brisbane," 148.

78. For Brisbane's motivation, see *Mental Biography*, 209–10, 250.

79. Parke Godwin to Charles A. Dana, 14 February [1845], B-G Collection; George Ripley to ?, [1843], quoted in Octavius Brooks Frothingham, *George Ripley* (Boston: Houghton Mifflin, 1883), 148–49.

80. [Ralph Waldo Emerson and Albert Brisbane], "Fourierism and the Socialists," *Dial* 3 (July 1842): 86; W. H. Channing, *Present* 1 (15 December 1843): 210. For a sampling of Associationist articles, see Noyes, *American Socialisms*, 541–50.

81. Channing, "Fourier and Swedenborg," *Present* 1 (1 April 1844): 431; Godwin, *Popular View*, 106.

82. [Charles J. Hempel], *The True Organization of the New Church* (New York: Wm. Radde, 1848). For the official New Church response to Fourierism, see Marguerite Beck Block, *The New Church in the New World: A Study of Swedenborgianism in America* (New York: Holt, Rinehart & Winston, 1932), 154–58.

83. Channing to Dwight, 8 November 1846, JSD Collection.

84. William Henry Channing, *The Gospel of To-day* (Boston: Crosby & Nichols, 1847), esp. 9; Dana, *Lecture*, 30, 33; J. S. Dwight, "Association the Body of Christianity," *Harbinger* 2 (21 February 1846): 175–76.

85. *Phalanx* 1 (20 April 1844): 104, 113; Noyes, *American Socialisms*, 219.

86. Address before the Philadelphia Sunday School Union, quoted in Clifford S. Griffin, "Religious Benevolence as Social Control, 1815–1860," *Mississippi Valley Historical Review* 44 (1957): 439. See also M'Laren, *Boa-Constrictor*, 24. For a liberal Protestant critique, see James Freeman Clarke, "Fourierism," *Christian Examiner* 37 (July 1844): 76–78.

87. R.H.M., "The Influence of Evil," *Harbinger* 6 (18 March 1848): 154. See also Brownson, "Church Unity," 314–16.

88. Brisbane, *Social Destiny*, 243; Brisbane, "The Religious Movement in Germany," *Harbinger* 2 (28 February 1846): 191.

89. Parke Godwin, "The Christian Examiner on the Doctrine of Fourier," *Phalanx* 1 (24 August 1844): 251–52; J. S. Dwight, "The American Review's Account of the Religious Union of Associationists," *Harbinger* 5 (19 June 1847): 30; Dwight, Reply to *Congregationalist, Boston Daily Chronotype*, 28 December 1849.

90. H. H. Van Amringe, *Nature and Revelation* (New York: R. P. Bixby, 1843), 7; Charles Dana, Reply to *Universalist Quarterly*, *Phalanx* 1 (3 May 1845): 328–29.

91. Parke Godwin, "A Letter to Joseph Mazzini on the Doctrines of Fourier," *Harbinger* 4 (15 May 1847): 366; "Social Reform," *Harbinger* 2 (28 March 1846), 250–55; Godwin, "The *Univercoelum*," *Harbinger* 6 (26 February 1848): 133.

92. Parke Godwin, "Influence of Evil," *Harbinger* 6 (18 March 1848): 155.

93. Wilkinson to Henry James, Sr., August 1846, quoted in Clement John Wilkinson, *James John Garth Wilkinson: A Memoir of His Life, with a Selection from His Letters* (London: Kegan Paul, Trench, Trubner, 1911), 55.

94. Frothingham, *George Ripley*, 148–49.

CHAPTER 5. THE UTOPIAN ALTERNATIVE

1. Karl Marx and Friedrich Engels, "Manifesto of the Communist Party," in *Basic Writings on Politics and Philosophy*, ed. Lewis S. Feuer (Garden City, N.Y.: Doubleday Anchor, 1959), 38, 37. See also Feuer, "The Influence of the American

Communist Colonies on Marx and Engels," *Western Political Quarterly* 19 (September 1966): 456–74.

2. Arthur Bestor, "The Communitarian Point of View," in *Backwoods Utopias: The Sectarian Origins and Owenite Phase of Communitarian Socialism in America, 1663–1829,* 2d ed. (Philadelphia: University of Pennsylvania Press, 1970), 1–19; T. D. Seymour Bassett, "The Secular Utopian Socialists," in *Socialism and American Life,* ed. Donald Drew Egbert and Stow Persons (Princeton, N.J.: Princeton University Press, 1952), 1:160.

3. Parke Godwin, *A Popular View of the Doctrines of Charles Fourier* (New York: J. S. Redfield, 1844), 110, 27.

4. Nicholas V. Riasnovsky, *The Teaching of Charles Fourier* (Berkeley: University of California Press, 1969), 43; Hubert Bourgin, *Fourier: Contribution à l'étude du socialisme français* (Paris: Société Nouvelle de Librairie et d'Edition, 1905), 287–88.

5. Brisbane, *Social Destiny,* 346–47; Brisbane, *Association; or, A Concise Exposition of the Practical Part of Fourier's Social Science* (New York: Greeley & McElrath, 1843), 16, 51, 77; "Spread of the Doctrine of Association and Practical Trials," *Phalanx* 1 (5 October 1843): 15.

6. Horace Greeley, *Recollections of a Busy Life* (New York: J. B. Ford, 1868), 149; E. F. Underhill to the *New York Times,* 25 June 1858.

7. Brisbane, *Association,* 78, 16.

8. See Brisbane, *Social Destiny,* 362–75; "Grand Unitary Edifice," *New York Tribune,* 13 August 1842; and *Constitution of the Philadelphia Unitary Building Association* (Philadelphia: U.S. Job Printing Office, 1849).

9. Brisbane, *Social Destiny,* 362–65. In 1845 Brisbane toured New England lecture halls with drawings and plans brought back from France. See John Orvis, "Lectures in Newburyport," *Harbinger* 4 (30 January 1847): 127–28; and "Lectures on Association in Boston," *Harbinger* (6 March 1847): 201–2.

10. Brisbane, *Association,* 24. See John F. C. Harrison, *Quest for the New Moral World: Robert Owen and the Owenites in Britain and America* (New York: Scribner, 1969), 57; Kenneth Roemer, *The Obsolete Necessity: America in Utopian Writings, 1888–1900* (Kent, Ohio: Kent State University Press, 1977), 153–62.

11. Brisbane, *Association,* 74–75; Brisbane, *Social Destiny,* 347–48; Parke Godwin, *Popular View,* 77–78. Demonstrating the Americans' progressive outlook, Brisbane wrote Fourier asking for more information about cities in Harmony; see Brisbane to Fourier, 1 April 1834, FNA (10 AS 36, doss. 11).

12. Luther Bernard, "Early Utopian Social Theory in the United States (1840–1860)," *Northwest Missouri Teachers College Studies* 2 (1938): 79. Dolores Hayden, *Seven American Utopias: The Architecture of Communitarian Socialism, 1790–1975* (Cambridge, Mass.: MIT Press, 1976), 150–55, contrasts Fourier's lively and socially sensitive plan with the "inappropriate, rigid architecture" (p. 154) of his disciples, particularly Victor Considerant.

13. On modernization and antebellum institutional reform, see David J. Rothman, *The Discovery of the Asylum: Social Order and Disorder in the New Republic* (Boston: Little, Brown, 1971); David B. Tyack, *The One Best System: A History of American Urban Education* (Cambridge, Mass.: Harvard University Press, 1974); and Richard D. Brown, *Modernization: The Transformation of American Life, 1600–1865* (New York: Hill & Wang, 1976). Mary P. Ryan, *Cradle of the Middle Class: The Family in Oneida County, New York, 1790–1865* (Cambridge: Cambridge University Press, 1981), 105–44, interprets antebellum voluntary associations as transitional mediating institutions between the increasingly isolated family and "the frenzy of a rapidly growing market town" (p. 143).

14. Riasnovsky, *Teaching of Fourier,* 198; *The Utopian Vision of Charles Fourier,*

ed. and trans. Jonathan Beecher and Richard Bienvenu (Boston: Beacon Press, 1971), 32–34.

15. "Letter from Mr. Brisbane to the New York Tribune," *Phalanx* 1 (24 August 1844): 260; Brisbane, *Association*, 16, 51; Noyes, *American Socialisms*, 264.

16. "Mr. Allen's Second Lecture in Cincinnati," *Harbinger* 6 (11 March 1848): 148; W. H. Channing, "Peace the Principle and Policy of Associationists," *Harbinger* 2 (30 May 1846): 394; Macdaniel, "Annual Report of the Commissioner of Patents," *Phalanx* 1 (1 June 1844): 153–54.

17. Albert Brisbane, "Mr. Etzler," *Phalanx* 1 (4 November 1843): 30; Osborne Macdaniel, "Etzler's Machinery," *Harbinger* 1 (22 November 1845): 383; "Mr. Allen's Second Lecture," 149. See Brisbane, "Plan of the Transitional Organization of Industry," MS, January 1868, AB-IHS, in which he described a "*vast Joint Stock Farm in the West,* worked by machinery and steam power" (p. 22). On Etzler's career, see Patrick R. Brostowin, "John Adolphus Etzler: Scientific-Utopian during the 1830s and 1840s" (Ph.D. diss., New York University, 1969). For Thoreau's review, see "Paradise (to be) Regained," *United States Magazine and Democratic Review* 13 (November 1843): 451–63.

18. Bernard, "Early Utopian Social Theory," 79; Leo Marx, *The Machine in the Garden: Technology and the Pastoral Ideal in America* (New York: Oxford University Press, 1964). For recent studies portraying nineteenth-century Americans' optimistic search for a middle ground between nature and technology, see Howard P. Segal, *Technological Utopianism in American Culture* (Chicago: University of Chicago Press, 1985); Thomas Bender, *Toward an Urban Vision: Ideas and Institutions in Nineteenth-Century America* (Lexington: University Press of Kentucky, 1975); Cecelia Tichi, *New World, New Earth: Environmental Reform in American Literature from the Puritans through Whitman* (New Haven, Conn.: Yale University Press, 1979); and Donald C. Burt, "Utopia and the Agrarian Tradition in America, 1865–1900" (Ph.D. diss., University of New Mexico, 1973). Daniel W. Howe, *The Political Culture of the American Whigs* (Chicago: University of Chicago Press, 1979), 193–94, finds Horace Greeley's Fourierism comparable to the Lowell mills as an expression of modernization.

19. See the section "Groups and Series" translated from Fourier in Brisbane, *Social Destiny*, 115–56. For a clear overview of Fourier's work arrangements, see Jonathan Beecher, *Charles Fourier: The Visionary and His World* (Berkeley: University of California Press, 1986), 274–96.

20. Brisbane, *Social Destiny*, 166–74, 181–89.

21. Ibid., 443–51.

22. Ibid., 127–31; Godwin, *Popular View*, 78–79.

23. See, e.g., Alan Dawley, *Class and Community: The Industrial Revolution in Lynn* (Cambridge, Mass.: Harvard University Press, 1976), 64.

24. J. S. Dwight, "The Good Time Coming," *Harbinger* 5 (14 August 1847): 156; Godwin, *Popular View*, 68.

25. Riasnovsky, *Teaching of Fourier*, 61; Beecher, *Charles Fourier*, 279–80.

26. Brisbane, *Association*, 60, 36, 62. See also Marx Edgeworth Lazarus, *Passional Hygiene and Natural Medicine* (New York: Fowlers & Wells, 1852), 267–68.

27. Horace Greeley, *Hints toward Reforms* (New York: Harper, 1850), 9; Howe, *Political Culture*, 192; Glyndon G. Van Deusen, *Horace Greeley, Nineteenth-Century Crusader* (Philadelphia: University of Pennsylvania Press, 1953), 67.

28. See, e.g., *Constitution of the Brook Farm Association, for Industry and Association* (Boston: I. R. Butts, 1844), 10.

29. Beecher, *Charles Fourier*, 247–48.

30. Horace Greeley, quoted in Howe, *Political Culture*, 193; Godwin, *Popular View*, 70; [J. S. Dwight], "Equality," *Boston Daily Chronotype*, 28 December 1849;

Harbinger 2 (14 February 1846): 148. It is worth noting that Godwin's translation deleted three paragraphs in which Renaud denounced equality of condition as a "monstrous idea." Compare Godwin, *Popular View*, 70, and Hippolyte Renaud, *Solidarité: Vue synthétique sur la doctrine de Fourier* (Paris: Librairie de l'Ecole Sociétaire, 1842), 133.

31. Brisbane, *Association*, 4, 35; Dana, *A Lecture on Association, in Its Relation to Religion* (Boston: B. H. Greene, 1844), 26; George Ripley, "Christianity and Socialism," *Harbinger* 7 (9 September 1848): 148.

32. See J. G. A. Pocock, *The Machiavellian Moment: Florentine Political Thought and the Atlantic Republican Tradition* (Princeton, N.J.: Princeton University Press, 1975); and Stow Persons, "The Cyclical Theory of History in Eighteenth-Century America," *American Quarterly* 6 (1954): 147–63.

33. W. H. Channing, "Objections to Association—No. 1," *Harbinger* 3 (11 July 1846): 79; Channing, "Association in the United States," *Harbinger* 1 (20 September 1845): 239.

34. J. S. Dwight, "Objections to Association—No. VII," *Harbinger* 3 (10 October 1846): 285–87; Beecher, *Charles Fourier*, 253–55.

35. Godwin, *Popular View*, 65, 75–77; Brisbane, *Association*, 71–73.

36. Emerson, "Historic Notes of Life and Letters in New England," in *The Complete Works of Ralph Waldo Emerson*, ed. Edward Waldo Emerson (Boston: Houghton, Mifflin, 1904), 10:354. The best account of Fourier's "new amorous world" is Beecher, *Charles Fourier*, 297–317. For translated excerpts from Fourier's notebooks, see Beecher and Bienvenu, *Utopian Vision*, 329–95.

37. W. H. Channing, "Othello—Jealousy," *Harbinger* 5 (25 September 1847): 254; Brisbane, *Social Destiny*, 293; George Ripley, "Influence of Association upon Woman," *Harbinger* 3 (27 September 1846): 252–53.

38. Riasnovsky, *Teaching of Fourier*, 210 n.47; Bourgin, *Fourier*, 356.

39. George Ripley, "New Light," *Harbinger* 4 (3 December 1846): 48; W. H. Channing, "Woman," *Present* 1 (December 1843): 165; Ripley, "Influence," 253; J. S. Dwight, "How Stands the Cause?" *Harbinger* 3 (7 November 1846): 350.

40. Noyes, *American Socialisms*, 23; Brisbane, *Social Destiny*, 397.

41. For Fourier's educational scheme, see Riasnovsky, *Teaching of Fourier*, 70–81; Beecher, *Charles Fourier*, 259–73; Jean Dautry, "Fourier et les questions d'éducation," *Revue Internationale de Philosophie* 16 (1962): 234–60; and David Zeldin, *The Educational Ideas of Charles Fourier (1772–1837)* (London: Cass, 1969).

42. Brisbane, *Social Destiny*, 392–442.

43. J. S. Dwight, "The American Review's Account of the Religious Union of Associationists,—No. IV," *Harbinger* 5 (10 July 1847): 74; Dwight, *A Lecture on Association, in Its Connection to Education* (Boston: B. H. Greene, 1844), 11, 13; Dwight, "Integral Education," *Harbinger* 5 (17 July 1847): 108; Greeley, *Hints toward Reforms*, 223, 70.

44. *Harmonian Man: Selected Writings of Charles Fourier*, ed. Mark Poster (Garden City, N.Y.: Doubleday, 1971), 99.

45. Lazarus, *Passional Hygiene*, iv, 265, 40–77, 23–25; Lazarus, *Comparative Psychology and Universal Analogy* (New York: Fowler & Wells, 1851), 260–62. See also Lazarus, *Homeopathy: A Theoretic Demonstration* (New York: Wm. Radde, 1851). For Lazarus's background, see Clement Eaton, *Freedom of Thought in the Old South* (Durham, N.C.: Duke University Press, 1940), 322; Mordecai Papers; and "Short Autobiography of Marx Edgeworth Lazarus," Labadie Collection.

46. Godwin, *Popular View*, 82–84; Lazarus, *Passional Hygiene*, 254–65.

47. Riasnovsky, *Teaching of Fourier*, 81–86; H. H. Van Amringe, *Nature and Revelation* (New York: R. P. Bixby, 1843), 7; J. S. Dwight, "Democracy *versus* Social Reform," *Harbinger* 5 (16 October 1847): 302.

48. Bestor, "Communitarian Point of View," 1–19.

49. Albert Brisbane, *A Concise Exposition of the Doctrine of Association* (New York: J. S. Redfield, 1844), 73–74. On Fourier and "partial" phalanxes, see Riasnovsky, *Teaching of Fourier*, 132–34; and Bourgin, *Fourier*, 369.

50. See esp. C. S. Griffin, "Everyman a Reformer—and a Conservative?" in *The Ferment of Reform, 1830–1860* (New York: Crowell, 1967), 28–31; and Ronald G. Walters, *The Anti-Slavery Appeal: American Abolitionism after 1830* (Baltimore, Md.: Johns Hopkins University Press, 1976).

51. Greeley quoted in Brisbane, *Concise Exposition,* cover and title page.

52. J. S. Dwight, "Fourier's Birthday in Boston," *Harbinger* 6 (15 April 1848): 188; T.C.P. [Thomas C. Palmer], *A Plain Lecture on Association* (Boston: Crosby & Nichols, 1847), 3; Brisbane, *Social Destiny,* 26.

53. Hugh Doherty, "Robert Owen, St. Simon, and Fourier," *Phalanx* 1 (28 May 1845): 341–42. On the widespread identification of "socialism" with Owen, see Arthur Bestor, "The Evolution of the Socialist Vocabulary," *Journal of the History of Ideas* 9 (June 1948): 263, 293. Ironically, almost immediately after Fourierists accepted the term, they were forced to avoid it because of the connotations of violence and state control it picked up in the 1848 revolutions.

54. Brisbane, *Association,* 27–28.

55. George Ripley, "Relation of Associationists to Civilization," *Harbinger* 6 (4 December 1847): 36–37.

56. See W. H. Channing, "Letter to Associationists," *Spirit of the Age* 1 (10 November 1849): 297–99 (criticism of Fourier); J. S. Dwight, review of Carlyle's *Cromwell, Harbinger* 2 (3 January 1846): 56–57; Parke Godwin, "Ralph Waldo Emerson," *People's Journal* 4 (1847): 305–8.

57. J. S. Dwight, "The Idea of a Divine Social Order," *Harbinger* 6 (11 April 1848): 170; Godwin, *Popular View,* 27.

58. See Charles Crowe, "Transcendentalist Support of Brook Farm: A Paradox?" *Historian* 21 (May 1959): 286, on Ripley's nostalgia for his native village of Greenfield, Massachusetts.

59. Stephen E. Maizlich, "Republicanism and the Whigs," *Reviews in American History* 15 (March 1987): 26–31; Sean Wilentz, *Chants Democratic: New York City and the Rise of the American Working Class, 1788–1850* (New York: Oxford University Pres, 1984).

60. R. Jackson Wilson, *In Quest of Community: Social Philosophy in the United States, 1860–1920* (New York: Oxford University Press, 1968), 15–18.

61. John Raymond Wennersten, "A Reformer's Odyssey: The Public Career of Parke Godwin of the New York *Evening Post,* 1837–1870" (Ph.D. diss., University of Maryland, 1970), 43; Hecker to Orestes Brownson, 15 July 1844, Brownson Papers; J. S. Dwight, "Meeting of the 'American Union of Associationists' in Boston," *Harbinger* 3 (27 June 1846): 47; "The Festival," *Phalanx* 1 (20 April 1844), 116; William Henry Channing, *The Gospel of To-day* (Boston: Crosby & Nichols, 1847), 19.

62. Diary II, 90; Lindsay Swift, *Brook Farm: Its Members, Scholars, and Visitors* (New York: Macmillan, 1900), 94–109; Isaac Hecker to Orestes Brownson, 21 January 1844, Hecker Papers.

63. Marx Edgeworth Lazarus, *The Zend-Avesta, and Solar Religions* (New York: Fowlers & Wells, 1852), 89–90; and Lazarus, *Passional Hygiene,* 236–38. *Zend-Avesta* credited Hugh Doherty and Charles Dupuis (author of *L'origine de tous les cultes ou religion universelle,* 1795) as well as Emerson. For Transcendentalist interest in the Orient, see Frederick Ives Carpenter, *Emerson and Asia* (Cambridge, Mass.: Harvard University Press, 1930).

64. Marx Edgeworth Lazarus, *The Solar Ray* (New York: Fowlers & Wells,

1851), sec. 2, p. 13; Lazarus, *Comparative Psychology*, xii, 134; and Lazarus, *The Human Trinity; or, Three Aspects of Life* (New York: Fowlers & Wells, 1851), 8–9. For references to Melville, see Lazarus, *Passional Hygiene*, 216, 239; *Solar Ray*, sec. 1, p. 7; and *Human Trinity*, 116–17.

65. Brisbane, *Mental Biography*, 229–31; Brisbane to Dwight, 2 December 1845, Dwight Brook Farm Collection; Bassett, "Secular Utopian Socialists," 196–97. Brisbane's Paris notebook, containing musical fragments, is in AB-IHS.

66. [Ralph Waldo Emerson and Albert Brisbane], "Fourierism and the Socialists," *Dial* 3 (July 1842): 86–89; Horatio Greenough, "Fourier et hoc genus omne," *Crayon* 1 (13 June 1855): 371–72.

67. For an excellent if highly idiosyncratic account of this shift, see Wilson Carey McWilliams, *The Idea of Fraternity in America* (Berkeley: University of California Press, 1973), esp. 94–111.

68. John L. Thomas, "Romantic Reform in America, 1815–1865," *American Quarterly* 17 (Winter 1965): 677.

69. Brisbane, *Association*, 35; "Letter from Mr. Brisbane," *Boston Quarterly Review* 4 (October 1841): 501; Riasnovsky, *Teaching of Fourier*, 52.

70. George Corselius, *Hints toward the Devlopment of a Unitary Science, or Science of Universal Analogy* (Ann Arbor, Mich.: S. B. McCracken, 1846), 19. For the Brook Farmers, see Chapter 4, above.

71. Albert Brisbane, "Interest on Capital," *Harbinger* 3 (18 July 1846): 94. C. M. Macpherson, *The Political Theory of Possessive Individualism* (London: Cambridge University Press, 1962), describes the linkage between freedom and property-holding in Anglo-American thought.

72. In a different context, Alfred Chandler has used this phrase to describe the development of research, planning, and marketing apparatus in capitalist corporations; see *The Visible Hand: The Managerial Revolution in American Business* (Cambridge, Mass.: Belknap Press of Harvard University Press, 1977).

73. Howe, *Political Culture*, 194.

74. Osborne Macdaniel, "The Right of Man to the Soil," *Phalanx* 1 (10 August 1844): 229, 231.

75. Leon Fink, "The New Labor History and the Power of Historical Pessimism: Consensus, Hegemony, and the Case of the Knights of Labor," *Journal of American History* 75 (June 1988): 123, persuasively argues against relying on broad and static antitheses such as "capitalism versus socialism" to assess dissenting ideologies. Howe, *Political Culture*, 193–94, suggests that early capitalism and utopian socialism were both agents of modernization.

76. Marx and Engels, "Manifesto," 38; Brisbane, *Association*, 4.

77. Brisbane, *Association*, 10; [American Union of Associationists], *Industrial Association: An Address to the People of the United States* (Boston: AUA, [1850]), 21.

78. Dana, *Lecture*, 29, 40–41. See also the numerous writings under the heading "The Religious Question" in AB-IHS.

79. Dana, *Lecture*, 40–41; Henry James, "Theological Differences in Association," *Harbinger* 6 (29 April 1848): 204.

80. Dana, *Lecture*, 26, 40; J. S. Dwight, "Convention of Associationists in Boston," *Harbinger* 4 (5 June 1847): 409–10; and Dwight, "Democracy *Versus* Social Reform," 302.

81. Among many Associationist disclaimers, see Charles Dana, "The Translator of the Wandering Jew," *Harbinger* 1 (8 November 1845): 350; and George Ripley, "The Democratic Review and Association," *Harbinger* 2 (3 January 1846): 60–62. French Associationists took the same stand. See Victor Considerant, *Immoralité de la doctrine de Fourier* (Paris: Les Marchands de Nouveautés, [1841]), 36–37.

82. Charles Dana, "Civilization: The Isolated Family," *Harbinger* 1 (27 September 1845): 251–53; Albert Brisbane, "Government—The Church—Marriage," *Harbinger* 3 (28 November 1846): 398; *Harbinger* 4 (19 December 1846): 25; *Phalanx* 1 (10 August 1844): 234–36.

83. Letter from Mary S. Gove, *New York Weekly Herald*, 15 March 1845, reprinted in *DocHist* 7:280; *Phalanx* 1 (1 April 1844): 93n.

84. Van Amringe, *Nature and Revelation*, 147–48; Greeley, *Recollections*, 589; Albert Brisbane, "Government—The Church—Marriage," *Harbinger* 3 (26 September 1846): 255; Parke Godwin, "The Advent of Robert Owen," *Phalanx* 1 (7 October 1844): 277–80.

85. Brisbane, *Association*, 9–10. See also "Letter from an Associationist to a Friend," *Phalanx* 1 (8 February 1845): 317–20.

86. Brisbane, "Government—The Church—Marriage," (November), 398; Godwin, "Advent of Owen," 377–80; Dwight, *Lecture*, 19–20.

87. Godwin, *Popular View*, 112–13.

88. Fourier, quoted in Beecher, *Charles Fourier*, 320. Frank E. Manuel makes the distinction between traditional ahistorical utopias and the dynamic "euchronias" that began to appear in the nineteenth century. The latter were presented as the culmination of "a long prior historical series." Fourier's utopia was a transitional type. While placing the phalanx at the distant end of a long historical process, Fourier also thought of human nature as unchanging and asserted that a successful trial phalanx had been possible for two millennia. See Manuel, "Toward a Psychological History of Utopia," in *Utopias and Utopian Thought*, ed. Frank E. Manuel (Boston: Beacon Press, 1967), 79; and Beecher, *Charles Fourier*, 319. According to Hubert Bourgin, Fourier believed that a model phalanx could transform the world within five years; Riasnovsky quotes a passage in which Fourier predicted it would take only one year. See Bourgin, *Fourier*, 380; Riasnovsky, *Teaching of Fourier*, 135n.

89. "The Two Ways to the Phalanstery," trans. John Dwight, *Harbinger* 5 (11 September 1847): 221–22; Riasnovsky, *Teaching of Fourier*, 135–38, 204n; Godwin, *Popular View*, 41.

90. See, among many articles, George Ripley, "Forms of Guarantyism," *Harbinger* 3 (31 October 1846): 335–36; and "Guarantyism," *Harbinger* 4 (3 April 1847): 270.

91. George Ripley, "Rail Road to the Pacific," *Harbinger* 4 (19 December 1846): 30–31; Parke Godwin, *Democracy, Constructive and Pacific* (New York: J. Winchester, 1844), 27–30; Dwight, "Two Ways," 221–22.

92. Erik H. Erikson, *Childhood and Society*, 2d ed. (New York: Norton, 1963), 285.

93. Even Rush Welter, who argues for the idea of a popular "mind," casts his definition in dialogical form, with shared premises often leading to conflicting conclusions; see his "On Studying the National Mind," in *New Directions in American Intellectual History*, ed. John Higham and Paul Conkin (Baltimore, Md.: Johns Hopkins University Press, 1979), 79.

94. See esp. John Higham, "Hanging Together: Divergent Unities in American Culture," *Journal of American History* (June 1974): 5–23; and Rush Welter, *The Mind of America, 1820–1860* (New York: Columbia University Press, 1975). My analysis here is tentative and does not address the difficult historical and sociological issue of exactly what "characteristic" American beliefs were and how widespread was their appeal. But intellectual and cultural historians do more or less agree on central ideas or habits of thought common to articulate mid-nineteenth-century Americans. And the relationship of Fourierism to these is

so clear and striking that further refinements would not change its essential character.

95. See Bestor, "Communitarian Point of View," 16–19.

96. Among national character studies that adopt the dualistic mode are Michael Kammen's analysis of America as a "contrapuntal civilization," *People of Paradox: An Inquiry concerning the Origins of American Civilization* (New York: Knopf, 1972); Ralph Barton Perry, *Characteristically American* (New York: Knopf, 1949), 3–33; Erikson, *Childhood and Society*, 285–87; and Arthur Schlesinger, Jr., "America: Experiment or Destiny?" *American Historical Review* 82 (June 1977): 505–22.

97. T. J. Jackson Lears, "Power, Culture, and Money," *Journal of American History* 75 (June 1988): 139. Perry, *Characteristically American*, 3–33, touches upon Americans' optimistic paradoxes; Kammen, *People of Paradox*, adds several to the list. For the same mode in nineteenth-century social thought, see John Higham, *From Boundlessness to Consolidation* (Ann Arbor, Mich.: Clements Library, 1969); Marx, *Machine in the Garden*, 145–226; and Bender, *Urban Vision*, 19–51.

98. In addition to the works cited in the notes 96 and 97, see Leon Samson's classic polemic, *Toward a United Front: A Philosophy for American Workers* (New York: Farrar & Rinehart, 1935), which forcefully points out affinities between the goals of socialism and the American creed. Samson's notion of Americanism as a "substitutive socialism" has informed my discussion of Fourierism as an "alternative Americanism."

99. T. J. Jackson Lears, "The Concept of Cultural Hegemony: Problems and Possibilities," *American Historical Review* 90 (June 1985): 575–76.

100. Ibid; Alcander Longley, "Life in the North American Phalanx," *Social Record* 1 (September 1858): 31.

Chapter 6. The Communitarian Boom and Bust

1. Quoted in Noyes, *American Socialisms*, 268, 392. Noyes's book, by far the most complete survey available on the American phalanxes, is a colorful compilation from three sources: published accounts in newspapers and journals; firsthand reports gathered by A. J. Macdonald, a Scottish follower of Robert Owen who was writing a book on American communitarian experiments when he died of cholera in the mid-1850s; and Noyes's own shrewd commentary pressing his theories about socialism, religious history, and communal success. In this and the following chapter I cite the Macdonald Collection only for material not reprinted by Noyes.

2. Noyes, *American Socialisms*, 351, 249.

3. Arthur Bestor, "Patent-Office Models of the Good Society: Some Relations between Social Reform and Westward Expansion," in *Backwoods Utopias: The Sectarian Origins and the Owenite Phase of Communitarian Socialism in America, 1663–1829*, 2d ed. (Philadelphia: University of Pennsylvania Press, 1970), 235–36.

4. Noyes, *American Socialisms*, 235–38, 304–6.

5. See, e.g., Rochester Fourier Society, *Labor's Wrongs and Labor's Remedy* [Rochester, N.Y.: 1843]; and [John S. Williams], *The Detriments of Civilization, and Benefits of Association* (Cincinnati, Ohio: The Integral Phalanx, 1844).

6. S. M. Pedrick, "The Wisconsin Phalanx at Ceresco," *Proceedings of the State Historical Society of Wisconsin*, 1902, pp. 191–94; *Phalanx* 1 (5 February 1844): 70. The best source for the phalanx's origins in Southport is the Michael Frank Diary, entries of 21 November 1843 to 20 May 1844, W-CC Collection.

7. "The Sangamon Association," *Harbinger* 1 (11 October 1845): 288.

8. Macdonald Collection, pp. 228–30; *Phalanx* 1 (1 April 1844): 98.

9. David Brion Davis, "The Emergence of Immediatism in British and American Antislavery Thought," *Mississippi Valley Historical Review* 49 (September 1962): 209–30.

10. Grant to Brisbane, 26 September 1843; Grant to Brisbane, 10 September 1843; Grant to B. F. Williams, 9 October 1843; Grant to Henry Barnard, 6 December 1843; Grant to J. P. Stuart, 28 September 1843; Grant to Greeley, 12 February 1844; Grant to Brisbane, 30 June 1845—all in EPG Papers. For the Pittsburgh convention, see "Proceedings of the Western Fourier Convention," *Phalanx* 1 (4 November 1843): 19–22. The fullest account of Grant's experiment is Carlton Smith, "E. P. Grant and the Ohio Phalanx" (M.A. thesis, University of Chicago, 1950).

11. Albert Brisbane, "Spread of the Doctrine of Association," *Phalanx* 1 (5 December 1843): 34.

12. For the Rochester convention and its aftermath, see Noyes, *American Socialisms,* 269–72 (quotation, p. 272; Leland's report, p. 268); and Arthur Bestor, "American Phalanxes: A Study of Fourierist Socialism in the United States (with Special Reference to the Movement in Western New York)" (Ph.D. diss. Yale University, 1938), 1:38–40. American phalanx names reflected a group's special pretension to greatness (Integral, North American, Sylvania, Alphadelphia) or else a choice of county or state name in keeping with the Associationist idea that a federation of successful phalanxes could be overlaid on the American system (Bureau County, La Grange, Clermont, Wisconsin). Grant's community ran the gamut, beginning as the "American Phalanx," then retreating to "Western Phalanx" and finally "Ohio Phalanx."

13. "Association in Illinois," *Harbinger* 1 (6 December 1845): 406; Integral Phalanx legal records, Bestor Papers; *Phalanx* 1 (15 June 1844): 176.

14. Noyes, *American Socialisms,* 366–67.

15. Ibid., 367, 369.

16. At least twenty-five Wisconsin Phalanx men were listed in later censuses as farmers, more than six times the known number who entered the community as farmers. Several others became founding fathers of frontier towns. See Joan Elias, "The Wisconsin Phalanx: An Experiment in Association" (M.A. thesis, University of Wisconsin, 1968), 203–4, 214–17. I have been influenced here by J. F. C. Harrison's interpretation of American Owenite communities as "instrument[s] for tackling collectively the harsh realities of frontier life"; see his *Quest for the New Moral World: Robert Owen and the Owenites in Britain and America* (New York: Scribner, 1969), 178.

17. See Noyes, *American Socialisms,* 233–47 (quotations, p. 235) for Sylvania; 256–59 for Social Reform Unity.

18. Ibid., 19, 264.

19. Ibid., 257, 367–68, 364.

20. Ibid., 372, 257, 408, 395.

21. Ibid., 408–9; George Ripley, "Fire at Brook Farm," *Harbinger* 2 (14 March 1846): 221.

22. Noyes, *American Socialisms,* 263–64, 364–65.

23. See Carol Weisbrod, *The Boundaries of Utopia* (New York: Pantheon Books, 1980).

24. "Association in Ontario County, New York," *Harbinger* 1 (27 September 1845): 248.

25. Noyes, *American Socialisms,* 279, 282–83.

26. Ibid., 349; Lindsay Swift, *Brook Farm: Its Members, Scholars, and Visitors* (New York: Macmillan, 1900), 182–84.

27. For the Philadelphia Industrial Association, see T. G. Turner, *Gazetteer of*

the St. Joseph Valley, Michigan and Indiana (Chicago: Hazlitt & Reed, 1867), 47–49; for Macdonald's records of the other incidents, see Noyes, *American Socialisms*, 394, 448, 350–51.

28. Elias, "Wisconsin Phalanx," 103–4.

29. Noyes, *American Socialisms*, 307.

30. Ibid., 369.

31. Mary S. Gove, *New York Weekly Herald*, 15 March 1845, reprinted in *DocHist* 7:278–80 (quotation, p. 278).

32. Macdonald Collection, p. 350; Reports of the Council of Arbitration, 1844–45, AA Papers.

33. Lawrence Foster, *Religion and Sexuality: The Shakers, the Mormons, and the Oneida Community* (New York: Oxford University Press, 1981), 57.

34. Total Wisconsin Phalanx membership is computed from the community's records in W-CC Collection. For turnover at the North American Phalanx, see NAP Proceedings, 8 January 1855, NAP Collection.

35. "Correspondence," *Harbinger* 1 (27 September 1845): 254; and C. C. Bristol in *New York Tribune*, 7 August 1844. The following account is based largely on Arthur Bestor's careful history of Sodus Bay in "American Phalanxes," 1:98–263.

36. "Correspondence," *Harbinger* 1 (27 September 1845): 254.

37. John A. Collins, quoted in Noyes, *American Socialisms*, 288–89.

38. Collins, quoted in Noyes, *American Socialisms*, 290; Macdonald, quoted in Noyes, *American Socialisms*, 291.

39. Among histories of the NAP, I have found Herman J. Belz, "The North American Phalanx: An Experiment in Socialism," *Proceedings of the New Jersey Historical Society* 81 (October 1963): 215–46, the clearest and most succinct account of its origins. See also Norma Lippincott Swan, "The North American Phalanx," *Bulletin of the Monmouth County Historical Association* 1 (1935): 36–65; Edward K. Spann, "The Phalanx in Dream and Reality," in *Brotherly Tomorrows: Movements for a Cooperative Society in America 1820–1920* (New York: Columbia University Press, 1989), 101–21; and two memoirs: Charles Sears, *The North American Phalanx: An Historical and Descriptive Sketch* (Prescott, Wis.: John M. Pryse, 1886), and Julia Bucklin Giles, "The North American Phalanx," typescript address, 1922, in NAP Collection.

40. Charles Sears, quoted in Noyes, *American Socialisms*, 454; NAP Proceedings, 19 February 1844, NAP Collection.

41. Belz, "North American Phalanx," 229.

42. The membership list for the North American Phalanx was compiled from Noyes, *American Socialisms*, 467; the 1850 U.S. Census; and records in the NAP Collection. Names of Wisconsin Phalanx residents come from W-CC Collection, papers and microfilms; I have especially benefited from preliminary lists prepared by a research assistant for F. Gerald Ham, State Archivist of Wisconsin. Brook Farm membership was compiled from its constitution of February 11, 1844; minutes of meetings, 1841–45; and Journal B, 1844–46, in Brook Farm Papers. For another list of Brook Farmers, see Anne C. Rose, *Transcendentalism as a Social Movement, 1830–1850* (New Haven, Conn.: Yale University Press, 1981), 234–42. My membership figures differ from Rose's because I have (l) excluded members who left before Brook Farm converted to Fourierism in 1844, (2) included members' wives who did not sign the community's constitution but remained beyond the probationary period of two months, and (3) included several persons who became members after April 1845, the date of the last signature on the 1844 constitution.

43. Manuscript Census of 12 May 1845, AA Papers; Grant to S. Frey, 30 June

456   NOTES TO PAGES 168–72

1845, EPG Papers. T. D. Seymour Bassett, "The Secular Utopian Socialists," in *Socialism and American Life,* ed. Donald Egbert and Stow Persons (Princeton, N.J.: Princeton University Press, 1952), 1:177–78, makes a similar point about Yankee predominance among the Fourierists.

44. Noyes, *American Socialisms,* 262 (Leraysville); Rose, *Transcendentalism,* 151 (Trumbull); and *New York Weekly Tribune,* 4 July 1846, in *DocHist* 7: 281 (Integral). A religious poll of Brook Farmers found them overwhelmingly Unitarian; see RUA Records, 5 December 1847.

45. Quoted in Noyes, *American Socialisms,* 280.

46. George Kirchmann, "Unsettled Utopias: The North American Phalanx and the Raritan Bay Union," *New Jersey History* 97 (1979): 28.

47. Constitution of the Trumbull Phalanx [1844], in Macdonald Collection, 216. For the religious background of Shakers and Oneidans, see Louis J. Kern, *An Ordered Love: Sex Roles and Sexuality in Victorian Utopias* (Chapel Hill: University of North Carolina Press, 1981), 14; and Maren Lockwood Carden, *Oneida: Utopian Community to Modern Corporation* (Baltimore, Md.: Johns Hopkins Press, 1969), 25–26.

48. See Franklin G. Sherill to American Home Missionary Society, 16 January 1851, Pedrick Collection. The W-CC Collection reveals the following fragmentary denominational breakdown: 7 Methodists, 5 Baptists, 3 Presbyterians, 2 Spiritualists, 1 Episcopalian, 1 Congregationalist and 1 Swedenborgian. Warren Chase, in *The Life-line of the Lone One; or Autobiography of the World's Child* (Boston: Bela Marsh, 1858), records his spiritual odyssey and its impact on the phalanx.

49. Noyes, *American Socialisms,* 350; Grant to Albert Brisbane, 31 March 1845, and Grant to Horace Greeley, 11 August 1844, EPG Papers.

50. Lillian Syms and Travers Clement, *Rebel America: The Story of Social Revolt in the United States* (New York: Harper & Row, 1934), 50–77; Norman Ware, *The Industrial Worker, 1840–1860* (Boston: Houghton Mifflin, 1924), 163–79; Arthur Schlesinger, Jr., *The Age of Jackson* (Boston: Little, Brown, 1945), 363–68; and Bernard K. Johnpoll, *The Impossible Dream: The Rise and Fall of the American Left* (Westport, Conn.: Greenwood Press, 1981), 96. For Marx and Engels, see "Manifesto of the Communist Party," in *Basic Writings on Politics and Philosophy,* ed. Lewis S. Feuer (Garden City, N.J.: Doubleday Anchor, 1959), 38–39.

51. The categories follow Michael B. Katz, *The People of Hamilton, Canada West: Family and Class in a Mid-Nineteenth-Century City* (Cambridge, Mass.: Harvard University Press, 1975), 343–48, with a separate ranking added for farmers. Brook Farm, Wisconsin, and North American phalanx information was gathered primarily from community recordbooks, genealogical records, city directories, and the U.S. Census. Many Brook Farm occupations are listed next to members' names on the constitution of 11 Febrary 1844; these were supplemented with information from published memoirs and, for Wisconsin, the Pedrick Collection; Elias, "Wisconsin Phalanx," 211; and *The History of Fond du Lac County, Wisconsin* (Chicago: Western Historical Company, 1880), 881–912. Alphadelphia occupations are listed in Report of the Board of Directors, 2 May 1844, AA Papers.

52. Charlotte Havens to sister Hannah, 26 October 1848, W-CC Collection.

53. Rose, *Transcendentalism,* 152–61.

54. Belz, "North American Phalanx," 228; Bestor, "American Phalanxes," 1:48–53.

55. *New York Tribune,* 1 February 1844, quoted in Belz, "North American Phalanx," 227; Rose, *Transcendentalism,* 158.

56. Noyes, *American Socialisms,* 240. For Brook Farm's agricultural economy, see Swift, *Brook Farm,* 40–43.

57. Noyes, *American Socialisms,* 398–400, 403.

58. Schlesinger, *Age of Jackson*, 364–65; Johnpoll, *Impossible Dream*, 96.

59. Christopher H. Johnson, *Utopian Communism in France: Cabet and the Icarians, 1839–1851* (Ithaca: Cornell University Press, 1974), 156, contrasts Fourier's and Cabet's constituencies on the basis (for the Fourierists) of impressionistic evidence; one memoirist recalled that "the phalanstère scarcely found any partisans in the working class" (p. 156 n.13). When the social composition of French Fourierism is studied in detail, the results may well modify such generalizations. An inventory of 802 men recruited for Victor Considerant's Texas colony in 1855, for example, showed 218 farmers and many skilled artisans. See "Diverses statistiques sur les membres de La Réunion," in Considerant MSS (I am grateful to Rondel V. Davidson for calling my attention to this source).

60. List of Stockholders, 5 August 1850, NAP Collection; and Dolores Hayden, *Seven American Utopias: The Architecture of Communitarian Socialism, 1790–1975* (Cambridge, Mass.: MIT Press, 1976), 164–82.

61. E. S. Camp to Directors of the Alphadelphia Association, 6 May 1844, AA Papers; Marianne Dwight, *Letters from Brook Farm, 1844–1847*, ed. Amy L. Reed (Poughkeepsie, N.Y.: Vassar College, 1928), 161. See also, "A Boy's Recollection of Brook Farm," *New England Magazine*, n.s. 16 (May 1894): 310.

62. Quoted in Noyes, *American Socialisms*, 402–3.

63. Belz, "North American Phalanx," 231.

64. Georgianna Bruce Kirby, *Years of Experience* (New York: Putnam, 1887), 179; Dwight, *Letters from Brook Farm*, 104, 165.

65. Noyes, *American Socialisms*, 57; Rosabeth Moss Kanter, *Commitment and Community: Communes and Utopias in Sociological Perspective* (Cambridge, Mass.: Harvard University Press, 1972), 93–94.

66. Noyes, *American Socialisms*, 351.

67. Ibid., 352, 249.

68. Brisbane, *Mental Biography*, 212.

69. Noyes, *American Socialisms*, 352.

70. "The Sangamon Association," 288.

71. Kanter, *Commitment and Community*, 75–138.

72. Jon Wagner, "Success in Intentional Communities: The Problem of Evaluation," *Communal Societies* 5 (1985): 89–100.

CHAPTER 7. LIFE IN THE PHALANXES

1. Quoted in *American Socialisms*, 427.

2. Ibid., 247; Arthur Bestor, "American Phalanxes: A Study of Fourierist Socialism in the United States (with Special Reference to the Movement in Western New York)" (Ph.D. diss., Yale University, 1938), 1:210–11. Noyes immediately contradicted himself by admiring the "unmitigated Fourierism" of work arrangements in western New York phalanxes; see *American Socialisms*, 276.

3. George Ripley, "The Commencement of Association," *Harbinger* 1 (16 August 1845): 159–60.

4. Macdonald Collection, p. 233.

5. Bestor, "American Phalanxes," 189–211.

6. J.M.P. [Jean M. Palisse], "Failure of Success in Practical Association," *Spirit of the Age* 1 (17 November 1849): 315.

7. Quoted in Noyes, *American Socialisms*, 453–54.

8. Frederick Grimké to Sarah Grimké, 17 August 1855, Weld-Grimké Papers.

9. Noyes, *American Socialisms*, 338, 419. For other phalanxes' crops, see ibid.,

281, 402, 405; Report of the General Council, 10 March 1845, AA Papers; and Bestor, "American Phalanxes," 1:179.

10. Bestor, "American Phalanxes," 1:181; Dolores Hayden, *Seven American Utopias: The Architecture of Communitarian Socialism, 1790–1975* (Cambridge, Mass.: MIT Press, 1976), 161; George Kirchmann, "Why Did They Stay? Communal Life at the North American Phalanx," in *Planned and Utopian Experiments: Four New Jersey Towns*, ed. Paul A. Stellhorn (Trenton: New Jersey Historical Commission, 1980), 22–24. In using the name "Seristery," the Associationists transferred Fourier's label from the series' meeting halls to their workshops, as had Victor Considerant; see Considerant, "Architecture," *Harbinger* 1 (30 August 1845): 183.

11. Lindsay Swift, *Brook Farm: Its Members, Scholars, and Visitors* (New York: Macmillan, 1900), 34–35; *New York Herald*, 4 June 1853, clipping in Macdonald Collection, p. 329; Julia Bucklin Giles, "North American Phalanx," typescript address [1922], 17, NAP Collection; Considerant, Sketch of the North American Phalanx [1853], Considerant MSS.

12. Albert Brisbane, *A Concise Exposition of the Doctrine of Association* (New York: J. S. Redfield, 1844), 53; Anne C. Rose, *Transcendentalism as a Social Movement, 1830–1850* (New Haven, Conn.: Yale University Press, 1981), 153.

13. Noyes, *American Socialisms*, 337.

14. "North American Phalanx Bill of Fare, October 1, 1854," NAP-HL.

15. "Our Success," *Harbinger* 1 (4 October 1845): 270.

16. Quoted in Noyes, *American Socialisms*, 458.

17. Bestor, "American Phalanxes," 1:153–54, 165–66 (Sodus Bay); Noyes, *American Socialisms*, 343, 349 (Trumbull); J.M.P., "Failure," 315 (Sylvania).

18. Swift, *Brook Farm*, 27–40.

19. George Ripley, "Fire At Brook Farm," *Harbinger* 2 (14 March 1846): 221.

20. For the various phalansteries, see *Harbinger* 1 (18 October 1845): 304 (Philadelphia Industrial Association); A. D. P. Van Buren, "The Alphadelphia Association," *Michigan Pioneer and Historical Collections* 5 (1884): 410; Noyes, *American Socialisms*, 419 (Wisconsin), 397–98 (La Grange), 369 (Clermont); and Hayden, *Seven American Utopias*, 161–73 (NAP). My analysis is indebted to Hayden's sensitive, expert discussion of phalanx architecture.

21. Beecher quoted in Dolores Hayden, *The Grand Domestic Revolution: A History of Feminist Designs for American Homes, Neighborhoods, and Cities* (Cambridge, Mass.: MIT Press, 1981), 56.

22. Noyes, *American Socialisms*, 385; Hayden, *Seven American Utopias*, 182. See "Plan of an Edifice for the Integral Phalanx" [1845], Bestor Papers.

23. Horatio Greenough, "Fourier et hoc genus omne," *Crayon* 34 (13 June 1855): 372.

24. See esp. the valuable discussion in "Work in Harmony," chap. 14 of Jonathan Beecher's biography, *Charles Fourier: The Visionary and His World* (Berkeley: University of California Press, 1986), 274–96.

25. J. S. Dwight, "Musical Review," *Harbinger* 1 (14 June 1845): 13; *Constitution of the Brook Farm Association for Industry and Education* (Boston: I. R. Butts, 1844), 7, 17.

26. Albert Brisbane, *Association; or A Concise Exposition of the Practical Part of Fourier's Social Science* (New York: Greeley & McElrath, 1843), 60, 62; Parke Godwin, *A Popular View of the Doctrines of Charles Fourier* (New York: J. S. Redfield, 1844), 66–68, 117.

27. "Constitution of the Trumbull Phalanx," Macdonald Collection, p. 216; *Constitution of the Brook Farm Phalanx* (N.p., [1845]), 7; "Pictures of Progress"

(cartoon), *Yankee Doodle*, 19 December 1846; "Constitution of the Wisconsin Phalanx," *Southport Telegraph*, 19 March 1844.

28. MS fragment of Constitution of the Alphadelphia Association, sec. 3, AA Papers; "Constitution, &c." [of the Sylvania Association], Macdonald Collection, p. 368; "Roll of Female members reported ready to labor for the Association, with their choice of labor," AA Papers.

29. Noyes, *American Socialisms*, 344, 385.

30. *Harbinger* 5 (7 August 1847): 13; Record Book of the Wisconsin Phalanx, 23 March 1844–29 November 1847, entry of 15 December 1846; Record Book of the Wisconsin Phalanx, 13 December 1847–6 November 1852, bylaws adopted 21 February 1848, W-CC Collection. For a full chronicle of labor changes, see Joan Elias, "The Wisconsin Phalanx: An Experiment in Association" (M.A. thesis, University of Wisconsin, 1968), 138–54.

31. NAP Proceedings, 1844, 1848–49, NAP Collection; Charles Sears, *The North American Phalanx: An Historical and Descriptive Sketch* (Prescott, Wis.: John M. Pryse, 1886), [5–6]; Swift, *Brook Farm*, 45; John T. Codman, *Brook Farm: Historic and Personal Memoirs* (Boston: Arena, 1894), 86.

32. "Revised Constitution of the North American Phalanx, Adopted December 27, 1848," NAP Proceedings, 1 September 1849, NAP Collection; *Constitution of the Brook Farm Phalanx*, 5, 8–14; Clarence Gohdes, "A Brook Farm Labor Record," *American Literature* 1 (1929–30): 299–300.

33. Sears, *North American Phalanx*, [6].

34. Godwin, *Popular View*, 68; J. S. Dwight, "The Good Time Coming," *Harbinger* 5 (14 August 1847): 156.

35. Bestor, "American Phalanxes," 1:209; Sears, *North American Phalanx*, [6].

36. NAP Proceedings, 13 January 1848, NAP Collection; Karl Marx and Friedrich Engels, *The German Ideology*, in *Collected Works of Marx and Engels* (New York: International Publishers, 1976), 5:47. For glimpses of job rotation, see Charles Dana, "Brook Farm," reprinted in James Harrison Wilson, *The Life of Charles A. Dana* (New York: Harper & Row, 1907), 532; Swift, *Brook Farm*, 45–46; Codman, *Brook Farm*, 84–86; and Brook Farm Account Book, June 1844–April 1845, Brook Farm Papers.

37. Marianne Dwight, *Letters from Brook Farm, 1844–1847*, ed. Amy L. Reed (Poughkeepsie, N.Y.: Vassar College, 1928), 7–8.

38. H. A. Taylor Labor Book, 10 March–20 September 1845, AA Papers.

39. Dwight, *Letters from Brook Farm*, 81. For artisan labor records, see Printing Group Day Book, April 1846–June 1847, Brook Farm Papers; Blacksmith Shop Record Book, AA Papers; and the account of Clarkson Phalanx seamstresses and carpenters reprinted in Noyes, *American Socialisms*, 276–77. Codman, *Brook Farm*, 85, recalled that mechanical groups "were usually the same persons the year around." Beecher, *Charles Fourier*, 288–89, provides a succinct assessment of Fourier's attitude toward manufacturing.

40. For Brisbane's recommendation, see his *Association*, 62. Interest rates for the phalanxes were usually stipulated in their constitutions; for the Morehouse Union, see Noyes, *American Socialisms*, 305. Wisconsin's annual dividends to capital are listed in Elias, "Wisconsin Phalanx," 213.

41. Noyes, *American Socialisms*, 305, 401; Bestor, "American Phalanxes," 1:207–8; NAP Proceedings, January 1847, NAP Collection; and Elias, "Wisconsin Phalanx," 145–46.

42. Jonathan Grieg, quoted in Noyes, *American Socialisms*, 272.

43. Table reprinted in Noyes, *American Socialisms*, 276.

44. NAP Proceedings, 5 December 1849, NAP Collection; Sears, *North Ameri-*

can Phalanx, [7]; "Key to Scale of Primary Awards for Labor and the Use of Capital at the North American Phalanx, 1853," NAP-HL; Printing Group Day Book, Brook Farm Papers; and Frank Flower, "Fourierism in Wisconsin," *Magazine of Western History*, February 1887, p. 66, Pedrick Collection.

45. Noyes, *American Socialisms*, 419; *New York Tribune*, 23 October 1844. For the communities' profits, see Octavius Brooks Frothingham, *George Ripley* (Boston: Houghton Mifflin, 1882), 158; and *Exposé of the Condition and Progress of the North American Phalanx* (New York: Dewitt & Davenport, 1853), 19.

46. Quoted in Noyes, *American Socialisms*, 444, 454. John Codman (*Brook Farm*, 74) complained that Fourierist work arrangements at Brook Farm required "too much labor to keep the accounts of so complex an organization."

47. *Exposé*, 23; Norma Lippincott Swan, "The North American Phalanx," *Bulletin of the Monmouth County Historical Association* 1 (1935): 54; Dana, quoted in Noyes, *American Socialisms*, 224.

48. Alcander Longley, "Life in the North American Phalanx," *Phalansterian Record* 1 (May 1858): 21; Giles, "North American Phalanx," 8; [Frederick Law Olmsted], "The Phalanstery and the Phalansterians," *New York Tribune*, 24 July 1852; Kalikst Wolski, "A Visit to the North American Phalanx," trans. Marion M. Coleman, *Proceedings of the New Jersey Historical Society* 83 (July 1965): 156.

49. "Correspondence," *Harbinger* 1 (26 July 1845): 99.

50. Dwight, *Letters from Brook Farm*, 40–41. Cf. Rose, *Transcendentalism*, 148.

51. *Exposé*, 9–10.

52. Alcander Longley, "Life in the North American Phalanx," *Social Record* 1 (September 1858): 31.

53. Noyes, *American Socialisms*, 445. Brook Farm's 1845 constitution attempted to solve the problem of a double payment to shareholding residents: as an individual's capital stock increased, he or she lost a proportionate share of the allotment to labor. The complex scheme was explained in *Constitution of the Brook Farm Phalanx*, 13–14.

54. Farmer–artisan conflict can be glimpsed in "By-Laws of the Alphadelphia Association," sec. 13, AA Papers; Noyes, *American Socialisms*, 444 (Wisconsin); "Wisconsin Phalanx," *Spirit of the Age* 1 (8 December 1849): 364; and *Exposé*, 10–12 (NAP).

55. Dana, "Brook Farm," 532; Karl Marx, *The Grundrisse*, ed. and trans. David McLellan (New York: Harper & Row, 1971), 124.

56. Charles Lane, "Brook Farm," *Dial* 5 (January 1844): 357.

57. Noyes, *American Socialisms*, 460; *DocHist* 7:279.

58. For an alternative assessment of sexual and familial arrangements in the phalanxes, see Raymond Lee Muncy, *Sex and Marriage in Utopian Communities: Nineteenth-Century America* (Bloomington: Indiana University Press, 1973), 70–78, 81–88. A general but more sympathetic treatment is Robert H. Lauer and Jeanette C. Lauer, *The Spirit and the Flesh: Sex in Utopian Communities* (Metuchen, N.J.: Scarecrow Press, 1983).

59. Ripley to Ralph Waldo Emerson, 9 November 1840, quoted in Frothingham, *George Ripley*, 307–8. My comments on gender relations at Brook Farm are indebted to the shrewd discussion in Rose, *Transcendentalism*, 185–96.

60. Henry James to Edmund Tweedy, 5 September 1852, James Papers; *The Journals and Miscellaneous Notebooks of Ralph Waldo Emerson*, ed. William H. Gilman et al. (Cambridge, Mass: Harvard University Press, 1960–82), 8:391–92; Rose, *Transcendentalism*, 137–38.

61. Dwight, *Letters from Brook Farm*, 84; Swift, *Brook Farm*, 117; Dwight, *Letters from Brook Farm*, 90.

62. Noyes, *American Socialisms*, 23. The most detailed and successful account of the emergence of the privatized family in antebellum America is Mary P. Ryan, *Cradle of the Middle Class: The Family in Oneida County, New York, 1790–1865* (Cambridge: Cambridge University Press, 1981). Barbara Taylor, *Eve and the New Jerusalem: Socialism and Feminism in the Nineteenth Century* (New York: Pantheon Books, 1983), 244–46, suggestively relates Owenite communitarianism to the impact of the Industrial Revolution on British working-class families, though the spread of the factory system and female wage labor was much greater in Britain than in the United States in the 1840s.

63. J. S. Dwight, *Harbinger* 2 (31 January 1846): 116; Harriot Haven to Charlotte Mason, 10 March 1850, W-CC Microfilms.

64. Town quoted in "Reminiscences of Early Days," *Ripon Commonwealth*, 21 October 1904, Pedrick Collection.

65. For evidence of chain migrations and economic support among kin in nineteenth-century industrialization, see Michael Anderson, "Family, Household, and the Industrial Revolution," in *The American Family in Social-Historical Perspective*, ed. Michael Gordon, 2d ed. (New York: St. Martin's Press, 1978), 38–51; more specifically, Tamara Hareven, *Amoskeag: Life and Work in an American Factory-City* (New York: Pantheon Books, 1978); and Thomas Dublin, *Women at Work: The Transformation of Work and Community in Lowell, Massachusetts, 1826–1860* (New York: Columbia University Press, 1979).

66. Lane, "Brook Farm," 355–56.

67. Ibid.; Warren Chase, *The Life-line of the Lone One; or, Autobiography of the World's Child* (Boston: Bela Marsh, 1858), 114, 124. A similar gender gap of expectations existed in the Weld-Grimké family during their stay at Raritan Bay. Theodore Weld told a correspondent that life at Raritan Bay contained "elements of varied attractiveness constituting a high ideal, a *home*," whereas his sister-in-law Sarah Grimké confided that "a *Home* & an Association are wide asunder. Time, experience satisfy me that they are antagonisms." See Weld to James G. Birney, 21 July [1854]; Grimké to the Wattles family, 2 April 1854, Weld-Grimké Papers.

68. Noyes, *American Socialisms*, 243, 384; Lane, "Brook Farm," 355.

69. Van Buren, "Alphadelphia Association," 412.

70. Quoted in Noyes, *American Socialisms*, 506.

71. Noyes, *American Socialisms*, 430–31; Chase, *Life-line*, 123.

72. Quoted in Noyes, *American Socialisms*, 479.

73. Amelia Russell, "Home Life of the Brook Farm Association," *Atlantic Monthly* 60 (November 1878): 561.

74. Dana to Dwight, 12 March 1846, and Ripley to Dwight, 19 March 1846, quoted in Zoltan Haraszti, *The Idyll of Brook Farm* (Boston: Boston Public Library, 1937), 31, 35; Dwight, *Letters from Brook Farm*, 171.

75. Quoted in "Reminiscences of Early Days."

76. N. C. Meeker, quoted in Noyes, *American Socialisms*, 502–3. For the debate and complaints from parents at the North American Phalanx, see NAP Proceedings, 21 April 1848 and 10 September 1854, NAP Collection.

77. Macdonald Collection, p. 366; Van Buren, "Alphadelphia Association," 412.

78. Quoted in Noyes, *American Socialisms*, 172.

79. Information on Charlotte and Harriot Haven comes from their letters (1848–50) and Harriot's journal (1848), W-CC Microfilms; and extracts from family letters in "Six Years of Communal Life," a typescript history of the Wisconsin Phalanx by Frances Mason Allensworth, W-CC Collection. Quotations are

from "Journal of Harriot Haven," entries of 11 and 13 October 1848; Charlotte Haven to Hannah Haven, 26 October 1848; and Charlotte Haven to Isabella Haven, 20 February 1850.

80. Mary Paul to Bela Paul, 27 November 1853, 7 May and 2 October 1854, 3 March and 12 April 1855, in *Farm to Factory: Women's Letters, 1830–1860*, ed. Thomas Dublin (New York: Columbia University Press, 1981), 113–14, 118–21.

81. Eighty-one letters of Elizabeth Curson (seventeen from Brook Farm and sixty-four from Raritan Bay) are in the Curson Papers—next to Marianne Dwight's letters, the largest surviving correspondence from a phalanx resident. Quotations are from Dwight, *Letters from Brook Farm*, 171; Elizabeth Curson Hoxie to Margaret Curson, 7 November 1853, 28 March and 26 November 1854. For a capsule portrait of Curson, see Codman, *Brook Farm*, 137.

82. Elizabeth Hoxie to Margaret Curson, 26 November 1854, Curson Papers.

83. Francis G. Shaw, "The Women of the Boston Antislavery Fair," *Harbinger* 1 (4 October 1845): 269; J. S. Dwight, "How Stands the Cause?" *Harbinger* 3 (7 November 1846): 350. For nineteenth-century ideals of domesticity and woman's sphere, see, e.g., Barbara Welter, "The Cult of True Womanhood, 1800–1860," *American Quarterly* 18 (Summer 1966): 151–74; Kathryn Kish Sklar, *Catherine Beecher* (New Haven, Conn.: Yale University Press, 1973); Mary P. Ryan, "American Society and the Cult of Domesticity, 1830–1860" (Ph.D. diss., University of California, Santa Barbara, 1971); and Nancy F. Cott, *The Bonds of Womanhood: "Woman's Sphere" in New England, 1780–1835* (New Haven, Conn.: Yale University Press, 1977).

84. Louis J. Kern, *An Ordered Love: Sex Roles and Sexuality in Victorian Utopias— the Shakers, the Mormons, and the Oneida Community* (Chapel Hill: University of North Carolina Press, 1981), esp. 310. Carol A. Kolmerten, *Women in Utopia: The Ideology of Gender in the American Owenite Communities* (Bloomington: Indiana University Press, 1990), also finds patriarchal attitudes and practices pervading Owenism. Surveys of women's roles in nineteenth-century utopian groups include Muncy, *Sex and Marriage;* Judith Fryer, "American Eves in American Edens," *American Scholar* 43 (Spring 1974): 78–100; Jean Harvey Baker, "Women in Utopia: The Nineteenth-Century Experience," in *Utopias: The American Experience,* ed. Gardner B. Moment and Otto F. Kransher (Metuchen, N.J.: Scarecrow Press, 1980), 56–71; and Jeanette C. Lauer and Robert H. Lauer, "Sex Roles in Nineteenth-Century American Communal Societies," *Communal Societies* 3 (1983): 16–28.

85. Eleanor Flexner, *Century of Struggle: The Woman's Rights Movement in the United States,* rev. ed. (Cambridge, Mass.: Harvard University Press, 1975), 62–65.

86. *Constitution and Laws of the Social Reform Unity* (Brooklyn: Van Anden, 1842), 13, 18; [Georgianna Bruce Kirby], "Reminiscences of Brook Farm," *Old and New* 4 (September 1871): 349.

87. "Wisconsin Phalanx, Act of Incorporation and By Laws," Pedrick Collection; *Constitution of the Alphadelphia Association* (Ann Arbor: R. Thornton, 1844), 9; Bestor, "American Phalanxes," 1:108.

88. Dwight, *Letters from Brook Farm*, 64, 106. This corrects Anne Rose's assertion in *Transcendentalism*, 194, that there is no "solid evidence that . . . [Brook Farm women] attended . . . [Fourier or labor] conventions."

89. Kirchmann, "Why Did They Stay?" 22.

90. Gertrude Sears to Anna Q. T. Parsons, 23 January 1848, Abernethy Library; Dwight, *Letters from Brook Farm*, 167.

91. Fredrika Bremer, *The Homes of the New World: Impressions of America*, trans.

Mary Howitt (New York: Harper, 1853), 81; Sears to Anna Q. T. Parsons, 23 January 1848, Abernethy Library.

92. Account Slip of M. S. Paul, 30 September 1854–30 September 1855, NAP-HL.

93. NAP Proceedings, 13 January 1848, NAP Collection; Record Book of the Wisconsin Phalanx, 23 March 1844–29 November 1847, entry of 23 March 1846, W-CC Collection.

94. Rose, *Transcendentalism*, 196; *Constitution of the Brook Farm Phalanx*, 6–7.

95. Bestor, "American Phalanxes," 1:108; "Constitution, &c." in Macdonald Collection p. 368; NAP Proceedings, 12 December 1843, NAP Collection; "Report of Committee to Organize and Equalize Labor" [1844], AA Papers.

96. Dwight, *Letters from Brook Farm*, 8; Taylor, *Eve and the New Jerusalem*, 248. See also Kolmerten, *Women in Utopia*, 92–98.

97. [Kirby], "Reminiscences," 349.

98. See Paul to Bela Paul, 2 October 1854, in Dublin, *Farm to Factory*, 118; and Account Slip of M. S. Paul, NAP-HL; NAP Proceedings, 30 June 1848, NAP Collection. Gerda Lerner, "The Lady and the Mill Girl: Changes in the Status of Women in the Age of Jackson," *Midcontinent American Studies Journal* 10 (Spring 1969): 5–15, first examined status tensions between wage-earning and non-wage-earning women in antebellum America.

99. Dwight, *Letters from Brook Farm*, 32, 33, 71, 94, 102, 105, 168.

100. Codman, *Brook Farm*, 134; Bremer, *Homes of the New World*, 618; Henry D. Thoreau to Sophia Thoreau, 1 November 1856, in *Familiar Letters of Henry David Thoreau*, ed. F. B. Sanborn (Boston: Houghton Mifflin, 1894), 335.

101. Giles, "North American Phalanx," 8; Town quoted in "Reminiscences of Early Days."

102. Bremer, *Homes of the New World*, 619.

103. J. S. Dwight, *A Lecture on Association, in Its Connection with Education* (Boston: B. H. Greene, 1844), 14–22; Swift, *Brook Farm*, 69–82.

104. "Brook Farm School," *Harbinger* 2 (28 February 1846): 192.

105. Swan, "North American Phalanx," 58–59; *New York Daily Tribune*, 13 May 1851 and 29 July 1852; NAP Proceedings, 21 April 1848, NAP Collection.

106. For these communities, see Jayme A. Sokolow, "Culture and Utopia: The Raritan Bay Union," *New Jersey History* 94 (Summer–Fall 1976): 93–96; Noyes, *American Socialisms*, 330 (Trumbull); *Harbinger* 1 (12 July 1845): 80 (Trumbull); and S. M. Pedrick, "The Wisconsin Phalanx at Ceresco," *Proceedings of the State Historical Society of Wisconsin* (1902): 211.

107. Henri Desroche, *La société festive: Du Fouriérisme écrit aux Fouriérismes pratiqués* (Paris: Editions du Seuil, 1975); *OC* 6:66–74 and 7:209–20.

108. Swift, *Brook Farm*, 53–55, 79.

109. Albert Brisbane, "Co-operation in America," *Christian Socialist* 2 (27 September 1851): 203; Noyes, *American Socialisms*, 498.

110. Alcander Longley, "Life in the North American Phalanx," *Social Record* 1 (August 1858): 26; "A Week in the Phalanstery," *Life Illustrated*, 11 August 1855.

111. Giles, "North American Phalanx," 16.

112. Stephen Nissenbaum, *Sex, Diet, and Debility in Jacksonian America: Sylvester Graham and Health Reform* (Westport, Conn.: Greenwood Press, 1980); and Martha Verbrugge, *Able-Bodied Womanhood: Personal Health and Social Change in Nineteenth-Century Boston* (New York: Oxford University Press, 1988), explore the ambiguous relation between nineteenth-century health reform and the evangelical sensibility.

113. Dwight's musical criticism is analyzed by George Willis Cooke, *John Sulli-*

van Dwight, Brook-Farmer, Editor, and Critic of Music (Boston: Small, Maynard, 1898), 48–145; Irving Lowens, "Writings about Music in the Periodicals of American Transcendentalism (1835–1850)," *Journal of the American Musicological Society* 10 (1957): 71–85; and Sterling F. Delano, *The Harbinger and New England Transcendentalism: A Portrait of Associationism in America* (Rutherford, N.J.: Fairleigh Dickinson University Press, 1983), 125–47. For Associationist literary criticism, see Delano, *Harbinger*, 65–110; and Clarence L. F. Gohdes, *The Periodicals of American Transcendentalism* (Durham, N.C.: Duke University Press, 1931), 83–131. Among artists, Story contributed several poems and reviews to *The Harbinger*, Lane was counted among Boston-area contributors to the AUA, and Sartain designed a "grand unitary edifice" for the Fourierist "Philadelphia Unitary Building Association" and also was included in Marcus Spring's abortive plans to form a utopian village on Staten Island. For Lane, see attached list of subscribers in Recordbook, BRUA Records. For Sartain, see *Constitution of the Philadelphia Unitary Building Association* (Philadelphia: U.S. Job Printing Office, 1849), lithograph insert; and Sartain to John S. Dwight, 6 April 1849, Dwight Collection. Sartain was probably the "well-known engraver in Philadelphia" who "wished to reside at the [North American] Phalanx" but did not join because he would have to do farm work, according to Alfred Cridge; see Noyes, *American Socialisms*, 498. The young landscape painter Lilly Martin Spencer may have lived for a time at the Trumbull Phalanx with her emigré French parents; see H. U. Johnson, "History of the Trumbull Phalanx," *Western Reserve Chronicle*, 5 May 1897.

114. N. C. Meeker's "Adventures of Captain Armstrong" reportedly described fictional communitarian settlements by South Pacific islanders. See David Boyd, *A History: Greeley and the Union Colony of Colorado* (Greeley, Colo.: Tribune Office, 1890), 15. The most Fourierist of George Lippard's sensationalized novels was *New York: Its Upper Ten and Lower Million* (Cincinnati: H. M. Rulison, 1853). Explicitly Fourierist utopias published in the period were the anonymous *Henry Russell; or, The Year of Our Lord Two Thousand* (New York: William H. Graham, 1846); and Jane Sophia Appleton's "Sequel to the Vision of Bangor in the Twentieth Century" (see Chapter 10, note 68). Delano, *Harbinger*, 111–24 surveys Associationist poetry.

115. Swift, *Brook Farm*, 66; Dwight, *Letters from Brook Farm*, 175–76; *New York Daily Tribune*, 5 August 1851.

116. Giles, "North American Phalanx," 9; *New York Daily Tribune*, 13 May 1851.

117. "The Fourth of July at Woburn," *Harbinger* 1 (12 July 1845): 80; Longley, "Life in the North American Phalanx" (August), 26.

118. "Celebration of Fourier's Birthday at Brook Farm," *Phalanx* 1 (3 May 1845): 336–37; "Celebration of Fourier's Birthday in New York," *Harbinger* 4 (24 April 1847): 314, 317.

119. Noyes, *American Socialisms*, 239–45, 307–8, 349–51, 394–96, 447–48; Van Buren, "Alphadelphia Association," 412; "Chester Adkins and the Ceresco Community," *Ripon Commonwealth*, 27 January 1904; Hunter quoted in "Reminiscences of Early Days."

120. Quoted in Swan, "North American Phalanx," 63.

121. "Historic Notes of Life and Letters in New England," in *The Complete Works of Ralph Waldo Emerson*, ed. Edward Waldo Emerson (Boston: Houghton Mifflin, 1903–4), 10:368–69.

CHAPTER 8. ORGANIZING A NATIONAL MOVEMENT

1. Ripley to Hecker, 18 September 1843, Hecker Papers, quoted in Edith R. Curtis, *A Season in Utopia: The Story of Brook Farm* (New York: Thomas Nelson,

1961), 152. For Ripley's oblique but public critique of New Yorkers, see "Associationists in New York," *Harbinger* 2 (30 May 1846): 397–98.

2. Godwin to Charles Dana, [24 October 1845], B-G Collection; James Kay, Jr. to J. S. Dwight, 2 March 1846, JSD Collection.

3. Godwin to Dana, 14 February [1845], B-G Collection.

4. E. P. Grant to Albert Brisbane, 26 September 1843 and 31 March 1845, EPG Papers.

5. Ripley to John S. Dwight, 26 March and 6 September 1849, JSD Collection.

6. Dana to Elizur Wright, Jr., 8 March 1850, Wright Papers.

7. Ripley, "Associationists in New York," 398. Macdaniel himself was far less popular at Brook Farm than his sisters, according to Marianne Dwight, *Letters from Brook Farm, 1844–1847*, ed. Amy L. Reed (Poughkeepsie, N.Y.: Vassar College, 1928), 134.

8. Lawrence Goodwyn, *Democratic Promise: The Populist Moment in America* (New York: Oxford University Press, 1976).

9. Dwight, *Letters from Brook Farm*, 73–74.

10. "Proceedings of the Western Fourier Convention," *Phalanx* 1 (4 November 1843): 19–22.

11. For a typical western complaint, see "Aid for the West," *Harbinger* 4 (12 December 1846): 15.

12. On Brisbane's tour, see *Phalanx* 1 (4 November 1843): 22, and (5 December 1843): 34. For the American Industrial Union, see *Phalanx* 1 (15 June 1844): 176–78; Arthur Bestor, "American Phalanxes: A Study of Fourierist Socialism in the United States (with Special Reference to the Movement in Western New York)" (Ph.D. diss., Yale University, 1938), 1:84–96; and American Industrial Union, *Articles of Confederation* (Rochester: C. S. McConnell, 1844).

13. Adin Ballou, *History of the Hopedale Community*, ed. William S. Heywood (Lowell: Thompson & Hill, 1897), 131–32; Dwight, *Letters from Brook Farm*, 27, 47.

14. *Phalanx* 1 (5 January 1844): 45; *Constitution of the Brook Farm Association, for Industry and Education, West Roxbury, Mass.* (Boston: I. R. Butts, 1844), 4–5. For the two tracts, see John S. Dwight, *A Lecture on Association, in Its Connection with Education* (Boston: B. H. Greene, 1844); and Charles Dana, *A Lecture on Association, in Its Connection with Religion* (Boston: B. H. Greene, 1844).

15. "General Convention of the Friends of Association in the United States," *Phalanx* 1 (20 April 1844): 106.

16. Ibid.

17. Ibid., 106, 114.

18. Brisbane, *Mental Biography* 218, 229. John R. Wennersten, "Parke Godwin, Utopian Socialism, and the Politics of Antislavery," *New-York Historical Society Quarterly* (July–October 1976): 119–20, claims that Godwin engineered Brisbane's removal from the scene, but there is no evidence to support this assertion.

19. *Phalanx* 1 (4 November 1843): 19; Grant to Brisbane, draft, c. 1 April 1844, EPG Papers; *Phalanx* 1 (8 February 1845): 314.

20. Parke Godwin, *A Popular View of the Doctrines of Charles Fourier* (New York: J. S. Redfield, 1844); Godwin to Dana, 14 February [1845], B-G Collection. For Godwin's political activities in 1843–44, see John R. Wennersten, "A Reformer's Odyssey: The Public Career of Parke Godwin of the New York *Evening Post*, 1837–1870" (Ph.D. diss., University of Maryland, 1970), 51–53.

21. *Phalanx* 1 (10 August 1844): 238–39n; "Fourier Clubs," *Phalanx* 1 (18 May 1844): 148; "Fund for the Propagation of the Doctrines of Association," *Phalanx* 1 (1 June 1844): 164.

22. "Suggestions in Reference to a Union of Associations," and "Meeting of the American Industrial Union," *Phalanx* 1 (15 June 1844): 167–69, 176–78.

23. Charles Dana, "A Visit to the Associations in Western New-York," and "Convention of Associations," *Phalanx* 1 (9 December 1844): 293–94, 294–96.

24. Godwin to Dana, 8 November 1844, B-G Collection.

25. For his studies in Paris, see Brisbane, *Mental Biography*, 229–44. His notebook (labeled "Cercle d'étude" across the pages) [1844] and manuscript fragments in AB-IHS, contain numerous translations from Fourier, musical studies, and mathematical notations. For his triumphant report, see *Phalanx* 1 (8 February 1845): 324.

26. Brisbane, *Mental Biography*, 246.

27. Dana to Godwin, n.d., B-G Collection; Dwight, *Letters from Brook Farm*, 54–55.

28. *Phalanx* 1 (8 February 1845): 324.

29. Dana to Godwin, 20 November 1844, B-G Collection; Dwight, *Letters from Brook Farm*, 52.

30. "Convention of the New England Fourier Society," *Phalanx* 1 (8 February 1845): 314. On John Dwight's studies, see Dwight, *Letters from Brook Farm*, 78; and Christopher List to J. S. Dwight, 14 March 1845, JSD Collection. For the Fourier classes, see Dwight, *Letters from Brook Farm*, 101, 106. On Ripley's translation work, see *Harbinger* 1 (12 July 1845): 80.

31. *Phalanx* 1 (8 February 1845): 314, 310; Dwight, *Letters from Brook Farm*, 81–82.

32. John S. Williams to Parke Godwin, 10 March 1845, B-G Collection.

33. Circular from the "Central Executive Committee of the Associationists of the United States," March 1845, B-G Collection, reprinted in *Phalanx* 1 (3 May 1845): 33; *Harbinger* 1 (28 June 1845): 48.

34. Deliberations about moving *The Phalanx* to Brook Farm can be followed in Dana to Godwin, n.d. and 20 February 1845; Godwin to Dana, 14 February [1845], "Monday 17" [March 1845] (quotation), and [21 March 1845], B-G Collection. See also Dwight, *Letters from Brook Farm*, 78, 81–82.

35. Dwight, *Letters from Brook Farm*, 78. *The Phalanx*'s last issue was dated 22 May 1845; *The Harbinger* first appeared on 14 June 1845.

36. *Harbinger* 1 (12 July 1845): 79. The fullest study of the new weekly is Sterling F. Delano, *The Harbinger and New England Transcendentalism* (Rutherford, N.J.: Fairleigh Dickinson University Press, 1983). See also Clarence Gohdes, *The Periodicals of American Transcendentalism* (Durham, N.C.: Duke University Press, 1931), 102–9.

37. Dwight, *Letters from Brook Farm*, 137.

38. Brisbane to Ripley, 9 December 1845, reprinted in Octavius Brooks Frothingham, *George Ripley* (Boston: Houghton Mifflin, 1882), 181–85 (quotation, p. 184). See also Edmund Tweedy to J. S. Dwight, 18 April 1846, JSD Collection.

39. *Harbinger* 2 (21 February 1846): 175, and 2 (7 March 1846): 205–7.

40. Dwight, *Letters from Brook Farm*, 145–55; Ripley, "Fire at Brook Farm," *Harbinger* 2 (14 March 1846): 220–22; J. S. Dwight to George Ripley, 16 March 1846, JSD Collection.

41. "Celebration of Fourier's Birthday in New York," *Harbinger* 2 (18 April 1846): 302.

42. George Ripley, "The Associative Movement," *Harbinger* 2 (9 May 1846): 346–47; Ripley "Associationists in New York," 397–99.

43. "Convention in Boston—Organization of 'The American Union of Associationists,' " *Harbinger* 2 (6 June 1846): 410–11. The AUA constitution of 1846 is reprinted in Delano, *Harbinger*, 162–67.

44. Ripley, "Associative Movement," 346–47; Ripley, "Conditions and Prospects of the Associative Cause," *Harbinger* 4 (3 April 1847): 267–68; Ripley, "New Associations," *Harbinger* 2 (17 March 1846): 207–8.

45. J. S. Dwight, "Meeting of the 'American Union of Associationists' in Boston," *Harbinger* 3 (27 June 1846): 47.

46. Charles Dana, "The Campaign Begun!" *Harbinger* 3 (11 July 1846): 80; George Ripley, "Association Meeting at Hingham, Mass." *Harbinger* 3 (1 August 1846): 127.

47. John Orvis to Marianne Dwight Orvis, 31 August 1847, Abernethy Library.

48. John Allen to Marianne Dwight, 15 January 1846, Henry S. Borneman Papers, IHS.

49. Orvis to Marianne Dwight, February 1846, in Curtis, *A Season in Utopia*, 273–74; Allen to Marianne Dwight, 13 February and 9 March 1846, Abernethy Library.

50. Orvis to John S. Dwight, 9 December 1846, JSD Collection, quoted in Zoltan Haraszti, *The Idyll of Brook Farm* (Boston: Public Library, 1937), 44–45.

51. Orvis to J. S. Dwight, 16 January 1847, and Orvis to Marianne Dwight Orvis, 8 March 1847, Abernethy Library; "Our Lectures," *Harbinger* 4 (17 April 1847): 302–3; and "Lectures in Providence," *Harbinger* 4 (1 May 1847): 335–36. For the Rhode Island Fourierists, see Charles R. Crowe, "Utopian Socialism in Rhode Island, 1845–1850," *Rhode Island History* 18 (January 1959): 20–26.

52. "Lectures on Association in Boston," *Harbinger* 4 (16 January 1847): 96; 4 (30 January 1847): 128; 4 (13 February 1847): 159–60; 4 (27 February 1847): 192; and "Lectures in New York," *Harbinger* 4 (27 February 1847): 192.

53. For lecture totals, see *Harbinger* 4 (29 May 1847): 388. For the West, see Ripley, "Aid from the West," *Harbinger* 4 (12 December 1846): 15; and John Allen to J. S. Dwight, 27 April 1848, JSD Collection.

54. J. S. Dwight, "Suggestions to Affiliated Societies," *Harbinger* 4 (27 March 1847): 254–55.

55. Boston Union membership figures are from "Annual Meeting of the American Union of Associationists," *Harbinger* 7 (13 May 1848): 12–13. Thomas Palmer, *Plain Lecture on Association*, and W. H. Channing, *The Gospel of To-day*, were published in Boston in 1847 by Crosby & Nichols.

56. Recordbook [1846–48], 21–23, 46, 51, BUA Records.

57. "Annual Meeting of the American Union of Associationists," *Harbinger* 7 (13 May 1848): 12–13; "Doings in Albany," *Harbinger* 6 (22 January 1848): 93; "Correspondence" (Lowell), *Harbinger* 5 (7 August 1847): 129.

58. Telegram to James T. Fisher, 9 April 1850, JTF Papers.

59. *Harbinger* 7 (12 May 1848): 12, lists twenty-one of the approximately thirty New Yorkers involved at one time or another in the New York Union; for Providence, see p. 13. For Philadelphia, see *Harbinger* (27 January 1849): 103.

60. "Our Lecturers in the State of New York," *Harbinger* 5 (18 September 1847): 238; "The Seventh of April in Cincinnati," *Harbinger* 7 (6 May 1848): 4–6.

61. Names of members were gathered from the Recordbook [1846–1848] and Treasurer's Account [1847–50], BUA Records. Occupational information comes primarily from the U.S. Census and Boston-area city directories, supplemented by information in manuscript collections. See Appendix Table 12, for an occupational analysis of three affiliated unions.

62. "Our Prospects in New York," *Harbinger* 5 (9 October 1847): 285–86.

63. James Kay to James T. Fisher, 26 November 1847, JTF Papers; "Dedicatory Festival of the Philadelphia Union of Associationists," *Harbinger* 7 (27 May 1848): 28; "Third Quarterly Report of the Group of Practical Affairs of the

Philadelphia Union, *Harbinger* 7 (16 December 1848): 50–51; *Constitution of the Philadelphia Unitary Building Association* (Philadelphia: U.S. Job Printing Office, 1849).

64. "A Woman's Call to Women," *Harbinger* 4 (8 May 1847): 351; W. H. Channing, "Woman's Function in the Associative Movement," *Harbinger* 3 (18 July 1846): 95.

65. "Meeting in New York," *Harbinger* 5 (24 July 1847): 111.

66. Recordbook, 51, BUA Records.

67. [Joseph Cooke] to [James T. Fisher], [1847], JTF Papers. See Kay's report to the Boston Union, in Recordbook, 36, BUA Records.

68. Elizabeth Blackwell, *Pioneer Work in Opening the Medical Profession to Women* (London: J. M. Dent, 1914), 10–11, 47.

69. For Blackwell's stay in Philadelphia, see her *Pioneer Work*, 44–50; and Nancy Sahli, "A Stick to Break Our Heads With: Elizabeth Blackwell and Philadelphia Medicine," *Pennsylvania History* 44 (1977): 335–47. The Blackwell family's interest in Fourierism is noted throughout Elinor Rice Hays, *Those Extraordinary Blackwells: The Story of a Journey to a Better World* (New York: Harcourt, Brace & World, 1967), but can be more clearly traced in the Blackwell Papers. Elder joined the Philadelphia Union in January 1848 and within a year became its "Chief of the Group of Indoctrination"; see Minutes of the Philadelphia Union of Associationists, Sartain Collection. His role in publicizing Fourierism is suggested in William Elder, *The Enchanted Beauty and Other Tales, Essays, and Sketches* (New York: J. C. Derby, 1855).

70. James Kay to [James T. Fisher], 26 November 1847, JTF Papers. See also *Harbinger* 7 (24 June 1848): 64, which lists Blackwell as an officer of the Philadelphia Union.

71. *Harbinger* 8 (30 December 1848): 72 (Maine); *Harbinger* 7 (13 May 1848): 10 (Cincinnati); *Harbinger* 5 (7 August 1847): 129 (Lowell).

72. "Celebration of Fourier's Birthday in New York," *Harbinger* 4 (24 April 1847): 316; "Correspondence," *Harbinger* 6 (25 March 1848): 166; "Convention of Associationists," *Harbinger* 4 (5 June 1847): 410.

73. Marianne Dwight Orvis to Anna Q. T. Parsons, 17 May 1847, Brook Farm Papers; "Union of Women for Association," *Harbinger* 5 (12 June 1847): 14–16; Boston Women to Women of the Trumbull Phalanx, 27 May 1847, Spencer Papers.

74. "Correspondence," *Harbinger* 5 (7 August 1847): 130.

75. Ibid., 131. For other responses, see "Letter to Women of the Boston Union of Associationists," *Harbinger* 5 (17 July 1847): 81–82; and Marianne Dwight Orvis to Mrs. Isaiah Ray, 25 July 1847, Ray Correspondence.

76. "First Annual Report of 'The Woman's Associative Union,'" *Harbinger* 7 (24 June 1848): 61.

77. Blackwell to Anna Q. T. Parsons, 29 October 1847, Abernethy Library; Blackwell, *Pioneer Work*, 76.

78. *La Phalange* (Paris), n.s. 1 (January–February 1845): 129–42.

79. "Organization in France," *Harbinger* 4 (6 March 1847): 205–6; Ripley, "The French School of Association," *Harbinger* 5 (7 August 1847): 139–40. For French Fourierists and phalanx experiments, see Hubert Bourgin, *Fourier: contribution à l'étude du socialisme française* (Paris: Société Nouvelle de Librairie et d'Edition, 1905), 462–65, 483–84; Henri Desroche, *La société festive: Du Fouriérisme ecrit aux Fouriérismes pratiqués* (Paris: Editions du Seuil, 1975), 248–54; and Rondel Van Davidson, *Did We Think Victory Great? The Life and Ideas of Victor Considerant* (Lanham, Md.: University Press of America, 1988), 54.

80. *Harbinger* 5 (21 August 1847): 171, and 4 (29 May 1847): 400; American

Union of Associationists, *Association, as Illustrated by Fourier's System* (Boston: Crosby & Nichols, 1847). The Americans published translations of works by Fourier, Matthew Briancourt, Felix Cantagrel, Alphonse Constant, Victor Hennequin, and Charles Pellarin. Special mention should also be made of George Sand's novel *Consuelo* (1842), first translated in *Harbinger* 1 (14 June 1845)–3 (20 June 1846).

81. Doherty to Parke Godwin, 17 August 1847, B-G Collection; Jules Duval to ? , 1 July 1844, FNA (10 AS 38, doss. 5). French Fourierist articles on the American movement are listed in Maurice Buchs, "Le Fouriérisme aux Etats–Unis; Contribution à l'étude du socialisme américaine" (Thèse du doctorat, Université de Paris, 1948), 209–12.

82. *La Phalange*, n.s. 1 (January–February 1845): 141, 138–39.

83. Agreement of 25 November 1844, signed by Albert Brisbane and Victor Considerant, FNA (10 AS 36, doss. 11).

84. For opposition to Considerant's central control, see Bourgin, *Fourier*, 468–70; Emile Poulat, *Les cahiers manuscrits de Fourier* (Paris: Entente Communautaire, 1957), 42; Desroche, *La société festive*, 164–77, 248–54; Davidson, *Did We Think Victory Great?*, 50–55, 118 (quotation).

85. On the interest of Marx and Engels in the United States, see R. Laurence Moore, *European Socialists and the American Promised Land* (New York: Oxford University Press, 1970), 3–24; and in greater detail, Robert Weiner, "Marx's Vision of America: A Biographical and Bibliographical Sketch," *Review of Politics* 42 (October 1980): 465–503.

86. Davidson, *Did We Think Victory Great?* 236.

87. *La Phalange*, n.s. 1 (January–February 1845): 132–33.

88. Private suggestions for an American colony included P. Malgoratt to Fourier, 15 July 1833, and George Mascard to editor of *Démocratie Pacifique*, 4 November 1845, FNA (10 AS 40, doss. 1). For the Texas venture of 1839–40, see Desroche, *La société festive*, 237. On Cabet's decision to migrate, see Christopher H. Johnson, *Utopian Communism in France: Cabet and the Icarians, 1839–1851* (Ithaca: Cornell University Press, 1974), 207–59. For rumors concerning a trial phalanx in the United States, see Jules Duval to ?, 13 August 1844, FNA (10 AS 38, doss. 5).

89. Brisbane's report of this letter is in Recordbook, entry of 31 January 1847, RUA Records.

90. On this "Union Industrielle du Sahy" (1841–45), see Desroche, *La société festive*, 262–65.

Chapter 9. The Problem of Slavery

1. Charles Dain, *De l'abolition de l'esclavage* (Paris: Bureau de la Phalange, 1836), 25; Albert Brisbane and Osborne Macdaniel, "Dangers Which Threaten the Future," *Phalanx* 1 (4 November 1843): 19; Horace Greeley, "Slavery at Home," *New York Daily Tribune*, 20 June 1845. Dain reprinted (pp. 43–54) Fourier's major statement on slavery, "Remède aux divers esclavages." Brisbane was familiar with Dain's work: an advertisement in *Phalanx* 1 (15 June 1844): 180, listed it among French Fourierist treatises available from the New York editor.

2. Charles Dana, "Cassius M. Clay—Slavery," *Harbinger* 1 (6 September 1845): 205.

3. Abbé de Lamennais, *The People's Own Book* (Boston: Little, Brown, 1839); Lamennais, *Modern Slavery* (London: J. Watson, 1840). For Associationist interest in Lamennais, see Octavius Brooks Frothingham, *Memoir of William Henry Channing* (Boston: Houghton Mifflin, 1886), 202–3; Parke Godwin, *A Popular View of*

the Doctrines of Charles Fourier (New York: J. S. Redfield, 1844), 27n; and Godwin, "An Hour with Lamennais," *Putnam's Magazine* 3 (May 1854): 466–73. Orestes Brownson quoted Lamennais on the wage system in "American Literature," *Boston Quarterly Review* 3 (January 1840): 75, and reviewed *The People's Own Book* in the same issue (pp. 117–27). For "wage slavery" rhetoric among the Owenites, see J.F.C. Harrison, *Quest for the New Moral World: Robert Owen and the Owenites in Britain and America* (New York: Scribner, 1969), 72.

4. [John S. Williams], *The Detriments of Civilization, and Benefits of Association* (Cincinnati: Integral Phalanx, 1844), 7; Brisbane, *Social Destiny,* 109, 112; "W. H. Channing on Association," *Harbinger* 1 (19 July 1845): 95–96.

5. Dana, "Cassius M. Clay," 205; Greeley, "Slavery at Home."

6. Albert Brisbane, "The Organization of Labor—No.III," *Harbinger* 3 (25 July 1846): 108n; George Ripley, "White Slavery," *Harbinger* 5 (14 August 1847): 160; Brisbane, *Social Destiny,* 93–114.

7. William H. Pease and Jane H. Pease, *Black Utopias: Negro Communal Experiments in America* (Madison: University of Wisconsin Press, 1963), 14. Abolitionist support of self-help and competitive capitalism is analyzed by Eric Foner, "Abolitionism and the Labor Movement in Ante-bellum America," in *Politics and Ideology in the Age of the Civil War* (New York: Oxford University Press, 1980), 57–76; Aileen S. Kraditor, *Means and Ends in American Abolitionism: Garrison and His Critics on Strategy and Tactics, 1834–1850* (New York: Random House, 1969), 244–55; and Jonathan A. Glickstein, " 'Poverty Is Not Slavery': American Abolitionists and the Competitive Labor Market," in *Antislavery Reconsidered: New Perspectives on the Abolitionists,* ed. Lewis Perry and Michael Fellman (Baton Rouge: Louisiana State University Press, 1979), 195–218.

8. Brisbane, "Organization of Labor," 108n.

9. Brisbane and Macdaniel, "Dangers," 19.

10. Greeley, "Slavery at Home;" Godwin to Charles Dana, 8 September 1845, B-G Collection; [Williams], *Detriments,* 25.

11. Albert Brisbane, "The Question of Slavery," *Harbinger* 1 (21 June 1845): 30. On workers' and especially labor leaders' indifference to abolitionists, see Joseph Rayback, "The American Workingman and the Anti-slavery Crusade," *Journal of Economic History* 3 (November 1943): 152–63; Willis H. Lofton, "Abolition and Labor," *Journal of Negro History* 33 (July 1948): 249–83; and Bernard Mandel, *Labor, Free and Slave: Workingmen and the Anti-Slavery Movement in the United States* (New York: Associated Authors, 1955), 61–95. More recently, however, scholars have found that there was a sizable working-class constituency among the antislaveryites; see Edward Magdol, *The Antislavery Rank and File: A Social Profile of the Abolitionists' Constituency* (Westport, Conn.: Greenwood Press, 1986).

12. Kraditor, *Means and Ends,* 251; Glickstein, "Poverty Is Not Slavery," 212–13.

13. On Collins, see John L. Thomas, "Antislavery and Utopia," in *The Antislavery Vanguard: New Essays on the Abolitionists,* ed. Martin Duberman (Princeton, N.J.: Princeton University Press, 1965), 254–59. For Orvis, see Lindsay Swift, *Brook Farm: Its Members, Scholars, and Visitors* (New York: Macmillan, 1900), 175; John Orvis, "Our Lectures in the State of New York," *Harbinger* 5 (18 September 1847): 239. For Spring, see Dale Warren, "Uncle Marcus," *New England Galaxy* 9 (Summer 1967): 16–26.

14. For Wright, see Kraditor, *Means and Ends,* 71–72, n.61; and Lawrence B. Goodheart, *Abolitionist, Actuary, Atheist: Elizur Wright and the Reform Impulse* (Kent, Ohio: Kent State University Press, 1990).

15. "Lectures in Providence," *Harbinger* 4 (1 May 1847): 335–6. Charles R.

Crowe, "Utopian Socialism in Rhode Island, 1845–1850," *Rhode Island History* 18 (January 1959): 23–25; and John S. Gilkeson, Jr., *Middle-Class Providence, 1820–1940* (Princeton, N.J.: Princeton University Press, 1987), 47–48.

16. Kraditor, *Means and Ends*, 244–46; Foner, "Abolitionism and the Labor Movement," 65–67 (quotation, p. 65); George Frederickson, *The Black Image in the White Mind* (New York: Oxford University Press), 32–34.

17. Foner, "Abolitionism and the Labor Movement," 65; Dana, "Cassius M. Clay," 205; "The Associationists and the Abolitionists," *National Anti-Slavery Standard*, 14 October 1847, p. 78. For a revealing comparison of abolitionist and labor-reform attitudes toward freedom, wage labor, and northern society, see Glickstein, "Poverty Is Not Slavery," 206–17.

18. Wendell Phillips in *Liberator*, 9 July 1847, reprinted in *Harbinger* 5 (17 July 1847): 87; see also *Harbinger* 5 (12 June 1847): 16; *Harbinger* 5 (17 July 1847): 92–93.

19. *Liberator*, 9 July 1847.

20. Wendell Phillips, *Speeches, Lectures, and Letters*, 2d ser. (Boston: Lee & Shepard, 1894), 152. For Phillips's participation in Gilded Age labor reform, see James Brewer Stewart, *Wendell Phillips: Liberty's Hero* (Baton Rouge: Louisiana State University Press, 1986), 258–63, 296–302; and David Montgomery, *Beyond Equality: Labor and the Radical Republicans, 1862–1872* (New York: Random House, 1967), 265, 269–70, 373, 413–14.

21. Eric Foner, "The Causes of the American Civil War: Recent Interpretations and New Directions," in *Politics and Ideology*, 24. See David Brion Davis, *The Problem of Slavery in the Age of Revolution, 1770–1823* (Ithaca: Cornell University Press, 1975). A penetrating forum on capitalism and antislavery, with articles by Davis, Thomas L. Haskell, and John Ashworth, appeared in *American Historical Review* 92 (October 1987): 797–878.

22. Even David Brion Davis concedes this point; see his "Reflections on Abolitionism and Ideological Hegemony," *American Historical Review* 92 (October 1987): 807.

23. Godwin to Charles Dana, 24 October 1845, B-G Collection; W. B. Greene to John S. Dwight, 22 October 1849, JSD Collection; [Williams], *Detriments*, 25.

24. Julia Bucklin Giles, "North American Phalanx," typescript address [1922], 7, NAP Collection; Norma Lippincott Swan, "The North American Phalanx," *Monmouth County Historical Association Bulletin* 1 (May 1935): 50–51; U.S. Census MSS. A few blacks did attend social functions at Brook Farm. See John Allen, "Fifth Lecture in Cincinnati," *Harbinger* 6 (22 April 1848): 197.

25. Channing to Maria Weston Chapman, 29 September 1846, Weston Collection, Boston Public Library.

26. Georgianna Bruce Kirby, *Years of Experience: An Autobiographical Narrative* (New York: Putnam, 1887), 183; Swift, *Brook Farm*, 122, 256; Samuel Gridley Howe to James T. Fisher, 26 September 1846, JTF Papers.

27. W. H. Channing, "The Plot to Annex Texas," *Present* 1 (15 November 1843): 137–41; Channing to Julia Channing, 7 August and 25 September 1845, Allen Correspondence; Channing, "Cassius M. Clay's Appeal," *Harbinger* 1 (20 October 1845): 318.

28. *Liberator*, 5 June 1846. See also Massachusetts Anti-Slavery Society, *Fifteenth Annual Report* (Boston, 1847), 93.

29. Garrison to Henry C. Wright, 1 June 1846, Antislavery Collection.

30. "Ode Inscribed to W. H. Channing," in *The Complete Works of Ralph Waldo Emerson*, ed. Edward Waldo Emerson (Boston: Houghton Mifflin, 1903), 9:76–79. See also Len Gougeon, "The Anti-Slavery Background of Emerson's 'Ode Inscribed to W. H. Channing,'" in *Studies in the American Renaissance 1985*, ed.

Joel Myerson (Charlottesville: University of Virginia Press, 1985), 63–77; and Frothingham, *Memoir of Channing*, 464–65.

31. W. H. Channing, "Peace the Principle and Policy of Associationists," *Harbinger* 2 (30 May 1846): 395; "Convention in Boston—Organization of 'The American Union of Associationists,'" *Harbinger* 2 (6 June 1846): 411.

32. "Lectures in Providence," 336; Marcus Spring to John S. Dwight, 29 May 1846, JSD Collection; "Convention in Boston," 411.

33. Godwin to Charles Dana, [5 June] 1846, B-G Collection. For Godwin's political evolution, see John Raymond Wennersten, "A Reformer's Odyssey: The Public Career of Parke Godwin of the New York *Evening Post*, 1837–1870" (Ph.D. diss., University of Maryland, 1970); for his earliest denunciation of slavery as "a gross and indefensible violation of right," see "The Slavery Question," *Pathfinder*, 29 April 1843, p. 145.

34. John R. Wennersten, "Parke Godwin, Utopian Socialism, and the Politics of Antislavery," *New-York Historical Society Quarterly* 60 (July–October 1976): 123; Godwin to Dana, [5 June] 1846, B-G Collection.

35. Godwin to Charles Dana, 17 [March 1845]; Godwin to Dana, 24 October 1845; Godwin to George Ripley, 1845, B-G Collection.

36. Godwin to Dana, [5 June] 1846; Dana to Godwin, 18 August 1846, B-G Collection; "Convention in Boston," 411.

37. Channing to Julia Channing, 1 January 1850, Allen Correspondence. For a later Channing-Godwin dispute—this time over Fourier's alleged "pantheism"—see the exchange in *Spirit of the Age* 1 (10 November and 1, 8, 14 December 1849): 297–99; 345–48, 360–62, 376–77.

38. For the AUA resolution, see "The Convention in Boston," *Harbinger* 4 (9 January 1847): 78; for Channing's petition see BRUA Records, 21 November 1847. Dana's peacemaking efforts can be glimpsed in Dana to Godwin, 18 August 1846, B-G Collection. John Dwight developed a neutral-sounding analysis blaming the Mexican War, and all contemporary wars, on competitive Civilization, condemning its cruelty and waste rather than slavery; see Dwight, "The War—Its Poetry and Its Piety," *Harbinger* 3 (5 December 1846): 412.

39. Godwin to James T. Fisher, 14 February [1847], JTF Papers; Thomas J. Durant to Albert Brisbane, 6 June 1847, Durant Papers.

40. Information on Macdaniel's background is scarce. Brook Farm records indicate that his sisters were born in Georgetown in 1815 and 1824, and Brook Farmers referred to his family as "Southern." See constitutions and minutes, Brook Farm Papers; and Marianne Dwight, *Letters from Brook Farm, 1844–1847*, ed. Amy L. Reed (Poughkeepsie, N.Y.: Vassar College, 1928), esp. 14, 126–28. As early as June 1841 Macdaniel was a member of the "Fourier Association of the City of New York"; see *Future* 1 (12 June 1841).

41. Brisbane and Macdaniel, "Dangers," 17–19; Osborne Macdaniel, "The Daily Delta," *Harbinger* 1 (8 November 1845): 352; *Harbinger* 3 (20 June 1846): 17.

42. *Phalanx* 1 (5 January, 1 March, 1 June 1844): 45, 80, 164; *Harbinger* 2 (18 April and 2 May 1846): 300, 336; George Ripley, "Another Good Movement," *Harbinger* 4 (6 February 1847): 142; Thomas J. Durant to Wilkins, 22 March 1845, Durant Papers. For biographical information on Wilkins, see Glenn R. Conrad's series "Virginians in the Teche Country," *Attakapas Gazette* 17 (Spring–Summer 1982): 8–18, 53–64.

43. *Harbinger* 6 (15 January 1848): 85; Grant to Wilson, 28 March 1844, EPG Papers. For Wilson's reports of Macdaniel's visit, see *Planters' Banner* (Franklin, La.), 6, 13, 20 May 1847.

44. Durant to Albert Brisbane, 24 March 1847, Durant Papers; Kirby, *Years of Experience*, 178.

45. See Joseph G. Tregle, Jr., "Thomas J. Durant, Utopian Socialism, and the Failure of Presidential Reconstruction in Louisiana," *Journal of Southern History* 45 (November 1979): 485–512; letters in Durant Papers and AB-IHS; Robert C. Reinders, "T. Wharton Collens: Catholic and Christian Socialist," *Catholic Historical Review* 52 (July 1966): 212–33; and Collens, "The Era of Guarantism," *Harbinger* 7 (12 August 1848): 114. On general interest in Fourier in New Orleans, see "New Orleans," *Harbinger* 2 (4 April 1846): 271.

46. "The Associationists and the Abolitionists."

47. Durant to John D. Wilkins, 1 April 1847, Durant Papers.

48. Macdaniel to E. P. Grant, 13 August 1847, EPG Papers.

49. On McDonogh, see Carl N. Degler, *The Other South: Southern Dissenters in the Nineteenth Century* (New York: Oxford University Press), 41–46, and the biographies it cites.

50. Macdaniel to E. P. Grant, 8 July and 13 August 1847 (quotations, next two paragraphs), EPG Papers.

51. E.g., the Owenite Frances Wright's Nashoba Community in Tennessee and McDonogh's system at McDonoghville. See O. B. Emerson, "Frances Wright and Her Nashoba Experiment," *Tennessee Historical Quarterly* 6 (1947): 291–314; and Helen Elliot, "Frances Wright's Experiment with Negro Emancipation," *Indiana Magazine of History* 36 (1939): 141–57.

52. "Letter from Mr. Brisbane," *Harbinger* 4 (22 May 1847): 375–76.

53. See "Abolition of Slavery, By a Carolinian" (bylined "Edgeworth"), *Spirit of the Age* 1 (10 November 1849): 291–93; Marx Edgeworth Lazarus, *Comparative Psychology and Universal Analogy* (New York: Fowlers & Wells, 1851), 49.

54. *Harbinger* 5 (25 September 1847): 248–49.

55. "The Associationists and the Abolitionists"; Janet Sharp Hermann, *Pursuit of a Dream* (New York: Oxford University Press, 1981), 3–34.

56. *Harbinger* 5 (25 September 1847): 249–50.

57. Durant to Brisbane, 6 June 1847, Durant Papers.

58. See Degler, *The Other South*, 41–46, 49–53, 90–91.

59. Macdaniel to E. P. Grant, 13 August 1847, EPG Papers; *Harbinger* 5 (25 September 1847): 248–49; Marx Edgeworth Lazarus, *Passional Hygiene and Natural Medicine* (New York: Fowlers & Wells, 1852), 436.

60. For the endorsement, see "Abolition of Slavery. No. 2," *Boston Daily Chronotype*, 9 January 1850. Lazarus repeated his plan in "Abolition of Slavery. By a Carolinian. Number Two," *Spirit of the Age* 1 (17 November 1849): 308–9; *Comparative Psychology*, 49; and *Passional Hygiene*, 369–70. In 1852 he projected a book to be titled "Slavery: A Clear Method of Annulling Its Evils, and Rendering the Relations of the White and Black Races Mutually Beneficient," but it was not published; see the announcement in *Passional Hygiene*, 439.

61. "Association at the South," *New York Daily Tribune*, 6 November 1850; Conrad, "Virginians in the Teche Country," 63.

62. F. L. Macdaniel to E. P. Grant, 12 December 1847; Osborne Macdaniel to E. P. Grant, 26 July 1848, EPG Papers; *Harbinger* 5 (25 September 1847): 256; *Boston Daily Chronotype*, 9 January 1850.

63. "Annual Meeting of the American Union of Associationists," *Harbinger* 4 (29 May 1847): 389.

64. J. L. Clarke, "Mr. Macdaniel's Lecture," *Harbinger* 5 (19 June 1847), 19; "Our Policy—Slavery—Letter from Mr. Macdaniel," *Harbinger* 5 (17 July 1847): 82–83; "Slavery," *Harbinger* 5 (14 August 1847): 150–51. Macdaniel's speech

was reported in *Planters' Banner,* 20 May 1847, and excerpted in "Lecture on Association," *Harbinger* 4 (5 June 1847): 407–8.

Chapter 10. The Movement Retreats

1. See "Statement of the 'American Union of Associationists' with Reference to Recent Attacks," *Harbinger* 3 (10 August 1846): 153–55 (no copies of the separate pamphlet are extant, to my knowledge); *Association, as Illustrated by Fourier's System* (Boston: Crosby & Nichols, 1847); and *Industrial Association: An Address to the People of the United States* (Boston: AUA, [1850]).

2. Tweedy to J. S. Dwight, 23 August 1847, Borneman Papers. Shaw translated works by Briancourt, Cantagrel, Constant, Pellarin, and George Sand.

3. Godwin to Charles Dana, 18 November 1846, B-G Collection. For the permanent fund, see "Circular" (August 1846), JFT Papers; and Albert Brisbane to Horace Greeley, [1846], Greeley-LC.

4. Godwin to Dana, [6 January 1846], B-G Collection; Grant to Brisbane, 5 February 1846, EPG Papers.

5. *Harbinger* 3 (13 June 1846): 12; "Meeting of the American Union of Associationists in Boston," *Harbinger* 3 (27 June 1846): 48. For details of the paper's financial history, see Sterling F. Delano, *The Harbinger and New England Transcendentalism* (Rutherford, N.J.: Fairleigh Dickinson University Press, 1983), 25–29.

6. "Meeting of the American Union of Associationists," *Harbinger* 4 (29 May 1847): 385–86.

7. "The Meetings in Boston," *Harbinger* 5 (23 October 1847): 316; "Office of the American Union," *Harbinger* 6 (6 November 1847): 7; Ripley to J. S. Dwight, 8 November [1847], JSD Collection.

8. Dwight, "How Stands the Cause?" *Harbinger* 3 (7 November 1846): 348–51; Ripley, "North American Phalanx," *Harbinger* 4 (13 March 1847): 222; "Model Phalanx in the West," *Harbinger* 4 (3 April 1847): 258–59; "Correspondence," *Harbinger* 5 (18 September 1847): 232.

9. Godwin to Charles Dana, 12 June, 12 August 1846, B-G Collection. See also E. P. Grant to Dana, 8 December 1846, EPG Papers.

10. Godwin to Dana, 12 June 1846, B-G Collection.

11. George Ripley, "Model Phalanx," *Harbinger* 4 (16 January 1847): 94–95; "Letter from Mr. Brisbane," *Harbinger* 4 (22 May 1847): 375–76.

12. *Harbinger* 4 (2 January 1847): 63.

13. "Annual Meeting of the American Union of Associationists," *Harbinger* 4 (29 May 1847): 385–92; "Meeting in New York," *Harbinger* 5 (24 July 1847): 111.

14. John Orvis, "The Committee of Thirteen," *Harbinger* 5 (7 August 1847): 144; Recordbook, 18 August 1847, BUA Records; Orvis to Isaiah C. Ray, 6 August 1847, Ray Correspondence; Joseph Cooke to *New York Daily Tribune,* 28 August 1847, reprinted in Noyes, *American Socialisms,* 428–30.

15. "The Meetings in Boston," *Harbinger* 5 (23 October 1847): 317.

16. "Annual Meeting of the American Union of Associationists," *Harbinger* 7 (13 May 1848): 12–14. The 1850 annual meeting did form a committee to raise $50,000 for improvements at the North American Phalanx, but its appeal for funds was probably absorbed into the Phalansterian Realization Fund Society appeal of the same year. See "Anniversary of the American Union of Associationists," *Protective Union* 1 (8 June 1850): 211–12.

17. Articles of Agreement, *Record of the PRFS,* PRFS Records.

18. Marcus Spring to James T. Fisher, 16 March 1848, JTF Papers; *Record of*

the PRFS, 9 May 1848, PRFS Records; NAP Proceedings, 24 March, 12 and 21 May 1848, NAP Collection. The society's dealings with the NAP are described somewhat differently in Dolores Hayden, *Seven American Utopias: The Architecture of Communitarian Socialism, 1790–1975* (Cambridge, Mass.: MIT Press, 1976), 164, 172; and Herman J. Belz, "The North American Phalanx: Experiment in Socialism," *Proceedings of the New Jersey Historical Society* 81 (October 1963): 233–36. I have based my account on the original PRFS and NAP records.

19. "North American Phalanx," *Harbinger* 4 (13 March 1847): 222; NAP Proceedings, 4 June, 23 June 1848, NAP Collection.

20. Hayden, *Seven American Utopias,* 172.

21. *Circular. To the Associationists of the United States,* 1 September 1850, JTF Papers.

22. Menu, Banquet of 6 May 1851, JTF Papers, cited in Hayden, *Seven American Utopias,* 173–74.

23. See the numerous plans and proposals in AB-IHS.

24. R. W. Emerson, "Fourierism and the Socialists," *Dial* 3 (July 1842): 88–89.

25. Noyes, *American Socialisms,* 662–63, 667–68.

26. Ibid., 671.

27. See Albert Brisbane, *Association; or, A Concise Exposition of the Practical Part of Fourier's Social Science* (New York: Greeley & McElrath, 1843), 4, 9, 31.

28. J. S. Dwight, "The Shakers at New Lebanon," *Harbinger* 5 (21 August 1847): 176.

29. See J. S. Dwight, "The American Review's Account of the Religious Union of Associationists," *Harbinger* 5 (19 June–10 July 1847): 28–30, 43–46, 58–60, 73–76; Hosea Ballou, "Fourierism and Similar Schemes," *Universalist Quarterly and General Review,* January 1845; and Donald C. M'Laren, *Boa-Constrictor; or, Fourier Association Self-Exposed as to Its Principles and Aims* (Rochester, N.Y.: Canfield & Warren, 1844), 16, 20.

30. "The Democratic Review and Association," *Harbinger* 2 (3 January 1846): 60–62; "The New York Observer on Association," *Harbinger* 3 (15 August 1846): 155–57. The series "Objections to Association" ran 11 July to 17 October 1846, encompassing eight articles in response to criticism in the *Oberlin Review.*

31. "Statement of the 'American Union of Associationists,'" 153–55.

32. Dana to Parke Godwin, 18 August 1846, B-G Collection; Grant to Fanny Macdaniel, 15 November 1846, and Grant to Charles Dana, 8 December 1846 (both in Pitman shorthand), EPG Papers.

33. Raymond to James Marsh, 14 January 1841, in *Coleridge's American Disciples: The Selected Correspondence of James Marsh,* ed. John J. Duffy (Amherst: University of Massachusetts Press, 1973), 246. For Raymond's biography, see Augustus Maverick, *Henry J. Raymond and the New York Press for Thirty Years* (New York: A. S. Hale, 1870).

34. Horace Greeley and Henry J. Raymond, *Association Discussed; or, The Socialism of the Tribune Examined* (New York: Harper, 1847), 39, 33, 56, 69. For the most extensive account of the debate, see James Parton, *The Life of Horace Greeley* (New York: Mason, 1855), 205–17. Daniel Walker Howe, *The Political Culture of the American Whigs* (Chicago: University of Chicago Press, 1979), 29, notes the Whigs' and Greeley's adherence to faculty psychology, which preached balance and restraint rather than indulgence of instincts.

35. Parton, *Greeley,* 205.

36. "Celebration of Fourier's Birthday in New York," *Harbinger* 4 (24 April 1847): 317. See also Glyndon Van Deusen, *Horace Greeley, Nineteenth-Century Crusader* (Philadelphia: University of Pennsylvania Press, 1953), 80.

37. Arthur Bestor, "American Phalanxes: A Study of Fourierist Socialism in the United States (with Special Reference to the Movement in Western New York)" (Ph.D. diss., Yale University, 1938), 1:260.

38. *Harbinger* 4 (29 May 1847): 391.

39. *Harbinger* 5 (18 September 1847): 238–39, and 5 (9 October 1847): 285; Bestor, "American Phalanxes," 1:277–78.

40. *Harbinger* 5 (9 October 1847): 285.

41. Warren Chase, *The Life-line of the Lone One; or, Autobiography of the World's Child* (Boston: Bela Marsh, 1858), 122.

42. Brisbane, *Mental Biography*, 246, 250; *Harbinger* 4 (29 May 1847): 390–91.

43. See Bryan R. Wilson, *Sects and Society* (Berkeley: University of California Press, 1961).

44. J. F. C. Harrison, *Quest for a New Moral World: Robert Owen and the Owenites in Britain and America* (New York: Scribner, 1969), 135–39; Christopher H. Johnson, *Utopian Communism in France: Cabet and the Icarians, 1839–1851* (Ithaca: Cornell University Press, 1974), 207–54; Frank E. Manuel, *The Prophets of Paris* (New York: Harper & Row, 1965), 149–93.

45. Jonathan Beecher, *Charles Fourier: The Visionary and His World* (Berkeley: University of California Press, 1986), 497–98; Charles Fourier, *Pièges et charlatanisme des deux sectes Saint-Simon et Owen* (Paris: Bossange, 1831).

46. See Beecher, *Charles Fourier*, 497–98; Rondel Van Davidson, *Did We Think Victory Great? The Life and Ideas of Victor Considerant* (Lanham, Md.: University Press of America, 1988), 46–48.

47. See, e.g., *Phalanx* 1 (20 April 1844): 104, 133; and Marianne Dwight, *Letters from Brook Farm, 1844–1847*, ed. Amy L. Reed (Poughkeepsie, N.Y.: Vassar College, 1928), 144.

48. Channing to John S. Dwight, 8 November 1846, JSD Collection, in Zoltan Haraszti, *The Idyll of Brook Farm* (Boston: Public Library, 1937), 42–43. Channing to James T. Fisher et al., 4 December 1845, JTF Papers.

49. Parke Godwin, *A Popular View of the Doctrines of Charles Fourier* (New York: J. S. Redfield, 1844), 114–15.

50. Noyes, *American Socialisms*, 550; Marguerite Beck Block, *The New Church in the New World: A Study of Swedenborgianism in America* (New York: Holt, Rinehart & Winston, 1932), 156–58; Ophia D. Smith, "The Rise of the New Church in Ohio," *Ohio State Archaeological and Historical Quarterly* 61 (October 1952): 405.

51. This discussion of Brook Farm's religious life and the section on the Religious Union of Associationists that follows are indebted to Charles Crowe's sensitive article "Christian Socialism and the First Church of Humanity," *Church History* 35 (March 1966): 93–106.

52. "Letter from Charles A. Dana," *Phalanx* 1 (24 August 1844): 256; Dwight, *Letters from Brook Farm*, 73–75, 96.

53. Crowe, "Christian Socialism," 97; "Celebration of Fourier's Birthday at Brook Farm," *Phalanx* 1 (3 May 1845): 336–37.

54. Crowe, "Christian Socialism," 98; Dwight, *Letters from Brook Farm*, 115–16, 122–24.

55. "Statement of Faith and Purpose," BRUA Records. The RUA Recordbook has been published by Sterling F. Delano as "A Calendar of the Meetings of the 'Boston Religious Union of Associationists,' " in *Studies in the American Renaissance 1985*, ed. Joel Myerson (Charlottesville: University of Virginia Press, 1985): 187–267.

56. *The Religious Union of Associationists*, printed circular dated 20 November 1848, in BRUA Records.

57. Crowe, "Christian Socialism," 99–102.

58. Recordbook, 24 January 1848 and 3 June 1849, BRUA Records; Allen to J. S. Dwight, 27 April 1848, JSD Collection; "Church of Humanity" (Pittsburgh), *Harbinger* 7 (22 July 1848): 94.

59. Though several sources exist, the most reliable membership evidence is the handwritten list, mostly signatures, appearing after the "Statement of Faith and Purpose" in the BRUA Records. Members' occupations were compiled from census, city directory, and manuscript materials. Nonjoining subscribers were identified through lists in the BRUA Records and JTF Papers; and the Treasurer's Account Book, RUA Records.

60. For the religious poll, see Recordbook, 5 December 1847, BRUA Records. On the social homogeneity of sects in their initial phase, see Bryan J. Wilson, "An Analysis of Sect Development," *American Sociological Review* 24 (February 1959): 3–15.

61. Although Crowe, "Christian Socialism," 103, says that the church "expired in 1854," the final entry in the Treasurer's Account Book, RUA Records, is dated 11 November 1852, and there is no evidence that the group met after May 1853. Channing assumed a Unitarian ministry in Rochester, New York, in 1852.

62. "Our Prospects in New York," *Harbinger* 5 (9 October 1847): 286; Orvis to Marianne Dwight Orvis, 9 December 1847, Abernethy Library.

63. [Charles Julius Hempel], *The True Organization of the New Church as Indicated in the Writings of Emmanuel Swedenborg, and Demonstrated by Charles Fourier* (New York: Wm. Radde, 1848), 57; Godwin, "What Associationists Propose," *Harbinger* 6 (8 January 1848): 76. Among many articles endorsing such measures, see George Ripley, "Forms of Guarantyism," *Harbinger* 3 (31 October 1846): 335–36; and "Guarantyism," *Harbinger* 4 (3 April 1847): 270.

64. J. S. Dwight, "Suggestions to Affiliated Unions," *Harbinger* 4 (27 March 1847): 254–55; "Convention of Associationists in Boston," *Harbinger* 4 (5 June 1847): 409–10; "Annual Meeting of the American Union of Associationists," *Harbinger* 7 (13 May 1848): 13.

65. "Annual Meeting [1848]," 13; "Ceresco Mercantile Protective Union," *Protective Union* 1 (13 April 1850): 145; BRUA Records; Philadelphia Union of Associationists, *Constitution of the Group of Actuation* (Philadelphia, n.d.).

66. Beecher, *Charles Fourier*, 244–46. See *Journals and Miscellaneous Notebooks of Ralph Waldo Emerson*, ed. William H. Gilman et al. (Cambridge, Mass.: Harvard University Press, 1960–82), 7:407–8; and Domingo Faustino Sarmiento, *Travels in the United States in 1847*, trans. Michael Aaron Rockland (Princeton, N.J.: University Press, 1970), 144.

67. For Daly's analysis of nineteenth-century architecture, see Ann Lorentz Van Zanten, "Form and Society: César Daly and the Revue Générale de l'Architecture," *Oppositions* 1 (Spring 1977): 136–45; and Donald J. Olsen, *The City as a Work of Art: London, Paris, Vienna* (New Haven, Conn.: Yale University Press, 1986), 114–22, 300–304.

68. *Communitist* 2 (9 October 1845): 38–39 (Rochester boarding-house); *Constitution of the Philadelphia Unitary Building Association* (Philadelphia: U.S. Job Printing Office, 1849); "Annual Meeting [1845]," 12 (Cincinnati plan); and BUA Records, 19, 23 August and 30 September 1847. For an endorsement of such dwellings for non-Fourierists, see Parke Godwin, "The Tenants' League," *Harbinger* 6 (11 March 1848): 148. A Fourierist-inspired fictional utopia written in 1848 by Jane Sophia Appleton portrayed cooperative eating houses and laundries, arcaded buildings, and model tenements in the Bangor, Maine, of 1978; see "Sequel to the Vision of Bangor in the Twentieth Century," reprinted in *American Utopias: Selected Short Fiction*, ed. Arthur O. Lewis (New York: Arno Press, 1971), 243–65.

69. See Helen Dwight Orvis, "A Note on Anna Q. T. Parsons," in Dwight, *Letters from Brook Farm*, xv; George Willis Cooke, *John Sullivan Dwight, Brook Farmer, Editor, and Critic of Music* (Boston: Small, Maynard, 1898), 129–30; William Henry Channing to Julia Channing, 29 November 1848, Allen Correspondence; and Parsons to Angélique Martin, November 1848, Spencer Papers. The first (Parson's) household included John Dwight and his fiancée Mary Bullard; the two Brook Farm couples in the second were the Sawyers and Butterfields; see U.S. Census MSS, Suffolk County, Massachusetts.

70. See J. Owen Stalson, *Marketing Life Insurance: Its History in America* (1942; rpt. Bryn Mawr, Pa.: McCahan Foundation, 1969), 82–125; and Charles K. Knight, *The History of Life Insurance in the United States to 1870* (Philadelphia, 1920).

71. "Annual Meeting of the American Union of Associationists," *Harbinger* 4 (29 May 1847): 387; Durant to Robert Wilson, 4 June 1847, Durant Papers; *Circular. To the Associationists of the United States*, 1 September 1850, JTF Papers.

72. For an Associationist tribute to Wright, see *Harbinger* 5 (17 June 1847): 52. For Wright's attendance, see "Celebration of Fourier's Birthday in Boston," *Harbinger* 4 (17 April 1847): 297–98.

73. See Philip G. Wright and Elizabeth Q. Wright, *Elizur Wright, the Father of Life Insurance* (Chicago: University of Chicago Press, 1937); and Lawrence B. Goodheart, *Abolitionist, Actuary, Atheist: Elizur Wright and the Reform Impulse* (Kent, Ohio: Kent State University Press, 1990). A sparkling summary of Wright's work in insurance reform is in Daniel J. Boorstin, *The Americans: The Democratic Experience* (New York: Random House, 1974), 175–80.

74. Madeleine B. Stern, *The Pantarch: A Biography of Stephen Pearl Andrews* (Austin: University of Texas Press, 1968), 52–54, 58–72. For Andrews's Fourierist phase (of which Stern appeared unaware), see "Celebration of Fourier's Birthday in Boston," *Harbinger* 4 (17 April 1847): 298; and T.C. Leland, "Individual Sovereignty," *American Socialist* 1 (1 June 1876): 73, and 2 (12 July 1877): 221. Andrews was elected the first president of the Boston Union of Associationists in November 1846 but declined to serve. See BUA Records, 30 November and 7 December 1846.

75. Charles Dana, Review of *The Complete Phonographic Class Book*, *Harbinger* 1 (29 November 1845): 394; Stern, *Pantarch*, 105–6, 155–56.

76. Stern, *Pantarch*, 62; Dwight, *Letters from Brook Farm*, 87–88; *Harbinger* 4 (2 January 1847): 62. Grant's letters are in Letterbook III, EPG Papers.

77. Stern, *Pantarch*, 70.

78. Charles Dana, *Proudhon and His "Bank of the People"* (New York: Benjamin Tucker, 1896), 34, 49–53; Dana, "The Bank of the People," *Spirit of the Age* 1 (1 December 1849): 358; Dana to John S. Dwight, 5 September 1849, JSD Collection. Most of Dana's series, which appeared from 6 October to 1 December 1849 in *Spirit of the Age*, was published as a pamphlet during the 1896 presidential election by the anarchist Benjamin Tucker. Tucker slyly countered the aged Dana's attacks on William Jennings Bryan and silverite monetary reform by bringing to light Dana's early interest in currency reform.

79. "Mutual Bank of Discount and Deposit," *Spirit of the Age* 1 (10 November 1849): 293–94; "H.M.P." [Henry M. Parkhurst], "A New Currency," *Boston Daily Chronotype*, 15 October 1849, p. 1.

80. Brisbane, *Mental Biography*, 294; Brisbane, "The Mutualist Township," *Spirit of the Age* 2 (23 and 30 March 1850): 179–83, 200–202; J. K. Ingalls, "A Practical Movement for Transition," *Spirit of the Age* 2 (30 March 1850): 202–4.

81. George Ripley, "Proudhon's Financial Schemes," *Harbinger* 7 (26 August 1848): 132; "Fourier and His School," *Harbinger* 7 (28 October 1848): 202. See

"Letters on Capital and Interest" in the *Boston Daily Chronotype* from 20 October to 4 December 1849; the Lazarus quotation is from 9 November 1849, p. 1.

82. E. W. Parkman, quoted in BUA Records, 29 November 1848; Philadelphia Union, *Constitution of the Group of Actuation.*

83. *Practical Christian* 19 (1858–59): 69; Jon Wagner, "Success in Intentional Communities: The Problem of Evaluation," *Communal Societies* 5 (1985): 96–98.

84. *Harbinger* 7 (13 May 1848): 13; BUA Records, 21 April 1847; *Harbinger* 7 (27 May 1848): 30; Ripley to J. S. Dwight, 8 and 22 November 1847, JSD Collection. For documents relating to Ripley's New York experience, see Joel Myerson, "New Light on George Ripley and the *Harbinger*'s New York Years," *Harvard Library Bulletin* 33 (Summer 1985): 313–36.

85. Godwin to J. S. Dwight, 8 December 1848; Ripley to Dwight, 7 December 1847 and 18 October 1848, JSD Collection; Ripley to Dwight, 10 April 1849, Borneman Papers.

86. Ripley to J. S. Dwight, 28 August 1848 and [December 1848], JSD Collection; "An Announcement," *Harbinger* 8 (10 February 1849): 116.

87. *To the Associationists of the United States,* printed circular [1849], JTF Papers; *Boston Daily Chronotype,* 23 August 1849, p. 1.

88. Ripley to J. S. Dwight, 26 March 1849, JSD Collection; Godwin to [James T. Fisher], 29 March 1849, JTF Papers; W. H. Channing, "End of Volume First," *Spirit of the Age* 1 (29 December 1849): 406.

89. Ripley to J. S. Dwight, [December 1848], JSD Collection; W. H. Channing, "To Meet Again!" *Spirit of the Age* 2 (27 April 1850): 264. For the Channing-Godwin dispute, see Channing, "Letter to Associationists," *Spirit of the Age* 1 (10 November 1849): 297–99; and "Criticism of Fourier Criticized," *Spirit of the Age* 1 (1, 8, 14 December 1849): 345–48, 360–62, 376–77.

Chapter 11. Campaigns with Labor

1. Norman F. Ware, *The Industrial Worker, 1840–1860* (Boston: Houghton Mifflin, 1924). For a more moderate formulation, see John R. Commons et al., *History of Labour in the United States* (New York: Macmillan, 1918), 1:575–786; and Henry Pelling, *American Labor* (Chicago: University of Chicago Press, 1960), 36–38. Even Marxist Philip S. Foner echoes this interpretation in his *History of the Labor Movement in the United States* (New York: International Publishers, 1962), 1:188–90.

2. The following paragraphs develop a critique, suggested by recent scholarship, of Ware's worker-reformer dichotomy. See Anne C. Rose, *Transcendentalism as a Social Movement, 1830–1850* (New Haven, Conn.: Yale University Press, 1981), 156; Jama Lazerow, "Religion and Labor Reform in Antebellum America: The World of William Field Young," *American Quarterly* 38 (Summer 1986): 283 n.13; and esp. Frances H. Early, "A Reappraisal of the New England Labour-Reform Movement of the 1840s: The Lowell Female Labor Reform Association and the New England Workingmen's Association," *Histoire Sociale/Social History* 13 (May 1980): 34–35, 53–54.

3. Ware, *Industrial Worker*, 22–23; Lazerow, "Religion and Labor Reform," 285 n.37.

4. Alan Dawley, *Class and Community: The Industrial Revolution in Lynn* (Cambridge, Mass.: Harvard University Press, 1976), 65.

5. Ware, *Industrial Worker*, 22, 239; Glyndon G. Van Deusen, *Horace Greeley, Nineteenth-Century Crusader* (Philadelphia: University of Pennsylvania Press, 1953), 77–78.

6. See, e.g., Parke Godwin, "Wages Slavery," *Harbinger* 6 (25 March 1848): 164.

7. Lazerow, "Religion and Labor Reform," 279–80.

8. Hewitt, quoted in Philip S. Foner, "Journal of an Early Labor Organizer," *Labor History* 10 (Spring 1969): 221–22.

9. Sean Wilentz, *Chants Democratic: New York City and the Rise of the American Working Class, 1788–1850* (New York: Oxford University Press, 1984); Dawley, *Class and Community*; Paul G. Faler, *Mechanics and Manufacturers in the Early Industrial Revolution: Lynn, Massachusetts, 1786–1860* (Albany: State University of New York Press, 1981), Bruce Laurie, *Working People of Philadelphia, 1800–1850* (Philadelphia: Temple University Press, 1980); Thomas Dublin, *Women at Work: The Transformation of Work and Community in Lowell, Massachusetts, 1826–1860* (New York: Columbia University Press, 1979); and Steven J. Ross, *Workers on the Edge: Work, Leisure, and Politics in Industrializing Cincinnati, 1788–1890* (New York: Columbia University Press, 1985). For the influence of religion, see Teresa Murphy, "Labor, Religion, and Moral Reform in Fall River, Massachusetts, 1800–1845" (Ph.D. diss., Yale University, 1982); and Jama Lazerow, "A Good Time Coming: Religion and the Emergence of Labor Activism in Antebellum New England" (Ph.D. diss., Brandeis University, 1983).

10. Wilentz, *Chants Democratic*, 339.

11. *Harbinger* 7 (13 May 1848): 12, lists twenty-one members of the New York Union; my research has added seven names. Of the twenty-eight, only two were workingmen, Ryckman (by then returned to New York) and James P. Decker, a self-employed cooper who later joined the North American Phalanx.

12. Horace Greeley, "The Relations of Learning to Labor," in *Hints toward Reforms* (New York: Harper, 1850), 132–34; John R. Wennersten, "Parke Godwin, Utopian Socialism, and the Politics of Antislavery," *New-York Historical Society Quarterly* 60 (July–October 1976): 115; Godwin to Dana, 8 November 1844, 26 April 1845, and 1 August 1845, B-G Collection; Greeley, "The Emancipation of Labor," in *Hints toward Reforms*, 48. For Godwin's speeches of early 1845, see "The Organization of Labor," and "Labor Because It Is Paid for by Wages Is a Species of Slavery," Godwin Papers.

13. Teresa Murphy, "Work, Leisure, and Moral Reform: The Ten-Hour Movement in New England, 1830–1850," in *Worktime and Industrialization: An International History*, ed. Gary Cross (Philadelphia: Temple University Press, 1988), 66.

14. Among accounts of the NEWA, see Commons et al., *History of Labour*, 1:537–39; Ware, *Industrial Worker*, 202–13, 218–22; and Early, "Reappraisal," 38–53.

15. "Circular of the Fall River Mechanics," *DocHist* 8:86; Foner, "Journal," 207.

16. "New England Working Men's Association, First Convention, Boston, October, 1844," *DocHist* 8:98.

17. "Workingmen's Convention," *Phalanx* 1 (9 December 1844): 304; Dana to Parke Godwin, 30 October 1844, B-G Collection; "Convention of the New England Fourier Society," *Phalanx* 1 (8 February 1845): 310–11.

18. Ware, *Industrial Worker*, 206–8; Osborne Macdaniel, "The Ten Hour System," *Phalanx* 1 (18 May 1844): 139. For the full slate of resolutions, see "Lowell Convention, March, 1845, Preamble and Resolutions," *DocHist* 8:99–106.

19. "Lowell Convention," 103–5; Rose, *Transcendentalism*, 156. Ryckman outlined his early reform career to an Associationist audience in 1847; see "Celebration of Fourier's Birthday in New York," *Harbinger* 4 (24 April 1847): 317.

20. "First Annual Meeting [of the NEWA]," *DocHist* 8:106–11.

21. *Voice of Industry*, 17 July, 12 June 1845, quoted in *DocHist* 7:233–34. For the Associationists' reply, see "Means and Measures," *Harbinger* 1 (12 July 1845): 78.

22. "New England Workingmen's Convention," *Harbinger* 1 (27 September 1845): 255–56; *Voice of Industry*, 7 November 1845; Early, "Reappraisal," 42–43. For the Fourierists' frustration with indifferent NEWA workers, see "The Working Men of New England," *Harbinger* 1 (26 July 1845): 112.

23. Ware, *Industrial Worker*, 134–45; Early, "Reappraisal," 45–46.

24. George Ripley, "Guarantyism," *Harbinger* 3 (24 October 1846): 319–20.

25. Ware, *Industrial Worker*, 219–20; Early, "Reappraisal," 49; *DocHist* 8:125–26.

26. Early, "Reappraisal," 50–51, 53; Ware, *Industrial Worker*, 221–22; Commons et al., *History of Labour*, 1:539. Charles Hosmer presented his address—privately published as *The Condition of Labor* (Boston, 1847)—to the LRL in January 1847. However, after Trask reported his participation to the BUA, they rejected an alliance with land reformers and decided not to send a delegate to the July 1847 LRL meeting. See BUA Records, 30 March 1847 and 8 July 1847.

27. Philip S. Foner, *Women and the American Labor Movement: From Colonial Times to the Eve of World War I* (New York: Free Press, 1979), 60. For accounts of the LFLRA, see Dublin, *Women at Work*, 108–31; Foner, *Women and the Labor Movement*, 55–84; and Early, "Reappraisal," 43–52. Madeleine B. Stern, *We the Women: Career Firsts of Nineteenth-Century America* (New York: Burt Franklin, 1975), 79–94, gathers information on Bagley; but for her doings after 1846, see various letters to Angélique Martin in the Spencer Papers.

28. Dublin, *Women at Work*, 116–20.

29. Ibid., 113–16.

30. *Voice of Industry*, 5 June, 10 July 1845, reprinted in *The Factory Girls*, ed. Philip S. Foner (Urbana: University of Illinois Press, 1977), 61, 109; George Ripley, "Brook Farm Lecturers," *Harbinger* 2 (21 February 1846): 175; Dublin, *Women at Work*, 117–18; Charles Dana, "The Campaign Begun!" *Harbinger* 3 (11 July 1846): 80.

31. "Correspondence," *Harbinger* 5 (7 August 1847): 129. For the officers in 1846, see Charles Dana, "The Lowell Union of Associationists," *Harbinger* 3 (29 August 1846): 191.

32. *Voice of Industry*, 18 September and 19 June 1846.

33. For the lectures, see *Voice of Industry*, 3, 9, 16 April 1847. Kennison had been an operative at the Merrimack Mill before joining the NAP at age twenty-six. See NAP Collection and the 1850 U.S. Census. Mary Paul joined at twenty-four after laboring on and off in the mills for four years. For her letters, see Thomas Dublin, ed., *Farm to Factory: Women's Letters, 1830–1860* (New York: Columbia University Press, 1981), 97–130.

34. Early, "Reappraisal," 51–52; Dublin, *Women at Work*, 121.

35. Edwin Charles Rozwenc, *Cooperatives Come to America: The History of the Protective Union Store Movement, 1845–1867* (1941; rpt. Philadelphia: Porcupine Press, 1975), 62; Dublin, *Women at Work*, 121. For a list of Lowell stores and officers, see *Protective Union* 1 (2 February 1850): 75.

36. Sarah Bagley to Angélique Martin, 28 March [1847], and Mary Emerson to Angélique Martin, April 1849, Spencer Papers; "Correspondence," *Harbinger* 5 (7 August 1847): 129; *Harbinger* 6 (6 November 1847): 7; Ware, *Industrial Worker*, 213.

37. In this and the following paragraph I have benefited from the excellent discussion in Rose, *Transcendentalism*, 157–59, on Brook Farm's artisans. Membership was compiled from the constitution of February 11, 1844; minutes of meet-

ings, 1841–45; and Journal B, 1844–46 in the Brook Farm Papers, supplemented by information from city directories. For differences between my data and Rose's, see Chapter 6, note 42.

38. Hewitt quoted in Foner, "Journal," 222. Boston Union membership was compiled from the List of Members to November 1848 and the Treasurer's Account, November 1847–January 1850, BUA Records, supplemented by U.S. Census and city directory information.

39. Helene Sara Zahler, *Eastern Workingmen and National Land Policy, 1829–1862* (New York: Columbia University Press, 1941), 35–36.

40. Osborne Macdaniel, "The Right of Man to the Soil," *Phalanx* 1 (10 August 1844): 229; Charles Dana, "Young America—Anti-Rentism," *Harbinger* 1 (23 August 1845): 174–75; "Convention of the New England Fourier Society," *Phalanx* 1 (8 February 1845): 316.

41. Horace Greeley, "Land Reform," in *Hints toward Reforms*, 311–17; *Harbinger* 4 (3 April 1847): 257; Zahler, *Eastern Workingmen*, 38, 54.

42. Letter to *Young America*, 28 February 1846, reprinted in *DocHist* 7:343–44; Lewis Ryckman, "Address to the Workingmen of New England," *Harbinger* 1 (21 June 1845): 22; Albert Brisbane, "What Do the Workingmen Want?" *Harbinger* 1 (5 July 1845): 61–62.

43. "Lowell Convention," *DocHist* 8:104; Zahler, *Eastern Workingmen*, 46; Ware, *Industrial Worker*, 219; Greeley, "Land Reform," 317.

44. *Harbinger* 1 (9 August 1845): 144.

45. For the 1845 Industrial Congress, see *DocHist* 8:26–27; and *New York Daily Tribune*, 14 October 1845. For 1846 and 1847, see Ware, *Industrial Worker*, 223–25. On Fourierists' participation in 1848 and 1849, see *DocHist* 8:22, 28; and *Spirit of the Age* 1 (14 July 1849): 25.

46. For Van Amringe and Hine, see Zahler, *Eastern Workingmen*, 46–47. Charles Dana, "The Industrial Congress," *Harbinger* 1 (1 November 1845): 335, complained that the congress gathered few of "the various classes immediately connected with labor." Zahler, *Eastern Workingmen*, 69, though defending the congresses as the legitimate voice of labor, admits that "organized labor as such had scant representation."

47. On Owenism and cooperation, see J. F. C. Harrison, *Quest for the New Moral World: Robert Owen and the Owenites in Britain and America* (New York: Scribner, 1969), 197–216; and G. D. H. Cole, *A Century of Cooperation* (London: Allen & Unwin, [1944]). For the strong Fourierist influence on cooperatives in France, see Charles Gide, *Fourier, précurseur de la coopération* (Paris: Association pour l'Enseignement de la Coopération, 1924); and esp. Jean Gaumont's monumental *Histoire générale de la coopération en France* (Paris: Fédération Nationale des Coopératives de Consummation, 1924), 1:160–227. According to Rozwenc, *Cooperatives*, 117, Associationists played "the paramount role" in creating an American cooperative movement.

48. Rozwenc, *Cooperatives*, 23–24, 29–30. For the influence of Fourierist lectures, see Albert Brisbane, "Co-Operation in America," *Christian Socialist* 2 (27 September 1851): 203. For Trask's account, see BUA Records, 23 March 1847.

49. Rozwenc, *Cooperatives*, 30–33, 36–37.

50. Ware, *Industrial Worker*, 187; "New England Protective Union," *Spirit of the Age* 1 (6 October 1849): 220. For Blacker's testimony, see Records of Group of Study and Indoctrination, 22 November 1848, BUA Records. Rozwenc, whose *Cooperatives* is the definitive monograph on protective unions, was unaware of Trask's and Blacker's Fourierist backgrounds.

51. *Voice of Industry*, 28 November 1845; "Convention of the New England Fourier Society," *Phalanx* 1 (8 February 1845): 315; "New England Workingmen's

Convention," *Harbinger* 1 (27 September 1845): 255; Osborne Macdaniel, "The Workingmen's Protective Union," *Harbinger* 2 (13 December 1845): 15.

52. Rozwenc, *Cooperatives*, 36, 39.

53. George Ripley, "Protective Unions," *Harbinger* 5 (16 October 1847): 304; *New York Daily Tribune*, 10 August 1846; Rozwenc, *Cooperatives*, 48.

54. "Convention of Associationists in Boston," *Harbinger* 4 (5 June 1847): 409–10; "Annual Meeting of the American Union of Associationists," *Harbinger* 7 (13 May 1848): 13; "Ceresco Mercantile Protective Union," *Protective Union* 1 (13 April 1850): 145.

55. "Correspondence," *Harbinger* 8 (20 January 1849): 94; "Sayings and Doings in Providence," *Harbinger* 6 (15 January 1848): 85; Charles R. Crowe, "Utopian Socialism in Rhode Island, 1845–1850," *Rhode Island History* 18 (January 1959): 26; "An Appeal," *Harbinger* 8 (9 December 1848): 43; "Anniversary of the American Union of Associationists," *Protective Union* 1 (8 June 1850): 211. On trade with the North American Phalanx, see Rozwenc, *Cooperatives*, 68.

56. Records of the Group of Study and Indoctrination, 22, 29 November 1848, BUA Records. See also BRUA Records, Minutes of 12 December 1847.

57. For Orvis and Allen's lectures, see "Our Prospects in New York," *Harbinger* 5 (9 October 1847): 286; and "Protective Unions," *Harbinger* 7 (23 September 1848): 161. For Brown, Merriam, and White, see *Protective Union* 1 (2 February, 20 April, and 12 October 1850): 75, 157, 356.

58. The most complete list of officers is in *Protective Union* 1 (2 February 1850): 75; among the officers were a carriage builder, a journeyman carpenter, a merchant, mill overseers, operatives, a painter, and foundry workers. Kaulback was quoted in Records of the Group of Study and Introduction, 22 November 1848, BUA Records. On the name change, see Rozwenc, *Cooperatives*, 60.

59. Rozwenc, *Cooperatives*, 94.

60. "New England Protective Union—Quarterly Report," *Protective Union* 1 (3 August 1850): 276; Brisbane, "Co-Operation in America," 204.

61. Rozwenc, *Cooperatives*, 97–115.

62. Wilentz, *Chants Democratic*, 366.

63. "New England Workingmen's Association," *DocHist* 8:97; *Fall River Mechanic*, 4 January 1845.

64. Trask, quoted in "New England Protective Union," *Spirit of the Age* 1 (6 October 1849): 220; Rozwenc, *Cooperatives*, 59.

65. *New York Daily Tribune*, 1 June 1850; 1, 13, 15, 26 July 1850, and 13 August 1850.

66. Bernard H. Moss, *The Origins of the French Labor Movement, 1830–1914: The Socialism of Skilled Workers* (Berkeley: University of California Press, 1976), 4–47; and esp. Gaumont, *Histoire générale de la coopération* 1:160–227.

67. "Associative Establishments in Paris" (reprinted from *Boston Chronotype*), *Harbinger* 8 (4 November 1848): 2; James Harrison Wilson, *The Life of Charles A. Dana* (New York: Harper, 1907), 89; Albert Brisbane, "Associations of Workingmen in Paris," *Boston Daily Chronotype*, 17 September 1849. Dana's support for cooperatives was linked to his championing of Proudhon, for he envisioned producers' associations eventually exchanging goods through the medium of the "Bank of the People." See Dana, *Proudhon and His "Bank of the People"* (New York: B. R. Tucker, 1896), 54.

68. For representative articles and speeches by Greeley, see *New York Daily Tribune*, 30 January, 1 March, and 24 April 1850; "Strikes and Their Remedy" and "The Organization of Labor," *Hints toward Reforms*, 364–66; 196–205. For Charles Sully, see *New York Daily Tribune*, 13 February 1851; and his *Associative Manual* (New York: Dewitt & Davenport, 1851). For Brisbane, see "Co- Operation

in America," 203; and "Letter from Mr. Brisbane," *Boston Daily Chronotype*, 5 January 1850. Dana's lectures are noted in Carl Bode, *The American Lyceum: Town Meeting of the Mind* (New York: Oxford University Press, 1956), 144–45.

69. "The Seventh of April in Cincinnati," *Harbinger* 7 (6 May 1848): 4–6; "The Cincinnati Molders," *DocHist* 8:309–14; "Correspondence," *Protective Union* 1 (19 January 1850): 59; and James T. Fisher, "Journeymen's Union Foundry," *Protective Union* 1 (16 February 1850): 95.

70. Ross, *Workers on the Edge*, 160–61.

71. "Boston Tailors' Associative Union," *DocHist* 8:279–85; "Address of the Boston Associationists to the Boston Tailor's Associative Union," *Protective Union* 1 (5 January 1850): 46. Brisbane's series appeared in the *Boston Daily Chronotype*, 12, 13, 15, and 17 September 1849. On the constitution, see Dana to Dwight, 5 September 1849, JSD Collection. For Associationist financial contributions, see *Boston Daily Chronotype*, 6 December 1849.

72. "The Jour Printers," *Boston Weekly Chronotype*, 22 December 1849; "The Dividend to Labor," *Boston Daily Chronotype*, 25 December 1849. For Manning, see *Protective Union* 1 (15 December 1849): 18. The *Protective Union* ran from 1 December 1849 to 9 November 1850; after April it was published by the Boston Printers' Cooperative Company, with Treanor among the proprietors.

73. See, for the seamstresses and machinists, *Protective Union* 1 (27 April and 21 September 1850): 164, 332. On meetings and lecture tours, see *Protective Union* 1 (1 December 1849): 3; (13 and 27 April, 3 and 31 August 1850): 145, 164, 276, 305. For the AUA endorsement, see *Protective Union* 1(8 June 1850): 211.

74. "New England Protective Union," *Spirit of the Age* 1 (6 October 1849): 220; Rozwenc, *Cooperatives*, 67–68; *New Era of Industry*, 13 July 1848.

75. Rozwenc, *Cooperatives*, 64–65.

76. By far the best account of New York's labor crisis of 1850 is Wilentz, *Chants Democratic*, 363–89 (quotation, p. 369); but see also Ware, *Industrial Worker*, 229–38. Dana's editorial was "The Carpenters' Strike," *New York Daily Tribune*, 12 March 1850.

77. Wilentz, *Chants Democratic*, 366; Stanley Nadel, "From the Barricades of Paris to the Sidewalks of New York: German Artisans and the European Roots of American Labor Radicalism," *Labor History* 30 (Winter 1989): 48–64.

78. "The Pittsburgh Congress," *Protective Union* 1 (27 April 1850): 164; *DocHist* 8:331–33; "The Ball is Moving (Cincinnati), *Boston Daily Chronotype*, 27 December 1849 and 4 January 1850.

79. "Trades Delegate Meeting in Boston," *Protective Union* 1 (18 May 1850): 188; "The New England Industrial League," *Protective Union* 1 (1 June and 13 July 1850): 201, 252; "The Workingmen's Convention," *Protective Union* 1 (19 October 1850): 361. Without access to copies of the *Protective Union*, Norman Ware misconstrued the League as a revival of the NEWA's ten-hour coalition rather than a congress of worker cooperatives; subsequent commentators followed his lead. See Ware, *Industrial Worker*, 155–58; and, among others, Joseph G. Rayback, *A History of American Labor* (New York: Free Press, 1966), 95.

80. Wilentz, *Chants Democratic*, 375–84 (quotation, p. 383). For Brisbane's speech, see *Protective Union* 1 (3 August 1850): 271. Henry Hoagland noted the difficulty Fourierists encountered in having the New York Congress actively support producer cooperatives, even though "the followers of Greeley and Brisbane," according to his estimate, made up over 20 percent of the delegates in mid–1850; see Commons et al., *History of Labour* 1:554–55.

81. Albert Brisbane, "Co-Operation in America," *Christian Socialist* 2 (4 October 1851): 219; *New York Daily Tribune*, 8 July 1850. Commons et al., *History of Labour* 1:568–71, reviews the many problems producers' associations faced. For the

Boston printers, see *Boston Weekly Chronotype*, 22 December 1849; for the Cincinnati iron-molders, see *DocHist* 8:312–14, and Ross, *Workers on the Edge*, 160.

82. Moss, *Origins of the French Labor Movement*, 22.

CHAPTER 12. THE LAST COMMUNITIES

1. For the phalanx building program, see Dolores Hayden, *Seven American Utopias: The Architecture of Communitarian Socialism, 1790–1975* (Cambridge, Mass.: MIT Press, 1976), 164–74. The revised constitution, approved 27 December 1848, was copied on 1 September 1849 into the NAP Proceedings, NAP Collection. For the net profit in 1851, see *Exposé of the Condition and Progress of the North American Phalanx* (New York: Dewitt & Davenport, 1853), 28.

2. NAP Proceedings, 8 January 1855, NAP Collection.

3. N. C. Meeker, quoted in Noyes, *American Socialisms*, 506. For typical complaints from parents, see NAP Proceedings, 21 April 1848 and 9 October 1854, NAP Collection.

4. *Exposé*, 10–15; Noyes, *American Socialisms*, 498.

5. Noyes, *American Socialisms*, 449.

6. Published histories include Maud Honeyman Greene, "Raritan Bay Union, Eagleswood, New Jersey," *Proceedings of the New Jersey Historical Society* 68 (January 1950): 1–20; Jayme A. Sokolow, "Culture and Utopia: The Raritan Bay Union," *New Jersey History* 94 (Summer–Fall 1976): 89–100; and George Kirchmann, "Unsettled Utopias: The North American Phalanx and the Raritan Bay Union," *New Jersey History* 97 (Spring 1979): 25–36. The best account of its emergence out of discord at the North American Phalanx is Herman J. Belz, "The North American Phalanx: An Experiment in Socialism," *Proceedings of the New Jersey Historical Society* 81 (October 1963): 236–44. The RBU collection contains a small but important file of correspondence and documents relating to the community.

7. Dale Warren, "Uncle Marcus," *New England Galaxy* 9 (Summer 1967): 16–26.

8. By 1850, Spring was the largest single stockholder in the NAP, with 527 shares, purchased at $10 per share. See List of Stockholders of the North American Phalanx, 5 August 1850, NAP Collection.

9. Fredrika Bremer, *Homes of the New World: Impressions of America*, trans. Mary Howitt (New York: Harper, 1853), 81–82; Marcus Spring to James T. Fisher, 16 March 1848, JTF Papers; Noyes, *American Socialisms*, 491–92. Charles Sears's response to this faction was published after the split as *Socialism and Christianity: Being a Response to an Inquirer concerning Religion and the Observance of Religious Forms at the North American Phalanx* (Monmouth Co., N.J.: NAP, 1854). Personality conflicts between Arnold and Sears helped fuel the dispute. See Rebecca Spring to Marcus Spring, 29 April 1853, RBU collection.

10. Noyes, *American Socialisms*, 498, 494; Spring to James T. Fisher, 16 March 1848, JTF Papers; Brisbane, *Mental Biography*, 213–14.

11. Clement Read to Marcus and Rebecca Spring, 19 June 1853; and "Provisional Prospectus of the Raritan Bay Union" [November 1852], photocopy, RBU Collection (original of prospectus in Emerson Papers).

12. Bremer, *Homes of the New World*, 612.

13. John Gray to Macdonald, quoted in Noyes, *American Socialisms*, 483–84.

14. John Sartain to John S. Dwight, 6 April 1849, JSD Collection.

15. For the directors and initial stockholders, see Greene, "Raritan Bay Union," 7.

16. Macdonald, quoted in Noyes, *American Socialisms*, 489; "Provisional Prospectus of the Raritan Bay Union."

17. The clearest description of the Union's economic arrangements is "Split among the Fourierites . . . ," *New York Herald*, 4 June 1853, clipping in the Macdonald Collection, p.329, excerpted in Noyes, *American Socialisms*, 487–88.

18. Spring's plan for a gigantic phalanstery 2,400 feet long is described in *New York Herald*, 4 June 1853.

19. Henry David Thoreau to Sophia Thoreau, 1 November 1856, in Thoreau, *Familiar Letters*, ed. F. B. Sanborn (Boston: Houghton Mifflin, 1894), 335. Thoreau surveyed the community's grounds during his stay, and his map (original in the Concord, Massachusetts Free Library) shows some individually owned plots but no houses on them.

20. Noyes, *American Socialisms*, 488; Belz, "North American Phalanx," 242; Charles Sears, *The North American Phalanx: An Historical and Descriptive Sketch* (Prescott, Wis.: J. M. Pryse, 1886), 16. A description of the stone mill is in the Raritan Bay Union Directors' Report of 7 January 1854, HL.

21. Sokolow, "Culture and Utopia," 93–96. See Gerda Lerner, *The Grimké Sisters from South Carolina* (New York: Schocken Books, 1971), 316–39; Katherine Du Pré Lumpkin, *The Emancipation of Angelina Grimké* (Chapel Hill: University of North Carolina Press, 1974), 200–214; and Robert Abzug, *Passionate Liberator: Theodore Dwight Weld and the Dilemma of Reform* (New York: Oxford University Press, 1980), 259–74. Parke Godwin sent his son Bryant to the school; see Godwin to Theodore Weld, 3 August 1858, Weld-Grimké Papers.

22. Quoted in Octavius Brooks Frothingham, *Memoir of William Henry Channing* (Boston: Houghton Mifflin, 1886), 241–42.

23. On one such trip to Brussels in 1853, Spring celebrated the Fourth of July with Victor Considerant; in Paris the following year he planned "to dip into the study of Fourier, a little." See Spring to James T. Fisher, 2 October 1854, JTF Papers.

24. Sarah Grimké to Harriot K. Hunt, 20 December 1854, and Grimké to the Wattles family, 12 November 1853, Weld-Grimké Papers; Elizabeth Hoxie to Margaret Curson, October 22, 1854, Curson Papers.

25. Marcus Spring to Ralph Waldo Emerson, 25 January 1857, Emerson Papers; Bronson Alcott to Mrs. Alcott, 21 October 1856, in *The Letters of Bronson Alcott*, ed. Richard C. Hernstadt (Ames: Iowa State University Press, 1969), 203–4.

26. Raritan Bay Union Circulars of 1 May 1857 and 15 May 1857, photocopies, RBU Collection (originals in Huntington Library, San Marino, California).

27. Kirchman, "Unsettled Utopias," 35.

28. For proposals to end most "guarantees" at the phalanx, see NAP Proceedings, 15 February 1855, NAP Collection.

29. Noyes, *American Socialisms*, 501–2.

30. Belz, "North American Phalanx," 244–45.

31. See "Summary of the Annual Statement of the North American Phalanx. Approved January 8th, 1855," MHS Broadside. For the New Yorkers, see NAP Proceedings, 20 May 1855, NAP Collection.

32. Arthur Young to Amédée Simonin, 30 July 1855, Simonin Papers; Young to Messrs. Bureau, Guillon, and Godin, 19 January 1856, FNA (10 AS 42, doss. 15). Marcus Spring suggested that the phalanx sell its property and that its members migrate with the proceeds to Considerant's colony; see Spring to James T. Fisher, 2 October 1854, JTF Papers.

33. For the division of lots, see "Positive Sale of the Domain of the Phalanx," Broadside, HL. For Young's plan, see Circulars of 17 October 1855 and 19 October 1855, HL; and James T. Fisher to Amédée Simonin, 3 November 1855, Simonin Papers. On the community after 1855, see George Kirchmann, "Why

Did They Stay? Communal Life at the North American Phalanx," in *Planned and Utopian Experiments: Four New Jersey Towns,* ed. Paul A. Stellhorn (Trenton: New Jersey Historical Commission, 1980), 14, 24; and Edwin Hoyt, *Alexander Woolcott: The Man Who Came to Dinner* (New York: Abelard-Schuman, 1968), 25–33.

34. For the Fourier Phalanx, see Alcander Longley's articles in *Phalansterian Record* 1 (January–December 1858): 8, 11–12, 19, 28. For his later efforts, see Chapter 16.

35. This account of La Réunion is based on the following sources: Russell M. Jones, "Victor Considerant's American Experience (1852–1869)," *French-American Review* 1 (Winter 1976–Spring 1977): 65–94, 124–50; Rondel V. Davidson, *Did We Think Victory Great? The Life and Ideas of Victor Considerant* (Lanham, Md.: University Press of America, 1988), 237–85; Davidson, "Victor Considerant and the Failure of La Réunion," *Southwestern Historical Quarterly* 76 (January 1973): 277–96; William J. Hammond and Margaret F. Hammond, *La Réunion: A French Settlement in Texas* (Dallas: Royal, 1958); "Documents pour une biographie complète de J. B.-A. Godin," *Le Devoir* 22–25 (1898–1901); Considerant's published writings on the colony; manuscripts in FNA and Considerant MSS; JTF Papers; and Simonin Papers.

36. For Brisbane's campaign in Paris and Belgium, see Guillon to Considerant, 30 December 1851, in FNA (10 AS 38, doss. 16); and Cantagrel to Godin, 29 May 1852, reprinted in *Le Devoir* 22 (1898): 261.

37. For the Swiss plan, see Considerant to Alllyre Bureau, 2 April 1852, Considerant MSS.

38. The best sources for Considerant's 1853 American trip are his letters to his wife Julie and French Fourierist colleagues, now in FNA, and Considerant MSS. Jones, "Considerant's American Experience," uses these to provide the most detailed published account available. See also Sterling F. Delano, "French Utopianism on American Soil: Six Unpublished Letters by Victor Considerant," *Nineteenth-Century French Studies* 13 (1985): 59–65. Considerant later described the trip in *Au Texas* (Paris: Librairie Phalanstérienne, 1854).

39. Victor Considerant, *The Great West: A New Social and Industrial Life in Its Fertile Regions* (New York: Dewitt & Davenport, 1854), 4–5, quoted in Davidson, *Did We Think Victory Great?,* 238. This pamphlet was an abridged translation of *Au Texas.*

40. Considerant, *The Great West,* 9–10; Considerant to Allyre Bureau, 20 July 1853, Considerant MSS.

41. Considerant to Allyre Bureau, 20 September 1852, FNA (10 AS 28, doss. 9); Considerant to James T. Fisher, 11 August 1853, JTF Papers; Considerant to Bureau, 27 May 1853, Considerant MSS.

42. Considerant, *Au Texas,* 33. I have used the translation in Jones, "Considerant's American Experience," 83–84.

43. Considerant, *Au Texas,* 17–18 and Part III.

44. *Bulletin de la Société de Colonisation Européo-Américaine au Texas,* January 1855, cited in *Le Devoir* 24 (1900): 6.

45. Davidson, "Considerant and the Failure of Réunion," is the best overall analysis of the colony's rapid collapse, although Jones, "Considerant's American Experience," adds an important emphasis on the ideological dilemma of capitalist venture versus Fourierist phalanx.

46. *Texas State Gazette,* 17 February and 11 August 1855, quoted in Hammond and Hammond, *La Réunion,* 68, 73 (pp. 68–84 detail the attitudes of Texans toward the colony).

47. Victor Considerant, *European Colonization in Texas: An Address to the American People* (New York: Baker, Godwin, 1855), 35–38. John Allen spread word among

American Fourierists that the Réunion colony would include "lots of slaves to be carried and educated and work out their freedom." See Elizabeth Hoxie to Margaret Curson, December 1853, Curson Papers.

48. For La Réunion's scattered property, see "Plan des terres appartenant à la Société de Colonisation Européo-Américaine dans le Comté de Dallas, Texas," reproduced in Hayden, *Seven American Utopias*, 182.

49. Davidson, "Considerant and the Failure of La Réunion," 287. According to Colonization Society records, over two hundred farmers officially applied to emigrate to Réunion; but few apparently made the journey; see "Diverses statistiques sur les membres de Réunion," 31 March 1855, Considerant MSS.

50. James T. Fisher to Amédée Simonin, 25 May and 7 June 1855; Benjamin Urner to Simonin, 5 May 1855, Simonin Papers. Lazarus invested $500 in Réunion. See Considerant to Allyre Bureau, 17 July 1854, FNA (10 AS 28, doss. 9).

51. See Notebook entries of 14 and 17 July 1855, Trist Papers; and Trist to Amédée Simonin, 9 July 1856, Simonin Papers. Trist's sympathy with Owenism was noted in Louis Martin Sears, "Nicholas P. Trist: A Diplomat with Ideals," *Mississippi Valley Historical Review* 11 (June 1924): 90, but not his connection with Brisbane and the Fourierists.

52. *Bulletin of the Texas Emigration Union* 1 (August 1855).

53. Hammond and Hammond, *La Réunion*, 117–25, include nineteen Americans in a partial list of the settlers.

54. In 1861, Considerant sued Brisbane for the remaining $13,000 and won a judgment, but he was still trying to collect it seven years later; eventually Brisbane settled the claim. See François Cantagrel to Amédée Simonin, 6 June 1868, Simonin Papers, and Account Book, pp. 13–15, AB-IHS. For Brisbane's rival plan, see Brisbane to Nicholas P. Trist, 6 June [1855], Trist Papers.

55. Davidson, "Considerant and the Failure of La Réunion," 292–93; Jones, "Considerant's American Experience," 132, 144–45.

56. Considerant, *Du Texas: Première rapport à mes amis* (Paris: Librairie Phalan-stérienne, 1857).

57. Augustin Savardan, *Un naufrage au Texas: Observations et impressions recuilliés pendant deux ans et demi au Texas et à travers les Etats-unis d'amérique* (Paris: Garnier Frères, 1858).

CHAPTER 13. THE FADING OF THE UTOPIAN DREAM

1. John Higham, *From Boundlessness to Consolidation: The Transformation of American Culture, 1848–1860* (Ann Arbor, Mich.: Clements Library, 1969).

2. "Sympathy with the French Revolution in Boston," *Harbinger* 6 (22 April 1848): 195. For the New York speeches, see "Response to the French Revolution," *Harbinger* 6 (8 April 1848): 179–81.

3. Hugh Doherty described his activities on February 23–25 in the *New York Daily Tribune*, 25 September 1849. Quotations are from Godwin, "American Sympathy with France," *Harbinger* 6 (8 April 1848): 179.

4. George Ripley, "The Harbinger," *Harbinger* 6 (15 April 1848): 187; Parke Godwin, "The Newspapers and the French Revolution," *Harbinger* 7 (20 May 1848): 20.

5. James Harrison Wilson, *The Life of Charles A. Dana* (New York: Harper, 1907), 63.

6. The account in Brisbane's *Mental Biography*, 267–71, must be compared with letters written immediately after the episode by Brisbane ("An Inside View of the Parisian Revolt") and by Garth Wilkinson ("Letter from London"); see *Harbinger* 7 (5 August 1848): 105–6, 109–11.

7. Quotations from "Editorial Correspondence," *Harbinger* 7 (5 August 1848): 109. Dana's letters are summarized in Wilson, *Dana*, 61–93.

8. Brisbane, *Mental Biography*, 273; Dana, obituary of Karl Marx, *New York Sun*, 16 March 1883, quoted in Morton Borden, "Some Notes on Horace Greeley, Charles Dana, and Karl Marx," *Journalism Quarterly* 34 (Fall 1957): 462. For the Marx-*Tribune* connection, see also William Harlan Hale, "When Karl Marx Worked for Horace Greeley," *American Heritage* 8 (April 1957): 20–25, 110–11; and, from Marx's viewpoint, David McClellan, *Karl Marx: His Life and Thought* (New York: Harper & Row, 1974), 284–89.

9. Wilson, *Dana*, 63. Dana's letter of 10 November from Vienna in *Harbinger* 8 (16 December 1848): 52–53, indicates visits also to Dresden and Prague, contrary to Wilson's surmise that "he gave up his proposed trip to those regions" (p. 86).

10. Fisher to John S. Dwight, 9 August 1848, JSD Collection; "Records of the Group of Study and Indoctrination," BRUA Records (comments on Parisian architecture); and Recordbook, Minutes of 12 November 1848, BRUA Records (ceremony at Fourier's grave).

11. Recordbook, Minutes of 12 November 1848, BRUA Records.

12. Charles Dana, "Parisian Insurrection," *Harbinger* 7 (22 July 1848): 89; Fisher to John S. Dwight, 9 August 1848, JSD Collection. The French Fourierists' role in the 1848 revolution is described in Hubert Bourgin, *Fourier: Contribution à l'étude du socialisme français* (Paris: Société Nouvelle de Librairie et d'Edition, 1905), 497–501, 531–33; Jean-Marcel Jeanneney, "Les disciples de Fourier et la révolution de 1848," *Revue des Sciences Politiques* 56 (January–March 1933): 91–110; and Félix Armand, *Les Fouriéristes et les luttes révolutionnaires de 1848 à 1851* (Paris: Presses Universitaires de France, 1948). Considerant's role is detailed in Rondel Van Davidson, *Did We Think Victory Great? The Life and Ideas of Victor Considerant* (Lanham, Md.: University Press of America, 1988), 143–219.

13. Brisbane, *Mental Biography*, 271; Charles Dana, "The European Revolution," *Spirit of the Age* 1 (18 August 1849): 98.

14. Hugh Doherty, letter of 8 August 1849 to the *New York Tribune*, reprinted in *Boston Daily Chronotype*, 7 September 1849, p. 1.

15. Clement John Wilkinson, *James John Garth Wilkinson* (London: Kegan Paul, Trench, Trubner, 1911), 60.

16. George Ripley, "European Affairs," *Harbinger* 7 (15 July 1848): 81; Parke Godwin, "The French Outbreak," *Harbinger* 7 (22 July 1848): 92; Recordbook, Minutes of 12 November 1848, BRUA Records.

17. See *Harbinger* 7 (22 and 29 July 1848): 92–93, 100.

18. W. H. Channing, "Victor Considerant," *Spirit of the Age* 1 (11 August 1849): 89–90; Dwight, *Boston Daily Chronotype*, 23 August 1849, p. 1.

19. Brisbane, *Mental Biography*, 272–90 (quotations, pp. 272, 282, 290). In Rome, Brisbane visited the Brook Farmers' Transcendentalist friend Margaret Fuller, who by then had married an Italian nobleman, shed her independent stance toward social reform, and thrown her support to the Roman revolution under Giuseppi Mazzini's leadership. See Margaret Fuller to Arthur B. Fuller, 20 January 1849, in *The Letters of Margaret Fuller*, ed. Robert N. Hudspeth (Ithaca: Cornell University Press, 1988), 5:185–86. Ironically, Fuller's thinking evolved in a direction opposite to Brisbane's and Dana's: her appreciation of Fourierist communitarianism increased as she studied social conditions and revolutionary politics in Europe. In 1845 she had criticized Fourier's view that humankind could be changed through new institutions; by 1848 she was proclaiming herself "as great an Associationist as W. Channing himself, . . . as firm a believer that the next form society will take in remedy of the dreadful ills that now consume it will be voluntary association in small communities." See Fuller, *Woman in the Nineteenth*

Century (1845; Boston: J. P. Jewett, 1855), 123–25; and Margaret Fuller to Mary Rotch, 29 May 1848, in *Letters of Margaret Fuller*, 5:71.

20. Brisbane, *Mental Biography*, 296–99 (quotation, p. 297). Brisbane's speech was reprinted in *Démocratie Pacifique*, 27 February 1849; a typescript transcription is in AB-IHS. See also "Mr. Brisbane Ordered to Quit France," *New York Daily Tribune*, 28 April 1849.

21. "Letter from Mr. Brisbane," *New York Daily Tribune*, 9 March 1849, p. 1.

22. Brisbane, *Mental Biography*, 271; Brisbane, "Co-Operation in America," *Christian Socialist* 2 (27 September 1851): 202–4.

23. Allan Nevins made a similar assessment in his excellent biographical sketch in the *Dictionary of American Biography*, s.v. "Dana, Charles Anderson."

24. "Parisian Insurrection," *Harbinger* 7 (22 July 1848): 89; Wilson, *Dana*, 74, 77, 86; "Editorial Correspondence," *Harbinger* 7 (12 August 1848): 117.

25. Dana to Elizur Wright, 15 February 1849, May Collection.

26. W. H. Channing, "Revolution—Reaction—Reorganization," *Spirit of the Age* 1 (14 July 1849): 26; Charles Dana, "The European Revolutions," *Spirit of the Age* 1 (18 August 1849): 98; Dana to Karl Marx, 15 July 1850, quoted in Morten Borden, ed., "Five Letters of Charles A. Dana to Karl Marx," *Journalism Quarterly* 36 (Summer 1959): 315.

27. Dana, "European Revolutions," 98.

28. "Response to the French Revolution," *Harbinger* 6 (8 April 1848): 180–81; *New York Daily Tribune*, 7 September 1849.

29. Charles Dana, "Socialism," *New York Daily Tribune*, 12 November 1852, p. 4; Dana to Elizur Wright, 15 February 1849, May Collection.

30. Dana, quoted in Candace Stone, *Dana and the Sun* (New York: Dodd, Mead, 1938), 14–15; Wilson, *Dana*, 135.

31. These are the titles of E. J. Hobsbawm's two volumes covering the period: *The Age of Revolution: Europe, 1789–1848* (New York: Praeger, 1962), and *The Age of Capital, 1848–1875* (London: Weidenfield & Nicholson, 1975). For a similar invocation of Hobsbawm for the American 1850s, see Anne C. Rose, *Transcendentalism as a Social Movement, 1830–1850* (New Haven, Conn.: Yale University Press, 1981), 207.

32. Parke Godwin, "How They Manage in Europe," *Putnam's Monthly* 1 (April 1853): 432; Godwin, "The Future Republic," B-G Collection.

33. "The Golden Age," *Harbinger* 8 (16 December 1848): 52.

34. H. U. Johnson, "History of the Trumbull Phalanx," *Western Reserve Chronicle*, 5 May 1897.

35. Phalansterian Company, *Constitution* (N.p., [1849]), 1, 9; NAP Proceedings, 3 February, 21 July, and 20 October 1849, NAP Collection. Among identifiable Associationists who joined the gold rush were Peter Baldwin of Brook Farm, Richard Thorn and Russell Robertson of the North American Phalanx, and Job Bennett and Matthew Limbert of the Wisconsin Phalanx. For gold fever at the Wisconsin Phalanx, see S. T. Kidder's 1906 interview with Mrs. R. D. Mason, "Recollections of Early Settlers," 263, W-CC Collection.

36. Warren Chase, *Life-line of the Lone One; or, Autobiography of the World's Child* (Boston: Bela Marsh, 1858), 129.

37. Horace Greeley, *Recollections of a Busy Life* (New York: J. P. Ford, 1868), 157. See also George Ripley, "Rail Road to the Pacific," *Harbinger* 4 (19 December 1846): 30–31; and Horace Greeley, *The Crystal Palace and Its Lessons* (New York: Dewitt & Davenport, 1852).

38. Macdonald, quoted in Noyes, *American Socialisms*, 448; see also, p. 498.

39. Henry James, Sr. to James T. Fisher, 7 June 1849, JTF Papers. For Sears, see Sears to E. P. Grant, 23 August 1871, EPG Papers; for Kaulback, see Edwin

C. Rozwenc, *Cooperatives Come to America: The History of the Protective Store Movement, 1845–1867* (1941; rpt. Philadelphia: Porcupine Press, 1975), 114; For Orvis, see Russell Duino, "Utopian Theme with Variations: John Murray Spear and His Kiantone Domain," *Pennsylvania History* 29 (April 1962): 148–49.

40. Greeley, *Recollections*, 158; Noyes, *American Socialisms*, 480.

41. For Dwight's career, see George Willis Cooke, *John Sullivan Dwight; Brook Farmer, Editor, and Critic of Music* (Boston: Small, Maynard, 1898); and Walter L. Fertig, "John Sullivan Dwight: Transcendentalist and Literary Amateur of Music" (Ph.D. diss., University of Maryland, 1952).

42. James Parton, *The Life of Horace Greeley* (New York: Mason, 1855), 404–5. For Dana's career on the *Tribune*, see Wilson, *Dana*, 94–177; and Richard Kluger, *The Paper: The Life and Death of the New York Herald Tribune* (New York: Knopf, 1986), 70–73, 94–96, 106–7.

43. Mid-nineteenth-century changes in journalism are colorfully summarized in Gunther Barth, "Metropolitan Press," chap. 4 of *City People: The Rise of Modern City Culture in Nineteenth-Century America* (New York: Oxford University Press, 1980), 58–109.

44. Dana to James S. Pike, 9 February [1852], microfilm copy, Alderman Library, University of Virginia (originals in Calais Free Library, Calais, Maine); Dana, quoted in Stone, *Dana and the Sun*, 31.

45. Parton, *Greeley*, 404. For Ripley's career as a man of letters, see Henry L. Golemba, *George Ripley* (Boston: Twayne, 1977), 112–49; and, more fully, Octavius Brooks Frothingham, *George Ripley* (Boston: Houghton Mifflin, 1882), 199–305.

46. Ripley to Ralph Waldo Emerson, 9 November 1840, quoted in Frothingham, *George Ripley*, 307–8; Whitman, "Democratic Vistas," in *The Collected Writings of Walt Whitman: Prose Works of 1892*, ed. Floyd Stovall (New York: New York University Press, 1964), 2:361–426; "The Genteel Tradition in American Philosophy" (1911), in *The Genteel Tradition: Nine Essays by George Santayana*, ed. Douglas L. Wilson (Cambridge, Mass.: Harvard University Press, 1967), 37–64.

CHAPTER 14. NEW DIRECTIONS OF THE 1850S

1. Thomas Low Nichols and Mary S. Gove Nichols, *Marriage: Its History, Character, and Results*, rev. ed. (Cincinnati, Ohio: V. Nicholson, 1855), 412–26; Thomas Nichols, "The Progressive Union," *Nichols' Monthly* (June 1855): 53–59.

2. *Nichols' Monthly*, 1856, quoted in Bertha-Monica Stearns, "Two Forgotten New England Reformers," *New England Quarterly* 6 (March 1933): 77.

3. See [Horace Greeley], "Modern Spiritualism," *Putnam's Magazine* 1 (January 1853): 59–64; Greeley, *Recollections of a Busy Life* (New York: J. B. Ford, 1868), 234–41; Herbert W. Schneider and George Lawton, *A Prophet and Pilgrim* (New York: Columbia University Press, 1942), 22; Brisbane, *Mental Biography*, 336–7, 339. Brisbane and Victor Considerant attended a séance among Fourierist friends in Cincinnati in 1853 while on their way west; see Considerant to Julie Considerant, 3 May 1853, FNA (10 AS 28, doss. 9).

4. George Ripley, Review of *The Principles of Nature, Harbinger* 5 (28 August 1847): 177–84. For the séance at Griswold's, see "An Evening with the Spirits," *New York Daily Tribune*, 8 June 1850, p. 4; and N. P. Willis, *The Rag-Bag: A Collection of Ephemera* (New York: Scribner, 1855), 185–94.

5. Octavius Brooks Frothingham, *Memoir of William Henry Channing* (Boston: Houghton Mifflin, 1886), 271; Lindsay Swift, *Brook Farm: Its Members, Scholars, and Visitors* (New York: Macmillan, 1900), 224.

6. For NAP, see Olmsted to Charles Loring Brace, 26 July 1852, in *The Papers*

of Frederick Law Olmsted, ed. Charles Capen McLaughlin (Baltimore, Md.: Johns Hopkins University Press, 1977–), 1:375. For Raritan Bay, see Elizabeth Hoxie to Margaret Curson, 12 May 1854, Curson Papers. For Brook Farm, see Marianne Dwight, *Letters from Brook Farm, 1844–1847,* ed. Amy L. Reed (Poughkeepsie: Vassar College, 1928), xiv, 181–91. For Wisconsin, see Warren Chase, *The Lifeline of the Lone One* (Boston: Bela Marsh, 1858), 112–13, 167; Chase, *Forty Years on the Spiritual Rostrum* (Boston: Colby & Rich, 1888), 23. For the phalanxes as "incubators" of reform fads, see T. D. Seymour Bassett, "The Secular Utopian Socialists," in *Socialism and American Life,* ed. Donald Drew Egbert and Stow Persons (Princeton, N.J.: Princeton University Press, 1952), 1:192.

7. Greeley, *Recollections,* 235, 240; Frothingham, *Memoir of Channing,* 271–72.

8. For spiritualists' religious liberalism and interest in Swedenborg, see R. Laurence Moore, *In Search of White Crows: Spiritualism, Parapsychology, and American Culture* (New York: Oxford University Press, 1977), 9–12, 56–61. For their relation to science, see Moore, "Spiritualism and Science: Reflections on the First Decade of the Spirit Rappings," *American Quarterly* 24 (October 1972): 474–500.

9. A. J. Davis, *The Principles of Nature, Her Divine Revelations, and A Voice to Mankind* (New York: S. S. Lyon and William Fishbough, 1847), 735–40. Moore, *White Crows,* chap. 3, downplays spiritualists' involvement in reform; a more positive account is Robert W. Delp, "American Spiritualism and Social Reform," *Northwest Ohio Quarterly* 44 (Fall 1972): 85–99. On spiritualist feminism, see Moore, *White Crows,* 116–21.

10. Schneider and Lawton, *A Prophet and a Pilgrim,* 166, 455–56; Robert V. Hine, *California's Utopian Colonies* (New Haven, Conn.: Yale University Press, 1966), 28; Noyes, *American Socialisms,* 565. For Harris's role in the AUA, see "Annual Meeting of the American Union of Associationists," *Harbinger* 4 (29 May 1847): 385.

11. Chase, *Life-line,* esp. 18, 19, 168, 170, 162, 171; Chase, *Forty Years,* 52.

12. Moore, *White Crows,* 88.

13. Ibid., 97; John C. Spurlock, *Free Love: Marriage and Middle-Class Radicalism in America, 1825–1860* (New York: New York University Press, 1988), 89–90; Noyes, *American Socialisms,* 374.

14. Bassett, "Secular Utopian Socialists," 193; Russell Duino, "Utopian Theme with Variations: John Murray Spear and His Kiantone Domain," *Pennsylvania History* 29 (April 1962): 148–49; William McDiarmid, *The Organization of Labor: Showing How to Acquire True Independence of Character* (Cincinnati: Times Office, 1863), 9. For more information on Spear, see Hal D. Sears, *The Sex Radicals: Free Love in High Victorian America* (Lawrence: Regents Press of Kansas, 1977), 16–19. Spear's group purchased John Allen's farm in Patriot, Indiana, as a western outpost; see Ernest C. Miller, "Utopian Communities in Warren County, Pennsylvania," *Western Pennsylvania Historical Magazine* 49 (October 1966): 309. The Fourierist minister S. C. Hewitt also became a devotee of Spear; see S. C. Hewitt, ed., *Messages from the Superior State; Communicated by John Murray, through John M. Spear, in the Summer of 1852* (Boston: Bela Marsh, 1852).

15. Frothingham, *Memoir of Channing,* 272; Henry James, "Modern Diabolism," *Alantic Monthly* 32 (August 1873): 219–24; Slater Brown, *The Heyday of Spiritualism* (New York: Hawthorn Books, 1970), 208–9.

16. W. S. Courtney, quoted in Moore, *White Crows,* 81; "Our Plans for Social Reform" (response to the *Univercoelum*), *Harbinger* 6 (18 March 1848): 155.

17. Taylor Stoehr, *Hawthorne's Mad Scientists: Pseudoscience and Social Science in Nineteenth-Century Life and Letters* (Hamden, Conn.: Archon Books, 1978); [Orestes Brownson], *The Spirit Rapper: An Autobiography* (Boston: Little, Brown, 1854);

Howard Kerr, *Mediums and Spirit Rappers and Roaring Radicals: Spiritualism in American Literature, 1850–1900* (Urbana: University of Illinois Press, 1972), 13–14, 82–107; "The Free Love System: Origin, Progress, and Position of the Anti-Marriage Movement," *New York Times*, 8 September 1855, p. 2.

18. Spurlock, *Free Love*, 139–46; "Free Love System," 2.

19. John Humphrey Noyes set the pattern when he traced the history of the Modern Times community through Josiah Warren and Robert Owen but not through Fourierists Stephen Pearl Andrews and the Nicholses; see *American Socialisms*, 94. The Fourierists' role in the controversy has recently been highlighted by Taylor Stoehr, *Free Love in America: A Documentary History* (New York: AMS Press, 1979); Charles Shively's introduction to Stephen Pearl Andrews, ed., *Love, Marriage, and Divorce, and the Sovereignty of the Individual: A Discussion by Henry James, Horace Greeley, and Stephen Pearl Andrews* (1853; rpt. Weston, Mass.: M&S Press, 1975), 1–13; and, most fully, Spurlock, *Free Love*, 56–72, 107, 146.

20. E. F. Underhill, quoted in *New York Times*, 25 June 1858, p. 2.

21. Godwin publicly disavowed any connection with free-love advocates; see letter from Henry Clapp, Jr., *New York Times*, 23 October 1855, p. 3. Dana, Ripley, and Channing never endorsed free love, though Channing argued for more liberal divorce laws.

22. [Charles Julius Hempel], *The True Organization of the New Church, as Indicated in the Writings of Emmanuel Swedenborg and Demonstrated by Charles Fourier* (New York: Wm. Radde, 1848), 339–44, (quotation, p. 342).

23. Victor Hennequin, *Love in the Phalanstery* (New York: Dewitt & Davenport, 1848); "The *Observer* and Hennequin," *Harbinger* 7 (21 October 1848): 197.

24. Hennequin, *Love in the Phalanstery*, ix; *Harbinger* 8 (2 December 1848): 37.

25. "The *Observer* and Hennequin," 197. For the debate, see articles by "A.E.F." and "Y.S." [Henry James] in *Harbinger* 8 (1848–49): 12–13, 36–37, 44–45, 53–54, 60–61, 68–69; and Sidney Ditzion, *Marriage, Morals, and Sex in America: A History of Ideas* (New York: Norton, 1978), 147–51.

26. Helen Beal Woodward, *The Bold Women* (New York: Farrar, Strauss & Young, 1953), 160. For Mary Gove Nichols, see John B. Blake, "Mary Gove Nichols, Prophetess of Health," *Proceedings of the American Philosophical Society* 106 (June 1962): 219–34; Spurlock, *Free Love*, 182–201; and Janet Hubly Noever, "Passionate Rebel: The Life of Mary Gove Nichols, 1810–1884" (Ph.D. diss., University of Oklahoma, 1983). Stearns, "Two Forgotten New England Reformers," is the most informative source on Thomas Nichols.

27. "The Literati of New York City," in *Complete Works of Edgar Allan Poe*, ed. James A. Harrison (New York: Crowell, 1902), 15:61.

28. Irving T. Richards, "Mary Gove Nichols and John Neal," *New England Quarterly* 7 (June 1934): 346; Blake, "Mary Gove Nichols," 226, 230; *Phalanx* 1 (5 February 1844): 64–65; and letter to the *New York Weekly Herald*, 15 March 1845, reprinted in *DocHist* 7: 277–80.

29. Thomas Low Nichols, *Woman in All Ages and Nations* (New York: H. Long, 1849), 108, 106, 214.

30. Noyes, *American Socialisms*, 481; [Mary Gove Nichols], *Mary Lyndon; or, Revelations of a Life* (New York: Stringer & Townsend, 1855), 284 (in this autobiographical *roman à clef*, Lazarus is depicted as "Dr. Mark Ellery").

31. Marx Edgeworth Lazarus, *Love vs. Marriage: Part I* (New York: Fowlers & Wells, 1852), 233, 235, 89.

32. Ibid., 236, 139–40, 250.

33. Ibid., 55.

34. Spurlock, *Free Love*, 139–63.

35. For James's review of Lazarus's book, see *New York Daily Tribune*, 18 Sep-

tember 1852. For Greeley's position, see Andrews, *Love, Marriage, and Divorce* (quotation, *New York Daily Tribune*, 24 December 1852). The Nicholses' charge against Greeley is in their *Marriage*, 145. For Victorian imagery of "spending" and "saving" applied to sex, see Ben Barker-Benfield, "The Spermatic Economy: A Nineteenth-Century View of Sexuality," *Feminist Studies* 1 (1972): 45–74.

36. Madeleine B. Stern, *The Pantarch: A Biography of Stephen Pearl Andrews* (Austin: University of Texas Press, 1968).

37. Andrews, *Love, Marriage, and Divorce*, 46–50.

38. Thomas Low Nichols, *Forty Years of American Life* (London: J. Maxwell, 1864), 2:42; Moncure Conway, "Modern Times, New York," *Fortnightly Review* 1 (1 July 1865): 421. The most carefully researched history of Modern Times provides a useful corrective to nineteenth-century sensationalized reports; see Roger Wunderlich, " 'Low Living and High Thinking' at Modern Times, New York (1851–1864)" (Ph.D. diss., State University of New York, Stony Brook, 1986).

39. "Free Love System," 2.

40. Spurlock, *Free Love*, 146.

41. Chase, *Life-line*, 250, advocated what today would be called no-fault divorce—mutually agreed-upon and legally granted with no need to reveal the cause—not as a license for promiscuity but to "release only the sufferers" to find their ideal mates. As an itinerant lecturer he was widely suspected of harboring "a wife in every Spiritualist port," as Benjamin Hatch put it (quoted in Moore, *White Crows*, 118) but Chase protested that his meetings with women were public and decorous (pp. 147–49).

42. Spurlock, *Free Love*, 2; Sears, *Sex Radicals*, esp. 4–5, 26–27, 272–73; Stephen Nissenbaum, *Sex, Diet, and Debility in Jacksonian America* (Westport, Conn.: Greenwood Press, 1981).

43. *Harbinger* 8 (16 December 1848): 53.

44. Lazarus, *Love vs. Marriage*, ii, 54. On Lazarus's marriage, see Stoehr, *Free Love* in America, 272–76.

45. *New York Times*, 19 October 1855, p. 4; "The Free-Lovers' Troubles," *New York Times*, 20 October 1855, p. 2. Information about Brisbane's private life in this paragraph has been pieced together from papers in *Lodoiska M. Brisbane v. Albert Brisbane*, 1883–85, in AB-IHS; the summary of testimony in the *New York Times*, 30 May 1883; a typescript biography of Brisbane by Michael McCrary in AB-Syr; and an account of the divorce trial in Richard Norman Pettitt, Jr., "Albert Brisbane: Apostle of Fourierism in the United States, 1834–1890" (Ph.D. diss., Miami University [Ohio] 1982), 305–19. Brisbane mentioned women named "Helen" and "Agnes" as former lovers in a letter to Redelia Brisbane, 12 November 1875, AB-IHS.

46. Marx Edgeworth Lazarus, *The Zend-Avesta, and Solar Religions* (New York: Fowlers & Wells, 1852), 60.

47. Albert Parry, *Garrets and Pretenders: A History of Bohemianism in America* (New York: Dover, 1960), 38–48.

48. Nichols and Nichols, *Marriage*, 228–31; Stern, *Pantarch*, 83–92.

49. "The Unitary Household," *New York Times*, 26 September 1860, p.2. Also see Chapter 16, n. 44.

50. Nichols and Nichols, *Marriage*, 13, 16.

51. On the Nicholses' plans, see "Institute of Desarollo" and "Our School of Life," reprinted in Nichols and Nichols, *Marriage*, 428. Other quotations are from Wunderlich, "Low Living and High Thinking," 244, 245, 263. For the Nicholses' later ventures, see Stearns, "Two Forgotten New England Reformers"; "Memnonia: The Launching of a Utopia," *New England Quarterly* 15 (June 1942): 281–

95; and Philip Gleason, "From Free Love to Catholicism: Dr. and Mrs. T. L. Nichols at Yellow Springs," *Ohio Historical Quarterly* 71 (October 1961): 283–307.

52. Spurlock, *Free Love*, 124–25, 147; E. L. Allen to G. W. Mordecai, 15 January 1860, Mordecai Papers; Richmond L. Hawkins, *Positivism in the United States (1853–1861)* (Cambridge, Mass.: Harvard University Press, 1938), 198 n.3; Wunderlich, "Low Living and High Thinking," 267.

53. Edger to Auguste Comte, [21 July 1854], reprinted in Hawkins, *Positivism,* 134.

54. Spurlock, *Free Love*, 155–57; S. M. Pedrick, "The Free Love Movement in Ceresco," *Ripon Commonwealth*, 16 February 1906, Pedrick Collection.

55. Unidentified newspaper clipping, Macdonald Collection, quoted in Noyes, *American Socialisms*, 99.

56. William Bailie, *Josiah Warren—The First American Anarchist* (Boston: Small, Maynard, 1906), 3–7 (quotation, p. 6).

57. Josiah Warren, *Equitable Commerce* (1846; rpt. New York: Fowlers & Wells, 1852); Bailie, *Warren*, 50–53; Noyes, *American Socialisms*, 97–99.

58. Nichols and Nichols, *Marriage*, 386; Stephen Pearl Andrews, *The Science of Society—No. 1: The True Constitution of Government* (New York: W. J. Baner, 1851), 35; Andrews, Editor's Preface in Warren, *Equitable Commerce*, vi.

59. Stephen Pearl Andrews, *The Science of Society—No.2: Cost the Limit of Price* (New York: W. J. Baner, 1851), 64; Warren, *Equitable Commerce*, 26.

60. Nichols and Nichols, *Marriage*, 18.

61. Marx Edgeworth Lazarus, *Passional Hygiene and Natural Medicine* (New York: Fowlers & Wells, 1852), 427; "Short Autobiography of Marx Edgeworth Lazarus," 4, Labadie Collection.

62. Andrews, *Science of Society—No.2*, 182–84.

63. Andrews, *Science of Society—No.1*, 13, 17; Andrews, *Science of Society—No. 2*, 41.

64. Andrews, *Science of Society.—No. 2*, 210–11, 65, 67; Nichols and Nichols, *Marriage*, 358. On the close connection between American anarchism and laissez-faire capitalism, see David DeLeon, *The American as Anarchist* (Baltimore, Md.: Johns Hopkins University Press, 1978).

65. Spurlock, *Free Love*, 202–5. In their individualistic assumptions, insistence on the right of self-ownership, and opposition to human government, the anarchists and free-lovers were in fact closer to radical abolitionists than to Fourierists. Most followed the abolitionists in accommodating the violence of the Civil War. For a thoughtful assessment of the relation between abolitionism and anarchism, see Lewis Perry, *Radical Abolitionism: Anarchy and the Government of God in Antislavery Thought* (Ithaca: Cornell University Press, 1973). Thomas Low Nichols extolled the unprecedented freedom of the antebellum North but believed it subversive of anarchist principles to coerce the South back into the Union; he and Mary Gove Nichols left for wartime exile in England.

66. John Higham, *From Boundlessness to Consolidation: The Transformation of American Culture, 1848–1860* (Ann Arbor, Mich.: Clements Library, 1969); John L. Thomas, "Antislavery and Utopia," in *The Antislavery Crusade: New Essays on the Abolitionists*, ed. Martin Duberman, (Princeton, N.J.: Princeton University Press, 1965), 240–65.

CHAPTER 15. FOURIERISM AND THE COMING OF THE CIVIL WAR

1. Edward Bellamy, "Progress of Nationalism in the United States," *North American Review* 154 (June 1892): 743.

2. Eric Williams, *Capitalism and Slavery* (Chapel Hill: University of North Carolina Press, 1944); David Brion Davis, *The Problem of Slavery in the Age of Revolution, 1770–1823* (Ithaca: Cornell University Press, 1975); Davis, "Reflections on Abolitionism and Ideological Hegemony," *American Historical Review* 92 (October 1987): 797. Among the most important works in the extensive literature are Howard Temperly, "Capitalism, Slavery, and Ideology," *Past and Present* 75 (1977): 94–118; Seymour Drescher, *Capitalism and Antislavery: British Mobilization in Comparative Perspective* (New York: Oxford University Press, 1987); Barbara Solow and Stanley L. Engerman, eds., *British Capitalism and Caribbean Slavery* (New York: Cambridge University Press, 1987); and Betty Fladeland, *Abolitionists and Working-Class Problems in the Age of Industrialization* (Baton Rouge: Louisiana State University Press, 1984). A valuable exchange on the relation of antislavery to capitalism, with contributions from Davis, Thomas L. Haskell and John Ashworth, appeared in *American Historical Review* 92 (October 1987): 797–878.

3. *OC*, 6:387.

4. "Slavery in New Mexico," *Harbinger* 6 (25 March 1848): 168; Parke Godwin, "The New-York Election," *Harbinger* 6 (6 November 1847): 6.

5. Godwin, "New-York Election," 6; Godwin, "Our Politics," *Harbinger* 7 (17 June 1848): 52; "The Presidential Election," *Harbinger* 8 (4 November 1848): 4.

6. "State Election," *Boston Daily Chronotype*, 12 November 1849.

7. W. H. Channing, "The First of August," *Spirit of the Age* 1 (18 August 1849): 104; Channing, "Compromise—Disunion—The Union of Freemen," *Spirit of the Age* 2 (23 February 1850): 122.

8. William Francis Channing, "The Free Soil Party," *Boston Daily Chronotype*, 10 November 1849; Russell M. Jones, "A Letter from Dr. William Francis Channing to Louis Kossuth," *New England Quarterly* 39 (March 1966): 92.

9. [J. S. Dwight], "Wage-Slavery and Chattel-Slavery," *Boston Weekly Chronotype*, 20 October 1849; Parke Godwin, "Free Trade, Free Soil, Free Labor, and Free Speech," *Harbinger* 6 (13 November 1847): 12; "State Election," *Boston Daily Chronotype*, 12 November 1849.

10. Dwight, "Free Soil," *Boston Daily Chronotype*, 8 November 1849.

11. Parke Godwin, "Kossuth and Hungary," *New York Daily Tribune*, 5 December 1851.

12. *New York Evening Post*, 10 December 1851; Parke Godwin, "Louis Kossuth," *Commemorative Addresses* (New York: Harper, 1895), 141–42. For Kossuth's tour, see John H. Komlos, *Kossuth in America, 1851–1852* (Buffalo, N.Y.: East European Institute, 1973); Reinhard H. Luthin, "A Visitor from Hungary," *South Atlantic Quarterly* 47 (January 1948): 29–34; and Asa E. Martin, "Louis Kossuth, Guest of the Nation," in *Essays in Honor of A. Henry Espenshade* (New York: Thomas Nelson, 1937), 182–208.

13. Parke Godwin, "Our Foreign Influence and Policy," in *Political Essays* (New York: Dix, Edwards, 1856), 115–18; Carl David Mead, *Yankee Eloquence in the Middle West: The Ohio Lyceum, 1850–70* (East Lansing: Michigan State University Press, 1951), 96–97, 254–55.

14. Godwin, "Foreign Influence," 93–94, 101, 105–6.

15. Godwin, "Louis Kossuth," 139–41; Godwin, "Foreign Influence," 101–2; Godwin, "American Despotisms," *Putnam's Monthly* 4 (November 1854): 524–31, reprinted in *Political Essays*, 57–88, as "The Vestiges of Despotism"; Godwin, "Kansas Must Be Free," and Godwin, "Northern or Southern, Which?" *Political Essays*, 329–30, 296. Other northerners agreed that the "Slave Power" was undermining America's mission to save the world. See David Brion Davis, *The Slave Power Conspiracy and the Paranoid Style* (Baton Rouge: Louisiana State University Press, 1970), 72–78.

16. The following two paragraphs are based on the discussion of Greeley's

antislavery views in Glyndon G. Van Deusen, *Horace Greeley: Nineteenth-Century Crusader* (New York: Hill & Wang, 1964); and Jeter Allen Isely, *Horace Greeley and the Republican Party, 1853–1861* (Princeton, N.J.: Princeton University Press, 1947).

17. *New York Daily Tribune*, 9 March 1849.

18. Horace Greeley, *Glances at Europe* (New York: Dewitt & Davenport, 1851), 83–86; "Anti-Slavery Lectures," *New York Times*, 25 January 1855.

19. Thomas Bender, *New York Intellect: A History of Intellectual Life in New York City, from 1750 to the Beginnings of Our Own Time* (New York: Knopf, 1987), 167; George Haven Putnam, *Memoirs of a Publisher, 1865–1915* (New York: Putnam, 1915), 12–13. See Parke Godwin, "Calhoun on Government," and "The Coming Session," *Putnam's Monthly* 7 (January 1856): 90–100; and 6 (December 1855): 644–49. In his discussion of the 1856 platform, on the other hand, William E. Gienapp, *The Origins of the Republican Party, 1852–1856* (New York: Oxford University Press, 1987), 334–37, attributes key roles to Preston King, David Wilmot, and Joshua Giddings but does not mention Godwin.

20. Isely, *Greeley and the Republican Party*, 290. Greeley served on the resolutions committee at the Chicago convention and boasted that the Homestead endorsement was "a plank . . . which I fixed exactly to my own liking." See Greeley to Schuyler Colfax, 20 June 1860, Greeley-NYPL.

21. Eric Foner, "Abolitionism and the Labor Movement," in *Politics and Ideology in the Age of the Civil War* (New York: Oxford University Press, 1980), 74. Foner's *Free Soil, Free Labor, Free Men* (New York: Oxford University Press, 1970) is the best description of Republican Party ideology.

22. Octavius Brooks Frothingham, *Memoir of William Henry Channing* (Boston: Houghton Mifflin, 1886), 333; Henry James, Sr., to James John Garth Wilkinson, 20 January 1863, James Papers.

23. John C. Calhoun, speech of 10 January 1838, in *Slavery Defended: The Views of the Old South*, ed. Eric L. McKitrick (Englewood Cliffs, N.J.: Prentice-Hall, 1963), 19; Richard Hofstadter, *The American Political Tradition* (1948; rpt. New York: Vintage Books, 1973), 86–117.

24. Godwin to William Cullen Bryant, 26 February 1840, B-G Collection; *Pathfinder*, 6 May 1843, p. 163; Brisbane, *Mental Biography*, 222.

25. George Fitzhugh, *Cannibals All! or, Slaves without Masters*, ed. C. Vann Woodward (Cambridge, Mass.: Belknap Press of Harvard University Press, 1960), 18; Fitzhugh, *Sociology for the South*, in *Ante-Bellum: Writings of George Fitzhugh and Hinton Rowan Helper on Slavery*, ed. Harvey Wish (New York; Capricorn, 1960), 59.

26. Fitzhugh, *Cannibals*, 192, 93, 101.

27. Fitzhugh, *Sociology*, 65, 69; Fitzhugh, *Cannibals*, 261.

28. Fitzhugh, *Cannibals*, 50. See especially Louis Hartz, *The Liberal Tradition in America* (New York: Harcourt, Brace & World, 1955), 146–48; and Eugene Genovese, *The World the Slaveholders Made* (New York: Vintage Books, 1971), 118–234.

29. Fitzhugh, *Cannibals*, 189, 6; Genovese, *Slaveholders*, 224.

30. Woodward, "George Fitzhugh, *Sui Generis*," in *Cannibals*, vii–xxix.

31. George Frederick Holmes, "Greeley on Reforms," *Southern Literary Messenger* 17 (May 1851): 257–80; Edmund Ruffin, quoted in Wish, *Ante-Bellum*, 8; Ruffin, *The Political Economy of Slavery* (Washington, D.C.: Lemuel Towers, 1853),; William Grayson, "The Hireling and the Slave," *De Bow's Review* 21 (September 1856): 248–56; James Hammond, "Speech on the Admission of Kansas," 4 March 1858, quoted in McKitrick, *Slavery Defended*, 123; Henry Hughes, *A Treatise on Sociology* (Philadelphia: Lippincott, Grambo, 1854).

32. See esp. Drew Gilpin Faust, *A Sacred Circle: The Dilemma of the Intellectual*

in the Old South (Baltimore, Md.: Johns Hopkins University Press, 1977), 112–31. For other works stressing the proslavery argument's significance for southerners, see Ralph E. Morrow, "The Proslavery Argument Revisited," *Mississippi Valley Historical Review* 47 (June 1961): 79–93; and David Donald, "The Proslavery Argument Reconsidered," *Journal of Southern History* 37 (1971): 4–18.

33. Garrison, quoted in Woodward, "Fitzhugh," xxix; Lydia Maria Child, *The Patriarchical Institution as Described by Members of Its Own Family* (New York: American Anti-Slavery Society, 1860); Wish, *Ante-Bellum,* 14. For the critical reception of Fitzhugh's writings in the North, see Harvey Wish, *George Fitzhugh, Propagandist of the Old South* (Baton Rouge: Louisiana State University Press, 1943), 113–25, 150–59, 195–99.

34. For the *Harbinger* as "proslavery," see Maria Weston Chapman to Caroline Weston, Anti-Slavery Collection. For Ballou and Weld, see John L. Thomas, "Antislavery and Utopia," in *The Antislavery Vanguard: New Essays on the Abolitionists,* ed. Martin Duberman (Princeton, N.J.: Princeton University Press, 1966), 249–54, 262–64, 266.

35. Olmsted to Charles Loring Brace, 26 July 1852, in *The Papers of Frederick Law Olmsted,* ed. Charles Capen McLaughlin (Baltimore, Md.: Johns Hopkins University Press, 1977–), 1:375; Laura Wood Roper, *FLO: A Biography of Frederick Law Olmsted* (Baltimore, Md.: Johns Hopkins University Press, 1973), 84–85, 90–91, 113; Olmsted, *A Journey in the Seabord Slave States* (New York: Dix & Edwards, 1856), 701–15. It was in 1853 that Olmsted met Victor Considerant and encouraged the French Fourierist to locate a colony in Texas; see Roper, *FLO,* 104.

36. W.G.C., "Socialism and Slavery," *Boston Daily Chronotype,* 17 November 1849; *Harbinger* 5 (17 July 1847): 82.

37. Eric Foner, "The Causes of the American Civil War: Recent Interpretations and New Directions," in Foner, *Politics and Ideology,* 24.

38. Yehoshua Arieli, *Individualism and Nationalism in American Ideology* (Baltimore, Md.: Penguin Books, 1966), 179–241. For Brisbane and the Fourierists' use of the term, see Carl J. Guarneri, "Utopian Socialism and American Ideas: The Origins and Doctrine of American Fourierism, 1832–1848" (Ph.D. diss., Johns Hopkins University, 1979), 105–8.

39. Foner, *Free Soil, Free Labor, Free Men,* 11–39.

40. See Woodward, "Fitzhugh," xxx; and Wish, *George Fitzhugh,* 150–59, for the "house divided" episode.

41. Speech at Kalamazoo, Michigan, 27 August 1856, and speech at New Haven, 6 March 1860, in *The Collected Works of Abraham Lincoln,* ed. Roy P. Basler (New Brunswick, N.J.: Rutgers University Press, 1953–55), 2:364, 4:24–25; Hofstadter, "Abraham Lincoln and the Self-Made Myth," in *American Political Tradition,* 152–53.

42. Jayme A. Sokolow, "Culture and Utopia: The Raritan Bay Union," *New Jersey History* 94 (Summer–Fall 1976): 98–99.

43. Lindsay Swift, *Brook Farm: Its Members, Scholars, and Visitors* (New York: Macmillan, 1900), 256, 40; Maude Honeyman Greene, "Raritan Bay Union, Eagleswood, New Jersey," *Proceedings of the New Jersey Historical Society* 68 (January 1950): 12–13.

CHAPTER 16. THE FOURIERIST LEGACY

1. Andrews, "Weekly Bulletin of the Pantarchy," *Woodhull and Claflin's Weekly* 3 (8 June 1871): 10, quoted in Dolores Hayden, *The Grand Domestic Revolution: A History of Feminist Designs for American Homes, Neighborhoods, and Cities* (Cambridge, Mass.: MIT Press, 1981), 102.

2. John F. C. Harrison, *Quest for the New Moral World: Robert Owen and the Owenites in Britain and America* (New York: Scribner, 1969), 245; Arthur Bestor, "Patent-Office Models of the Good Society: Some Relationships between Social Reform and Westward Expansion," in *Backwoods Utopias: The Sectarian Origins and the Owenite Phase of Communitarian Socialism in America, 1663–1829*, 2d ed. (Philadelphia: University of Pennsylvania Press, 1970), 251.

3. Paul and Percival Goodman, *Communitas: Means of Livelihood and Ways of Life* (New York: Vintage Books, 1960), 109.

4. Edward K. Spann, *Brotherly Tomorrows: Movements for a Cooperative Society in America, 1820–1920* (New York: New York University Press, 1989), 130.

5. Brisbane to Redelia Brisbane, 7 April 1875, AB-IHS. Brisbane's post–Civil War activities can be traced through hundreds of letters, clippings, and manuscript articles in the AB-IHS, the FNA, and the EPG Papers. For Brisbane's "method of study," see Brisbane to Considerant, 29 December 1872, FNA (10 AS 36, doss. 11); Brisbane to Redelia Brisbane, 28 October 1875, and "Method of Study; or, Investigation and Discovery," MS, both in AB-IHS. This collection also contains documents relating to Brisbane's numerous patents; for the inventions, see Richard Norman Pettitt, Jr., "Albert Brisbane: Apostle of Fourierism in the United States, 1834–1890" (Ph.D. diss., Miami University [Ohio], 1982), 256–84. Brisbane's pledge to use the profits for Association is in his letter to Victor Considerant, 25 April 1870, FNA (10 AS 36, doss. 11). For the reunion with Considerant in 1877, see Brisbane, *Mental Biography*, 23. Brisbane's most ambitious publication of the postwar years was *General Introduction to Social Science* (New York: C. P. Somerby, 1876). A perceptive discussion of the elderly Brisbane's cast of mind is Michael Fellman, *The Unbounded Frame: Freedom and Community in Nineteenth-Century American Utopianism* (Westport, Conn.: Greenwood Press, 1973), 16–18.

6. William H. Muller, *New Departure: A Description of Pacific Colony* (New York: Credit Foncier, 1886). For Young and Leland, see Bestor, *Backwoods Utopias*, 56–57; for Harris, Herbert W. Schneider and George Lawton, *A Prophet and a Pilgrim* (New York: Columbia University Press, 1942); for Joslin, Albert Shaw, *Icaria: A Chapter in the History of Communism* (New York: Putnam, Sons, 1884), 185; for Macdaniel, Elizabeth Cady Stanton, *Eighty Years and More (1815–1897): Reminiscences of Elizabeth Cady Stanton* (London: T. Fisher Unwin, 1898), 449. It is also worth noting that just after Brisbane moved to France, several former Associationists proposed to establish a "Hotel and Cottage Association" on his former estate near Fanwood, New Jersey; see William Alfred Hinds, *American Communities* (Oneida, N.Y.: Office of *American Socialist*, 1878), 155.

7. For this "Potomac phalanx," see Hinds, *American Communities*, 155; *American Socialist* 2 (1877): 10, 11, 19, 24; and Joel Ellis to Edward Daniels, 11 January 1879, Durant Papers. In the 1870s, Durant proposed a scheme for cooperative colonies to be established under the auspices of the federal government; see Thomas J. Durant, *Some Remarks on the Subject of Home Colonization* (Washington, D.C., [1874?]). In addition to the communities already noted, a Fourierist communal household nestled in the redwoods north of San Francisco was described by a magazine writer in 1873, but it appears to have been a fictional creation. See [Noah Brooks], "The San Raphael Phalanstery," *Scribner's Monthly* 5 (February 1873): 453–60.

8. Albert Brisbane, "The Organization of Industry: Plan of a Great Joint-Stock Farm in the West," clipping from *New York Tribune* [1868]; Brisbane, "Plan of the Transitional Organization of Industry," January 1868, AB-IHS; E. P. Grant to Thomas J. Durant, 20 December 1868, EPG Papers. Information on de Boissiere and Silkville not otherwise attributed is from Garret R. Carpenter,

"Silkville: A Kansas Attempt in the History of Fourierist Utopias, 1869–1892," *Emporia State Research Studies* 3 (December 1954): 3–29.

9. Grant to Thomas J. Durant, 3 October 1868 and 22 January 1869, EPG Papers.

10. Grant to Thomas J. Durant, 3 July 1869; Grant to Brisbane, 9 February 1869; Brisbane to Grant, 7 February 1869, EPG Papers; and *Articles of Association of the Kansas Co-operative Farm* (Canton, Ohio, 1869). De Boissiere objected to Brisbane's "free love life," Grant to his lack of "practical business capacity." As early as 1854, in pledging support to Considerant's Texas colony, de Boissiere had expressed the hope that its preparations would be "directed by a more practical man than our friend Brisbane." Boissiere to ?, 17 May 1854, FNA (10 AS 36, doss. 8). Durant was offered the presidency of the colony; though he refused, he publicized the experiment and sent advice; see Grant to Durant, 25 November 1868, EPG Papers.

11. E. P. Grant publicized the Kansas colony in *Co-Operation; or, Sketch of the Conditions of Attractive Industry, and Outline of a Plan for an Organization of Labor* (New York: American News Company, 1870). Grant returned to Silkville in August 1872 and stayed until early 1874.

12. Brisbane to Considerant, 19 February 1869, FNA (10 AS 36, doss. 11); "Communism in Kansas," Oneida *Circular*, n.s. 7 (26 December 1870): 322–23.

13. Sears to E. P. Grant, 12 May 1870, 23 August 1871, EPG Papers. Boissiere's visit to the North American Phalanx is referred to in A. Bureau to North American Phalanx [c.1853], FNA (10 AS 36, doss. 12). In 1870, Sears was an agent for the National Land Company, which was helping to settle the semi-Fourierist Union Colony in Colorado. See Barbara Smith, *1870–1970, The First Hundred Years: Greeley, Colorado* (Greeley, Colo.: Centennial Commission, 1970), 15.

14. *The Prairie Home: Association and Co-operation Based on Attractive Industry* (Williamsburg, Kan., [1873]).

15. See the recollections of de Boissiere by former residents recorded in Paul I. Wellman, "Only Mulberry Trees Outlive the Colony of Good Dreams," *Kansas City Star*, 19 April 1942. (My thanks to Timothy Miller of the University of Kansas for this reference.)

16. Alcander Longley, "Life in the North American Phalanx," *Social Record* 1 (September 1858): 31–32; Collins, quoted in Noyes, *American Socialisms*, 290.

17. Longley, quoted in H. Roger Grant, "Missouri's Utopian Communities," *Missouri Historical Review* 66 (October 1971): 39. The fullest account of Longley's career is Hal D. Sears, "Alcander Longley, Missouri Communist: A History of Reunion Community and a Study of the Constitutions of Reunion and Friendship," *Bulletin of the Missouri Historical Society* 25 (January 1969): 123–37.

18. The following account of Greeley is based primarily on Dolores Hayden, *Seven American Utopias: The Architecture of Communitarian Socialism, 1790–1975* (Cambridge, Mass.: MIT Press, 1976), 260–87, and the sources it cites. The most complete historical treatment of the colony, written by a former member, is David Boyd, *A History: Greeley and the Union Colony of Colorado* (Greeley, Colo.: Greeley Tribune Press, 1890).

19. N. C. Meeker, "Post Mortem and Requiem, by an old Fourierist," *New York Tribune*, 3 November 1866, in Noyes, *American Socialisms*, 499–507 (quotations, pp. 506–7).

20. "A Western Colony," *New York Tribune*, 4 December 1869; Hayden, *Seven American Utopias*, 262, 270, 273–74; Spann, *Brotherly Tomorrows*, 134. Evidently, Meeker believed that temperance was the "moral stethoscope to test human character" that Horace Greeley had sought for the phalanxes of the 1840s. See Greeley to A. L. West, 15 April 1845, Greeley-NYHS.

21. Meeker quoted in Hayden, *Seven American Utopias*, 273.

22. Ibid., 284.

23. William McDiarmid, *The Organization of Labor: Showing How to Acquire True Independence of Character* (Cincinnati: Times office, 1863), 4; David Montgomery, *Beyond Equality: Labor and the Radical Republicans, 1862–1872* (1967; rpt. New York: Vintage Books, 1972), 387–424 (quotation, p. 411).

24. Montgomery, *Beyond Equality*, 442, 425–47; Irwin Unger, *The Greenback Era: A Social and Political History of American Finance, 1865–1879* (Princeton, N.J.: Princeton University Press, 1964), 94–114.

25. Brisbane, *Mental Biography*, 201; Considerant to General Grant, 27 December 1868, FNA (10 AS 28, dossier 11); Victor Considerant, *Three Hundred Millions of Dollars Saved in Specie by the Meaning of a Word* (New York: New York News, 1868); Brisbane to Considerant, 27 December 1867 and 5 February 1869, FNA (10 AS 36, doss. 11); Unger, *Greenback Era*, 110, 305, 373n, 377. See Albert Brisbane, *The Philosophy of Money* (N.p., 1863); Charles Sears, *Representative Money* (Ottawa, Kan., 1878); and Thomas J. Durant, *Free Money, Free Credit, and Free Exchange* (Washington, D.C.: Gibson, 1874).

26. See esp. Brisbane, *Mental Biography*, 202–3; Brisbane to Considerant, 5 February 1869, FNA (10 AS 36, doss. 11).

27. Montgomery, *Beyond Equality*, 246.

28. Ibid., 410; John R. Commons et al., *History of Labour in the United States* (New York: Macmillan, 1918), 2:138; E. P. Grant to Thomas J. Durant, 16 February 1869, EPG Papers; Martin Henry Blatt, *Free Love and Anarchism: The Biography of Ezra Heywood* (Urbana: University of Illinois Press, 1989), 49–50.

29. Montgomery, *Beyond Equality*, 415–21; Samuel Bernstein, *The First International in America* (New York: Augustus M. Kelly, 1962), 112–19; Brisbane to Considerant, 28 April 1872, FNA (10 AS 36, doss. 11).

30. For a biographical sketch of Orvis, see Lindsay Swift, *Brook Farm: Its Members, Scholars, and Visitors* (New York: Macmillan, 1900), 174–81.

31. John Orvis, "Social Transition," *Nationalist* 3 (August 1890): 8.

32. Swift, *Brook Farm*, 179; Commons et al., *History of Labour*, 2:173; Montgomery, *Beyond Equality*, 414; Arthur Mann, *Yankee Reformers in the Urban Age: Social Reform in Boston, 1880–1900* (1954; New York: Harper & Row, 1966), 178–84. For his program in the Sovereigns of Industry, see John Orvis, *A Plan for the Organization and Management of Co-operative Stores and Boards of Trade under the Auspices of the Order of the Sovereigns of Industry* (Worchester, Mass.: Sovereigns of Industry, 1876). Butterfield is listed as secretary of the National Council of the Sovereigns in Edwin M. Chamberlin, *The Sovereigns of Industry* (Boston: Lee & Shepard, 1875), addenda, xvii. For the Knights of Labor and cooperatives, see Commons et al., *History of Labour*, 2:430–38; and Florence E. Parker, *The First Hundred Years: A History of Distributive and Service Cooperation in the United States* (Superior, Wis., 1956), 17–23.

33. See Charles P. Le Warne, "Labor and Communitarianism, 1880–1900," *Labor History* 16 (Summer 1975): 393–407. For individual communities, see Robert Hine, *California's Utopian Colonies* (1953; New York: Norton, 1973), 101–31, 142–44; Le Warne, *Utopias on Puget Sound, 1885–1915* (Seattle: University of Washington Press, 1975); Howard H. Quint, *The Forging of American Socialism: Origins of the Modern Movement* (Indianapolis, Ind.: Bobbs-Merrill, 1964), 189–94; James Dombrowski, *The Early Days of Christian Socialism in America* (New York: Columbia University Press, 1936), 132–70; Bernard J. Brommel, "Debs's Cooperative Commonwealth Plan for Workers," *Labor History* 12 (February 1971): 560–69; Nick Salvatore, *Eugene V. Debs: Citizen and Socialist* (Urbana: University of Illinois Press, 1982), 162–67; and Spann, *Brotherly Tomorrows*, 235–42.

34. Montgomery, *Beyond Equality*, 415–16; Quint, *Forging*, 192. See William H. Muller, *Socialism in a Nutshell* (Ruskin, Tenn., 1898).

35. For the larger context of this development, see Daniel Bell, *Marxian Socialism in the United States* (Princeton, N.J.: Princeton University Press, 1967), 45–55.

36. Woodhull, quoted in Emanie Sachs, *"The Terrible Siren" Victoria Woodhull (1838–1927)* (New York: Harper, 1928), 135. For Andrews's side of the partnership, see Madeleine B. Stern, *The Pantarch: A Biography of Stephen Pearl Andrews* (Austin: University of Texas Press, 1968), 103–21.

37. *Protective Union* 1 (7 September 1850): 317; *Proceedings of the Woman's Rights Convention, Held at Worcester, October 23rd and 24th, 1850* (Boston: Prentiss & Sawyer, 1851), 18–19.

38. Madeleine B. Stern, "William Henry Channing's Letters on 'Woman in Her Social Relations,' " *Cornell Library Journal* 6 (August 1968), 54–62; Fredrika Bremer, *The Homes of the New World: Impressions of America*, trans. Mary Howitt (New York: Harper, 1853), 614–15.

39. William Leach, *True Love and Perfect Union: The Feminist Reform of Sex and Society* (New York: Basic Books, 1980), 203; *Provisional Prospectus of the Raritan Bay Union* [1852], photocopy in RBU Collection.

40. Sarah Moore Grimké to the Wattles family, 12 November 1853; Sarah to Harriot K. Hunt, 20 December 1854, Weld-Grimké Papers.

41. Stanton, *Eighty Years and More*, 134, 147.

42. Norma Lippincott Swan, "The North American Phalanx," *Bulletin of the Monmouth County Historical Association* 1 (May 1935): 60–61; Stanton to Paulina Davis, 6 December 1852, RBU Collection; Elisabeth Griffith, *In Her Own Right: The Life of Elizabeth Cady Stanton* (New York: Oxford University Press, 1984), 68.

43. Stanton, *Eighty Years and More*, title page. Cf. Charles Fourier: "The extension of the privilege of women is the fundamental cause of all social progress," *OC*, 1:133.

44. See Hayden, *Grand Domestic Revolution*, 95–96; Spann, *Brotherly Tomorrows*, 127–28; Stern, *Pantarch*, 93–97; Laura Stedman and George M. Gould, *Life and Letters of Edmund Clarence Stedman* (New York: Moffat, Yard, 1910), 1:151–77; *New York Times*, 22 and 25 June 1858, 21 and 26 September 1860.

45. Quoted in Hayden, *Grand Domestic Revolution*, 102.

46. For Howland's career, see ibid., 91–113; Spann, *Brotherly Tomorrows*, 165–75; Robert Fogarty, introduction to Marie Howland, *The Familistère* (1874; rpt. Philadelphia: Porcupine Press, 1975); and Paul M. Gaston, *Women of Fair Hope* (Athens: University of Georgia Press, 1984), 19–65. Entitled *Papa's Own Girl* in the first and second editions (1874 and 1885), Howland's novel was called *The Familistère* in the third (1918). For Godin's experiment at Guise, see Marie Moret, *Documents pour une biographie complète de J.-B. A. Godin*, 3 vols. (Guise: Familistère, 1897–1901); Jules Prudhommeaux, *Les experiences sociales de J.-B. A. Godin* (Paris: Imprimerie Nouvelle, 1919); Léon Durand, *Le Familistère de Guise* (Geneva: University of Geneva, 1933); and Annick Brauman, *Le Familistère de Guise ou les equivalents de la richesse* (Brussels: Editions des Archives d'Architecture, 1976). For Topolobampo, see Ray Reynolds, *Cat's Paw Utopia* (El Cajon, Calif., 1972).

47. Hayden, *Grand Domestic Revolution*, 80, 77, 119. See N. C. Meeker, "Cooperation: Model Tenement Houses and Cooperative Housekeeping," *New York Tribune* (semiweekly), 31 August 1869; and John Codman, "Co-operation," *Woman's Journal* 11 (9 October 1880).

48. Hayden, *Grand Domestic Revolution*, 51, 173, 168.

49. Ibid., 108; Jonathan Beecher, *Charles Fourier: The Visionary and His World* (Berkeley: University of California Press, 1986), 461, 465–67; Considerant to Julie Considerant, 3 May 1853, FNA (10 AS 28, doss. 9).

50. See Hayden, *Grand Domestic Revolution*, 108; and Kenneth M. Roemer, *The Obsolete Necessity: America in Utopian Writings, 1888–1900* (Kent, Ohio: Kent State University Press, 1976), 153–70.

51. Hayden's pathbreaking *Grand Domestic Revolution* defines and surveys the "material feminist" tradition (pp. 4–29), then unearths dozens of plans for clubs, houses, and towns with socialized domestic arrangements. I have borrowed several examples with Fourierist ancestry for this section. Hayden presents her arguments for a new feminist architecture in *Redesigning the American Dream: The Future of Housing, Work, and Family Life* (New York: Norton, 1984).

52. Fourier's influence in Europe is suggested by Leonardo Benevolo, *The Origins of Modern Town Planning* (Cambridge, Mass.: MIT Press, 1967), 56–75. For Oneida's adoption of Fourierist architectural ideas, see Hayden, *Seven American Utopias*, 196–97. For Fourier's influence on Le Corbusier, see Peter Serenyi, "Le Corbusier, Fourier, and the Monastery of Ema," *Art Bulletin* 49 (December 1967): 267–86.

53. Olmsted to John Olmsted, 11 August 1850, in *The Papers of Frederick Law Olmsted*, ed. Charles Capen McLaughlin (Baltimore, Md.: Johns Hopkins University Press, 1977–), 1:355; [Olmsted], "The Phalanstery and the Phalansterians," *New York Tribune*, 24 July 1852; Laura Wood Roper, "Frederick Law Olmsted and the Western Texas Free-Soil Movement," *American Historical Review* 56 (1950): 60.

54. See the suggestive analyses of Albert Fein in "Fourierism in Nineteenth-Century America: A Social and Environmental Perspective," in *France and North America: Utopias and Utopians*, ed. Mathé Allain (Lafayette: University of Southwestern Louisiana, 1978), 133–48; and Fein, *Frederick Law Olmsted and the American Environmental Tradition* (New York: Braziller, 1972), 8–10, 15–19, 57–61.

55. Olmsted, "Public Parks and the Enlargement of Towns" (1870), in *Civilizing American Cities: A Selection of Frederick Law Olmsted's Writings on City Landscapes*, ed. S. B. Sutton (Cambridge, Mass.: MIT Press, 1971), 75.

56. On Curtis, see Fellman, *Unbounded Frame*, 89–103. For the ASSA, see Luther Bernard and Jessie Bernard, *Origins of American Sociology: The Social Science Movement in the United States* (New York: T. Y. Crowell, 1943), 527–67; Thomas Haskell, *The Emergence of Professional Social Science: The American Social Science Association and the Nineteenth-Century Crisis of Authority* (Urbana: University of Illinois Press, 1977); and Leach, *True Love and Perfect Union*, 292–346.

57. *New York Tribune*, 19 June, 6 and 8 July 1867. Without noting its Fourierist affiliations, Haskell, *Emergence*, 118, dismisses the New York branch of the ASSA as short-lived.

58. Haskell, *Emergence*, 119, 82.

59. See Sylvia E. Bowman, *The Year 2000: A Critical Biography of Edward Bellamy* (New York: Bookman, 1958); and *Edward Bellamy Abroad: An American Prophet's Influence* (New York: Twayne, 1962).

60. Bowman, *The Year 2000*, 91–92; Charles H. Brown, *William Cullen Bryant: A Biography* (New York: Scribner, 1971), 495–96; Arthur E. Morgan, *Edward Bellamy* (New York: Columbia University Press, 1944), 369; Oliver Carlson, *Brisbane: A Candid Biography* (New York: Stackpole, 1937), 82.

61. Edward Bellamy, "Progress of Nationalism in the United States," *North American Review* 154 (June 1892): 743.

62. The influence of Fourier was strangely overlooked by Arthur Morgan, who undertook an otherwise exhaustive analysis of Bellamy's possible sources in *Bellamy*, 204–22, 235–44. Brisbane was preoccupied with his transport system of spherical containers sent through pneumatic tubes at the time he and Bellamy met. He had petitioned Congress to incorporate the company promoting his

invention, and in 1872 Congress appropriated $15,000 to build a pilot system underground between the Capitol and the Government Printing Office. The tube collapsed, however, and construction was not completed before the deadline set by the House Appropriations Committee. See Brisbane, "To the Honorable the [sic] Members of the Senate and House of Representatives of the United States," printed broadside [c. 1870]; Pettitt, "Albert Brisbane," 278–83; and Brisbane to Victor Considerant, 29 December 1872 and 9 February 1874, FNA (10 AS 36, doss. 11).

63. Edward Bellamy, *Looking Backward: 2000–1887* (1888; rpt. Cambridge, Mass.: Harvard University Press, 1967), 124–25.

64. John L. Thomas, introduction to Bellamy, *Looking Backward*, 13.

65. The following comments are based on a comparison of "The Religion of Solidarity," in *Edward Bellamy: Selected Writings on Religion and Society*, ed. Joseph Schiffman (New York: Liberal Arts Press, 1955), 3–27, and Pierre Leroux's *De l'humanité* (Paris: Perrotin, 1840).

66. Brisbane, "The Religion of the Future," MS, April 1871 (quotation, p. 5), and E. P. Grant to Charles Sears, 14 June 1870, both in EPG Papers.

67. Here and in the following paragraph my discussion is indebted to Thomas's critique of the "dystopian features of Bellamy's ideal society" in his introduction to *Looking Backward*, 63–66.

68. Bellamy to William Dean Howells, 17 June 1888, Bellamy Manuscripts, HL, quoted in Fellman, *Unbounded Frame*, 122.

69. See especially Hine, *California's Utopian Colonies*, 162–63.

70. Edward Bellamy, "Concerning the Founding of Nationalist Colonies," *The New Nation* 3 (23 September 1893): 434, quoted in Fellman, *Unbounded Frame*, 106.

A Bibliography
of American Fourierism

For an excellent bibliography of works by and about Charles Fourier, see Jonathan Beecher, *Charles Fourier: The Visionary and His World* (Berkeley: University of California Press, 1986), 571–85. The best general bibliography of the international Fourierist movement can be found in I. I. Zilberfarb, *The Social Philosophy of Charles Fourier* [in Russian] (Moscow: Izdatel'stvo Nauka, 1964), 460–532. Anyone working on American Fourierism is indebted to the pioneering research and bibliographic work of Arthur Bestor. Bestor intended to provide an exhaustive catalogue of works on American Fourierism in "American Phalanxes: A Study of Fourierist Socialism in the United States," (Ph.D. diss., Yale University, 1938), vol. 2, but the dissertation was submitted with an incomplete bibliography. It can be supplemented with the numerous bibliographic lists Bestor later deposited at the Illinois Historical Survey, University of Illinois, though even these lists generally extend only into the 1940s and do not include the many secondary titles and manuscript sources that have become available since then. For Brook Farm, there exists a comprehensive published bibliography: Joel Myerson, ed., *Brook Farm: An Annotated Bibliography and Resource Guide* (New York: Garland, 1978). Three additional bibliographies gather important published primary sources: Bestor, "American Phalanxes," 2:28–43, lists Albert Brisbane's Fourierist columns in the *New York Tribune*, 1842–43; Sterling F. Delano, *The Harbinger and New England Transcendentalism: A Portrait of Associationism in America* (Cranbury, N.J.: Associated University Presses, 1983), 168–204, lists all original articles in the Fourierists' official journal; and Maurice Buchs, "Le Fouriérisme aux Etats-Unis; Contribution à l'étude du socialisme américain" (Thèse du doctorat, Université de Paris, 1948), 209–12, lists articles about American Fourierism which appeared in French Fourierist periodicals.

The following bibliography does not repeat all the references cited in the book; readers looking for more detailed information should consult the extensive chapter notes. Instead, it lists the most important titles and manuscripts that relate directly to American Fourierism, including a few sources consulted in preparation for the book but not specifically cited in the chapter notes.

PRIMARY SOURCES

Manuscripts

Abernethy Library of American Literature Miscellaneous Manuscripts. Middlebury College, Vermont.
Allen, William, Family Correspondence. Houghton Library, Harvard University
Alphadelphia Association Papers. Bentley Historical Library, University of Michigan.
Antislavery Collection. Boston Public Library.
Archives Sociétaires, Fonds Fourier et Considerant. French National Archives, Paris.
Bestor, Arthur, Papers. Illinois Historical Survey, University of Illinois (including copies of archival records of Brook Farm, Sodus Bay Phalanx, and Wisconsin Phalanx, and chapter drafts for "Backwoods Utopias," vol. 2).
Birney, James G., Papers. William Clements Library, University of Michigan.
Blackwell Family Papers. Library of Congress, Washington, D.C.
Borneman, Henry S., Papers. Illinois Historical Survey, University of Illinois.
Boston Religious Union of Associationists Records. Massachusetts Historical Society, Boston.
Boston Union of Associationists Records. Houghton Library, Harvard University.
Brisbane, Albert, Papers. George Arents Research Library, Syracuse University.
Brisbane, Albert, Papers. Illinois Historical Survey, University of Illinois.
Bristol, Cyrenius C., Papers. University of Rochester.
Broadside Collection. Massachusetts Historical Society, Boston.
Brook Farm Papers. Massachusetts Historical Society, Boston.
Brown, John Stillman, Family Papers. Kansas State Historical Society, Topeka.
Brownson, Orestes, Papers. University of Notre Dame Archives.
Bryant, William Cullen, and Parke Godwin Collection. New York Public Library.
Considerant, Victor, Manuscripts. Ecole Normale Supérieure, Paris.
Cranch, Christopher P., Papers. Massachusetts Historical Society, Boston.
Curson Family Papers. Houghton Library, Harvard University.
Durant, Thomas J., Papers. New-York Historical Society, New York City.
Dwight, John S., Collection. Boston Public Library.
Dwight Brook Farm Collection, Boston Public Library.
Emerson, Ralph Waldo, Papers. Houghton Library, Harvard University.
Fisher, James T., Papers. Massachusetts Historical Society, Boston.
Fruitlands Museum Archives. Harvard, Massachusetts.
Godwin, Parke, Papers. Princeton University.
Grant, Elijah P., Papers. University of Chicago Library.
Greeley, Horace, Papers. Library of Congress, Washington, D.C.
Greeley, Horace, Manuscripts. New-York Historical Society, New York City.
Greeley, Horace, Papers. New York Public Library.
Hecker, Isaac, Papers. Archives of the Paulist Fathers, New York.
Hinds, William A., *American Communities* Collection. George Arents Research Library, Syracuse University.

Houghton Library Miscellaneous Manuscripts and Autograph File. Harvard University.

James, William, Papers. Houghton Library, Harvard University.

Labadie Collection. Division of Rare Books and Special Collections, University of Michigan Library.

Macdonald, A. J., Collection. Beinecke Rare Book and Manuscript Library, Yale University.

May, Samuel J., Collection. Cornell University Library.

Mordecai, G. W., Papers. Southern Historical Collection, University of North Carolina at Chapel Hill.

North American Phalanx Manuscript Collection. Monmouth County Historical Association, Freehold, N.J.

North American Phalanx Records and Miscellaneous Papers. Houghton Library, Harvard University

Paul, Mary, Correspondence. Vermont Historical Society, Montpelier.

Pedrick, Samuel M., Collection. State Historical Society of Wisconsin, Madison.

Phalansterian Realization Fund Society Records. Houghton Library, Harvard University.

Raritan Bay Union Collection, New Jersey Historical Society, Newark.

Ray, Isaiah C., Correspondence. Slavery in the United States Collection, American Antiquarian Society, Worcester, Massachusetts.

Religious Union of Associationists Records. Houghton Library, Harvard University.

Ripley, George, Papers. Massachusetts Historical Society, Boston.

Santerre, George Henry (La Réunion Colony), Papers. Dallas Public Library.

Sartain, Harriet, Collection. Historical Society of Pennsylvania, Philadelphia.

Simonin, Amédée, Papers. Library of Congress, Washington, D.C.

Sodus Bay Phalanx Collection. Rochester Historical Society.

Spencer, Lilly Martin, Family Papers. Campus Martius Records, Ohio Historical Society, Columbus.

Throop, George A., Papers. Local and Regional History Collection, Cornell University.

Trist, Nicholas, Papers. Library of Congress, Washington, D.C.

U.S. Census, Manuscript Population Schedules of the Seventh Census (1850).

Weld-Grimké Papers. William Clements Library, University of Michigan.

Western Historical Manuscripts Collection (including microfilms from Archives Sociétaires). University of Missouri, Columbia.

Weston Collection. Boston Public Library.

Wisconsin Phalanx Collection, Ceresco Community Papers and Microfilms. State Historical Society of Wisconsin, Madison.

Wright, Elizur Jr., Papers. Library of Congress, Washington, D.C.

Newspapers and Periodicals

Boston Daily Chronotype. 1849–50.

Bulletin du Mouvement Sociétaire en Europe et en Amérique. Brussels, 1857–60.

Bulletin of the Texas Emigration Union. August 1855.

The Future. New York, 1841.

The Harbinger. Boston and New York, 1845–49.

New York Daily Plebian. 1842–43.

New York Daily Tribune. 1842–55.

Phalansterian Record. Cincinnati, 1857–58 (called *Social Record,* 1858–59).

The Phalanx. Buffalo, 1840.

The Phalanx. New York, 1843–45.
The Present. New York, 1843–44.
Protective Union. Boston, 1849–50.
The Spirit of the Age. New York, 1849–50.
The Voice of Industry. Fitchburg, Lowell, and Boston, Mass. 1845–49.

Books and Pamphlets

This section comprises publications (including translations) of American Fourier-ist groups and individuals; autobiographies, memoirs, and critical works; and titles relating to the French-American colony of La Réunion. Constitutions, by-laws, circulars, and broadsides—of which dozens were printed—have been omitted.

American Union of Associationists. *Association, as Illustrated by Fourier's System.* Boston: Crosby & Nichols, 1847.

——. *Industrial Association. An Address to the People of the United States.* Boston: AUA, [1850].

Andrews, Stephen Pearl, ed. *Love, Marriage, and Divorce, and the Sovereignty of the Individual: A Discussion by Henry James, Horace Greeley, and Stephen Pearl Andrews.* New York: Stringer & Townsend, 1853; rpt. Weston, Mass.: M&S Press, 1975.

Bremer, Fredrika. *Homes of the New World: Impressions of America.* Trans. Mary Howitt. New York: Harper, 1953.

Briancourt, Mathieu. *The Organization of Labor and Association.* Trans. Francis George Shaw. New York: William H. Graham, 1847.

Brisbane, Albert. *Association; or, A Concise Exposition of the Practical Part of Fourier's Social Science.* New York: Greeley & McElrath, 1843.

——. *A Concise Exposition of the Doctrine of Association.* New York: J. S. Redfield, 1844.

——. *General Introduction to Social Science.* New York: C. P. Somerby, 1876.

——. *Social Destiny of Man; or, Association and Reorganization of Industry.* Philadel-phia: C. F. Stollmeyer, 1840.

——. *Theory of the Functions of the Human Passions, Followed by an Outline View of the Fundamental Principles of Fourier's Theory of Social Science.* New York: Miller, Orton & Mulligan, 1856.

——. *Treatise on the Functions of Human Passions; An Outline of Fourier's System.* New York: Dewitt, 1857.

Brisbane, Redelia. *Albert Brisbane: A Mental Biography; with a Character Study by His Wife Redelia Brisbane.* Boston: Arena, 1893.

Calvert, George H. *Introduction to Social Science.* New York: J. S. Redfield, 1856.

Cantagrel, F. F. *The Children of the Phalanstery.* Trans. George Shaw. New York: W. H. Graham, 1848.

Channing, William Henry. *The Christian Church and Social Reform.* Boston: Crosby & Nichols, 1848.

——. *The Gospel of To-day.* Boston: Crosby & Nichols, 1847.

Chase, Warren. *Forty Years on the Spiritual Rostrum.* Boston: Colby & Rich, 1888.

——. *The Life-line of the Lone One; or, Autobiography of the World's Child.* Boston: Bela Marsh, 1852.

Codman, John Thomas. *Brook Farm: Historic and Personal Memoirs.* Boston: Arena, 1894.

Considerant, Victor. *Au Texas.* Paris: Librairie Phalanstérienne, 1854.

——. *Du Texas: Premier rapport à mes amis.* Paris: Librairie Phalanstérienne, 1857.

——. *European Colonization in Texas: An Address to the American People.* New York: Baker, Godwin, 1855.

——. *The Great West: A New Social and Industrial Life in Its Fertile Regions.* New York: Dewitt & Davenport, 1854.

Constant, Alphonse. *The Last Incarnation: Gospel Legends of the Nineteenth Century.* Trans. Francis George Shaw. New York: W. H. Graham, 1847.

Corselius, George. *Hints toward the Development of a Unitary Science, or Science of Universal Analogy.* Ann Arbor, Mich.: S. B. McCracken, 1846.

Dana, Charles. *A Lecture on Association, in Its Connection with Religion.* Boston: B. H. Greene, 1844.

——. *Proudhon and his "Bank of the People."* New York: B. R. Tucker, 1896.

Durant, Thomas J. *Some Remarks on the Subject of Home Colonization.* Washington, D.C., [1874?]

Dwight, John S. *A Lecture on Association, in Its Connection with Education.* Boston: B. H. Greene, 1844.

Elder, William. *The Enchanted Beauty, and Other Tales, Essays, and Sketches.* New York: J. C. Derby, 1855.

Exposé of the Condition and Progress of the North American Phalanx, Being a Reply to Horace Greeley. New York: Dewit & Davenport, 1853.

Fourier, Charles, *Oeuvres complètes de Charles Fourier.* 12 vols. Paris: Editions Anthropos, 1966–68.

——. *Social Destiny of Man; or, Theory of the Four Movements.* Trans. by Henry Clapp, Jr., and Albert Brisbane. New York: Dewitt, 1856.

——. *Social Science. The Theory of Universal Unity by Charles Fourier.* Ed. by Albert Brisbane. New York: American News Company, 1877.

Godin, Jean-Baptiste André. *Social Solutions.* Trans. Marie Howland. New York: John W. Lovell, 1886.

Godwin, Parke. *Democracy, Constructive and Pacific.* New York: J. Winchester, 1844.

——. *A Popular View of the Doctrines of Charles Fourier.* New York: J. S. Redfield, 1844.

[Godwin, Parke]. *Phalansterian Association. An Address to the People of the United States, by the American Union of Associationists.* Philadelphia, 1850. (Same as American Union of Associationists, *Industrial Association.*)

Grant, E. P. *Co-Operation; or, Sketch of the Conditions of Attractive Industry.* New York: American News, 1870.

Greeley, Horace. *Hints toward Reforms.* New York: Harper, 1850.

——. *Recollections of a Busy Life.* New York: J. B. Ford, 1868.

Greeley, Horace, and H. J. Raymond. *Association Discussed; or, The Socialism of the Tribune Examined.* New York: Harper, 1847.

[Hempel, Charles Julius]. *The True Organization of the New Church, as Indicated in the Writings of Emmanuel Swedenborg, and Demonstrated by Charles Fourier.* New York: Wm. Radde, 1848.

Hennequin, Victor. *Love in the Phalanstery.* [Trans. Henry James, Sr.] New York: Dewitt & Davenport, 1849.

Henry Russell; or, The Year of Our Lord Two Thousand. New York: W. H. Graham, 1846.

[Hosmer, Charles]. *The Condition of Labor: An Address to the Members of the Labor Reform League of New England, by One of the Members.* Boston, 1847.

Howland, Marie. *The Familistère, A Novel.* 1874; rpt. Philadelphia: Porcupine Press, 1975.

Ingles, Thomas, Jr. *The Destiny of the Human Race on Earth, and the Means for Its Attainment.* Cincinnati, Ohio: Wright, Fisher, 1849.

James, Henry, [Sr.]. *Moralism and Christianity; or, Man's Experience and Destiny.* New York: J. S. Redfield, 1850.

——. *Tracts for the New Times. No. 1: Letter to a Swedenborgian.* New York: John Allen, 1847.

Kirby, Georgianna Bruce. *Years of Experience: An Autobiographical Narrative.* New York: Putnam, 1887.

Lazarus, Marx Edgeworth. *Comparative Psychology and Universal Analogy.* New York: Fowlers & Wells, 1851.

——. *Homeopathy: A Theoretic Demonstration, with Social Applications.* New York: Wm. Radde, 1851.

——. *The Human Trinity; or, Three Aspects of Life: The Passional, the Intellectual, the Practical Sphere.* New York: Fowlers & Wells, 1851.

——. *Love vs. Marriage: Part I.* New York: Fowlers & Wells, 1852.

——. *Passional Hygiene and Natural Medicine: Embracing the Harmonies of Man with His Planet.* New York: Fowlers & Wells, 1852.

——. *The Solar Ray.* New York: Fowlers & Wells, 1851.

McDiarmid, William. *The Organization of Labor: Showing How to Acquire True Independence of Character.* Cincinnati: Times Office, 1863.

M'Laren, Donald C. *Boa Constrictor; or, Fourier Association Self-Exposed as to Its Principles and Aims.* Rochester, N.Y.: Canfield & Warren, 1844.

W.H.M. [Muller, William H.] *There Exists a Social Law; or A Divine Order of Human Society.* Pittsburgh, Pa.: Johnston & Stockton, 1849.

[Nichols, Mary Gove]. *Mary Lyndon; or, Revelations of a Life.* New York: Stringer & Townsend, 1855.

Nichols, Thomas Low. *Woman in All Ages and Nations.* New York: H. Long, 1849.

Nichols, Thomas Low, and Mary Gove Nichols. *Marriage: Its History, Character, and Results.* Cincinnati, Ohio: V. Nicholson, 1855.

T.C.P. [Palmer, Thomas C.] *A Plain Lecture on Association.* Boston: Crosby & Nichols, 1847.

Pellarin, Charles. *The Life of Charles Fourier.* 2d ed. Trans. Francis George Shaw. New York: W. H. Graham, 1848.

Rochester Fourier Society. *Labor's Wrongs and Labor's Remedy.* Rochester, 1843.

Russell, Amelia. *Home Life of the Brook Farm Association.* Boston: Little, Brown, 1900.

Salisbury, Annie. *Brook Farm.* Marlborough, Mass.: W. B. Smith, 1898.

Savardan, Augustin. *Un naufrage au Texas: Observations et impressions recuilliés pendant deux ans et demi au Texas et à travers les Etats-unis d'amérique.* Paris: Garnier Frères, 1858.

Schroder, J. P. *The System of Association, by Charles Fourier, Attested by Nature and Revelation.* Cincinnati, Ohio, 1844.

Sears, Charles. *The North American Phalanx: An Historical and Descriptive Sketch.* Prescott, Wis.: J. M. Pryse, 1886.

[Sears, Charles]. *Socialism and Christianity: Being a Response to an Inquirer concerning Religion and the Observance of Religious Forms at the North American Phalanx.* Freehold, N. J.: NAP, 1854.

Sears, John Van der Zee. *My Friends at Brook Farm.* New York: Desmond, Fitzgerald, 1912.

Sully, Charles. *Associative Manual.* New York: Dewitt & Davenport, 1851.

Toussenel, Alphonse. *Passional Zoology: or, Spirit of the Beasts of France.* Trans. Marx Edgeworth Lazarus. New York: Fowlers & Wells, 1852.

Two Essays on the Social System of Charles Fourier, being an Introduction to the constitution of the Fourienne Society of New York. New York: H. D. Robinson, 1838.

Van Amringe, H. H. *Association and Christianity.* Pittsburgh, Pa.: J. W. Cook, 1845.

——. *Nature and Revelation.* New York: R. P. Bixby, 1843.

"What Is Association?" Tract No. 1. Cincinnati Branch of the American Union of Associationists. Cincinnati, Ohio, [1847].

[Williams, John S.]. *The Detriments of Civilization, and Benefits of Association.* Cincinnati, Ohio: Integral Phalanx, 1844.

Published Letters and Documents

Commons, John R., et al., eds. *A Documentary History of American Industrial Society.* Vols. 7 and 8, *Labor Movement, 1840–1860.* New York: Russell & Russell, 1958.

Curtis, George W. *Early Letters to John S. Dwight, Brook Farm and Concord.* Ed. G. W. Cooke. New York: Harper, 1898.

Delano, Sterling, F. "A Calendar of the Meetings of the 'Boston Religious Union of Associationists.' " In *Studies in the American Renaissance 1985,* ed. Joel Myerson, 187–267. Charlottesville: University of Virginia Press, 1985.

——. "French Utopianism on American Soil: Six Unpublished Letters by Victor Considerant." *Nineteenth-Century French Studies* 13 (1985): 59–65.

Dublin, Thomas, ed. *Farm to Factory: Women's Letters, 1830–1860.* New York: Columbia University Press, 1981.

Dwight, Marianne. *Letters from Brook Farm, 1844–1847.* Ed. Amy L. Reed. Poughkeepsie, N.Y.: Vassar College, 1928.

Emerson, Ralph Waldo. *The Journals and Miscellaneous Notebooks of Ralph Waldo Emerson.* Ed. Ralph H. Orth et al. Vols. 8 and 9. Cambridge, Mass.: Harvard University Press, 1960–82.

——. *The Letters of Ralph Waldo Emerson.* Ed. Ralph L. Rusk. Vols. 2 and 5. New York: Columbia University Press, 1939.

Fuller, Margaret. *The Letters of Margaret Fuller.* Ed. Robert N. Hudspeth. Vols. 4 and 5. Ithaca: Cornell University Press, 1987–88.

Gohdes, Clarence. "Three Letters by James Kay Dealing with Brook Farm." *Philological Quartlery* 17 (October 1938). 377–88.

Haraszti, Zoltan. *The Idyll of Brook Farm as Revealed by Unpublished Letters in the Boston Public Library.* Boston: Public Library, 1937.

Miller, Perry, ed. *The Transcendentalists: An Anthology.* Cambridge, Mass.: Harvard University Press, 1950.

Moret, Marie. *Documents pour une biographie complète de J.-B. A. Godin.* 3 vols. Guise: Familistere, 1877–1901.

Myerson, Joel, ed. *The Brook Farm Book.* New York: Garland, 1987.

Olmsted, Frederick Law. *The Papers of Frederick Law Olmsted.* Ed. Charles Capen McLaughlin et al. Vol. 1. Baltimore, Md.: Johns Hopkins University Press, 1977.

Sams, Henry W., ed. *Autobiography of Brook Farm.* Englewood Cliffs, N.J.: Prentice-Hall, 1958.

Stedman, Laura, and George Gould, eds. *Life and Letters of Edmund Clarence Stedman.* 2 vols. New York: Moffat, Yard, 1910.

Stoehr, Taylor, ed. *Free Love in America: A Documentary History.* New York: AMS Press, 1979.

Wilkinson, Clement John. *James John Garth Wilkinson: A Memoir of His Life, with a Selection from His Letters.* London: Kegan Paul, Trench, Trubner, 1911.

SECONDARY SOURCES

Unpublished Works

Bestor, Arthur. "American Phalanxes: A Study of Fourierist Socialism in the United States (with Special Reference to the Movement in Western New York)." Ph.D. diss., Yale University, 1938.

Buchs, Maurice. "Le Fouriérisme aux Etats-Unis: Contribution à l'étude du socialisme américain." Thèse du doctorat, Université de Paris, 1948.

Earl, Lloyd Rohler, Jr. "The Utopian Persuasion of Albert Brisbane, First Apostle of Fourierism." Ph.D. diss., Indiana University, 1977.

Elias, Joan. "The Wisconsin Phalanx: An Experiment in Association." M.A. thesis, University of Wisconsin, 1968.

Glynn, Lawrence, E., Jr. "Alphadelphia Association: A Michigan Communitarian Experiment, 1843–1848." M.A. thesis, Wayne State University, 1964.

Guarneri, Carl J. "Utopian Socialism and American Ideas: The Origins and Doctrine of American Fourierism, 1832–1848." Ph.D. diss., Johns Hopkins University, 1979.

Koretsky, Cecilia. "Horace Greeley and Fourierism in the United States." M.A. thesis, University of Rochester, 1952.

Noever, Janet Hubly. "Passionate Rebel: The Life of Mary Gove Nichols, 1810–1884." Ph.D. diss., University of Oklahoma, 1983.

Pettitt, Richard Norman, Jr. "Albert Brisbane: Apostle of Fourierism in the United States, 1834–1890." Ph.D. diss., Miami University (Ohio), 1982.

Schirber, Eric R. "The North American Phalanx, 1843–1855." M.A. thesis, Trinity College (Hartford, Connecticut), 1972.

Smith, Carlton. "Elijah P. Grant and the Ohio Phalanx: A Study in Utopian Socialism." M.A. thesis, University of Chicago, 1950.

Wennersten, John Raymond. "A Reformer's Odyssey: The Public Career of Parke Godwin of the New York *Evening Post*, 1837–1870." Ph.D. diss., University of Maryland, 1970.

Books

Arieli, Yehoshua. *Individualism and Nationalism in American Ideology*. Cambridge, Mass.: Harvard University Press, 1964.

Barkun, Michael. *Crucible of the Millennium: The Burned-Over District of New York in the 1840s*. Syracuse, N.Y.: Syracuse University Press, 1986.

Beecher, Jonathan. *Charles Fourier: The Visionary and His World*. Berkeley: University of California Press, 1986.

Bernard, L. L. and Jessie Bernard. *Origins of American Sociology: The Social Science Movement in the United States*. New York: T. Y. Crowell, 1943.

Bestor, Arthur. *Backwoods Utopias: The Sectarian Origins and the Owenite Phase of Communitarian Socialism in America, 1663–1829*. 2d ed. Philadelphia: University of Pennsylvania Press, 1970.

Block, Marguerite Beck. *The New Church in the New World: A Study of Swedenborgianism in America*. New York: Holt, Rinehart & Winston, 1932.

Bourgin, Hubert. *Fourier: Contribution à l'étude du socialisme français*. Paris: Société Nouvelle de Librairie et d'Édition, 1905.

Carpenter, Garrett R. *Silkville: A Kansas Attempt in the History of the Fourierist Utopias, 1869–1882*. Emporia, Kan.: Kansas State Teachers College, 1954.

Commons, John R., et al. *History of Labour in the United States*. Vol. 1. New York: Macmillan, 1918.

Cooke, George Willis. *John Sullivan Dwight: Brook Farmer, Editor, and Critic of Music*. Boston: Small, Maynard, 1898.

Cross, Whitney R. *The Burned-Over District: The Social and Intellectual History of Enthusiastic Religion in Western New York, 1800–1850*. Ithaca: Cornell University Press, 1950.

Crowe, Charles. *George Ripley, Transcendentalist and Utopian Socialist*. Athens: University of Georgia Press, 1967.

Curtis, Edith R. *A Season in Utopia: The Story of Brook Farm*. New York: Thomas Nelson, 1961.

Davidson, Rondel Van. *Did We Think Victory Great? The Life and Ideas of Victor Considerant* (Lanham, Md.: University Press of America, 1988).

Delano, Sterling F. *The Harbinger and New England Transcendentalism: A Portrait of Associationism in America*. Cranbury, N.J.: Associated University Presses, 1983.

Desroche, Henri. *La société festive: Du fouriérisme écrit aux Fouriérismes pratiqués*. Paris: Editions du Seuil, 1975.

Fellman, Michael. *The Unbounded Frame: Freedom and Community in Nineteenth Century American Utopianism*. Westport, Conn.: Greenwood Press, 1973.

Fogarty, Robert S. *Dictionary of American Communal and Utopian History*. Westport, Conn.: Greenwood Press, 1980.

Frothingham, Octavius Brooks. *George Ripley*. Boston: Houghton Mifflin, 1882.

——. *Memoir of William Henry Channing*. Boston: Houghton, Mifflin, 1886.

Golemba, Henry. *George Ripley*. Boston: Twayne, 1977.

Hammond, William J., and Margaret F. Hammond. *La Réunion: A French Settlement in Texas*. Dallas: Royal, 1958.

Hayden, Dolores. *The Grand Domestic Revolution: A History of Feminist Designs for American Homes, Neighborhoods, and Cities*. Cambridge, Mass.: MIT Press, 1981.

——. *Seven American Utopias: The Architecture of Communitarian Socialism, 1790–1975*. Cambridge, Mass.: MIT Press, 1976.

Howe, Daniel Walker. *The Political Culture of the American Whigs*. Chicago: University of Chicago Press, 1979.

Kanter, Rosabeth Moss. *Commitment and Community: Communes and Utopias in Sociological Perspective*. Cambridge, Mass.: Harvard University Press, 1972.

Manuel, Frank E., and Fritzie P. Manuel. *Utopian Thought in the Western World*. Cambridge, Mass.: Harvard University Press, 1979.

Montgomery, David. *Beyond Equality: Labor and the Radical Republicans, 1862–1872*. New York: Knopf, 1967.

Muncy, Raymond Lee. *Sex and Marriage in Utopian Communities: Nineteenth-Century America*. Bloomington: Indiana University Press, 1973.

Noyes, John Humphrey. *History of American Socialisms*. Philadelphia: Lippincott, 1870.

Riasnovsky, Nicholas. *The Teaching of Charles Fourier*. Berkeley: University of California Press, 1969.

Rose, Anne C. *Transcendentalism as a Social Movement, 1830–1850*. New Haven, Conn.: Yale University Press, 1981.

Rozwenc, Edwin C. *Cooperatives Come to America: The History of the Protective Store Movement, 1845–1867*. Mt. Vernon, Iowa: Hawkeye-Record Press, 1941; Rpt. Philadelphia: Porcupine Press, 1975.

Spann, Edward K. *Brotherly Tomorrows: Movements for a Cooperative Society in America, 1820–1920*. New York: Columbia University Press, 1988.

——. *Ideals and Politics: New York Intellectuals and Liberal Democracy, 1820–1880*. Albany: State University of New York Press, 1972.

Spurlock, John C. *Free Love: Marriage and Middle-Class Radicalism in America, 1825–1860*. New York: New York University Press, 1988.

Stern, Madeleine. *The Pantarch: A Biography of Stephen Pearl Andrews*. Austin: University of Texas Press, 1968.

Stoehr, Taylor. *Hawthorne's Mad Scientists: Pseudoscience and Social Science in Nineteenth-Century Life and Letters*. Hamden, Conn.: Archon Books, 1978.

Swift, Lindsay. *Brook Farm: Its Members, Scholars, and Visitors*. New York: Macmillan, 1900.

Van Deusen, Glyndon G. *Horace Greeley: Nineteenth-Century Crusader*. Philadelphia: University of Pennsylvania Press, 1953.

Ware, Norman F. *The Industrial Worker, 1840–1860.* Boston: Houghton Mifflin, 1924.

Warren, Austin. *The Elder Henry James.* New York: Macmillan, 1934.

Wilson, James H. *Life of Charles A. Dana.* New York: Harper, 1907.

Wisbey, Herbert, Jr. *The Sodus Bay Shaker Community.* Lyons, N.Y.: Wayne County Historical Society, 1982.

Zahler, Helene Sara. *Eastern Workingmen and National Land Policy, 1829–1862.* New York: Columbia University Press, 1941.

Zilberfarb, I. I. *Sotsialnaia filosofia Sharlia Fure i ee mesto v istorri sotsialisticheskoi mysli pervoi poloviny XIX veka. (The social philosophy of Charles Fourier and its place in the history of socialist thought in the first half of the nineteenth century).* Moscow: Izdatel'stvo Nauka, 1964.

Articles

Bassett, T. D. Seymour. "The Secular Utopian Socialists." In *Socialism and American Life,* ed. Donald Drew Egbert and Stow Persons, 1:155–211. Princeton, N.J.: Princeton University Press, 1952.

Belz, Herman. "The North American Phalanx: An Experiment in Socialism." *Proceedings of the New Jersey Historical Society* 81 (October 1963): 215–47.

Bernard, L. L. "Early Utopian Social Theory in the United States (1840–1860)." *Northwest Missouri State Teachers College Studies* 2 (1938): 71–94.

Bestor, Arthur. "Albert Brisbane—Propagandist for Socialism in the 1840s." *New York History* 28 (April 1947): 128–58.

——. "The Evolution of the Socialist Vocabulary." *Journal of the History of Ideas* 9 (June 1948): 259–302.

——. "Fourierism in Northampton: A Critical Note." *New England Quarterly* 13 (March 1940): 110–22.

Blake, John B. "Mary Gove Nichols, Prophetess of Health." *Proceedings of the American Philosophical Society* 106 (June 1962): 219–34.

Borden, Morten. "Some Notes on Horace Greeley, Charles Dana, and Karl Marx." *Journalism Quarterly* 34 (Fall 1957): 457–65.

Crowe, Charles R. "Christian Socialism and the First Church of Humanity." *Church History* 35 (March 1966): 93–106.

——. "Fourierism and the Founding of Brook Farm." *Boston Public Library Quarterly* 12 (April 1960): 79–88.

——. "This Unnatural Union of Phalansteries and Transcendentalists." *Journal of the History of Ideas* 20 (October–December 1959): 495–502.

——. "Transcendentalist Support of Brook Farm: A Paradox?" *Historian* 21 (May 1959): 281–295.

——. "Utopian Socialism in Rhode Island, 1845–1850." *Rhode Island History* 18 (January 1959): 20–26.

Davidson, Rondel V. "Victor Considerant and the Failure of La Réunion." *Southwestern Historical Quarterly* 76 (January 1973): 277–96.

Dawson, George E. "The Integral Phalanx." *Transactions of the Illinois State Historical Society,* 1907, pp. 85–98.

Delano, Sterling F., and Rita Colanzi. "An Index to Volume VIII of *The Harbinger.*" *Resources for American Literary Study* 10 (Autumn 1980): 173–86.

Early, Frances H. "A Reappraisal of the New England Labour-Reform Movement of the 1840s: The Lowell Female Labor Reform Association and the New England Workingmen's Association." *Histoire Sociale/Social History* 13 (May 1980): 33–54.

Fein, Albert. "Fourierism in Nineteenth-Century America: A Social and Environmental Perspective." In *France and North America: Utopias and Utopians*, ed. Mathé Allain, 133–48. Lafayette: University of Southwest Louisiana, 1978.

Feuer, Lewis. "The Influence of the American Communist Colonies on Engels and Marx." *Western Political Quarterly* 19 (September 1966): 456–74.

Foner, Philip S. "Journal of an Early Labor Organizer." *Labor History* 10 (Spring 1969): 205–27.

Francis, Richard. "The Ideology of Brook Farm." In *Studies in the American Rennaissance 1977*, ed. Joel Myerson, 1–48. Boston: Twayne, 1978.

Gohdes, Clarence. "A Brook Farm Labor Record." *American Literature* 1 (November 1929): 297–303.

Greene, Maud Honeyman. "Raritan Bay Union, Eagleswood, New Jersey." *Proceedings of the New Jersey Historical Society* 67 (January 1950): 2–20.

Guarneri, Carl. "The Associationists: Forging a Christian Socialism in Antebellum America." *Church History* 52 (March 1983): 36–49.

———. "Importing Fourierism to America." *Journal of the History of Ideas* 43 (October–December 1982): 581–94.

———. "Two Utopian Socialist Plans for Emancipation in Antebellum Louisiana." *Louisiana History* 24 (Winter 1983): 5–24.

———. "Who Were the Utopian Socialists? Patterns of Membership in American Fourierist Communities." *Communal Societies* 5 (1985): 65–81.

Johnson, H. U. "History of the Trumbull Phalanx." *Western Reserve Chronicle* 81 (5 May 1897).

Jones, Russell M. "Victor Considerant's American Experience (1852–1869)." *French–American Review* 1 (1976–77): 65–94, 124–50.

Jordan, Philip D. "The Iowa Pioneer Phalanx." *Palimpsest* 16 (July 1935): 211–25.

Kirchmann, George. "Unsettled Utopias: The North American Phalanx and the Raritan Bay Union." *New Jersey History* 47 (Spring 1979): 25–36.

———. "Why Did They Stay? Communal Life at the North American Phalanx." In *Planned and Utopian Experiments: Four New Jersey Towns*, ed. Paul A. Stellhorn, 11–28. Trenton: New Jersey Historical Commission, 1980.

Lauer, Jeanette C., and Robert H. Lauer. "Sex Roles in Nineteenth-Century American Communal Societies." *Communal Societies* 3 (1983): 16–28.

Lazerow, Jama. "Religion and Labor Reform in Antebellum America: The World of William Field Young." *American Quarterly* 38 (Summer 1986): 265–86.

Morris, James M. "Communes and Cooperatives: Cincinnati's Early Experiments in Social Reform." *Cincinnati Historical Society Bulletin* 33 (Spring 1975): 57–80.

Myerson, Joel. "New Light on George Ripley and the *Harbinger's* New York Years." *Harvard Library Bulletin* 33 (Summer 1985): 313–36.

Okugawa, Otohiko. "Intercommunal Relationships among Nineteenth–Century Communal Societies in America." *Communal Societies* 3 (1983): 68–82.

Pedrick, S. M. "The Wisconsin Phalanx at Ceresco." *Proceedings of the State Historical Society of Wisconsin,* 1902, pp. 190–226.

Prieur, Vincent. "Un syncrétisme utopique: Le cas du Fouriérisme Américain (1840–50)." In J. Bartier et al., *1848: Les utopismes sociaux*, 261–72. Paris: S.E.D.E.S., 1981.

Robinson, David. "The Political Odyssey of William Henry Channing." *American Quarterly* 34 (Summer 1982): 165–84.

Schafer, Joseph. "The Wisconsin Phalanx." *Wisconsin Magazine of History* 19 (June 1935): 454–74.

Sears, Hal. "Alcander Longley, Missouri Communist: A History of Reunion Community and a Study of the Constitutions of Reunion and Friendship." *Missouri Historical Society Bulletin* 25 (1969): 123–37.

Shively, Charles. Introduction. In Stephen Pearl Andrews, *Love, Marriage, Divorce, and the Condition of Woman.* New York: M & S Press, 1975.

Sokolow, Jayme A. "Culture and Utopia: The Raritan Bay Union." *New Jersey History* 94 (Summer–Fall 1976): 93–100.

Stearns, Bertha-Monica. "Two Forgotten New England Reformers [Thomas Low Nichols and Mary Gove Nichols]." *New England Quarterly* 6 (March 1933): 59–84.

Swan, Norma Lippincott. "The North American Phalanx." *Monmouth County Historical Association Bulletin* 1 (May 1935): 35–63.

Thomas, John L. "Antislavery and Utopia." In *The Antislavery Vanguard: New Essays on the Abolitionists,* ed. Martin Duberman. Princeton, N.J.: Princeton University Press, 1966.

——. "Romantic Reform in America, 1815–1865." *American Quarterly* 17 (Winter 1965): 656–81.

Thomas, N. Gordon. "The Alphadelphia Experiment." *Michigan History* 55 (Fall 1971): 205–16.

Tregle, Joseph G., Jr. "Thomas J. Durant, Utopian Socialism, and the Failure of Presidential Reconstruction in Louisiana." *Journal of Southern History* 45 (November 1979): 485–512.

Van Buren, A. D. P. "The Alphadelphia Association." *Michigan Pioneer and Historical Collections* 5 (1884): 406–12.

Wennersten, John R. "Parke Godwin, Utopian Socialism, and the Politics of Antislavery." *New-York Historical Society Quarterly* 60 (July–October 1976): 107–27.

Index

517